COMMON LAW CONSTITUTIONAL RIGHTS

There is a developing body of legal reasoning in the United Kingdom Supreme Court in which members of the senior judiciary have asserted the primary role of common law constitutional rights and critiqued legal arguments based first and foremost on the Human Rights Act 1998. Their calls for a shift in legal reasoning have created a sense amongst both scholars and the judiciary that something significant is happening. Yet despite renewed academic and judicial interest we have limited insight into what common law constitutional rights we have, how they work and what they offer. This book is the first collection of its kind to systematically explore both the content and role of individual common law constitutional rights alongside the constitutional significance and broader implications of these developments. It therefore contributes not only to our understanding of what the common law might be capable of offering in terms of the protection of rights, but also to our understanding of the nature of the constitutional order of which such rights are an integral part.

Common Law Constitutional Rights

Edited by
Mark Elliott
and
Kirsty Hughes

·HART·
OXFORD · LONDON · NEW YORK · NEW DELHI · SYDNEY

HART PUBLISHING

Bloomsbury Publishing Plc

Kemp House, Chawley Park, Cumnor Hill, Oxford, OX2 9PH, UK

1385 Broadway, New York, NY 10018, USA

HART PUBLISHING, the Hart/Stag logo, BLOOMSBURY and the Diana logo are
trademarks of Bloomsbury Publishing Plc

First published in Great Britain 2020

A catalogue record for this book is available from the British Library.

Library of Congress Cataloging-in-Publication data

Names: Elliott, Mark, 1975- editor. | Hughes, Kirsty, editor.

Title: Common law constitutional rights/edited by Mark Elliott and Kirsty Hughes.

Description: Oxford ; New York : Hart, 2020. | Includes bibliographical references and index.

Identifiers: LCCN 2019051347 (print) | LCCN 2019051348 (ebook) |
ISBN 9781509906864 (hardback) | ISBN 9781509906888 (Epub)

Subjects: LCSH: Constitutional law—Great Britain. | Common law—England.

Classification: LCC KD3989.A2 C58 2020 (print) | LCC KD3989.A2 (ebook) |
DDC 342.4208/5—dc23

LC record available at https://lccn.loc.gov/2019051347

LC ebook record available at https://lccn.loc.gov/2019051348

ISBN: HB: 978-1-50990-686-4
       ePDF: 978-1-50990-687-1
       ePub: 978-1-50990-688-8

Typeset by Compuscript Ltd, Shannon
Printed and bound in Great Britain by CPI Group (UK) Ltd, Croydon CR0 4YY

To find out more about our authors and books visit www.hartpublishing.co.uk.
Here you will find extracts, author information, details of forthcoming events
and the option to sign up for our newsletters.

FOREWORD

ROBERT REED*

Towards the end of 2010, or early in 2011, I was sitting on a criminal appeal in Scotland which concerned the admission of evidence that the police had obtained irregularly. It would have been a routine appeal but for the fact that counsel argued it entirely on the basis of article 6 of the European Convention on Human Rights, and the jurisprudence of the European Court on Human Rights. When I pointed out that this was a question on which there was a wealth of domestic case law, counsel's response was striking. There was, she said, no need to look at domestic case law. Either it was in accordance with article 6, in which case it added nothing, or it was not in accordance with article 6, in which case it should be disregarded, so as to avoid an incompatibility with Convention rights. The court did not accept that argument, but I was struck by what seemed to me to be a misunderstanding of the relationship between the Convention and the national legal systems of the contracting parties.

I had also been struck by some decisions of the House of Lords not long before, which displayed a reluctance to develop the common law in areas where the Convention applied, on the basis that such matters were better dealt with under the Human Rights Act. Although I accepted that there were limits to judicial development of the common law, and that some developments would indeed have to be addressed under the Human Rights Act, a general refusal to develop the common law in the light of the Convention seemed to me to be an inappropriate restriction of its natural dynamism, and of its openness to influence from international law.

Not long afterwards, in March 2011, I was invited, along with Lord Hope of Craighead (standing in at short notice for Lord Rodger of Earlsferry, who had been taken ill as a consequence of the illness which was to cause his death three months later) and Sir Nicolas Bratza, to give a lecture at a seminar in Parliament House in Edinburgh on the relationships between the Strasbourg Court, the Supreme Court and the Scottish courts. I decided to speak about the place of the Convention in domestic law, about the extent to which the rights protected by the Convention were immanent in, and protected by, domestic law, and about the ways in which the Convention might influence the development of domestic law. In doing so I was influenced by my experience as counsel for the Government in a number of

* Lord Reed is the President of the United Kingdom Supreme Court.

Strasbourg cases, and as an ad hoc judge on the Strasbourg court: roles in which it is necessary to explain to the court how Convention rights are protected in the United Kingdom, in the absence of a written constitution or bill of rights, by the common law and statute.

About two years later, having succeeded Lord Rodger as a Justice of the Supreme Court, I was sitting on the case of *R (Osborn) v Parole Board*[1] when I experienced a sense of déjà vu. The case concerned the right to a fair hearing: a topic on which English administrative law is highly developed. Counsel for the appellants chose, however, to argue the appeal almost entirely on the basis of Strasbourg judgments concerned with article 5(4) of the Convention. I remember rather impatiently asking counsel, as we were taken through a seemingly endless catalogue of cases concerned with proceedings of various kinds in Russia and Ukraine, whether Wade and Forsyth's *Administrative Law* and De Smith's *Judicial Review of Administrative Action* were to be consigned to the wastepaper basket. When I was asked to write the judgment of the court, I looked out the lecture I had given in Edinburgh two years earlier, and it formed the basis of some remarks about the relationship between Convention rights and the common law: remarks which developed some observations that I had made in an earlier case,[2] and which I repeated in some later cases.[3]

I was not the only judge to be concerned about the way in which the relationship between the Convention and the common law was developing. Remarks along similar lines to my own were also made in other cases by Lord Mance[4] and by Lord Justice Toulson,[5] as he then was, and their cumulative effect began to influence advocacy before the court and the thinking of our colleagues. Over time, the idea that statutory provisions and the common law protected underlying values or principles became linked with three other ideas: first, the principle of legality, expressed by Lord Bridge of Harwich in *Ex parte Pierson*[6] and by Lord Hoffmann in *Ex parte Simms*;[7] secondly, the idea of constitutional statutes, developed by Sir John Laws in *Thoburn*[8] and other cases; thirdly, the idea that *Wednesbury* unreasonableness was a ground of review of variable intensity, depending on the subject matter of the act or decision being considered; and fourthly, the related idea, developed particularly by Professor Paul Craig, that review on that ground might not be fundamentally different from the concept of proportionality, and that the latter facilitated a more structured and transparent exercise of the court's supervisory jurisdiction.

---

[1] [2013] UKSC 61, [2014] AC 1115.

[2] *R (Sturnham) v Parole Board* [2013] UKSC 23, [2013] 2 AC 254.

[3] For example, *A v BBC* [2014] UKSC 25, [2015] AC 588.

[4] See *Kennedy v Charity Commission* [2014] UKSC 20, [2015] 2 AC 455.

[5] See *R (Guardian News and Media Ltd) v City of Westminster Magistrates' Court* [2012] EWCA Civ 420, [2013] QB 618.

[6] *R v Secretary of State for the Home Department, Ex parte Pierson* [1998] AC 539.

[7] *R v Secretary of State for the Home Department, Ex parte Simms* [2000] 2 AC 115.

[8] *Thoburn v Sunderland City Council* [2002] EWHC 195 (Admin), [2003] QB 151.

Over time, these related ideas bore fruit in a number of decisions of the Supreme Court concerned particularly with constitutional law, of which *HS2*,[9] *UNISON*[10] and *Miller 2*[11] are perhaps the most significant. This development in judicial thinking also generated a considerable amount of academic commentary, which in turn fed into the further evolution of judicial thinking. The commentary has been extremely varied in tone. Some commentators have responded positively and have regarded the developing case law as evidence of the continued vigour of the common law and of judicial creativity. Others have deplored what they regard as constitutionally inappropriate meddling by the courts in the political realm. Some commentators have made large, and possibly over-stated, claims for the significance of common law constitutional rights, as they have come to be called. Others have questioned what all the fuss is about.

The implications of the idea of common law constitutional rights are still being examined by the courts in a range of situations, and it will be some time before the law becomes settled. In those circumstances, it is particularly important that academic lawyers should analyse what is going on in the courts, identify the strengths and weaknesses of judicial reasoning, and point out possible ways forward for courts seeking to steer a course between the Scylla of sterility and passivity, and the Charybdis of instability and uncertainty.

I therefore welcome this volume of essays on the content, role and potential of common law constitutional rights. I have been using the book in manuscript while writing some recent judgments, and can testify to the quality of the analyses it contains. It will be of assistance both to judges who are sometimes too busy dealing with the cases before them to have much time to stand back and reflect on the bigger picture, and to lawyers who are looking for analyses of the case law which will provide them with guidance as to where the law stands and ideas about where it might be heading. Above all, it is a timely and valuable analysis of an important recent development in the law, which deserves, and receives, thoughtful academic study.

The Supreme Court of the United Kingdom
February 2020

---

[9] *R (Buckinghamshire County Council) v Secretary of State for Transport* [2014] UKSC 3. [2014] 1 WLR 324.

[10] *R (UNISON) v Lord Chancellor* [2017] UKSC 51, [2017] 3 WLR 409.

[11] *R (Miller) v Prime Minister* [2019] UKSC 4, [2019] 3 WLR 589.

TABLE OF CONTENTS

LIST OF CONTRIBUTORS

Tom Allen is Professor of Law at Durham University.

Joanna Bell is an Associate Professor of Law at the University of Oxford and a Fellow of St Edmund Hall, Oxford.

Brice Dickson is Emeritus Professor of International and Comparative Law at Queen's University Belfast.

Mark Elliott is Professor of Public Law at the University of Cambridge and a Fellow of St Catharine's College, Cambridge.

Thomas Fairclough is a barrister at 2TG.

Kirsty Hughes is a Senior Lecturer in Law at the University of Cambridge and a Fellow of Clare College, Cambridge.

Natasa Mavronicola is a Reader in Law at the University of Birmingham.

Colm O'Cinneide is Professor of Human Rights Law at University College London.

Gavin Phillipson is Professor of Law at the University of Bristol.

Jacob Rowbottom is an Associate Professor of Law at University of Oxford and a Fellow of University College, Oxford.

Se-shauna Wheatle is an Associate Professor of Law at Durham University.

Alison Young is the Sir David Williams Professor of Public Law at the University of Cambridge and a Fellow of Robinson College, Cambridge.

1

The Nature and Role of Common Law Constitutional Rights

MARK ELLIOTT AND KIRSTY HUGHES

I. Common Law Constitutional Rights on the Agenda

This book was first conceived following a raft of United Kingdom Supreme Court judgments championing common law constitutional rights. Cases such as *Osborn v Parole Board*,[1] *Kennedy v Charity Commissioner*[2] and *A v BBC*[3] all saw judges turning to common law constitutional rights. At that time various members of the senior judiciary asserted the *primary* role of common law constitutional rights and critiqued legal arguments based first and foremost on the Human Rights Act 1998 (HRA). For example, in *Osborn* Lord Reed declared that the HRA

> does not supersede the protection of human rights under the common law or state, or create, a discrete body of law based upon the judgments of the European court. Human rights continue to be protected by our domestic law, interpreted and developed in accordance with the Human Rights Act when appropriate.[4]

Equally in *Kennedy v Charity Commissioner* Lord Mance critiqued what he regarded as a tendency following the enactment of the HRA 'to see the law in areas touched on by the Convention solely in terms of the Convention rights'.[5] In his view 'the Convention rights represent a threshold protection' but 'especially in view of the contribution which common lawyers made to the Convention's inception, they may be expected, at least generally even if not always, to reflect and to find their homologue in the common or domestic statute law'.[6] Indeed Lord Mance asserted that 'the natural starting point in any dispute is to start with domestic law, and it is certainly not to focus exclusively on the Convention rights, without

---

[1] [2013] UKSC 61, [2014] AC 1115.
[2] [2014] UKSC 20, [2015] 2 AC 455.
[3] [2014] UKSC 25, [2015] AC 588.
[4] *Osborn* (n 1) [57].
[5] *Kennedy* (n 2) [46].
[6] Ibid, [46].

surveying the wider common law scene.[7] Lord Toulson joined in lamenting the 'baleful and unnecessary tendency to overlook the common law', declaring that '[i]t needs to be emphasised that it was not the purpose of the Human Rights Act that the common law should become an ossuary'.[8]

The combined effect of these dicta was to create a sense amongst both scholars and the judiciary that something significant was happening, that there was a shift occurring in judicial reasoning and that this was intended to stimulate common law arguments in legal submissions in order to reinvigorate the common law.[9] At the time both the President and Deputy President of the Supreme Court acknowledged this sense of movement, appearing to signify judicial engagement with and a willingness to return to the common law. Indeed Lady Hale went as far as to deem this development evidence of 'UK constitutionalism on the march'.[10] Meanwhile, Lord Neuberger acknowledged that judges 'have tried to bring the common law back to centre stage',[11] expressing the view that there are 'now two separate seams, common law rights and Convention rights, which can overlap, but each of which also has its own different area of exclusivity'.[12] Certainly this renewed focus upon common law rights appeared to present itself across the Supreme Court. Consequently, five years ago, common law constitutional rights appeared to be in receipt of extensive judicial support at the highest level both in Supreme Court judgments and in extra-judicial addresses.

Scholars offered various explanations for this development, one of which was that this was a strategic judicial move to prepare English law for the possible repeal of the HRA. Others identified renewed emphasis on the common law as part of a broader development of common law reasoning. In any event academics differed on the implications of this move. Scholars such as Masterman and Wheatle highlighted the 'resurgence' of the common law and its potential to operate as an 'independent source of rights', taking this as a sign 'not only of [the common law's] resilience but also of its continuing ability to recalibrate itself in the face of new challenges and current needs'.[13] Equally Stephenson suggested that these

---

[7] Ibid, [2014] UKSC 20; [2014] 2 WLR 808, [46].

[8] Ibid, [2014] UKSC 20; [2014] 2 WLR 808, [133].

[9] See, eg, R Masterman and S Wheatle, 'A Common Law Resurgence in Rights Protection?' [2015] *European Human Rights Law Review* 57; R Clayton, 'The Empire Strikes Back' [2015] *Public Law* 3.

[10] Lady Hale, keynote address to the Constitutional and Administrative Law Bar Association, 'UK Constitutionalism on the March?', 12 July 2014 www.supremecourt.uk/docs/speech-140712.pdf.

[11] Lord Neuberger at a conference at the Supreme Court of Victoria, Melbourne 'The role of judges in human rights jurisprudence: a comparison of the Australian and UK experience', 8 August 2014 (www.supremecourt.uk/docs/speech-140808.pdf) at [29].

[12] Lord Neuberger at a conference at the Supreme Court of Victoria, Melbourne 'The role of judges in human rights jurisprudence: a comparison of the Australian and UK experience', 8 August 2014 (www.supremecourt.uk/docs/speech-140808.pdf) at [30]. See also Lord Neuberger, President of the Supreme Court 'What's in a name?' – Privacy and anonymous speech on the Internet Conference5RB Keynote speech, 30 September 2014 (www.supremecourt.uk/docs/speech-140930.pdf) at [38], and Lord Neuberger The Conkerton Lecture 2014, Liverpool Law Society The Supreme Court and the Rule of Law (www.supremecourt.uk/docs/speech-141009-lord-neuberger.pdf).

[13] Masterman and Wheatle (n 9) 64–65.

cases 'suggest that the common law remains a dynamic and important source of rights protection in the UK and may, in some circumstances, even provide more protection for rights than the HRA.'[14] Whilst another scholar asserted that it is now evident 'that the common law has developed its protection of fundamental rights in a way that cannot be deprecated as being no more than a domestic hand-maiden to the HRA'[15] others, however, were more wary about the likely impact of these cases in domestic law, cautioning that such rights were unlikely to repli-cate the rights protected by the HRA and that it was 'premature to argue that "the force is with us" in developing common law rights, unless and until some underly-ing principles are modified'.[16] Indeed one of us noted at the time that it would be 'unrealistic to argue that domestic law in this area is so extensive, rigorous, and resilient as to render the HRA–ECHR [regime] essentially redundant, such that (for instance) repeal of the former and withdrawal from the latter are prospects that can be met with utter equanimity'.[17]

Although the flurry of Supreme Court cases explicitly engaging with the primary role of common law constitutional rights has arguably dissipated in the last two or three years, there have nevertheless been significant further develop-ments. Two Supreme Court cases in particular are worth emphasising here and are discussed further in various chapters throughout this book, namely *Unison*[18] and *Privacy International*.[19] In *Unison* the Supreme Court held that the imposition of fees on those wishing to bring claims to the Employment Tribunal effectively denied access to justice to potential claimants. In coming to the decision that the Fee Orders were unlawful Lord Reed emphasised that 'the right of access to justice is not an idea recently imported from the continent of Europe, but has long been deeply embedded in our constitutional law'.[20] He also noted that *Unison* was 'argued primarily on the basis of the common law right of access to justice';[21] an indication that at least in the access to justice context counsel are heeding judicial calls to bring the common law centre stage.

The landmark Supreme Court decision in *Privacy International* also brought to the fore the role of the common law. In determining that section 67(8) of the Regulation of Investigatory Powers Act 2000 does not oust the supervisory juris-diction of the High Court over decisions of the Investigatory Powers Tribunal,

---

[14] S Stephenson 'The Supreme Court's Renewed Interest in Autochthonous Constitutionalism' [2015] *Public Law* 394, 399.

[15] E Bjorge 'Common Law Rights: Balancing Domestic and International Exigencies' (2016) 75 *CLJ* 220, 221.

[16] Clayton (n 9) 3.

[17] M Elliott 'Beyond the European Convention: Human Rights and the Common Law' (2015) 68 *Current Legal Problems* 85, 88.

[18] *R (Unison) v Lord Chancellor* [2017] UKSC 51, [2017] 3 WLR 409.

[19] *R (Privacy International) v Investigatory Powers Tribunal* [2019] UKSC 22, [2019] 2 WLR 1219.

[20] *Unison* (n 18) [64].

[21] Ibid, [64].

Lord Carnwath stated (albeit obiter, but with Lady Hale and Lord Kerr in concurrence) that there is

> a strong case for holding that, consistently with the rule of law, binding effect cannot be given to a clause which purports wholly to exclude the supervisory jurisdiction of the High Court to review a decision of an inferior court or tribunal, whether for excess or abuse of jurisdiction, or error of law. In all cases, regardless of the words used, it should remain ultimately a matter for the court to determine the extent to which such a clause should be upheld, having regard to its purpose and statutory context, and the nature and importance of the legal issue in question; and to determine the level of scrutiny required by the rule of law.[22]

This dictum, albeit obiter, has been seized upon as further evidence of the common law turn in English law. It is relevant to one of the core questions surrounding the potential potency of common law constitutional rights: namely, the extent to which they are subordinate to parliamentary sovereignty. Thus although there have arguably been fewer explicit calls for the primacy of common law constitutional rights since the renewed interest that seemed to peak in 2014, the common law tide has not turned.

When we commenced this project we were interested in what these common law constitutional rights were, how they work, what they offer and what they might mean for the protection of rights in English law. Those questions remain pertinent today. However, since we began this project the need to take a hard look at these rights has become ever more pressing. Part of the initial impetus for our inquiry was the fact that repeal of the HRA had been favoured in certain political quarters for some time.[23] That remains the case today. In the past, comfort was often sought (by those who view the prospect of HRA repeal with horror) in the notion that even without the HRA the UK would likely remain a member of the European Convention on Human Rights (ECHR) and thus bound to act compatibly with those rights in international law. Indeed a sense of security was provided by the notion that it was doubtful that the UK would seek to withdraw from the ECHR altogether given that there is, at the very least, considerable uncertainty as to whether it would be possible to remain a member of the European Union following such a step.[24] Any perceived EU/ECHR safeguard was however, dealt a fatal blow by the Brexit referendum in 2016. The obligations of EU membership are no longer any obstacle to ECHR withdrawal, while very little imagination is needed in order to envisage the ECHR entering, in short order, into the crosshairs of those who advocated Brexit. The future of the ECHR/HRA regime for the protection of rights in domestic law is consequently far more precarious and contingent upon political developments than it has been since the HRA's enactment.

---

[22] *Privacy International* (n 19) [144].

[23] The Conservative Party included the repeal of the Human Rights Act 1998 in their 2010 and 2015 general election manifestos. See also Conservative Party 'Protecting Human Rights in the UK: The Conservatives' Proposals for Changing Britain's Human Rights Laws' (2014).

[24] House of Commons Library, 'Is Adherence to the European Convention on Human Rights a Condition of European Union Membership?' (Standard Note Sn/IA/6577).

A further impetus for exploring the offerings and prospects of common law constitutional rights that has come to the fore in the intervening period is the growing backlash against human rights at the international level.[25] Enforcement of international human rights judgments remains problematic both as a matter of political will and through the invocation in some states of national law as a justification for failure to implement. Hence the most recent annual report of the Council of Europe Committee of Ministers emphasises 'persistent shortcomings in the effective national implementation of the Convention' and the need to reaffirm the 'unconditional character of the obligation to fully execute the Court's judgments … against the temptation to put forward domestic or international obstacles'.[26] Meanwhile, the Council of Europe Commissioner for Human Rights also highlights the problems of non-implementation (more than 7,000 judgments were awaiting full implementation at the end of 2017), a tendency for states to 'cherry-pick' judgments depending on their acceptance by political authorities, and the use of political rhetoric that delegitimises the Court.[27] The rise of far right populist parties and politicians across Europe (and elsewhere) also suggests that we should be cautious about the resilience of European (and other international) human rights instruments in what may turn out to be a post-European framework. Indeed, in the midst of the political and legal uncertainty that the UK now faces, it is imperative that we take a realistic look at what the common law would or could offer in the event that reliance can no longer be placed upon the protections afforded by international law under the post-war settlement.

If we turn to consider common law constitutional rights it is evident that despite renewed academic and judicial interest we have limited insight into what rights we have, how they work and what they offer. Common law constitutional rights tend to be considered as a species focusing upon their interface with parliamentary sovereignty and their role in administrative law,[28] or as individual rights in isolation, for example the common law constitutional right to freedom of expression or access to the courts. It is however, crucial to any discourse about common law constitutional rights that we seek to develop a clear sense of which rights exist, what they consist of, what can be done with such rights, how such rights come into existence, their similarities and differences and how they relate to one another. Although one scholar suggests that instead of considering 'the potentially differing

---

[25] A Gilmore, UN Assistant Secretary-General for Human Rights 'The Global Backlash Against Human Rights', University of California, Berkeley and McGeorge School of Law, Sacramento, 12 and 13 March 2018.

[26] Council of Europe Committee of Ministers *Supervision of the Execution of Judgments and Decisions of the European Court of Human Rights: 12th Annual Report of the Committee of Ministers* (Strasbourg, Council of Europe, 2019).

[27] See Council of Europe Commissioner for Human Rights 'Maintaining the Independence and Effectiveness of the European Court of Human Rights is a Matter for Us All' Speech by Council of Europe Commissioner for Human Rights (26 November 2018). CommDH/Speech(2018)12. For discussion of some core examples of these practices see K Dzehtsiarou and DK Coffey 'Suspension and Expulsion of the Members of the Council of Europe: Difficult Decisions in Troubled Times' (2019) 68(2) *ICLQ* 443.

[28] See, eg, the articles cited at n 13–17 above.

level of protection offered to different rights … it is arguably more useful to focus instead on the systemic feature which is the test that the courts apply in relation to interferences with the right at issue', this is premised upon his determination that 'common law rights and HRA rights alike are protected through judicial reliance on the proportionality inquiry (or a rationality inquiry which amounts in substance to the same test)',[29] which he asserts 'is no less rigorous at common law than it is under the HRA.[30] The reality, however, is somewhat more nuanced than this. First, because in order to know whether we apply proportionality analysis we need to know whether, to begin with, a relevant right is applicable. Second, not all rights are subject to proportionality analysis. Third, it is questionable whether domestic proportionality analysis is as rigorous in domestic law as it is in Strasbourg jurisprudence, as indicated by the fact that the Strasbourg Court continues to find violations of the Convention in cases where UK courts have deemed interferences to be proportionate. Fourth, it is necessary to bear in mind that how and to what extent rights are protected vary not only across rights and frameworks but within individual rights. Common law constitutional rights are thus not a homogenous species that can be simply considered en masse.

We thus need both an overarching study of the role of common law constitutional rights at a conceptual level, as well as a detailed and comparative analysis of the content of individual rights. Unfortunately, as Tugendhat J acknowledged in *AKJ*, these rights are not easy to identify because they have not been codified and because for a long period fundamental rights were eclipsed by philosophical ideas that were inconsistent with natural rights and by the concept of absolute parliamentary sovereignty.[31] He noted that a 'further complication for lawyers in presenting cases based on the fundamental rights recognised by the common law is that the names of the torts by which fundamental rights are protected under the common law bear little relationship to the rights themselves.[32] All of these difficulties have been encountered in putting together this book. Although the first part of the book offers detailed analysis of the content and role of individual common law constitutional rights in judicial decision-making, the scope of the book evidently meant that choices had to be made as to which rights to include and how to approach such rights. One option would have been to seek to work through the full catalogue of ECHR rights and look to see whether they are replicated in the common law. Another option would have been to seek to exhaustively catalogue the rights that exist in the common law and then compare those rights to the ECHR. In fact, we elected to use something of a hybrid model in this book, clustering rights thematically and examining the role of the common law and the ECHR vis-à-vis those values and interests. Inevitably this means that the scope

---

[29] Bjorge (n 15) 222.
[30] Ibid, 222.
[31] *AKJ and others* v *Commissioner of Police of the Metropolis* [2013] EWHC 32 (QB), [2013] 1 WLR 2734, [63].
[32] Ibid, [65].

of the book is not comprehensive and that there is further work to be done in this vein. We hope, however, that this book will stimulate further discourse within both the academic and judicial community, and we offer the book in the hope that, while it does not amount to an exhaustive evaluation of the whole rights frame-work, it will provide insight into the nature of common law constitutional rights and the values that they seek to protect.

II. Themes

It will be apparent from what has already been said that an underlying premise of this book is that the issues raised by the subject of common law constitutional rights are many and cross-cutting. Correspondingly, a rich variety of themes arise from and are explored in the contributions to this volume. Inevitably, such themes can be extracted and understood in different ways, and readers will form their own views about what the critical themes are, about the relationships with one another, and about their relative importance. In what follows, however, we offer some thoughts on what appear to us to be the key themes to emerge from the essays found in subsequent chapters, and the agendas that they set for further scholarship in this field.

A. The Catholicity of Common Law Constitutional Rights

We have already noted that it is a mistake to suppose that common law constitu-tional rights can fruitfully be understood or interrogated as an undifferentiated mass. This is not, of course, to deny that such rights lack sufficient commonality to warrant regarding them as a meaningful category. But the examination of clus-ters of rights in the first part of the book, sheds light on the offerings, potential and limitations of existing common law rights, demonstrating that not all of the rights falling under the common law constitutional umbrella have been developed, employed and entrenched to the same extent. This underlines the importance of approaching common law constitutional rights with due sensitivity to the catholic-ity of that broad category, and requires us to confront the extent to which, properly understood, such rights differ from or resemble human rights as they are other-wise conceived. After all, understood in spheres other than the common law, it is uncontroversial and widely acknowledged that human rights have developed as different categories of rights with varying kinds of obligations from negative to positive, and diverging degrees of enforcement from absolute rights to aspirational rights. Of course, such understandings of human rights are, taken at face value, crude, and have long invited criticism for (among other things) their arbitrary and politically determined distinctions. Nevertheless, general recognition of the differentiated nature of human rights stands in stark contrast to the tendency to regard common law constitutional rights in more homogenous terms. Against this background, one of the key points to emerge from the chapters in the first part of this book, in which clusters of rights are examined, is the high degree of variation that is apparent in terms of both the degree to which different rights are acknowledged at common law and the extent to and the ways in which they are liable to be upheld judicially. It is, for instance, noteworthy that even rights that are often identified as the best established at common law – such as freedom of expression, access to court and the right to property – are subject to significant limitations, while other significant rights that are generally clearly acknowledged in Bills or Treaties of rights – such as privacy and voting rights – remain largely absent at common law. Meanwhile, the degree of protection offered to rights that are acknowledged differs in ways and to degrees that in many respects render common law rights a *more* differentiated category than human rights generally, particularly rigorous judicial safeguarding of (some aspects of) the right of access to justice being a case in point.

B. Negative and Positive Rights

As noted above, the catholicity of common law constitutional rights counteracts a tendency to address common law constitutional rights as a homogenous category. It is nevertheless clear throughout the rights-focused chapters offered by this book that, in stark contrast to human rights, which have been developed as different categories of rights with varying kinds of obligations from negative to positive, the common law falls far short of the HRA/ECHR when it comes to positive obligations. Indeed, most of the chapters highlight the fundamental role of the distinction between negative restrictions on state powers and positive duties as a core feature that continues to shackle the development of common law rights.

C. The Role of Common Law Constitutional Rights in the Face of Constitutional Uncertainty

This interest in the differences between the two systems and the potential of the common law is particularly pertinent in the face of the possibility of repeal of the HRA and withdrawal from the ECHR. Certainly the prospect of a loss of such rights would explain a desire to embed in the common law a set of rights and values that could withstand this change. The content of those rights and the role that such rights would play in the UK's constitutional framework would therefore be a question of paramount importance. Fundamental to such discourse is not only a consideration of whether those in the UK would continue to enjoy the same rights that they had under the HRA, but also whether common law rights have the capacity to withstand change.

The chapters that form the first part of this book indicate that as things stand, whilst there may be some overlap between the common law and ECHR/HRA rights, it is highly doubtful that the full content of the rights protected by the HRA would be found within the common law if the HRA were to be repealed. Moreover, in looking to the potential to develop further rights in that environment such a move would be likely to run counter to Parliament's presumed intent in the event that it had repealed human rights legislation. The book thus looks at the role of common law constitutional rights in the UK's constitutional framework and their capacity to withstand political change. In that regard, a further form of uncertainty must be negotiated when the potential of common law constitutional rights is assessed – namely, their legal security in the light of the doctrine of parliamentary sovereignty. As many of the chapters acknowledge, this takes us into deep constitutional waters by raising questions about nature and extent of Parliament's authority with respect to the limitation of rights. Taken in combination, these various forms of uncertainty – respectively concerning the possibility of HRA repeal and legislation that conflicts with common law rights – coalesce into a single, overarching issue concerning the extent to which fundamental rights are an embedded feature of the UK constitution as distinct from an aspect of it that is ultimately subject to legislative control.

D. Common Law Constitutional Rights and the Role of Judicial Preference

A further and related issue is whether common law constitutional rights are more subject to judicial preferences than the rights protected under the HRA. Whilst the rights protected under that Act come with a semi-defined set of obligations and roles for the judiciary – given the textual starting-point afforded by the ECHR and the substantial body of jurisprudence of the Strasbourg Court – common law constitutional rights in theory have the potential for far greater radical or conservative interpretation. That is so in part because, in many respects, they are far less developed – including in terms of precedent – than Convention rights, and in part because the absence of any textual framework would suggest that the judiciary begins with a freer hand. This potential, however, has to be considered alongside the evidence of traditional restraint on the part of our judiciary provided by the chapters offered in the first part of this book as well as the considerable scope and open-textured nature that is afforded to the ECHR rights by the living instrument approach.

The evolution of common law rights it thus likely to be highly dependent upon judicial perceptions of the relationship between the Judiciary, Parliament and the Executive. Bearing in mind their differing views as to the proper remit of judicial decision-making, it seems implausible that members of the Supreme Court will develop a united view on the extent and role of such rights. The different judicial philosophies on display in *Nicklinson* amply attest to this.[33] Such judicial philosophies are likely to affect the sources that judges turn to in contemplating

---

[33] [2014] UKSC 38; [2014] 3 WLR 200.

common law rights, the extent to which they focus on historic domestic precedent, look to other common law systems, use international law sources, or engage in deeper normative analysis of the conceptual underpinnings of rights. The composition of judicial views and approaches to the judicial task is thus likely to determine whether a more radical or conservative approach will prevail in the longer term, and thus ultimately whether common law constitutional rights develop into an effective and expansive means of protecting rights or whether they are destined to remain – as they are at least in part at present – a relatively rhetorical device with limited practical bite.

In addition to differences of judicial philosophy at apex court level, it is also worth considering the extent to which differences may emerge in other judicial tiers. Whilst the HRA provides an explicit statutory remit for the High Court and the Court of Appeal – which, along with the Supreme Court, are permitted to issue declarations of incompatibility[34] – it is less clear that common law constitutional rights will be developed and applied with the same vigour by these courts. Are such arguments likely to be advanced by counsel, and accepted by judges, or will they – at least at the formative stage – be largely the preserve of the Supreme Court? What will this mean for litigation and the development and enforcement of these rights? The historical reflections on the use of common law constitutional rights by judges in the pre-HRA era offered in subsequent chapters aid in informing this debate.

E. Common Law Rights in Relationship with Convention Rights

Thus far the role of common law constitutional rights have been considered from the perspective of their function in a post-HRA era. However, regardless of whether repeal becomes a reality there is a sense that common law rights have a continuing role to play in the UK's constitutional framework; this is evident in Lord Neuberger's reference, noted earlier, to 'two separate seams' of judicial decision-making in the rights context.[35] Thus it is important to consider the relationship between these two conceptions of rights and the extent to which they undermine or support each other. Whilst Supreme Court judges have called for a renewed focus on the primary role of the common law, many contributors to this book conclude that those calls have not been universally heeded in the context of all rights. There are some cases in which matters are primarily or even exclusively litigated through the HRA and others in which the common law is more dominant. Moreover, some common law developments derive from the HRA rights, for

---

[34] HRA, s 2(5).

[35] Neuberger, 'The role of judges in human rights jurisprudence: a comparison of the Australian and UK experience' (n 12).

example the evolution of the law of misuse of private information and the possible recognition of a common law right to informational privacy. Meanwhile, other cases such as *Kennedy*[36] pull in different directions, on the one hand suggesting that the courts will use the common law to provide a further mode of protection, on the other suggesting that common law rights may not necessarily result in greater, or indeed any real judicial enforcement of citizens' interests and may in fact undercut the protection afforded under the statutory scheme. The flexibility that this affords means that the relationship between the two systems is relatively undefined. It is, however, possible to imagine scenarios in which a renewed focus on the common law could lead to the two rights' frameworks pulling in opposite directions, particularly in cases involving conflicts of rights where the scope and or weight accorded to one right under the common law may differ from that afforded by the ECHR/HRA. In other words, the more that common law rights are articulated, the more likely it is that any differences with the ECHR/HRA rights will need to be confronted.

This possibility was recognised by Lord Reed in *A v BBC* where he noted that 'although the Convention and our domestic law give expression to common values, the balance between those values, when they conflict, may not always be struck in the same place under the Convention as it might once have been under our domestic law'.[37] He suggested that in those situations 'effect must be given to the Convention rights in accordance with the Human Rights Act'.[38] That view is in line with the notion that parliamentary sovereignty is the ultimate constitutional principle, such that in the event of tension between the common law and HRA regimes, it is the latter, which exists in the form of legislation enacted by Parliament, that must prevail. However, the picture changes if, as some of the chapters in this book contemplate, common law constitutional rights are embedded in the constitutional framework to an extent that challenges orthodox accounts of parliamentary sovereignty.

F. Empirical Inquiry v Potential

This book considers the empirical track record of common law rights alongside theoretical accounts of the potential of common law constitutional rights. To date, a good deal of the debate regarding common law constitutional rights has focused on analysing what the common law actually does in terms of recognising and protecting rights emphasising the common law's poor historical track record in this regard.[39] Clearly, there is great merit in examining the law

---

[36] *Kennedy* (n 2).
[37] *A v BBC* [2014] UKSC 25, [2015] AC 588, [57].
[38] Ibid, [57].
[39] See, eg, C Gearty, *On Fantasy Island: Britain, Europe and Human Rights* (Oxford, Oxford University Press, 2016).

as it is, and in thus engaging in a form of empirical inquiry about common law constitutional rights. Indeed, precisely such an inquiry forms part of the focus of the chapters that make up the first part of this book. However, others argue that the potential of the common law should not be judged principally – or perhaps even at all – by reference to the current state of jurisprudence in this area. On this view, the potential of the common law is to be judged not by what has been achieved but by reference to the underlying principles that animate common law rights jurisprudence. This, in turn, raises fundamental questions about how the potential of the common law can be best assessed – and, in particular, about the extent to which such assessments should be informed by empirical analysis as distinct from being undertaken by reference to underpinning constitutional norms.

G. The Nature of Common Law Constitutional Rights – Principles, Values or Rights

This leads on to a further, and closely related, theme that emerges from the book. Whatever view one takes in respect of the matter canvassed in the previous paragraph – that is, whether the common law's potential in this area falls to be determined through principally empirical or principally normative analysis – it is difficult to argue against the proposition that common law constitutional rights exist in relationship with what might loosely be termed constitutional principles. It is, for instance, evident that at least some of the rights that enjoy particular prominence and especially rigorous protection at common law derive from or give effect to (the nature and direction of the relationship themselves being debatable) well-established constitutional principles. It is, for instance, surely no accident that the common law constitutional right of access to courts, which benefits from a particular high degree of judicial protection, sits in close relationship with aspects of the rule of law and the separation of powers that are well acknowledged as normative facets of the UK's constitutional arrangements. Indeed, this raises the further question as to whether common law constitutional rights are in fact 'rights' at all or whether they are instead 'values' or 'principles', or whether some are rights whilst others are values or principles. This raises important questions, which are explored throughout this book, about whether common law constitutional rights are likely to 'succeed', in the sense of securing clear recognition and strong protection of the interests of individuals, or whether they are destined to remain anchored to and thus limited to the protection of constitutional structures and institutional relationships. Indeed, as noted above, where the common law protects such rights, the question arises: to what extent are such rights likely to be conferred a 'constitutional' status in the absence of ties to well-established constitutional institutional principles?

III. Structure of the Book

A. The Content of Common Law Constitutional Rights

The first part of the book consists of seven chapters each of which explores a cluster of rights. In Chapter 2 Natasa Mavronicola offers analysis of the protection afforded to bodily integrity. Although she identifies 'a vast landscape' of legal protection for bodily integrity within domestic law she cautions that there is a 'certain "mythology" surrounding the constitutional protection of bodily integrity' which belies 'the uncertainty and potential vulnerability of some of these rights, as well as the vulnerability of the bodies that stand to benefit from them'. Indeed following detailed analysis of the right to life and the right not to be subjected to torture or to inhuman or degrading treatment or punishment she concludes that both rights raise such serious concerns about the 'certainty, content, and normative force' of common law constitutional rights 'that there is little cause for complacency or reassurance in respect of the common law constitution's guarantee of rights to bodily integrity'.

Although the focus of Se-shauna Wheatle's analysis in Chapter 3 is the well-established common law constitutional right to access to justice she is also cautious about the nature of this right. Wheatle highlights the centrality of access to justice to the common law and the multiple roles that it plays: serving to ensure individual access to the legal process; operating as a gateway to development of common law rights; and as a tool of judicial self-defence. She suggests that through these roles it builds upon significant features of the 'constitutional structure of the state, including respect for the rule of law, judicial independence, accountability and good governance, and enforcement of individual rights and obligations'. She argues, however, that if access to justice is to truly flourish as a right we need to shift the normative focus from judicial empowerment to public empowerment. Although she identifies some signs of a shift towards this in the case law she also identifies a number of constraints on such a development including a 'failure to account for status-based restrictions on access to justice and the need for obligations on the state to take action to remove limitations on access'. In particular she suggests that both the division between negative and positive duties and the failure to attend to 'a broad range of bases of exclusion and disempowerment' continue to shackle the development of access to justice. Consequently it is evident from Wheatle's chapter that even in the context of what is arguably the most developed of all common law constitutional rights there is considerable need for further evolution and doubt as to the extent to which such developments will be forthcoming.

One of the most potent criticisms of the common law focuses upon the nature of the rights that judges elect to protect. Scholars have long lamented what they regard as the common law's fixation on property as opposed to other more fundamental rights.[40] However, Tom Allen suggests in Chapter 4 that whilst a right to property may seem 'relatively unimportant when set beside rights relating to liberty, freedom of expression and religion', history demonstrates that disputes over property can provoke serious political conflict. He thus explores whether there is a right to property under the common law constitution. He begins by considering whether Parliament acts on the basis that its powers are limited by a constitutional right to property, highlighting a long line of writers, including Grotius, Locke and Blackstone who have stated that there are constitutional limits on the sovereign power over private property. Yet Allen notes that to the extent that Parliament operates in this way, this may stem from political pragmatism rather than constitutional obligation. Indeed he concludes that although there is evidence that both Parliament and the courts recognise limits on state power over property, the picture is murky such that at best we 'say that there are practices that would be compatible with a right to property, should one be introduced'.

Conversely, in Chapter 5, Kirsty Hughes examines an area in which there has historically been no common law right – privacy. Whilst acknowledging the long-standing protection that the common law affords to the home, privilege and confidentiality and the more recent recognition of a common law right to informational privacy, Hughes argues that there is no indication of judicial appetite for the recognition of a broader common law constitutional right to privacy. In particular she highlights the continuing silence of the common law in Supreme Court privacy cases, including during the most recent judicial turn to common law rights, as well as a series of cases in which the European Court of Human Rights (ECtHR) has found privacy violations against the UK where domestic courts had previously found no violation or held that the right to privacy was inapplicable. Exploring the ways in which common law rights come into existence she offers potential means of developing a common law constitutional right or cluster of rights to privacy, advocating far greater normative engagement with the conceptual values underpinning the right. Ultimately, however, she concludes that even if we can overcome longstanding common law reluctance to recognise a right to privacy, it is highly likely that any such right would be far more restrictively interpreted and would carry less weight than the Convention right. She thus cautions against any assumption 'that without the HRA the common law would rise like a phoenix from the ashes to replace the Convention right'.

In Chapter 6, the focus shifts to expressive rights, including the right to vote and freedom of expression. Jake Rowbottom notes that as these rights form the core of a democratic society it might be assumed that they have a particular significance in the common law constitutional model. As Rowbottom notes, however, it is perhaps surprising then that the two rights have such vastly different histories and statuses in the common law. Whilst freedom of expression has long been offered the protection of the common law there remains 'considerable doubt and

---

[40] See, eg, Gearty (n 39).

debate about the extent to which the right to vote is protected under the common law (if at all). Rowbottom highlights the different ways in which the common law protects freedom of expression alongside the challenges associated with protecting the right to vote at common law. In a similar fashion to Wheatle's chapter on access to justice he highlights the important role of the distinction between negative restrictions on state powers and positive duties as a core factor in shaping the development of the common law rights, including both the limitations on freedom of expression and the reluctance to recognise the right to vote. As to the former, his examination of the case law reveals that despite its prominence in the common law in practice 'the courts simply borrow from the ECHR jurisprudence' such that whilst 'freedom of speech is one of the most well established common law rights, its historical foundation is more precarious than sometimes acknowledged and its content less than certain'.

In Chapter 7 Gavin Phillipson explores rights connected to freedom of association and assembly. In examining the impact of the common law he proposes a taxonomy by which the role played by the common law in relation to fundamental rights in any particular case may be analysed and classified. Applying this to assembly and association he argues that 'the differences between the two regimes (common law and ECHR) are so profound that loss of HRA-ECHR protection would amount to a radical diminution in the potential for their judicial protection'. Similar to Hughes's analysis of privacy his analysis of association and assembly reveals that in many cases the common law remains completely silent on these rights. A further problem that emerges in this context is the role of the common law in 'undercut[ting] – or deny[ing] access to – the protection provided by statute'. Like Wheatle and Rowbottom he suggests that this is partly attributable to a failure to develop the common law beyond a mere negative liberties model. Moreover, like Mavronicola and Hughes he concludes that the common law comes nowhere close to offering either the range nor depth of protection offered by the ECHR. Indeed he suggests that to even 'speak of its possible *resilience* against incursion would be premature' as 'the rights themselves must first start to take real shape in the common law' a prospect that he regards as very far away.

In Chapter 8, the final chapter in the first part of the book, Colm O'Cinneide examines equality. He argues that although equality has 'acquired a much more tangible status within UK public law, and is now generally acknowledged to be an important constitutional value' a closer examination reveals that it is 'qualified in significant ways'. He highlights the inclination to regard it as a mere consideration to be subsumed within rationality and a reluctance to recognise either equality as a free-standing ground of review or non-discrimination as a free-standing right. Consequently he notes that at best both equality and non-discrimination are the subject of indirect protection through the common law and that neither are currently addressed adequately through rationality. In a similar fashion to Wheatle's analysis of access to justice and Hughes's analysis of the right to privacy, O'Cinneide argues that if the courts are to develop the common law there needs to be far greater engagement with the underlying concept, in his case more 'equality' than there has been to date. In developing this he suggests that 'different types of differential treatment should attract different standards of review – depending on the extent to which equality of status is undermined by the type of treatment under review'.

Throughout the first part of the book it is thus evident time and time again that there are significant limitations to the way that common law constitutional rights have functioned in the past and the way that they operate today. There are some rights that have not been recognised or developed in the common law at all, whilst even the most well established of the common law rights' constitutional rights are revealed to be highly limited in some respects. The overall picture that emerges from this collection of essays is of a patchy and limited framework for rights protection.

B. The Role and Potential of Common Law Constitutional Rights

The second part of the book offers a number of lenses through which to examine overarching issues concerning the role and potential of common law constitutional rights. It is thus concerned not with whether the common law does or does not recognise a particular right, but with more cross-cutting issues concerning the potential of the common law – and, more generally, of the UK's particular constitutional system – to afford meaningful protection to common law rights.

In Chapter 9 Mark Elliott considers the extent to which common law rights in the UK can meaningfully be said to enjoy the status of 'fundamental' rights. In doing so, he considers what it means for rights to have such a legal status and to what extent rights may properly be said to be 'fundamental' in a system in which the legislature's authority is legally unbounded. Elliott uses three sets of distinctions in order to explore this question. First, he distinguishes between 'theoretical' and 'operational' forms of fundamentality, noting that while there is judicial rhetoric to the effect that certain common law rights are immune from legislative infraction, the operational reality of judicial practice paints a rather different picture. Second, he contrasts 'hard' and 'soft' forms of fundamentality, arguing that even if common law rights in the UK do not operate as absolute trumps that are impervious to conflicting legislation, other, softer forms of protection should not readily be dismissed as insufficient to warrant the characterisation of common law rights as meaningfully fundamental. Third, Elliott distinguishes between the breadth of common law rights as a category and the depth of protection afforded to different rights, suggesting that the latter is a variable phenomenon, with the greater protection being afforded to an elite subset of common law rights.

Alison Young's chapter focuses on the relationship between common law constitutional rights and legislation, paying particular attention to the principle of legality. In Chapter 10, she addresses the constitutional underpinnings of that principle, noting that it is often understood by reference to a perceived tension between parliamentary sovereignty and the rule of law. Looked at in this way, Young notes, the potency of the principle of legality turns upon the relative weight that is ascribed to those two underlying constitutional principles. Young challenges this understanding of the principle of legality, offering in its place a more subtle account that views the capacity of the principle to protect a given right as a function of the context-sensitive interaction of democratic- and rule of law-based considerations. Building on this approach, Young goes on to argue that it is necessary to disaggregate accounts of the principle of legality, on the one hand, and the possibility of the disapplication of legislation, on the other. In advocating this distinction, she argues that it is necessary further to distinguish between common law constitutional rights that are concerned with human rights and civil liberties, and those that are concerned with foundational matters such as establishing and maintaining the distinct constitutional roles of different institutions of government. Young concludes that the interpretive protection of human rights and civil liberties is the domain of the principle of legality, while the possibility of disapplication of legislation arises in relation to the preservation of the very foundations of the constitution.

The focus then shifts from legislative to executive action in Chapter 11. In examining the relationship between common law constitutional rights and judicial review of executive action, Joanna Bell addresses three key issues that arise from the very notion of 'common law constitutional rights'. First, she asks the extent to which judicial review can, in the first place, properly be regarded as an exercise in developing the common law, noting that legal adjudication in this field is deeply pluralistic, the common law being one, but only one, of several layers of legal norms that often fall to be navigated in judicial review cases. Second, Bell considers the extent to which judicial review is concerned with the protection of rights, concluding that while common law constitutional rights are an important part of the picture, they can be regarded as no more than that. Finally, she examines two distinct but closely related questions: namely, whether judicial review or any of the grounds of judicial review can properly be regarded as 'constitutional'. Here, she notes that the position is both complex and ambiguous: on a specific level, it seems clear that Parliament is capable, through sufficiently specific provision, of displacing at least some grounds of judicial review. Meanwhile, although at an overarching level, dicta can be pointed to that suggest that the common law affords strong protection to judicial review as a broader phenomenon, Bell notes that the significance of such dicta is uncertain given their ultimately untested nature.

Chapter 12 concerns the extent to which the concept of common law constitutional rights is a viable one viewed from the perspective of the devolved levels of the UK constitution. Brice Dickson's assessment of this matter is largely in the negative. His ultimate conclusion – reached on the basis of a detailed assessment of relevant jurisprudence in relation to Northern Ireland, Scotland and Wales – is that while common law constitutional rights bear upon devolved institutions to the extent that they can be considered to be 'baked into' the devolution settlements as general limits on competence, there is little evidence to support the proposition that any locally specific common law constitutional rights operate within the UK's three devolved territories. Nevertheless, Dickson considers that there may be two exceptions to this general point. First, drawing on the *AXA* case, he argues that legislation proposed or enacted by a devolved legislature may be open to challenge on the ground that it is contrary to a common law constitutional right that is a relevant aspect of the rule of law. Dickson treats this as a phenomenon that would be specific to the devolved jurisdictions on account of the fact that there is no clear authority to the effect that common law constitutional rights can operate equivalently upon the UK Parliament. This, then, is not a case of distinct *rights* taking effect in devolved territories, but of rights being *applicable* in devolved contexts in a way that differs from their applicability at a UK level. Second, Dickson canvasses the possibility of a common law constitutional right vesting in those who live in the devolved regions that might be breached if the UK Parliament were to legislate in a way that compromised the permanency of the devolved institutions. In this way, argues Dickson, the common law may supplement – and even overshadow – the merely declaratory statements as to the permanence of devolved institutions found in the relevant legislation.[41]

All of the case studies offered in the first part of the book consider the current offerings of common law constitutional rights and the prospect of depending upon such rights, often sounding notes of caution about the latter bearing in mind the limitations of the former. However, in the final chapter, Chapter 13, a different perspective is adopted. Thomas Fairclough offers an alternative, more optimistic vision of common law constitutional rights. He argues that an empirical approach to questions about common law constitutional rights is flawed because it 'ignores the dynamic, principle-orientated approach that the common law should and does take'. He goes on to say that 'the principles underlying rights that have already been explicitly recognised can equally account for other rights'. This leads him to conclude that that there is considerable *potential* for the development of common law constitutional rights, and to argue that the limited progress that the common law has actually made to date should not be understood to be determinative of what the common law is capable of in this regard. Indeed, contrary to the views expressed in the first part of the book, he suggests that when we examine the common law from a rule of law perspective 'there is little to choose between' the common law and HRA models, such that 'repeal of the HRA would not fundamentally narrow the range of human rights available in the domestic legal system'.

IV. Concluding Remarks

We began our introductory chapter by noting that plans for this book were first made in the wake of a series of UK Supreme Court judgments that reinvigorated

---

[41] Scotland Act 1998, s 63A; Government of Wales Act 2006, s A1.

the notion of common law constitutional rights after a period when the HRA, following its enactment, had very much occupied the centre stage. The return of the common law to the limelight reignited debate in this area, encouraging reflection on both where the common law presently stands and on what its potential might be – questions whose relationship is, as we have just seen, open to discussion. But it is not only jurisprudence, whether from the Supreme Court or elsewhere, that renders the question of common law constitutional rights such a live issue today. In the early to mid-2010s, when this book was conceived, the political environment in the UK was radically different in some respects from that which exists today. It was certainly not the case then that the UK constitution was a paragon of stability: the issue of Scottish independence was very much on the agenda, and the prospect of the repeal of the HRA was a very real one. In such circumstances, reflection upon what (if anything) exists at the level of constitutional bedrock – of what is inherent and innate, and so perhaps immune or at least resistant to the winds of political change and legislative intervention – is both inevitable and necessary. One of the hallmarks of the British constitution is often considered to be the fact that so much is 'up for grabs', and thus vulnerable to alternation or evisceration by whoever is capable, at any given time, of commanding the confidence of the House of Commons and thus the critical constitutional lever afforded by the principle of parliamentary sovereignty.

Five or more years later, the constitutional picture has in some respects changed almost beyond recognition – and yet, in some senses at least, the position remains a familiar one. The picture has changed, of course, principally as a result of the Brexit referendum in 2016 and the period of political instability and constitutional uncertainty that the outcome of that plebiscite precipitated. The degrees of instability and uncertainty that have been experienced since 2016 undeniably eclipse – perhaps by several orders of magnitude – the ramifications of the debate in the mid-2010s concerning the possibility of repealing the HRA. However, in at least three respects, the debates concerning Brexit and the future of the HRA – and thus the potential of common law rights – exhibit notable parallels.

The first, that each concerns the UK's fraught relationship with 'Europe', is obvious but nevertheless important: among other things, it goes to fundamental questions about the extent to which the UK legal, constitutional and political orders are receptive to influences from elsewhere. Against this background, it is relevant that one of the principal driving forces in the debate about the HRA has been the perceived 'otherness' of the ECHR rights to which that legislation gives domestic effect, a phenomenon that perhaps reached its zenith – or, depending on one's perspective, nadir – in proposals for a 'British Bill of Rights'.[42] That this has been one of the underpinnings of the debate is potentially significant. On the one hand, it suggests that if there is substantial alignment between the ECHR and common law rights, the practical effect of HRA repeal and/or ECHR withdrawal

---

[42] Commission on a Bill of Rights, *A UK Bill of Rights? The Choice Before Us* (2012).

would be relatively small, and that those who favour judicial protection of fundamental rights could meet such a prospect with relative equanimity. On the other
hand, if there are in fact significant differences between the respective capacities
of the common law and the HRA/ECHR to protect rights, the debate concerning repeal/withdrawal assumes an altogether more critical character. Either way,
however, it is imperative that the debate takes place on the basis of an accurate
understanding of the similarities and differences between the two systems.

The debate about the future of human rights protection in the UK echoes the
broader debate about Britain's relationship with Europe in a second important
respect. This is not to suggest that ECHR rights have a status or effect in domestic
law that precisely mirrors the domestic status that the European Communities
Act 1972 accorded to EU law. Most significantly, the HRA explicitly denies UK
judges any power to disapply Acts of Parliament that are incompatible with
Convention rights. Nevertheless, the HRA gives effect in domestic law to a set
of rights that are anchored in an international legal framework that is binding
upon the UK as a state. Against this background, it is often difficult, when analysing criticism of the HRA system, to disentangle dissatisfaction with the perceived
'otherness' of the ECHR rights, which we noted in the previous paragraph, from
unhappiness with the fact that such rights are ultimately vouchsafed by an international legal framework that declines to bend its knee to the domestic notion of
legislative supremacy. To put the matter more provocatively, it is not always easy to
determine whether criticism of the HRA – and of the ECHR framework to which
the HRA gives certain domestic effects – is animated by concern about the domestic imposition of (what are perceived to be) foreign values, or whether the true
objection is to the judicial curation of legal norms that, as a matter of international
law, do not yield to the will of Parliament. Be that as it may, unease in the human
rights context is undoubtedly attributable, at least in part, to the UK's international
ECHR obligations, just as unease, at least in some quarters, about EU membership
has been driven partly by concern about the capacity of EU law to take precedence
over domestic legislation, parliamentary sovereignty notwithstanding. In this way,
an important element of the debate about 'Europe' is in fact a debate about the
extent to which it is normatively desirable or acceptable to embrace ways of doing
things that sit in tension with the notion that the UK Parliament has unlimited
legislative authority.

Once again, however, it is crucial for this debate to take place on the basis of
an accurate understanding of the reality of the UK's innate constitutional arrangements. Viewed in simplistic terms, arguments about what might be termed the
de-Europeanisation of the UK's legal and constitutional order may appear to offer
the possibility of swapping rule by foreign judicatures for rule by domestic politicians (and, in particular, legislators) freed from the shackles of binding international
legal norms. But this narrative presupposes a particular view of the common law
constitution – and of the place within it of common law rights – that is, at the very
least, both contestable and contested. If the debate about de-Europeanising UK
human rights law is to be a meaningful one, an accurate appreciation of that which

is inherent within the domestic constitutional order is imperative: and, as more than one contribution to this book attests, it is at least arguable that the common law constitution does not afford legislators the blank canvas of Eurosceptics' and of rights-sceptics' dreams.

This all leads on to a third, and overarching, point: namely, that the debate about the merits or otherwise of HRA repeal and/or ECHR withdrawal, like the broader debate about the UK's relationship with 'Europe', is (or ought to be) as much about what would remain if such European influences were stripped away as it is about the nature and implications of those influences to begin with. As far as the topic of human rights is concerned, the possibility of ridding the UK legal system of such European influences necessarily invites – indeed, demands – reflection upon what is inherent within the domestic constitutional order. It follows that, as the UK stands at a crossroads in terms of its relationships with the European legal orders, it is necessary critically and carefully to examine the innate capacity – and limitations – of the UK constitution itself.

That task can, and ought to be, undertaken in a variety of ways. Attentiveness to the track-record of the common law must necessarily be part of the analysis, alongside consideration of whatever might be its as yet unrealised potential. Examination of extant jurisprudence is clearly imperative, but so too is analysis of the framework of constitutional theory within which that jurisprudence sits and which will shape the trajectory of the courts' curation of common law rights into the future. And it is essential that relevant matters are considered at both the micro- and macro-levels: thus, while it is necessary to interrogate the common law's achievements and potential in respect of specific rights, it is equally necessary to appreciate the opportunities and the limitations that arise from the UK's unusual constitutional architecture. Reflection on such matters serves an obviously practical purpose if, as it may well be in the foreseeable future, the common law's capacity to go it alone in this sphere is ever tested. But in fact reflection on such matters also serves a deeper, if less immediately practical, objective, for it requires us to confront questions about the essence of the British constitution: questions about what would be left were potentially transitory legislative frameworks and institutional schemes to fall away. Thus it is hoped that, by subjecting the notion of common law constitutional rights to critical scrutiny, this book contributes not only to our understanding of what the common law might be capable of in this sphere, but also to our understanding of the nature of the constitutional order of which such rights are an integral part.

PART I

The Content of Common Law
Constitutional Rights

2

The Mythology and the Reality of Common Law Constitutional Rights to Bodily Integrity

NATASA MAVRONICOLA

I. Introduction

Bodily integrity may be best understood by recognising the body as the 'point of integration of the subject and the objective world'.[1] Our legal understanding of bodily integrity, and of impermissible infractions thereon, tends to take shape in light of this duality, and is preoccupied therefore not just with corporeal 'encounters', but with whether they occur in a way which is fundamentally respectful of the subject. Rights of bodily integrity are understood chiefly as protecting persons' exclusive use and control over their body and casting interferences with one's body as illegitimate where they are unwanted or otherwise improper.[2] As Jonathan Herring and Jesse Wall have argued, '[i]t is because the body is where we experience states of well-being, it is the way in which we flourish as humans, it is the medium through which we interact with others, and it is the way in which we execute our agency, that we have such a broad and all-encompassing right over our own bodies'.[3]

With this starting point, we come upon a vast landscape of legal protections of bodily integrity within the UK, provided through common law and statute, protections whose scope, implications and interconnections are intricate and multi-faceted. These protections encompass duties on state agents and private individuals to respect bodily integrity by refraining from unwanted interference with a person's body in most (but not all) circumstances, duties 'whose transgression

---

[1] J Herring and J Wall, 'The Nature and Significance of the Right to Bodily Integrity' (2017) 76 *CLJ* 566, 581.

[2] D Feldman, *Civil Liberties and Human Rights in England and Wales*, 2nd edn (Oxford, Oxford University Press, 2002), 241.

[3] Herring and Wall (n 1) 580 (citations omitted).

generates a distinctive range of responses'.[4] They also encompass positive obligations on the state to take measures to protect persons' bodily integrity in various ways, including through legislative and operational measures.

Looking at the European Convention on Human Rights (ECHR), we find many relevant rights, including the right to life (Article 2), the right not to be subjected to torture or inhuman or degrading treatment or punishment (Article 3), the prohibition of slavery and forced labour (Article 4), the right to liberty (Article 5), and the right to private life (Article 8).[5] These provisions, particularly Articles 2, 3, 5 and 8,[6] have been the subject of rich jurisprudential output by the European Court of Human Rights (ECtHR). They vary in content and character, but invariably make demands not only of non-interference but also of active legal and operational protection, and have had a substantial impact in domestic jurisprudence over the years since the enactment of the Human Rights Act 1998 (HRA).[7]

In this chapter, I consider how far the common law can be taken to safeguard rights relating to bodily integrity as constitutional rights, and the extent to which the protection of rights to bodily integrity in the UK is imperilled by the prospect of repeal of the HRA and a withdrawal from the ECHR. I find that, while the centrality of bodily integrity to the UK constitution has been lauded, it is difficult, out of the vast domestic common law and legislative landscape, to delineate (common law) *constitutional* rights to bodily integrity. This stems in no small part from the elusive distinction between (common law) constitutional rights of bodily integrity and more transient or vulnerable legal protections, and is compounded by the fact that the protection of bodily integrity is specifically legislated for in many concrete settings, such as the regulation of the use of force by law enforcement agencies[8] and the criminalisation of violent offences.[9] Ultimately, I argue that the 'mythology' surrounding the constitutional protection of bodily integrity is belied by the uncertainty and potential vulnerability of some of these rights,[10] as well as the vulnerability of the bodies that stand to benefit from them. While the evaluative endeavour undertaken must be tempered by a sense of its speculative quality and a recognition of the 'necessarily obfuscatory effect' of the HRA's

---

[4] Ibid, 584.

[5] Herring and Wall tie 'bodily integrity' to a narrower set of rights, notably Art 3 and Art 8 ECHR: Herring and Wall (n 1) 574–575.

[6] For an excellent overview of the more limited but growing case law under Art 4 ECHR, see V Stoyanova, *Human Trafficking and Slavery Reconsidered. Conceptual Limits and States' Positive Obligations* (Cambridge, Cambridge University Press, 2017).

[7] See, eg, B Dickson, *Human Rights in the UK Supreme Court* (Oxford, Oxford University Press, 2013) chs 4, 5, 6, 8.

[8] See, eg, Criminal Law Act 1967, s 3, Police and Criminal Evidence Act 1984, s 117, and Criminal Justice and Immigration Act 2008, s 76(7).

[9] See, eg, the Offences against the Person Act 1861.

[10] Brendan Lim describes as 'vulnerable' those rights 'which the ordinary political process may be inapt to protect': B Lim, 'The Normativity of the Principle of Legality' (2013) 37 *Melbourne University Law Review* 372, 395.

enduring presence,[11] the chapter concludes with the pessimistic view that there is little cause for complacency or reassurance in respect of the common law constitution's guarantee of rights to bodily integrity. Lastly, I suggest, looking ahead, that the demands of the specification of rights of bodily integrity militate against insularity in judicial reasoning.

In view of space constraints, the analysis and argument in this chapter concentrates on the right to life and the right not to be subjected to torture or to inhuman or degrading treatment or punishment, and is focused on issues of certainty, content, and normative force in the protection of these rights within the common law constitution.

II. Conceptual Starting Points: Rights as Distinct from Values

Mark Elliott has rightly cautioned against conflating rights, which constitute legally enforceable entitlements, with values, which are altogether more fluid in substance and function.[12] He has argued that:

> It is true that the Convention embodies rights that amount to specific manifestations of values that, at some level of abstraction, are reflected in the English common law tradition. However, it does not follow from this that the common law did, or does, contain a catalogue of rights that equates to the body of rights found in the Convention.[13]

Alan Gewirth, writing on absolute rights, highlighted that meaningful absolute rights operate in the intermediate space between highly abstract principle and individualised concrete findings. He referred to this space as 'rule absolutism' – where a 'specific rule can be stated describing the content of the right and the correlative duty'.[14] His insight is important in conveying that loose allusions to ideas such as human dignity or even to rights to bodily integrity offer little if they do not go some way towards specifying the precise contours of the entitlement and its correlative duty or duties. Gewirth was referring to Wesley Hohfeld's model of claim-rights: entitlements to the performance of correlative duties, which the right-holder(s) can enforce against the duty-bearer(s).[15] The relevant duties may be negative, amounting to duties to refrain from a particular act, or positive, requiring particular action. On the other hand, values, or highly abstract conceptions of

---

[11] M Elliott, 'Beyond the European Convention: Human Rights and the Common Law' (2015) 68 *Current Legal Problems* 85, 95.

[12] Ibid, 89–90, 96.

[13] Ibid, 89.

[14] A Gewirth, 'Are There Any Absolute Rights?' (1981) 31 *Philosophical Quarterly* 1, 4.

[15] W Hohfeld, *Fundamental Legal Conceptions as Applied in Judicial Reasoning* (New Haven, Yale University Press, 1919).

'rights' which do not specify relevant duties, may inform adjudication in more fluid ways but only solidify into concrete entitlements in particular circumstances.[16]

The analysis below proceeds on the Hohfeldian understanding of claim-rights. While it is important to acknowledge that theorists and jurists may adopt the language of rights more loosely to identify important interests or values,[17] it is equally crucial to recognise that these looser invocations may not substantiate enforceable duties in the same manner that a Hohfeldian claim-right does.[18] As Gewirth highlighted, the idea of a right is meaningful where we can identify right-holders and duty-bearers, and the entitlement and correlative duty that are being claimed.[19] This is the terrain in which Hohfeldian claim-rights operate and it is within these parameters that we can speak of constitutionally protected common law rights: where one can effectively assert an entitlement to the performance of a correlative duty by public authorities. This approach to the concept of common law rights is particularly important in view of assertions that common law rights may provide equivalent protections to Convention rights, given that the latter are quintessential examples of Hohfeldian claim-rights.

III. The Ubiquity, and Fluidity, of Bodily Integrity Protections

From this conceptual starting point, we can locate a range of protections including claim-rights, often by observing their correlative duties, emerging out of a constellation of legal provisions and common law precedent protecting bodily integrity. These protections span various areas of law, and do not necessarily represent rights in the public law or human rights sense. Duties to refrain from certain behaviour often correspond with a right in tort law. For example, unwanted physical interference with someone is seen as tortious in principle, entitling the victim to damages under the common law.[20] Putting someone in fear of violence may constitute an assault and unwanted touching may constitute a battery in tort law, while the same acts may also amount to criminal offences. The consent of the person whose bodily integrity is at stake generally vitiates the act's wrongfulness, in view of the significance of the will of the subject in delineating bodily integrity. The legitimation of such interference can also occur through statutory provision, as is the case in

---

[16] Elliott (n 11) 96.

[17] J Varuhas, 'The Reformation of English Administrative Law? "Rights", Rhetoric and Reality' (2013) 72 *CLJ* 369, 396.

[18] Ibid, 396–413.

[19] Gewirth (n 14) 3–4.

[20] D Feldman, *Civil Liberties and Human Rights in England and Wales*, 2nd edn (Oxford, Oxford University Press, 2002) 241.

respect of the legally authorised deployment of coercive force by law enforcement officials.[21] The physical prevention of any person from moving or leaving any place can constitute false imprisonment, which under English law attracts substantial damages on account of the importance of safeguarding liberty.[22] To put the example of false imprisonment in a Hohfeldian claim-right perspective, in light of the conceptual starting points set out above, we might say (refining Jason Varuhas' formulation[23]) that X has a right that Y not confine her except in a limited range of legally ordained circumstances, while Y bears a corresponding duty to X not to confine her except in a limited range of legally ordained circumstances.[24]

There are, therefore, numerous claim-rights across various areas of law that we may consider to be protecting bodily integrity. Moreover, the ubiquity of bodily integrity entails that we can conceive of much of the law governing our physical interactions with one another and with the state as being infused with respect for the value of bodily integrity, or even governed by what some may abstractly conceive of as an overarching 'right to bodily integrity' – an abstract notion which operates at a level of generality that largely elides Hohfeld's claim-right category.

On the other hand, the concrete implications, in terms of *constitutionally* protected Hohfeldian claim-rights, of the various legal protections available and of the pervasive significance of bodily integrity are debateable. While the constellation of legal safeguards that protect bodily integrity is vast and rich, 'there is little guidance on the content or nature of the right'.[25] The issues of 'content' and 'nature' are interrelated: even if we may be able to enumerate all the specific instantiations of the legal protection of bodily integrity, what is crucial for our purposes is that the line between the more robust (common law) constitutional right(s) to bodily integrity and more transient legal protections is elusive; and vague references to bodily integrity's significance do not necessarily amount to the recognition of *concrete* (common law) constitutional *claim*-rights. Insofar as we seek to speak of a (common law) constitutional right to bodily integrity, therefore, 'it is far from clear what the contours of the right are'.[26]

On occasion, the umbrella notion of a 'right to bodily integrity' is cited with concrete implications. For example, Lady Hale's view, albeit obiter and in a dissenting judgment, that 'the common law has always regarded the right to freedom

---

[21] Ibid. David Feldman cites the prime example of using force if necessary to make an arrest: see ss 24 and 116 of the Police and Criminal Evidence Act 1984.

[22] See J Varuhas, 'False Imprisonment of Prisoners: Lawful Authority, Omissions and Damages' (2010) 69 *CLJ* 438, 440.

[23] Varuhas (n 17) 398.

[24] See further J Varuhas, 'The Concept of "Vindication" in the Law of Torts: Rights, Interests and Damages' (2014) 34 *OJLS* 253, 264–265. On the remedy of habeas corpus, see M Tugendhat, *Liberty Intact: Human Rights in English Law* (Oxford, Oxford University Press, 2016) 91; see, too, *Belhaj v Straw* [2017] UKSC 3, [2017] 2 WLR 456, [272] (Lord Sumption).

[25] Herring and Wall (n 1) 575.

[26] Ibid, 575.

from physical coercion, sometimes referred to as the right to bodily integrity, as the most important of civil rights',[27] concretely entailed that a Parole Board decision on whether to order the claimant's re-release from prison engaged his civil rights and triggered a fair hearing under Article 6 ECHR.[28] Ultimately, however, this did not substantiate a precise entitlement but rather operated as a gateway to the application of Article 6 ECHR. This example therefore highlights an interplay between common law rights reasoning and Convention rights but does not specify the (common law) constitutional right(s) to bodily integrity in a way that takes us beyond the fluidity and open texture we may more readily ascribe to values.

This fluidity and uncertainty do not necessarily dissipate when we zoom in on more specific allusions to particular rights to bodily integrity. In the following sections, I explore how the – questionable – content and nature of (common law) constitutional rights to bodily integrity fare in relation to Convention rights, with a focus on the right to life and the right not to be subjected to torture or inhuman or degrading treatment or punishment. Consideration is given to issues of certainty, substance, and normative force.

IV. Comparing the Common Law and the Convention on the Right to Life and the Right not to be Subjected to Torture or Ill-Treatment[29]

The idea of a 'right to life' or specific duties associated with it has surfaced in common law precedent and has been included in the list of common law constitutional rights provided in *De Smith's Judicial Review*.[30] The 'right to life' was mentioned in pre-HRA case law such as *Bugdaycay*, where Lord Bridge, in assessing the determination of individuals' asylum applications in view of an alleged risk to life upon expulsion, indicated that 'the most fundamental of all human rights is the individual's right to life and when an administrative decision under challenge is said to be one which may put the applicant's life at risk, the basis of the decision must surely call for the most anxious scrutiny'.[31] Post-HRA, in *Amin*, which concerned the adequacy of investigative steps taken after the killing of Zahid Mubarek in prison by his racist cellmate, the duty at common law to investigate the

---

[27] *R (on the application of Justin West) v The Parole Board* [2002] EWCA Civ 1641, [2003] 1 WLR 705, [49] (Hale LJ in dissent).

[28] Ibid.

[29] The term 'ill-treatment' is employed here to signify cruel, inhuman or degrading treatment or punishment. Although the term 'cruel' is not included in Article 3 ECHR, it is found in other relevant domestic and international instruments.

[30] H Woolf et al, *De Smith's Judicial Review*, 7th edn (London, Sweet & Maxwell, 2013) 265. See also E Bjorge, 'Common Law Rights: Balancing Domestic and International Exigencies' (2016) 75 *CLJ* 220, 222.

[31] *R v Home Secretary, ex parte Bugdaycay* [1987] AC 514, 531 (Lord Bridge).

death of anyone who dies in prison was mentioned,[32] though the case was decided primarily with reference to the demands of Article 2 ECHR.[33]

In the 1995 case of *ex parte B*, a first instance judgment in favour of the provision of experimental medical treatment for a young girl suffering from non-Hodgkins lymphoma on the basis of a 'right to life' was overturned in the Court of Appeal, which opted not to frame the issue in terms of the right to life and referred instead to the value of life.[34] The difference between the approach at first instance and that adopted on appeal is instructive in terms of the distinction between upholding a right and asserting an underlying or overarching value. At the heart of Laws J's first instance judgment in *ex parte B* was the idea that certain rights protected both under the ECHR and within the common law, including the right to life, are 'not to be perceived merely as moral or political aspirations', but should be seen as conferring duties on public bodies not to infringe the right 'unless [they] can show a substantial objective justification on public interest grounds'.[35] He found that the Cambridge Health Authority had failed to show adequate justification for infringing the right to life, something he believed the court was tasked with assessing in order to vindicate the right. On the other hand, at the Court of Appeal, where what was taken to be at issue was the *value* of human life in the context of the medical treatment, rather than the infringement of the right to life in the denial of medical treatment, the public authority's decision was found to fall within its discretion in respect of the allocation of limited resources. The Court was not in a position to second-guess it. Sir Thomas Bingham MR, as he then was, put it thus: 'Difficult and agonising judgments have to be made as to how a limited budget is best allocated to the maximum advantage of the maximum number of patients. That is not a judgment which the court can make.'[36] The appellate judgment did not therefore proceed on an understanding that the authority was under a duty not to infringe the right to life by denying the relevant treatment, or to provide substantial objective justification, as assessed by the Court, for doing so. What was at stake, in the Court of Appeal's view, was a 'decision affecting human life', and while the Court of Appeal recognised that 'a very high value is put on human life',[37] this did not entail the close judicial scrutiny applied at first instance.

Today, while the right to life has been given the label of common law constitutional right by some, it is unclear to what extent this rhetoric is reflected in judicial practice, what content we can convincingly ascribe to this right, and what its demands are in particular situations. Indeed, as Brice Dickson has observed, there has been reluctance, particularly in the UK's apex court, to frame the protection of life as a common law constitutional right in key judgments,[38] with the UK's

---

[32] *R (Amin) v Secretary of State for the Home Department* [2004] 1 AC 653, [16] (Lord Bingham).
[33] Ibid, [18]–[38] (Lord Bingham), [40]–[48] (Lord Slynn), and [50]–[53] (Lord Steyn).
[34] *R v Cambridge DHA, ex parte B (No 1)* [1995] 1 WLR 898, 904 (Sir Bingham MR).
[35] *R v Cambridge Health Authority, ex parte B* [1995] 1 FLR 1055, 1060.
[36] *Ex parte B* (n 34) 906.
[37] Ibid, 905.
[38] Dickson (n 7) 101.

top judges generally tending to allude to the sanctity of life as a value or principle rather than to present the right to life as a legal entitlement.[39] In substantive terms, the application of Convention rights has taken the demands made of the state substantially beyond what was otherwise required under domestic common law and statute.[40] Dickson has suggested that the UK's top judges have preferred to 'work with traditional legal categories and to allow the European Court of Human Rights to take the lead on the right to life per se'.[41] It is possible that any impetus there may have been to grapple with the right to life at common law by the 1990s – with (relatively infrequent) invocations in domestic courts – was superseded by the advent of the HRA.

The right not to be subjected to torture or ill-treatment or, at least, the prohibition of torture, has been put forward as a central tenet of the common law,[42] though *De Smith* only cites the 'prohibition on the use of evidence obtained by torture'[43] rather than a broader prohibition of torture and ill-treatment. The landmark House of Lords judgment in *A (No 2)*[44] is cited in *De Smith* as the judgment underpinning the prohibition's status. *A (No 2)* concerned the consideration by the Special Immigration Appeals Commission (SIAC), in respect of the detention of terrorist suspects under the Anti-terrorism, Crime and Security Act 2001, of evidence obtained through torture in a foreign state without the proven involvement of the UK Government. The House of Lords found that evidence obtained by the torture of a suspect or witness could not lawfully be admitted into SIAC proceedings, irrespective of who had inflicted the torture. In making this finding, the Law Lords applied the principle of legality in respect of the exclusionary rule, to conclude that the SIAC's powers to consider a wide range of evidence did not include a power to admit evidence obtained by torture. In applying the principle of legality, Lord Bingham forcefully rejected what he considered to be the approach of lower courts, namely that 'this deeply-rooted tradition and an international obligation solemnly and explicitly undertaken can be overridden by a statute and a procedural rule which makes no mention of torture at all'.[45] Lord Carswell described the common law as a 'freshly growing fabric',[46] and reasoned:

> We have long ceased to give credence to the fiction that the common law consists of a number of pre-ordained rules which merely require discovery and judicial enunciation.

---

[39] Ibid, 108. See, in this regard, *R (Amin) v Secretary of State for the Home Department* [2004] 1 AC 653, [30] (Lord Bingham); see, too, the judgment of Hoffmann LJ, as he then was, in the Court of Appeal, and the judgment of Lord Keith in the House of Lords in *Airedale v Bland* [1993] 2 WLR 316; [1993] AC 789.

[40] Dickson (n 7) 101.

[41] Ibid.

[42] See, eg, Bjorge (n 30) 222.

[43] *De Smith* (n 30) 266.

[44] *A and others v Secretary of State for the Home Department (No 2)* [2005] UKHL 71, [2006] 2 AC 221.

[45] Ibid.

[46] Ibid, [152] (Lord Carswell), citing F Pollock, *Oxford Lectures and Other Discourses* (MacMillan 1890) at 111.

Two centuries ago Lord Kenyon recognised that in being formed from time to time by the wisdom of man it grew and increased from time to time with the wisdom of mankind … I am satisfied that, whether or not it has ever been affirmatively declared that the common law declines to allow the admission of evidence obtained by the use of torture, it is quite capable now of embracing such a rule. If that is any extension of the existing common law, it is a modest one, a necessary recognition of the conclusions which should be drawn from long established principles. I accordingly agree with your Lordships that such a rule should be declared to represent the common law.[47]

Lord Hope reasoned that the common law already cohered with Article 15 of the United Nations Convention against Torture (UNCAT), which contains the exclusionary rule:

I would hold that the formal incorporation of the evidential rule into domestic law was unnecessary, as the same result is reached by an application of common law principles. The rule laid down by article 15 was accepted by the United Kingdom because it was entirely compatible with our own law. The use of such evidence is excluded not on grounds of its unreliability-if that was the only objection to it, it would go to its weight, not to its admissibility-but on grounds of its barbarism, its illegality and its inhumanity. The law will not lend its support to the use of torture for any purpose whatever. It has no place in the defence of freedom and democracy, whose very existence depends on the denial of the use of such methods to the executive.[48]

Lord Bingham sought to show the embeddedness of the prohibition of torture within the common law, suggesting that 'the English common law has regarded torture and its fruits with abhorrence for over 500 years, and that abhorrence is shared by over 140 countries which have acceded to the Torture Convention'.[49] He characterised the condemnation of torture as a 'constitutional principle'.[50] Lord Nicholls similarly indicated that the common law had 'for centuries … set its face against torture'.[51]

The standard for proving that evidence was tainted by torture would be – according to the majority, with Lords Bingham, Nicholls and Hoffmann dissenting – the 'balance of probabilities', determined by such inquiry as practicable to carry out in the circumstances.[52] The Law Lords also found that the Secretary of State had not acted unlawfully in relying on such tainted material when certifying, arresting and detaining persons under the 2001 Act.[53]

The strong, quotable messages of *A (No 2)* cannot be taken, without more, to represent the recognition of a robust prohibition of torture (and other ill-treatment) at common law. While providing a 'template' for specifying claim-rights out of

---

[47] *A (No 2)* (n 44), [152] (Lord Carswell).
[48] Ibid, [112] (Lord Hope).
[49] Ibid, [51] (Lord Bingham).
[50] Ibid, [12] (Lord Bingham).
[51] Ibid, [64] (Lord Nicholls).
[52] Ibid, notably [116]–[121] (Lord Hope); cf [55]–[62] (Lord Bingham).
[53] See ibid, [47] (Lord Bingham).

the common law's fundamental commitments in their specification of a duty to refrain from using evidence obtained by torture, the apex court's findings are nonetheless characterised by both considerable uncertainty and substantive limitations. There is, to begin with, enduring uncertainty as to whether the judges were simply recognising or actively incorporating the exclusionary rule within the fabric of the common law. In addition, it cannot be disregarded that judges such as Lord Bingham did not rely solely on the common law, but sought reinforcements by citing the UK's commitment, alongside a substantial number of states, to the prohibition at international law. The notion that the common law so zealously safeguards the prohibition of torture is also blunted by the significant limitations in the judgment's substance, not least the qualified guarantees the judgment ultimately offers in respect of evidence obtained by torture. The executive's use of tainted evidence and resulting 'market' for the fruit of torture[54] is upheld, reinforcing the hollow purity of the common law, which 'boasts' that torture has traditionally been an instrument of state and not of law.[55] In addition to this, with the balance of probabilities test, the SIAC is invited, even if in doubt, to err on the side of using potentially tainted evidence: 'if SIAC is left in doubt as to whether the evidence was obtained in this way, it should admit it', as Lord Hope put it.[56] Furthermore, the judgment does not necessarily thwart the admissibility of real evidence discovered on the basis of statements obtained through torture – the 'fruit of the poisoned tree';[57] premised largely on the comparative reliability of real evidence over *statements* obtained through torture,[58] this casts a utilitarian shadow over the lofty principle conveyed. Lastly, the judgment's focus on *torture* leaves room for contemplating that inhuman or degrading treatment might bear distinct, lesser implications, and for the kind of tinkering with the threshold between torture and other ill-treatment that has particularly plagued the prohibition after 9/11.[59]

Other statements of principle in respect of the condemnation of torture have pushed towards positive outcomes by way of accountability and redress for torture, as was the case in *Pinochet (No 3)*,[60] which concerned the extradition to Spain of former dictator of Chile Augusto Pinochet Ugarte, and the recent extraordinary rendition case of *Belhaj v Straw*.[61] In *Belhaj*, the Supreme Court found that claims against UK officials for complicity in acts of torture overseas could proceed to

---

[54] Report submitted by the Special Rapporteur on torture and other cruel, inhuman or degrading treatment or punishment, Juan E Méndez, 3 February 2011, UN doc. A/HRC/16/52, para 53.

[55] E Black, 'Torture under English Law' (1927) 75 *University of Pennsylvania Law Review and American Law Register* 344, 344.

[56] *A (No 2)* (n 44), [118] (Lord Hope).

[57] But see the controversial approach taken on this issue in *Gäfgen v Germany* (2011) 52 EHRR 1.

[58] See, eg, *A (No 2)* (n 44), [88] (Lord Hoffmann).

[59] See, in relation to this, WB Wendel, 'The Torture Memos and the Demands of Legality' (2009) 12 *Legal Ethics* 107. See the interesting assessment of the significance of the distinction between torture and other ill-treatment in *Belhaj* (n 24), [280] (Lord Sumption).

[60] *R v Bow Street Metropolitan Stipendiary Magistrate and others, ex parte Pinochet Ugarte (No 3)* [2000] 1 AC 147, [1999] 2 WLR 827.

[61] *Belhaj* (n 24).

trial, dismissing the defendants' appeals to state immunity and the doctrine of foreign act of state. Lord Mance's dismissal of the latter in particular relied on the fact that 'torture has long been regarded as abhorrent by English law [citing *A (No 2)*] … and individuals are unquestionably entitled to be free of deliberate physical mistreatment while in the custody of state authorities'.[62] This militated against judicial abstention in the case at hand. Meanwhile Lord Sumption's reasoning, which relied on *jus cogens*, was buttressed by the conviction that 'English law's rejection of torture … is an essential feature of our constitutional order'.[63]

It is nonetheless hard to shake the sense that, in some of the strongest messages of the condemnation of torture and ill-treatment outlined above, such condemnation is orientated towards protecting the integrity of the law itself, rather than the integrity of the persons that stand to be ill-treated. The implications of this can be significant, as the misgivings shared above in relation to *A (No 2)* indicate. More broadly, allusions to the common law's condemnation of problematic practices and the sketched contours of a common law right to life and respect for the prohibition of torture and ill-treatment ultimately look thin in comparison to the wealth of principles and concrete findings that have emerged out of hundreds of ECtHR judgments on Article 2[64] and Article 3 ECHR,[65] building up a body of jurisprudence which has been treated widely as *res interpretata*.[66] Many key cases, involving significant findings and vital specification of the rights, concern the UK. Such cases include, in respect of Article 3 ECHR, the finding that life imprisonment must be reducible de jure and de facto in order to be compatible with Article 3,[67] the frequently affirmed *non-refoulement* duty under Article 3,[68] and the protection of mentally ill persons in detention from being exposed to substantial suffering or humiliation through conventional or harsh detention regimes.[69] Also worthy of note in this regard are cases concerning the UK arising under

---

[62] *Belhaj* (n 24), [98] (Lord Mance); see, too, ibid, [107] (Lord Mance).

[63] *Belhaj* (n 24), [272] (Lord Sumption, with whom Lord Hughes agreed). See also ibid, [168] (Lord Neuberger, with whom Baroness Hale, Lord Wilson, and Lord Clarke agreed), tying 'public policy' both to international law and to domestic principle.

[64] By the end of 2018, there had been over 1,300 findings of violation of Art 2 ECHR. See COE, Annual Report: European Court of Human Rights (2018), available at: www.echr.coe.int/Documents/Annual_report_2018_ENG.pdf.

[65] By the end of 2018, there had been over 3,200 findings of violation of Art 3 ECHR. See COE, Annual Report: European Court of Human Rights (2018), available at: www.echr.coe.int/Documents/Annual_report_2018_ENG.pdf. On the body of ECtHR doctrine on Art 3 see, inter alia, H Bakirci and U Erdal, *Article 3 of the European Convention on Human Rights: A Practitioner's Handbook* (OMCT, 2006).

[66] On *res interpretata* and ECtHR pronouncements, see OM Arnardóttir, 'Res Interpretata, Erga Omnes Effect and the Role of the Margin of Appreciation in Giving Domestic Effect to the Judgments of the European Court of Human Rights' (2017) 28 *European Journal of International Law* 819; on the significance of the ECtHR's pronouncements on Art 3 in respect of the s 2 HRA 1998 duty, see B Malkani, 'A rights-specific approach to section 2 of the Human Rights Act' (2012) *European Human Rights Law Review* 516, 519–521.

[67] *Vinter v United Kingdom* (2016) 63 EHRR 1.

[68] *Soering v United Kingdom* (1989) 11 EHRR 439; *Chahal v United Kingdom* (1997) 23 EHRR 413.

[69] *Keenan v United Kingdom* (2001) 33 EHRR 38; *MS v United Kingdom* (2012) 55 EHRR 23.

Article 2 ECHR, notably those elucidating the duty to investigate suspicious deaths with a view to establishing the circumstances in which they occurred and whether the Convention was violated and, where appropriate, identifying and punishing those responsible.[70] ECtHR doctrine has shaped domestic judgments since the advent of the HRA and continues to make a significant mark on some of the most compelling questions surrounding takings of life and torture and ill-treatment, with prominent though by no means uncontroversial cases in this regard being *Keyu*,[71] on the question of the duty to investigate the mass killing of civilians by British officers in a former colony in 1948, and *D v Commissioner of Police of the Metropolis*,[72] regarding the police response to complaints of assault and rape at the hands of serial abuser John Worboys.

The positive obligations emerging out of Articles 2 and 3 ECHR, in particular, have made considerable demands of the laws and practices of state authorities across the Council of Europe. Given that the general, or framework, positive duties require law and enforcement mechanisms which adequately protect life and safeguard people from torture, inhumanity and degradation,[73] many elements of the UK's current law and enforcement framework are effectively rendered not only desirable but essential for compliance with the ECHR. State authorities are also under a duty to take operational measures to protect someone liable to be killed or to be subjected to torture or inhuman or degrading treatment, insofar as they know or ought to know of a real and immediate risk to this person.[74] There are also extensive and robust requirements of investigation and redress imposed under what is often referred to as the 'procedural' positive obligation to investigate suspicious deaths and alleged or suspected torture or ill-treatment.[75] All of these positive duties, which are interlinked, entail that states are required not only to put in place legal frameworks which adequately protect persons from ill-treatment such as rape and sexual assault and other infringements of bodily integrity, but also to enforce such laws rigorously. Such rigorous implementation encompasses the adequate investigation of complaints, as was made clear in the recent Supreme Court judgment concerning failings in the police response to complaints regarding serial rapist John Worboys.[76] It bears highlighting, in this context, that positive duties under Article 2 ECHR – notably general duties to protect life and duties to investigate suspicious deaths – have been key towards ensuring a rigorous

---

[70] *McCann and others v United Kingdom* (1996) 21 EHRR 97; *Jordan v United Kingdom* (2003) 37 EHRR 2; *McKerr v United Kingdom* (2002) 34 EHRR 20.

[71] *Keyu v Secretary of State for Foreign & Commonwealth Affairs* [2015] UKSC 69, [2015] 3 WLR 1665; see the interesting comment in Bjorge (n 30) 237.

[72] *D v Commissioner of Police of the Metropolis (Liberty and others intervening)* [2018] UKSC 11.

[73] See, ie, *MC v Bulgaria* (2005) 40 EHRR 20.

[74] See, ie, *Osman v United Kingdom* (2000) 29 EHRR 245; *Opuz v Turkey* (2010) 50 EHRR 28.

[75] See, ie, *Jordan v United Kingdom* (2003) 37 EHRR 2.

[76] *D v Commissioner of Police of the Metropolis (Liberty and others intervening)* [2018] UKSC 11.

process of accountability in the aftermath of the devastating Grenfell Tower fire, as illustrated in a spate of relevant contributions by the Equality and Human Rights Commission.[77]

It is difficult to conclude or even imagine that, absent the HRA, the courts would recognise common law protections which resemble the multi-faceted demands of positive obligations under the relevant Convention rights, as elaborated in the rich jurisprudence of the ECtHR. It is, after all, well established that the UK's top court has been 'prompted into action by decisions of the European Court of Human Rights', for example, in the realm of positive duties to protect against known risks to life and to investigate suspicious deaths.[78]

Furthermore, insofar as rights of bodily integrity that align with the right not to be ill-treated may be secured through tortious liability under the common law, the recent Supreme Court judgment concerning the systemic failings in the police response to complaints about Worboys constitutes an interesting development. In particular, it was key to the majority judgments that a relevant exemption from liability of the police at common law was irrelevant to claims advanced under the HRA, as the two involved distinct spheres of liability and policy.[79] Distinguishing the common law duty of care from the relevant positive duty under human rights law, Lord Kerr (with whom Baroness Hale agreed) indicated that:

> In as much as it was considered that the common-law duty should not be adapted to harmonise with the perceived duty arising under ECHR, so should the latter duty remain free from the influence of the pre-HRA domestic law. Alternatively, it requires, at least, to be considered on its own merits, without the encumbrance of the corpus of jurisprudence under common-law.[80]

The judgment confirms that common law liability on the one hand, and ECHR positive obligations under rights such as Articles 2 and 3 ECHR on the other, operate on distinct planes; and the latter may make considerably more substantial demands of state authority action than the former.[81]

---

[77] See, inter alia, EHRC, *In the Public Inquiry into the Fire at Grenfell Tower: Equality and Human Rights Commission Submissions Following Phase 1 of the Inquiry* (January 2019), www.equalityhumanrights.com/sites/default/files/grenfell-inquiry-phase-1-submissions-january-2019.pdf; EHRC, *Following Grenfell: the right to life* (2018), www.equalityhumanrights.com/sites/default/files/following-grenfell-the-right-to-life_0.pdf. See, further, EHRC, 'Following Grenfell: why is the Commission involved?', www.equalityhumanrights.com/en/following-grenfell/following-grenfell-why-commission-involved.

[78] Dickson (n 7) 128.

[79] *D v Commissioner of Police of the Metropolis (Liberty and others intervening)* [2018] UKSC 11, [68] (Lord Kerr).

[80] Ibid. See the inverse point, to the effect that the ECHR's positive obligations do not require the expansion of common law liability, in *Van Colle v Chief Constable of Hertfordshire* [2008] UKHL 50, [2009] AC 225, [138] (Lord Brown).

[81] See the critical analysis in J Morgan, 'Parallel Lines that Never Meet: Tort and the ECHR Again' (2018) 77 *CLJ* 244.

V. Constitutional Legislation

One way in which the common law could protect rights of bodily integrity is *directly* – that is, by means of embodying and giving effect to such rights, including as interpretive constructs via the principle of legality (discussed further below). An alternative way in which the common law might protect such rights is *indirectly*, by means of ascribing a privileged status to legislation that itself acknowledges or establishes such rights. The recognition, at common law, of a statute as constitutional protects it from implied repeal.[82] As such, the substantial extent to which protection of bodily integrity is secured through legislation compels the question: are rights to bodily integrity entrenched through constitutional legislation? The issue is complicated by the contestation surrounding the means of identifying constitutional legislation, not least because the process of identifying such legislation brings up the thorny question of what constitutions are for – what, in other words, is their 'core function'.[83] The answer to this is, at best, elusive. The well-known *Thoburn* formulation, according to which 'a constitutional statute is one which (a) conditions the legal relationship between citizen and state in some general, overarching manner, or (b) enlarges or diminishes the scope of what we would now regard as fundamental constitutional rights',[84] is open-ended, such that the specification of constitutional legislation requires a substantial interpretive leap. For the purposes of discerning the constitutional protection of rights to bodily integrity, its reliance on the notion of 'fundamental constitutional rights' begs the question.

Judicial pronouncements also provide an indication of particular statutes which are considered to be of constitutional character, including the Magna Carta, the Petition of Right 1628, the Bill of Rights and (in Scotland) the Claim of Rights Act 1689, the European Communities Act 1972, the Human Rights Act 1998 and the Constitutional Reform Act 2005.[85] Yet, as David Feldman rightly highlights, '[m]any statutes deal with a variety of matters, some but not all of which are constitutional',[86] so that it may be more appropriate, in certain instances, to distinguish as constitutional particular legislative provisions rather than entire statutes, keeping in mind that provisions of constitutional status are likely to be 'scattered through legislation of all kinds'.[87] If so, the search for the constitutional right(s) to

---

[82] *Thoburn v Sunderland City Council* [2003] QB 151 [63] (Laws LJ). But see the nuanced discussion in F Ahmed and A Perry, 'The Quasi-Entrenchment of Constitutional Statutes' (2014) 73 *CLJ* 514.

[83] D Feldman, 'The nature and significance of "constitutional" legislation' (2013) 129 *LQR* 343, 357.

[84] *Thoburn v Sunderland City Council* [2003] QB 151 [62] (Laws LJ).

[85] *R (HS2 Action Alliance Ltd) v Secretary of State for Transport (HS2)* [2014] UKSC 3, [2014] 1 WLR 324, [207] (Lord Neuberger and Lord Mance).

[86] Feldman (n 83) 352. See also M Elliott, 'Constitutional Legislation, European Union Law and the Nature of the United Kingdom's Contemporary Constitution' (2014) 10 *European Constitutional Law Review* 379, 386.

[87] Ibid, 357.

bodily integrity in statute must be both wide and laser-like in order to determine the constitutional character of specific provisions.

As mentioned above, an array of legal provisions encompass duties which might be conceived as correlative to the right to life and the right to be free from torture and ill-treatment, including the criminal law on homicide as well as the defence of self-defence, offences against the person, and sexual offences, the regulation of the use of force by law enforcement authorities, the law regulating prisons, the law on immigration and asylum, and the law pertaining to the investigation of suspicious deaths or incidents of alleged or suspected ill-treatment. By way of more specific legislative provision, torture is criminalised under section 134 of the Criminal Justice Act 1988, with the maximum penalty being life imprisonment,[88] and a prohibition on torture and related ill-treatment can be traced back to at least the Bill of Rights of 1689, which banned 'cruell and unusuall punishments', and has been adopted across multiple jurisdictions since.[89]

Yet while we may readily assume the constitutional status of the prohibition on cruel and unusual punishment in the Bill of Rights and even section 134 of the 1988 Act, for example, it is not clear that more 'conventional' statutory protections of bodily integrity would be thus immunised from implied repeal, or that those that might pass the constitutionality test could be said to protect the equivalent of the rich content of rights such as Articles 2 and 3 ECHR. In addition, even if courts were to hand-pick some statutory provisions which delineate fundamental rights to bodily integrity, such as section 76 of the Police and Criminal Evidence Act 1984, or provisions which together set up legal regimes which serve such rights, such as the legal framework on inquests,[90] it is actually doubtful whether such an approach would protect bodily integrity in the most fruitful way. After all, progressive reform of relevant legal provision(s) or entire regimes of protection may be compelled by a range of factors, such as new empirical insights or technological developments, and immunising them from implied repeal may impede such reforms' effectiveness. What works better is, unsurprisingly, what the HRA currently offers: a guarantee of non-regression – admittedly still qualified by the HRA's preservation of parliamentary sovereignty – while the capacity for progressive reform remains largely unconstrained.

VI. Optimism, Mythology, and their Limits

The question of the constitutional protection of rights of bodily integrity in the absence of the HRA is a speculative assessment. If rose-tinted spectacles are

---

[88] See also Mental Health Act 1983, s 127, and Children and Young Persons Act 1933, s 1.

[89] See, eg, the Eighth Amendment to the US Constitution: 'Excessive bail shall not be required, nor excessive fines imposed, nor cruel and unusual punishments inflicted.'

[90] On the lineage and import of this regime, see *R (Amin) v Secretary of State for the Home Department* [2004] 1 AC 653, [16]–[17] (Lord Bingham).

employed in conducting this assessment, one might imagine domestic courts developing or reading into the common law protections equivalent to those offered by Convention rights. Domestic courts might openly or clandestinely embrace the 'internalisation' of Convention rights,[91] or they may, with interpretivist flair, 'discover' that much that is equivalent to the ECHR's protection of bodily integrity is already part and parcel of the common law constitution. Courts might, in doing so, resort to abstract fundamentals, such as autonomy, the sanctity of life, the idea of bodily integrity itself or loose references to a right of bodily integrity, the umbrella notion of human dignity,[92] or the common law's 'abhorrence' towards certain wrongs, and concretise such abstract concepts into Hohfeldian claim-rights. Such a method would not be entirely at odds with the way in which constitutional rights have so far taken hold and taken shape within the common law, for instance in respect of the right of access to justice.[93]

Yet an interpretivist reading of the common law constitution as guaranteeing the rich tapestry of Convention rights to bodily integrity may have to rely on a glorification bordering on mythology. Lord Bingham's view, as expressed in *A (No 2)*, of the common law's abhorrence towards torture was grounded in the 'received opinion' of a formidable line of jurists attesting to the common law's rejection of such cruelty and contrasting it with practices prevailing in continental Europe – though he simultaneously conceded that their sources were of 'doubtful validity'.[94] Lord Carswell's readiness, in *A (No 2)*, to find in (a natural extension of) the common law's requirements what he considered to be a clear moral imperative emerged out of a very particular value judgement on the polity and legal system celebrated by Tennyson as:

A land of settled government,
A land of just and old renown,
Where Freedom slowly broadens down
From precedent to precedent.[95]

This vision of the common law's ever-larger freedom might be more sceptically seen as nothing but a 'myth of the marvellous past';[96] but more importantly, it raises the question of 'whose freedom we are concerned with, what sort of freedom we have in mind, and which English people it is of whose virtue the common law

---

[91] V Fikfak, 'English Courts and the "Internalisation" of the European Convention of Human Rights? – Between Theory and Practice' (2015) 5 *UK Supreme Court Annual Review* 188.

[92] See, eg, D Friedman, 'A Common Law of Human Rights: History, Humanity and Dignity' [2016] *European Human Rights Law Review* 378.

[93] See R Clayton, 'The Empire Strikes Back: Common Law Rights and the Human Rights Act' [2015] *Public Law* 3, 4–7.

[94] *A (No 2)* (n 44), [11] (Lord Bingham).

[95] Alfred, Lord Tennyson, 'You Ask Me, Why, Tho' Ill at Ease' (1842), cited in *A (No 2)* (n 44), [152] (Lord Carswell).

[96] C Gearty, *On Fantasy Island: Britain, Europe, and Human Rights* (Oxford, Oxford University Press, 2016) ch 2.

is the legal embodiment'.[97] It is worth contemplating in particular the distribution of freedom, or freedom from harm, that would emerge in a future without the HRA, not least in view of the contemporary precarity of the 'human' in human rights. Mark Elliott has observed that the depletion of public and political support towards human rights in the UK is marked by 'a scepticism about the universalist nature of human rights', leading to arguments in the vein of '"British rights for good British citizens"', which he rightly considers to be irreconcilable with any conception of universally applicable *human* rights.[98] 'Whose freedom' is a vital question to ask – it is chiefly the 'others' of the political community, like prisoners, asylum-seekers, immigrants, women, persons of colour, disabled persons, whose rights and whose bodies stand to be impinged upon in a future where human rights protections are not as robustly guaranteed, and it is those whose protection through the HRA attracts considerable wrath by some sections of the media.[99]

Moreover, it bears highlighting that the common law may be no stranger to politics, ideologies or less vocalised hegemonic norms which set certain persons apart in according fundamental protections. While there are frequent allusions to the common law's egalitarian credentials,[100] one can hardly neglect earlier decisions of common law courts holding that the notion of a 'person' in legislative provisions did not include women,[101] and legitimately consider that those among us who are systemically or structurally othered from the category of 'person' may be a shifting rather than obsolete category under the common law.[102]

This is relevant to rights of bodily integrity in concrete terms. To give just a few examples in respect of Article 3 ECHR in particular, it is not clear how far the full scope of the *non-refoulement* duty under Article 3, or the duty to provide a meaningful prospect of release for persons on whole life sentences rather than to treat them as 'human waste',[103] or certain high standards for the protection of mentally unwell persons in custody, would survive repeal of the HRA. There is ample basis to ground the argument that the HRA and the Convention rights it transposes have protected 'people whose tenuous connection with the mainstream has left them vulnerable to being passed over by conventional legal frameworks

---

[97] Ibid 22.

[98] M Elliott, 'A Damp Squib in the Long Grass: The Report of the Commission on a Bill of Rights' [2013] *European Human Rights Law Review* 137, 141.

[99] See Gearty (n 96) 152–160; L Gies, 'Human Rights, the British Press and the Deserving Claimant' in KS Ziegler, E Wicks and L Hodson (eds), *The UK and European Human Rights: A Strained Relationship?* (Oxford, Hart Publishing, 2015).

[100] On equality in the common law, see, eg, Lord Steyn, 'Dynamic Interpretation Amidst an Orgy of Statutes' (2004) 35 *Ottawa Law Review* 163, 171; *De Smith* (n 30) 620.

[101] A sobering reminder of this is offered in M Kirby, 'Legal obligations. Legal revolutions' (2018) 134 *LQR* 43, 51–52; see, eg, *Nairn v University of St Andrews* [1909] AC 147.

[102] See, eg, the often damning insights provided in R Hunter, C McGlynn and E Rackley (eds), *Feminist Judgments: From Theory to Practice* (Oxford, Hart Publishing, 2010).

[103] *Murray v Netherlands* (2017) 64 EHRR 3, Partly Concurring Opinion of Judge Pinto de Albuquerque, para 21.

of support',[104] and good reason to fear that the removal of this human rights framework and its humanist egalitarian underpinnings may precipitate a new approach to rights (and responsibilities) in which a criterion other than humanity is key.[105] The bodies whose integrity will be on the front line in such developments will most likely be those of non-citizens or 'quasi-citizens' on the margins of public, political and judicial goodwill. The UK's already 'hostile environment', for example, so starkly exposed in the detention and deportation of members of the Windrush generation,[106] may well be emboldened and exacerbated in the absence of clear human rights protections which protect even those cast as 'citizens of nowhere'.[107]

All this is not to say that Convention rights are free from problems and warranted criticism. There remains significant criticism, contestation and uncertainty regarding the contours of the relevant Convention rights' substantive scope and precise demands in the range of circumstances in which they apply.[108] Nonetheless, they encompass enumerated enforceable entitlements whose correlative duties are based on a rich conception of bodily integrity. Moreover, while it is important not to overstate the clarity and ex ante guidance offered by these enumerated Convention rights and Strasbourg pronouncements, neither should it be underplayed.[109] The difficulty in delineating the precise scope of the constitutional protection of bodily integrity in domestic law heightens the significance of enumerated and richly elaborated human rights to bodily integrity under the Convention. Moreover, while we might, within common law's past, present, and future, find what Danny Friedman calls 'invented traditions' and 'necessary mythologies'[110] that may be deployed to provide protections which align or go beyond those demanded by the ECHR, it is impossible to pronounce this to be guaranteed or even likely. Convention rights are, although not perfect or perfectly ascertained, both more substantial and better substantiated than the common law constitution's equivalent guarantees.

---

[104] Gearty (n 96) 131.

[105] A similar argument is made, in relation to the current state of affairs and in the spirit of 'dignifying' the UK rights model, in B Douglas, 'Undignified rights: the importance of a basis in dignity for the possession of human rights in the United Kingdom' [2015] *Public Law* 241.

[106] See, for example, Joint Committee of Human Rights, *Windrush generation detention* (June 2018), https://publications.parliament.uk/pa/jt201719/jtselect/jtrights/1034/1034.pdf.

[107] 'Theresa May's keynote speech at Tory conference in full', *The Independent*, 5 October 2016, www.independent.co.uk/news/uk/politics/theresa-may-speech-tory-conference-2016-in-full-transcript-a7346171.html.

[108] On Art 3, for example, see Dickson (n 7) 129; N Mavronicola, 'What is an "absolute right"? Deciphering Absoluteness in the Context of Article 3 of the European Convention on Human Rights' (2012) 12 *Human Rights Law Review* 723, 739–758.

[109] P Sales, 'Rights and Fundamental Rights in English Law' (2016) 75 *CLJ* 86, 95.

[110] Friedman (n 92).

VII. Normative Force and Resilience

The normative implications of (common law) constitutional rights are chiefly shaped by the interpretive principles of legality and anxious scrutiny.[111] As developed in the years prior to the enactment of the HRA, the principle of legality provides that '[f]undamental rights cannot be overridden by general or ambiguous words'.[112] This principle does not make it unlawful per se for a public authority to act in contravention of a (common law) constitutional right; rather, it amounts to an 'interpretive presumption against legislative abrogation' of such rights.[113] Thus, fundamental rights offer porous shields against the excesses of executive power on the basis of principles of legal interpretation. Statutory authorisation for their infringement can be provided expressly or by necessary implication. On the other hand, section 3 of the HRA amounts to a more stringent 'interpretive command'[114] to courts and, alongside section 6 of the HRA, offers both sword and shield to victims of human rights violations.

The principle of 'anxious scrutiny' associated with common law constitutional rights chiefly took hold in the common law as a 'heightened rationality review',[115] bringing *Wednesbury* unreasonableness closer to the proportionality test in respect of interferences with fundamental rights or interests. Anxious scrutiny is directed at the justification which it is incumbent on the state to provide for such interferences: 'The more substantial the interference with human rights, the more the court will require by way of justification before it is satisfied that the decision is reasonable', goes its classic formulation.[116] Such an approach largely coheres, even if it does not necessarily align,[117] with the approach taken to determining violations of qualified Convention rights – that is, those that allow for lawful interferences insofar as these are in accordance with the law and 'necessary

---

[111] M Fordham, 'Common Law Rights' [2011] *Judicial Review* 14. It is, at the same time, worth noting that they may also carry particular implications in the delineation of common law doctrines such as that of foreign act of state – see *Belhaj* (n 24).

[112] *R v Secretary of State for the Home Department, ex parte Simms* [2000] 2 AC 115, 131 (Lord Hoffmann).

[113] B Lim, 'The Normativity of the Principle of Legality' (2013) 37 *Melbourne University Law Review* 372, 373.

[114] Sales (n 109) 95; P Sales, 'A Comparison of the Principle of Legality and Section 3 of the Human Rights Act 1998' (2009) 125 *LQR* 598, 607–611, 615.

[115] P Craig, 'Judicial review and anxious scrutiny: foundations, evolution and application' [2015] *Public Law* 60, 63.

[116] *R v Ministry of Defence ex parte Smith* [1996] QB 517 at 554 (Sir Thomas Bingham MR, adopting David Pannick QC's formulation).

[117] Indeed, the proportionality test applied by the ECtHR in *Smith and Grady v UK* (2000) 29 EHRR 493 was decisively more demanding than the Court of Appeal's anxious scrutiny, and the judgment in *Smith* encompassed a finding of a violation of Art 13 ECHR due to the inadequacy of judicial review in protecting the right to private life (see *Smith v UK*, paras 135–138).

in a democratic society' in pursuit of an enumerated legitimate aim, triggering a proportionality assessment.[118]

This formulation of anxious scrutiny is not, however, readily applicable in the specification of rights which admit of no lawful state infringement, such as the right not to be subjected to torture or ill-treatment.[119] Moreover, anxious scrutiny as enhanced rationality review does not necessarily promise the rigour of assessment demanded by the 'absolute necessity' test in respect of the state's deployment of (potentially) lethal force, given that '"absolutely necessary" … indicates that a stricter and more compelling test of necessity must be employed from that normally applicable when determining whether State action is "necessary in a democratic society" under paragraph 2 of Articles 8 to 11 of the Convention …'.[120]

Paul Craig has suggested that after the enactment of the HRA, anxious scrutiny operates to intensify factual assessments that trigger demands under Convention rights,[121] notably questions of risk of ill-treatment in particular circumstances, such as the placing of a former police informer in prison,[122] or the return of a person to a state where they may be in danger of being tortured or otherwise attacked.[123] Indeed, this is the form that 'most anxious scrutiny' took in *Bugdaycay*.[124] Yet even if anxious scrutiny has evolved, post-HRA, without being parasitic on reasonableness, its re-fashioning casts it as a tool whose relevance hinges on substantive demands (such as the principle of *non-refoulement* under human rights law and refugee law[125]) which may not be guaranteed in a different legal landscape in which the HRA is absent.

Moreover, while the transposition of Convention rights and the extent to which they are implemented within the UK is subject to the legislative supremacy of Parliament, and to that extent they lack any special 'resilience' above and beyond common law protections, the picture changes when we shift perspective onto the international plane to find that they are binding upon all state authorities;[126] and, indeed, that some of them are absolute or non-derogable. Where rights face 'adverse legislative or administrative action',[127] the Convention and ECtHR

---

[118] On proportionality, see the particularly incisive critical analysis in A Young, 'Proportionality is Dead: Long Live Proportionality!' in G Huscroft, BW Miller and G Webber (eds), *Proportionality and the Rule of Law: Rights, Justification, Reasoning* (Cambridge, Cambridge University Press, 2014).

[119] Mavronicola (n 108) 723–738.

[120] *McCann v United Kingdom* (1996) 21 EHRR 97, [149]. But see the critique of recent developments in N Mavronicola, 'Taking Life and Liberty Seriously: Reconsidering Criminal Liability under Article 2 of the ECHR' (2017) 80 *MLR* 1026.

[121] Craig (n 116) 64–67.

[122] See, eg, *R (on the application of Bloggs 61) v Secretary of State for the Home Department* [2003] EWCA Civ 686; [2003] 1 WLR 2724.

[123] See, eg, *RB (Algeria) v Secretary of State for the Home Department* [2008] EWCA Civ 290; [2010] 2 AC 110, [221] (Lord Hope).

[124] *Bugdaycay* (n 31) at 531 (Lord Bridge).

[125] See K Wouters, *International Legal Standards for the Protection from Refoulement* (Antwerp, Intersentia, 2009).

[126] Elliott (n 11) 110.

[127] Ibid 85.

themselves feature in the dynamics that determine their resilience. The ECHR binds the UK at international law, whereas common law rights remain exclusively within 'the same, domestic, constitutional space as the doctrine of parliamentary sovereignty' and are therefore, as Elliott argues, more vulnerable to abrogation.[128] It should not be overlooked, therefore, that Convention rights carry a special normative force which compels non-regression, not only in terms of the concrete legal protections of bodily integrity they consist of, but also in respect of the egalitarian humanist essence which underpins them. This layer of resilience is particularly significant where human rights make demands which have the counter-majoritarian qualities of being unpopular or politically unprofitable, and is most vital to those whose bodily integrity is on the front line.

VIII. Looking Outward and the Threat of Insularity

A word is also warranted on the spectre of insularity that currently haunts the UK. A significant dimension of human rights protecting bodily integrity is the distillation of particular, often highly specific, requirements and concrete outcomes out of abstract fundamentals.[129] This process of specification is characterised by uncertainty and contestation. It is one thing to say that the right to be free from torture and inhuman or degrading treatment or punishment is recognised at common law and the Convention alike, and another to establish whether the right protects a person with certain mental health problems from being placed in solitary confinement, for example,[130] or left in regular detention for a number of hours in a situation of escalating distress and self-harm.[131] The hard questions raised in the course of the process of specification demand rigorous first-order reasoning, which can be boosted by looking outward: that is, beyond one's jurisdictional boundaries.[132]

Looking outward encompasses more than merely ascertaining the state of customary international law and its implications.[133] Rather, as I understand it, it

---

[128] Ibid 111. But on the neutralisation of rights-infringements by legislative interpretation, see ibid, 111–115.

[129] On the significance of levels of abstraction and specification see, in respect of absolute rights: Mavronicola (n 108) 739–748; and in respect of qualified or limitable rights, A Young, 'Proportionality is Dead: Long Live Proportionality!' in Huscroft et al (n 118) 52–58.

[130] See, eg, *Keenan* (n 69); for an analysis of some of the ECtHR's reasoning in this area, see N Mavronicola, 'Crime, Punishment and Article 3 ECHR: Puzzles and Prospects of Applying an Absolute Right in a Penal Context' (2015) 15(4) *Human Rights Law Review* 721.

[131] See, eg, *MS v United Kingdom* (2012) 55 EHRR 23.

[132] For an interesting argument on the reflective model of according value to foreign law, and its limits, see B Tripkovic, 'The Morality of Foreign Law' (2019) *ICON* (forthcoming, on file with author). On the 'dialogic' enterprise among courts, see R Teitel, 'Book Review: Comparative Constitutional Law in a Global Age' (2004) 117 *Harvard Law Review* 2570.

[133] On this aspect of 'comparative' legal reasoning, see Friedman, 'A Common Law of Human Rights: History, Humanity and Dignity' (2016) *European Human Rights Law Review* 378, 387.

involves a reflective enterprise which takes into consideration relevant reasoning and deliberative outcomes on the substantive questions to which answers are being sought. To address the example of solitary confinement, these questions would include: what does solitary confinement involve and what kind of suffering can it cause? What vulnerabilities might arise in certain cases and what would they entail in respect of impact and necessary safeguards? How is human dignity affected by deprivation of sensory stimulation and social interaction? The vast corpus of relevant human rights findings, standards, guidelines and analytical and critical literature contains insights based on close deliberation on the very same questions that UK courts are, or ought to be, grappling with in delineating wrongs such as torture and related ill-treatment. They are therefore at least capable of offering illuminating insights into the ways that a person's body and psyche may be violated in specific instances, but also towards a broader conceptual understanding of ideas such as human dignity and its antithesis.[134]

There is, accordingly, much to be gained not only from the 'transnationalization of constitutional argument'[135] which UK courts have already embraced to a certain extent, with predominant focus on common law jurisdictions,[136] but more broadly from remaining vigilant, reflective, and open to any well-reasoned legal and extra-legal deliberations and findings on such challenging questions.[137] Insularity or 'sovereigntist myopia'[138] is not an option: rights to bodily integrity are about humanity. It is to be hoped, therefore, that, whatever the future might hold, judicial deliberation on rights to bodily integrity will remain open to 'taking notice'[139] of insights that emerge from deliberations occurring beyond the confines of the common law.

IX. Conclusion

In sum, there is little doubt that the common law and legislation offer guarantees of bodily integrity, and it may be ventured that the status of some of these guarantees (both common law and legislative) may be considered 'constitutional'. Nonetheless, the above assessment, with a focus on the right to life and the right not to be subjected to torture or related ill-treatment, indicates that there is little

---

[134] See E Webster, 'Interpretation of the Prohibition of Torture: Making Sense of "Dignity" Talk' (2016) 17 *Human Rights Review* 371.

[135] B Flanagan and S Ahern, 'Judicial Decision-Making and Transnational Law: A Survey of Common Law Supreme Court Judges' (2011) 60 *International and Comparative Law Quarterly* 1, 2.

[136] H-R Zhou, 'A Contextual Defense of "comparative constitutional common law"' (2014) 12 *International Journal of Constitutional Law* 1034.

[137] But note the reservation expressed in W Sadurski, 'Judicial Review and the Protection of Constitutional Rights' (2002) 22 *OJLS* 275, 292.

[138] N Walker, 'Setting English Judges to Rights' (1999) 19 *OJLS* 133, 139.

[139] See Sedley J in *R v Secretary of State for the Home Department ex parte McQuillan* [1995] 4 All ER 400, 422.

basis for viewing the prospect of losing the rich and robust protections offered by the ECHR with equanimity. While bodily integrity, and, in particular, life and freedom from torture and ill-treatment, may be protected currently by a panoply of legal provisions and precedent, there are good reasons to rest unassured that the common law constitution offers the same or equivalent guarantees, particularly against regressive developments, as those provided by the HRA. First, it is hard to pinpoint a set of entitlements and correlative duties which definitively constitute the relevant rights. Second, there are sound reasons not to assume that the substantive scope of common law protections currently overlaps or will be interpreted as overlapping with the substantive scope of negative and positive obligations that make up the rich content of Convention rights protecting bodily integrity such as Articles 2 and 3 ECHR. Third, it is seriously questionable whether protection by way of constitutional legislation can deliver the content, as well as the safety net and 'upward' flexibility, offered by the HRA. Finally, that the UK is bound by the ECHR at international law further insulates rights of bodily integrity from abrogation. Losing this added layer of protection could cause considerable detriment, not least to those whose bodily integrity is, or might be, on the margins of mainstream regard, or indeed on the front line of attack by various policies, practices, and anti-human rights rhetoric. Retaining the HRA, remaining bound by the ECHR, maintaining an outward-looking stance, and resisting the politics of othering which has infiltrated UK 'rights talk' is vital towards safeguarding bodily integrity and human dignity for all.

3

Access to Justice:
From Judicial Empowerment
to Public Empowerment

SE-SHAUNA WHEATLE*

I. Introduction

The common law right of access to justice serves as a protective mechanism that facilitates public access to courts while also having wider import for the common law and constitutionalism in the UK. The doctrine's reach and significance are seen in the multiple roles it plays: it serves to ensure individual access to the legal process, as a gateway to development of common law rights and as a tool of judicial self-defence. These roles rest on several rationales that are embedded in the constitutional structure of the state, including respect for the rule of law, judicial independence, accountability and good governance, and enforcement of individual rights and obligations. One path towards the full flourishing of access to justice as a right and a constitutional principle is to de-emphasise the role of the doctrine as a bastion for judicial empowerment and to refocus access to justice as a tool for public empowerment. De-emphasising the institutional empowerment rationale of the doctrine and highlighting its other valuable contributions to the constitution can serve to enhance opportunities for a wider range of communities to access the levers of justice and encourage positive action by the state to reduce limitations on access to justice.

The chapter begins by outlining the current uses and normative value of access to justice. These include access to justice providing a gateway to a larger family of common law rights, a path for vulnerable or marginalised individuals to gain entry to the justice system and a trigger for strong(er) judicial interpretive powers. I then go on to analyse the dominant rationales for access to justice,

* I am grateful to Dr Ruth Houghton, Professor Roger Masterman and Bethany Shiner for helpful discussions on this topic and to Mark Elliott and Kirsty Hughes for helpful comments on earlier drafts.

arguing that while there is value in justifying robust protection of access to justice as a concomitant of the judicial function of upholding the rule of law, this vision of access to justice suffers from institutional insularity that side-lines the public-facing element implied in the very idea of access to justice. I argue that the right ought to be reframed as a tool of public empowerment. The term 'public' in this sense encompasses both the individual litigant who benefits from adjudication of her case and the community that benefits from the resulting enforcement of legal norms, accountability and good governance. Public empowerment requires a realistic approach to both economic and status-based disempowerment and exclusion as well as positive obligations on the state to redress limitations on access to justice. A turn towards empowerment through positive obligations would require courts to re-evaluate the traditional common law conception of rights as negative duties. Yet it is by focusing the conceptualisation and rationale of access to justice on public empowerment that the right, its place in the constitutional milieu and its transformative potential can be better developed.

II. The Normative Value of Access to Justice

In UK common law rights jurisprudence, access to justice is understood in terms of access to courts and tribunals.[1] The right surfaces in a multiplicity of ways in the constitutional system, supporting both broader rights protection and constitutional development. This section outlines the value that access to justice adds to common law rights adjudication and discourse. At a basic level, the right functions as a means of accessing other common law rights as it enables individuals to invoke their rights claims before a court of law. In a fundamental sense, this represents the core value of access to justice to both the individual and the edifice of rights protection within the constitution. The constitutional importance of access to justice further contributes to robust claims to strong judicial interpretive powers that test the traditional institutional boundaries within the constitution. Finally, both the practical and more principled facets of access to justice are seen in the opportunities the doctrine provides for the disempowered to engage in the legal system. While the right furthers both individual and institutional concerns within the constitutional state, it is through a focus on the individual – by widening access for the marginalised or disenfranchised – that the current contribution and potential of the right can be fully realised.

---

[1] See discussion of the meanings and components of access to justice in W Lucy, 'The Normative Standing of Access to Justice: An Argument from Non-Domination' (2016) 33 *Windsor Yearbook of Access to Justice* 231, 234–39.

A. Gateway to Common Law Rights

Access to justice provides a gateway to other common law rights in two respects. First, by accessing courts, individuals are able to advance rights claims and to seek and obtain relief for breaches of those rights. Protection of access to justice is thereby instrumentally supportive of other rights. Judicial enforcement has become a central feature of modern rights protection, providing a means for relief or remedy where other means have failed.[2] The availability of access to the courts therefore emerges as a *sine qua non* of rights enforcement in a more general sense. In this way, access to justice resonates beyond the terms of the right itself; it becomes part of the structure of fundamental rights in the state. Second, from the view of doctrinal development, access to justice is among the most regularly identified and defended common law rights and has facilitated a burgeoning common law rights discourse. It has been said, in this vein, that 'the impetus for constitutional common law rights is rooted in the right of access to the courts'[3] and that access to justice is 'the wellspring for the modern jurisprudence on fundamental common law rights'.[4] Indeed, access to courts largely accounted for the emerging constitutional rights jurisprudence prior to the Human Rights Act 1998 (HRA).[5] Moreover, it was in landmark access to justice cases such as *ex p Witham*,[6] *ex p Leech*[7] and *ex p Simms*[8] that the limbs of the fledgling common law rights movement were advanced. This line of case law cemented fundamental facets of common law rights doctrine, including that a statute will be presumed not to authorise violation of a constitutional right unless clear words are used,[9] that a power conferred by Parliament does not authorise the donee of that power to contravene rights unless expressly permitted by Parliament[10] and that limitations on a right must represent the minimum interference necessary to achieve the claimed objectives.[11]

The gateway function of access to justice has been further bolstered by the substantive and normative force applied to the right through the HRA. The European Convention on Human Rights (ECHR) and the HRA have facilitated

---

[2] T Ginsburg, 'The Global Spread of Constitutional Review' in K Whittington and D Kelemen (eds) *Oxford Handbook of Law and Politics* (Oxford, Oxford University Press, 2008) 87–89.

[3] R Clayton, 'The empire strikes back: common law rights and the Human Rights Act' [2015] *PL* 3, 4.

[4] T Hickman, *Public Law after the Human Rights Act* (Oxford, Hart Publishing, 2010) 298.

[5] M Elliott, 'Beyond the European Convention: Human Rights and the Common Law' (2015) 68 *CLP* 85.

[6] *R v Lord Chancellor, ex p Witham* [1998] QB 575.

[7] *R v Secretary of State for the Home Department, ex p Leech* [1994] QB 198 (CA).

[8] *R v Secretary of State for the Home Department, ex p Simms* [2000] 2 AC 115 (UKHL).

[9] *Simms* (n 8) 131.

[10] *Raymond v Honey* [1983] 1 AC 1 (UKHL) 12–13, 15; *Witham* (n 6) 585.

[11] *Leech* (n 7) 217.

the development of access to justice in several ways. First, by empowering the judiciary to enforce rights through statutory construction, the HRA has contributed to a newly empowered judiciary. The conferral of strong interpretive powers on the courts by section 3 of the HRA, along with section 4's conferral of the power to issue declarations of incompatibility, have been central to the reputed 'juridification' of the UK constitution. By enlarging judicial powers, particularly in assessing government action for rights consistency, the HRA has buttressed and reinforced the institutional capacity of the courts to interpret and adjudicate rights claims.

Second, litigation and discourse resulting from the HRA have affected the culture of adjudication and review in the UK legal system. Commentators have described the HRA as encouraging a 'culture of justification'[12] through expanded judicial review, under which executive acts are understood to be generally reviewable by the courts and thereby subject to not only administrative but also constitutional – including rights-based – standards. Consequently, the potential impact of engaging the courts has been substantially increased as higher standards of review are applied and a wider range of activities is challenged. Moreover, there has been an evolution of the courts' self-perception and their role in shaping the constitutional conversation and decision-making, due in no small part to the enhanced interpretive and declaratory powers conferred under sections 3, 4 and 6 of the HRA. The HRA powers thereby helped to stimulate discourse about the evolution of the UK Supreme Court into a 'proto constitutional' court, engaged in constitutional review.[13] Lord Steyn has maintained that the 'European Convention on Human Rights as incorporated into our law by the Human Rights Act, 1998, created a new legal order'.[14] In a wider sense, the strong interpretive powers conferred on the courts by section 3 of the HRA have arguably contributed to heightened judicial assertiveness. Judicial experience with interpretive techniques such as the strong interpretive presumption of consistency with the ECHR accompanied by the remedial power to alter the meaning of legislation to achieve consistency,[15] have affected constitutional culture and will likely have lasting impact beyond statute. The effect on judicial culture has been acknowledged by Lord Neuberger, who observed that 'the introduction of the Convention into UK law' has made the judiciary 'more questioning about our accepted ideas and assumptions.'[16] The institutional cultural changes occasioned in part by the HRA

---

[12] See, eg, M Hunt, 'Sovereign's Blight: Why Contemporary Public Law Needs the Concept of "Due Deference"' in N Bamforth and P Leyland (eds), *Public Law in a Multi-Layered Constitution* (Oxford, Hart Publishing, 2003), 342; Lord Steyn, 'The New Legal Landscape' [2000] *EHRLR* 549, 552.

[13] R Masterman and J Murkens, 'Skirting Supremacy and Subordination: The Constitutional Authority of the UK Supreme Court' [2013] *PL* 800.

[14] *R (Jackson) v AG* [2005] UKHL 56, [2006] 1 AC 262 [102] (Lord Steyn).

[15] See, eg, *Ghaidan v Godin-Mendoza* [2004] UKHL 30, [2004] 3 All ER 411 (HL).

[16] Lord Neuberger, 'The role of judges in human rights jurisprudence: a comparison of the Australian and UK experience' (8 August 2014) [31].

have the potential to take root in the common law and thereby survive the possible repeal of the HRA.[17]

Third, it is certainly arguable that fair trial rights, as provided under Article 6 ECHR and interpreted by both the European Court of Human Rights (ECtHR) and UK courts, added content to the concept of access to justice that had thus far been expressed in the common law sphere. The reasoning in *ex p Witham* points to a similarity of content between the common law and Convention rights, with both common law courts and the ECtHR holding that there must be an effective right to access the courts and that barriers to court must be justified.[18] However, evidence of the European influence on the mechanism for protecting the common law right has come into sharper focus in recent case law. In *R (UNISON) v Lord Chancellor* Lord Reed makes clear that even if the court finds that legislation expressly authorises an intrusion on the right of access to justice, the extent of the permissible intrusion falls to be determined by reference to a proportionality assessment. Accordingly, the statute will be 'interpreted as authorising only such a degree of intrusion as is reasonably necessary to fulfil the objective of the provision in question.'[19] As Lord Reed acknowledged in *UNISON*, this language is analogous to the requirements of the proportionality test employed by the ECtHR and, in more general terms, 'the case law of the Strasbourg court concerning the right of access to justice is relevant to the development of the common law.'[20]

Domestic rights jurisprudence both pre-and post-HRA owes much to the concept of access to justice. Doctrinally, it is one of the more fully developed rights at common law, and has been connected to the right of prisoners to contact journalists[21] and the right to access legal advice.[22] Perhaps more significantly, in methodological terms, access to justice case law has shown its constitutional mettle by concretising the judicial method for application and enforcement of constitutional rights. Through the distinctly common law requirement of clear wording to authorise rights infringement and the articulation of an assessment akin to the European proportionality test to determine whether breach of a right is justified, access to justice has led to maturation of the methodology of common law rights and indeed common law constitutionalism. Crucially then, access to justice has been a route not only to doctrinal realisation of a specific right but in various ways, has enabled the very idea and methods of common law rights to flourish.

---

[17] See the Conservative Party proposals to repeal the HRA: The Conservative Party, *Protecting Human Rights in the UK: The Conservatives' Proposals for Changing Britain's Human Rights Laws* (October 2014).

[18] T Eicke, 'Speaking in UNISON? Access to Justice and the Convention' [2018] *EHRLR* 22, 25.

[19] *R (UNISON) v Lord Chancellor* [2017] UKSC 51 [80].

[20] *UNISON* (n 19) [89].

[21] *Simms* (n 8) 130.

[22] *R v Secretary of State for the Home Department, ex p Anderson* [1984] QB 778 (UKHL) 790.

B. Trigger for Strong Judicial Interpretive Powers

Alongside its operation as a distinct right that can be raised against the state, access to justice also has a broader conditioning effect upon the constitution. Underpinning this wider constitutional role is the conceptualisation of access to justice as 'inherent in the rule of law'.[23] A dramatic constitutional impact of viewing access to justice as a fundamental feature of the rule of law is that threats to access to justice may trigger strong judicial interpretive powers. In this sense, potential contraventions of access to justice are perceived as potential contraventions of the rule of law itself, which therefore provoke controversial judicial interpretations that challenge accepted understandings of the boundaries of judicial interpretation.

The shot across the bow issued by Lady Hale and Lord Steyn in *Jackson*, warning the government and Parliament against broad ousters of judicial review over substantial areas of executive decision-making, have been extensively deconstructed.[24] However, in the context of common law rights, it is worth revisiting the centrality of access to justice to the cautions issued by both judges. Thus, for Lady Hale, heightened interpretive scepticism or legislative rejection by the courts can be provoked by statutory provisions that purport to remove judicial supervision of alleged violations of rights.[25] Similarly, the 'exceptional circumstances' that Lord Steyn envisioned as triggering a judicial reformulation of parliamentary supremacy involved 'an attempt to abolish judicial review or the ordinary role of the courts'.[26]

It is unsurprising that the confrontation between parliamentary sovereignty and the rule of law as envisioned in *Jackson* centred on a possible removal of the power to review governmental activity affecting the individual. There is a history of judicial activity testing constitutional boundaries by appearing to regulate – rather than interpret – constitutional language resting on challenges to judicial review. *Anisminic* stands as a powerful example.[27] A clause in the Foreign Compensation Act 1950 purported to insulate decisions of the Foreign Compensation Commission by providing that 'The determination by the Commission of any application made to them under this Act shall not be called in question in any court of law'. The House of Lords was able to restrict the effect of this section by holding that a 'determination' did not include a decision made outside the Commission's jurisdiction. Such decisions were a nullity and therefore did not constitute determinations. In so holding, the courts retained authority to review 'purported' determinations that resulted from an error of law. The spectre of an administrative agency acting outside its powers and private individuals and bodies having no avenue

---

[23] *UNISON* (n 19) [66] (Lord Reed).
[24] *Jackson* (n 14). See also ch 10.
[25] *Jackson* (n 14) [159].
[26] *Jackson* (n 14) [102].
[27] *Anisminic Ltd v Foreign Compensation Commission* [1969] 2 AC 147 (UKHL).

for relief prompted the court – in the view of some commentators – to frustrate Parliament's intention.[28] *Anisminic* therefore represented an interpretation prompted by 'a particularly strong presumption in favour of securing access to a court for resolution of a legal dispute.'[29]

The Supreme Court furthered this judicial posture in *Privacy International* by restrictively interpreting a provision in the Regulation of Investigatory Powers Act 2000 which stated that 'decisions of the [Investigatory Powers] Tribunal (including decisions as to whether they have jurisdiction) shall not be subject to appeal or be liable to be questioned in any court.'[30] Noting the 'obvious parallel' with the ouster clause in *Anisminic*, the Court concluded that the controlling principle is 'the common law presumption against ouster',[31] which could only be displaced by 'the most clear and explicit words.'[32] The formulation in the statute was again not clear enough to exclude judicial intervention where decisions were based on errors of law. The fact that judicial supervision was retained despite 'a more elaborate attempt to exclude judicial review' has been described as 'challenging the legislature's legally unlimited law-making authority.'[33] Yet, the Court's interpretive approach reflects the constitutional importance of judicial assessment of questions of law and oversight of executive bodies. The normative weight of this principle thereby shifts construction outside the realms of 'ordinary statutory interpretation.'[34]

The constitutional paramountcy of preserving access to the courts similarly triggered strong judicial interpretation in *Evans*,[35] which was also seen as straining the boundaries of judicial power. On its face, the case did not raise access to justice issues. Government departments denied a Freedom of Information request from a journalist for communications between the Prince of Wales and government ministers. Those refusals were upheld by the Information Commissioner, but the Upper Tribunal overturned this decision, finding that public interest weighed in favour of releasing the communications. The Attorney General responded by overriding the Tribunal's decision; in doing so he relied on section 53 of the Freedom of Information Act, which allowed him to override disclosure notices if 'he has on reasonable grounds formed the opinion' that failure to disclose did not violate the Act. It was in the Court's interpretation of section 53 that the access to justice implications of the override became apparent. In concluding that section 53

---

[28] A Tucker, 'Parliamentary Intention, *Anisminic*, and the Privacy International Case (Part One)', UK Constitutional Law Blog (18 December 2018) (available at https://ukconstitutionallaw.org/); B Schwartz, '*Anisminic* and Activism-Preclusion Provisions in English Administrative Law' (1986) 38 *Administrative Law Review* 33, 48–49.

[29] P Sales, 'The common law: context and method' [2019] *LQR* 47, 65, fn 75.

[30] *R (Privacy International) v Investigatory Powers Tribunal* [2019] UKSC 22.

[31] *Privacy International* (n 30) [107].

[32] *Privacy International* (n 30) [111].

[33] M Gordon, '*Privacy International*, Parliamentary Sovereignty and the Synthetic Constitution', UK Constitutional Law Blog (26 June 2019) (available at https://ukconstitutionallaw.org/).

[34] *Privacy International* (n 30) [107].

[35] *R (Evans) v Attorney General* [2015] UKSC 21.

should not be interpreted as permitting override of a judicial decision – including the decision of the Upper Tribunal – the majority of the Supreme Court maintained that the override 'cut across two constitutional fundamentals'. The first was that a decision of a court is binding but the second was 'that decisions and actions of the executive are, subject to necessary well established exceptions (such as declarations of war), and jealously scrutinised statutory exceptions, reviewable by the court at the suit of an interested citizen'.[36] The override was perceived as undermining citizens' ability to avail themselves of the courts; if judicial decisions could be overridden by the executive, the very value of accessing the courts would be rendered nugatory. The Supreme Court's decision that the wording of section 53 was not sufficiently clear to indicate parliamentary intention to allow override of the Upper Tribunal's decision has been described 'as a soft form of judicial strike-down'.[37] Yet, this interpretation can be perceived as further proof that judges will go to great constitutional lengths in order to preserve supervisory jurisdiction and the role of the courts in standing between the citizen and the state.

The line of case law regarding supervisory jurisdiction of the court does reveal some potential for the common law to continue to exert influence on legislation in the event of a repeal of the HRA. The courts' determination to maintain their role as arbiter of rights and mediator between the individual and the state, takes roots beyond the confines of legislative conferrals of judicial power. Judges have founded their role in delivering justice and the individual's access to judicial protection firmly in the rule of law. By further applying these requirements through the common law presumption embedded in the principle of legality, courts have developed a means for the common law to condition the meaning and impact of legislation, even without the textual affirmation of the HRA. It is in the ability to channel traditional acceptance of access to justice through the methodological funnel of the principle of legality that access to justice has a special capacity to flourish. While there is a general criticism that common law method outstrips the development of the content of common law norms,[38] as one of the more commonly invoked rights, access to justice has experienced substantial doctrinal development as well as strong normative application. The extent to which access to the courts is embedded within the constitutional system of the UK, and its ability to challenge traditional institutional boundaries makes access to justice well-equipped to weather legislative changes.

However, this representation of access to justice on the constitutional stage, while enabling citizen action, appears centred on the role of the court within the state. Judicial empowerment emerges as a central theme of the strong interpretive

---

[36] *Evans* (n 35) [52].

[37] M Elliott, 'A Tangled Constitutional Web: the black-spider memos and the British constitution's relational architecture' [2015] *PL* 539, 549.

[38] R Masterman and S Wheatle, 'Unity, Disunity and Vacuity: Constitutional Adjudication and the Common Law' in M Elliott, J Varuhas and S Wilson-Stark (eds), *The Unity of Public Law? Doctrinal, Theoretical and Comparative Perspectives* (Oxford, Hart Publishing, 2018).

powers triggered by governmental (or parliamentary) erosions of access to justice in *Anisminic, Privacy International, Evans* and *Jackson*. Yet, access to justice can- and to some extent does- serve to empower the citizen as well as the institutions of state. The following section highlights the use of access to justice to empower the disempowered.

C. Access for the Disempowered: Vulnerability, Marginalisation and Exclusion

Disempowerment and exclusion in the social, economic and political spheres create conditions that elevate the necessity for reliance on the legal system. These sources of disadvantage and marginalisation tend to give rise to legal problems in relation to exclusion from majoritarian institutions, provision of public services and provision of services by private persons and bodies. Research has shown, for instance, that those living in poverty 'experience more legal difficulties than the average [person]'.[39] Further, persons who lack socio-economic or political influence are less able to generate private solutions to their problems or prevail upon political bodies to address their issues and protect their interests. They are therefore more reliant on the legal system – including the system of fundamental rights enforcement – which rests on non-majoritarian imperatives.[40] Yet, the very conditions that produce the need for the legal system – exclusion, vulnerability or marginalisation – can also prevent or impede their access to that system.

The crux of defining and protecting access to justice as a right turns on whether there is a hindrance or impediment to access and whether that hindrance is justified. Despite the apparently blanket statement in *Pyx Granite Co Ltd v Ministry of Housing and Local Government* that 'the subject's right of recourse to Her Majesty's courts for the determination of his rights' is 'not by any means to be whittled down',[41] it is clear that not every hindrance in the ordinary sense of the word would constitute a hindrance in the eyes of the law. The necessity for an individual to engage and pay for transportation to law offices or the courts could be seen as an impediment in the ordinary sense of the word. Without the assistance of transportation, she would be unable to attend court proceedings or assist in her legal representation. Yet it is unlikely that the need to pay for such transportation would be deemed an infringement of the right. The cases therefore often turn on what constitutes an *impermissible* hindrance, which includes, first, the types of barriers that can be hindrances and, second, assessment of the extent or impact of the hindrance.

---

[39] DL Rhode, *Access to Justice* (Oxford, Oxford University Press, 2004) 103; JA Leitch, 'Having a Say: Access to Justice as Democratic Participation' (2015) 4 *UCL Journal of Law and Jurisprudence* 76, 78.

[40] See discussion of the importance of Bills of Rights for political minorities in *National Coalition for Gay and Lesbian Equality v Minister of Justice* [1998] ZACC 15, 1998 (12) BCLR 1517 (SACC) [25] (Ackermann J).

[41] [1960] AC 260 (HL) 286.

Hindrances may take the form of specific procedural impediments to initiating litigation, the complexity of the legal process, bars to the award of a remedy, financial conditions for the pursuit of litigation and, potentially, the withdrawal of legal aid. The hindrance must not have the impact of completely depriving the individual of the right; the core of the right must be retained. Following a review of the authorities in *UNISON*, Lord Reed devised a three-stage test for determining whether there has been an unconstitutional impediment to access to justice. First, 'any hindrance or impediment requires clear authorisation by Parliament'.[42] Second, even if such statutory authorisation for an impediment exists, the courts will interpret the statute 'as authorising only such a degree of intrusion as is reasonably necessary to fulfil the objective of the provision in question'.[43] Third, the measure imposed 'will be ultra vires if there is a real risk that persons will effectively be prevented from having access to justice'.[44]

The vulnerable status of claimants has provided context for judgments rebuffing governmentally erected roadblocks to accessing courts. The *UNISON* case called for contemplation of vulnerability in determining whether the imposition of fees for access to employment tribunals and employment appeal tribunals undermined access to justice. Lord Reed opened the discussion by reflecting on 'the vulnerability of employees to exploitation, discrimination, and other undesirable practices, and the social problems which can result' as the driving force behind the enactment of statutory rights for employees.[45] This mirrors similar concerns regarding workers' rights expressed by Chief Justice McLachlin of the Canadian Supreme Court in *Trial Lawyers Association of British Columbia v British Columbia*.[46] Thus, judges have, with increasing confidence, come to grapple with the economic context of claimants and the impact of government policies on the financial capabilities of potential litigants. However, empowerment must resonate not only in a financial sense but in other important aspects of people's lives.

While access to justice discourse often centres on economic disempowerment, disempowerment and exclusion exist in a variety of forms that resonate in the justice system. Alongside economic disadvantage, disempowerment and exclusion can result from minority status (including ethnic and sexual minority status) and from social and political exclusion (including through refugee, asylum or immigration status). To truly empower the public through access to justice, there must be engagement with a wide range of realistic hindrances to access to justice, through frank acknowledgement of societal identity-based grounds of inclusion and marginalisation. As is discussed in Part III below, while the courts have recognised economic-based disempowerment within access to justice analysis, they have been less responsive to status-based impediments to access.

---

[42] *UNISON* (n 19) [78].
[43] Ibid, [80].
[44] Ibid, [86].
[45] Ibid, [6].
[46] *Trial Lawyers Association of British Columbia v British Columbia* [2014] 3 SCR 31.

D. Access to What End? The Rationales of Access to Justice

As the normative importance of access to justice manifests in various forms within the constitution, this suggests that the rationale of access to justice is itself varied. Indeed, it suggests a need to inquire into multiple rationales underpinning the right, rather than a single rationale. This part of the chapter examines the rationales of access to justice, noting rationales that highlight institutional imperatives on the one hand and those geared towards public empowerment on the other. I advocate emphasis on a public empowerment rationale, recognising signs that the courts have tentatively taken in that direction and the scope for further orientation towards a public facing vision of the right.[47]

The strength and influence of access to justice lie in part in its multiple rationales and objectives, including pursuit of individual interests and fundamental rights, respect for the rule of law, judicial independence, support for administration of justice and accountability in government. Future development of the doctrine ought to be guided by interrogation of the imperatives protected by these multiple rationales, with thoughtful assessment of the relative importance of these pursuits. In short, we must take stock of why this doctrine matters, whom it serves and how its objectives can best meet the needs of our constitutional democracy. Such a frank assessment should influence the dominant roles played by the doctrine in the future as well as the terms in which courts communicate with the state and the public about access to justice. It is argued that in advancing these rationales, more emphasis should be placed on the public facing imperatives of the doctrine and less on the institutional priorities served by ensuring access to courts. Such emphasis would serve to bolster access to justice as a bastion for defence of individual interests and fundamental rights, and a support mechanism for public engagement in governance. As is argued in further detail below, emphasising public facing rationales has the advantage of highlighting and giving effect to the value of access to courts as a right of and for the public.

III. Institutional Rationales and the Role of the Judiciary

Where the judiciary has sought to explain the foundation and rationale for protecting access to justice, while the interests of the individual do not escape mention, the first port of call is often the institutional interests of the judicial branch of state.

---

[47] The concept of legal empowerment has become ascendant in development literature, and is understood as 'the use of law to specifically strengthen the disadvantaged': Stephen Golub, 'What is Legal Empowerment? An Introduction' in S Golub (ed), *Legal Empowerment: Practitioners' Perspectives* (International Development Law Organization 2013) 13. Crucially, 'the disadvantaged' encompasses the poor, minorities, defendants in criminal cases and other groups affected by societal injustice. See also B Van Rooij, 'Bringing Justice to the Poor, bottom-up legal development cooperation' [2012] *Hague Journal on the Rule of Law* 286.

The current dominant framing of access to justice starts from the centrality of access to justice to the fulfilment of the judicial function. Thus, the celebrated defence of access to justice in *Pyx Granite Co Ltd v Ministry of Housing and Local Government* was arrived at because, in the words of Lord Jenkins: 'I cannot find any sufficient indication that it was intended to oust the jurisdiction of the court.'[48] This dynamic is not limited to the UK and can be seen in the approach of the Supreme Court of Canada. Accordingly, the primary flaw with the hearing fees imposed by the province of British Columbia in *Trial Lawyers Association* was that 'the legislation at issue bars access to the superior courts ... by imposing hearing fees that prevent individuals from having their private and public law disputes resolved by the courts of superior jurisdiction- the hallmark of what superior courts exist to do'.[49] The principal concern, as in UK jurisprudence, is with the position and jurisdiction of the court, whereas the rights and engagement of the public appear to be secondary, albeit important.

While access to justice is sometimes presented as being grounded in the rule of law, rule of law justifications for a right of access to courts are themselves often couched in exclusively or predominantly institutional terms. After anchoring the right in the rule of law, Lord Reed's *UNISON* judgment cast the importance of the rule of law in terms of the departments of state:

> At the heart of the concept of the rule of law is the idea that society is governed by law. Parliament exists primarily in order to make laws for society in this country. Democratic procedures exist primarily in order to ensure that the Parliament which makes laws includes Members of Parliament who are chosen by the people of this country and are accountable to them. Courts exist in order to ensure that the laws made by Parliament, and the common law created by the courts themselves, are applied and enforced. That role includes ensuring that the executive branch of government carries out its functions in accordance with the law. In order for the courts to perform that role, people must in principle have unimpeded access to them.[50]

In this framing, the public are beneficiaries of the protection and defence of the right but they play a secondary role in the narrative; it is the institutions of state that take centre stage. Lord Reed advances a vision of institutional interaction facilitated by the settlement of disputes in courts. The institutional narrative presented by Lord Reed is one of collaboration and mutual problem-solving, rather than institutional confrontation and antagonism. The court must be commended for articulating the challenge before it in these terms, rather than conjuring up the image of a battle. A battle narrative would legitimise the sometimes unspoken assumption of political constitutionalist judicial review sceptics that there is a power struggle between the judiciary and political actors. The undercurrent of battle is, for instance, revealed in Ekins and Forsyth's response to the UK Supreme Court's

---

[48] *Pyx Granite* (n 41) 304.
[49] *Trial Lawyers Association* (n 46) [35].
[50] *UNISON* (n 19) [68] (Lord Reed).

restrictive interpretation of the Freedom of Information Act 2000 in *Evans*.[51] Ekins and Forsyth characterise *Evans* as an 'expansion of judicial power' and accuse the judges of 'suppressing the Minister's statutory power and undercutting the scheme Parliament enacted'.[52] This posture is maintained in their consequent advice to Parliament to respond to the judgment by enacting legislation expressly conferring on the Attorney General the power to override the decision of the Upper Tribunal and 'standing ready to reverse other judgments that overstep the mark'.[53] The battle narrative is an outgrowth of the debate sparked during the twentieth century between legal and political constitutionalists, which has been criticised for its polarising nature and its slowness to account for new models of inter-institutional exchange.[54] The terms of the political versus legal constitutionalism discourse are emblematic of an adversarial construction of constitutionalism, thereby ignoring the potential for collaborative engagement. This framing ought to be dispensed with, in favour of a more collaborative understanding of constitutional relationships, such as that envisioned by Lord Reed.

A collaborative model of constitutionalism would eschew fixations on duelling legal and political visions of the constitution and, as a result, reject strictly hierarchical institutional orderings.[55] Collaborative constitutionalism, as described by Eoin Carolan, encourages 'fruitful conflict' and mutual constructive engagement between institutions with differing priorities and perspectives. Though conflict remains a feature of constitutionalism under this model, there is no expectation that conflict will result in battle or lead to a final winner-takes-all result. Rather, constitutional collaboration 'discourages the anthropomorphism that sometimes reduces constitutionalism to a conflict between the Politician and the Judge and instead encourages awareness of the role of institutions as transactional sites for interplay between different views'.[56] This proposed reformulation of constitutional interactions would sound in access to justice reasoning by fostering cooperative and participatory language, envisioning public use of the court system as a means of stimulating collaborative problem-solving between the institutions of state. Lord Reed's language in *UNISON* is therefore a step in the right direction, but to be sufficiently collaborative, and more effective at problem-solving, the vision of

---

[51] *Evans* (n 35).

[52] R Ekins and C Forsyth, 'Judging the Public Interest: The Rule of Law v The Rule of Courts' (Policy Exchange, Judicial Power Project) 5.

[53] Ekins and Forsyth (n 52) 5.

[54] See generally, S Gardbaum, *The New Commonwealth Model of Constitutionalism: Theory and Practice* (Cambridge, Cambridge University Press, 2013).

[55] E Carolan, 'Dialogue isn't working: the case for collaboration as a model of legislative-judicial relations' (2015) 36 *LS* 209, 224–26. See also A Bogg, 'The Common Law Constitution at Work: *R (on the application of UNISON) v Lord Chancellor*' (2018) 81 *MLR* 509, 514.

[56] Carolan (n 55) 226. See also feminist theory advanced by scholars such as Benhabib and Fredman, which proposes deliberation and participation as pinnacles of democratic constitutionalism. See, eg, S Benhabib, 'Deliberative Rationality and Models of Democratic Legitimacy' (1994) 1 *Constellations* 26, 31–35; S Fredman, 'From Dialogue to Deliberation: Human rights adjudication and prisoners' rights to vote' (2013) *PL* 292, 294–45.

constitutionalism presented by the Supreme Court must also be public-focused, encouraging and highlighting public participation instead of being consumed by institutional interplay. While the court may be moving towards more collaboration between institutions, there remains outsized focus within access to justice reasoning on justifying and buttressing the court's position within the state. The importance of protecting access to the justice system would be better understood in the context of the entire constitutional framework as a route to empowering the public to participate more closely in governance.

IV. Beyond Judicial Empowerment to Public Empowerment

There are two primary reasons for deemphasising the judicial empowerment rationale in access to justice reasoning. First, the full societal impact of the right of access to justice can be seen more thoroughly through the individual and communitarian objectives it serves, not the institutional benefit it brings to the judiciary. Certainly, judges have stressed that in securing the role of the judiciary in reviewing governmental action and holding the state to account, the courts are thereby ensuring that the state remains within and subject to the law and that the judicial branch serves as a forum for the individual to be heard and have their interests protected.[57] Nonetheless, this is a formulation that pivots around the courts and rule of law concerns in a limiting manner, and sidelines wider reflections on the requirements, objectives and aspirations of constitutional rights. Second, rights are fundamentally about the person, seeking to respect their dignity and enhance their capabilities. Institutional benefits that may accrue in the process of rights protection are secondary. It is this understanding of the rights protection dynamic that ought to inform access to justice reasoning.

Public empowerment has two constituents: the individual and the community. The individual dimension requires that each person can access courts, receive adjudication and rely upon the outcome of that adjudication. Within the individual imperative of the doctrine exists a need to protect the jurisdictional attributes of courts – such as the independence of the judiciary and the impartiality of individual judges – and the finality of the judicial settlement. Understood in this way, the institutional protection offered by access to justice is not the end, but a means to an end. The communitarian dimension exists in the claim that the proper administration of justice and accountability of state organs to the people is served by preserving avenues to the courts. In this sense, the accessibility of the legal process provides a means of holding government (if not the legislature) to account, ensuring a route for the public to challenge and obtain justification for executive

---

[57] Se, eg, *Jackson* (n 14) [159].

decision-making. The intertwined individual and communitarian imperatives of securing access to courts are well-represented in Lord Diplock's words in *Attorney General v Times Newspapers Ltd* that:

> The due administration of justice requires first that all citizens should have unhindered access to the constitutionally established courts ..., secondly that they should be able to rely upon obtaining in the courts the arbitrament of a tribunal which is free from bias and whose decision will be based upon those facts only that have been proved in evidence before it in accordance with the procedure adopted in courts of law, and thirdly that, once the dispute has been submitted to a court of law, they should be able to rely upon there being no usurpation by any other person of the function of that court.[58]

The communitarian import has garnered some recognition in case law. The UK Supreme Court's recent rejection of 'the idea that bringing a claim before a court or a tribunal is a purely private activity, and the related idea that such claims provide no broader social benefit' offers powerful support to a communitarian potential for the right.[59] In finer detail, the social benefits of individual access to courts were identified in *UNISON* as (i) judicial decisions on matters of general importance,[60] (ii) the provision of an impetus for the enforcement of rights and a deterrent to breaches of obligations, buttressed by security in the knowledge of an avenue for protection of those rights and obligations[61] and (iii), which is closely related to (ii), a buffer against the effects of power imbalances which would, if unrestrained, inevitably favour 'the party in the stronger bargaining position'.[62] By highlighting the public good served by access to justice, not only in its individual but also in its communitarian dimensions, *UNISON* marks a welcome turn towards a public empowerment rationale of access to justice. A public empowerment understanding of the doctrine is particularly encouraged by recognition of the social benefit of a 'fair and just system of adjudication'[63] as a bulwark against power imbalances.

There are signs of an emerging public empowerment understanding of the right as courts have become increasingly engaged with, and responsive to, economic hindrances to access to justice. This engagement, which has been fostered by realistic assessment of the impact of governmental policies on 'behaviour in the real world',[64] speaks to the public facing perspective of access to justice. Yet, despite the courts' robust acknowledgement of the social purpose of the right, a public empowerment approach must also address (i) the need for positive action to redress limitations on access to justice and (ii) the need for equality of access across both economic and status-based differences. The following sections discuss the courts'

---

[58] [1974] AC 273, 309.
[59] *UNISON* (n 19) [67] (Lord Reed).
[60] Ibid, [69]–[70].
[61] Ibid, [71].
[62] Ibid, [72].
[63] Ibid, [72].
[64] Ibid, [93].

embrace of realism but argue that the law should also recognise status-based limitations on access to justice and the need for positive obligations on the state.

V. Realism and the Need for Positive Action

Enhancement of equal access to justice is being shepherded along by a pragmatic approach that assesses individuals within their economic context. This approach is consistent with UK courts' growing preference for realistic over formalist reasoning. The realistic turn in judicial reasoning is seen most resoundingly in *Miller v Secretary of State for Exiting the European Union*,[65] with the Supreme Court rejecting the government's argument that as UK domestic law is the source of EU law within the UK, the status of EU law in the UK does not change without a change in domestic law by domestic actors. The majority considered that in 'a more realistic sense, where EU law applies in the UK, it is the EU institutions which are the relevant source of that law' with the consequence that a notification of withdrawal from the EU would effect a change in domestic law and therefore require prior parliamentary approval.[66] Realism is similarly becoming prominent in the UK's access to justice jurisprudence, in relation to state imposition of financial conditions on access to courts. Early signs of a pragmatic approach to access to justice have been evident since *Witham*.[67] The Court's view that the Lord Chancellor's discretion to set fees under the Supreme Court Act 1981 was subject to fundamental rights, with the effect that he could not 'exercise his power in such a way as to deprive the citizen of … his constitutional right of access to the courts', was fueled by a practical assessment of the potential economic impact of the fees order. A guiding principle has evolved that the impact of disputed measures 'must be considered in the real world', in the words of Dyson LJ in *R (Hillingdon Borough Council) v Lord Chancellor*.[68] Following this principle, the Supreme Court's *UNISON* judgment 'brought a dose of realism to its task',[69] taking stock of statistics reflecting the impact of the fees order. Such data included a 66–70 per cent decrease in the number of claims pursued in Employment Tribunals, evidence of a fall in claims for lower or no financial remedies, and a smaller than expected proportion of claimants receiving a remission of fees. The belief that realism points the way forward for protecting access to justice is mirrored across the Atlantic in the Canadian Supreme Court. In the *Trial Lawyers Association* judgment McLachlin CJ took account of evidence comparing hearing fees with the median incomes of households, to arrive at the conclusion that to bring a claim, many litigants would have to sacrifice

---

[65] [2017] UKSC 5, [2018] AC 61.
[66] *Miller* (n 65) 61.
[67] Eicke, 'Speaking in UNISON?' (n 18) 24–25.
[68] [2008] EWHC 2683 (Admin), [2009] CP Rep 13 [61].
[69] Bogg, 'The Common Law Constitution at Work' (n 55) 510.

'reasonable expenses'. The hearing fees were accordingly deemed unaffordable for middle-income households and an unconstitutional barrier to access to the courts.[70]

Though barriers to access to justice are being challenged by the judiciary's willingness to take account of economic realism, the full potential of the right is nonetheless hampered by the traditional common law conception of rights as negative. Thus, in traditional common law theory, rights are understood as freedoms from state power and intrusion and do not readily encompass positive demands on the state to take action that protects fundamental rights.[71] Indeed, the exhortation in *UNISON* regarding access to 'a fair and just system of adjudication' and enforcement of rights and obligations has been described by one commentator as reflective of the 'common law's concern with freedom as independence'.[72] The idea of freedom as independence reflects an embedded negative conception of rights, which prioritises governmental restraint rather than governmental action. Accordingly, to perceive access to justice as a representation of freedom as independence is to conceive of access to justice in purely negative terms without the space for positive obligations on the state.

The traditional reluctance to interpret the fundamental right of access to justice – and fundamental rights in general – as capable of imposing positive obligations on the state is also bound up with the view that public spending priorities are par excellence executive and legislative decisions that require deference on the part of the courts. Accordingly, in the context of governmental regulation of the justice system, a lack of legal aid funding is a softer target than the imposition of court fees and charges. For instance, despite the robust account in *UNISON* of the public good served by access to justice, the Court avoided any intimations that the state had a duty to fund access to justice for persons who could not otherwise afford it.[73] In both *ex p Witham* and *Public Law Project* Laws LJ was more explicit on the boundaries of positive obligations and resource implications; in the latter judgment, he explained that:

> there is a profound difference between on the one hand the state's duty to ensure fair and impartial procedures and to avoid undue legal obstacles to access to the courts, and on the other a putative duty to fund legal representation. In *R v Lord Chancellor, Ex p Witham [1998] QB 575*, 586 in the Divisional Court, in a judgment with which Rose LJ agreed, I said:
>
>> "Mr Richards submitted that it was for the Lord Chancellor's discretion to decide what litigation should be supported by taxpayers' money and what should not.

---

[70] *Trial Lawyers Association* (n 46) [52]–[59].

[71] P Bowen, 'Does the Renaissance of Common Law Rights mean that the Human Rights Act 1998 is now Unnecessary?' [2016] *EHRLR* 361, 369.

[72] Bogg, 'The Common Law Constitution at Work' (n 55) 513.

[73] A Higgins, 'The Supreme Court turns the judicial rhetoric on access to justice up to 11 as it strikes down unaffordable and disproportionate employment tribunal fees, but key questions about the funding of civil justice remain: *R (on the application of UNISON) v Lord Chancellor* [2017] UKSC 51' [2018] *Civil Justice Quarterly* 1, 9–10.

As regards the expenses of legal representation, I am sure that is right. Payment out of legal aid of lawyers' fees to conduct litigation is a subsidy by the state which in general is well within the power of the Executive, subject to the relevant main legislation, to regulate. But the impost of court fees is, to my mind, subject to wholly different considerations. They are the cost of going to court *at all*, lawyers or no lawyers. They are not at the choice of the litigant, who may by contrast choose how much to spend on his lawyers."

If I may say so that still seems to me to be correct and I am not aware that it has been contradicted.[74]

The resource allocation implications in *Public Law Project* therefore led Laws LJ and the remainder of the Bench of the Court of Appeal to uphold the Lord Chancellor's proposed amendment to the Legal Aid, Sentencing and Punishment of Offenders Act 2012. The amendment would have excluded those who failed a residency test from eligibility for civil legal aid under the statute, except in exceptional circumstances. The Supreme Court maintained wider access to courts by reversing the Court of Appeal decision, but did so on the ground that the order was ultra vires the statutory power to 'vary or omit services' as it sought to limit legal aid on bases 'which have nothing to do with the nature of the issue or services involved or the individual's need, or ability to pay, for the services'.[75] In arriving at that conclusion, the Justices skirted the issue whether and in what circumstances access to justice can necessitate changes in government spending priorities.

If the negative view of access to justice holds, the common law right falls short of fair trial obligations under the ECHR. The ECtHR's ruling in *Airey v Ireland* set a standard that even in civil cases, where there is no express Convention right to legal assistance, 'Article 6(1) may sometimes *compel* the state to provide for the assistance of a lawyer when such assistance proves indispensable for an effective access to court'.[76] The significance of the *Airey* ruling must not be overstated; it does not require states to provide a legal aid system and does not require legal aid or representation in all cases.[77] Yet the *Airey* conceptualisation of access to courts undoubtedly goes further than the view of the right espoused by Laws LJ, as the Strasbourg Court was guided by the principle that 'fulfilment of a duty under the Convention on occasion necessitates some positive action on the part of the State' and that in such cases "'there is ... no room to distinguish between acts and omissions"'.[78]

A change may, however, be on the horizon. On the issue of legal aid, the traditional reluctance to derive positive obligations from the right of access to justice gave way to a broader conceptualisation in *The Law Society v The Lord Chancellor*.[79] The High Court's judgment in that case accepted that 'the right of those accused

---

[74] *R (Public Law Project) v Lord Chancellor* [2015] EWCA Civ 1193 [44].
[75] *R (Public Law Project) v Lord Chancellor* [2016] UKSC 39 [29] (Lord Neuberger).
[76] *Airey v Ireland* (1979) 2 EHRR 305 [26] (emphasis added).
[77] J McBride, 'Access to Justice and Human Rights Treaties' (1998) *Civil Justice Quarterly* 235, 259–62.
[78] *Airey* (n 76) [25].
[79] *The Law Society v The Lord Chancellor* [2018] EWHC 2094 (Admin).

of criminal offences to be given publicly funded legal advice, assistance and representation when they cannot afford to pay for such services, if the interests of justice require it' forms part of Article 6 ECHR and should also be seen as part of the common law constitutional right of access to justice.[80] While ultimately concluding that, applying the *UNISON* test, the evidence did not establish a real risk that defendants would be denied access to justice, the embrace of positive duties arising from access to justice is significant. It remains to be seen whether higher courts will adopt this position as an extension of the turn towards realism in access to justice claims. However, movement in this direction would be consistent with related case law such as *Howard League for Penal Reform v Lord Chancellor*, which holds that the common law duty of fairness in proceedings may require the provision of legal aid.[81] The Court of Appeal in *Howard League* held that regulations removing legal aid for certain categories of prisoners were unlawful as they created an inherently unfair system.[82] While *Howard League* was concerned with the fairness of legal proceedings rather than access to court, the Court of Appeal's approach should be relevant to determining whether the very avenues to court have been foreclosed by the unavailability of legal aid.

The *Howard League* and *Law Society* cases might herald a new direction in access to justice case law. Indeed, recognition of positive duties arising from the right of access to justice would accord with both the realistic turn in access to justice case law and the embrace of ECHR influence. For this new approach to become accepted and established, it would however, have to overcome the traditional common law reticence towards positive duties.

VI. Status-based Exclusion and Access to Justice

As a further extension of the realistic approach, meaningful realisation of the full potential of the right of access to justice must respond to both economic and status-based disempowerment. Through taking account of financial as well as identity-based grounds of marginalisation and disempowerment, access to justice has the potential to perform an empowering and equalising role. Certainly, these bases of disempowerment are intersectional and there is a strong likelihood that financial barriers to accessing courts would have a more deleterious impact on already disempowered status groups. One way of understanding this differential impact is that persons disempowered due to their identity are likely to be over-represented in groups disempowered by reason of socio-economic status. Evidence of such impact appears in witness statements referred to in the Justice Committee's report on *Courts and Tribunal Fees*, which spoke to the special impact

---

[80] *The Law Society* (n 79) [129].
[81] *R (Howard League for Penal Reform) v Lord Chancellor* [2017] EWCA Civ 244; [2017] 4 WLR 92.
[82] *Howard League* (n 81) [98]–[109].

of employment tribunal fees on pregnant women and new mothers.[83] Yet, despite the *UNISON* Court's pragmatic examination of the impact of employment tribunal fees, hints of intersectional and contextual reasoning in *UNISON* featured not in analysis of the right of access to justice, but in analysis of discrimination on the ground of protected characteristics under the Equality Act 2010. Lady Hale's conclusion that levying higher fees for discrimination claims is indirectly discriminatory against women and others with protected characteristics who bring such claims was not seen to influence the determination of the access to justice issue.[84] Such dissociation between the two lines of analysis misleadingly suggests that analysis of the access right is complete without attention to the implications for discrimination on identity grounds. Decoupling status-based marginalisation from economic marginalisation removes some of the useful context that should inform understanding of the impact of governmental policies on access to justice. Treating access to justice separately from identity-based disempowerment would also limit the avenues to obtaining legal remedies for persons who fall outside the protected characteristics of relevant discrimination legislation.

While there are statutory protections for equality and non-discrimination – including the Equality Act 2010 and Article 14 ECHR as applied through the HRA – these statutory protections are attended by limitations on their effectiveness and reach. For instance, the right to non-discrimination under Article 14 ECHR can only be successfully claimed if it engages another Convention right. While Protocol 12 to the ECHR makes the right to non-discrimination a free-standing right, the UK has not ratified the Protocol, and its absence from Schedule 1 to the HRA means that it falls outside the corpus of rights protected by that legislation. Moreover, reliance on equality legislation to protect against status-based exclusions or differential hindrances to access restricts courts to the protected characteristics specified in the legislation. This inhibits an evolving realistic appreciation of the actual ways in which policies in the justice sector may affect different groups in society. In this light, one of the benefits of using common law rights is the adaptability of the common law to changes in society and changing conceptions of justice. This adaptability would enable judges to acknowledge discriminatory impact on groups identified by characteristics not listed in equality or human rights legislation.

A more fulsome approach to access for the disempowered would be informed by both attention to economic vulnerability, as in *Unison*, and consideration of wider contextual factors as done by the Court of Appeal in *R (Medical Justice) v Secretary of State for the Home Department*.[85] At issue in that case was the reduction of a standard 72-hour notice period between notification of an order of removal from the country and the actual removal. The Court of Appeal endorsed

---

[83] House of Commons Justice Committee, *Courts and Tribunal Fees* (HC 167, 2016) 28.
[84] *UNISON* (n 19) [132]–[134].
[85] [2011] EWCA Civ 1710.

the view that a person served with an order of removal from the UK would, under the constitutional right of access to justice, 'need to have a reasonable opportunity to obtain legal advice and assistance if they wished to do so'.[86] Critically, in determining whether a reasonable time was available, the Court noted that English will not be the first language of many returnees and that they will often be restricted by being held in detention.[87] This approach incorporates concerns arising from status-based disadvantage into a claim of unconstitutional limits on access to justice. The case, admittedly, does not engage with familiar protected characteristics or specifically address discrimination as a sub-concept within access to justice. It does, however, contribute to the doctrine by applying a realistic assessment to non-economic disempowerment, and in that sense, it is a welcome step in the right direction.

The pragmatic or realistic ethos in access to justice reasoning has the potential to foster a turn towards a public empowerment understanding of the right at common law. A public empowerment framing of access to justice would encourage greater reflection on the public benefits accruing from the right and its importance to the public – in both its individual and communitarian dimensions. Such a shift in focus would also move the discussion away from the power that defence of access to justice either grants or removes from the organs of state. There are some hints of a public facing orientation – interspersed with the traditional institutional orientation – of the right in the approach of the Supreme Court in *Unison*. However, to fulfil its public empowerment potential, access to justice adjudication ought to address access in a holistic sense. This requires attention to the full range of restrictions on access – whether arising from economic or status-based concerns – and the steps necessary to make access to justice effective- including positive obligations on the state.

VII. Conclusion

As a right that has been central to the growth of common law rights in the UK, access to justice serves multiple constitutional imperatives. It offers a bridge to other common law rights, by preserving avenues for the public to lay claim to fundamental rights in courts and by furthering the doctrinal and methodological development of common law rights adjudication. Through access to justice, the disempowered or marginalised in society have a route to defend their interests, make their voices heard and hold the state to account. In the institutional sense, access to justice has repeatedly been a trigger for controversially strong powers of judicial interpretation. This is bound up with the focus on institutional dynamics

---

[86] *Medical Justice* (n 85) [20].
[87] Ibid.

as the dominant rationale of access to justice. The right is commonly justified by courts on the basis of the core judicial roles of resolving disputes, interpreting the law and upholding the rule of law. This leads to a conceptualisation of access to justice as a judicial empowerment doctrine.

There are some indications of a turn towards a public empowerment rationale, which highlights the public good that access to justice serves for the individual and the wider community. However, remaining constraints on the full blossoming of the public empowerment rationale lie in a failure to account for status-based restrictions on access to justice and the need for obligations on the state to take action to remove limitations on access. If the traditional divide, or perception of a divide, between negative and positive duties continues to restrict access to justice jurisprudence, the pragmatic approach necessary for fulfilment of equal access will be stymied. Similarly, the public empowerment goal of equal access to adjudication to enforce rights and obligations cannot be achieved without attention to a broad range of bases of exclusion and disempowerment.

4

A Constitutional Right to Property?

TOM ALLEN

I. Introduction

This chapter asks whether there is a right to property under the common law constitution. A right to property may seem relatively unimportant when set beside rights relating to liberty, freedom of expression and religion. Indeed, it hardly features in debates on the repeal of the Human Rights Act 1998.[1] However, history shows that disputes over property can provoke serious political conflict. In the UK, for example, the rejection of the tax and redistributive provisions of the People's Budget by the House of Lords eventually led to the Parliament Act 1911.[2] Elsewhere, the judicial protection of property produced serious constitutional deadlocks in the United States in the 1930s[3] and in India in the 1970s.[4] While such episodes are not echoed in recent British history, if the pendulum swings back to greater state involvement in the economy (as the Labour Party has suggested), the repeal of the Human Rights Act 1998 could change matters.

The chapter begins by considering whether Parliament has acted on the basis that its powers are limited by a constitutional right to property. It is deliberately selective in its scope, as it concentrates on rights to compensation on an expropriation. As such, it does not consider the procedural aspects of grants or exercises of statutory powers, or the purposes for which property may be taken or regulated;

---

[1] Conservative Party, *Protecting Human Rights in the United Kingdom: The Conservatives' Proposals for Changing Britain's Human Rights Laws* (2014). The 2017 Conservative Manifesto states that the consideration of the human rights framework would be delayed until after Brexit, and the UK would remain signatory to the Convention for the duration of the next Parliament: Conservative Party, *Forward, Together: Our Plan for a Stronger Britain and a Prosperous Future* (2017), 37.

[2] I Packer, *Lloyd George, Liberalism and the Land* (Woodbridge, Suffolk, Boydell & Brewer, 2001), 54–64; B Short, *Land and Society in Edwardian Britain* (Cambridge, Cambridge University Press, 1997), 9–37.

[3] L Kalman, 'The Constitution, the Supreme Court, and the New Deal', (2005) 110 *American Historical Review* 1052; VF Nourse, 'A Tale of Two Lochners: The Untold History of Substantive Due Process and the Idea of Fundamental Rights', (2009) 97 *California LR* 751.

[4] T Allen, 'The Revival of the Right to Property in India' (2015) 10 *Asian J Comparative L* 23.

neither does it examine the discriminatory aspects of property law and welfare rights.[5] Limitations of space make it necessary to be selective, but there is sound reason to concentrate on compensation: comparative and international law show that it is the issue that provokes the most contentious disputes, both in the drafting of rights to property and in their interpretation by the courts.[6] Hence, it is likely to be the issue that will dominate any future development of a right to property in the UK.

A long line of writers, including Grotius,[7] Locke[8] and Blackstone[9] have stated that there are constitutional limits on the sovereign power over private property. On the face of it, the durability of private property seems to confirm the existence of some form of limit. JW Gough and Susan Reynolds have found that, in the pre-industrial age, it was taken for granted that compensation would be paid on the taking of land.[10] Of course, property may owe its protection to political pragmatism rather than constitutional obligation, and a practice is not the same as a binding principle.[11] Moreover, the durability of property may not be quite as strong as thought: Daniel Bogart and Gary Richardson, and Julian Hoppitt, argue that Britain's industrialisation may have been hastened by Parliament's regular restructuring and redistribution of property rights.[12] The first section therefore examines the legislative practice and debates for evidence that Parliament has regarded itself as bound by substantive constitutional obligations regarding property and compensation.

---

[5] On these topics, see M Taggart, 'Expropriation, Public Purpose and the Constitution' in C Forsyth and I Hare (eds), *The Golden Metwand and the Crooked Cord: Essays on Public Law in Honour of Sir William Wade QC* (Oxford, Clarendon, 1998), 91; EJL Waring, 'The Prevalence of Private Takings' in N Hopkins (ed), *Modern Studies in Property Law, Volume 7* (Oxford, Hart Publishing, 2016) 419; L Lammasniemi, 'Welfare, Anti-austerity and Gender: New territory and new sources of hostility for the Human Rights Act' in F Cowell (ed), *Critically Examining the Case Against the 1998 Human Rights Act* (Abingdon-on-Thames, Routledge, 2017) 151.

[6] AWB Simpson, *Human Rights and the End of Empire: Britain and the Genesis of the European Convention* (Oxford, Oxford University Press, 2001), 754–807; T Allen, *Property and the Human Rights Act 1998* (Oxford, Hart Publishing, 2005), 16–38; Allen, 'Revival', (n 4); Kalman (n 3); Nourse (n 3).

[7] H Grotius, *De Jure Belli ac Pacis* (first published 1625, Francis Kelsey tr, Oxford, Clarendon, 1925), 807.

[8] J Locke, *Two Treatises of Government* (first published 1689; Fenn, 1821), 308–309.

[9] 1 Bl Comm 135.

[10] S Reynolds, *Before Eminent Domain: Toward a History of Expropriation of Land for the Common Good* (North Carolina, U North Carolina Press, 2010), 7; JW Gough, *Fundamental Law in English Constitutional History* (Oxford, Clarendon, 1955), 2, 54; FA Mann, 'Outlines of a History of Expropriation' (1959) 75 *LQR* 188.

[11] J Murkens, 'The Quest for Constitutionalism in UK Public Law Discourse' (2009) 29 *OJLS* 427, 446–450; see below, text accompanying notes 21–30; P McAuslan and J McEldowney, 'Legitimacy and the Constitution: the Dissonance between Theory and Practice' in P McAuslan and J McEldowney (eds), *Law, Legitimacy, and the Constitution: Essays Marking the Centenary of Dicey's Law of the Constitution* (London, Sweet & Maxwell, 1985) 1, 8.

[12] D Bogart and G Richardson, 'Property Rights and Parliament in Industrializing Britain', National Bureau of Economic Research, Working Paper No 15697 (Cambridge, MA, 2010); J Hoppit, 'Compulsion, Compensation and Property Rights in Britain, 1688–1833' (2011) 210(1) *Past & Present* 93.

The chapter then considers the relationship between statutory interpretation and constitutional rights. Rupert Cross and Francis Bennion have stated that general presumptions of statutory interpretation protect 'fundamental principles' or 'constitutional rights'.[13] Lord Hoffmann in *Simms* and Lord Steyn in *Anufrijeva* expressed similar views;[14] Ivor Jennings and John Willis observed a comparable practice between the World Wars (although they were more critical of it).[15] In relation to property, however, the chapter shows that the judges have not spoken with one voice. At least since World War II, the dominant view has been that the presumptions of interpretation do not provide even a weak restraint on Parliament's powers over property, but merely an aid to discovering its 'true' intentions. However, there are some recent cases where judges have used the presumptions as strongly as that which derives from section 3 of the Human Rights Act, and for the similar purpose of protecting a right to property.

The domestic picture is therefore one in which there is evidence that might suggest that Parliament and the courts recognise limitations on state power over property. However, the picture is unclear; probably, at most, we can say that there are practices that would be compatible with a right to property, should one be introduced. The final section therefore examines the Conservative proposals for a new human rights bill, and specifically the implications of seeking to retain the Convention rights whilst weakening links with the European Court of Human Rights.[16] It considers the aim that a new bill would restore the 'original meaning' and 'mainstream understanding'[17] to the Convention rights, as it shows that there have been three markedly different interpretations of the right to property of Article 1 of the First Protocol ('A1P1').

II. Parliament and a Right to Property

The political power of property owners is often enough to persuade governments and MPs to exercise restraint in promoting policies that involve taking or regulating property. Hence, it can be difficult to distinguish between restraint by Parliament that is exercised for political reasons and restraint that anticipates or

---

[13] R Cross, *Statutory Interpretation*, 3rd edn by J Bell and G Engle (Oxford, Oxford University Press, 1995) 166; O Jones and F Bennion, *Bennion on Statutory Interpretation: A Code* 5th edn (London, LexisNexis, 2010), 773.

[14] *R v Secretary of State for the Home Department, ex p Simms* [2000] 2 AC 115, 131; *R v Secretary of State for the Home Department, ex p Anufrijeva* [2003] UKHL 36 [27].

[15] WI Jennings, 'Courts and Administrative Law – The Experience of English Housing Legislation' (1935–36) 49 *Harvard LR* 429; J Willis, 'Statutory Interpretation in a Nutshell' (1938) 16 *Canadian Bar Review* 1, 17–18; J Willis, 'Administrative Law and the British North America Act', (1939) 53 *Harvard LR* 251.

[16] Conservative Party, *Protecting Human Rights* (n 1) 5.

[17] Ibid.

responds to constitutional obligations.[18] One writer who sought to separate political from constitutional restraint in property cases is Michael Taggart.[19] He argued that, as both Parliament and the courts have consistently required the promoter to identify a public interest in support of the grant or use of a power of compulsory purchase, legislation authorising compulsory purchase would be unconstitutional if it were not in the public interest. If, as Taggart argues, a consistent legislative and judicial practice establishes a constitutional obligation, one could argue that the regular payment of compensation for the expropriation of land suggests that there is also a constitutional right to compensation.[20]

Paul Scott has considered Taggart's evidence, but he doubts whether it is sufficient to establish a constitutional obligation: 'Taggart's ostensibly normative "constitutional principle" is as much a description of political practice as it is the practice of the courts on those rare occasions where Parliament's statutory outputs might be plausibly interpreted as permitting interference in contravention of Taggart's principle.'[21] In relation to compensation, Scott notes that the consistency of the practice has been questioned. He cites the eighteenth-century debate in Parliament over its power to impose taxes in America.[22] Lord Camden asserted that Parliament 'cannot enact any thing against the divine law'; specifically, it 'cannot take away any man's private property without making him a compensation.' This, he argued, was proved by 'the many private bills, as well as public, passed every session.'[23] Lord Mansfield challenged Camden's reliance on divine law as 'simply not applicable to the present question'. In any case, the practice was not as clear as Camden suggested: 'I deny the proposition that parliament takes no man's property without his consent: it frequently takes private property without making what the owner thinks a compensation.'[24] Indeed, depending on the meaning of 'taking' property, it can seem that compensation is denied more often than it is provided. For example, there is no consistency in the provision of compensation for destruction of property or the extinction of rights of property. Thus the Slavery Abolition Act 1833 set aside £20 million to compensate former owners of slaves, but this was attributable to a political compromise rather than a settled moral or constitutional principle.[25] In more recent years, full compensation was provided for the destruction of cattle in the foot-and-mouth outbreak of 2001, but the rules were later re-written to limit liability and deal with the moral hazards created by full compensation.[26] In addition, compensation is not normally paid for losses caused

---

[18] Murkens (n 11); McAuslan and McEldowney (n 11).

[19] Taggart (n 5).

[20] Reynolds (n 10), 7, 34–46; Gough (n 10), 2, 54.

[21] P Scott, 'Entick v Carrington and the Legal Protection of Property', in A Tomkins and P Scott (eds), Entick v Carrington: *250 Years of the Rule of Law* (Oxford, Hart Publishing, 2015), 131, 158.

[22] Ibid, 137–39.

[23] *Cobbett's Parliamentary History*, XVI, 167 (1766).

[24] Ibid, 172 (1766).

[25] See especially ss 24 and 45 and Hoppit (n 12) 115–120.

[26] See *R v Secretary of State for Environment, Food and Rural Affairs, ex p Partridge Farms* [2009] EWCA Civ 284, on steps taken by DEFRA to address over-compensation for diseased animals.

by the regulation of property, or for losses arising from changes to the private law of contract. For example, landowners are not normally compensated for losses caused by environmental controls; neither are suppliers for consumer protection laws.

Arguably, these examples do not disprove the constitutional principle; at most, they show that compensation is only required in the specific case of compulsory purchase.[27] Even here, however, the practice has been quite fluid. Early UK legislation provided very little guidance on the valuation of property; instead, the issue was referred to a disinterested jury or commission, which set compensation on the tort basis.[28] The application of tort principles meant that compensation reflected the owner's loss, rather than the taker's gain (or loss).[29] This remains the governing principle, but Parliament has regularly adjusted the nature of losses for which the owner may claim compensation. This often reflects concerns over compensation for unearned or undeserved values. For example, housing laws of the later nineteenth and early twentieth century denied compensation for uninhabitable homes on land that was taken for slum clearance.[30] The Leasehold Enfranchisement Act 1967 allowed tenants to purchase the freehold of their property, without compensation for the value of the building. This was justified by reference to the tenant's obligation of repair: in most cases, the tenants on a long lease would have effectively paid for the cost of the building by the end of the term.[31] Parliament has also approached general issues of quantum and valuation with a degree of flexibility. The Acquisition of Land (Assessment of Compensation) Act 1919 took a step away from the tort measure, as it treated the owner as a 'willing seller', thereby denying compensation for the losses that an 'unwilling seller' would experience for being forced to sell at an inopportune time.[32] Another important step was taken with the enactment of the Town and Country Planning Act 1947. Under the Act, an owner's right to develop land was expropriated, and thereafter compensation

---

[27] Even so, there has been inconsistency in laws for the acquisition of easements and wayleaves: see N Hutchison and J Rowan-Robinson, 'Utility wayleaves: a compensation lottery?', (2002) 20 *J Property Investment & Finance* 159, 166 ('The different measures of compensation provided in law for compulsory access by the utilities to private land is both surprising and confusing.').

[28] This continued with the Land Clauses Consolidation Act 1845: see FA Sharman, 'The History of the Land Clauses Consolidation Act, 1845' (1986) 7 *Statute LR* 13, 17–18.

[29] Blackstone stated that Parliament strikes a bargain between owner and promoter, on terms giving the owner 'a full indemnification and equivalent for the injury thereby sustained.' 1 Bl Comm 135. There were some exceptions: enclosures and the adjustment of rights in settled estates usually provided that those who held rights in the common land or the estate would retain an interest in the land or estate, and hence there was the possibility of sharing in any gains: see Reynolds (n 10), 42–43. On the implications of the 'value to the owner' principle, see BP Denyer Green, 'The *Pointe Gourde* Principle – 1', (1978) 8 *Kingston LR* 101, 109–112; Law Commission, *Towards a Compulsory Purchase Code (I) Compensation Final Report*, Appendix D, 171–220 (Law Com No 286, 2003).

[30] JA Yelling, *Slums and Slum Clearance in Victorian London* (Oxford, Oxford University Press, 1986).

[31] In *James v UK* (1986) Series A No 98, the European Court of Human Rights held that the Act did not violate the Convention.

[32] Acquisition of Land (Assessment of Compensation) Act 1919, s 2(1), (2).

excluded planning gains.[33] Planning decisions were made by the community, for the benefit of the community; so far as the owner was concerned, there was no moral claim to any increment in market value accruing from the grant of planning permission.[34] Recently, both Labour and Conservative party members have raised the possibility of denying compensation for the element of the value of land that is attributable to the grant of planning permission.[35] The core principle of compensating for loss would remain in place, but Parliament would remain free to determine the types of loss that should be compensated.

To summarise: Parliament regularly legislates for the compulsory redistribution of property, on the basis that the owner should be compensated for its loss. However, the practice would not support the case for a rigid right to compensation at market value, as Parliament has varied in its view of the 'loss' that should be compensated. This therefore brings us back to the core question of Taggart and Scott: does a practice, even if consistent over time, amount to a constitutional principle? A consistent practice may be a necessary criterion, but – if a constitutional principle really is at work – there should also be some evidence that Ministers, when framing legislation, and MPs, when scrutinising it, have a common means of identifying and using precedents so as to determine what the constitutional principle requires in the particular context. In effect, Parliament must have its own principles of constitutional interpretation. However, as a general rule, Parliamentary debates rarely exhibit a concern with precedent, or with the appropriate ways of reasoning from precedent. Moreover, even where Ministers and MPs reflect on legislative precedent, they may do so for a variety of reasons. They may, for example, wish to draw on precedent to make pragmatic arguments that a proposed course of action is likely to be successful (or not). By contrast, constitutional reasoning would explore precedent for evidence that a proposed course of action is within limits on its powers that Parliament has previously observed. Taggart found this in the private bill procedures of the nineteenth century; Scott questioned whether the practice had developed into a binding constraint, especially in relation to compensation.

One specific example of constitutional reasoning concerns debates on the extinction of property rights by retrospective legislation. As a matter of convention, Law Officers must consent to the introduction of bills with retrospective provisions. The Law Officers, or relevant Ministers, often acknowledge that there are constitutional restrictions on retrospection, and refer to legislative precedent to show that the provisions in question are compatible with these restrictions. For example, in the debate on the War Damage Bill of 1966 (reversing the judgment

---

[33] The Town and Country Planning Act 1959 shifted the emphasis back to market value compensation.

[34] KC Clark, 'The British Labor Government's Town and Country Planning Act: A Study in Conflicting Liberalisms' (1951) 66 *Political Science* Q 87; M Grant, 'Compensation and Betterment' in B Cullingworth (ed), *British Planning: 50 Years of Planning and Regional Policy* (Oxford, Athlone, 1999).

[35] 'Labour's housebuilding plan labelled "deeply sinister" by Tory minister', *The Guardian*, 2 Feb 2018, at www.theguardian.com/society/2018/feb/02/labours-housebuilding-plan-labelled-deeply-sinister-by-tory-minister.

in *Burmah Oil v Lord Advocate*[36]), the Attorney General acknowledged that retrospective laws are 'in general wrong and contrary to the rule of law', but may be legitimate if the affected individuals were warned of the possibility of retrospection, and that retrospection was needed to achieve fairness for all individuals in a similar position. Both elements, he argued, were present in respect of the Bill and therefore established its constitutionality.[37] These principles were further explored in debates on retrospective tax laws. Similarly, in the debates on the retrospective tax provisions in the Chancellor's budget proposals for 1978, Peter Rees MP identified core principles for provisions aimed at plugging unintended gaps and loopholes in taxing provisions.[38] The principles were primarily concerned with Parliamentary procedures, but still echoed the substantive points regarding warnings and fairness that were made by the Attorney General in relation to the War Damage Bill. Moreover, they were derived from a similar interpretive process, leading Geoffrey Howe MP to say that the 'Rees Rules' stood on 'a firm foundation of practice and constitutional convention.'[39]

Retrospection provides an example of Parliamentary constitutional interpretation, but it is a fairly narrow one. It is only in the debates on Irish home rule that Parliament has taken a general view of legislative practice and interpretation in relation to a putative right to property. In response to fears that an Irish legislature would confiscate the property of landlords, the second Home Rule Bill (1893) provided that the new legislature would not have the power to enact laws 'Whereby any person may be deprived of life, liberty or property without due process of law … or whereby private property may be taken without just compensation.'[40] The government claimed that the clause imported principles that were already recognised under the common law constitution, except that the courts would now have the power to strike down legislation that violated them. In response, the opposition argued that there were no precedents by which the courts could derive standards that would allow them to judge whether legislation secured 'due process' or 'just compensation'. The Attorney General, Charles Russell, countered that 'due process

---

[36] [1965] AC 75.

[37] HC Deb 12 May 1965, vol 712, col 600; see also HC Deb 25 June 2007, vol 462, cols 48–49, 57, 59. To support his argument, the Attorney General referred to the Indemnity Act 1920, the War Charges Validation Act 1925; the Charitable Trusts (Validation) Act 1954, the Wireless Telegraphy (Validity of Charges) Act 1954 and the Finance Act 1960, s 39.

[38] A Seely, 'Retrospective taxation: earlier debates', House of Commons Library Standard Note SN04369, 18 July 2012; O Gay, 'Retrospective legislation', House of Commons Library Standard Note SN/PC/06454, 14 June 2013; A Seely, 'Retrospective taxation: section 58 of the *Finance Act 2008*', House of Commons Library Standard Note SN6361, 28 Aug 2013.

[39] HC Deb 12 July 1978, vol 953, col 1642. Rees and Howe were in the opposition; they objected to the extent of retrospectivity in the tax avoidance provisions in the proposed budget.

[40] Government of Ireland Bill (1893); see T Allen, 'Constitutional Rights in the Irish Home Rule Bill of 1893' (2018) 39 *Journal of Legal History* 187; J Jaconelli, 'Human Rights Guarantees and Irish Home Rule', (1990–91) 25–27 *Irish Jurist* NS 181; R Keane, 'Fundamental Rights in Irish Law: A Note on the Historical Background' in J O'Reilly (ed) *Human Rights and Constitutional Law: Essays in Honour of Brian Walsh* (Dublin, Round Hall, 1992), 25–35.

of law is where the process of law follows settled principles of judicial procedure, or where such process follows sound precedent applicable to the subject-matter and the circumstances affecting it.'[41] He did not, however, identify the source or nature of the 'settled principles' or 'sound precedent' that would guide the legislature or the courts.[42] In relation to the takings clause, the Solicitor General argued that '"just compensation" must be measured by what the Irish and English laws at the present time think to be just'.[43] The debate therefore asked whether practices could be the foundation of a constitutional right to property.

Russell did not explain why practices would provide this foundation. He may have adapted his argument from the Fur Seal arbitration, where he argued that consent of nations was the foundation of international law; crucially, he claimed that evidence of consent could only be found in practice where states had regarded themselves as bound.[44] It seems that he simply adapted his argument to the constitutional debate. In the home rule debates, the issue was not whether practice should prevail over natural law, but whether it provided any sort of law or binding principle at all.[45] On this point, the opposition borrowed from AV Dicey's separation of constitutional history and constitutional law.[46] Dunbar Barton argued that 'In no country had historical precedents been used in deciding legal questions', and hence it was impossible to say that the clause would provide any real protection for property owners.[47] George Wyndham reprised Mansfield's speech of over a century earlier, as he said that 'The Imperial Parliament was every day engaged in passing laws, extinguishing the rights of property in a manner some believed to be due and others believed to be undue.'[48] In effect, Wyndham argued that Parliament's respect for private property was a product of political morality rather than binding obligation. Questions regarding process and compensation were inherently political and moral; no institutional structure could capture Parliament's sense of political morality in a way that could be transferred to an Irish legislature.[49] The 1893 Bill eventually passed the Commons, but it was defeated by a large margin in the Lords. It is safe to say that there was no consensus on the existence of a right to property and, in particular, whether or how it could be derived from the legislative practice.

---

[41] HC Deb 15 June 1893, series 4, vol 13, col 1116.

[42] Ibid.

[43] HC Deb 11 April 1893, series 4, vol 11, col 112.

[44] Fur Seal Arbitration, Proceedings of the Tribunal of Arbitration, United States v Great Britain, Washington, 1895. Vol XIII, 7–11, 265–268.

[45] Ibid; the American lead counsel in the arbitration, James Carter, argued that principles of international law could be deduced from natural law and moral principles.

[46] AV Dicey, *Lectures Introductory to the Study of the Law of the Constitution* 4th edn (London, MacMillan, 1893).

[47] HC Deb 16 June 1893, series 4, vol 13, cols 1209–10.

[48] HC Deb 15 June 1893, series 4, vol 13, col 1129.

[49] See authorities cited at (n 46).

The UK Government did not include the due process and takings clauses in the Government of Ireland Act 1914,[50] for reasons that would become standard in British constitutional drafting until the 1960s that is, fundamental rights could not be expressed in a form that courts could interpret consistently and, in any case, constraints should not be imposed on legislatures with responsible government.[51] Subsequently, the government was persuaded to include takings clauses in the Government of Ireland Act 1920 and the Government of India Act 1935.[52] With the latter, the right was very limited: the legislature was required to set out the basis for determining compensation on a taking of land, but there was no minimum standard for compensation. In effect, the legislature was required to limit the risk of arbitrary executive action, but that was all. This view of compensation was also evident in the UK position on the inclusion of a right to property in the Convention. The UK ratified the Protocol, but only after A1P1 was stripped of any hint of a compensation guarantee.[53] Even so, the government delayed its acceptance of the jurisdiction of the European Court of Human Rights and the right of individual petition until after the War Damage Act 1966 came into effect.[54] Later cases suggest that it is quite possible that the Act would have satisfied the Convention, but it was very much an open question at the time.[55]

In summary, there is enough in the historical record to support arguments that there is a legislative practice of compensating for property, but it is debateable that it constitutes an obligation binding on Parliament. Whether it is explained by political pragmatism or a constitutional obligation, one point is clear: if a new bill of rights includes a right to property, with a substantive guarantee of compensation, it would only be consistent with tradition and practice if it allowed Parliament some latitude to determine the types of loss that should be compensated.

III. The Courts and a Right to Property

In 1610, the Court of Common Pleas stated in *Sir Francis Barrington's Case* that 'when an Act makes any conveyance good against the King, or any other person or persons in certain, it shall not take away the right of any other, although there be not

---

[50] A narrower version of the right, only dealing with takings and compensation, was incorporated in the Government of Ireland Act 1920, but only by a private member's amendment and after initial resistance by the Government: Allen, 'Constitutional Rights' (n 46).

[51] On Ireland, see authorities cited (n 46); on the colonies, see COH Parkinson, *Bills of Rights and Decolonization* (Oxford, OUP, 2009); Simpson (n 6) 1–54.

[52] Allen (n 4).

[53] Simpson (n 6) 754–807; Allen, *Property and the Human Rights Act 1998* (n 6) 16–38.

[54] A Lester, 'UK Acceptance of the Strasbourg Jurisdiction: What went on in Whitehall in 1965' [1998] *PL* 237.

[55] *National & Provincial Building Society v UK* (1998) 25 EHRR 127; *Jahn v Germany* [2004] ECHR 36.

any saving in the Act.'[56] *Barrington's Case* was cited in *Western Counties v Windsor and Annapolis*, which is one of a number of cases where courts have stated that an Act does not take away or extinguish rights of property unless it clearly provides that it does.[57] If, as Cross and Bennion argue, presumptions protect rights, it would seem that there is a constitutional right to property.[58] Moreover, it may incorporate a substantive right to compensation. One frequently quoted statement is that of Brett LJ in *AG v Horner*, where he said that 'it is a proper rule of construction not to construe an Act of Parliament as interfering with or injuring persons' rights without compensation, unless one is obliged to so construe it.'[59] In *De Keyser's Hotel*, Lord Atkinson stated that 'unless the words of the statute clearly so demand, a statute is not to be construed so as to take away the property of a subject without compensation.'[60]

Cross and Bennion may be correct in respect of presumptions relating to liberty or access to the courts; certainly, Lord Hoffmann in *Simms* and Lord Steyn in *Anufrijeva* suggest that the courts use the presumptions to protect fundamental rights.[61] However, in relation to property, the courts have not reached a consensus on the use of presumptions as restraints on Parliament. The judicial statements in the preceding paragraph can be contrasted with Bowen LJ's dicta in *London and North Western Railway v Evans*, where he said that the presumption against a deprivation of property was nothing more than a doctrine 'of sound sense and obvious justice'.[62] Similarly, in the first edition of *Law of the Constitution*, AV Dicey acknowledged that, in cases of doubt, judges apply the meaning that is 'consistent with the doctrines both of private and of international morality', but he denied that interpretation operated as a substantive limit on Parliament.[63] Indeed, in 1915, in *Local Government Board v Arlidge*, on the powers of local authorities over housing, Lord Haldane suggested that the presumptions were out of date. Whilst he agreed that rights of property and liberty 'are not to be affected unless Parliament has said so', he continued by observing that 'Parliament, in what it considers higher interests than those of the individual, has so often interfered with such rights on other occasions, that it is dangerous for judges to lay much stress on what a hundred years ago would have been a presumption considerably stronger than it is to-day.'[64]

---

[56] (1610) 8 Co Rep 136b, 138; 77 ER 681, 684.
[57] (1882) 7 App Cas 178, 188; *London and North-Western Railway Co v Evans* [1893] 1 Ch 16, 27; *Mayor of Yarmouth v Simmons* (1879) 10 Ch D 518, 527; *Jones v Cleanthi* [2006] EWCA Civ 1712; *In the matter of Peacock* [2012] UKSC 5.
[58] Cross (n 13); Bennion (n 13).
[59] (1884) 14 QBD 245, 257; *Commissioner of Public Works (Cape Colony) v Logan* [1903] AC 355, 363–364.
[60] [1920] AC 508, 542.
[61] *Simms* (n 14); *Anufrijeva* (n 14).
[62] *London and North Western Ry Co v Evans* [1893] 1 Ch 16, 28.
[63] Dicey, *Lectures Introductory to the Study of the Law of the Constitution* (London, Macmillan, 1885), 58–59.
[64] [1915] AC 120, 130.

About 20 years after *Arlidge*, Ivor Jennings noted a shift in interpretation, at least in relation to housing laws and the delegation of power over compulsory purchase to local authorities.[65] Judges were now much more restrictive: 'the rules of interpretation permit, and the judges in recent years have been unconsciously led by social conditions to exhibit, a bias against social reform'.[66] In 1930, in *Minister of Health v R (ex p Yaffe)* (another housing case), Scrutton LJ stated that the delegation of power to condemn housing to local authorities was a matter of 'constitutional importance', as it appeared to exclude the authority of the courts.[67] Writing extra-judicially, Gordon Hewart, the Lord Chief Justice, attacked the breadth of executive powers of new social legislation in *The New Despotism*.[68] Jennings argued that these attacks demonstrated that the turn to restrictive interpretation was motivated by an antipathy to social reform, and that the presumptions were being applied improperly. In his view, there was no ambiguity in the language of the relevant statutes; indeed, the judges were deliberately frustrating the clear aim of the law: 'to interfere with common law rights'.[69] John Willis also argued that the presumptions were not invoked as an aid to discovering Parliament's intentions from ambiguous language, but as a means for avoiding those intentions where expressed in clear language. For Willis, the judges were using the presumptions to construct a common law bill of rights, which they used to obstruct social legislation, not unlike the way that the Supreme Court had done in the US.[70]

The Donoughmore Committee dismissed Hewart's criticisms, although it did not specifically comment on presumptions and statutory interpretation.[71] After World War II, judges returned to the language of Bowen LJ, as they framed the presumptions in terms of discovering Parliament's intentions. In *Secretary of State for Defence v Guardian Newspapers Ltd*, Lord Scarman stated that

> there certainly remains a place in the law for the principle of construction … that the courts must be slow to impute to Parliament an intention to override property rights in the absence of plain words to that effect. But the principle is not an overriding rule of law: it is an aid, amongst many others, developed by the judges in their never ending task of interpreting statutes in such a way as to give effect to their true purpose.[72]

A similar view applies to the related presumption concerning retrospectivity. In 1892, in *Lauri v Renad*, on the International Copyright Act 1886, Lindley LJ stated

---

[65] Jennings (n 15) 443.
[66] Ibid, 452.
[67] [1930] 2 KB 144, 148.
[68] G Hewart, *The New Despotism* (Benn 1929).
[69] Jennings (n 15) 437.
[70] Willis 'Statutory Interpretation' (n 15); Willis 'Administrative law' (n 15).
[71] *Report of the Committee on Ministers' Powers* (Cmd 4060, 1932), 54–55. The *Report* did include a separate Note by Harold Laski, one of the Committee members, that recommended a fresh approach to statutory interpretation. 'Note by Professor Laski on the Judicial Interpretation of Statutes', Annex V, *Report of the Committee on Ministers' Powers*, 135–137.
[72] [1985] AC 339, 363 (dissenting on another point).

that 'It is a fundamental rule of English law that no statute shall be construed so as to have a retrospective operation unless its language is such as plainly to require such a construction.'[73] In 1994, in *L'Office Cherifien des Phosphates v Yamashita-Shinnihon Steamship*, on amendments to the Arbitration Act 1950, Lord Mustill denied that the presumption reflected higher constitutional principles: 'since it is rightly taken for granted that Parliament will rarely wish to act in a way which seems unfair it is sensible to look very hard at a statute which appears to have this effect, to make sure that this is what Parliament really intended. This is, however, no more than common sense ...'[74] More recently, in *Odelola v Secretary of State for the Home Department*, an immigration case, Lord Neuberger described the presumption against retrospectivity as a 'rule of construction, or, perhaps more accurately, a factor to be taken onto account when interpreting a statute or rule.'[75] He was clear that 'It is not some sort of substantive, or even procedural, legal right.'[76]

These cases suggest that the presumptions relating to property are now treated as aids to interpretation, rather than devices enabling courts to protect property. The picture is not entirely clear, however. In 2006, in *Jones v Cleanthi*, Jonathan Parker LJ referred to Brett LJ's reasoning in *Horner*, and stated that an Act can only take away a right of property 'by plain enactment or necessary intendment'. Moreover, he stated that this is 'a principle which largely reflects article 1 of the First Protocol to the European Convention on Human Rights, incorporated into domestic law by the Human Rights Act 1998.'[77] Some judges have also suggested that the presumption is now as strong as that which is created by section 3 of the Human Rights Act 1998. In *Peacock*, the Supreme Court considered whether section 16(2) of the Drug Trafficking Act 1994 authorised the forfeiture of assets that had been lawfully obtained after conviction, in addition to the assets obtained from criminal activity.[78] Section 16(2) stated that confiscation orders were limited to the value of unlawfully obtained assets, but it did not say, explicitly, that the orders could only be satisfied from the assets. Nevertheless, the claimant argued that the general presumption against deprivations of rights should apply.[79]

---

[73] [1892] 3 Ch 402, 421; *In re Athlumney, Ex parte Wilson* [1898] 2 QB 547, 552; *Yew Bon Tew v Kenderaan Bas Mara* [1983] 1 AC 553, 558; *Pearce v Secretary of State for Defence* [1988] AC 755, 802. Note that the presumption does not apply to procedural rights: *Arnold v Central Electricity Generating Board* [1988]. AC 228, 275.

[74] [1994] 1 AC 486, 525.

[75] [2009] UKHL 25 [55].

[76] Ibid. Hence, the presumption should not be applied mechanically: the more unfair and harsh the impact of an interpretation, the less likely it is that it reflects Parliament's intention and the courts should opt for the less intrusive meaning: *L'Office Cherifien des Phosphates* [1994] 1 AC 486, 525; *Wilson v Secretary of State for Trade and Industry* [2003] UKHL 40, [18]–[20], [98], [187]–[199].

[77] [2006] EWCA Civ 1712 [82].

[78] *Re Peacock* [2012] UKSC 5.

[79] The claimant took his case to Strasbourg but it was dismissed for the failure to exhaust domestic remedies, because he had not pleaded or argued his Convention rights before the national courts: *Peacock v UK* (2016) 62 EHRR SE14.

Hence, he argued that the court should opt for the interpretation that was less intrusive, with the result that lawfully obtained assets would not be subject to confiscation. The majority rejected this argument, on the basis that there was no ambiguity in section 16(2): the plain language ruled out any restriction to unlawfully obtained assets and there was no room to consider the presumption. It is interesting to note, however, that Lord Hope, dissenting, with Lady Hale concurring, took the view that the presumption should be applied, because 'it is not necessary to read section 16 as extending to after acquired property to make sense of it.'[80] He did not suggest that the provision was ambiguous; instead, it was enough that the provision would still have some effect if it were read more narrowly. In essence, he followed the approach of section 3 of the Human Rights Act 1998.[81] His view did not carry the majority, but nonetheless it indicates that some judges are prepared to apply a very strong presumption in favour of property rights. Even among the majority, Lord Walker took the same view as Jonathan Parker LJ in *Jones v Cleanthi*, as he referred to 'the well-established principle of statutory construction that property rights are not to be taken away without compensation unless Parliament's intention to expropriate them has been expressed in clear and unambiguous terms', and stated that 'The principle is in no doubt.'[82] He was not prepared to go as far as Lord Hope or Lady Hale, but arguably they differed only in the scope of presumptions, rather than the legitimacy of using them to protect an underlying constitutional right.

The potential impact of the use of strong presumptions is demonstrated by developments in Canada. The seminal case is *Manitoba Fisheries v R*.[83] The Canadian Parliament passed legislation which was intended to nationalise the fish marketing industry, which it did by setting up a state corporation with the exclusive right to export fish from those provinces that chose to participate in the scheme.[84] Manitoba joined the scheme; as a result, the plaintiff, a Manitoba fish exporter, was put out of business.[85] The legislation did not require Canada to compensate fish exporters. Instead, it provided that compensation would be paid by each participating province, at rates determined by the province. Manitoba agreed to pay compensation for the value of redundant physical assets, but not for the goodwill. The plaintiff claimed that goodwill was a type of property, and hence he had a right to compensation for it.

---

[80] *Peacock* (n 84) [65].

[81] See A Kavanagh 'What's so Weak about "Weak-form Review"? The case of the UK Human Rights Act 1998' (2015) 13 *International Journal of Constitutional Law* 1008.

[82] *Peacock* (n 84) [33].

[83] (1978) 88 DLR (3d) 462; see PA Warchuk, 'Rethinking Compensation for Expropriation,' (2015) 48 *University of British Columbia Law Review* 655 for Canadian developments subsequent to *Manitoba Fisheries*.

[84] The Canadian federal system only allows the Canadian Parliament to pass fisheries legislation, but its Freshwater Fish Marketing Act, R.S.C. 1970, c. F-13 enabled provinces to form state monopolies in their jurisdiction.

[85] Private operators were prohibited from exporting fish without a licence or exemption; the plaintiff's requests for one were refused.

On compensation, Ritchie J, for the Supreme Court of Canada, referred to Lord Atkinson's statement in *AG v De Keyser's Royal Hotel*.[86] After stating that goodwill is a form of property, he said that 'There is nothing in the Act providing for the taking of such property by the Government without compensation and as I find that there was such a taking, it follows, in my view, that it was unauthorized having regard to the recognized rule [in *De Keyser's Hotel*]'.[87] It is worth noting that Ritchie J did not suggest that there was a general principle against creating state monopolies; hence, the taking was only 'unauthorised' because compensation was not paid. However, this right to compensation did not arise under the Act. Indeed, the Act provided that any compensation would be paid by the provincial government. However, under the federal system, Canada had no power to require Manitoba to pay compensation. *Manitoba Fisheries* therefore stands for the principle that a property owner has a right to compensation that exists outside the statute that authorises the taking. Ritchie J stated that the legislature can exclude the right, but held that Canada had not done so in this case. Given the clarity of the statutory provisions stating that Canada would not pay compensation, it is clear that only the strongest language would exclude the right to compensation.

In conclusion, the judicial view on the relationship between the presumptions and a right to property is mixed. Judges look for interpretations that avoid harsh or unfair treatment, but only some of them use the presumptions as a limitation on legislative power (even if only in a weak form). Hence, the court's interpretive practices seem to provide no more clarity than Parliament's legislative practices.

IV. Property and Repeal of the Human Rights Act

If Parliament repealed the Human Rights Act and enacted a new law to 'restore' British ideas of civil liberties, what form would it take? In 2014, the Conservative Party's *Protecting Human Rights in the United Kingdom: The Conservatives' Proposals for Changing Britain's Human Rights Laws*, proposed to replace the Act with a new Act, without repealing or denouncing the Convention rights themselves.[88] The intention is to incorporate the original text of the Convention, to 'restore common sense', and 'ensure that they [the Convention rights] are applied in accordance with the original intentions for the Convention and the mainstream understanding of these rights'.[89]

This raises interesting questions relating to the 'original intentions' and 'mainstream understandings' of the right to property. A1P1 was written to avoid any kind

---

[86] *De Keyser's* (n 66).
[87] *Manitoba Fisheries* (n 89), 473.
[88] Conservative Party, *Protecting Human Rights* (n 1).
[89] Ibid (n 1), 5; see H Fenwick and R Masterman, 'The Conservative Project to "Break the Link between British Courts and Strasbourg": Rhetoric or Reality?' (2017) 80 *MLR* 1111.

of substantive guarantee relating to compensation.[90] When the Convention was drafted, the UK, and several other states, insisted that the right to property should not incorporate any form of guarantee of compensation. As a result, A1P1 does not include the language importing the proportionality test, as found in other Convention rights: an interference with the enjoyment of possessions must be lawful, and in the public or general interest, but there is no requirement that it should be 'necessary in a democratic society'. The right to property therefore seemed to focus more on observance of the rule of law and freedom from discrimination.[91] Supporting this interpretation of A1P1 could therefore put a Conservative Government in the potentially awkward position of defending the dilution of the right to property.[92] In any case, the position under the A1P1 changed in 1982, with *Sporrong and Lönnroth v Sweden*.[93] The European Court of Human Rights stated that an interference with the enjoyment of possessions would comply with A1P1 only if 'a fair balance was struck between the demands of the general interest of the community and the requirements of the protection of the individual's fundamental rights.'[94] Following *Sporrong*, the Court held that the fair balance would normally require compensation for a taking of property, but exceptions could be made for social justice or economic restructuring.[95] For example, in *James v UK*, it was held that the compensation provisions of the Leasehold Enfranchisement Act 1967 were not contrary to A1P1, even though the payment for the freehold excluded the value of the buildings.[96] In *Lithgow v UK*, it declared that states may depart from the usual compensation standard when engaged in restructuring on a large scale, as in the case of a nationalisation of an industry.[97] This flexibility also applied in regulatory cases: in *Mellacher v Austria*, the Court found no violation in respect of rent controls that, according to the applicant, made it difficult to cover the maintenance costs of the property.[98] These cases – all decided in the 1980s – indicate that A1P1 imposed substantive obligations on states, but they were flexible enough to accommodate the kinds of policies that the UK sought to protect when the Convention was being drafted.

The *Sporrong* interpretation does not reflect the original intention but, to return to the Conservative proposals, it probably reflects the 'mainstream understanding' of the right to property. However, it is not clear that the European Court of Human Rights still follows the flexible approach of *Sporrong, Mellacher, James*

---

[90] Simpson (n 6), 754–807; Allen (n 6), 16–38; T Allen, 'Liberalism, Social Democracy and the Value of Property under the European Convention on Human Rights' (2010) 59 *ICLQ* 1055.

[91] See, eg, *Handyside v UK* (1976) Series A no 24.

[92] Although, of course, it would provide more latitude in changing social welfare benefits: see Lammasniemi (n 5).

[93] (1982) Series A No 52.

[94] Ibid.

[95] *James* (n 37) [54].

[96] *James* (n 37).

[97] *Lithgow v UK* (1986) Series A No 102 [120].

[98] *Mellacher v Austria* (1989) Series A No 169 [55]–[56].

and *Lithgow*. Proportionality remains the central principle, but it is now sometimes interpreted within an ordoliberal, social market economy framework.[99] The key case is *Hutten-Czapska v Poland*, where the Court declared that A1P1 provides landlords with an 'entitlement to derive profit from their property', with the result that rents cannot be controlled indefinitely.[100] Plainly, the Court has become much more willing to intervene in regulatory cases than the states would have expected when A1P1 came into force. The Court's judgments suggest two reasons for this. First, the Court seems to challenge the idea that property may be subject to social obligations in favour of vulnerable groups. In *Radovici and Stănescu v Romania*,[101] it said that it is legitimate for the state to ensure that individuals have access to affordable housing, but the burden of making that provision cannot be imposed on landlords: 'the legitimate interests of the community in such situations call for a fair distribution of the social and financial burden involved in the transformation and reform of the country's housing supply. *This burden cannot, as in the present cases, be placed on one particular social group, however important the interests of the other group or the community as a whole …*'.[102] Presumably, the burden would be shared through taxation or other general revenues; crucially, it is unfair to put the obligation on the shoulders of property owners as parties to the contract.

The second reason focusses on the market itself, rather than the protection of vulnerable groups. In *Hutten-Czapska*, the Court was concerned that the control of rents made it impossible for the landowner to earn a profit. However, *Radovici* suggests that the focus is not so much on earning a profit, but on the freedom to set a price. It is less about the enjoyment of property generally, and more about the specific freedoms associated with market activity. In most cases, these would be the same. Nevertheless, there is a difference. For example, if the state sought to set prices so as to allow both suppliers and buyers in a particular sector to earn a reasonable profit, it might be able to justify its policy under *Hutten-Czapska*. However, *Radovici* suggests that, if either party thought they could get a better price without controls, they could complain that they were being forced to bear a cost that should be more widely distributed.

This position is also evident in cases on expropriation. As noted above, the Court initially allowed compensation to fall below the market value where justified by social justice or economic restructuring. As explained above, in the UK, this has usually turned on finding that an element of the market value was not attributable to the investment of the owner.[103] Full market value is now normally required even for owners that did not make any investment in the land, and even if the state argues that the current value is attributable to the investment of the

---

[99] Allen, 'Liberalism' (n 96).
[100] *Hutten-Czapska v Poland* ECHR 2006-VIII [239]; *Radovici and Stănescu v Romania* App No 68479/01, 71351/01 and 71352/01 (ECtHR, 2 November 2006).
[101] *Radovici*, ibid.
[102] Ibid [88] (emphasis added).
[103] See text accompanying (n 36)–(n 41).

tenants or the public sector.[104] This was the theory behind the compensation provisions of the Town and Country Planning Act 1947: the uplift in value arising from the grant of planning permission was not due to the investment or work of the landowner, and hence the uplift should belong to the community.[105] However, in *Kozacioğlu v Turkey*[106] and *Urbárska v Slovakia*,[107] the Court found violations of A1P1 where national law excluded compensation for values that were not attributable to the applicants' own investment in their property. This is highly significant, as it challenges the logic behind the Town and Country Planning Act and the earlier housing laws that denied compensation for the value of residential buildings that were unfit for occupation.[108] This is another aspect of ordoliberalism or social market economy, in its rejection of policies for solidarity and redistribution that operate by modifying private rights of property and contract.[109] It is not an outright rejection of solidarity or redistribution, but it accepts them only when the cost is shared widely, as through general taxation. Moreover, it does not reject state interventions in private law, provided they are aimed at ensuring that autonomy in transactions can be realised and protected. Indeed, it may require them. Nevertheless, *James* and *Mellacher* might now be decided differently, as landlords were stripped of their property rights for reasons that did not relate to the recognition or protection of the autonomy of tenants.

Parliamentary practice suggests that the narrower, social market version of proportionality would not be as compatible with the UK practice as the *Sporrong* version. Indeed, the UK courts have not followed the more recent Strasbourg case on this point. This is apparent from *Axa General Insurance v Lord Advocate*, in which insurance companies argued that their rights under A1P1 were violated by legislation that retroactively expanded the types of disease that constituted actionable injuries.[110] The legislation was prompted by the Supreme Court's judgment in *Rothwell v Chemical & Insulating Co Ltd*,[111] where it held that asymptomatic pleural plaques did not constitute an injury that would support a claim in negligence. Many insurance companies had already paid against claims for pleural plaques, and there were discussions in Edinburgh and London over the response to *Rothwell*. In England and Wales, public funds were used to compensate anyone with pleural plaques. However, the Scottish Parliament enacted the Damages (Asbestos-related Conditions) (Scotland) Act 2009, which reversed the judgment by declaring that the development of asymptomatic pleural plaques had

---

[104] Allen, 'Liberalism' (n 96), 1070–1078.

[105] Above, text and references accompanying (n 40).

[106] App No 2334/03 (ECtHR, 19 February 2009).

[107] App No 74258/01 (ECtHR, 27 November 2007); see Allen, 'Liberalism' (n 96) 1070–76.

[108] See text accompanying (nn 37–41).

[109] A Somma, 'At the roots of European private law: social justice, solidarity and conflict in the proprietary order', in H-W Micklitz (ed), *The Many Concepts of Social Justice in European Private Law* (Cheltenham, Elgar, 2011), 188.

[110] [2011] UKSC 46.

[111] [2007] UKSC 39.

constituted an actionable injury and continued to do so. In effect, it adopted the approach that, in very broad terms, was condemned in *Radovici*, as it required a selected group of private persons to bear the cost of benefiting a vulnerable class. Moreover, the contrasting position in England suggests that direct compensation was a viable alternative. The insurers of the employers therefore argued that the Act amounted to a violation of A1P1, as it would affect the amount that would be payable to their policyholders. The Court also rejected arguments that it was improper to look to the employers or insurers to compensate for these injuries. Lord Reed recognised that there was an argument that compensation should have come from the public treasury, as in England and Wales, but 'the fact that a publicly-funded scheme would avoid any burden being placed on insurers [does not] entail that a scheme which imposes such a burden is disproportionate'.[112] Furthermore, Lord Hope stated that the pursuit of social justice could justify both the provision of compensation for the employees and the imposition of the burden on the negligent employers (and through them, their insurers).[113] Moreover, the extension of liability was not merely a means of supporting a vulnerable group; it also reflected the legislature's legitimate belief that it was appropriate to make the employers liable for the cost. This is consistent with the earlier approach of the European Court of Human Rights in cases such as *James* and *Mellacher*, and the long tradition in the UK of the adjustment of the rules of private law by Parliament, but not with some of the later cases from Strasbourg.

V. Conclusion

The Conservative Party's *Protecting Human Rights* cited a number of decisions of the European Court of Human Rights to show that the Strasbourg jurisprudence had exceeded 'common sense'.[114] None of these concerned A1P1, perhaps because UK legislation and practice has been largely compatible with its requirements. In particular, the UK, like most other jurisdictions, normally requires compensation based on the value to the owner on a compulsory purchase or its equivalent. Hence, as a practical matter, the enactment of a bill to replace the Human Rights Act would probably not make a significant change to the UK's practices, even if it did not include a right to property. If a new Act did include a property right, its impact would depend on the degree of latitude it allowed Parliament. The Conservative proposal would leave this point open, as it would incorporate A1P1 but break the link to the European Court of Human Rights. However, it is not clear how it would deal with the changes in the interpretation of A1P1 since its ratification. Which, if any, judgments of the European Court of Human Rights on property 'exceed

---

[112] [2013] UKSC 3 [130].
[113] Ibid, [33].
[114] Conservative Party, *Protecting Human Rights* (n 1).

common sense', and therefore represent the direction that the UK courts should not take? Would it be the *Sporrong, James* and *Lithgow* judgments, where the Court imported the proportionality standard, and the compensation principles that flow from it, but left the states with considerable latitude to depart from market value compensation? Or its more recent judgments, starting with *Hutten-Czapska*, that narrowed the latitude? The Conservative proposals also refer with approval to the 'UK courts' careful applications of Convention rights':[115] perhaps this would favour the Supreme Court's reading of A1P1 in *Axa General Insurance*, which, like *James*, does allow scope for legislation that adjusts property rights to bring about greater social justice.

The Conservative proposals also criticise the European Court of Human Rights' application of the 'living instrument doctrine':[116] perhaps this would lead us back to the post-World War II Labour Government, which took the view that ratifying a right to property that guaranteed anything more than a basic standard of legality and due process would go too far, because it would not reflect the British practice or its constitutional values. This was not merely a matter of preserving Parliamentary supremacy in the abstract, but a practical reality, as it was feared that binding the UK to a right to compensation would not allow for the kind of restructuring of property rights that had occurred with the Town and Country Planning Act 1947 and nationalisations of industry, or similar restructurings that could occur in future. Earlier, the home rule debates in 1893 show that there was no consensus across Parliament on the existence or content of a common law right to property, or, if there was such a right, the manner of determining how it should be applied to a specific issue. The Conservative proposals do not go as far as they might have done, as they do not require Parliament to consider a new draft of a right to property. Nevertheless, if implemented, they will require the courts to consider how they will adapt the existing jurisprudence on A1P1 to a constitutional picture that is hazy and largely incomplete.

[115] Ibid, 3.
[116] Ibid.

5

A Common Law Constitutional Right to Privacy – Waiting for Godot?

KIRSTY HUGHES*

I. Introduction

Common law rights have a noble reputation. Indeed in 1762 when the King's messengers broke into John Entick's home to search for seditious writings it was the common law that boldly ruled that lawful executive power ended at Entick's door.[1] The common law has also long proffered other essential privacy related rights such as the right to privilege.[2] The significance of which was evident in *Secretary of State for the Home Department, ex parte Daly* where Lord Cooke of Thorndon, prefiguring the more recent judicial turn to common law rights, emphasised that it was of 'great importance that the common law by itself is being recognised as a sufficient source of the fundamental right', as 'some rights are inherent and fundamental to democratic civilised society. Conventions, constitutions, bills of rights and the like respond by recognising rather than creating them.'[3] Yet whilst the common law evidently offered some significant fundamental rights it repeatedly declined to recognise a general right to privacy in English law.[4] This refusal was said to be due to difficulties that judges would encounter in defining privacy and establishing

---

* I am grateful to Mark Elliott for his insightful comments on an earlier draft. Any remaining errors are, of course, mine alone.

[1] *Entick v Carrington* (1765) 2 Wils KB 275. For discussion of the importance of the case see A Tomkins and P Scott (eds) *Entick v Carrington 250 Years of the Rule of Law* (Oxford, Hart Publishing, 2015).

[2] For discussion of the protection that the common law offered to privacy see D Feldman *Civil Liberties and Human Rights* (Oxford, Oxford University Press, 2002) Pt III.

[3] *Secretary of State for the Home Department, ex parte Daly* [2001] UKHL 26; [2001] 3 All ER 433; [2001] 2 WLR 1622 at [30].

[4] For discussion of the absence of a right to privacy in domestic law and the piecemeal development of privacy laws see D Seipp 'English Judicial Recognition of the Right to Privacy' (1983) 3 *OJLS* 325; Lord Neuberger *Privacy in the 21st Century*, (28 November 2012) speech at the UK Association of Jewish Lawyers and Jurists' Lecture; and H Fenwick *Fenwick on Civil Liberties and Human Rights* (Abingdon-on-Thames, Routledge, 2017) pp 689–690.

necessary limits; a right to privacy was therefore deemed to be beyond the reach of the common law.[5] Consequently whilst the common law precluded state boots from trampling the threshold of the Englishman's castle, it did not extend to other types of intrusion. Its impotence meant that in the heyday of common law rights the state could tap your telephone, use listening devices, or compel you to remove your clothes for a strip search, without the inconvenience of a legal framework, limits or safeguards.[6] Equally, you could be resting up in your hospital bed in a state of semi-consciousness after brain surgery, whilst the paparazzi were free to storm your hospital room and publish the resulting photographs.[7] The common law's rejection of a right to privacy in the face of such shortcomings should ring a note of caution to those enticed by the golden allure of common law rights as a superior or even viable alternative to human rights.

This chapter examines the prospect of the common law proffering a right to privacy in the event that we no longer have the benefit of Article 8 of the European Convention on Human Rights (ECHR). Unfortunately this is no mere academic exercise in the present political climate. Clearly repeal of the Human Rights Act 1998 (HRA) has been a desire in certain political quarters for some time.[8] In the past some comfort may have been sought in the notion that even without the HRA the UK would likely remain a member of the ECHR and thus bound to act compatibly with those rights in international law. It was doubted that the UK would seek to withdraw from the ECHR altogether given that there is, at the very least, considerable uncertainty as to whether it would be possible to remain a member of the European Union following such a step.[9] Any perceived EU/ECHR safeguard was however, dealt a fatal blow by the Brexit Referendum in 2016. In the midst of political and legal uncertainty it is now imperative that we take a realistic look at why our courts historically refused to recognise a right to privacy, and whether there is any indication in the post-HRA case law that the common law could fill the lacuna left by repeal of the HRA. Sadly, both past and present judicial practices suggest that there is little basis for putting our faith in the common law.

If we compare the common law and the Convention is it evident that there is a vast abyss between the two legal frameworks. Article 8 ECHR expressly provides for rights to respect for private life, family life, home and correspondence – there are thousands of Article 8 ECHR judgments and decisions and even a cursory glance at the case law indicates that many aspects of Article 8 ECHR have no obvious parallel in traditional common law rights. When it comes to

---

[5] *Malone v Metropolitan Police Commissioner* [1979] ch 344.

[6] *Ibid, R v Khan (Sultan)* [1996] UKHL 14, [1997] AC 558 and *Wainwright v Home Office* [2003] UKHL 53, [2004] 2 AC 406.

[7] *Kaye v Robertson* [1990] EWCA Civ 21, [1991] FSR 62.

[8] The Conservative Party included repeal of the Human Rights Act 1998 in their 2010 and 2015 general election manifestos. See also Conservative Party 'Protecting Human Rights in the UK: The Conservatives' Proposals for Changing Britain's Human Rights Laws' (2014).

[9] House of Commons Library *Is Adherence to the European Convention on Human Rights a Condition of European Union Membership?* Standard Note Sn/IA/6577.

Article 8 ECHR it is commonly acknowledged that of all the Convention rights it 'has by far the widest scope',[10] and that it is 'the least defined and most unruly' of the Convention rights.[11] The right thus reaches far beyond what has been deemed the 'anglo-saxon or french notion of the right to privacy'.[12] As such the broader Article 8 ECHR right embraces a right 'to establish and to develop relationships with other human beings, especially in the emotional field for the development and fulfilment of one's own personality',[13] 'physical and moral integrity' or 'physical and psychological integrity',[14] a 'zone of interaction of a person with others, even in a public context, which may fall within the scope of private life',[15] 'reputation',[16] and 'personal autonomy'.[17] Consequently Article 8 ECHR encompasses not only interferences with correspondence,[18] state surveillance,[19] wiretapping,[20] police registers,[21] recordings of conversations,[22] searches of homes,[23] strip searches,[24] DNA databases,[25] retention of fingerprints,[26] registers of sex offenders,[27] and forced medical examinations;[28] but also the criminalisation of homosexuality,[29] gender recognition,[30] euthanasia and assisted dying,[31] in-vitro fertilisation treatment,[32]

---

[10] A Lester and D Pannick *Human Rights Law and Practice* 3rd edn (London, LexisNexis, 2009) p 359.

[11] *R (Wright) v Secretary of State for Health* [2006] EWHC 2886 (Admin), cited with approval in the House of Lords [2009] UKHL 3 at [30].

[12] *X v Iceland* (1976) 5 DR 86, EComm HR.

[13] Ibid.

[14] See, eg, *X. and Y. v Netherlands* (1986) 8 EHRR 235 'physical and moral integrity' at [22]; *Mikulic v Croatia* [2002] 1 FCR 720 'physical and psychological integrity' at [53]; *Bevacqua v Bulgaria* [2008] ECHR 498 'physical and psychological integrity' at [65]; *Y.F. v Turkey* (2004) 39 EHRR 34 'physical and psychological integrity' at [33]; *Wainwright v United Kingdom* (2007) 44 EHRR 40 'physical and moral integrity' at [43]; *Pfeifer v Austria* [2007] ECHR 935, 'physical and psychological integrity' at [33].

[15] See, eg, *Peck v United Kingdom* (2003) 36 EHRR 41 at [57] and *Von Hannover v Germany* (2005) 40 EHRR 1 at [50].

[16] See, eg, *Chauvy v France* (2005) 41 EHRR 29 and *Delfi v Estonia* (2016) 62 EHRR 6 Grand Chamber.

[17] See, eg, *Pretty v United Kingdom* (2002) 35 EHRR 1 at [61].

[18] A right to respect for correspondence is expressly listed in the text of Article 8 ECHR. There is a vast body of case law on this element of the Convention right, in particular on interferences with prisoners' correspondence. See, eg, *Golder v United Kingdom* (1975) 1 EHRR 524.

[19] See, eg, *Klass v Germany* (1978) 2 EHRR 214; *Malone v United Kingdom* (1985) 7 EHRR 14; *Liberty v United Kingdom* (2009) 48 EHRR 1; *Kennedy v United Kingdom* (2011) 52 EHRR 4; *Szabó and Vissy v Hungary* (2016) 63 EHRR 3; *Big Brother Watch v United Kingdom* (App No 58170/13) available on HUDOC.

[20] See, eg, *Malone v United Kingdom*, ibid.

[21] See, eg, *Rotaru v Romania* (2000) 8 BHRC 449.

[22] See, eg, *PG and JH v United Kingdom* (2008) 46 EHRR 51.

[23] The right to respect for the home is expressly listed in the text of Article 8 ECHR. See, eg, *Keegan v United Kingdom* (2007) 44 EHRR 33.

[24] See, eg, *Wainwright v United Kingdom* (n 14).

[25] See, eg, *S and Marper v United Kingdom* (2009) 48 EHRR 50.

[26] Ibid.

[27] See, eg, *Gardel v France* (App No 16428/05) available on HUDOC.

[28] See, eg, *Storck v Germany* (2005) 43 EHRR 96.

[29] See, eg, *Dudgeon v United Kingdom* (1981) 4 EHRR 149.

[30] See, eg, *Christine Goodwin v United Kingdom* (2002) 35 EHRR 447.

[31] See, eg, *Pretty v United Kingdom* (n 17).

[32] See, eg, *Evans v United Kingdom* (2006) 43 EHRR 21.

restrictions on home births[33] and restrictions on accessing abortion rights.[34] This is a non-exhaustive list. Indeed, as David Feldman has noted, the content of Article 8 ECHR is 'dynamic and continuous, so any account is only a snapshot of a developing process caught at a single moment'.[35]

The stark gulf between the common law and the ECHR is evident in the fact that the Strasbourg Court has found Article 8 ECHR violations against the UK on more than 70 occasions.[36] These include, amongst others, a violation for discriminating against homosexuals in the armed forces,[37] failing to provide an adequate legal framework for surveillance,[38] a failure to legally recognise a change of gender,[39] the use of broad stop and search powers that were neither sufficiently circumscribed nor subject to adequate legal safeguards against abuse,[40] blanket powers of retention of fingerprints, cellular samples and DNA profiles of persons suspected but not convicted of offences,[41] the distribution of CCTV footage of a suicidal man,[42] and the retention of a legal framework that criminalised homosexuality in Northern Ireland.[43] Given the extraordinary breadth of Article 8 ECHR there is little point in simply seeking to enumerate the myriad ways in which the common law does not extend to the vast range of interests that have been brought within the scope of the Convention right. That is self-evident. Instead this chapter focuses on the common law's historic rejection and, I argue, continuing disregard for a right to privacy, as well as the conservative approach of our domestic judges to even some of the core aspects of the right to privacy under Article 8 ECHR when compared with their European counterparts. This difference in judicial perception is apparent in the fact that even with the HRA the Strasbourg Court continues to find violations in cases where our domestic courts have held that UK practices are compatible with the Convention right.[44] That is a difference that would doubtless be important if we ever had to rely exclusively upon the common law for protection.

None of this is to suggest that there would be no privacy law at all without Article 8 ECHR and the HRA. Indeed, it is clearly not the case that all privacy laws would come crashing down with repeal of the HRA. The longstanding protection that the common law offers to the home, privilege and confidentiality preceded the

---

[33] See, eg, *Dubská and Krejzová v Czech Republic* (2017) 65 EHRR 5 Grand Chamber.

[34] See, eg, *Tysiąc v Poland* (2007) 45 EHRR 42.

[35] D Feldman *Civil Liberties and Human Rights in England and Wales* 2nd edn (Oxford, Oxford University Press, 2002) p 527.

[36] There are currently 71 cases available in the European Court of Human Rights case law database (HUDOC) in which the Court has found a violation of Article 8 ECHR.

[37] *Smith and Grady v United Kingdom* (2000) 29 EHRR 493.

[38] *Malone v United Kingdom* (1985) 7 EHRR 14; *Liberty v United Kingdom* (2009) 48 EHRR 1; *Big Brother Watch v United Kingdom* (n 14).

[39] *Goodwin v United Kingdom* (2002) 35 EHRR 18.

[40] *Gillan v United Kingdom* (2010) 50 EHRR 45.

[41] n 25.

[42] *Peck v United Kingdom* (2003) 36 EHRR 41.

[43] *Dudgeon v United Kingdom* (1981) 3 EHRR 40.

[44] See discussion below at pp 107–112.

HRA, whilst other privacy-related laws such as data protection are not contingent on the HRA either. Although the HRA played a pivotal role in the creation of the common law of misuse of private information[45] it is likely that this too would survive repeal of the HRA. Indeed 20 years after the enactment of the HRA the privacy law landscape is remarkably different from the pre-HRA era. Yet what we are interested in is not simply whether there are common law or legislative means of protecting privacy in our domestic legal framework, but rather whether *special protection* is, or would be, afforded to privacy in the form of a *constitutional common law right.* There was certainly no such right prior to the HRA.

Post-HRA, although there are signs that the courts may recognise a *common law right to informational privacy,*[46] one that exists alongside misuse of private information, it is not apparent that this has a constitutional status, nor are there signs of judicial appetite for a broader right to privacy. On the contrary, although the Supreme Court has determined a spate of Article 8 ECHR privacy cases in recent years, including during the period in which there has arguably been a judicial turn to common law rights, the common law has remained silent on privacy.[47] This may in part be explained by the fact that these cases have almost certainly been litigated solely through Article 8 ECHR, a strategy that would make sense given the vast body of Article 8 ECHR jurisprudence and the speculative nature of any endeavour to invoke a common law right. Indeed Tugendhat J acknowledged the difficulty of seeking to litigate common law rights in *AKJ* when he noted that

---

[45] The House of Lords decision in *Campbell v MGN* [2004] UKHL 22 famously recognised a cause of action for misuse of private information. Lord Nicholls declaring that '[t]he time has come to recognise that the values enshrined in articles 8 and 10 are now part of the cause of action for breach of confidence' and that '[t]he essence of the tort is better encapsulated now as misuse of private information' at [17] and [14]. For discussion of the evolution of breach of confidence and the law of misuse of private information see H Fenwick *Civil Liberties and Human Rights* (Abingdon-on-Thames, Routledge, 2016) ch 10, H Fenwick and G Phillipson *Media Freedom under the Human Rights Act* (Oxford, Oxford University Press, 2006), N Moreham 'Breach of Confidence and the Misuse of Private Information – How do the Two Actions Work Together' (2010) 15 *Media and Arts Law Review* 265, N Moreham 'The Protection of Privacy in English Common Law: A Doctrinal and Theoretical Analysis' (2005) *LQR* 628, G Phillipson 'Privacy: the Development of Breach of Confidence – the Clearest Case of Horizontal Effect' in D Hoffman (ed) *The Impact of the UK Human Rights Act on Private Law* (Cambridge, Cambridge University Press, 2011), G Phillipson 'The Common Law, Privacy and the Convention' in H Fenwick et al (eds) *Judicial reasoning under the UK Human Rights Act* (Cambridge, Cambridge University Press, 2007), G Phillipson 'The Right of Privacy in England and Strasbourg Compared' in A Kenyon and M Richardson (eds) *New Dimensions in Privacy law: International and Comparative Perspectives* (Cambridge, Cambridge University Press, 2006). G Phillipson 'Judicial Reasoning in Breach of Confidence Cases under the Human Rights Act: Not Taking Privacy Seriously?' (2003) *EHRLR* 54, G Phillipson 'Transforming Breach of Confidence? Towards a Common Law Right of Privacy under the Human Rights Act' (2003) *MLR* 726, K Hughes 'Parliament Reports on Privacy and Injunctions' (2012) *Journal of Media Law* 17.

[46] *Khuja v Times Newspapers Ltd* [2017] UKSC 49.

[47] *Catt v Association of Chief Police Officers of England Wales and Northern Ireland* [2015] UKSC 9, [2015] 1 AC 1065, [2015] 2 All ER 727; *In the Matters of an Application by JR38 for Judicial Review (Northern Ireland)* [2015] UKSC 42, [2016] AC 1131; *Beghal v DPP* [2015] UKSC 49, [2016] 1 All ER 483, [2015] 3 WLR 344, [2016] AC 88; and *Gaughran v CC of Northern Ireland Police* [2015] UKSC 29, [2016] AC 345, [2015] 2 WLR 1303.

it is not easy to identify common law rights because they have not been codified and because for a long period fundamental rights were eclipsed by philosophical ideas that were inconsistent with natural rights and by the concept of absolute parliamentary sovereignty.[48] However, the fact that cases may be litigated using Convention rights alone has not precluded the courts from invoking the common law in other contexts where counsel have focused upon the ECHR rights.[49]

A further reason for doubting the prospects of the common law is the afore-mentioned conservative manner with which our domestic judges often approach Article 8 ECHR when compared with their European counterparts. A difference in perception of the scope and importance of privacy is evident in the fact that the European Court of Human Rights (ECtHR) continues to find privacy violations against the UK in cases where our own courts have found no violation and even in cases where our own courts have held that the right to privacy is inapplicable.[50] Hence even if our judges overcome longstanding common law reluctance to recognise a right to privacy, and this chapter considers possible means of doing so, it is highly likely that that any such right would be far more restrictively interpreted and would carry less weight than the Convention right. It is worth emphasising for the avoidance of doubt that I am referring here not to the inevitable failure to recognise a common law equivalent to the full gamut of Article 8 ECHR interests, that really goes without saying, but rather to the weaker approach that would likely be employed by our courts in what may be regarded as even paradigm privacy cases such as those relating to police powers. We thus cannot assume that without the HRA the common law would rise like a phoenix from the ashes to replace the Convention right.

II. Privacy and the Common Law Prior to the Human Rights Act 1998

We are sometimes led to believe that privacy has not in any way been protected in English law: that 1998 was for privacy, to use Larkin's famous words, what 1963 … was for sexual intercourse, *"the time when it all began"*. Well, 1998 was no more when privacy began in English law than 1963 was when sexual intercourse began.

Lord Neuberger, 2012[51]

As Lord Neuberger colourfully indicates even prior to the HRA there were various ways in which the law protected particular privacy-related interests, including

---

[48] *AKJ and others v Commissioner of Police of the Metropolis* [2013] EWHC 32 (QB), [2013] 1 WLR 2734, at [63].

[49] *Osborn v Parole Board* [2013] UKSC 61, [2014] AC 1115; and *Kennedy v Charity Commissioner* [2014] UKSC 20, [2015] 1 AC 455.

[50] See discussion below at pp 107–109.

[51] Lord Neuberger *Privacy in the 21st Century* (n 4). For more detailed discussion see D Seipp (n 4).

amongst other things trespass to the home, privilege and the equitable doctrine of confidentiality.[52] Yet despite a long history of piecemeal protection there was no right to privacy.[53] This was not a mere oversight, nor was it a result of a lack of opportunity. On the contrary, prior to the HRA our domestic courts faced numerous calls to recognise a right to privacy, and yet they consistently declined do so. The rationale for refusing to recognise a right was famously set out by Robert Megarry VC in *Malone*.[54] Megarry VC rejected Malone's claim that police interception of his telephone violated a common law right to privacy on the basis that: (i) a right to privacy would raise numerous definitional problems; and (ii) ultimately 'no new right in the law, fully-fledged with all the appropriate safeguards, can spring from the head of a judge deciding a particular case'.[55] These concerns over the potential reach of any privacy right and the need for, and difficulty in identifying, safeguards represent the heart of common law resistance. The vital role that Article 8 ECHR has played in filling that gap is demonstrated by the fact that when Malone took his case to Strasbourg the Court held that the UK had violated Article 8 ECHR, a decision that compelled the UK to put in place a legislative framework.[56]

The 1990 case of *Kaye v Robertson* offers further insight into the woeful inadequacies of the pre-HRA common law.[57] Kaye, a well-known actor, suffered a serious head injury after a piece of wood fell through his car windscreen during a storm. Following extensive surgery journalists gained unauthorised access to his hospital room and purported to interview and take photographs of him. His state of health was such that shortly afterwards he had no recollection of the journalists' visit. As English law knew of no cause of action in privacy the Court was unable to offer a remedy for the intrusion into the hospital room, nor could it prohibit a tabloid newspaper from publishing the material. In fact all the Court could do was turn to the law of malicious falsehood to issue an injunction prohibiting the newspaper from publishing any material which implied that Kaye had voluntarily permitted the photographs to be taken and/or participated in the interview.[58] This left the newspaper free to publish the photographs and the interview – a position that was highly unsatisfactory, as Bingham LJ (as he then was) highlighted:

> The defendants' conduct towards the plaintiff here was "a monstrous invasion of his privacy" … If ever a person has a right to be let alone by strangers with no public interest to pursue, it must surely be when he lies in hospital recovering from brain surgery and in no more than partial command of his faculties. It is this invasion of his privacy

---

[52] On the need for a right of privacy see D Eady 'A Statutory Right of Privacy' [1996] *EHRLR* 243 and T Bingham 'Should there be a Law to Protect Rights of Personal Privacy?' [1996] *EHRLR* 450.

[53] For discussion see Lord Neuberger *Privacy in the 21st Century* (n 4) at [11], Feldman (n 2), Seipp (n 4), Fenwick *Fenwick* (n 4) pp 689–690.

[54] *Malone v Metropolitan Police Commissioner (No.2)* [1979] ch 344.

[55] Ibid, p 372.

[56] *Malone v United Kingdom* (1985) 7 EHRR 14 at [64].

[57] *Kaye v Robertson* [1990] EWCA Civ 21, [1991] FSR 62.

[58] Ibid, pp 67–68.

which underlies the plaintiff's complaint. Yet it alone, however gross, does not entitle him to relief in English law.[59]

Yet whilst all three Court of Appeal judges deeply regretted the failure of the common law to deal with these 'monstrous violations' each held that a right to privacy was beyond the reach of the common law. Leggatt LJ noted that the 'right has so long been disregarded here that it can be recognised now only by the legislature',[60] whilst Glidewell LJ declared that '[t]he facts of the present case are a graphic illustration of the desirability of Parliament considering whether and in what circumstances statutory provision can be made to protect the privacy of individuals.'[61]

In 1997 the House of Lords in *Khan* considered whether the law should recognise a right to privacy when the police fixed a listening device to the outside of the defendant's house.[62] On that occasion the Law Lords declined to determine the matter concluding that even if such a right existed, the evidence obtained by the device would remain admissible. The fact that they did not outright reject a right to privacy perhaps suggests that they were more open to the prospect than Megarry VC had been in *Malone*.[63] Certainly Lord Nicholls of Birkenhead preferred to 'leave open for another occasion the important question whether the present, piecemeal protection of privacy has now developed to the extent that a more comprehensive principle can be seen to exist.'[64] A different note was, however, struck by Lord Nolan who noted that 'under English law, there is in general nothing unlawful about a breach of privacy.'[65] In any event the matter went to the ECtHR where the Strasbourg Court held that the UK had yet again violated Article 8.[66]

Wainwright v Home Office was the last case in which the Lords had to consider a potential invasion of privacy without the benefit of Article 8 ECHR and the HRA.[67] Although the proceedings took place in 2003 the incident itself had taken place prior to the HRA coming into force and thus the matter did not fall within the scope of the HRA. The Lords were therefore required to consider once more whether the common law could protect privacy. The case related to an incident in a prison during which visitors (a mother and her disabled son) were required to undergo a strip search. There was no statutory authority for the strip search, but there was also no common law remedy. Lord Scott of Foscote explained that:

> whatever remedies may have been developed for misuse of confidential information, for certain types of trespass, for certain types of nuisance and for various other situations

---

[59] Ibid, p 70.
[60] Ibid, p 71.
[61] Ibid, p 66.
[62] *R v Khan (Sultan)* [1996] UKHL 14, [1997] AC 558.
[63] n 54.
[64] n 62, p 582.
[65] n 62, p 581.
[66] *Khan v United Kingdom* (2000) 31 EHRR 45 at [26]–[28].
[67] *Wainwright v Home Office* [2003] UKHL 53, [2004] 2 AC 406.

in which claimants may find themselves aggrieved by an invasion of what they conceive to be their privacy, the common law has not developed an overall remedy for the invasion of privacy.[68]

Once more the matter ended up before the ECtHR and once more the Strasbourg Court held that the UK had violated Article 8 ECHR.

This brief look at privacy prior to the HRA reveals that the common law routinely failed to protect privacy as evidenced by the experiences of those who found themselves with no means of redress in the face of media intrusions into hospital bedrooms, unauthorised strip searches, and surveillance. History thus dictates that we should be deeply cautious about the claims of those drawn to the tantalising allure of the *potential* of common law rights.

Before turning to the post-HRA case law I wish to pause to consider one further pre-HRA case. That case is the 1980 House of Lords decision in *Morris v Beardmore*, a judgment that contains several references to privacy rights in the home as well as a reference to a right to personal privacy.[69] At the heart of *Morris* was the principle developed in *Entick v Carrington*, namely that the state cannot enter the home without legal authority.[70] *Morris v Beardmore* is of interest because it demonstrates how common law rights may be framed in broad terms even if in reality they have a narrow sphere of application; it thus provides a useful comparator for some of the contemporary judicial rhetoric that we will return to later. Indeed, despite the broader references to a right to privacy in the home and a right to personal privacy it is evident that the Lords did not intend to develop a new privacy right in *Morris*, nor to expand the existing rights. We should therefore be cautious about giving too much weight to isolated judicial rhetoric.

The background to the case was that following a road traffic accident the police had entered Beardmore's home to demand a breath test, Beardmore had refused on the basis that the police were trespassing, and he was arrested. The Law Lords had to determine whether the actions of the police were lawful, they held that in the absence of an express statutory provision Parliament had not authorised what would otherwise be a trespass, thus applying *Entick v Carrington*. In making that assessment, however, they made several references to a common law right to *privacy in the home*. For example, Lord Edmund Davies concluded that: 'to reject the appeal would entitle a constable who, *in deliberate violation of a householder's right, forcibly invades his privacy*, thereafter to put the machinery of section 8 into operation'.[71] Lord Scarman was even more explicit venturing to explain that he deliberately described 'the right of privacy as "fundamental"' based in part on the protection afforded by the ECHR, but also due to the 'importance attached by the *common law to the privacy of the home*'.[72] Yet whilst the judges referred to a right to

---

[68] Ibid at [62]. See also Lord Hoffmann's analysis at [15]–[35].
[69] *Morris v Beardmore* [1981] 1 AC 446, [1980] 3 WLR 283.
[70] n 1.
[71] n 69, pp 461–462 (emphasis added).
[72] n 69, p 464 (emphasis added).

privacy in the home in general terms their reasoning can only be reconciled with *Malone* (and more importantly for the purposes of precedent with the later House of Lords decision in *Khan*) if the right to privacy in the home is limited to *Entick v Carrington*-style physical trespasses. Certainly it had only been a year earlier that Sir Robert Megarry VC had been resolute in *Malone* that there is no right to privacy in English law a judgment that would of course not have bound the House of Lords, but was not even cited in *Morris v Beardmore*. Perhaps this was because *Malone* was not as well known in 1980 as it would later become, or because arguments based on telephone tapping were not seen as relevant to the scope of police powers to enter the home to carry out breath tests. More significantly, however, if *Morris* had recognised a right to privacy in the home that extended beyond physical trespasses then this should have been considered in *Khan* when the House of Lords declined to consider such a right in a case in which a listening device had been installed outside the defendant's home.[73] Yet there was no reference to *Morris* in *Khan* either, suggesting that despite the broader reference to 'privacy in the home' in *Morris* the right was indeed limited to physical entries into the home.

It is also worth noting that Lord Keith of Kinkel alluded to another type of privacy right in *Morris*. In contemplating the process of being compelled to provide a breath test he noted that the road traffic legislation already 'authorised serious invasions of … *personal privacy*', a reference that seems to invoke a bodily integrity conception of privacy[74] and bears some similarities to the right to personal security that has been invoked more recently in post-HRA cases (discussed further below).[75] Eight years later, however, Lord Keith declared that the law should also protect a 'right to personal privacy' vis-à-vis revelations of details of a person's private life, a move that suggests that (at least his conception of) personal privacy was not limited to bodily integrity.[76] It might therefore be tempting to try to pull together these isolated strands of dicta to argue for the recognition of a cluster of common law privacy rights or even a broader general right to privacy. Yet it is important to note that when Lord Keith was given the opportunity to consider whether the common law recognised a general right to privacy in *Khan*, he followed the lead of the other judges and declined to comment.[77]

It is therefore worth reiterating that although we occasionally encounter common law rights presented in broader, more general terms there is no evidence that such rights have been realised in practice, despite the fact that there have been, as we have already seen, cases that provided both the opportunity and an impetus for doing so. Certainly *Khan* would have provided a test case for a broader right

---

[73] *R v Khan (Sultan)* [1996] UKHL 14, [1997] AC 558.
[74] Ibid, p 462.
[75] See p 104.
[76] *AG v Guardian (No.2)* [1990] 1 AC 109, 255.
[77] n 62, p 570.

to privacy in the home, whilst *Wainwright* would have been an opportunity for recognising a right to personal privacy. We should therefore exercise caution in examining and overemphasising fleeting judicial references to potentially broader rights. This is an important consideration as we turn to the post-HRA case law.

III. Are there Any Signs of a Constitutional Common Law Right to Privacy Emerging Post-HRA?

In the two decades that have followed the coming into force of the HRA it is evident that privacy law has fundamentally changed and that human rights law has been a major part of that evolution.[78] One of the most significant developments has, of course, been the recognition of the tort of misuse of private information.[79] Although the HRA was an important catalyst for the tort there are a number of reasons for concluding that it is not dependent upon the HRA for its survival. First, the early development of misuse of private information occurred even before the ECtHR had confirmed that Article 8 ECHR requires states to offer protection vis-a-vis the press.[80] This is an indication of the eagerness of our domestic judiciary to develop a common law remedy and the extent to which they are likely to resist a return to pre-HRA confidentiality. Second, whilst it is true that misuse of private information embodies the same values as Article 8 ECHR, operates within a similar structure, and that the courts often tackle the common law and the Convention right in tandem without necessarily demarcating distinct bodies of law, this does not deny the independent existence of the common law cause of action.[81] Indeed the fact that there are two bodies of law was noted in *Richard v BBC* where it was acknowledged that, strictly speaking, the complaint against the police was a direct complaint under the HRA whilst the complaint against the BBC was based in tort.[82] For these reasons we can be confident that although the two bodies of law are conjoined, the common law tort would survive severance. It is, of course, possible that without the HRA our domestic courts may amend misuse of private information altering the degree of protection afforded to privacy vis-à-vis freedom of expression, but as the Strasbourg Court already offers a

---

[78] Obviously data protection law has also played a fundamental role and is not contingent upon the survival of the HRA 1998.

[79] *Campbell v MGN* (n 45) at [17]. For discussion see literature cited at n 45.

[80] G Phillipson 'Transforming Breach of Confidence? Towards a Common Law Right of Privacy under the Human Rights Act' (n 45), p 729.

[81] This is evident in the structure and content of the court's analysis in *Richards v BBC* [2018] EWHC 1837 (Ch) [267]–[322], which replicates the same structure and factors identified in the Strasbourg case law: see *Von Hannover v Germany (No.2)* (2012) 55 EHRR 15; *Axel Springer v Germany* (2012) 55 EHRR 6; and *Couderc and Hachette Filipacchi Associés v France* (Grand Chamber) [2016] EMLR 19.

[82] *Richard v BBC*, ibid at [259].

relatively wide margin of appreciation the presence or otherwise of the HRA is arguably not hindering such a move.[83]

The evolution of the law of misuse of private information is also important because it may have given the courts the impetus to recognise a common law right to informational privacy. The notion that a common law right exists alongside the law of misuse of private information appears in Lord Sumption's declaration in *Khuja* that the House of Lords in *Campbell* recognised a 'qualified common law right of privacy' when it absorbed the Convention rights into breach of confidence.[84] Yet whilst he phrased this as a 'right of privacy' both *Campbell* and *Khuja* were concerned with publication of information, thus as with the dicta in *Morris* discussed above, we should be cautious about assuming that the right has a broader remit outside the informational privacy context. Further, albeit perfunctory references to a right to privacy appear in cases such as *Dr DB v The General Medical Council*,[85] which concerned whether a private report should be released in response to an FOI request, and *W v Secretary of State for Health*, which concerned the transfer of personal information from the NHS to the Home Office.[86] It is therefore worth emphasising three points. First, if there is a move to recognise a common law right to informational privacy the HRA has been a catalyst for this as this was not previously evident in the common law. Second, if there is a common law right it seems to be limited to informational privacy as there is no indication that the courts are developing a broader right to privacy. Indeed whilst these judicial references to a common law right may lend credence to the idea that the common law recognises a right to informational privacy, one that exists alongside misuse of private information and Article 8 there is no indication that a common law right to privacy is being applied in other contexts. I will return to the continuing absence of a broader right shortly. The third point to note is that there is no evidence that the purported common law right to informational privacy has a constitutional status. Indeed it is perfectly possible that the right that Lord Sumption referred to in *Khuja* is simply a recognition of the fact that a right emerges from the duties imposed by the law of tort. Clearly if the right is a mere common law right as opposed to a common law constitutional right then its capacity to protect privacy in the event that the HRA is repealed is limited. Whereas if the right takes on a constitutional status there may be a deeper penetration of public law through, for example, the operation of the principle of legality in interpreting the powers conferred by legislation. Depending on how one views the constitutional role of common law constitutional rights such a right may also act as a more robust bulwark against even parliamentary intrusion. We thus need far

---

[83] The Strasbourg Court gives states a margin of appreciation on these matters provided that they fall within the parameters of the criteria it established in *Von Hannover v Germany (No.2)* (n 81) and *Axel Springer v Germany* (n 81).

[84] *Khuja v Times Newspapers Ltd* [2017] UKSC 49; [2019] AC 161 at [21].

[85] *Dr DB v The General Medical Council* [2016] EWHC 2331 (QB); (2016) 152 BMLR 106.

[86] *W v Secretary of State for Health* [2015] EWCA Civ 1034, [2016] 1 WLR 698 at [26].

greater clarity as to both the scope and the status of any purported privacy rights before we can be confident that they could offer significant protection.

Returning then to the question of scope it is striking that whilst there have been a raft of Supreme Court Article 8 ECHR decisions since the recent judicial turn to common law rights, there has been no pull towards a common law right to privacy in our highest court. In fact not a single reference to a common law right to privacy is to be found in cases such as *Catt v Association of Chief Police Officers of England Wales and Northern Ireland* (police database of protestors),[87] *Re JR38* (images of child involved in rioting released to and published in local newspaper to assist police in identifying participants),[88] *Beghal v DPP* (stop and search powers at ports),[89] *Gaughran v Chief Constable of Northern Ireland Police* (indefinite retention of DNA samples of those who had been convicted of an offence),[90] and *T v CC Greater Manchester* (criminal records checks).[91] This is despite the fact that in each of these cases it was determined that there was no violation of Article 8 ECHR. Of course, a common law right may well have led to the same result, but if such a right exists it would surely have been worthy of consideration. Moreover, in some of these cases other common law rights *were* addressed alongside their Convention right counterparts. For example, in *Beghal* although privacy was litigated exclusively through the framework of Article 8 ECHR the privilege against self-incrimination was considered under both the common law and Article 6 ECHR.[92] Equally in *Catt* the right to protest was referred to as a 'basic right which the common law has always recognized', whilst there was no mention of a common law privacy right.[93] As noted earlier, the likely explanation for this is that these cases were pleaded solely as Article 8 ECHR cases, however, as also noted earlier, this has not precluded judges from reaching for the common law in other contexts.

A rare nod to a general common law right to privacy outside the informational privacy context can be found in Tugendhat J's first instance judgment in *AKJ*, a case that concerned the legality of undercover police officers forming sexual relations with the political activists they were investigating.[94] The matter before the Court was whether (due to provisions of the HRA and RIPA) the Investigatory Powers Tribunal (IPT) was the only appropriate tribunal to hear the claimants' human rights claims, and if so whether any common law claims should also be heard by the IPT. In discussing the common law arguments advanced by the claimants Tugendhat J commented that 'the right to privacy is ... one of the rights which has the longest history of recognition by the common law, although that has

---

[87] n 47.
[88] n 47.
[89] n 47.
[90] n 47.
[91] [2014] UKSC 35; [2015] AC 49.
[92] n 47.
[93] n 47.
[94] *AKJ and others v Commissioner of Police of the Metropolis* [2013] EWHC 32 (QB), [2013] 1 WLR 2734.

not always been appreciated'.[95] He then went on, however, to substantiate this by reference to the right to privacy of the home and correspondence and a right to privacy in information.[96] Thus, once more, we see that despite an initial framing of the right as a general right to privacy on closer inspection it appears in fact to be a cluster of narrower privacy-related rights. Moreover, on appeal the Court of Appeal made no reference to a common law right to privacy at all, instead turning to a right to personal security.[97]

The relationship between privacy and this common law right to personal security is also potentially interesting and worthy of further discussion as it feeds into a consideration of where and how the courts may be able to develop common law rights. Indeed, the right to personal security is a constitutional common law right, whereas, as discussed above, the status of the right to informational privacy is less clear cut. The notion of a right to personal security can be seen in Blackstone's Commentaries on the Laws of England in 1766.[98] As noted above, in *AKJ* it was this right that was invoked by the Court of Appeal to declare that 'establishing and/or maintaining an intimate sexual relationship for the covert purpose of obtaining intelligence is a seriously intrusive form of investigatory technique ... [and] that [this] amounts to an invasion of an individual's common law right to personal security'.[99] The right to personal security also made an appearance in *Secretary of State for the Home Department v GG*, a case concerning the legitimacy of a control order requiring the subject of the order to submit to bodily searches.[100] In that case counsel notably did not argue that there was a common law right to privacy, nor did he rely upon Article 8, but instead argued that 'the value which the law of battery and trespass to the person has historically aimed to protect is the right to freedom from deliberate physical interference, not least on the part of the state'.[101] Consequently 'if Parliament is to abrogate or limit that right it must make it plain beyond doubt that that is its intention'.[102] Sedley LJ agreed declaring that it is 'axiomatic that the common law rights of personal security and personal liberty prevent any official search of an individual's clothing or person without explicit statutory authority'.[103] The right to personal security was thus employed in *GG* to hold that the powers conferred by the terrorism legislation did not extend to requiring a person subject to a control order to submit to a search of his or her body or clothing.

---

[95] Ibid at [70].
[96] Ibid at [71]–[72].
[97] *AJA v Commissioner of Police of the Metropolis* [2013] EWCA Civ 1342; [2014] 1 WLR 285.
[98] D Lemmings (ed) *The Oxford Edition of Blackstone: Commentaries on the Laws of England Volume 1: Of the Rights of Persons* (Oxford, Oxford University Press, 2016) pp 88. The Commentaries state that '[t]he right of personal security consists in a person's legal and uninterrupted enjoyment of his life, his limbs, his body, his health, and his reputation' at p 88.
[99] n 97 at [22].
[100] *Secretary of State for the Home Department v GG* [2009] EWCA Civ 786, [2010] QB 585.
[101] Ibid at [9].
[102] Ibid.
[103] Ibid at [12].

There may therefore be some potential in the common law for drawing upon these rights to provide constitutional protection for some privacy-related interests. Before turning to consider this further, however it is worth reiterating the current position of the common law. It is evident that there are a number of long-established common law constitutional rights which may offer some protection for privacy-related interests, including privacy of the home (vis-à-vis physical trespasses), privilege and even a right to personal security or liberty. It is also possible that the common law provides a right to informational privacy, albeit that it is not yet clear whether that right has a constitutional status. There are, however, no signs that the courts are eager to recognise a general constitutional common law right to privacy, nor is there a clear indication that the courts are eager to develop the cluster of existing rights to offer greater protection for privacy. Thus leaving aside the development of informational privacy, the common law has not progressed significantly further than it had prior to the HRA, nor is there a clear indication that the courts are making any moves in this direction.

IV. How could a Constitutional Common Law Right to Privacy Come into Existence?

Having concluded that neither a general constitutional common law right to privacy, nor a broader cluster of constitutional common law privacy-related rights has emerged in the post-HRA case law I now turn to consider how such a right or rights could come into existence in the event that domestic judges are, contrary to past and present practices, willing to grasp the nettle. In contemplating the prospect of the common law developing further rights it is important to consider how such a right or rights could come into existence. Certainly Lord Sumption in *Khuja* and Tugendhat J in *AKJ* appear to differ as to how and when they think that a right to informational privacy came into existence in the common law. In *Khuja* Lord Sumption regarded the common law right as one that is 'relatively new to English law' and one that was brought into existence by the House of Lords in *Campbell* under the influence of the HRA.[104] This perspective differs from that of Tugendhat J who looked beyond the HRA to connect the right to privacy to the historic protection that the common law has provided for other aspects of privacy such as the home.[105] These perceptions are significant in thinking about potential growth and the status of such rights.

The right identified by Lord Sumption appears to be governed by the capacity of the common law to absorb Convention rights into private law thus rendering it contingent upon the extent of the HRA's indirect horizontal effect and the

---

[104] n 84 at [21].
[105] n 97 at [70].

permanency of that process of absorption.[106] On this view, as the love child of the Convention and the common law torts, the right would appear to be limited by that parental relationship, such that although the Article 8 ECHR right is broad only a limited element of that right may be embedded in domestic law due to the need for a domestic law parent. If this is the case then the right to privacy is unlikely to expand beyond the information law context as it has taken root in the law of misuse of private information. Moreover, although such a right could take on a constitutional form, it may also remain a mere common law right.

Conversely the right to privacy identified by Tugendhat J appears to depend upon the capacity of existing common law rights to cross-fertilise and give birth to new rights. Certainly in his eyes the informational privacy right appears to have had a longer history in domestic law, one that stems from the evolution of other common law rights.[107] Following this approach development of a common law right is not contingent upon the contours of existing common law causes of action and their interface with the Convention and therefore in theory the common law could perhaps evolve to offer a broader common law right or cluster of rights. Moreover, by linking the development of the right to existing constitutional common law rights such as the right to the home it seems more likely that the right is intended to have a constitutional status. If our courts are willing to develop the cluster of common law privacy rights using this approach then potential avenues for further development could be the right to personal privacy noted in *Morris* and the rights to personal security and liberty identified in *AKJ* and *GG*. Those rights could then offer a means of accommodating bodily privacy, including matters such as strip searches, breath tests or DNA tests. Equally a broader development of the right to privacy in the home could expand beyond physical trespasses to include other interferences with the home such as the use of wiretapping listening devices or heat detection devices. Finally a right to informational privacy could be applicable in cases concerning matters such as collection and retention of data on police databases. Developing a cluster of rights in this vein would not encompass all aspects of a right to privacy, nor would it replicate all aspects of the Article 8 right; decisional privacy would certainly be lacking,[108] whilst it is possible that

---

[106] There is a vast body of literature on the horizontal effect of the HRA including the following: M Hunt 'The Horizontal Effect of the HRA' [1998] *PL* 423; W Wade 'Horizons of Horizontality' (2000) 116 *LQR* 217, R Buxton 'The Human Rights Act and Private Law' (2000) 116 *LQR* 48; D Pannick and A Lester 'The Impact of the Human Rights Act on Private Law: The Knight's Move' (2000) *LQR* 623; N Bamforth 'The True Horizontal Effect of the HRA 1998' (2001) *LQR* 34, G Phillipson 'Privacy: the Development of Breach of Confidence – the Clearest Case of Horizontal Effect?' (n 45), A Williams and G Phillipson 'Horizontal Effect and the Constitutional Constraint' (2011) 74(6) *MLR* 878–910, G Phillipson 'The Human Rights Act, the Common Law and 'Horizontal Effect: A Bang or a Whimper?'' (1999) 62(6) *MLR* 824–84, A Young 'Mapping Horizontality' in D Hoffman (ed) *The Impact of the UK Human Rights Act on Private Law* (Cambridge, Cambridge University Press, 2011) and A Young 'The Human Rights Act 1998, Horizontality and the Constitutionalisation of Private Law' in K Ziegler and P Huber (eds) *Current Problems in the Protection of Human Rights* (Oxford, Hart Publishing, 2013).

[107] n 97.

[108] The premise of decision-making privacy is that there are certain realms of life into which the state should not interfere; it protects decisions that one is entitled to take without being dictated to, or

some aspects of privacy, such as stop and search powers in public places may be deemed to fall outside the scope of these rights.[109] In the event that the courts are willing to embark on this path then this cluster of common law privacy rights could be the ultimate destination of the common law, or, in theory at least, it could be a step towards the recognition of a broader common law right. The long-standing resistance to developing a broader common law right to privacy would, however, suggest that if the courts are willing to develop rights at all it is likely to be a cluster of clearly defined rights relating to particular interests that emerges. Moreover, with only a few oblique references in the case law to such potential rights, none of which engaged in extensive discussion, we have to recognise that the prospect of such rights providing a vehicle for further development is highly speculative at best.

V. Any Constitutional Common Law Right to Privacy it is Likely to be Weaker than the Convention Right

Finally I argue that even if the common law were to proffer such rights it is likely that those rights would be more limited and less potent than their Article 8 ECHR counterpart. Certainly, under the HRA we have seen that our domestic courts have often been inclined to a more conservative approach than their European counterparts. This is evident in a number of cases in which our domestic courts have doubted whether Article 8 ECHR is even engaged, before going on to determine that even if the right is applicable the purported interference is a minimal one that is easily justified. That reasoning contrasts sharply with that of the Strasbourg Court which in the same proceedings has held that the right clearly applies and that the UK is in breach of the Convention. An example of this is *Marper* where the House of Lords held that even if the indefinite retention of fingerprints and DNA samples on a police database engaged Article 8 ECHR (which they doubted) it was a modest interference with the right and plainly justified.[110] Conversely the European Court of Human Rights held that the database clearly fell within the parameters of the right and that the UK had violated Article 8 due to the 'blanket and indiscriminate nature of the powers of retention'.[111] The same chasm in reasoning arose in

influenced, by the state. The idea is that there are certain realms where the citizen can say to the state 'this matter is none of your business, I can do what I want'. Decision-making privacy may therefore encompass matters such as contraception or abortion. For discussion of different types of privacy see D Solove *Understanding Privacy* (London, Harvard University Press, 2008).

[109] See the House of Lords reasoning in *R (on the application of Gillan and Quinton) v Commissioner of Police of the Metropolis* [2006] UKHL 12, [2006] 2 AC 307, discussed below at p 108, where the Lords doubted that stop and search powers engaged Article 8 ECHR.

[110] *R (on the application of S and Marper) v Chief Constable of South Yorkshire & Another* [2004] UKHL 39, [2004] 1 WLR 2196.

[111] n 25 at [125].

Gillan where the Law Lords doubted that Article 8 was engaged by police stop and search powers.[112] In that case even Lord Bingham doubted 'whether an ordinary superficial search of the person can be said to show a lack of respect for private life' and inclined 'to the view that an ordinary superficial search of the person and an opening of bags, of the kind to which passengers uncomplainingly submit at airports, for example, can scarcely be said to reach' the level required to constitute an interference with the right.[113] Once again the Strasbourg Court took a very different approach, finding that Article 8 was clearly engaged and that it had been violated.[114] In response to the suggestion that Article 8 was not applicable, the Court commented that 'the use of the coercive powers conferred by the legislation to require an individual to submit to a detailed search of his person, his clothing and his personal belongings amounts to a clear interference with the right to respect for private life.'[115] The Court went on to find that the stop and search powers violated Article 8.[116] The Supreme Court's judgment in *Kinloch*, in which it held that Article 8 was not engaged when the police created a surveillance log that was later used in criminal proceedings, is a further example of this trend.[117] Lord Hope (giving the single unanimous judgment of the Court) held that the claimant had no reasonable expectation of privacy as he was in a public place in public view and '[h]e took the risk of being seen and of his movements being noted down. The criminal nature of what he was doing, if that was what it was found to be, was not an aspect of his private life that he was entitled to keep private'[118] – a determination that neglects the fact that observing an individual in a public place is not the same as covert planned state surveillance.[119]

As noted above, one way in which our domestic courts may limit the scope of privacy under the common law is through the recognition of a cluster of privacy-related interests as opposed to the development of a general right to privacy. An alternative possibility is that our courts recognise a general right to privacy but more tightly control when that right is applicable than the ECtHR currently does. Certainly if the common law recognised a general right to privacy it is likely that

---

[112] n 109.
[113] Ibid at [28].
[114] n 40.
[115] Ibid at [63].
[116] Ibid at [87].
[117] *Kinloch v HM Advocate* [2012] UKSC 62; [2013] 2 AC 93.
[118] Ibid at [21].
[119] Although the more recent case of *JR38* (n 47) offered a more nuanced approach to privacy in public as some of the judges were willing to find that the Convention right was applicable when a child was engaged in criminal activity in public, this was premised upon the fact that the case concerned the publication of photographs of a child, and so the factual matrix was different from *Kinloch*, the Supreme Court justices did not dispute that *Kinloch* was rightly determined. Indeed even Lord Kerr who concluded that Article 8 ECHR applied in *JR38* did not suggest that *Kinloch* was wrong, on the contrary he noted that such persons 'could not have a reasonable expectation of privacy for his criminal activity' and that 'consideration may occupy a position of such importance in the question of whether particular circumstances come within the ambit of article 8, that no other factor could outweigh it' at [54].

the threshold for determining the applicability of that right would be a reasonable expectation of privacy test.[120] In various jurisdictions a reasonable expectation of privacy test is used to determine whether a right to privacy is applicable or whether there is a viable cause of action in tort. Indeed in English law the reasonable expectation of privacy test is used to determine whether there is a claim under the law of misuse of private information[121] and in Article 8 ECHR cases to determine whether the right is applicable.[122] The reasonable expectation of privacy test is also the touchstone for privacy-related laws in other common law jurisdictions. In the US it was first developed in *Katz v United States*, a case that concerned the legality of wiretapping[123] and since then the test has been the touchstone for Fourth Amendment jurisprudence. In Canada, it is used in the jurisprudence of section 8 of the Canadian Charter of Rights and Freedoms and its remit is similar to the US Fourth Amendment in that it is concerned with searches and seizures. In both of those jurisdictions, however, a number of scholars have expressed concerns about the use of the test. Daniel Solove explains that whilst 'at first glance' the test 'seems quite sensible', it 'has failed to live up to its aspirations' as that 'the Supreme Court adopted a conception of privacy that countless commentators have found to be overly narrow, incoherent, short-sighted, deleterious to liberty, and totally out of touch with society'.[124] Canadian scholars have expressed similar concerns.[125] Thus whilst the development of a common law right to privacy underpinned by a reasonable expectation of privacy is a possible way forward, it runs the risk that such a right may be narrowly interpreted.

The approach taken by the ECtHR is different, although it too refers to 'reasonable expectations of privacy' it is less clear that it operates as a threshold for engaging the Convention right. In fact the phrase 'reasonable expectation of privacy' only appears in a small subset of the ECHR case law.[126] Given the

---

[120] Note in *JR38* (n 47) there was some disagreement amongst the judges as to whether the reasonable expectation of privacy test is a factor or the sole factor in determining the application of Art 8 ECHR.

[121] See *Campbell v MGN* (n 45), and *Murray v Big Pictures Limited* [2008] EWCA Civ 446; [2008] 3 WLR 1360, at [35]–[36]. See also discussion in K Hughes 'A Behavioural Understanding of Privacy and its Implications for Privacy Law' (2012) 75(5) *MLR* 806, 827–828.

[122] See for example *Catt* (n 47).

[123] In *Katz v United States* 389 US 347 (1967) the Supreme Court held that wiretaps were covered by the Fourth Amendment and developed the reasonable expectation of privacy test. Although the test did not feature in the Opinion of the Supreme Court in *Katz*, the first judicial uttering of the concept appeared in the concurring opinion of Justice Harlan.

[124] D Solove, 'Fourth Amendment Pragmatism' (2010) *Boston College Law Review* 1511, 1519.

[125] Ian Kerr has highlighted how the Canadian courts have interpreted the reasonable expectation of privacy test in a restrictive manner which cannot accommodate the threats posed by modern technology. See I Kerr, M Binnie and C Aoki, 'Tessling on My Brain: The Future of Lie Detection and Brain Privacy in the Criminal Justice System' (2008) 50 *Canadian Journal of Criminology and Criminal Justice* 367; and I Kerr and J McGill, 'Emanations, Snoop Dogs and Reasonable Expectation of Privacy' (2007) 52 *Criminal Law Quarterly* 392.

[126] See discussion in K Hughes (n 121). For examples of the cases where the phrase has appeared see *Halford v United Kingdom* (1997) 24 EHRR 523, *PG and JH v United Kingdom* (2008) 46 EHRR 51, *Peck v United Kingdom* (2003) 36 EHRR 41, *Perry v United Kingdom* (2004) 39 EHRR 3, *Von Hannover v Germany* (2005) 40 EHRR 1, *Copland v United Kingdom* (2007) 45 EHRR 37, *Gillan and Quinton v United Kingdom* (n 40), *Axel Springer v Germany* (n 81), and *Von Hannover v Germany (No.2)* (n 81).

common law origins of the 'reasonable expectation of privacy' formulation it is perhaps not surprising that it first appeared in a case against the UK,[127] and that almost all of the early cases in which it appeared also concerned the UK.[128] The ECtHR has not, however, sought to identify a single test for determining the applicability of the Convention right, instead routinely declaring that private life 'is a broad concept, not susceptible to exhaustive definition'.[129] This enables the ECtHR to avoid clearly demarcating a binary distinction between what is public and what is private. Thus contrary to notions of privacy that centre upon the hermit, the home and private places the ECtHR has instead recognised that there is 'a zone of interaction of a person with others, even in a public context, which may fall within the scope of private life'.[130] As a result the Convention right to privacy does not cease whenever we leave our homes or interact with others, a feature that reflects a more contemporary understanding of privacy.[131] In fact the ECtHR very rarely finds that Article 8 (1) ECHR does not apply to a given set of facts. It often regards the applicability of the right as self-evident and even where there is some doubt the ECtHR may elect to proceed on the assumption that it applies. Consequently out of thousands of Article 8 ECHR judgments there are only a handful in which the ECtHR has declared that the right does not apply at all.[132]

It is this approach to the scope and applicability of the right that is likely to be very different under any common law right. At present when our domestic courts apply the reasonable expectation of privacy test they are guided by the Article 8 ECHR jurisprudence in determining the parameters of what is private. As Lord Sumption noted in *Catt*, under the HRA 'the test cannot be limited to cases where a person can be said to have a reasonable expectation about the privacy of his home or personal communication' as the Convention jurisprudence offers an 'expanded concept of private life' which extends to 'every occasion on which a person has a reasonable expectation that there will be no interference with the broader right of personal autonomy recognised in the case law of the Strasbourg court'.[133] Yet even with this jurisprudence we have, as noted above, seen signs that our own courts tend towards a more conservative approach and are much more inclined to the view that there was no reasonable expectation of privacy. Without Strasbourg guidance they may thus be far more inclined to determine that no reasonable expectation of privacy has been established.

---

[127] *Halford v United Kingdom*, ibid.
[128] n 126.
[129] See, eg, *Couderc* (n 81) at [83].
[130] Ibid.
[131] For discussion of different conceptions of privacy see K Hughes 'A Behavioural Understanding of Privacy' (n 121).
[132] For discussion see K Hughes *The Elusive Right to Privacy* (Oxford, Hart) forthcoming.
[133] n 47, at [4].

Moreover, even where our domestic courts are willing to accept that Article 8 ECHR is applicable they may be more likely to deem those interferences trivial and/or easily justified. This is evident in *Catt* where the majority of the judges determined that the collation of information on protestors' public activities by the police was a 'comparatively minor interference' with private life.[134] Lord Toulson was alone in his recognition that such intrusions are significant 'because in modern society the state has very extensive powers of keeping records on its citizens'.[135] The approach of the majority of the Supreme Court Justices was thus in stark contrast to the approach taken by the ECtHR which held that 'personal data revealing political opinion falls among the special categories of sensitive data attracting a heightened level of protection'.[136] A further concern is whether our domestic courts may be inclined to ascribe greater weight to other competing interests. This is evident in *Beghal* where the importance of national security was emphasised such that it was held that 'a court should be circumspect before upholding any challenge to such legislative powers, when that challenge is based on necessity or disproportionality'.[137] On that occasion Lord Kerr was alone in emphasising that this was a significant interference and that the state had failed to make the case for why it was necessary.[138] It is of course important to acknowledge that the ECtHR can also be extremely deferential to claims to national security, see, for example its reasoning in *Big Brother Watch v United Kingdom*,[139] but in *Beghal* itself the ECtHR found that the provisions lacked the necessary safeguards and were thus violated the Convention.[140]

We should therefore be cautious about the scope and strength of any constitutional common law right that is not shaped by the Convention jurisprudence. Indeed if domestic judges are inclined to doubt that a right to privacy is engaged by state retention of DNA data, coercive stop and search powers, and surveillance logs, or to perceive such interferences as trivial and easily displaced by other interests, then the prospect of a constitutional common law right to privacy offering substantial protection seems slim indeed. Thus even if the common law finally recognises a constitutional right to privacy or enhanced cluster of privacy-related rights, we may well need to convince our domestic judges of the normative reach and significance of those rights. A way forward in that regard would be to take a deeper look at how we experience privacy and why it is important. Elsewhere I have explained how privacy forms an important part of social interaction, how this can be accommodated in a reasonable expectation of privacy test and why

---

[134] n 47, at [26] and [29].
[135] n 47, at [69].
[136] n 47, at [112].
[137] n 47, at [75].
[138] n 47, at [127]–[128].
[139] n 19.
[140] *Beghal v United Kingdom* (App No 4755/16) 28 February 2019.

privacy is important to both the individual rights-holder and society.[141] Indeed if we engage further with the underlying privacy concept and the values that it promotes it is perfectly possible to develop an approach centred upon the reasonable expectation of privacy test that is not contingent upon binary notions of what is public and private or limited to private spaces, that, however, has not been the natural inclination of our common law judges. Thus whilst there is always the potential for development we have to be realistic about what the common law has offered to date and how our judges approach privacy.

VI. Conclusion

In conclusion, whilst privacy law has evolved significantly over the last 20 years considerable doubt remains as to whether the common law will ever recognise a general constitutional right to privacy or even an enhanced cluster of common law privacy-related rights. Certainly *if* the common law is in a position to give birth to such a right then this is likely to be due to the influence of the rights culture that the HRA and Convention have spurred and the value accorded to privacy in both ECHR and European Union law. Such a development is, however, by no means certain: although the courts have begun to recognise a common law right to privacy in informational privacy cases, there is no guarantee that this is a constitutional right, nor that a common law right will emerge to protect privacy outside of the informational privacy context. The lack of clarity as to the capacity and direction of the common law means that we may well be waiting for Godot in looking for a case in which non-informational aspects of privacy are litigated using both the common law and Article 8 ECHR. It is far easier for counsel to turn to Article 8 ECHR and the courts do not appear to be encouraging them to do otherwise. It is however, only in such a case that we will see if the courts are finally willing to overcome longstanding common law resistance to a right to privacy. Yet as things stand their track record even on some of the core aspects of Article 8 privacy rights does not bode well. It is therefore likely that even if a constitutional common law right to privacy finally appears that it would be narrower in scope and less weighty than the Convention right. We thus should not underestimate what the HRA offers. Indeed without it we may well find that the common law continues, as it consistently did prior to the HRA, to fall woefully short for even core elements of a right to privacy.

---

[141] K Hughes 'A Behavioural Understanding of Privacy' (n 121).

6

Freedom of Expression and the Right to Vote: Political Rights and the Common Law Constitution

JACOB ROWBOTTOM*

This chapter will look at the protection of the right to vote and freedom of expression under the common law. The two rights lie at the core of a democratic society. Freedom of expression is a form of participation that is crucial to opinion formation, for the persuasion of others and the general scrutiny of government. The right to vote is a form of direct power that reflects the equal status of citizens, provides the means for people to direct the legislature and discipline public officials. The two are connected. The right to vote would be pretty meaningless if people lacked the freedom to engage in advocacy, to discuss political matters and receive diverse content. The democratic justifications for free speech assume some mechanism (such as voting) for people to channel their views and priorities to public officials. Despite this close connection, the two rights have different histories in the common law. Freedom of speech (and liberty of the press) has long been recognised and offered some piecemeal protection under the common law. Free speech is frequently said to be one of the most obvious candidates for common law protection.[1] By contrast, there remains considerable doubt and debate about the extent to which the right to vote is protected under the common law (if at all).

This chapter will begin by considering why the right to vote and freedom of expression are valued and given constitutional status. The discussion will then look at the ways in which the rights are protected under the common law. Given the strong emphasis placed on freedom of expression, greater attention will be given to that right. The discussion of expression rights will show that there are different ways that the common law is thought to protect that right. The shortcomings and limits of the various methods of protection will be noted.

---

* With thanks to Heather Green for comments on an earlier draft of this chapter.
[1] See M Elliott, 'Beyond the European Convention: Human Rights and the Common Law' (2015) 65 *Current Legal Problems* 85, 88.

The discussion will then examine the treatment of the right to vote, and the challenges in protecting that right under the common law. One challenge is historical, given that the universal franchise has not enjoyed such longstanding recognition and is a product of legislation. The UK's transition to a modern democracy was a result of political pressure that was sometimes resisted by the common law. A further challenge is that the right to vote demands greater positive protection, as an election requires considerable state machinery and expense. These expenses include staffing polling stations and policing the election campaign rules. The right to vote also entails difficult questions of design in the electoral system. These qualities make the protection harder to secure under the common law, given that common law rights tend to focus on negative restrictions on state power primarily through the means of statutory interpretation. Consequently, common law rights may offer less protection for those rights that entail positive steps to be taken by a public body.

I. Free Speech and the Vote as Fundamental Constitutional Rights

The common law recognises certain rights that are of fundamental status, for which the protection is a matter of constitutional importance. Lord Steyn has noted that to categorise a right as 'fundamental' is to emphasise its 'higher normative force'.[2] An initial challenge is to identify those rights that are deserving of such heightened protection. A starting point is to look at those rights that have some obvious connection with the constitutional system of government. As Lord Cooke explained in *R (Daly) v Secretary of State for the Home Department*, 'some rights are inherent and fundamental to democratic civilised society'.[3] If the connection with a democratic society is the key criterion, then the rights to expression and to vote are obvious candidates for inclusion in the constitutional framework. In *Animal Defenders International* (an Article 10 of the European Convention on Human Rights (ECHR) case), Baroness Hale referred to the 'the two most important components of a democracy: freedom of expression and voter equality'.[4] The two are political rights that enable citizens to influence and exercise some control over government decisions.

The precise role that voting plays in conferring democratic legitimacy to a system of government will vary according to different democratic theories. However, for present purposes, it is enough to note that voting is a key component in any democratic system. At its most basic, a system of representative government cannot describe itself as democratic if citizens do not have the means to choose the

---

[2] Lord Steyn in *Reynolds v Times Newspapers* [2001] 2 AC 127, 207.

[3] *R (Daly) v Secretary of State for the Home Department* [2001] UKHL 26, [2001] 2 AC 532, [30].

[4] *R (Animal Defenders International) v Secretary of State for Culture, Media and Sport* [2008] UKHL 15, [2008] 1 AC 1312, [49].

public officials that hold the ultimate decision-making power. In most representative systems, that will be reflected in the election of members to the legislature.

With freedom of expression, the right can be justified for many reasons, including those with no connection with democratic debate.[5] However, in the domestic and Strasbourg jurisprudence, the courts have justified the constitutional protection of the right in terms of its importance in a democracy. The protection of expression is often taken to be what separates a democratic and non-democratic regime. In *Spycatcher*, Lord Bridge famously stated that:

> Freedom of speech is always the first casualty under a totalitarian regime. Such a regime cannot afford to allow the free circulation of information and ideas among its citizens. Censorship is the indispensable tool to regulate what the public may and what they may not know.[6]

More broadly, in *ex parte Simms*, Lord Steyn referred to a range of justifications for freedom of expression and noted that 'freedom of speech is the lifeblood of democracy' and the 'free flow of information and ideas informs political debate.'[7] The role of freedom of expression in facilitating democratic participation and an informed citizenry has been repeated on many occasions.[8]

By taking a largely election-centric view of expression rights, a connection is made with voting rights in which the free dissemination of ideas, facts and opinions enables the vote to be exercised in an informed way. Along these lines, Lord Nicholls in *Reynolds* stated:

> At a pragmatic level, freedom to disseminate and receive information on political matters is essential to the proper functioning of the system of parliamentary democracy cherished in this country. This freedom enables those who elect representatives to Parliament to make an informed choice, regarding individuals as well as policies, and those elected to make informed decisions.[9]

The dominant view (though not the sole view) is that freedom of speech is valued for its service to a democratic society.

For present purposes, the crucial point is that both the right to vote and freedom of expression are regarded as core democratic rights. Both therefore qualify for elevated protection within a constitutional system. These points do not mean that all aspects of the rights must be judicially protected, and there may be other methods of protection. The discussion will explore a particular type of legal protection and consider how both have enjoyed different status under the common law. It will be considered whether that difference sheds any light on the capacity of the common law to protect constitutional rights more generally.

---

[5] For an overview, see E Barendt, *Freedom of Speech* (Oxford, Oxford University Press, 2005) ch 1.

[6] *Attorney General v Newspapers Ltd (No 1)* [1987] 1 WLR 1248, 1286.

[7] *R v Secretary of State for the Home Department, ex parte Simms* [2000] 2 AC 115, 126.

[8] See Lord Kerr in *R (Lord Carlile of Berriew QC) v Secretary of State for the Home Department* [2014] UKSC 60, [2015] AC 945, [172], describing freedom of speech as a 'cornerstone of our democracy'.

[9] *Reynolds* (n 2) 200. See also *McCartan Turkington Breen v Times Newspapers Ltd* [2001] 2 AC 277, 290–291 (Lord Bingham).

II. Freedom of Speech and the Common Law

The courts recognised the importance of freedom of speech and freedom of the press on numerous occasions prior to the Human Rights Act 1998.[10] In *Broome v Cassell*, the court referred to 'a constitutional right to free speech'.[11] In *Spycatcher*, Lord Goff stated that 'we may pride ourselves on the fact that freedom of speech has existed in this country perhaps as long as, if not longer than, it has existed in any other country in the world.'[12] In *Verrall*, Watkins J described freedom of speech as 'a fundamental freedom which this country has prided itself on maintaining, and for which much blood has been spilt over the centuries.'[13] Such self-congratulatory statements possibly overlook the long history of censorship and control of publication (which helped to generate the various campaigns for free speech).[14] Notwithstanding this qualification, the common law has recognised the importance of free speech (even if it has not always secured strong protection). The discussion will explain three ways that the common law can be said to protect expression rights. The first is the Diceyan view that the ordinary common law method has features that will generally support expression rights. The second is that the substance of the doctrines in the ordinary common law function to protect expression rights in practice. The third is the development of a specific constitutional branch of the common law that recognises an abstract right to freedom of expression, which has distinct legal consequences, such as informing the interpretation of legislation.

A. The Common Law Method Itself is Conducive to Free Speech

The first line of argument is that the common law method protects freedom of expression through the ordinary operation of the rule of law. The term 'common law method' is used here not just to refer to judge-made law, but also the fact that such laws are founded in precedent and applied by the ordinary courts. While the common law method is not necessary to meet the basic requirements of legality under the rule of law, Dicey's work strongly suggests these features of the

---

[10] For the purposes of this discussion, I use freedom of speech to include the common law protection of press freedom, despite the differences in the content of either right. See J Rowbottom, *Media Law* (Oxford, Hart Publishing, 2018) ch 1.

[11] *Broome v Cassell & Co Ltd* (No 1) [1972] AC 1027, 1133. However, this was qualified by the statement that the right has been in place 'at least since the European Convention was ratified'.

[12] *Attorney General v Guardian (No 2)* [1990] 1 AC 109.

[13] Watkins J in *Verrall v Great Yarmouth Borough Council* [1981] 1 QB 202, 205.

[14] Measures ranging from the licensing of the press, the law of seditious libel, various powers of search, government secrecy, and controls on public protests, to name but a few, show how there has also been a strong tradition of restriction.

common law are particularly well suited to fulfilling those demands.[15] Along these lines, Dicey wrote that 'the so-called liberty of the press is a mere application of the general principle, that no man is punishable, except for a distinct breach of the law'.[16] That principle thereby supports a presumption against prior restraints that stop a publication taking place in advance of any wrongdoing. The common law method also stresses the role of the ordinary courts in developing and applying the law. Under this view, legal restrictions on expression or publication are adjudicated before an ordinary court, rather than a specialist tribunal. Speech rights are therefore not at the mercy of administrative discretion. Dicey accordingly noted that the right to trial by jury in a libel case means that 'it is impossible that the Crown or the Ministry should exert any stringent control over writings in the press, unless (as indeed may sometimes happen) the majority of ordinary citizens are entirely opposed to attacks on the government'.[17] Taking the application of the law out of the hands of government, and into those of judges and juries, was thought to reduce the ability of government officials to selectively censor content. The hostility to the 'exceptional authority' of government and the principle that no man is punished except where there is a breach of the law was thought to preclude a system of government licensing of the press. The absence of such a system of licensing was a key part of the ideal of press freedom at the time.

The approach taken by Dicey suggests that expression rights are protected as a consequence of these methods and processes found in the common law, which reflected the principles in his account of the rule of law. In Dicey's view, the protection of the right did not depend on the judge's enthusiasm for freedom of expression. The thinking was that free speech would be protected even in a system where many people 'hated toleration and cared little for freedom of speech'.[18] Instead, the requirements of the rule of law simply made arbitrary and discretionary restrictions on expression harder to implement. That, however, reflects a very limited view of freedom of expression, which sees the main threat in terms of prior restraints imposed by administrative discretion. That approach does not offer much of a safeguard from restraints imposed through the ordinary law, such as defamation or controls to preserve public order. As Ewing and Gearty wrote, the protection offered to political liberties under this method was 'insecure' in so far as there was 'no fixed definition of what constitutes unlawful action'.[19]

---

[15] See discussion in TRS Allan, 'The rule of law as the rule of reason: consent and constitutionalism' (1999) 115 *LQR* 221, 242, noting that 'Dicey's analysis of the rule of law should be understood chiefly as an account of the common law's contribution to constitutional government'.

[16] A V Dicey, *Introduction to the Study of the Law of the Constitution*, 8th edn (Liberty Fund reprint, 1982, originally Macmillan, 1915) 153.

[17] Ibid, 155. Though since the Defamation Act 2013, jury trials are no longer the norm in libel cases.

[18] Ibid, 166–67.

[19] K Ewing and C Gearty, *The Struggle for Civil Liberties: Political Freedom and the Rule of Law in Britain 1914–1945* (Oxford, Oxford University Press, 2000) 31.

Moreover, many commentators have disputed Dicey's description of the constitution, particularly the limits on specialist discretionary power. It is certainly not possible to maintain such a position today. The emphasis on the ordinary law stands in stark contrast to various specialist administrative systems that regulate expression rights, such as broadcast regulation, the classification of films and the regulation of certain internet content. From these examples, we can see that the elements of the rule of law that Dicey thought to be inherent in the common law offer limited protection for expression rights and in any event are not fully followed in the current system of communications regulation.

B. The Substance of the Common Law Protects Freedom of Expression

The second line of argument is that the substance of the ordinary common law offers protection for expression rights. Under this view, the common law does not need to enshrine an abstract right to freedom of expression that can be asserted against public bodies. Instead, the argument runs that existing doctrines in the common law have developed in a way that respects the right. This may, again, follow the Diceyan view that the law of the constitution is the product of the rights in the ordinary law that are 'defined and enforced by the Courts'.[20] The line of argument is also reflected in more recent statements, such as claims from the courts that the rights protected under the ECHR have long been protected under the common law.[21] The argument does not pretend the common law is comprehensive or that it provides complete protection for those rights found in the Convention. As a result, adjustments to the common law need to be made. However, the argument runs that the common law already goes some way towards meeting the obligations of the ECHR, and that such protection can be found in the free speech tradition. The common law protection for freedom of expression under this approach is piecemeal. Rather than having an overarching constitutional right to expression stated in the abstract, the various bits of ordinary common law doctrine add up to provide space for free speech.

Two examples show how the substance of the common law had carved out some protection for free speech long before the UK signed up to the ECHR.

---

[20] Dicey (n 16), 121.

[21] See, eg, *R v Central Criminal Court, ex parte Bright* [2001] 1 WLR 662, [87], 'we surely fully appreciate that the principles to be found in Articles 6 and 10 of the European Convention are bred in the bone of the common law'. The argument is used in relation to other rights. For example, Lord Bingham noted that 'the English common law has regarded torture and its fruits with abhorrence for over 500 years' in *A v Secretary of State for the Home Department (No 2)* [2006] 2 AC 221 at [51]. See also *R (on the application of Roberts) v Metropolitan Police Commissioner* [2015] UKSC 79, stating that 'the legal protection of the citizen pre-dates the Human Rights Act' and the common law rules provide the starting point.

In relation to defamation law, the rule in *Bonnard v Perryman* meant that an interim injunction would not be granted unless it could be shown that the defences would fail at trial.[22] The rule operated to protect free speech by imposing a high burden on a claimant seeking a restraint prior to trial. In *Bonnard*, Coleridge CJ stated that:

> The right of free speech is one which it is for the public interest that individuals should possess, and, indeed, that they should exercise without impediment, so long as no wrongful act is done; and, unless an alleged libel is untrue, there is no wrong committed; but, on the contrary, often a very wholesome act is performed in the publication and repetition of an alleged libel.[23]

Such reasoning is consistent with a fairly narrow view of free speech that is primarily concerned with the absence of prior restraints. The current justification for the rule reflects the importance of freedom of expression and the fact that reputation is normally restored through the award of damages post-publication.[24] The rule is, however, specific to defamation law and does stand as a general protection against prior restraints.

Another notable feature of the common law protection for free speech is the open justice principle, which allows the public to attend court proceedings and to report what happened in court. In the 1913 decision of *Scott v Scott*, Lord Shaw stated that the publicity of judicial proceedings was a matter of 'constitutional right' as opposed to 'judicial discretion'.[25] The freedom to report on matters in court is particularly important and in *Khuja* Lord Sumption stated that to impose a restriction on the reporting of what is said in court amounts to 'direct censorship'.[26] Jaconelli notes that the open justice principle is exceptional in so far as the common law requires a level of transparency in relation to the courts, which is not demanded of other areas of government activity.[27] Not only does the rule contrast with the tradition of government secrecy, but it also imposes a positive obligation on the courts to open its doors. The rule is not absolute and can be limited, for example where necessary for the attainment of justice. However, the principle stands out as an area where the courts have traditionally recognised the importance of free speech.

Both the rule in *Bonnard* and open justice show two areas where the common law has traditionally applied relatively strong protection for certain speech rights. There has been concern that such common law rules could be weakened through

---

[22] *Bonnard v Perryman* [1891] 2 ch 269.

[23] Ibid, 284.

[24] See Lord Sumption in *Khuja v Times Newspapers Ltd* [2017] UKSC 49; [2017] 3 WLR 351, [19].

[25] *Scott v Scott* [1913] AC 417, 477.

[26] *Khuja* (n 24) [16]. The initial justification, to prevent the judge usurping the jury, no longer explains the rule following the presumption that defamation claims are heard by a judge under the Defamation Act 2013.

[27] J Jaconelli, *Open Justice: A Critique of the Public Trial* (Oxford, Oxford University Press, 2002) 1–2.

the application of the ECHR under the Human Rights Act 1998 (HRA).[28] For example, the ECHR provides a basis for restricting the reporting of court proceedings. Newspapers may be prohibited from reporting certain details in a trial, where it would put a person's life at risk or disproportionately invade privacy rights.[29] Similarly, the rule in *Bonnard* has come under challenge on the basis that it is inconsistent with the ECHR, in so far as it represents a prioritisation of expression rights over rights to reputation that are protected under Article 8.[30] Instead, the critics argue that reputation and expression rights should be given equal weight, and that there should not be such a strong presumption in favour of one right.

The examples highlight a key difference between the piecemeal protection of the rights in the substance of the common law and comprehensive systems of rights protection (such as the ECHR). Under the common law, protection is offered to certain rights (or aspects of a right), but not others. By contrast, a comprehensive system offers protection to a wide range of rights, which are broadly defined and cast in general terms. In such a system, various fundamental rights may be in tension with one another, and require the courts to resolve the conflict. In some cases, this will involve a compromise in which one right is qualified in order to protect another. Consequently, those rights that were offered stronger protection under the common law may be more easily limited by the wider range of rights recognised in a comprehensive system of protection.

One obvious criticism of the piecemeal protection in the common law is that it is patchy and inconsistent. There are parts of the common law that carve out space for the right, but there are others that permit or impose restrictions. One example can be found in the common law of contempt of court prior to 1981. In the famous *Sunday Times* decision, the House of Lords upheld an injunction to restrain the publication of an article criticising the conduct of the manufacturer of the drug Thalidomide in the course of negligence litigation.[31] The common law permitted the prior restraint and the judges sought to prevent the media usurping the court and conducting 'trial by media'. The decision of the House of Lords was found to be a violation of Article 10 by the European Court of Human Rights (ECtHR).[32] The shortcoming of the common law was subsequently addressed through legislative reform.

The common law provided the basis for restraining the publication of *Spycatcher* in the UK in the 1980s. The common law also allowed for considerable

---

[28] G Robertson and A Nicol, *Media Law*, 5th edn (London, Sweet and Maxwell, 2007) 15–18.
[29] *A v BBC* [2014] UKSC 25, [2015] AC 588.
[30] See A Mullis and R Parkes (eds), *Gatley on Libel and Slander*, 12th edn (London, Sweet and Maxwell, 2013) [25.22]. In *Greene v Associated Newspapers* [2004] EWCA Civ 1462, [2005] QB 972, an argument that s 12 of the Human Rights Act 1998 reduces the threshold for an interim injunction to a 'more likely than not' standard was rejected on the basis that s 12 was not intended to lower the protection for freedom of expression.
[31] *Attorney-General v Times Newspapers Ltd* [1974] AC 273.
[32] *Sunday Times v UK* (1979–80) 2 EHRR 245.

prior controls to be imposed on the right to assemble and protest.[33] Until statutory reform, blasphemy was a common law offence. Under the common law, relatively little protection was afforded to journalists' confidential sources. In 1980, Lord Wilberforce stated that the issue of source protection 'does not touch upon the freedom of the press even at its periphery'.[34] That approach contrasts sharply with the position of the ECtHR, which has held that source protection is a basic condition of press freedom.[35] The position was changed by legislation in 1981, which created a statutory presumption against source disclosure. Under the piecemeal protection, the common law offered protection for some aspects of speech rights, but not others. The protection was haphazard and dependent on the cause of action, rather than reflecting any clear principled basis for protecting expression rights.

A further criticism of the piecemeal approach is that the patchy protection of free speech is not a matter of chance, but depends on whether the right is aligned or set against those interests that are more highly prized in the common law.[36] Along these lines, critics have argued that the common law was often concerned with the protection of property related interests, and that the protection for expression rights (or rights of assembly) was largely incidental.[37] For example, in the case of *Verrall v Great Yarmouth BC*, the court ruled that a Labour council could not cancel an agreement to allow the National Front to host its conference at a hall owned by the public authority.[38] The ruling was based on specific performance of a contract. While the decision made reference to the right of free speech, the decision was grounded in protecting the interest in property that had been created through a contractual licence.

This criticism runs that the right is placed in a precarious position when it comes into tension with a property right. A well-known illustration is where people seek to communicate or distribute leaflets on publicly accessible land that is privately owned, but are refused permission by the landowner. In such cases, the court has ruled that the right of the landowner prevails, as part of the right to exclude that forms a key part of a property right.[39] This is not to say that free speech requires access to privately owned spaces in all cases (and the matter is subject to debate). However, the point shows that free speech has sometimes been protected simply because it was aligned with other more prized interests. Where the interest in expression ran contrary to such interests (whether property, the

---

[33] *Moss v McLachlan* (1985) 149 JP 167.
[34] *British Steel v Granada* [1981] AC 1096, 1168.
[35] *Goodwin v United Kingdom* (1996) 22 EHRR 123.
[36] Ewing and Gearty (n 19) 31–32, referring to protection by virtue of a 'happy coincidence'.
[37] Ibid.
[38] *Verrall* (n 13).
[39] See, eg, *CIN Properties v Rawlins* [1995] 39 EG 148 and *Appleby v United Kingdom* (2003) 37 EHRR 38. For discussion see J Rowbottom, 'Property and Participation: A Right of Access for Expressive Activities' [2005] *European Human Rights Law Review* 186. The case of *Appleby* shows how expression rights can be trumped by property rights under the ECHR framework.

authority of the courts, the interest in reputation), then it traditionally received limited protection.

Despite the criticism of the common law, there are some cases that cannot be so easily written off and have resulted in significant changes to the substance of the law. Two examples from defamation law illustrate the point.[40] The first is the landmark decision in *Derbyshire County Council v Times Newspapers*, where the House of Lords ruled 'that under the common law of England a local authority does not have the right to maintain an action of damages for defamation'.[41] Lord Keith stated that he had reached his conclusion based on the common law of England without relying on the European Convention.[42] Lord Keith stated:

> I regard it as right for this House to lay down that not only is there no public interest favouring the right of organs of government, whether central or local, to sue for libel, but that it is contrary to the public interest that they should have it. It is contrary to the public interest because to admit such actions would place an undesirable fetter on freedom of speech.[43]

The line of argument emphasises the importance of allowing the scrutiny and criticism of government. A significant part of the reasoning also lay in the fact that the government body does not have the same interest in protecting its reputation as a human. On this view, the actions of a public body should serve the public interest and the reputation of the public body should therefore yield to the public interest in free discussion. The ruling cannot be characterised simply as private law incidentally protecting free speech. Freedom of speech featured prominently in Lord Keith's reasoning and was used to resolve an uncertainty in the law of defamation. At the same time, it was not clear what the legal effects of the common law right were, or how that free speech principle might be invoked in later cases. The reference to the common law right paved the way for the right to be developed in a more systematic fashion in later cases, but the ruling did not provide a framework for a generalised principle applicable to other areas of law.

A second example is the decision in *Reynolds v Times Newspapers*, in which the House of Lords developed the defence of qualified privilege in defamation to protect statements on matters of public interest that met the standards of responsible journalism.[44] This marked a change from the earlier law, where it was difficult for statements to the world at large to fulfil the requirements for common law qualified privilege. In developing the defence, Lord Nicholls stated that his 'starting

---

[40] The discussion is not exhaustive. For an example in relation to assembly rights, *see DPP v Jones* [1999] 2 AC 240 and on public order see *Redmond-Bate v DPP* (1999) 7 BHRC 375.

[41] *Derbyshire CC v Times Newspapers* [1993] AC 534.

[42] Ibid, 460.

[43] Ibid, 549.

[44] *Reynolds* (n 2).

point is freedom of expression', and the question is then what constraints on that right 'are fairly and reasonably necessary for the protection of reputation'.[45] The responsible journalism test thereby sought to strike a balance that protected serious reporting, but which did not give a licence to tear down reputations with scant evidence. The reasoning of the court anticipated the effect of the Human Rights Act 1998, which was soon to come into force.[46] However, the court used the 'elasticity of the common law principle' in defamation law to accommodate the expression rights. Along with the *Derbyshire* decision, the ruling shows how the courts refer to freedom of expression, but the decisions rest on common law doctrines in defamation rather than a generally applicable legal principle of freedom of expression.

The discussion has shown that sometimes the substance of the law secured the protection of certain aspects of freedom of expression. Two earlier examples (the rule in *Bonnard v Perryman* and the open justice principle) were discussed, as well as two more recent examples in relation to defamation law. The protection offered in those examples were specific to the legal doctrines in question and did not provide a generalised framework that could protect expression rights in other contexts. The rulings do not outline the scope of the right or explain the permissible limits of the right. Moreover, there were many areas in which the common law did not offer protection and sometimes imposed a restriction on the right. In some cases, the limits of the protection offered under the common law had to be changed through statute. The protection for free speech in the substance of the common law doctrines has been sporadic and piecemeal, rather than systematic. However, some of the rulings laid the foundations for the evolution of a constitutional branch of the common law, which will be considered next.

C. Common Law Constitutional Rights

The third approach sets out constitutional principles recognised in the common law that embody and protect certain rights. This establishes a type of constitutional common law that is distinct from the ordinary doctrines that make up the various legal causes of action. This approach takes the sporadic references to freedom of speech (and other rights) that were noted in the previous section and uses them as a foundation for a more systematic method of protection. Accordingly, in *Derbyshire*, Lord Keith cited Lord Goff's congratulatory remarks in *Spycatcher*

---

[45] Ibid, 201.

[46] The point is also noted in *Flood v Times Newspapers* [2012] UKSC 11, [2012] 2 AC 273 at [46], 'the creation of *Reynolds* privilege reflected a recognition on the part of the House of Lords that the existing law of defamation did not cater adequately for the importance of the article 10 right of freedom of expression.'

concerning the English free speech tradition as authority for a common law right.[47] In *ex parte Simms*, both those rulings were then cited as authority for the common law protection of free speech, which in turn was relied on to develop a more general system of constitutional protection.[48] Under the approach of common law constitutionalism, the ideal is not simply to protect rights where they overlap with common law doctrines or where courts sometimes choose to develop the common law. Instead, the ideal is for the rights themselves to have their own free standing legal status and consequences, and to take a more central place in the court's analysis.

This approach builds on the Diceyan tradition of protecting residual liberties, in which people are free to do that which is not restricted by law. Earlier it was outlined that under the Diceyan approach, a person cannot be punished unless there has been a breach of the law. The operation of this approach depends on the courts being able to identify where the law restricts a liberty, which will sometimes depend on the interpretation of the statute in question. The presence of a common law right will direct the court to choose an interpretation that does not restrict a right (or is least restrictive of the right), unless the restriction is the clear intention of the legislature. This approach is labelled the 'principle of legality'.[49]

While the principle is well established, it requires the court to determine the scope of the right and when it is engaged. For example, the ruling in *Simms* was not a straightforward free speech case concerning a publication to the public or a punishment for something said. Instead, *Simms* concerned a restriction preventing a prisoner being interviewed in person with a journalist. To deal with this issue, the court therefore had to form a view on whether the measure engaged the right and whether the right deserved protection. To address these issues, Lord Steyn placed considerable weight on the role of investigative journalism in uncovering miscarriages of justice. The issue of free speech was connected with an interest in the administration of justice. Lord Steyn explained that the ruling did not provide a general right for prisoners to conduct interviews on any matter: 'no prisoner would ever be permitted to have interviews with a journalist to publish pornographic material or to give vent to so-called hate speech.'[50] In such cases, he stated, the right to free speech would be outweighed. The reasoning shows that the system of common law rights requires the court to develop variable weightings depending on the importance of the expression right in question. It also requires a method for determining when the right is outweighed.[51] These raise difficult methodological questions, but the approach taken appears to mirror that found under the ECHR.

---

[47] See (n 12).

[48] *Simms* (n 7), 126. See also *ex p Bright* (n 21) at [100].

[49] For discussion, see the introductory chapter to this volume.

[50] *Simms* (n 7), 127.

[51] In *Pham v Secretary of State for the Home Department* [2015] UKSC 19, [2015] 1 WLR 1591, Lord Reed stated that in such cases the court 'has adopted an approach amounting in substance to a requirement of proportionality, although less formally structured than under the Human Rights Act'.

D. Post-Human Rights Act 1998

While the common law right to freedom of expression developed prior to the Human Rights Act 1998, it was not clear what future there was for common law rights after that statute was enacted. The common law could have become redundant, given that the courts could directly rely on the Convention rights. Many of the leading free speech cases focused primarily on the terms of Article 10, such as *ProLife Alliance*,[52] *Shayler*,[53] *Miss Behavin'*,[54] *Animal Defenders International*,[55] and *Carlile*.[56] However, the common law right to freedom of expression has continued to play a prominent role in some cases.

In particular, the courts have been clear that the common law has not been superseded by the Human Rights Act 1998 and that the two co-exist. In *Kennedy*, a journalist sought to access documents held by the Charity Commission in relation to an inquiry into an appeal by a charity. In interpreting the obligations under the Charities Act, Lord Mance stated that the domestic law is the natural starting point.[57] Lord Mance stated that 'there has too often been a tendency to see the law in areas touched on by the Convention solely in terms of the Convention rights'.[58] He noted that similar protections for rights are likely to be found in the domestic law, either in statute or common law. Similarly, in *A v BBC*, when considering whether to preserve the anonymity of a person subject to deportation, Lord Reed stated that 'the common law principle of open justice remains in vigour, even when Convention rights are also applicable'.[59] He expressed the view that the domestic law will 'normally meet the requirements of the Convention'.[60] However, he added that where the balance struck by the Convention conflicts with that under the common law, effect must be given to the Convention.[61] In *Rhodes*, Lord Neuberger also pointed to the co-existence of the common law and the Convention. However, he also noted that the latter can influence the former. Accordingly, he said that while the case involved 'a purely common law issue', 'the common law should be generally consistent with the Convention and it would be arrogant to assume that there may be no assistance to be gained from the Strasbourg jurisprudence'.[62]

The ECHR has had a direct influence on the content of some areas of the common law. As public authorities, the courts are required to act in compliance

---

[52] *R (ProLife Alliance) v BBC* [2003] UKHL 23, [2004] 1 AC 185.
[53] *R v Shayler* [2002] UKHL 11. [2003] 1 AC 247.
[54] *Belfast City Council v Miss Behavin' Ltd* [2007] UKHL 19, [2007] 1 WLR 1420.
[55] *Animal Defenders International* (n 4).
[56] *Carlile* (n 8).
[57] *Kennedy v Information Commissioner* [2014] UKSC 20; [2015] AC 455, [46].
[58] Ibid, [46].
[59] *A v BBC* (n 29) [56]. See also *Guardian News and Media Ltd v City of Westminster Magistrates' Court* [2012] EWCA Civ 420, [2013] QB 618, [88].
[60] *A v BBC* (n 30) [57].
[61] Ibid, [58].
[62] *O (A Child) v Rhodes* [2015] UKSC 32, [2016] AC 219 at [120].

with the Convention. This means that in 'developing the common law the courts as public authorities are obliged to have regard to the requirements of the Convention'.[63] The court has found that this obligation does not require the creation of any new causes of action, but applies in relation to the existing common law doctrines.[64] In the context of free speech, the issue has been most prominently developed in relation to privacy law.[65]

E. Summary on Freedom of Expression

The discussion has shown how the principle of free speech has been recognised in the common law. Freedom of speech often comes near the top of any list of common law rights, and it thereby provides a useful case study on the workings of common law rights more generally. However, the discussion has shown how its status is more precarious than often thought. The protection has not been consistent, and in some cases the common law permitted or mandated restrictions on expression. The discussion has shown the different ways the common law can support freedom of speech, with the protection evolving from various sporadic references to the right. This piecemeal protection has provided a basis for a more general framework of constitutional common law. While the courts attempt to provide a more systematic basis for protecting the right to expression, the workings and methodology of the framework (along with its relation to the ECHR) are still developing. Having set out the different aspects of the common law right to free speech, along with its shortcomings, the discussion will now turn to a right that has typically received less recognition in the common law, the right to vote.

III. The Right to Vote and the Common Law

The right to freedom of expression has been the subject of numerous cases, which have helped to illustrate the evolution of common law rights. The literature and case law on the right to vote under the common law is, however, more limited. An opportunity to consider common law protection of the right to vote has arisen with legal challenges relating to the rights of prisoners. The issue of prisoner voting rights became prominent following the ruling in Strasbourg in *Hirst* that the UK's blanket ban on prisoners voting in parliamentary or local elections violates the ECHR.[66] The *Hirst* decision led to a declaration of incompatibility in

---

[63] Flood (n 46) [46].
[64] See *Campbell v MGN* [2004] UKHL 22, [2004] 2 AC 457.
[65] See ch 5 for discussion.
[66] *Hirst v United Kingdom (No 2)* (2006) 42 EHRR 41.

the domestic court.[67] The failure of the government to rectify this breach led to a number of further challenges both in the domestic and Strasbourg Courts.[68] The challenges made to disenfranchisement in parliamentary or local elections were framed under Article 3 of Protocol No 1 of the ECHR, which provides that signatory states must 'hold free elections at reasonable intervals by secret ballot, under conditions which will ensure the free expression of the opinion of the people in the choice of the legislature'. This has been interpreted by the Strasbourg Court to protect both a right to vote and to stand for election.[69] As a result of these provisions, the challenges in relation to elections to a legislature did not need to rely on the common law.

The ECHR refers to the 'the choice of the legislature', and therefore does not obviously apply to mechanisms of direct democracy that do not involve the selection of representatives.[70] Consequently, when a challenge in *Moohan* was brought to legislation which prevented prisoners from voting in the referendum on Scottish independence, the applicants relied on a common law right to vote.[71] In the Outer House, Lord Glennie stated that 'the common law has developed to recognise the right to vote as a fundamental or constitutional common law right', and it had done so in tandem with the statutory extension of the franchise'.[72] The right would be protected against very severe restrictions. That did not, however, mean that there was a 'a constitutional right of universal suffrage for all purposes' and it did not extend to a right to vote in referenda.[73] Accordingly the claim was rejected. In the Inner House, the claim was also rejected. Lady Paton, however, was more dismissive of a common law right, stating that 'there is no clearly identifiable common law fundamental right to vote in the UK'.[74] According to Lady Paton, that something had been accepted as a 'constitutional right' did not mean that it was based in the common law, and the ECHR was the primary tool to protect voting rights.[75]

In the Supreme Court, the claim was also rejected. Lord Hodge stated that the common law had yet to recognise 'a right of universal and equal suffrage from which any derogation must be provided for by law and must be proportionate'.[76]

---

[67] *Smith v Scott* [2007] CSIH 9, 2007 SC 345.

[68] *R (Chester) v Secretary of State for Justice* [2013] UKSC 63, [2014] AC 271; *Greens v United Kingdom* (2011) 53 EHRR 21; *Shindler v United Kingdom* (2013) 58 EHRR 148; *Firth v United Kingdom* (2016) 63 EHRR 25.

[69] *Mathieu-Mohin and Clerfayt v Belgium* (1988) 10 EHRR 1, [51].

[70] Though see the subsequent decision in *Moohan and Gillon v United Kingdom* (App Nos 22962/15 and 23345/15, 13 June 2017) [42] leaving open the possibility that the right might be engaged in relation to referenda in certain conditions.

[71] The domestic court found that the provisions of the ECHR do not apply to referenda. See also *X. v the United Kingdom* (dec.), App No 7096/75, 3 October 1975, *Nurminen v Finland* (dec.), App No 27881/95, 26 February 1997, *Z. v Latvia* (dec.), App No 14755/03, 26 January 2006 and *Niedzwiedz v Poland* (dec.), App No 1345/06, 11 March 2008.

[72] *Moohan v Lord Advocate* [2013] CSOH 199, [71].

[73] Ibid, [71]–[72].

[74] *Moohan v Lord Advocate* [2014] CSIH 56, 2015 SC 1, [26].

[75] Ibid, [29].

[76] *Moohan v Lord Advocate* [2014] UKSC 67, [2015] AC 901, [34].

However, he did not rule out the potential for the right to vote to be developed in the common law, stating:

> I do not exclude the possibility that in the very unlikely event that a parliamentary majority abusively sought to entrench its power by a curtailment of the franchise or similar device, the common law, informed by principles of democracy and the rule of law and international norms, would be able to declare such legislation unlawful.[77]

A similar point was made by Lord Glennie in the Outer House.[78] Such comments add a further contribution to the debate about the potential for common law rights to restrict the legislature.[79] It is ironic that the extreme interference with the right to vote – which has questionable status in the common law – is cited as an example of where the common law may be invoked to directly challenge the legislature. This shows how the rights protected under the common law and weight assigned to such rights may vary depending on the legal consequences of a breach.

While Lord Kerr also rejected the claim in *Moohan*, he was not so quick to dismiss the role of the common law in such a case. Pointing out that the common law has developed to accommodate democratic rights, he stated that it is 'at least arguable that exclusion of all prisoners from the right to vote is incompatible with the common law'.[80] However, he stated that further argument would be necessary before he could express a 'final conclusion' on the issue. Following the reasoning in *Moohan*, Lord Dyson MR in *Shindler* stated that a common law challenge to the exclusion of UK citizens non-resident for more than 15 years from the referendum on EU membership was 'hopeless'.[81] Such an exclusion did not amount to an extreme or abusive restriction that Lord Hodge in *Moohan* had referred to as an exceptional case.[82]

While the courts in *Moohan* and *Shindler* rejected the applicants' common law claims, it is important to remember that the challenge was made to the terms of *legislation* restricting the franchise. In *Shindler*, the court was asked to declare that primary legislation enacted by Westminster, the European Union Referendum Act 2015, was unconstitutional. To entertain such a review of primary legislation under the common law would have abandoned the longstanding constitutional relationship between the courts and Westminster. In *Moohan*, the challenge was to legislation enacted by the Scottish Parliament, the Scottish Independence Referendum (Franchise) Act 2013. The potential to review statutes from a devolved legislature is less radical and was accepted in *AXA*, but is still one of

---

[77] Ibid at [35].
[78] *Moohan v Lord Advocate* [2013] CSOH 199, [78]: 'so much so that in the unlikely event of parliament now seeking to legislate to restrict it severely or to abolish it entirely, the question would again be raised as to whether there were any limits to the doctrine of parliamentary sovereignty'.
[79] For discussion, see chs 9, 11 and 13.
[80] *Moohan* (n 78) at [88].
[81] *Shindler v Chancellor of the Duchy of Lancaster* [2016] EWCA Civ 469, [50].
[82] Ibid.

the more far-reaching applications of common law rights.[83] The ruling in *Moohan* should not preclude the reliance on a common law right where the consequences are less far-reaching. The discussion below will explore some of the reasons why courts may nonetheless be reluctant to pursue such a path.

A. Historical Support

Given that voting stands alongside expression as a central political right in any democracy, this raises the difficult question of why those two rights appear to have different status in the common law. One possible reason is historical, as the right to vote was subject to a wide range of restrictions.[84] While the Victorian period saw a considerable extension of the franchise (alongside reforms of the electoral system more generally), property qualifications for the right to vote were only abolished in 1918. Women received the right to vote in 1918, and only on equal terms as men in 1928. Against this background, it is difficult to assert that the common law has long recognised a universal right to vote. The precedents suggest that for much of the UK's history restrictions were widely tolerated.

Dicta from some older cases may (at face value) appear to lend some support for a common law right to vote. In *Ashby v White*, an action was brought against a returning officer in a parliamentary election that had refused to allow the plaintiff to vote. The case raised a difficult issue relating to the jurisdiction of the court. At the time, the conduct of elections was governed by Parliament, so the claim faced the objection that it asked the courts to infringe parliamentary privilege. To avoid this consequence, in his dissent (which was subsequently upheld by the House of Lords), Justice Holt stated that the 'right of voting is a right in the plaintiff by the common law, and consequently he shall maintain an action for the obstruction of it'.[85] Holt described the right as a 'matter of property', which fits with property qualifications that were required to vote at the time.[86] By characterising the right as a matter of property, it fell within the jurisdiction of the court (and not Parliament). Accordingly, when discussing the decision in *Watkins*, Lord Rodger explained that it should be understood as protecting a property interest rather than a constitutional right.[87] Lord Rodger also explained that the decision should not be remembered in 'purely legal terms', but as 'a set-piece battle in a war between

---

[83] *AXA General Insurance Ltd v Lord Advocate* [2011] UKSC 46, [2012] 1 AC 868. On the role of common law rights in the devolved context, see ch 12.

[84] For discussion of the development of the right to vote in UK law, see B Watt, *UK Election Law: A critical examination* (London, Glass House Press, 2006) ch 2.

[85] *Ashby v White* (1703) 2 Ld Raym 938: 'the plaintiff has a right and privilege to give his vote' and 'that if he be hindered in the enjoyment or exercise of that right, the law gives him an action against the disturber, and that this is the proper action given by the law'.

[86] See Watt (n 84) 34–37.

[87] *Watkins v Secretary of State for the Home Department* [2006] UKHL 17, [2006] 2 AC 395, [55]. Accordingly, Lord Rodger found that the decision does not support an action for damages for an infringement of a constitutional right without proof of special damage.

the two Houses of Parliament and between the Whigs and the Tories'.[88] Moreover, even though the decision refers to a common law right to vote, the decision says little about the content of such a right. More fundamentally, it is difficult to see a decision from the pre-democratic era providing much of a foundation for the right to vote in its modern sense, with its demand for equal weight and universal suffrage.

In the campaign for universal suffrage in the nineteenth century, appeals were sometimes made to ancient constitutional rights to vote. Such arguments formed part of the 'rhetoric of British radicalism' in the nineteenth century, and enabled the campaigners 'to argue that women' s enfranchisement also promised a return to the true basis of British democracy'.[89] However, whatever value such rhetoric had in organising the political movement, the arguments were based on the 'myth' of the 'freeborn Briton' rather than precedent.[90]

The status of the right to vote under the common law was considered in a number of legal challenges made as part of the campaign for universal suffrage. In these cases, the courts were invited to interpret the relevant statutes in a way that extended the right to vote to women. In *Chorlton v Lings*, the issue was the interpretation of the Second Reform Act of 1867, which provided that 'every man' shall be entitled to register as a voter in a borough constituency, as long as the relevant qualifications are fulfilled, which included the absence of any 'legal incapacity'.[91] The appellants argued that the term 'every man' should also include women, and that there was no legal incapacity. When addressing the question of incapacity, the judges rejected various older precedents provided by the appellants and found a lack of evidence to support the appellants claim that women enjoyed a common law right to the franchise. After reviewing the sporadic references to an ancient right in the common law, Bovill CJ stated 'these instances are of comparatively little weight' when compared with the practice of the restricted franchise that had been in place for several centuries.[92] Keating J also noted that Lord Coke had 'considered the law to be that women were disqualified at common law', and that the conclusion had been supported by centuries of practice.[93]

In *Nairn v University of St Andrews*, the House of Lords considered whether a provision of the Representation of the People Act 1868 that stated that 'every person' on the register of the University and not subject to any legal incapacity shall be entitled to vote in a parliamentary election.[94] A group of female graduates relied on the provision to argue that they were entitled to vote. The House of Lords

---

[88] Ibid, [51].
[89] S Holton, 'The making of suffrage history' in J Purvis and S Holton (eds), *Votes for Women* (London, Routledge, 2000) 13. See discussion in Watt (n 84) 45.
[90] Ibid.
[91] *Chorlton v Lings* (1868–69) LR 4 CP 374.
[92] Ibid, 383.
[93] Ibid, 396.
[94] *Nairn v University of St Andrews* [1909] AC 147.

rejected the argument, finding that the term 'persons' was intended to apply only to men. Lord Ashbourne stated that 'the parliamentary franchise was by constitutional principle and practice confined to men', and so the legislature would only have had men in contemplation when drafting the provision.[95]

Far from supporting voting rights, the common law imposed restrictions on the franchise. The common law provided that mental incapacity was a ground to legally disqualify a person from voting, until the Electoral Administration Act 2006 abolished any remaining common law rule.[96] In *Nairn*, Lord Loreburn held that the incapacity of women to vote was a matter of common law, and that it had been a 'constant tradition' and practice.[97] The incapacity was so firmly rooted in the constitution, that it could only be changed where Parliament's clear intention can be demonstrated.[98] Similarly Lord Ashbourne stated that if the statute 'was intended to make a vast constitutional change in favour of women graduates, one would expect to find plain language and express statement'.[99] The incapacity was therefore not just rooted in the common law, but elevated to constitutional principle, thereby reversing the assumption currently made under the principle of legality. Rather than the assumption lying with the right to vote, the common law constitution denied the vote to women and a clear intention was required to override that.

Even if the common law does not confer a right to vote, various parts of the common law can regulate the conduct of elections and the integrity of the process. Before statutory election offences were introduced, the common law provided for offences such as bribery, treating and undue influence in elections.[100] Some common law offences can continue to regulate the conduct of public officials that administer elections. For example, if a public official maliciously inhibits a person from exercising a vote, then it could constitute misconduct in public office. Now, however, the controls are largely statutory, and legislation provides a comprehensive framework governing the conduct of elections.

Given the history of voting rights and related decisions, it is easy to see why a common law right to vote has had a mixed reception (at best) in the courts. Despite this, the historical reservations about such a right are not a convincing reason against the recognition of such a right. Similar points can be made in relation to other common law rights. While there are various references to 'liberty of the press' and freedom of speech in earlier case law, the law tolerated far-reaching

---

[95] Ibid, 163.

[96] See Electoral Administration Act 2006, s 73. For the old common law on mental incapacity, see *Bedford County case, Burgess case* (1785) 2 Lud EC 381, cited in B Posner and L Footner (eds), *Schofield's Election Law* (London, Sweet & Maxwell, 2010) at [4-027]. See also Representation of the People Act 1983, s 3A.

[97] Ibid, 160.

[98] Ibid, 161, 'It would require a convincing demonstration to satisfy me that Parliament intended to effect a constitutional change so momentous and far-reaching by so furtive a process.'

[99] Ibid, 163, See also Lord Robertson.

[100] Posner and Footner (n 96) [13-001].

restrictions on the right in previous centuries. The earlier cases referring to that freedom are also from a pre-democratic era and do not provide precedent for freedom of speech in its current form. As Lord Kerr noted in *Moohan*, the common law rights and content of those rights evolve alongside the modern constitutional system.[101] The discussion above showed how the content of expression rights has developed from an absence of prior restraints to the broader protection of the right to criticise government and to make statements on matters of general interest. The focus on history and precedent may reflect a reticence for the courts to start recognising new constitutional rights. However, few would regard the right to vote as being a controversial candidate and history should not preclude the recognition of such a common law right.

B. Statutory Foundation

There are a number of other challenges facing the protection of the right to vote in the common law. In particular, the extension of the vote was not the product of common law decisions, but of legislation.[102] In *Moohan*, Lord Hodge stated that 'for centuries the right to vote has been derived from statute' and that the legislature 'has controlled and controls the modalities of the expression of democracy'.[103] Such rights can currently be found in statutes such as the Representation of the People Act 1983. Similarly, Lady Hale found that while a common law right to equal suffrage would be 'wonderful', the borough franchise was the product of a royal charter, and subsequent extensions of the franchise have been through legislation.[104]

The statutory roots of voting rights can pose a challenge in applying the principle of legality. Normally, the principle of legality is applied to statutes that confer a power in general terms which is used to restrict a pre-existing right. However, with the right to vote, the statute that grants the right may also include a number of restrictions. The provisions that have been subject to legal challenge, such as the exclusion of prisoners, are cast in clear terms as part of the legislative framework that defines voting rights and the conduct of elections.[105] It is hard to use the principle of legality to establish that a right should be conferred in defiance of any restrictions specified in a statute. However, the principle of legality can still have some application where a right to vote has been conferred in legislation.[106]

---

[101] *Moohan* in the Supreme Court (n 76) [86].
[102] Ibid, [34] (Lord Hodge).
[103] Ibid.
[104] Ibid, [56].
[105] For example, see *Chester* (n 68) [113].
[106] Lord Rodger stated that the principle of legality can protect the right to vote: *Watkins* (n 87) [61].

An example from the 2010 General Election provides a useful illustration. At the time, the Representation of the People Act 1983 provided that a poll should close at 10pm.[107] That provision raised the question of how the rule should be applied when people arrive at the polling station prior to 10pm, but have not had chance to cast their vote once that deadline has passed. In theory, the rule could be applied in a number of ways: (1) no further papers should be put in the ballot box after 10pm, or (2) those issued with a ballot paper prior to 10pm can still place the vote in the ballot box after that time or (3) anyone present or queuing at the polling station prior to 10pm for the purpose of voting can be issued with a ballot paper and place it in the box after that time. In 2010, people were still queueing outside some polling booths after 10pm and up 1,200 were unable to vote as a result.[108] The legislation did not provide for an extension of the polling hours in such circumstances, but did not specify how the cut off should be drawn. Citing legal precedent, the Electoral Commission stated that approach (2) is the correct rule and stated the election administrators had no discretion to apply it more flexibly.[109] By contrast, the House of Lord Constitution Committee found the law to be less certain and stated that 'even if it is the case that there is no express statutory provision for the extension of polling time other than in cases of riot etc, we do not think it follows that there is necessarily no discretion in certain circumstances to allow for this.'[110] This situation provides an example of where a person denied the vote could have relied on a constitutional right to vote, so that the legislation could be interpreted to allow the administrators to accommodate those queuing at the polling station (and thereby revise the earlier case law). The specific example has now been addressed by legislative amendment that permits ballot papers to be issued after 10pm in such circumstances.[111] However, the example illustrates the type of case where a principle of legality analysis could have been employed.[112]

Even if such an approach were taken, it is not clear that the interpretation of the statute is being driven by the common law. Instead, the constitutional right to vote may be based in statute, which in turn has constitutional status – along the lines set out in *Thoburn*.[113] However, the constitutional status of the right need not rest solely on the terms of the statute, but may reflect a common law presumption that any voting rights to certain offices or in referenda will have such status. Under this approach, a person cannot demand a constitutional right for certain

---

[107] See Representation of the People Act 1983, sch 1, r 1.

[108] House of Lords Select Committee on the Constitution, *Voting at the Close of Poll: Report* (2012, HL Paper 245).

[109] See ibid for the Electoral Commission's argument. *Islington* (1901) 5 O'M. & H. 120 and *In the Matter of the Parliamentary Election for Fermanagh and South Tyrone Held On 7 June 2001*.

[110] House of Lords Select Committee on the Constitution, ibid.

[111] Electoral Registration and Administration Act 2013, Pt 2, s 19(2).

[112] Though I make no claim as to whether the common law right would have led to a successful outcome for an applicant.

[113] *Thoburn v Sunderland City Council* [2002] EWHC 195 (Admin), [2003] QB 151.

office holders to be chosen by election (such as a police commissioner). However, the argument runs that once a decision is made to select that officer by election, a common law right is triggered. Accordingly, the statute granting the right to vote could then be interpreted to avoid (as far as possible) any arbitrary denial or restriction of the right. This may not result in a completely free standing common law right to vote, but could be characterised as a common law right that any votes granted by the legislature should be distributed on fair and equal terms. Such an approach could be characterised as having elements of both statute and common law. Consequently, it may be more useful to simply describe the right to vote as 'constitutional' without specifying the foundation.

Such an approach sketched above explains how the techniques found under principle of legality could be developed for some types of voting right case. However, it is not clear that such a development would be necessary. Ordinary principles of public law, such as the purposes doctrine, may already provide tools to ensure that legislation is interpreted compatibly with voting rights and to prevent any powers being abused.[114] However, the recognition of a constitutional right to vote may provide some support to such claims, for example in setting the standard of review or identifying the appropriate purposes of a relevant statutory power.

C. Positive Obligations and Questions of Design

Even if a right to vote could be protected in some cases along the lines suggested above, a further challenge lies in the questions of design. The right to vote is not something that can be secured through an absence of state action. As Lord Donaldson explained in *Hipperson*:

> Voting rights lie at the root of parliamentary democracy. Indeed many would regard them as a basic human right. Nevertheless they are not like the air we breathe. They do not just happen. They have to be conferred, or at least defined and the categories of citizen who enjoy them have also to be defined. Thus no one would expect a new-born baby to have voting rights or that citizens could vote in all constituencies or in that of their unfettered choice.[115]

The right to vote imposes a number of positive obligations on the state.[116] Ballot papers have to be issued, polling stations need to be set up and staffed, the secrecy of the ballot needs to be secured, votes have to be counted and finally the public body has to find a way to implement the electoral choice (such as translating votes into seats in the legislature). These factors all impose a cost on government. Above

---

[114] *Porter v Magill* [2001] UKHL 67, [2002] 2 AC 357.
[115] *Hipperson v Electoral Registration Officer for the District of Newbury* [1985] QB 1060, 1067.
[116] C Gearty, *Principles of Human Rights Adjudication* (Oxford, Oxford University Press, 2005) 34–35.

and beyond the basics, there are also obligations to secure conditions for free and fair elections. This includes rules on electoral spending, restrictions on government speech, and regulations on campaign publicity. All these rules require mechanisms of monitoring and enforcement. The right to vote cannot be understood in terms of government standing aside and leaving people to get on with their activity.

The point should not be overstated. There are some common law rights that demand positive protection.[117] However, such obligations tend to be the exception rather than the norm. The courts may require positive steps to be taken in the more extreme cases where a failure by the state would destroy the essence of the right. The courts will tend not to make detailed decisions on the allocation of resources. Such issues are no less fundamental, but tend to be addressed by the other branches of government.

Choices have to be made in relation to the right to vote, such as who should hold that right. To answer that question there are difficult issues in defining citizenship and also residence requirements. There are also age restrictions on voting, which require an act of line-drawing. In addition, there are further questions about the voting system. Some voting systems may respect the equal weighting of each vote, whereas others may be valued for being more likely to return a majority or develop a relationship between citizen and representative. There are also difficult questions in deciding how the geographical boundaries should be drawn when defining constituencies. These are all questions for which there are different choices, that can be defended from various democratic perspectives. For this reason, there are reasons why the courts may prefer to leave such matters to expert bodies.[118] This does not preclude a common law right (or legal right more generally), but it is likely to set only the outer boundary on the permissible choices of such questions of design.

Aside from such questions of design, there are also challenges in determining which decisions should be subject to a ballot. The ECHR refers to a right to vote for members of the legislature. However, even in that respect, it is important to recognise that one chamber in Westminster remains unelected. There is no right to a referendum in the UK. That means that the right to vote is understood in the context of a representative (as opposed to direct) democracy. None of these points defeat the case for a common law right to vote. For example, the right could be limited to the election of MPs and members of the devolved legislatures. Alternatively, along the lines suggested earlier, the right could be triggered only where the legislature has decided that a particular office or person should be put to a vote – thereby recognising a right to fair and equal votes, rather than an absolute right to vote. However, these examples show how there are difficult questions about the scope of the right, which again may make the courts reluctant to take the lead in developing common law protection.

---

[117] Such as open justice or certain obligations to protect speakers from a hostile audience.
[118] *R v Boundary Commission for England, ex parte Foot* [1983] QB 600, noting the 'heavy burden' to establish irrationality in relation to decisions concerning constituency boundaries.

IV. Conclusion

The discussion in this chapter has compared the protection of the right to free-dom of expression with that of the right to vote in the common law. Freedom of expression has long been cited as a clear example of a common law constitutional right, while the status of the right to vote is (at best) the subject of debate. Part of the appeal of a system of common law rights lies in its references to history and precedent.[119] Reliance on past cases shows that the protection of such rights is not a departure from traditional judicial functions or a radical innovation. Such an appeal to history is not an option with the right to vote, as the historical precedents often supported limits on the franchise. Even with the right to expres-sion, the history is mixed. For every *Bonnard* or *Scott v Scott*, there were common law rulings that would violate current understandings of freedom of expression. The discussion has shown how protection for expression in the substance of the common law was piecemeal and inconsistent. That did not stop the courts later drawing on dicta referring to the importance of free speech as a foundation for a more systematic protection as a common law constitutional right.

The current scheme of common law constitutional rights seeks to offer protec-tion through the interpretation of legislation and in setting the standard of review of executive action. There is further debate about whether this will develop into standards for the direct review of legislation. Even at this stage in the develop-ment, there are remaining questions about the scope of the common law right to free speech, its content and the methodology for weighing up competing interests. In practice, it is likely that the courts simply borrow from the ECHR jurispru-dence (which, in most free speech cases, has been the central focus of the courts' reasoning). However, the point goes to show that while freedom of speech is one of the most well established common law rights, its historical foundation is more precarious than sometimes acknowledged and its content less than certain.

If freedom of expression is now recognised as one of the key common law rights, it stands in contrast to the right to vote. While the right to vote is said to be of constitutional importance, considerable doubt has been expressed as to whether its foundations lie in the common law. One explanation for the differ-ence in treatment may be historical, given that voting was for centuries attached to property rights and the franchise restricted. However, the discussion has noted that the historical limits on free speech have not impeded its constitutional status in the common law. Moreover, there is no reason why the common law cannot evolve to rectify its earlier limits and recognise the constitutional status of the right to vote in current law.

---

[119] See discussion in T Poole, 'Back to the Future? Unearthing the Theory of Common Law Consti-tutionalism' (2003) 23 *OJLS* 435 on the use of historical arguments in relation to common law constitutionalism.

One possible explanation may be that the different treatment reflects a specific constitutional theory underpinning common law rights. Along these lines, Laws LJ – a judge frequently associated with common law constitutionalism – has written that the central goal of the constitution is 'the autonomy of every individual', which prioritises a principle of 'minimal interference'.[120] Under this view, free speech is not valued as a political right, but as an aspect of individual autonomy that is intrinsically worthy of protection. Laws LJ has also stated that freedom of speech is not a 'creature of democracy'.[121] Instead, he argued that the freedom 'belongs to every individual for his own sake' because 'free thought, which is a condition of every man's flourishing, needs free expression; and this is every person's birthright, in whatever polity he has to live.'[122] Under this view, free speech is itself a liberty and interference should be kept to a minimum. By contrast, democracy is valued instrumentally in promoting a person's autonomy.[123] Under some versions of this approach, the democratic process is valued in so far as it provides a check on government and helps to guard a person's rights.[124] Under this view, the right to expression may be placed high up in the hierarchy as a basic right, while voting is an instrumental right that does not enjoy the same status.

Such a constitutional vision may be contrasted with the central role for political rights if the main goal of a constitutional system is to facilitate representative democracy. Under this view, the democratic process is valued as a channel to express the popular will and to legitimate government. As Conor Gearty has written, the 'right to vote is the most important of all the civil liberties possessed by an individual in a representative democracy'.[125] Accordingly, the other civil liberties 'are valuable because they make meaningful the exercise of this core right to vote.'[126] Freedom of speech is not primarily valued as a basic liberty that limited government must respect. Instead, it is valued in so far as it creates an informed public and promotes the free scrutiny of government and other powerful institutions. The emphasis on democracy is often associated with the political constitutionalist. Under this view, the right to vote legitimates government, and the legitimacy it confers means that the decisions of a democratically elected body should not be readily challenged by the courts. Accordingly, the political constitutionalist may attack common law constitutionalism on the grounds that (a) it is a form of legal constitutionalism that fails to fully respect the legitimacy of the legislature

---

[120] J Laws, 'The constitution: morals and rights' [1996] *Public Law* 622.
[121] *R (Miranda) v Secretary of State for the Home Department* [2014] EWHC 255 (Admin), [2014] 1 WLR 3140.
[122] Ibid, [45]–[46].
[123] Laws (n 120). See discussion in Poole (n 119) 448.
[124] In *Reynolds v Sims* (1964) 377 US 533 (1964), the US Supreme Court referred to the value of the vote as a means to protect other liberties: 'the right to exercise the franchise in a free and unimpaired manner is preservative of other basic civil and political rights'.
[125] C Gearty, *Civil Liberties* (Oxford, Oxford University Press, 2007) 61.
[126] Gearty (n 116) 35.

conferred through voting, and (b) the lack of respect is further evidenced in the failure to recognise the right to vote in the common law.

The views sketched above suggest that the different treatment of the right to vote and freedom of speech may reflect the constitutional values underpinning the theory of common law constitutionalism. While some common law constitutionalists may prioritise free speech as a fundamental individual liberty over a collective right to vote, such a generalisation should be resisted. The discussion earlier showed that the common law right of free speech is most frequently justified in terms of its service to a democracy. As such, it is not valued over the right to vote, but stands alongside it as a political right to participate (and one that helps to inform the exercise of the vote). Moreover, a political constitutionalist, that largely calls for judicial restraint and deference to elected branches, may nonetheless see value in some judicial protection of core political rights (which themselves are key elements in a system of political accountability).[127]

The different levels of protection afforded to the two rights may be explained by more practical constraints. The cases that come before the court will be one factor. The right to freedom of expression has simply had more opportunities to be developed by the courts. By contrast, there are relatively fewer voting rights cases in the UK, and where such claims arise, there may be little need to resort to common law rights to resolve the issue, given the presence of various statutory rules and the right under the ECHR.

Another explanation for the different treatment may lie in the content of the two rights.[128] As was noted, the right to vote is largely secured through positive steps. While free speech has a positive element, an absence of interference plays an important part in its protection.[129] Given that common law rights typically operate by requiring a narrow construction of a statute or imposing a stronger burden of justification on government, the methodology is better suited to protecting the negative aspects of rights. Such techniques will be harder to invoke in relation to many aspects of the right to vote, such as how constituencies should be drawn, how frequent elections should be, how the votes should be counted, how election campaigns should be conducted and who holds the voting rights. As was argued, this should not preclude the common law being developed to protect the right to vote in some cases. These factors, however, suggest that such a common law right may have limited application in practice.

The discussion in this chapter provides us with a reminder of the limits of common law constitutional rights. Not every aspect of a right can be secured

---

[127] See also the discussion of common law employment rights and political constitutionalism in A Bogg, 'The Common Law Constitution at Work: R (on the application of UNISON) v Lord Chancellor' (2018) 81 *MLR* 509, 525–26.

[128] Gearty (n 116).

[129] On the limits of the positive protection, see J Rowbottom, 'Positive Protection for Speech and Substantive Political Equality' in A Kenyon and A Scott (eds), *Positive Free Speech: Rationales, Methods and Implications* (Oxford, Hart Publishing, forthcoming).

through the common law methods. There are other legal tools available that avoid heavy reliance being placed on the common law, including statute and the ECHR. Moreover, the protection of a right requires a degree of partnership between government and courts, with government taking action to secure some elements of a right and the courts protecting others.[130] This leaves open a number of questions, such as the appropriate division of labour between the branches of government in the protection of the rights – which in turn will depend the scope of the rights, the legal effects of the right, the methodology of balancing, etc. So far, the reliance on the ECHR has allowed some of the uncertainties to continue without posing practical problems. However, if greater reliance is placed on common law rights in future, these are the questions that will need to be addressed.

---

[130] A Kavanagh, 'Recasting the Political Constitution: From Rivals to Relationships' (2019) 30 *King's Law Journal* 43.

7

Searching for a Chimera? Seeking Common Law Rights of Freedom of Assembly and Association

GAVIN PHILLIPSON*

I. Introduction

The case for or against the record of the common law in protecting fundamental rights cannot be made either generally or in the abstract. Rather, it must be granular, nuanced and particular. It should clearly distinguish between instances in which the common law has made a major contribution to the protection or promotion of such rights and those where its effect has been minor, minimal or even negative. It must avoid generalised assessments and particularly the kind of wishful thinking encapsulated in Lord Donaldson's assertion that 'you have to look long and hard before you can detect any difference between the English common law and the principles set out in the [ECHR]'.[1] Thus, rather than making such sweeping claims, the enquiry should be 'empirical' in approach.[2]

It should also, so far as possible, be untainted by the enthusiasm or otherwise of the particular writer for the judicial role in protecting fundamental rights *in general*. The judicial record here has been much-debated between Bill of Rights enthusiasts and political constitutionalist sceptics,[3] but has often lapsed into what Colm O'Cinneide has neatly dubbed 'the war of examples'[4] in which each side

* The author would like to thank Alan Bogg for his extremely helpful comments and discussion on freedom of association and Alison Young, Robert Craig and the editors for their detailed and valuable comments on an earlier draft. The usual disclaimer applies.

[1] *R v Secretary of State for the Home Department, ex parte Brind* [1991] 1 AC 696, 717.
[2] M Elliott, 'Beyond the European Convention: Human Rights and the Common Law' (2015) 68 *PL* 85, 95.
[3] See, eg, A Tomkins (eds), *Sceptical Essays on Human Rights* (Oxford, Oxford University Press, 2001); KD Ewing, 'The futility of the Human Rights Act' [2004] *PL* 829.
[4] C O'Cinneide, 'Democracy, Rights and the Constitution – New Directions in the Human Rights Act Era' (2004) 57 *CLP* 175, 180.

focuses only on the instances that support their favoured stance. This chapter tries to avoid that tendency: while the author has been a strong supporter of the role of courts in protecting rights,[5] the analysis below eschews any idealisation of the judicial record in the fields under consideration in favour of a rigorous assessment of the case-law. As a way of structuring this assessment, it proposes a six-fold taxonomy by which the role played by the common law in relation to fundamental rights in any particular case may be analysed and classified.[6]

Mark Elliott has argued that there are two extreme analyses of this issue that should be rejected. It would be unrealistic, he claims, to contend that 'the common law is so extensive, rigorous and resilient as to render the ECHR-[Human Rights Act] essentially redundant.'[7] However Elliott says that 'it would be *equally* mistaken to suppose that the common law and HRA-ECHR regimes are so radically different that the absence of the [latter][8] would transform judicial protection of rights in the UK beyond all recognition.'[9] Applied to assembly and association rights, the author agrees that the first suggestion would indeed be unreal, but disagrees that the second would be equally wide of the mark. This chapter argues that the difference between the common law and HRA-ECHR approaches, at least to these two rights, are so profound that loss of the HRA-ECHR scheme would radically diminish the potential for their judicial protection.

While agreeing that in other areas of law the common law has provided 'glimpses' of its potential to protect rights[10] it contends that in this area these amount to little more than flickers of light in the dark.[11] In case after case, either the common law is completely silent on issues of principle – with analysis moving immediately from statutory provision to ECHR analysis – or serves actually to undercut, or deny access to, the protection provided by statute. It argues that this tendency has arisen principally from four causes. First, common law thinking in this area has barely progressed beyond the traditional approach whereby 'rights' of association or assembly figure as mere negative liberties – aspects of the general freedom to do that which the law does not forbid. Second in the field of protest rights, courts continue to pay often overwhelming deference to police decision-making, both on the ground and in relation to policing strategies more generally. Third, courts continue to place heavy weight on property and contractual rights – even when highly abstract. Fourth and most importantly, the common law itself continues to provide key police powers to curtail protest that are far broader and less well-defined than those set out in statute. As discussed below, this seems

---

[5] See, eg, G Phillipson 'Deference, 'Discretion and Democracy in the Human Rights Act Era' (2007) 60 *CLP* 40–78.

[6] Below at 143–45.

[7] Elliott (n 2) 88.

[8] The text (ibid at 88) says 'former' but the author has confirmed this is a typographical error.

[9] Ibid.

[10] Ibid, 90.

[11] See the like conclusion of D Mead: 'A seven (or so) year hitch: how has the Coalition's pledge to restore the right to non-violent protest fared?' (2018) 29(2) *King's Law Journal* 1, 8.

to encourage the courts to see the ECHR as the sole source of rights, with the common law figuring only as a potential means of *curtailing* them.

After first sketching the taxonomy referred to above, this chapter paints a brief historical overview of the largely negative or absent role of the common law in relation to freedom of association, before considering how far Alan Bogg's more optimistic analysis qualifies the historical verdict. Turning to freedom of assembly, it concentrates its attention on two areas in which the contribution of the common law has been critical. First, it considers the common law power to prevent anticipated breaches of the peace – a power of such breadth and controversy that it has given rise to most of the recent appellate decisions in this area, including *Laporte*,[12] *Austin*[13] and *Hicks*.[14] Second, it analyses the use of claimed common law powers to enable the surveillance of protestors and the placing of their personal data on police databases, something that has a significant chilling effect upon rights of public assembly and protest. In relation to these powers it argues that the common law has failed to comply with the basic rule-of-law requirements.

II. A Six-Fold Taxonomy

This section sketches a taxonomy, used throughout this chapter, of different roles that common law fundamental rights (CLFRs) or the common law more generally may play in rights cases, ranking them from the most to the least positive. In *category 1*, CLFRs play the role of *prime movers;* this encompasses two distinct situations. First, rights are used as a ground of review, to read down sharply even very broad statutory powers to make secondary legislation or rules so that they can no longer be used to invade the right in question. In the absence of express authorising words or a necessary implication that restrictions on the fundamental right in question are intended, the secondary rules that invade the right are thus found ultra vires. Examples include *Simms*,[15] *Witham*,[16] *Ahmed v HM Treasury*[17] and *UNISON*[18] (considered below), in which, as Alan Bogg puts it, 'the common law was positioned centre-stage'.[19] This approach, now well-known as the 'principle of legality', has *not* been used in either of the two fields that are the subject of this chapter.

---

[12] R. *(on the application of Laporte) v Chief Constable of Gloucestershire* [2007] 2 AC 105 (hereafter *'Laporte'*).

[13] *Austin v Commissioner of Police of the Metropolis* [2009] 1 AC 564.

[14] *Hicks v Commissioner of Police of the Metropolis* [2012] EWHC 1947 (Admin); [2017] UKSC 9; [2017] AC 256 (SC); (hereafter *'Hicks'*).

[15] R *v Secretary of State for the Home Department ex p Simms* [1999] 3 All ER 400.

[16] R *v Lord Chancellor ex p Witham* [1998] QB 575.

[17] [2010] UK SC 2.

[18] R *(UNISON) v Lord Chancellor* [2017] UKSC 51 (hereafter, *'UNISON'*).

[19] A Bogg 'The Common Law Constitution at Work' (2018) 81(3) *MLR* 509, 511.

Perhaps an equally important variant on category 1 – but involving more sustained judicial creativity – is where courts have engaged in *major common law development*, with the express purpose of giving effect to a fundamental right. Well-known examples are the development of the *Reynolds* defence in defamation,[20] designed to protect press freedom[21] and the development from breach of confidence of 'misuse of private information', with the aim of protecting the Article 8 ECHR right to respect for private life.[22] Here the imperative of rights protection drives major common law doctrinal development. Again, there are no examples in our two fields. Hence, we can already rule out the suggestion that the common law has played a *leading* role in protecting rights to freedom of association and assembly.

Category 2 encompasses cases in which CLRFs have had *significant influence*. Here we might see common law rights reasoning altering, to a greater or lesser extent, the interpretation of statute, or modifying common law doctrine; instances might include the tightening up of existing legal definitions to allow less intrusion into a right, or effecting the development of a defence or exclusion so as to give greater scope for the right.[23] The field of freedom of assembly may furnish two examples – *Redmond-Bates*,[24] and *Laporte*; in relation to freedom of association we identify one, the *Uber* case.[25] All are considered below.

Category 3 sees CLFRs having a *minor supportive role*; here the real driver is the ECHR rights, but judges find the right also to be protected by the common law. The role played may be largely rhetorical as opposed to substantive or significant, but it shows the courts starting to put in place the first tentative pieces in what *may* later become a meaningful structure of common law principle. Examples in the field of freedom of assembly include *DPP v Jones*[26] and, in relation to association, *UNISON*.

Category 4 encompasses cases characterised simply by *common law absence*: here CLFRs play no role at all, so that courts move straight from statutory interpretation to application of Convention rights under the HRA. As will appear below, most cases on freedom of assembly and freedom of association fall into this category.

In *category 5*, the common law features as a *negative interpretive factor*. This occurs where a particular interpretive choice is made, when construing a statute, common law precedents, or relevant Strasbourg authority, that tends to *expand* the ability of the law to interfere with the fundamental right in question or *restrict*

---

[20] Originating in *Reynolds v Times Newspapers Ltd* [1999] UKHL 45, [1999] 4 All ER 609.

[21] See J Rowbottom, 'Freedom of Expression and the Right to Vote: Political Rights and the Common Law Constitution' at 122–23 in this volume.

[22] See K Hughes, 'A Common Law Constitutional Right to Privacy – Waiting for Godot?' in this volume.

[23] *Derbyshire County Council v Times Newspapers* [1993] AC 534 held that central and local government could not bring actions in defamation.

[24] *Redmond-Bate v DPP* 163 JP 789, [1999] *Crim LR* 998.

[25] *Uber BV and others v Aslam and others* UKEAT/0056/17/DA.

[26] [1999] 2 WLR 625.

the scope or meaning of the right. There are several examples in our field: *Austin*[27] and *Hicks* show domestic courts engaged in novel readings of Article 5 ECHR that ensured the contested police action could not be found to have violated it. A further example is *Richardson*,[28] in which the Supreme Court actually expanded the reach of the much-criticised statutory offence of 'aggravated trespass',[29] thereby contracting the scope of protest rights. In relation to freedom of association, we consider below the example of *Smith v Carillion (JM) Ltd*.[30]

At the bottom of the scale come *category 6* cases in which courts apply or develop a common law power that the state uses to *curtail* the exercise of fundamental rights, notably breach of the peace and the general common law duty to prevent crime. Such powers not only restrict the right in question; they may also *undercut* the protective effect of statute, not through affecting its interpretation – as in category 4 – but simply by providing a kind of catch-all power that the police can turn to in order to *avoid* the more restrictive and tightly defined powers provided in legislation. The numerous examples in the field of freedom of assembly discussed below include *Catt*,[31] *Austin, Hicks, Wood*[32] and *Wright*.[33]

III. Freedom of Association at Common Law

A. The Traditional, Negative View

The predominant view of labour lawyers is clear and straightforward: the common law 'does not grant positive rights of association, enforceable against others', so that 'such positive rights to associate as there are in English law have been granted by statute'.[34] Fundamental rights are treated as 'belonging to a separate compartment of legal reasoning [the HRA and Article 11 ECHR], rather than as a seamless element integrated into general common law reasoning'.[35] A classic example of such absence is the well-known decision in *GCHQ*,[36] which concerned a direct restriction on freedom of association – the banning of trade unions at GCHQ. While the case was almost entirely concerned with the common law, freedom of

---

[27] Above, n 13.

[28] *Richardson and another v Director of Public Prosecutions* [2014] UKSC 8; [2014] AC 635.

[29] Criminal Justice and Public Order Act 1994, s 68; H Fenwick and ors, *Fenwick on Civil Liberties* 5th edn (London, Routledge, 2017) at 637.

[30] [2015] EWCA Civ 209, [2015] IRLR 467.

[31] *R. (on the application of Catt) v Association of Chief Police Officers* [2015] AC 1065 (hereafter 'Catt').

[32] [2009] EWCA Civ 414, [2010] 1 WLR 123.

[33] *Wright v Commissioner of Police of the Metropolis* [2013] EWHC 2739 (QB).

[34] A Baker, I Smith and O Warnock, *Smith & Wood's Employment Law* 13th edn (Oxford, OUP, 2017) at 668.

[35] A Bogg, 'Common Law and Statute in the Law of Employment' (2016) 69(1) *CLP* 67, 109–10.

[36] *Council of Civil Service Unions v Minister for Civil Service* [1985] AC 374.

association figures *only* in the summary of Counsels' argument in the Appeal Cases Report;[37] it goes wholly unmentioned by their Lordships. This theme of common law absence is evident in the way that leading texts on civil liberties, when they deal with association rights at all,[38] consider exclusively statutory provisions[39] and/or Article 11 jurisprudence.[40]

Labour lawyers have often regarded the common law not merely as absent but as actively hostile, a trend perhaps started by the House of Lords decision in *Amalgamated Society of Railway Servants v Osborne*,[41] described as dealing a 'heavy blow to freedom of association.'[42] As a result, labour law has been widely seen as the 'autonomous' creation of statute that had to be clearly hived off and protected from the reach of common law reasoning, which, with its attachment to 'property-based principles of liberty' would seek to attack and undermine it.[43] Moreover this 'regressive quality was presented as almost "hard-wired"' in the common law,[44] which 'often subverted the legislative purposes of protective statutes.'[45] So far did this tendency go that historically, employment lawyers were concerned that common law rights in this area were really '"employers' fundamental rights", to private property and freedom of contract.'[46]

B. A More Positive Perspective?

Alan Bogg has in recent years developed an alternative analysis under which the common law may be understood as operating *in support* of the almost entirely statutory rights of freedom of association. He readily concedes, however, that his enterprise is as much directed at encouraging possible future developments as finding clear existing evidence of such support.[47] An important recent case here is *UNISON*,[48] in which the Supreme Court struck down a regime whereby very

---

[37] Ibid, 383.

[38] David Feldman's *Civil Liberties and Human Rights in England and Wales* 2nd edn (Oxford, OUP, 2002) has no substantive treatment.

[39] S Bailey and N Taylor, *Bailey, Harris and Jones: Civil Liberties: Cases and Materials* 6th edn (Oxford, OUP, 2009), 287–91.

[40] Fenwick (n 29) 89–90; similarly, see C Gearty, *Civil Liberties* (Oxford, Clarendon, 2007) at 156–60.

[41] [1910] AC 87.

[42] See, eg, Ewing and Gearty's characterisation of this case: *The Struggle for Civil Liberties: Political Freedom and the Rule of Law in Britain 1914–1945* (Oxford, OUP, 1999) at 19, hereafter 'Struggle'.

[43] Ibid at 21. See the discussion in A Bogg, 'The Hero's Journey: Lord Wedderburn and the "Political Constitution" of Labour Law' (2015) 44 *Industrial Law Journal* 299, 307–09 and (critiquing the notion of autonomy) Bogg (n 40), 69–75.

[44] Bogg 'Hero's Journey', ibid, at 306.

[45] Above, n 22 at 525.

[46] Bogg, above, n 35, at 101 citing P Sales, 'Rights and Fundamental Rights in English Law' (2016) 75 *CLJ* 86, 87.

[47] Bogg (n 19) 525–26.

[48] On which see also analysis by S Wheatle in 'Access to Justice: From Judicial Empowerment to Public Empowerment' in this volume.

high fees had been imposed on those wishing to bring claims to the Employment Tribunal on the basis that this had functioned effectively to deny access to justice to potential claimants.[49] Given that a common law right acted as the 'prime mover' in this case, it is certainly a category 1 decision. However, as Bogg concedes, the Court relied solely on the well-established common law right of access to a court.[50] Nevertheless, he makes the bold claim that the decision 'may stand as the most important labour law judgment to be handed down by the Supreme Court in a generation.'[51]

This, however, must be read in light of Bogg's shrewd qualification that the judgment 'creates an *opening* for workers and trade unions to *argue for* a broader category of common law fundamental rights ... begin[ning] with the fundamental right to freedom of association',[52] revealing his evaluation to be directed mainly at the judgment's future potential. He contends that such potential may be seen in the 'horizontal application' of *UNISON* in the later 'gig economy' case on whether 'Uber' drivers should be classed are 'employees'.[53] As Bogg explains

> the common law determination of employment status is pivotal to the practical question of whether fundamental employment rights enacted through legislation, such as basic working time or minimum wage protections, are enforceable.[54]

Here the common law serves a 'gateway' function: satisfaction of its tests is required for claimants to access such legislated rights. However in contrast to the 'favourability principle', used to decide employment status in some civil law systems, whereby the norm most favourable to the worker is applied,[55] Bogg stresses that, 'Historically the common law ... rested upon the opposite axiom' whereby the law 'conceal[s] the realities of subordination behind the conceptual screen of contracts considered as concluded between equals.'[56]

UNISON's potential here lies in Lord Reed's departure from this historical approach; his Lordship recognised that 'relationships between employers and employees are generally characterised by an imbalance of economic power', leading to the 'vulnerability of employees to exploitation [and] discrimination'; hence the need for them to benefit from rights that are guaranteed by statute rather than being left 'to be determined by freedom of contract.'[57] Bogg hails this as an important step in the process whereby 'common law's principles and doctrines should

---

[49] *UNISON* at [39] and [87], per Lord Reed.
[50] Bogg (n 19) 514–15.
[51] Ibid, 524.
[52] Ibid, 515.
[53] Bogg (n 35).
[54] Bogg (n 19) 516.
[55] Ibid at 519, citing M Freedland and N Kountouris, *The Legal Construction of Personal Work Relations* (Oxford, OUP, 2011) 186–87.
[56] Ibid, citing PL Davies and MR Freedland (eds), *Kahn-Freund's Labour and the Law* 3rd edn (London, Stevens, 1983) 15.
[57] Ibid, citing *UNISON* [6] (Lord Reed).

be progressively refashioned so as to protect the weaker party in the contractual relation.'[58]

However, progress is distinctly patchy in this respect. The *Uber* case appears to fall into category 2 in that common law 'interpretive principles' had a significant effect on 'the construction of the specific contractual arrangements'[59] at issue, whilst other recent decisions evince a much more formalist approach.[60] In *Smith v Carillion (JM) Ltd*[61] the question was whether the claimant could claim the protective benefit provided by statute against the blacklisting of trade unionists. Such blacklisting is 'a serious violation of the very core of freedom of association';[62] however the claimant could only benefit from statutory protection if a contractual relationship between himself and the end user of his labour could be inferred.[63] The Court of Appeal declined to do this, instead applying a restrictive test that shut the gateway to the claimant. As Bogg comments, the 'consequences were catastrophic in destroying Mr Smith's ability to secure employment in his chosen occupation'.[64] Since the common law featured as a *negative* interpretive factor this puts *Smith* into category 5.

Vining[65] is a more encouraging judgment – but one that also shows how nascent and uncertain any recognition of association rights is in common law. The claimant, who was a member of the parks police force, complained that he and his colleagues had not been consulted before they were made redundant. Bringing them within the scope of the statutory provision that granted consultation rights[66] required re-reading it[67] under the HRA.[68] But this required first recognising that the claimed consultation right fell 'squarely within the "essential elements" protected by Article 11 ECHR'. This required some reasoning by analogy, given that none of the relevant Strasbourg authorities dealt specifically with the right to be consulted over proposed dismissals.[69] The Court readily undertook this reasoning, finding Article 11 squarely applicable and hence able to change the meaning and effect of the statute via the HRA.[70] Thus, in contrast to *Carillion*, in which the Court's common law reasoning *barred* the claimant from entry into the

---

[58] Ibid 520. He cites the insistence in *Autoclenz* [2011] UKSC 41, at [35] that relative bargaining power must be taken into account when construing contracts.

[59] Bogg (n 19) 516.

[60] See also *Pimlico Plumbers Ltd and another v Smith (Pimlico Plumbers)* [2017] EWCA Civ 51, at [143].

[61] [2015] EWCA Civ 209, [2015] IRLR 467.

[62] Bogg (n 19) 524.

[63] Smith had been employed in a triangular agency arrangement in the construction industry.

[64] Bogg (n 35) 110; for a similarly negative decision see *R (on the application of Independent Workers Union of Great Britain) v Central Arbitration Committee and Roofoods Ltd t/a Deliveroo* [2018] EWHC 3342; for comment see Bogg (2019) 135 *LQR* 219–26.

[65] *Wandsworth London Borough Council v Vining and others* [2017] EWCA Civ 109.

[66] Trade Union and Labour Relations (Consolidation) Act 1992, ss 188–192.

[67] Ibid, s 280.

[68] Whereby, per s 3(1), courts must 'so far as is possible' construe statutory provisions compatibly with Convention rights.

[69] Above, n 65, at [63].

[70] Ibid.

protective ambit of the statute, in *Vining* the Court did real work to bring the claimant *within* it. This was not, however, common law labour, but rather construction of *Strasbourg* caselaw under Article 11. In short, the Court's reasoning certainly advanced association rights – albeit for a very narrowly defined class of potential claimants[71] – but one can discern no role for the common law in doing so.[72] *Vining* thus falls squarely into category 4 – common law absence – demonstrating that as late as 2017, an appellate court, dealing with an 'essential' aspect of freedom of association, found no normative resource in the common law upon which to draw.

C. Conclusion on Freedom of Association

The analysis here has considered the innovative approach of Alan Bogg in order to give as fair a hearing as possible to the argument that the common law may have a positive role in protecting freedom of association. We have seen some glimmers of hope; however, we have also found recent examples of appellate decisions in which the common law outright obstructs the protection of freedom of association or simply has nothing to say about it. A fair-minded conclusion would not deny some hopeful signs for the future but must recognise that a common law right to freedom of association does not yet exist.

IV. Freedom of Assembly and the Common Law

A. The Traditional Common Law Approach

The historical approach to freedom of assembly is to view it simply as a familiar English negative liberty:[73] the common law traditionally '[did] not recognise any special right of public meeting for political or other purposes'.[74] *Beatty v Gillbanks*[75] – in which the High Court found that the Salvation Army could not lawfully be restrained from marching because of the fear that the Skeleton Army would violently disrupt their march – is often held up as a positive

---

[71] As Alan Bogg has pointed out: 'The Constitution of Capabilities: The Case of Freedom of Association' in B Langille, *The Capability Approach to Labour Law* (Oxford, OUP, 2019) at 261–62. And *cf* the narrow and negative approach to Art 11 taken in *Pharmacists' Defence Association Union v Boots Management Services Ltd* [2017] EWCA Civ 66; critiqued, A Bogg and R Dukes (2017) 46(4) *Industrial Law Journal* 543.

[72] It is mentioned only once in the judgment, as part of the basis for the powers of constables: above, n 65 at [10].

[73] Lord Bingham in *Laporte* at [34] describes the traditional common law approach as 'hesitant and negative'.

[74] *Duncan v Jones* [1936] 1 KB 218; Feldman (n 38) 1012. And see, similarly Dicey, *Introduction to the Study of the Constitution*, 10th edn by ECS Wade (London: Palgrave, 1959) 4.

[75] (1882) 9 QBD 308.

nineteenth-century decision. However, as Ewing and Gearty observe, far from recognising any *right* of freedom of assembly or protest, it merely protected the general 'right of the individual not to be restrained unless he or she has done something unlawful'.[76] Similarly, Lord Denning's oft-cited dicta in *Hubbard v Pitt*,[77] stressing 'the right to demonstrate and ... protest on matters of public concern'[78] were not only uttered in dissent (the majority mentioned no such principles) but closer examination reveals that his Lordship was talking *not* about a positive right at all. As he goes on to say, 'As long as all is done peaceably and in good order, without ... obstruction to traffic, *it is not prohibited*'.[79]

Moreover, while there is a long tradition of peaceful public protest in this country, there are also instances in which, not only have the police not hesitated to act against it, but courts have strongly upheld their actions.[80] In this respect, the 1930s decision in *Duncan v Jones*[81] still casts a long shadow. The police had insisted on moving the peaceful speaker, who wished to address the issue of unemployment, away from her chosen spot outside a training centre for the unemployed. They claimed the action was necessary to avoid an imminent breach of the peace; this was based on the fact that, following a meeting addressed by the claimant some *14 months ago*, a disturbance had taken place in the training centre. When Duncan refused to move on, she was arrested for obstructing a police officer in the course of his duty, a decision that the High Court strongly upheld. This refuted any notion that *Beatty v Gillbanks* had established a clear common law principle that peaceful protestors may not be arrested because of the feared reactions of others. Gearty describes such cases[82] as 'the forging of a repressive common law' that has been 'deployed to close down protest as key moments on a regular basis ever since'.[83] Thus under the historical view the common law generally plays no role in protecting protest rights (category 4); worse it often provides a basis to *attack* their exercise (category 6).

B. Recent 'Glimmers of Hope?'[84]

There are a few cases in which we see common law principle bearing on the outcome (category 2) or at least building up rights rhetorically (category 3). Some of these are well-known: Sedley LJ in *Redmond Bates* sought to resist the *Duncan v Jones* approach by suggesting clearer criteria to limit the power of police

---

[76] 'Struggle' at 31.
[77] *Hubbard v Pitt* [1976] QB 142, 178–79.
[78] Cited by Otton J in *Hirst v Chief Constable of West Yorkshire* (1986) 85 Cr App R 143, 151–152.
[79] (1882) 9 QBD 308 (emphasis added).
[80] Below at 156–59.
[81] [1936] 1 KB 218.
[82] See also *Thomas v Sawkins* [1935] 2 KB 249
[83] Gearty (n 40) 137.
[84] The phrase is from Mead (n 11) 8.

to arrest a person not themselves engaging in violence on the basis that others might may be provoked into violence,[85] stressing that:

> Free speech includes not only the inoffensive but the irritating, the contentious, the eccentric, the heretical, the unwelcome and the provocative, provided it does not tend to provoke violence.[86]

The House of Lords decision in *DPP v Jones* was another rare win for protestors; however the author's previous analysis found that, while it gave minor rhetorical recognition to common law rights (placing it in category 3) the actual decision protected freedom of assembly merely as a precarious negative liberty.[87]

A more recent positive example is *Boyd v Ineos Upstream Ltd*,[88] in which the Court of Appeal found that some of the injunctions sought by fracking companies at first instance against 'persons unknown' thought 'likely to become protesters at fracking sites' were too widely drafted, given that no unlawful conduct had yet happened. The judgment has been commended for giving weight to 'the potential "chilling effect" on the rights of freedom of expression and lawful assembly' of such pre-emptive injunctions.[89] However, the Court recognised no such 'rights': quoting Dicey, it noted that freedom of assembly was merely the liberty of individual persons 'to meet together in the open air' and 'say what [they] like'.[90] Hence the supposed group 'right to protest' was seen by the Court simply as several individuals exercising their negative freedoms together. Strikingly, Longmore LJ said: '[t]his neatly states the common law as it was in 1959 [and] I do not think it has changed since.'[91] The absence of meaningful common law rights thus puts this case in our now familiar category 4. Faint glimmers of hope indeed.

C. Breach of the Peace – Progress Squandered?

We may now return to the most significant contribution of the common law in this area – the doctrine of breach of the peace and its associated preventive police powers. The traditional test is that such a breach arises:

> whenever harm is actually done or is likely to be done to a person or in his presence to his property or a person is in fear of being so harmed through ... assault ... unlawful assembly or other disturbance.[92]

---

[85] As summarised in the later case of *Bibby v The Chief Constable of Essex Police* [2000] EWCA Civ 113, these were that: the conduct must clearly interfere with the rights of others; the natural consequence of the conduct must be violence from a third party that is not wholly unreasonable; the conduct of the person being arrested was unreasonable.

[86] [2007] EWHC 237 (Admin), at [32].

[87] H Fenwick and G Phillipson, 'Public Protest, the Human Rights Act and Judicial Responses to Political Expression' [2000] *PL* 627.

[88] [2019] EWCA Civ 515.

[89] C Gilmartin '*Boyd v Ineos*, "Persons unknown" injunctions against future protest action' (23 April 2019) available https://inforrm.org/.

[90] Above, n 88 at [36]. Although one line did mention 'the citizen's right of protest': ibid at [42].

[91] Ibid at [37].

[92] *Howell* [1982] QB 416 at 427.

Breach of the peace is not a criminal offence in English law but there is a power of arrest both in relation to an ongoing breach and in order to prevent one imminently apprehended; the police also have powers to take measures short of arrest, such as moving demonstrators on or preventing them from travelling. Hence this power exemplifies a crucial feature shared by the modern policing of protest – the highly controversial 'preventive' turn,[93] by which, rather than seeking to react to actual disorder or criminality, the police instead seek to pre-empt the possibility of it arising in the first place.[94] Because the common law here hands such broad preventive powers to the police, it often undercuts the modest degree of protection that Parliament has sought to bestow through the creation of specific public order powers and offences that at least provide a level of precision as to the criteria that must be satisfied to use them.[95]

Thus, breach of the peace cases in general tend to fall into category 6. However, the House of Lords decision in *Laporte* amounts to a major pushback against its repressive tendencies. Gearty, a fierce critic of the role of the courts in this area, claims *Laporte* is 'an immensely important' decision that could 'greatly reduce' the capacity of breach of the peace 'to do civil libertarian harm'.[96] This section considers whether this positive assessment has been borne out by subsequent events. In doing so the focus is not on the well-analysed issue of the positive role given to ECHR rights in the judgment,[97] but rather on the role of the common law.

D. 'Immensely Important' Progress? Laporte in the House of Lords

The claimants had been in three coachloads of protestors stopped by police on the basis that they included eight members of an anarchist group who had used violent tactics in the past. The police claimed that when those protestors arrived at the military base against which they wished to protest, a breach of the peace would *then* have become imminent. Instead of waiting for this to happen, however, they decided to intervene at an earlier point, sending the three coaches back to London, and ensuring no-one could leave them during the journey back. *Laporte* required reconsideration of the notorious 1980s decision in *Moss v McLachlan*,[98] in which the police had turned around a carload of striking miners to prevent them joining

---

[93] This is seen in many areas including counter-terrorism powers. See, eg, Lucia Zedner, 'Preventive Justice or Pre-punishment? The Case of Control Orders' (2007) 60 *CLP* 174

[94] Mead (n 11) 11.

[95] H Fenwick 'Marginalising Human Rights: Breach of the Peace, "Kettling", the Human Rights Act and Public Protest' [2009] *PL* 737–38.

[96] Gearty (n 40) 135.

[97] Fenwick (n 95); D Mead, *The New Law of Peaceful Protest* (Oxford, Hart Publishing, 2010) 335–348.

[98] [1985] IRLR 76.

a picket nearby. Under the *Moss* approach, the police could take 'reasonable' preventive measures, provided the senior officer 'honestly and reasonably' apprehended 'a real risk of a breach of the peace in close proximity both in place and time:[99] this clearly gave the police preventive powers of enormous and ill-defined scope. *Laporte* did two things here. First, the police had argued that action *short* of arrest (here, the turning around of the coaches) did *not* require that a breach of the peace was reasonably considered 'imminent'. The House rejected this, ruling that this 'imminence' requirement applied equally to arrest *and* to action short of arrest.[100] Second, *Laporte* tightened up the definition of 'imminent' itself; their Lordships rejected the contention that it meant only anticipating a breach of the peace as a real, not a remote possibility,[101] a definition that gave the police licence to intervene well before any immediate risk of violence had arisen. Imminence, the House said, meant, 'about to occur';[102] however given that the Court was not the primary decision maker, its role was limited to checking that the police had reasonably apprehended that this was the case.

What then was the role of the common law in the judgment? In the House of Lords, 'common law' is mentioned 33 times; in nearly all instances it refers to the common law's role in empowering the state to *restrict* rights through the breach of the peace doctrine. Thus, as the Divisional Court saw it, while rights of expression and assembly were of 'the greatest importance to the proper functioning of any democracy',[103] they were entitlements that arose solely under Articles 10 and 11 ECHR. Possible interferences with them – which must be 'jealousy scrutinised' – could come both from statute *and* 'the developing common law'.[104] This approach sees the common law solely as a means of *restricting* rights and would put *Laporte* in category 6. However, the approach of the House of Lords was a little more positive. Their Lordships found a breach of Articles 10 and 11 primarily because they considered that the common law provided no lawful basis for turning the coaches around, given that the 'imminence' test had not been satisfied. Hence these Convention rights had been violated because the restrictions imposed on them had not been 'prescribed by law'.[105] Thus while the common law featured almost exclusively as providing a police *power*, the tighter common law standard applied by the House of Lords operated in *support* of the Convention rights, instead of providing a means of undermining them. Hence *Laporte* can be put in category 2.

However, this still leaves *Laporte* some distance from a position in which the common law is itself seen a *source* of rights, as opposed to providing a possible basis for restricting them. For example, the key finding that it 'was wholly disproportionate' to restrict the rights of the claimant 'because she was in the company

---

[99] *Laporte* (CA) at [39].
[100] Fenwick (n 29) 647.
[101] Based on *Piddington v Bates* [1961] 1 WLR 162.
[102] *Laporte* at [29].
[103] [2004] EWHC 253, at [35].
[104] Ibid at [45].
[105] Ibid at [45].

of others, some of whom might … in … future, breach the peace' was expressed wholly in terms of 'rights under articles 10 and 11'.[106] Lord Mance's dictum that, 'both at common law and certainly since the [HRA], the court's scrutiny … should now be closer than … in *Moss v McLachlan*'[107] provided a small measure of category 3 rhetorical support for common law rights. However, such support was not provided by all their Lordships; Lord Carswell specifically contended that it was 'no longer necessary' in this area 'to debate' the traditional negative liberty approach because this 'has been overtaken by the provisions of the [HRA] ….[108] Like the Divisional Court view, this sees positive rights as emanating exclusively from the Convention and HRA.

Overall, then the common law in *Laporte* still functioned largely as the enabler of police action although its negative potential in this regard was at least recognised – and reduced. There was, however, no clear statement that the test for using breach of the peace would be stricter where it was being used to curb political protest as opposed, say, to dealing with rowdy late-night behaviour outside a pub. This forms a sharp contrast with what we see in category 1 cases like *UNISON*, in which it is common law fundamental rights that sharply narrow the scope of statutory powers so that they can no longer be used to interfere with the right in question. In *Laporte*, the House of Lords did narrow somewhat the permissive scope of the common law in a way that at first sight looks similar; however, the main reason given was not the demands of common law principle but simply that *existing authority* did not support the wider reading. Lord Bingham gave as an additional ground that to do otherwise risked undermining the efforts Parliament had made in crafting public order laws, to give the police only 'carefully defined powers' so as to be 'sensitive to the democratic values inherent in recognition of a right to demonstrate'. This recognition is welcome – but we should be clear about *what* is being recognised here: *not* the common law's ability actively to *protect* fundamental rights, but rather its potential to frustrate Parliament's attempts to do so.

E. *Laporte's* Promise Blighted?

As this next section demonstrates, subsequent cases have not only rowed back on the modest tightening up of imminence requirements in *Laporte* but expanded these common law powers in other ways. The rowing back was possible because, as Glover has noted,[109] the clarity of Lord Bingham's approach was undercut even in *Laporte* by that of Lord Rodger, who thought that 'imminence' did not necessarily mean that a breach of the peace was 'about to happen' but also where it was

---

[106] *Laporte*, at [55].
[107] Ibid at [150].
[108] Ibid at [93].
[109] R Glover, 'Keeping the peace and preventive justice – a new test for breach of the peace' [2018] *PL* 444, 450.

'likely to happen' in 'the near future.'[110] This ambiguity allowed two differently-constituted Courts of Appeal subsequently to diverge on the point:[111] the first, in *Austin*,[112] favoured Lord Bingham's view,[113] but the second in *Moos*[114] endorsed the looser 'likely to happen' approach.[115]

The subsequent House of Lords decision in *Austin*, was remarkable, not because it changed the test of imminence, but rather because it expanded the permissible scope of 'action short of arrest' that may be taken to prevent a breach of the peace to include de facto detention – the 'kettling' of hundreds of peaceful protestors for around seven hours. This was justified on the basis of the alleged violent conduct of *other* protestors so confined.[116] As in many other cases in this area, the role of the common law once again lay only in *empowering* the police; it provided no normative resource to challenge their actions. In a now familiar pattern, rights figured solely as *Convention* rights. And if the influence of common law values can be seen in how domestic judges approach the task of interpreting and applying ECHR rights then assessment of the case becomes even more negative. Despite the obvious chilling effect that indiscriminate kettling of peaceful and violent protestors alike might exert on peoples' willingness to engage in mass demonstrations, all the courts agreed that neither Article 10 nor Article 11 were even prima facie applicable. Moreover all three courts in *Austin* found different – and novel – ways of finding that that there had been no deprivation of liberty contrary to Article 5.[117] *Austin* thus saw the courts both using the common law to empower repressive police action (category 6) and undermine the application of Convention rights (category 5).

The decision in *Wright*[118] similarly belongs in category 6. The Court again sanctioned police action under breach of the peace powers to 'kettle' protestors, in this case for a much shorter time. Remarkably, the senior police officer openly admitted that he had used the common law power because, the risk of any disorder being so uncertain, 'he did not consider there was a risk of sufficient seriousness' to meet the statutory conditions for imposing restrictions on public assemblies.[119]

---

[110] See Lord Rogers in *Laporte* at [66]–[68]. Lord Mance also acknowledged that the test had to allow for 'flexibility': at [102]

[111] Glover (n 109) 150–51.

[112] [2007] EWCA Civ 989; [2008] QB 660.

[113] Ibid at [19]–[20]

[114] *R (on the application of Moos) v Commissioner of Police of the Metropolis* [2012] EWCA Civ 12 [36].

[115] Upholding [2011] EWHC 957 (Admin) at [56].

[116] Non-violent protestors, including those in urgent need, were not allowed to leave: Joint Committee on Human Rights, *Demonstrating Respect for Rights? Follow-up, 22nd Report of Session 2008–09*, HL 141; HC 522 at [20].

[117] [2005] EWHC 480; [2005] HRLR 20; (on which see Fenwick (n 95) 745); [2009] 1 AC 564 at [27]. As Mead notes, however, this 'idiosyncratic reasoning' was largely upheld by Strasbourg in *Austin v UK*, nos 39692/09, 40713/09 and 41008/09, 15 March, 2012): D Mead 'The Right To Protest Contained By Strasbourg' UK Const L Blog (16 March 2012) https://ukconstitutionallaw.org/.

[118] *Wright v Commissioner of Police of the Metropolis* [2013] EWHC 2739 (QB).

[119] Ibid, [48]. Namely serious public disorder, serious damage to property, serious disruption to the life of the community or intimidation of others (s 14(1)(a), Public Order Act 1986).

The common law's ability to undermine the statutory scheme – precisely what Lord Bingham had warned about in *Laporte* – could not have been more starkly displayed.

Our final decision here is *Hicks*, which concerned multiple challenges to decisions of the Metropolitan police to arrest and detain about 75 people in London around the time of the Royal Wedding of Kate and William for periods of between four and nine hours. The protestors were released once the wedding was over: none were charged or bound over. None were alleged to have engaged in any violent or disorderly conduct or to be in possession of any prohibited items; the police however argued that they reasonably believed the arrests necessary to prevent imminent breaches of the peace. The analysis below details the remarkable facts in order to reveal the flimsy nature of the evidence that the courts accepted as justification for the pre-emptive arrest and detention of wholly peaceful protestors.

Brian Hicks was known to the police as a republican anarchist, who had committed no offences for over 20 years; he was arrested and detained for six hours on the basis that he was heading to Trafalgar Square where he was thought likely to meet up with anarchist groups and possibly join in the disruption the police thought they were planning. The 'Starbucks protestors' – all of good character with no previous convictions – had planned to join a 'Queer Resistance' zombie picnic. When arrested they appeared to have abandoned this attempt and were having coffee together in Starbucks. Searches of them found nothing suspicious, but they were arrested and detained for around four hours on the basis of some uncertain intelligence that some 'zombie protestors' might intend to disrupt the wedding.[120] A further 'zombie' claimant was seemingly heading *away* from the protests, but was arrested on the grounds that she had momentarily partially covered her face (to avoid being photographed) 'and was in possession of anti-wedding literature'; this was said to provide 'a reasonable basis for apprehension of conflict with pro-wedding supporters'.[121] Nine other protestors were identified 'as part of a group who admitted to being anti-royalist'; they had placards and banners and what the police described as 'climbing equipment'.[122] The justification for their arrest and detention (in handcuffs!) for around five hours was either that they might be in some way associated with anarchist groups intent on causing disruption, or that if not, their open expression of anti-royal views meant that pro-royal spectators would likely attack them. Finally, a 16-year-old boy of good character carrying a megaphone was stopped and searched and found to have some marker pens.[123] He was arrested on suspicion of intent to cause criminal damage by way of graffiti; he was fingerprinted, photographed and his DNA samples taken, but subsequently released from police custody without charge.

---

120 [2012] EWHC 1947 (Admin), at [44]; [26].
121 Ibid, [168].
122 Ibid, [63].
123 Ibid, [80].

The Court's accommodating attitude to some of the flimsier 'evidence' proffered by the police was striking. One officer justified arrests as being partly to prevent 'damage to property'; this was based on possession of what was described as 'climbing equipment' – it was actually a cycle helmet.[124] Hicks was searched because the police suspected his 'bulging pockets' contained equipment to smash windows or spray graffiti. The searched produced only a packet of biscuits and a comb, but Hicks was arrested anyway.[125] A police office justified arresting the 16-year-old boy partly because he seemed anxious when stopped and told him that 'a judge had ruled that he was allowed to express his opinion', which was interpreted as 'defensive'.[126] An individual heading towards an area where there were anti-royal protestors provided grounds for suspicion because, together, they might cause disruption. But being near an area with pro-royal spectators *also* provided grounds to fear a breach of the peace, because spectators were said to be likely to attack anti-royal demonstrators, perhaps especially if they were dressed as zombies. Proximity to Trafalgar Square could conveniently give rise to suspicion for either or both reasons.[127] The Starbucks claimants were found chatting over coffee, but the police could still reasonably anticipate them causing an imminent breach of the peace: they had, after all, *intended* to go to 'a zombie event in Soho Square associated with possible disruptive activity'.[128] Possession of a megaphone apparently helped provide grounds to suspect an imminent breach of the peace but those without one were equally suspected.[129]

Instead of dismissing these almost farcical attempts to justify arresting peaceful protestors, the Court sided with the police in every single case. Lord Bingham's attempt in *Laporte* to insist that imminence must mean 'about to happen' was brushed aside; the Court preferred Lord Roger's view that it meant simply likelihood 'that a breach of the peace would occur sometime in the near future, if the protesters persisted ...'.[130] This was then applied to people who, far from 'persisting' in protest, were seeking to leave the area or were having coffee in Starbucks. Perhaps most problematic of all was the way the Court dealt with the arrest of several peaceful protesters, where the *sole ground* for anticipating a breach of the peace was the claim that pro-royal spectators would be likely to physically attack them for voicing anti-royal sentiments. The more restrictive criteria set out in *Redmond Bate* supposedly required to justify arresting peaceful protestors on the basis that *others* might be provoked to violence were ignored.[131] Police apprehension of an imminent breach of the peace is, in theory, required to be 'reasonable'; this generally requires some *evidence* to be adduced, to support the

---

[124] Ibid, [65].
[125] Ibid, [33].
[126] Ibid, [76].
[127] Ibid, [163] and [170].
[128] Ibid, [166].
[129] Ibid, [168].
[130] ibid, [132] citing Lord Roger at [69] in *Laporte*.
[131] Above, n 86.

police assessment. Hence, one might have expected the Court to demand hard evidence that pro-royal spectators really were likely to attack republican protestors, such as violent clashes or scuffles that had occurred elsewhere on the day or on previous occasions. No such evidence was provided: the police case here rested on pure assertion. But the Court never questioned the police's alleged belief that members of the British public – supposedly famous for their tolerance of dissent and eccentricity – would so readily resort to violence against peaceful protestors.

Hicks thus undercut the attempt made in *Redmond Bate* to restrict the scope of common law preventive police powers and failed to give any meaningful content to the common law's purported insistence that police apprehensions of a breach of the peace be reasonable. Importantly, this approach was implicitly endorsed by the Court of Appeal's refusal of leave to appeal on grounds of misuse of the police's breach of the peace powers. The Divisional Court also brushed aside the claimant's Article 11 arguments, asserted vigorously that the Convention rights of peaceful protestors could be suppressed 'entirely legitimately', to prevent *others* being provoked to violence.[132] As Fenwick and Hamilton comment,[133] this 'upends the core principle' established by Strasbourg that 'peaceful demonstrators ... should be protected from violence by others.'[134] Finally, what of the argument that, even if the police had reasonably feared a breach of the peace, pre-emptive arrest and detention was a disproportionate response? Proportionality, if properly applied, is meant to require state authorities to show that they have used the least intrusive means possible to achieve their objectives. In *Laporte*, Lord Bingham had excoriated as 'wholly disproportionate' measures taken against those *not* themselves suspected of violent intentions on the basis that they were in the company of others who might have them.[135] In *Hicks* those arrested were not even in such 'bad company'; several were arrested on the basis that they *might* be planning to join others who *might* later engage in violence or disruption; moreover the sanction of arrest and detention was considerably more draconian than the turning round of the coaches in *Laporte*. Moreover, as the claimants argued, the police have comprehensive *statutory* powers to impose conditions on protests, in order to keep rival protestors apart[136] and so prevent violence or disorder. Hence, less intrusive measures, such as diverting protestors to anti-royal areas, could have been used as alternatives to immediate arrest and detention. However, these arguments were brusquely dismissed by the Court as 'wholly unrealistic'.[137] The eventual appeal to the Supreme Court considered *only* the claim that the arrest and detention of

---

[132] Above, n 120, at [123].

[133] Fenwick and Hamilton (n 29) 650.

[134] *Plattform 'Ärzte für das Leben' v Austria* A 139 (1988) at para 38; *Steel v United Kingdom* (1999) 28 EHRR 603.

[135] *Laporte*, [55].

[136] Public Order Act 1986, s 12.

[137] Above, n 120, at [172].

the protestors breached Article 5; here by giving Article 5 a novel interpretation, arguably contrary to the Strasbourg caselaw, the Court managed again to protect the police.[138]

Hicks thus evidences three different kinds of *anti*-rights reasoning that combined the worst of categories 5 and 6. First, common law police powers were re-expanded to facilitate the suppression of peaceful protest; second, Lord Bingham's warning against allowing common law powers to undermine the protections devised by Parliament was ignored: the Divisional Court upheld as lawful at common law pre-emptive arrest and detention – something that could never have been justified under statute.[139] And third, the Court trampled on one of the core Strasbourg principles animating Article 11's protection for peaceful protest. Ewing and Gearty commented that the effect of notorious 1930 cases like *Duncan v Jones* was to give the police 'an unlimited power subject to minimal scrutiny by the courts' that could be used 'to selectively undermine political freedom'.[140] This case showed the common law facilitating exactly the same thing in the twenty-first century. *Hicks* buries the promise of *Laporte*.

F. Surveillance of Protestors: The Common Law as the Handmaiden of Broad, Preventive Police Powers

State surveillance of protestors and the storing of information about them on police databases is another example of 'preventive' policing. It was recently subject to challenge in two cases, *Wood*,[141] and *Catt*, both of which concerned peaceful, law-abiding protestors, who challenged the taking and retention of their photographs and other personal information under Article 8 ECHR. The privacy angle of the cases is not directly our concern here;[142] rather our first point of interest is the way in which the courts in each case almost entirely overlooked the 'chilling effect' this kind of policing has on public protest. *In Wood* neither the majority nor Laws LJ in dissent appeared to find anything especially untoward about an enormous police presence at a peaceful protest against the arms industry, nor in the initial surveillance of the protestors.[143] Laws LJ dismissed with obvious impatience the claims of violations of Articles 10 and 11 as 'fanciful', despite the fact that the entire point of attending the event in question was for the protestors to

---

[138] [2017] UKSC 9; [2017] AC 256. Strasbourg, however, found no breach of Art 5 in the subsequent *Renyard v UK* (2019) App no 57884/17.

[139] On this undermining effect see R Stone, 'Breach of the Peace: the case for abolition' [2001] 2 *Web Journal of Current Legal Studies*.

[140] 'Struggle', at 328.

[141] *R (Wood) v Commissioner of Police of the Metropolis* [2009] EWCA Civ 414, [2010] 1 WLR 123 (hereafter, 'Wood').

[142] It succeeded in *Wood* at [2] and [89] but failed in *Catt;* see n 22 above, at 111.

[143] *Wood* at [59].

further their political campaign against the arms trade.[144] In *Catt* the Article 8 claim failed in the Supreme Court, due essentially to a familiar story of heavy judicial deference to the police. The Court readily accepted that including details of wholly peaceful protestors on a database was valuable and that regularly reviewing it to remove the innocent would be too onerous a task. This was despite the fact that the police could point to no practical use that had ever been made of Mr Catt's information. Predictably, a less deferential Strasbourg subsequently found a violation of Article 8.[145]

What is of interest to us is *why* the Supreme Court demanded so little by way of justification for storing the data of even peaceful protestors. It did so at least partly because it found this to be only a 'minor'[146] interference with Article 8 rights, a finding that in turn was made partly because the Court barely glanced at the freedom-to-protest issue[147] and failed even to *mention* association rights. That many people would regard it as worrying and highly intrusive to have the police gather their personal details and place them on a 'National Extremism Database' due to their engagement in political protest did not appear to occur to the Court. In contrast, for Strasbourg, it was precisely the fact that the database implicated both freedom of assembly *and* association that made it of major concern in human rights terms.[148] This led directly to its conclusion that the UK had failed to justify 'the retention of the applicant's data, *in particular concerning peaceful protest*'.[149] This recognition of the close nexus between the privacy, association and protest rights at stake in such cases may also be seen in the warning by the US Supreme Court,[150] that 'Awareness the Government may be watching chills associational and expressive freedoms'. Similarly, Privacy International noted:

> The overt surveillance capabilities produced by such databases also permit the police to identify protestors and then to take practical steps in preventing them from attending demonstrations even before they have arrived at a protest site.[151]

Thus far then these cases tell a familiar story of common law absence from the discussion of all three relevant rights – association, assembly and privacy, fitting

---

[144] Ibid [61]. Though see some obiter expressions of concern: ibid, [92] and [100].

[145] *Catt v UK* (App no 43514/15), 24 January 2019, esp [119]–[128], finding that it was not necessary to retain the applicant's personal data on the database.

[146] Ibid, [26].

[147] Baroness Hale did note the 'potentially chilling effect on the right to engage in peaceful public protest' of the database: (*Catt* [51]). Lord Sumption noted in general terms that 'Political protest is a basic right which the common law has always recognised' (ibid, [19]).

[148] It noted Principle 2 of Recommendation R (87) 15 of the Committee of Ministers regulating the use of personal data in the police sector and its own decision in *Segerstedt-Wiberg v Sweden* App no 62332/00, § 73, ECHR 2006-VII; above, n 145 at [124].

[149] Ibid, emphasis added.

[150] *United States v Jones* 132 S Ct 945 (2012) at 956. For empirical findings to this effect, see V Ashton, *Conceptualising surveillance harms in the context of political protest: privacy, autonomy and freedom of assembly* (2019) PhD, UEA Law School, ch 2; similar concerns were expressed by the UN Special Rapporteur on the Rights to Freedom of Peaceful Assembly and of Association, A/HRC/23/39/Add.1, para 32.

[151] Above, n 145 at para 5.4.

them neatly into category 4. However, as the next section explains, the picture is bleaker than this: it was, once again, the common law that provided the power used to *restrict* the rights in question.

G. The Common Law as Providing a Broad Investigatory Police Power

We saw above how the ancient common law power of breach of the peace has survived – and often still overshadows – the dense web of public order powers and offences introduced by modern legislation.[152] Similarly, in relation to more general police powers, statutes – principally the formidable Police and Criminal Evidence Act 1984 – similarly lay out in exhaustive detail a comprehensive array of specific powers, while counter-terrorism legislation[153] adds a formidable battery of further powers. Yet, *Wood* and *Catt* show that, despite this huge array of statutory powers, police frequently fall back on a very general investigatory power provided by the *common law*. As the Court of Appeal observed in *Catt*, '[t]he [National Extremism] Database ... has no statutory foundation but is based on the common law powers of the police to obtain and store information likely to be of assistance in carrying out their duties'.[154] Not only is this power defined in the broadest terms but its relationship with breach of the peace is obscure: in *Wood* Laws LJ cited dicta from *Rice v Connolly* to the effect that the powers and obligations of a police constable include taking 'all steps which appear to him necessary for *keeping the peace*'.[155] However Counsel, when citing these dicta, took them as referring to general 'common law powers to detect and prevent crime'.[156] This might suggest that 'keeping the peace' includes both a broad, general power to prevent and detect crime *and* a more specific power to prevent an imminent breach of the peace. Alternatively, perhaps the two powers are wholly distinct; no-one seems to know.

In *Catt* the former power was defined as being to '*obtain and store* information for policing purposes, i.e. broadly speaking for the maintenance of public order and the prevention and detection of crime'.[157] However earlier cases show it to be considerably wider than this. In both *Hellewell v Chief Constable*[158] and *Thorpe*[159] it was found to extend also to sharing highly sensitive information about previous convictions with third parties in an attempt to forestall future feared

---

[152] Principally the Public Order Act 1986, as amended.
[153] Principally the Terrorism Act 2000, amended.
[154] *Catt* [2013] EWCA Civ 192, at [32].
[155] [1966] 2 QB 414, 419.
[156] *Wood*, [50].
[157] *Catt*, [7] (emphasis added).
[158] [1995] 1 WLR 804.
[159] *R v Chief Constable of North Wales ex parte Thorpe* [1998] 3 LWR 57.

criminal activity; in the latter case, Lord Woolf said it extended to making any 'reasonable use' of information for 'the purposes of the prevention ... of crime'.[160] This common law power then is broad, indistinct, and obscure. But where did it come from?

Wood traced it back to the decision in *Murray v UK*,[161] in which the Strasbourg Court accepted the finding of the trial court and Court of Appeal that the measures taken in that case (the photographing of a terrorist suspect) were lawful under common law. However, as the relevant judgments reveal, the domestic courts had found, not that there was a positive common law *power* to take this action, but that none was required. Domestic law at this point, prior to the HRA, recognised no general right to privacy; hence, the courts found that, since taking a photograph was not a prima facie wrong or interference with rights, it could be done on the simple basis that no law prohibited it.[162] The Strasbourg Court, however, appeared to mischaracterise the domestic judgments, finding that, '[t]he taking and ... retention of [the] photograph ... without consent had no statutory basis' but that, 'as explained by the trial court judge and the Court of Appeal, [they] were lawful under the common law.[163]

Strasbourg may simply have misread the domestic judgment here, conflating a mere finding that taking a photograph was *not tortious* and hence needed no positive legal authorisation, with a holding that the common law *provided* such authorisation. Alternatively, it may have failed at this point properly to distinguish its own role from that of the domestic courts. Under Article 8, a *positive* legal basis is required as the first of the steps by which an interference with private life may be justified under paragraph (2). Since domestic law provided no positive legal basis for the intrusive action undertaken in *Murray*, the result should have been the same as in the well-known decision in *Malone* concerning phone-tapping:[164] a finding that the interference with Article 8 rights was not 'in accordance with law' under paragraph (2). As *Malone* demonstrates, Article 8(2) can *never* be satisfied merely by the fact that the intrusive action does not amount to a legal wrong, domestically. There must not only be a positive legal power but one that satisfies the rule-of-law requirements of being sufficiently precise and certain that the individual may guide their conduct by it.[165] These factors were simply not considered in *Murray*; if they had been, it seems clear that the mere fact of the action not being unlawful in domestic law could not possibly have satisfied them. This failure may have come about because the national security/counter-terrorism context

---

[160] Ibid.

[161] (1994) 19 EHRR 193.

[162] The domestic courts found that 'According to the common law, *there is no remedy* if someone takes a photograph of another against his will'; cited in *Murray v UK* (1995) 19 EHRR 193 at 203 (emphasis added).

[163] Ibid, 218.

[164] *Malone v UK* (1985) 7 EHRR 14.

[165] *Sunday Times v UK* (1980) 2 EHRR 245.

of *Murray* resulted in Strasbourg applying an instinctively 'lighter touch' review across the board than it did in the more mundane context of *Malone*. Overall there was either a simple oversight by Strasbourg or a misreading of the domestic court judgments.

In *Wood*, Counsel, seeking to dispute the legal basis of similar police actions, sought to persuade the High Court that the decision in *Murray v UK* was 'wrong' on the above points. However, McCombe J said that he could not so 'dismiss' the finding of the Strasbourg court, because that 'would do quite inadequate respect for the decisions of that court, the ultimate arbiter of these matters.'[166] Strasbourg however is clearly not 'the ultimate arbiter' of the correct interpretation of English common law. No finding by Strasbourg can change a mere 'no tort' finding into a positive common law power: its status in this respect is a matter of *domestic* law, not the Convention. The High Court in *Wood* however, used Strasbourg's *Murray* decision as authority for the propositions (a) that the common law provided a positive police *power* to engage in surveillance and storage of protestors' personal information; and (b) that this, plus the safeguards provided by data protection law,[167] was capable of satisfying Article 8, now applicable in domestic law under the HRA. As seen, the Court added that neither of these findings could be questioned because they came from Strasbourg. The Court of Appeal agreed that 'the common law power' provided the necessary legal basis under Article 8(2) for the police action[168] and a like finding was made in *Catt*.[169] Hence a prior domestic-law finding that the police had committed no tort in photographing a suspect has somehow morphed into a positive 'common law power' to gather, store and distribute to others[170] the personal information of peaceful protestors, including their photographs, for the broad purpose of preventing and detecting crime. The extraordinary breadth of this power may be seen in the fact that, as *Catt* demonstrates, it has no requirement that the police reasonably suspect the individual in question of any criminal activity.

This saga in turn uncovers a deeper issue: a long-standing common law ambivalence about whether the rule of law places different requirements on public authorities, including the police, as compared to private citizens. Famously, in *Malone*, Megarry J collapsed the distinction between the two, holding that the state could tap phones because – just like any individual – it was free to do anything the law did not prohibit.[171] Strasbourg of course roundly condemned this notion as a wholly inadequate legal basis for interfering with Convention rights.[172]

---

[166] [2008] EWHC 1105 (Admin) at [70].
[167] Then the Data Protection Act 1998.
[168] Per Laws LJ at [55] and Dyson LJ at [98].
[169] Above, text to n 157.
[170] As in *Thorpe* and *Hellewell*.
[171] *Malone v Commissioner for the Metropolitan Police (No 2)* [1979] 2 All ER 620.
[172] *Malone v UK* (1985) 7 EHRR 14.

Moreover, Laws LL has famously condemned this kind of reasoning, insisting in *Fewings* that:

> For private persons, the rule is that you may do anything you choose which the law does not prohibit … The freedoms of the private citizen are not conditional upon some distinct and affirmative justification for which he must burrow in the law books … But for public bodies the rule is the opposite …: any action to be taken must be justified by positive law.[173]

There is considerable debate about how widely this principle sweeps. Some seek to confine it to statutory bodies, like local authorities, with which *Fewings* itself was concerned; they argue in particular that it cannot apply to central government, which wields the powers of the Crown. Thus the Court of Appeal recently cited with approval the proposition that '[a]t common law the Crown, as a corporation possessing legal personality, has the capacities of a natural person and thus the same liberties as the individual',[174] a principle sometimes known as the 'Ram' or 'third source powers' doctrine. This in turn raises the question of whether the powers of the police are governed by the *Fewings* doctrine or whether they are in some way akin to those of the Crown. Police constables are not 'Crown servants' as civil servants are, but they do swear an oath to the Crown[175] and the governmental view is that a Chief Constable 'holds office under the Crown'.[176] Moreover it may be that a constable's power to prevent a breach of the peace is a residue of the ancient prerogative power to keep the Queen's peace, so controversially asserted – or revived – in *Northumbria Police Authority*.[177]

There is a further strand of thinking that may encourage the notion of endowing police constables with the general liberties of the individual: the long-standing notion that police constables are merely 'citizens in uniform'. As a Royal Commission in 1929 said:

> … a policeman, in the view of the common law, is only "a person paid to perform, as a matter of duty, acts which if he were so minded, he might have done voluntarily."[178]

This view still finds strong expression in modern caselaw through the insistence that the power – and duty – to prevent a breach of the peace belongs to the ordinary citizen as well as the police officer.[179] Such a view may encourage the ready conflation that we saw in *Wood* of a mere liberty held by police officers with a

---

[173] *R v Somerset County Council ex parte Fewings and Others* [1995] 1 WLR 1037.
[174] *R v Secretary of State for Health ex p. C* [2000] 1 FLR 627; citing *Halsbury's Laws of England* vol 8 (2), at n 6 to para 101.
[175] The wording is traditional but set out at www.metfed.org.uk/support/uploads/1214552596Office%20Constable.pdf.
[176] Policing Protocol Order (2011) available at https://assets.publishing.service.gov.uk/government/uploads/system/uploads/attachment_data/file/117475/draft-police-protocol.pdf.
[177] *Northumbria Police Authority* [1988] 2 WLR 590. I owe this point to Robert Craig.
[178] Home Office, *Royal Commission on Police Powers and Procedure* (Cmd 3297 1929) at 6.
[179] See, eg, *Laporte*, [29], [46], [49], [61], [66], [110], [128], citing the strong finding to this effect by Lord Diplock in *Albert v Lavin* [1982] AC 546, 565.

positive police *power*, but it is surely suspect: given the formidable array of coercive powers the modern police force can deploy, it seems perverse to continue an historic legal fiction that treats police officers as merely a special kind of citizen. Moreover, in a case concerning the claimed 'third source' powers of the Crown, Lord Sumption expressed strong doubt as to whether:

> The analogy with a natural person is really apt in the case of public or governmental action, as opposed to purely managerial acts of a kind that any natural person could do, such as making contracts.[180]

Given that police powers are governmental powers par excellence, these dicta caution strongly against treating the police analogously to private citizens.

To sum up a long argument: we have seen that the notion of a general common law police *power* to gather, store and disseminate personal information for the purposes of crime prevention originated in the notion of a mere liberty to do that which the law did not forbid. Domestic law provides no clear answer as to whether the police enjoy such general liberties: the clarity of the *Fewings* principle is obscured by the traditional common law view of police officers as merely 'citizens in uniform'. However, even if the Ram doctrine or something like it *does* apply to the police, it is now clear that it does *not* empower state actors to do anything that interferes with the rights or liberties of the subject, including their ECHR rights.[181] Given that *Wood* and *Catt* agreed that the powers in question *do* constitute an interference with Article 8 rights, no such general liberty can now be relied upon to authorise such interference. Hence the police actions in *Wood* and *Catt* should have been held to be an unlawful interference with Article 8 rights, for the simplest of reasons: that they lacked a positive legal basis.[182] The failure to recognise this means that, far from bolstering the status of freedom of assembly, the common law has once again facilitated police action that chills and undermines that right and undercuts the protection afforded to it by statute.

V. Conclusion

Given the above analysis, the conclusions of this chapter can be briefly stated. There is no common law right to freedom of association or to freedom of assembly. Both freedoms remain mere liberties at common law; they rarely warrant a mention in the cases as anything other than *Convention* rights. The common law

---

[180] *R (on the application of New London College) v Secretary of State for the Home Department* [2013] UKSC 51, at [28].

[181] *Shrewsbury & Atcham Borough Council v Secretary of State for Communities and Local Government* [2008] EWCA Civ 148; *New College of Humanities*, ibid, at [28].

[182] In *Catt v UK* (above n 145) Strasbourg declined to determine whether the 'in accordance with law' test was satisfied.

has had a positive effect in a few cases but probably the most important – *Laporte* – seems already to have had its positive impact reversed, while the future potential of *UNISON* for labour rights remains at present uncertain. As such, it is impossible at this point to find a developed autonomous or even minor supportive role for the common law in protecting these rights. In relation to freedom of assembly indeed, its most important role has been to empower preventive policing, including its selective use against political protest.

Mark Elliott has argued that we should assess the performance of the common law in protecting fundamental rights across three vectors:[183] *normative reach* – are the two bodies of law co-extensive?; *protective rigour* – how *strong* is the protection afforded to a given right?; *constitutional resilience* – how far is the right protected against adverse incursion by statute or prerogative powers? Applying these, we may conclude that the common law governing rights of protest and association has as yet nothing close to the *normative reach* of Article 11 and nothing like its *protective rigour*. And even to speak of its possible *resilience* against incursion would be premature: the rights themselves must first start to take real shape in the common law. The grounds for hope that they will are not absent but faint. Real common law rights may eventually develop in this field, but at present that prospect seems distant indeed.

---

[183] Elliott, above n 2 above, at 87.

8

Equality: A Core Common Law Principle, or 'Mere' Rationality?

COLM O'CINNEIDE

In 1994, Jeffrey Jowell published a paper in that year's volume of *Current Legal Problems*, entitled 'Is Equality a Constitutional Principle?'[1] He began that paper by noting that equality was an oddly neglected topic in discussion of UK constitutional and administrative law, in contrast to its salience in other legal systems. He then argued that this neglect served to obscure the fundamental importance of equality – and in particular the 'fundamental precept' that persons should be treated as having 'equal worth' and not be discriminated against without adequate justification, which he argued was 'constitutive of democracy'.[2] He made the case that this 'equality principle' should be recognised as having constitutional status, and be expressly recognised by the courts to be a free-standing ground of judicial review – as distinct from being submerged within 'vague definitions of irrationality'.

Twenty-five years later, it is instructive to revisit Jowell's analysis. At first glance, much would appear to have changed. Equality has acquired a much more tangible status within UK public law, and is now generally acknowledged to be an important constitutional value – at a certain level of abstraction, at least.[3] The right of individuals to equality and non-discrimination, ie to be treated as enjoying equal worth in accordance with Jowell's equality principle, receives a degree of legal protection through the provisions of both the Human Rights Act 1998 ('HRA') and UK and EU anti-discrimination legislation.[4] Within the sphere of common law adjudication, the courts regularly acknowledge the fundamental importance of the equality principle, often quoting Jowell's 1994 paper with approval in so doing.[5]

---

[1] (1994) 47 *Current Legal Problems* 1–18.

[2] Ibid, 7.

[3] Bamforth has described anti-discrimination law as evolving out from its labour law roots and taking a 'constitutional turn': see N Bamforth, 'Conceptions of Anti-discrimination Law' (2004) 24 *OJLS* 693.

[4] The distinction between the scope and substance of these various legislative instruments as they apply to equality is outlined in Part II of this chapter, below.

[5] See, eg, *Matadeen v Pointu* [1999] 1 AC 98, as discussed below in Part IV of this chapter.

The courts have also exercised their common law powers of review to strike down a number of discriminatory decisions by public authorities. *De Smith*, the leading practitioner text in the field, states that the equality principle applies 'to the exercise of all public functions', and provides a long list of administrative law cases apparently illustrating the application of this principle.[6]

One might thus assume that Jowell's arguments have been vindicated, and the equality principle has put down deep roots in UK public law. However, a closer look complicates the picture. In actuality, the status of equality is qualified in significant ways. This is particularly true when it comes to the common law dimension of UK public/administrative law. Judges have repeatedly emphasised the constitutional significance of the equality principle. However, they have been reluctant to treat it as a free-standing ground of review. Instead, the courts have subsumed equality considerations within the general scope of rationality review, treating them in Lord Sumption's words in *R (Gallaher Group Ltd) v Competition and Markets Authority* as 'no more than a particular application of the ordinary requirement of rationality imposed on public authorities'.[7]

Thus, the core argument made by Jowell back in 1994, namely that the equality principle should be liberated from the confines of rationality review and acknowledged to be a core structural common law norm, has not become accepted orthodoxy. By extension, the courts have not recognised the existence of a common law right to non-discrimination: this right informs the application of rationality review, but beyond that receives at best indirect protection via the common law.

This is a sub-optimal situation. Equality concerns fit awkwardly within the framework of rationality review. The copiousness of this mode of review creates a risk that the normative specificity of the equality principle will be lost in its imprecision.[8] Furthermore, it is not clear what standard of scrutiny should be applied in subjecting potentially unequal treatment to rationality review: the relevant case-law in this regard is characterised by a high degree of vagueness, uncertainty and inconsistency. In general, the current legal status quo offers neither clarity nor consistency – and also arguably undervalues the constitutional importance of the equality principle.

Jowell's central argument in his 1994 paper – namely that the equality principle is too important to be left to the vagaries of rationality review – thus continues to have force. However, it is also important to recognise that equality is a notoriously abstract concept that is capable of being interpreted and applied in very different ways. As such, if the equality principle is to be liberated from the distorting framework of rationality review and treated as a free-standing ground of review in

---

[6] Lord Woolf et al, *De Smith's Judicial Review*, 8th edn (London, Sweet and Maxwell, 2018) [11.061]–[11.068].

[7] [2018] UKSC 25, [50].

[8] As McColgan has argued, much discrimination has been 'widely regarded as acceptable, even common-sensical' until prohibited by statute: its 'irrationality' has rarely been self-evident: A McColgan, *Discrimination, Equality and the Law* (Oxford, Hart Publishing, 2014) 12.

its own right, courts need articulate its scope and substance with a greater degree of precision than has hitherto been present in much of the relevant common law jurisprudence. A strong case can also be made for disaggregating the principle, and recognising that different types of differential treatment should attract different standards of review – depending on the extent to which equality of status is undermined by the type of treatment under review.

Part I of this chapter clarifies contemporary normative understandings of equality, with a particular emphasis on disentangling certain specific views of what respect for equality entails which are often bundled together under the generic term of 'equal treatment': clarifying some conceptual starting-points is a necessary first step in this context, before engaging with the relevant common law jurisprudence. Part II outlines how respect for 'equality of status' has come to be recognised as an important constitutional value. Part III analyses the arguments made by Jowell and others as to why respect for equal status should be elevated to the status of a free-standing ground of review – which would give it analogous status to recognised common law rights. Part IV examines the circumstances in which the courts have been prepared to review the actions of public authorities for conformity with the principle of equality – and analyses how this legal status quo falls short of the position Jowell argued for back in 1994. Part V critically examines the current legal position, identifying some significant areas of uncertainty and conceptual mismatch, while the Conclusion draws some wider lessons from the ambivalent status of equality within the common law with a view to proposing some necessary adjustments to the status quo. Throughout this chapter, the focus will be on public law: space permits detailed consideration of the interesting question of how the equality principle should influence the interpretation and application of relevant private law norms, although aspects of the public/private law interface in this context will be discussed.[9]

I. The Equality Principle Disaggregated: Equality of Status and its Formal/Substantive Aspects

Debates about equality are often muddled by conceptual confusion about the meaning of this term. As such, before turning to legal analysis, it is helpful to clarify what people mean when they talk about equality – especially in the context of its status as an important constitutional value.

Equality is an abstract term, capable of bearing multiple meanings. Some commentators have argued that this malleability indicates that equality is an 'empty' concept, ie that it lacks any substantive content or intrinsic value in its

---

[9] For detailed consideration of the private law dimension, see C McCrudden, 'Equality and Non-Discrimination' in D Feldman (ed), *English Public Law* (Oxford, Oxford University Press, 2004) 587.

own right.[10] However, as deployed in political and legal debate since the early modern (seventeenth and eighteenth centuries) period in Europe, the concept has come to be associated with a complex set of interlinked ideas clustered around a unifying core idea – namely that all persons should be treated as being equal in status (or as enjoying 'equal worth', as Jowell put it).[11]

Described by Waldron as reflecting the 'basic' notion that no morally signifi- cant differences exist between different classes of human being,[12] and shaped by a reaction against centuries-old practices of racism, patriarchial oppression and socio-economic class differentiation, the idea of equal status requires that all persons be treated as if they possess a shared degree of intrinsic dignity.[13] The concepts clustering around this foundational idea include notions such as 'equality before the law', 'equal protection of the law', 'equality in the law', and 'equal citizen- ship'. These concepts often overlap in scope and content, and are not always easy to disentangle. However, taken together, they are generally viewed as generating two distinct but inter-related sets of normative obligations – 'formal' and 'substantive' equality.[14]

Formal equality is generally associated with the concept of 'equality before the law'. It requires that persons 'who have equal status in at least one normatively relevant respect … must be treated equally with regard to this respect'.[15] In other words, it requires consistency of treatment: similarly situated persons should be treated in a similar manner, unless differential treatment can be shown to be clearly justified. Such consistency of treatment is widely viewed as an intrinsic good, on the basis that it manifests respect for equality of status.[16] Perhaps more convinc- ingly, it is also viewed as an instrumental good, as it limits the extent to which power can be exercised in an arbitrary and/or irrational manner – which is why formal equality tends to be viewed as an integral aspect of rule of law.[17]

In contrast, substantive equality requires that persons not be subject to treat- ment that denies or undermines their intrinsic equality of status, ie that they not

---

[10] See, eg, J Raz, *The Morality of Freedom* (Oxford, Oxford University Press, 1986) ch 9. See also P Westen, 'The Empty Idea of Equality' (1985) 95 *Harvard Law Review* 537.

[11] A wide range of different theorists have identified the key importance of equal status as an organ- ising concept in political and legal debate: see, eg, R Dahl, *On Political Equality* (New Haven, Yale University Press, 2006) 4; R Dworkin, *Taking Rights Seriously* (Cambridge, Harvard University Press, 1977) 272–273; NM Smith, *Basic Equality and Discrimination: Reconciling Theory and Law* (London, Routledge, 2011) 1.

[12] J Waldron, *One Another's Equals: The Basis of Human Equality* (Cambridge, Harvard University Press, 2017).

[13] Ibid. See also S Moreau, 'Equality and Discrimination', in J Tasioulas (ed), *The Cambridge Companion to Philosophy of Law* (Cambridge, Cambridge University Press, 2019).

[14] See in general S Fredman, *Discrimination Law* 2nd edn (Oxford, Oxford University Press, 2011).

[15] S Gosepath, 'Equality', *Stanford Encyclopaedia of Philosophy*, available at https://plato.stanford.edu/entries/equality/#ForEqu.

[16] T Allan, *Constitutional Justice: A Liberal Theory of the Rule of Law* (Oxford, Oxford University Press, 2001) 243–281.

[17] F Thomsen, 'Concept, Principle, and Norm – Equality before the Law Reconsidered' (2018) 24 *Legal Theory* 103.

be discriminated against on grounds that offend their dignity, or otherwise deny their 'equal worth'. This can include stereotyping, harassment, and other forms of unjustified discrimination which are predicated on assumptions about the lesser worth of particular social groups.[18]

Formal equality is thus essentially concerned with consistency of treatment, while substantive equality targets demeaning discrimination: the former seeks 'equal treatment' as a general rule, the latter is focused on redressing specific forms of injustice. Some commentators lump both types of obligation together into a single agglutinate mass, and slap the same 'equality' label on the resulting mush: others try to draw a bright-line distinction between the two.[19] However, their relationship is more complex than either of these approaches would suggest.

The two types of equality overlap: treatment may be inconsistent because it is based on demeaning assumptions, and vice versa. Indeed, substantive equality is best viewed as a fully fleshed-out, intensified application of the formal equality approach: it targets specific forms of status-denying differential treatment, while aiming to ensure comprehensive consistency of treatment for the individuals affected. However, while both types of equality require that differential treatment of similarly situated individuals be justified, substantive equality is generally understood to impose a more demanding justificatory burden.[20] In particular, it requires that compelling reasons be shown to justify the use of 'suspect' grounds of discrimination, such as race, sex or disability, which are linked to historic patterns of group subordination. In contrast, formal equality is less exacting, as a rule of thumb: in general, only differences in treatment which are clearly irrational or arbitrary will be viewed as breaching its requirements, reflecting the multitude of different situations where a reasonable case may be made for treating persons differently.[21]

The formal/substantive distinction is also important to bear in mind when considering the status of the human right to equality and non-discrimination. This right is prominent within the international human rights lexicon: it affirms the equal status of all humans, along with their entitlement not to be discriminated

---

[18] See in general T Khaitan, *A Theory of Discrimination Law* (Oxford, Oxford University Press, 2015).

[19] See, eg, Thomsen (n 17).

[20] Substantive equality also has a positive dimension: pre-emptive action in the form of reasonable accommodation measures and other positive steps may be required in certain circumstances to eliminate discriminatory obstacles. In contrast, formal equality is usually not conceptualised in positive terms, but instead solely as a negative constraint on inconsistent treatment. Similarly, substantive equality is viewed as 'biting' on both public and private actors, while formal equality tends to be viewed solely as an issue of public power – and thus as not translating over into the private sphere. See in general Khaitan (n 18).

[21] Lord Nicholls set out the distinction between these varying levels of scrutiny with admirable clarity in the HRA case of *Ghaidan v Godin-Mendoza* [2004] UKHL 30, [9]: 'In many circumstances opinions can differ on whether a suggested ground of distinction justifies a difference in legal treatment. But there are certain grounds of factual difference which by common accord are not acceptable, without more, as a basis for different legal treatment ... Unless good reason exists, differences in legal treatment based on grounds such as these are properly stigmatised as discriminatory.'

against in ways that deny their equality of status.[22] Every major international human rights treaty contains provisions requiring state parties to respect the equal status principle when giving effect to their provisions: examples include Article 2(1) of the International Covenant on Civil and Political Rights (ICCPR) and Article 14 of the European Convention on Human Rights (ECHR). The existence of a free-standing individual right to equality and non-discrimination is also affirmed, ie in Article 26 of the ICCPR and Protocol 14 of the ECHR. These abstract provisions are generally interpreted as covering both the formal and substantive dimensions of the equal status principle.[23] However, particular emphasis tends to be placed on the non-discrimination requirements of the latter.[24] International human rights bodies, along with national courts applying these provisions as part of domestic law, thus subject differential treatment based on 'suspect' grounds such as race, sex, religion or (increasingly) sexual orientation to demanding scrutiny, in contrast to the lighter touch applied to other forms of differential treatment.

In other words, the human right to equality and non-discrimination is largely interpreted in substantive terms – whereas formal equality tends to be a more peripheral concern.[25] 'Mere' inconsistent treatment, without the added 'substantive' ingredient of discrimination on suspect grounds, is generally not viewed as infringing upon human rights.[26] It may be concerning from a rule of law and/or good governance perspective – perhaps even seriously so – but it is usually not conceptualised as a violation of fundamental rights as such (with all that entails in terms of remedial expectations).

These distinctions between the formal and substantive dimensions to equality of status, and the relative 'demandingness' of the normative obligations they impose upon public authorities, are widely recognised in the academic literature.[27] However, they are not always disaggregated in judicial discussions of what 'equal treatment' entails (as outlined further below). This is unfortunate: equality is a complex idea, and the common law like other legal frameworks needs to reflect this complexity. In the subsequent parts of this chapter, the evolving status of equality within the constitutional and public law architecture of the UK, and in particular within the common law, are analysed with reference to these conceptual distinctions – which comprise the ideational grammar through which tangible expression is given to the notion of 'equality of status'.

---

[22] See, eg, Arts 1 and 2 of the Universal Declaration of Human Rights.

[23] The provisions of the EU Charter of Fundamental Rights are unusual in this respect, in that they explicitly recognise both the formal and substantive dimensions of equality. Art 20 guarantees 'equality before the law' while Art 21 protects against discrimination on an assortment of suspect grounds – thereby giving textual shape to the formal/substantive equality distinction.

[24] For the ECHR case-law in this regard, see J Gerards, 'The Discrimination Grounds of Article 14 ECHR' (2013) 13 *Human Rights Law Review* 99.

[25] See, eg *R (Carson) v Secretary of State for Work and Pensions* [2006] 1 AC 173; *Carson v United Kingdom* (2010) 51 EHRR 13.

[26] See, eg, *Springett and Others v United Kingdom*, App nos 34726/04, 14287/05 and 34702/05, Decision on Admissibility, 27 April 2010.

[27] See, eg, Fredman (n 14).

II. The Constitutional Status of Equality

When the modern language of equality first entered European political discourse, it was radical and destabilising. By affirming the equal status of all citizens, it posed a direct challenge to the notions of natural, God-ordained hierarchy that had hitherto shaped the political and social organisation of societies across Europe and beyond. However, with the gradual expansion of the franchise, the development of legal constraints on the arbitrary exercise of state power, and the emergence of modern constitutional democracies, this once radical notion became part of a new constitutional orthodoxy.

The concept of equal status – concisely encapsulated by the slogan 'one person, one vote' – now underpins contemporary forms of democracy, in both its representative and direct modes. The associated principle of 'equality before the law' has also become one of the integral elements of rule of law. It is now commonplace for national constitutional orders to treat equality as a foundational principle, and for the written texts of virtually all liberal democratic constitutions to recognise equality to be a fundamental right. Furthermore, national legal systems are increasingly giving legal effect to the formal and substantive dimensions of equality, through eg the developing case-law of national courts and the expanding scope of anti-discrimination legislation in both the public and private spheres.

The UK is no exception to these general trends. Much of its machinery of state was not originally designed with the equal status principle in mind.[28] However, over time, equality has become an animating value of the British constitutional order: strong expectations exist that its component parts should function in a manner broadly compatible with equality of status and its associated formal/substantive dimensions.

For example, representative democracy in the UK is now structured around the assumption that all citizens should enjoy 'political equality', ie formal equality of status as participants within the democratic process.[29] Key aspects of the UK's political system, such as the primacy of the Commons, the sovereign law-making authority of Parliament, and the functioning of its inter-institutional accountability mechanisms, are structured and justified by reference to this value.[30]

---

[28] It also retains certain elements, such as the monarchy and the House of Lords, which can be difficult to reconcile with a deep attachment to this notion.

[29] This does not necessarily translate into practical or substantive equality of status – as evidenced by, for example, the restrictions imposed on prisoner voting.

[30] As Gordon puts it, 'it is this notion of the political equality of citizens which gives force to, and is manifested by, the extra-constitutional and intra-constitutional aspects of democracy': M Gordon, *Parliamentary Sovereignty in the UK Constitution: Process, Politics and Democracy* (Oxford, Hart Publishing, 2015) 34. Respect for political equality generally plays out in formal terms, as for example reflected in the importance assigned to majoritarian decision-making. However, it is gradually acquiring a more substantive dimension, as evidenced by measures such as ss 104 and 106 of the Equality Act 2010 which are directed towards encouraging political parties to select more candidates from under-represented groups.

A commitment to formal equality of status also underpins contemporary understanding of what respect for the rule of law entails. Writing in 1885, Dicey famously argued that the equal application of the law to all persons, irrespective of their social or political status, was one of the defining features of the British rule of law tradition: '[h]ere every man, whatever be his rank or condition, is subject to the ordinary law of the realm and amenable to the jurisdiction of the ordinary tribunals'.[31] This was a highly formalist view of what respect for equal status entailed, which required little if anything more than the equal subjection to the jurisdiction of the courts.[32] However, Dicey's views have been revised and reworked by subsequent commentators. An expanded formalist interpretation of 'equality before the law', requiring consistency of treatment as between similarly situated persons, is now generally acknowledged to be a key element of the rule of law. For example, in his influential analysis of the rule of law, Lord Bingham argued that 'the laws of the land should apply equally to all, save to the extent that objective differences justify differentiation'.[33]

In line with formal equality reasoning more generally (as outlined in Part I above), this understanding of the notion of equality before the law is justified on the basis that it both manifests respect for equality of status and limits the potential for arbitrary exercise of power. It is also increasingly viewed as having a substantive dimension, ie as precluding the exercise of legal powers in a way that discriminates on grounds incompatible with equality of status.[34] As with other aspects of the rule of law, the exact parameters of 'equality before the law' remain a matter of debate. However, the general idea that law should respect equality of status, in both its formal and substantive dimensions, is widely accepted – and reflected in how legislators, administrators and judges go about the business of framing, interpreting and applying legal rules.[35]

The value assigned to equality of status is also reflected in the UK's ratification of all the core UN and Council of Europe treaty instruments guaranteeing the right to equality and non-discrimination, and the incorporation of Article 14 ECHR into domestic law via the HRA. Article 14 ECHR is a circumscribed equality guarantee, as it only prohibits discrimination against individuals on 'status' grounds such as race and sex when it comes to matters that come within the 'ambit'

---

[31] AV Dicey (ed ECS Wade), *An Introduction to the Study of the Law of the Constitution* 10th edn (London, Macmillan, 1959) 193.

[32] As Craig has argued, Dicey's analysis provides little if any insight as to when it will be legitimate to apply different rules to different groups of individuals, or when public authorities such as the police should benefit from special powers and privileges unavailable to others. See P Craig, 'Formal and Substantive Conceptions of the Rule of Law: An Analytical Framework' [1997] *PL* 467, 472–3.

[33] T Bingham, 'The Rule of Law' (2007) 66 *CLJ* 67, 73. See also Allan (n 16) 243–281.

[34] Bingham (n 33). See also T Bingham, *The Rule of Law* (London, Allen Lane, 2010).

[35] Thus, for example, Lord Bingham suggests that laws which discriminate on status grounds such as race and sex are not based on 'objective differences', and therefore contravene the rule of law: Bingham (n 33) 73.

of another Convention right. However, the Strasbourg Court has adopted a wide interpretation of what comes within the ambit of Convention rights, and also of what qualifies as a status ground. As a result, the scope of Article 14 as incorporated by the HRA is wide, and it has generated an extensive and influential case-law.[36] Differences in treatment of similarly situated persons that affect the enjoyment of other Convention rights, which are linked to a status ground, must be shown to be objectively justified in line with the standard proportionality approach of the Strasbourg Court – with differences of treatment based on 'suspect' grounds such as race attracting more intensive scrutiny from the courts. A failure to differentiate between differently situated individuals can also qualify as discrimination,[37] as can a failure on the part of public authorities to take positive steps to protect individuals against discriminatory treatment by employers and other private actors.[38]

The UK has also enacted detailed anti-discrimination legislation (prompted in part by the requirements of EU law). The Equality Act 2010 codified the law in this regard in Britain, after decades of incremental development.[39] Unlike Article 14 ECHR, which as mentioned above protects against all discrimination based on the open-ended grounds of 'personal status', anti-discrimination legislation only protects against discrimination based on a much narrower set of specified 'protected characteristics' such as race/ethnicity, sex, sexual orientation, disability and religion and belief.[40] However, anti-discrimination legislation regulates the conduct of both private and public bodies, unlike Article 14 ECHR, which via the HRA is only capable of exercising a qualified form of indirect horizontal effect on laws regulating the relationship between private parties.[41] It also imposes a positive duty on public authorities to eliminate discrimination and promote equality of opportunity in respect of all the protected characteristics[42] – thereby

---

[36] An arguable case can be made that Article 14 jurisprudence of the UK courts has generated more substantial changes to UK law than any other single element of the Convention rights incorporated by the HRA.

[37] *Thlimmenos v Greece* (2001) 31 EHRR 411.

[38] *Eweida v UK* (2011) ECHR 738.

[39] The 2010 Act does not apply to Northern Ireland, where discrimination law still consists of a complex mix of primary legislation and regulations implementing the various provisions of the EU equality directives.

[40] Within this narrower scope of application, the requirements of anti-discrimination legislation can be more demanding than those arising under the HRA. For example, most forms of direct discrimination based on protected characteristics is prohibited, without any possibility of showing objective justification: see s 13 of the Equality Act 2010.

[41] Formerly, UK public bodies were only bound by anti-discrimination legislation when they acted in their capacity as service providers or employers, ie in a manner analogous to private bodies. A number of legislative reforms, culminating in the provisions of s 29 of the 2010 Act read together with Schs 3, 22 and 23 of the Act, have now prohibited discrimination by public authorities in the performance of their public functions. However, Sch 23(1) of the 2010 Act exempts all acts done under authorisation by primary and secondary legislation: this constitutes a significant limitation on the scope of anti-discrimination legislation as it applies to public authorities.

[42] Equality Act 2010, s 149.

requiring public authorities to take procedural steps to give effect to substantive equality considerations in their policies and practices.

EU law has also been influential in extending legal protection against discrimination. Crucially, it has both a formal and a substantive equality element.[43] The Court of Justice of the EU (CJEU) has recognised the existence of a general principle of equal treatment.[44] Within the scope of application of EU law, differences in treatment of similarly situated persons must be objectively justified in line with the demands of formal equality – with this principle now acknowledged to be a 'right' by virtue of Article 20 of the EU Charter of Fundamental Rights. However, this principle of equal treatment also has a distinct substantive dimension, recognised by Article 21 of the EU Charter. Differences of treatment based on 'suspect' grounds such as sex and race will be subject to more demanding scrutiny. Furthermore, the detailed provisions of the EU equality directives, which require states to enact laws prohibiting discrimination on a number of specific grounds, are read by the CJEU as having direct horizontal effect by virtue of this general principle – while UK legislation must comply with their requirements.[45] In general, due to the supremacy and direct effect of EU law, its equality/non-discrimination dimension has been very influential in shaping key aspects of UK law, including the provisions of the Equality Act 2010. (Brexit will obviously impact on this, as discussed further below.)

Not every facet of UK public law animated by a concern with equality of status is 'constitutionalised', ie is acknowledged to form part of the core framework of legal and political norms that make up the UK's constitutional infrastructure. For example, the provisions of the Equality Act 2010 have no special constitutional status (even if important elements of the legislation are currently backstopped by the supremacy/direct effect requirements of EU equality law). However, on a general level, equality of status has become a key underpinning value of the UK's constitutional order. Writing in 1994, Jowell described respect for equal status as 'fundamental' to a rule of law-based democracy like the UK. Since then, its constitutional significance has, if anything, grown – due in particular to the new substantive dimension it has acquired via the incorporation of Article 14 ECHR. Strong expectations now exist that state institutions should respect both its formal and substantive dimensions – even if what such respect entails in practice is often a matter of debate.

---

[43] See in general E Ellis and P Watson, *EU Anti-discrimination Law* 2nd edn (Oxford, Oxford University Press, 2012).

[44] C O'Cinneide, 'The Constitutionalization of Equality within the EU Legal Order: Sexual Orientation as a Testing Ground' (2015) 22 *Maastricht Journal of European and Comparative Law* 370.

[45] Case C-144/04, *Mangold v Helm* [2005] ECR I-9981; Case C-388/07, *Age Concern England (Incorporated Trustees of the National Council for Ageing)*, [2009] ECR I-1569.

III. The Case for Recognising the Existence of the Equality Principle within the Common Law

Common law adjudication in fields as diverse as administrative law, tort law or employment law is informed by certain core values, such as respect for the principle of legality, legal certainty and individual autonomy.[46] Within public law, these values crystallise at times into free-standing 'principles' or 'common law rights', which impose specific constraints on government action that are distinguishable from irrationality and other grounds of review.[47] Public authorities are presumed to lack the power to act in contravention of such principles/rights, in the absence of clear statutory authorisation for their actions. These principles and rights are also taken into account in statutory interpretation, with legislation being interpreted subject to a presumption that Parliament did not intend to limit these principles/rights.[48]

So, given the constitutional significance of equal status, where does it fit into this picture? Whether, how and to what extent should courts take equality into account when developing the common law? Is equality a value that should inform the development of established common law norms? Or is it something more than that – a free-standing principle, on a par with access to justice and the other common law rights that have been recognised to constitute free-standing grounds of review within UK public law over the last few decades?

In asking this question, some historical context needs to be added to the picture. It has been long established that the courts can strike down decisions by public authorities which treat people in an unequal manner, if such decisions lack a 'reasonable' basis. In other words, as discussed further below, unequal treatment my fall foul of common law rationality review. However, beyond that, the common law has historically lacked a well-developed equality dimension.

For example, when litigants began to challenge race and sex discrimination by private employers and service providers from the 1940s onwards, they found

---

[46] D Oliver, *Common Values and the Public-Private Law Divide* (London, Butterworths, 1999).

[47] See, eg *R v Secretary of State for the Home Department, Ex p Simms* [2000] 2 AC 115; *R (Unison) v Lord Chancellor* [2017] UKSC 51. The UK courts do not appear to draw a sharp distinction between 'principles' and 'rights' in this context: see, eg, *R (Unison) v Lord Chancellor* [2017] UKSC 51, [65], where Lord Reed stated that the 'constitutional right of access to justice' was one of the 'constitutional principles' at play in that case. Within EU law, 'principles' are treated as objective norms of the EU legal order which primary and secondary legislation must respect – while 'rights' involve a crystallisation of such principles into the form of 'subjective' norms conferring specific legal entitlements upon individuals: see, eg, T Tridimas, 'Fundamental Rights, General Principles of EU Law, and the Charter' 16 *Cambridge Yearbook of European Legal Studies* 361. Lord Reed's above-cited comments in *Unison* indicates that an analogous relationship exists between the two concepts in the context of UK common law.

[48] See in general M Elliott, 'Beyond the European Convention: Human Rights and the Common Law' (2015) 68 *Current Legal Problems* 85.

common law causes of action to be of limited use. In 1944, the famous West Indian cricketer Learie Constantine successfully invoked the implied duty of an innkeeper to provide accommodation to guests on a reasonable basis in challenging a hotel's refusal to give him a room on the grounds of his race.[49] However, other attempts to invoke tort or contract law causes of action to challenge discrimination were generally unsuccessful – with the Court of Appeal in *Scala Ballroom (Wolverhampton) Ltd v Ratcliffe* acknowledging that there was no bar in law to the plaintiffs denying admittance to 'coloured people'.[50]

McColgan has characterised this historical approach of the common law to discrimination as displaying a 'marked lack of concern'.[51] A more charitable way of putting it would be that the common law lacked any articulated concept of equality, or any legal channel to vindicate claims of discriminatory treatment aside from rationality review in the case of public authorities – and, even in the latter case, the relevant case-law was often criticised for lacking coherence and consistency.[52]

Beginning with the Race Relations Act 1965, Parliament used anti-discrimination legislation to plug the gap left by the lack of a meaningful equality/non-discrimination dimension to the common law. Subsequently, much academic commentary questioned the capacity of the common law to engage meaningfully with equality and non-discrimination values – both on the basis of its lack of an articulated conception of equality, and also because of concern that the ideological biases of the judiciary would invariably infect any common law adjudication in this context.[53] Interestingly, the courts themselves also tended to adopt the position that legal developments in the equality/non-discrimination field had to be driven by legislation, because of the conceptual complexity of the issues involved. This view remains very influential: for example, as of 2003, Lord Hope in *Relaxion Group v Rhys-Harper plc* commented as follows:

> [A]lthough discrimination on whatever grounds is widely regarded as morally unacceptable, the common law was unable to provide a sound basis for removing it ... Experience has taught us that this is a matter which can only be dealt with by legislation, and that it requires careful regulation by Parliament ... The fact is that the principle of equal treatment is easy to state but difficult to apply in practice.[54]

However, this scepticism about the capacity of the common law to handle equality issues sits a little uncomfortably with how the common law has developed over the last few decades: the normative dimension of the common law has

---

[49] *Constantine v Imperial Hotels Ltd* [1944] KB 693.

[50] [1958] 3 All ER 220.

[51] McColgan (n 8) 11.

[52] In 1972 Lester and Bindman observed that 'apart from their disapproval of slavery, English judges have never declared that acts of racial discrimination committed in this country are against public policy': see A Lester & G Bindman, *Race and Law* (London, Penguin, 1972) 25. See also ibid, 34, referring to the case of *Santos v Illidge* (1859) 6 CB (NS) 841.

[53] See in general B Hepple, *Race, Jobs and the Law in Britain* (London, Penguin, 1970) 143; see also McColgan (n 8).

[54] [2003] UKHL 33, [78].

deepened considerably, in response to the 'rights revolution' and shifts in the UK's constitutional self-understanding. This is particularly marked when it comes to the development of common law rights jurisprudence since the early 1990s (as described in detail in the other chapters of this book). Given the importance of equal status as both a right and a constitutional bedrock, it would be an interesting exception for the common law's historically stunted equality dimension to remain untouched by this process.

Furthermore, as discussed in Part II of this chapter, equality in both its formal and substantive dimensions has acquired much greater salience within the UK constitutional order over the last few decades. In particular, the importance of substantive equality is now acknowledged in both the political and legal spheres, in a way that was not the case when cases like *Constantine* and *Scala Ballroom* were being decided in the 1940s and 50s – while the concept of 'equality before the law' is now much more articulated within rule of law theorising by academics and judges alike than was the case back then. As a result, the formal and substantive dimensions of equality have acquired much greater definition than was hitherto the case. Again, this raises the question of whether the common law should evolve in response.

Jowell's 1994 paper was an attempt to jump-start the development of the common law in this regard. In essence, he argued that equality of status had become such an established and sufficiently articulated value within the UK constitutional order that the courts should take it into account in developing the common law. More specifically, he argued that 'our constitution rests upon the assumption that government should not impose upon any citizen any burden that depends upon an argument that ultimately forces the citizen to relinquish her or his sense of equal worth', and that the common law should give effect to this 'equality principle' by restraining public authorities from acting in a way that failed to respect equality of status.[55] Furthermore, Jowell suggested this principle should be regarded as a free-standing ground of review, capable of being applied in its own right to invalidate government action which was incompatible with its requirements. This would ensure it was 'explicitly articulated and declared' within the framework of administrative law adjudication, rather than being treated as a 'well-disguised rabbit to be hauled occasionally out of the *Wednesbury* hat'.[56]

Other commentators have subsequently made similar arguments, making the case for the equality principle to be treated on a par with other fundamental rights and principles that have become free-standing grounds of review within administrative law – such as access to justice, or the principle of legality. In Trevor Allan's view, this would ensure that the common law kept fidelity with the normative requirements of rule of law.[57] For Paul Bowen QC, this would enhance the common law's ability to act as a guarantor of individual rights, by reinforcing

---

[55] Jowell (n 1) 18.
[56] Ibid, 14.
[57] Allan (n 16) 246.

the existing protection afforded by the HRA and the Equality Act 2010 to the right to equality and non-discrimination.[58]

Giving legal weight in this way to the equality principle would arguably enhance the capacity of the common law to protect individuals against unequal treatment, by establishing a clearly-defined, distinct ground of review. It also could provide a clear common law basis for interpreting and applying legislation and other legal rules in ways that reflect the normative demands of the formal and substantive dimensions of equal status. It would also be in tune with the wider legal trend of recognising the existence of fundamental common law principles, and of ensuring that the common law was capable of protecting basic rights.

However, it would also introduce a newly recognised ground of review into an already well-populated administrative law landscape. Furthermore, the scope of the equality principle as defined by Jowell and others is potentially very wide: it could open up any differential treatment of similarly situated individuals that is deemed to affect 'equal worth' to judicial scrutiny. The HRA and anti-discrimination legislation already provide relatively comprehensive protection against discrimination in both the public and private law contexts.

Arguments thus can be made both for and against judicial recognition of a distinct equality principle within the common law. It is thus unsurprising that the courts have trod with some caution in this area. Enthusiastic affirmation of the constitutional significance of the equality principle has gone hand-in-hand with a tendency to keep its actual legal effect corralled within the framework of rationality review.

IV. The Current Status of Equality within the Common Law

The courts have repeatedly acknowledged the fundamental importance of equality of status to democracy and rule of law. For example, in the HRA case of *Ghaidan v Godin-Mendoza*, Baroness Hale concisely outlined the deep connection between democracy and equality:

> Democracy is founded on the principle that each individual has equal value. Treating some as automatically having less value than others not only causes pain and distress to that person but also violates his or her dignity as a human being.[59]

Indeed, it has become common for judges to genuflect to the constitutional significance of equality of status, both in obiter comments in judgments and speaking extra-judicially.

---

[58] P Bowen, 'Lion under the Throne or Rabbit from a Hat? Equality as a constitutional right in the law of the United Kingdom', conference paper, JUSTICE Human Rights Conference, 14 October 2016, on file with the author.
[59] [2004] UKHL 30, [132].

The courts have also affirmed that some variant of the equality principle is immanent to the common law. Lord Hoffmann referred in *Arthur JS Hall v Simons* to 'the fundamental principle of justice which requires that people should be treated equally and like cases treated alike',[60] while Rault J in *Police v Rose* affirmed that '[e]quality before the law requires that persons should be uniformly treated, unless there is some valid reason to treat them differently'.[61] Similarly, in *Edwards v SOGAT*,[62] a case involving the withdrawal of trade union rights, Lord Denning said '[t]he courts of this country will not allow so great a power to be exercised arbitrarily or capriciously or with unfair discrimination, neither in the making of rules or in the enforcement of them' – while Lord Sumption in *R (Rotherham Metropolitan Borough Council) v Secretary of State for Business, Innovation and Skills* recently pronounced to the effect that the equality principle was 'fundamental to any rational system of law'.[63]

By extension, the courts have been prepared to treat the equality principle as informing the application of irrationality review. It is now well-established doctrine that differential treatment of similarly situated persons that lacks objective justi-fication may be struck down on the basis that it is *Wednesbury* unreasonable. Lord Russell CJ affirmed in *Kruse v Johnson* that byelaws could be struck down as 'unreasonable' if it they were 'partial and unequal in their operation as between different classes'.[64] This was cited by Simon Brown J in *R v Immigration Appeal Tribunal, ex p. Manshoora Begum*,[65] in concluded that a provision in the Immigra-tion Rules was 'manifestly unjust' on account of how it applied minimum income requirements for leave to enter in a discriminatory fashion as between inhabitants of poorer and more affluent states. Similarly, in *Middlebrook Mushrooms*,[66] Stanley Burton J ruled that the exclusion of mushroom pickers from a set minimum harvesting wage was a form of differential treatment that could not be objectively justified in the circumstances – and thus was irrational.[67]

Cases with a substantive equality dimension can also fall within rational-ity review. Thus, in *Gurung v Ministry of Defence*,[68] McCombe J concluded that unjustifiable distinctions based on racial or ethnic distinctions would be 'irra-tional and inconsistent with the principle of equality that is the cornerstone of our law', while concluding that the exclusion of Gurkha soldiers from the scheme of compensation payments awarded to former Japanese prisoners of war was

---

[60] [2002] 1 AC 615, 688–9. See also Lord Donaldson MR in *R (Cheung) v Hertfordshire County Council, The Times*, 4 April 1998: '[i]t is a cardinal principle of public administration that all persons in a similar position should be treated similarly', cited in *De Smith* (n 6) [13-041].

[61] [1976] MR 79, 81.

[62] [1971] Ch 354.

[63] [2015] UKSC 6, [26].

[64] [1898] 2 QB 91.

[65] [1986] Imm AR 385.

[66] [2004] EWHC 1447 (Admin).

[67] *R (Middlebrook Mushrooms Ltd) v Agricultural Wages Board of England & Wales* [2004] EWHC 1447 (Admin), [74], citing Lord Donaldson MR's comments in *Cheung* (n 60).

[68] [2002] EWHC 2463 (Admin).

irrational. Similarly, in *R (Limbu) v Secretary of State for the Home Department*,[69] another case concerning race and ethnicity discrimination claims related to the treatment of Gurkhas who had served in the armed forces, Blake J was of the view that this 'common law principle [of equality] is an important instrument whereby it can be determined whether a discretionary public law decision is rational' – even though he concluded on the facts that the treatment of Gurkhas by the immigration authorities under review in that case did not breach the principle.

The courts have also occasionally applied other common law grounds of review in a way that has given indirect effect to the equality principle. For example, De Smith cites a number of cases where unequal treatment fell foul of the procedural requirement to take relevant considerations into account.[70] However, in general, equality and discrimination claims have been argued and adjudicated by reference to the irrationality ground of review.

The assumption underpinning this approach is that differences in treatment that cannot be objectively justified lack rational foundation – with judges often classifying discriminatory behaviour as motivated by stereotyping, prejudice and other forms of 'bad faith' reasoning.[71] Indeed, the classic example of *Wednesbury* unreasonableness, as originally set out in Warrington LJ in *Short v Poole Corporation*[72] and subsequently cited by Lord Greene MR in *Wednesbury* itself, constitutes a flagrant breach of formal equality principle – namely 'the red-haired teacher, dismissed because she had red hair'.[73] Paul Daly has argued it is consistent with the 'internal logic and structure' of *Wednesbury* unreasonableness to treat differential treatment as one of the 'indicia' of irrationality, generating a presumption of unreasonableness unless objectively justified.[74]

However, framing breaches of the equality principle as instances of irrationality also generates some conceptual difficulties. Irrationality is a fluid and uncertain concept, which is inherently prone to subjective interpretation. Insofar as it has a conceptual core, it is structured round the idea of 'reasonableness': decisions by public authorities must usually be shown to be clearly unreasonable before a challenge on this ground can succeed. However, discriminatory practices are often based on received wisdom, or embedded assumptions about how particular matters should be handled. As a consequence, their unreasonableness is rarely self-evident.[75] Taken together with the inchoate nature of this test and its vulnerability to subjective interpretation, this means that rationality review has often proved to be a poor diagnostic tool for identifying breaches of the equality principle.

---

[69] [2008] EWHC 2261 (Admin), [50].
[70] *De Smith* (n 6) [11.061–11.068].
[71] B Hale, 'The Quest for Equal Treatment' [2005] *PL* 571–585.
[72] [1926] Ch 66, 90, 91.
[73] *Associated Provincial Picture Houses Ltd v Wednesbury Corporation* [1948] 1 KB 223, 229.
[74] P Daly, '*Wednesbury*'s Reason and Structure' [2011] *PL* 237.
[75] McColgan (n 8) 12.

Short v Poole Corporation, already cited above, illustrates this problem.[76] In that case, the Court of Appeal upheld that a decision by a public authority to terminate the employment contract of a teacher after it concluded that her husband would be able to 'maintain her'. The dismissed teacher had a husband to look after her, and her job could be given to another – meaning that, in the Court's view, the decision was not based on 'alien and irrelevant grounds'.[77] This conclusion would now be plainly incompatible with the requirements of the equality principle.[78] McCombe J acknowledged as much in *Gurung*: 'the facts [of *Short*] may well provide an example of a danger of decision makers today adopting a "rationality" based upon the criteria of yesterday'.[79]

Furthermore, rationality review focuses on the coherence of public authority decision-making, while the equality principle focuses on whether public authority decision-making shows sufficient respect for the concept of equal status. The two lines of analysis will often overlap. But there are times when discriminatory treatment will often be motivated by eminently rational concerns, which may nevertheless be insufficiently compelling to satisfy the demands of the equality principle. Thus, for example, the outcome of cases such as *Middlebury* and *Gurung* flow from the failure of public authorities to provide *adequate* justification for differential treatment, rather than from a failure to provide a rational justification as such for their actions. This makes rationality review an awkward receptacle for the equality principle: labels such as 'reasonableness' or 'irrationality' do not describe what is really driving the outcome of such judgments.

Perhaps conscious of these tensions, the courts have retooled aspects of rationality review to accommodate the equality principle. Case-law has clarified that 'flawed logic, more readily shown than a decision which simply defies comprehension, may breach the principle of rationality', as Ouseley J put it in *R (Gurung) v Secretary of State for Defence* (another equal treatment case involving the situation of Gurkha ex-soldiers.)[80]

Furthermore, the courts have sometimes been prepared to apply more intensive scrutiny in cases involved alleged infringements of the right to non-discrimination, and thus the substantive dimension of the equality principle – reflecting the 'anxious scrutiny' approach now applied to common law rights claims more generally.[81] There are even suggestions in the case-law that a similar intensity of review should be applied to common law equality claims as is applied to Article 14 ECHR claims. Thus Ouseley J in *R (Gurung) v Secretary of State for the Defence* indicated that when equality rights

> are interfered with, the greater the scrutiny to which the reason for the interference will be subjected … [T]he consideration of the human rights claim, which would

[76] [1926] ch 66.
[77] Ibid, 91 (Warrington LJ).
[78] The initial decision by the public authority would also now be an obvious breach of the sex discrimination provisions of the Equality Act 2010.
[79] [2002] EWHC 2463 (Admin), [35].
[80] [2008] EWHC 1496 (Admin).
[81] See Bingham MR (as he was then) in *R (Ministry of Defence), ex parte Smith* [1996] QB 517.

often require a more intrusive analysis of the basis of the claimed justification, is likely to be satisfied on the same basis as or in step with what would satisfy rationality in public law.[82]

Blake J in *Limbu* similarly took the view that 'the common law and Convention principle essentially walk hand in hand together, although the common law principle [of equality] has to be applied through the public law doctrine of rationality'.[83]

However this intensity of review is not always consistently applied across all common law cases with a substantive equality dimension. For example, McColgan has argued that a less exacting standard was applied in *ABCIFER v Secretary of State for Defence*.[84] This case concerned an irrationality challenge to the exclusion of British civilian subjects who were neither born in the UK nor had a parent or grandparent so born from a compensation scheme for civilians interned by the Japanese during the Second World War. In his judgment, Scott Baker J suggested it was 'reasonable' for the UK Government to distinguish between persons with a clear link to the territory of the UK and those who did not. As McColgan notes, it is debatable whether this conclusion is compatible with a rigorous application of anxious scrutiny review, especially if the purpose of the compensation scheme and the background historical context are taken into account.[85] Instead, the judgment in *ABCIFER* is probably best viewed as an application of the weaker reasonableness standard, which is more commonly applied in rationality review cases than intensive scrutiny. The language associated with this test – as distinct from the more demanding standard associated with rights review either under the ECHR or common law – has been used in subsequent judgments relating to race discrimination claims litigated through rationality review.[86]

Furthermore, uncertainty persists as to what level of scrutiny should be applied when it comes to cases involving an allegation of a breach of formal equality requirements – as distinct from the substantive equality issues at stake in cases like *ABCIFER* and *Gurung v Ministry of Defence*. This is evident from the judgment of the UK Supreme Court in *R (Rotherham Metropolitan Borough Council) v Secretary of State for Business, Innovation and Skills*,[87] the first case where the UK's apex court has taken account of the equality principle in an administrative law context. *Rotherham* involved a challenge to how the Secretary of State had allocated EU

---

[82] [2008] EWHC 1496 (Admin), [54], [60].

[83] [2008] EWHC 2261 (Admin), [50].

[84] [2002] EWHC 2119 (Admin).

[85] McColgan (n 8) 12.

[86] See, eg, Ouseley J's judgment in *R (Gurung) v Secretary of State for the Defence* [2002] EWHC 2119 (Admin): '[t]hat principle also requires a rational connection between the problem to be solved or aim to be advanced and the means chosen to solve the problem or to advance the aim. The [measure under challenge] comes well within the range of responses available to a reasonable decision-maker. I also accept that where, i.e. within the range of responses open to a reasonable decision maker'. See also *R (Mohammed) v Secretary of State for Defence* (2007) 104 LSG 32; *R (Mohammed Rafi Hottak and Al) v Secretary of State for Foreign and Commonwealth Affairs* [2016] EWCA Civ 438.

[87] [2015] UKSC 6.

structural funds to different regions across the UK, with the applicants arguing that this process had unjustly discriminated against certain regions in the north of England. The Supreme Court agreed that the differential treatment in question could be subject to rationality review under the common law, as well as under the general principle of equal treatment recognised in EU law. The majority of the Court then proceeded to apply a very light touch standard of review in concluding that the differential treatment in question was not unjust, as is usually the case when such decisions involve resource allocation. However, in dissenting, Lords Mance and Carnworth (with Lady Hale concurring) took the view that 'closer review' could be applied in cases such as this where there was a 'failure to treat like cases alike' – especially when the decision in question had been taken on an informal basis and without prior consultation.[88]

This 4-3 divide in *Rotherham* is striking, especially given the leeway normally given to resource allocation decisions by public authorities. The minority regarded such treatment as a pressing 'indicator' of unreasonableness (to use Daly's terminology), with the burden passing to the Secretary of State to show a clear justification. In contrast, the majority applied a much less demanding level of scrutiny, which was more in tune with the traditional light touch associated with *Wednesbury* unreasonableness.

These uncertainties relating to the appropriate standard of review, as well as to what qualifies more generally as 'irrational' behaviour, are symptoms of a wider problem – namely the inherent difficulties of accommodating the equality principle within the confines of rationality review. As originally set out in cases such as *Short* and *Wednesbury*, this ground of review was conceptualised as setting a forbiddingly high threshold for judicial intervention, only to be crossed in situations where public authorities had behaved in a manifestly irrational manner. However, these expectations sit uneasily with the value now assigned to the equality principle, and the widespread view that courts should play an active role in reviewing conformity with its normative demands.[89] Adjusting the standard template of rationality review to give effect to the principle, by for example applying heightened scrutiny in substantive equality cases, can help to reduce this inherent tension. However, this stretching of *Wednesbury* unreasonableness is problematic from the point of view of coherence and clarity. As Jowell argued in 1994, it risks turning the equality principle into a 'well-disguised rabbit' to be pulled periodically out of the *Wednesbury* hat as and when judges see fit.

Some commentators have taken the view that a better approach would be to classify the existing 'equality as rationality' jurisprudence as an aspect of a wider legal framework structured around the equality principle. They regard cases like *Middlebrook* and *Gurung* as in effect involving the direct application of the equality principle, with 'irrationality' simply serving as an artificial label for what is

---

[88] Ibid, [142] (Lord Mance), [167] (Lord Carnwath).
[89] I am grateful to Mark Elliott for this point.

really going on in these cases – namely the review of state action by reference to an overarching 'constitutional principle of equality' which also is protected by EU law and Article 14 ECHR.[90] However, this take on the status of the equality principle – which is for example adopted in De Smith – overeggs the current status quo. The courts have been slow to set the equality principle free from its irrationality shackles, reflecting their historic caution in this area.

Lord Hoffmann's judgment in the Privy Council case of *Matadeen v Pointu* has been a regular point of reference in this regard.[91] *Matadeen* concerned a challenge to a regulation introduced by the government of Mauritius, on the basis that it gave an unfair advantage in the university admissions exam process to secondary school students studying an Asian language. The Supreme Court of Mauritius interpreted sections 1 and 3 of the Mauritian Constitution, which taken together guarantee the enjoyment without discrimination of the protection of the law and other basic democratic rights and freedoms, as setting out a general justiciable principle of equality[92] – before proceeding to strike down the regulation at issue, on the basis it offended against this principle. In contrast, the Privy Council concluded that the provisions of the circumscribed non-discrimination clause set out in section 3 of the constitution, which was similar in substance to Article 14 ECHR, could not be read as establishing the existence of such a justiciable general equality principle. Giving the judgment of the Judicial Committee, Lord Hoffmann affirmed the importance of the equality principle to rule of law and constitutional democracy more generally – citing Jowell's 1994 paper in so doing. He also recognised that it could be invoked as a 'ground' of irrationality, thereby implicitly endorsing the expanded approach to rationality review that the lower courts have adopted with respect to the equality principle.[93] However, in a much-cited passage, he went on to express concern about the uncertain scope of the principle:[94]

> Their Lordships do not doubt that such a principle is one of the building blocks of democracy and necessarily permeates any democratic constitution. Indeed, their Lordships would go further and say that treating like cases alike and unlike cases differently is a general axiom of rational behaviour. It is, for example, frequently invoked by the courts in proceedings for judicial review as a ground for holding some administrative act to have been irrational: see Professor Jeffrey Jowell Q.C., *Is Equality a Constitutional Principle?* [1994] Current Legal Problems 1, 12–14 and De Smith, Woolf and Jowell, *Judicial Review of Administrative Action*, paras. 13-036 to 13-045.

---

[90] Lord Steyn in 2002 welcomed what he saw as the development by the UK courts of a domestic 'constitutional principle of equality', on the basis that it constituted a welcome 'organic development of constitutional rights', which complemented the less extensive protection provided by Art 14 ECHR with its limited scope of application: see Lord Steyn, Lecture on 18 September 2002 in honour of Lord Cooke of Thorndon, text cited by McCombe J in *Gurung* (n 68) [36].

[91] [1999] 1 AC 98.

[92] In so doing, the Mauritian Supreme Court said that 'the notion of equality ... is contained ... in the concept of democracy', noted that the 'principle of equality ... permeates the whole Constitution', and cited the provisions of Art 26 of the ICCPR in support of their interpretation: ibid, [7].

[93] [1999] 1 AC 98, 109.

[94] Ibid, 109.

But the very banality of the principle must suggest a doubt as to whether merely to state it can provide an answer to the kind of problem which arises in this case. Of course persons should be uniformly treated, unless there is some valid reason to treat them differently. But what counts as a valid reason for treating them differently? And, perhaps more important, who is to decide whether the reason is valid or not? ... The fact that equality of treatment is a general principle of rational behaviour does not entail that it should necessarily be a justiciable principle – that it should always be the judges who have the last word on whether the principle has been observed ...

Lord Hoffmann's comments about the uncertain scope of the equality principle relate specifically to the issues of constitutional interpretation at stake in *Matadeen* and the potential limits it might impose on the powers of the Mauritian legislature – an issue that is not directly relevant in the UK with its sovereign legislature. Furthermore, they relate to the formal dimension of the equality principle: section 3 of the Mauritian Constitution contains a specific non-discrimination clause prohibiting discrimination by the legislature on race, gender and other 'status' grounds.[95] However, Lord Hoffmann's concerns about the uncertain scope of the equality principle – and the potential scope it might open up for excessive judicial inference with executive and legislative decision-making – have nevertheless resonated.

This is evident in the most recent UK Supreme Court decision concerning the equality principle, namely *R (Gallaher Group Ltd) v Competition and Markets Authority*.[96] This case involved claims that the Office of Fair Trading (OFT) had subjected different parties caught up in a price-fixing investigation to unfair and unequal treatment. The Supreme Court reversed the Court of Appeal's finding that inter alia these other parties had been treated unequally without objective justification, concluding that the OFT had acted reasonably. However the most interesting element of the judgment was the Court's conclusion that the equality principle did not have free-standing status within the common law.

Giving the leading judgment, Lord Carnwath commented that '[w]hatever the position in European law or under other constitutions or jurisdictions, the domestic law of this country does not recognise equal treatment as a distinct principle of administrative law'.[97] He went on to state that '[c]onsistency ... is a generally desirable objective, but not an absolute rule', before citing Lord Hoffmann's comments in *Matadeen* as authority for the proposition that there was a need 'to distinguish between equal treatment as a democratic principle and as a justiciable rule of law'.[98] He concluded that issues of consistency of treatment would generally arise only 'as aspects of rationality'.[99]

---

[95] As noted by McCombe J in *Gurung* (n 68) [39].
[96] [2018] UKSC 25, [50].
[97] Ibid, [24].
[98] Ibid, [26].
[99] Ibid.

In his concurring judgment, Lord Sumption took a similar view. In so doing, he clarified his earlier judgment in *Rotherham*, where he had described the equality principle as 'fundamental to any rational system of law, and ... part of English public law since at least the end of the nineteenth century'.[100] That passage in *Rotherham* had contained no reference to the principle constituting an aspect of rationality: if anything, it seemed to suggest it was a free-standing element of administrative law. However, in *Gallaher*, he was at pains to put the principle back into its *Wednesbury* box:

> In public law, as in most other areas of law, it is important not unnecessarily to multiply categories. It tends to undermine the coherence of the law by generating a mass of disparate special rules distinct from those applying in public law generally or those which apply to neighbouring categories. To say that a decision-maker must treat persons equally unless there is a reason for treating them differently begs the question what counts as a valid reason for treating them differently. Consistency of treatment is, as Lord Hoffmann observed in *Matedeen v Pointu* [1999] 1 AC 98, at para 9 'a general axiom of rational behaviour'. The common law principle of equality is usually no more than a particular application of the ordinary requirement of rationality imposed on public authorities.[101]

Gallaher thus establishes that the equality principle is, for all its constitutional significance, just an 'aspect of rationality'.[102] Two sets of justifications are offered for this conclusion. Lord Carnwath cites Lord Hoffmann's concerns in *Matadeen* about the uncertain scope of the principle: Lord Sumption cites the need to avoid unnecessary multiplication of different categories of review. Taken together, these concerns are invoked to close down the argument that the equality principle should have free-standing status – and to affirm the traditional caution sown by the courts in giving effect to equality as a value through the common law.

However, while *Gallaher* may appear to settle this point, it may not generate the legal certainty and clarity that Lords Carnwath and Sumption are seeking to achieve. As already discussed, the equality principle fits awkwardly within rationality review. Indeed, if anything, *Gallaher* may add to this awkwardness. In his leading judgment, Lord Carnwath described the common law case-law and various HRA judgments involving Article 14 ECHR as reflecting a common commitment to rationality.[103] This could be read as suggesting that a broadly similar approach should be adopted in both Article 14 and at least some common law equality cases – despite the level and type (proportionality) of scrutiny applied in Article 14 claims being viewed as generally more demanding than the scrutiny standards applied in rationality claims. In turn, this suggests that the heightened

---

[100] Ibid, [26].

[101] Ibid, [50].

[102] *Gallaher* did not involve any 'status' ground of discrimination: however, there is no indication in any of the judgments that the Court intended to draw a distinction between the formal and substantive dimensions of the principle.

[103] See also *R (MM) v SSHD* [2014] EWCA Civ 985, [95], [153].

level of scrutiny applied in cases like *Gurung* is justified. This means that rationality review involving allegations of unequal treatment will continue to have teeth. However, it also means that the current problems of 'fit', clarity and coherence will continue to be a problem.

Gallaher also leaves other issues open. If equality is 'not a distinct principle of administrative law' or a 'justiciable rule of law' in its own right, but only a dimension of rationality, what if any role should it play in statutory interpretation? Legislation like the Equality Act 2010 will obviously be interpreted by reference to the underlying intention of Parliament to provide effective protection against discrimination. But should the constitutional significance of the equality principle be taken into account in interpreting other statutes, if for the purposes of the common law it is 'only' an aspect of rationality? There is nothing in *Gallaher* that necessarily closes off this possibility. However, the apparent downgrading of equality as compared to access to justice and other recognised free-standing common law principles does raise the question of what weight should be attached to it when it comes to interpreting statutes or reviewing secondary legislation.[104]

Finally, it should be borne in mind that the unequal treatment at issue in *Gallaher* did not generate any concerns from a substantive equality perspective. This leaves open the possibility that the Supreme Court's approach in *Gallaher* could be distinguished in future cases with a substantive equality dimension. However, there is no explicit basis in the *Gallaher* judgment for making such a distinction between formal and substantive equality cases. The Supreme Court did not engage in any substantive discussion of the differing normative requirements associated with these different component elements of the equality principle, beyond acknowledging the well-established rule that certain 'suspect' discrimination grounds such as race would attract more demanding scrutiny.

V. A Critical Analysis of the Status of Equality within the Common Law

The cautious approach traditionally adopted by the courts in giving effect to the equality principle in the common law is thus on full display in *Gallaher*. The judgment affirms the importance of the equality principle in the abstract, but denies it free-standing status.

Is this situation satisfactory? Lord Hoffmann's concerns in *Matadeen* have some validity: there are reasons to be wary of opening up government action to review

---

[104] Note that the Equality and Human Rights Commission argued in an intervention before the Supreme Court in the case of *P v Commissioner of Police of the Metropolis* [2017] UKSC 65 that the provisions of the Equality Act 2010 should be interpreted in a manner that reflected the constitutional significance of the equality principle. The subsequent judgment did not engage with this argument. (Full disclosure: the author provided assistance to Paul Bowen QC in framing this intervention.)

by reference to the equality principle, because of the width of its potential scope of application. As such, the status quo has the advantage of providing an indirect degree of common law protection for the equality principle, and by extension for the related individual right to equality and non-discrimination – while channelling legal challenges through the tried and trusted framework of rationality review.

However, it also has a down side. As discussed, the status quo generates a degree of doctrinal incoherence, and dilutes the status of equality as an important common law value. It also promises more legal certainty than it provides in practice. Jowell's concern that the equality principle would become a 'well-disguised rabbit', to be hauled out of the *Wednesbury* hat as and when judges deem it appropriate, is well-founded – as illustrated by the readiness of the courts to apply a level of scrutiny analogous to that applied under the HRA in cases such as *Gurung*, which would appear to go well beyond the less demanding standards normally applied in rationality review.

Furthermore, keeping equality subsumed within irrationality, while other foundational rights and principles such as access to justice are treated as freestanding common law norms, generates problems of conceptual consistency. It is striking that other core principles have been elevated to the status of common law rights/principles, while equality languishes within its irrationality box.

None of these issues were discussed in the Supreme Court's reasoning in *Gallaher*, which was rather perfunctory.[105] Lord Sumption's desire to prevent an 'unnecessary multiplication' of existing categories of administrative law review is understandable. However, as Mark Elliott has argued in response, 'concern about too much doctrine too many grounds of review must … be balanced with a countervailing concern about too little doctrine'.[106] Keeping the equality principle boxed up within rationality review for the sake of doctrinal simplification risks becoming counter-productive, if it has the effect of further diluting the clarity and coherence of the latter ground of review. Indeed, it may even open the door to the type of ad hoc judicial decision-making that both Lord Hoffmann in *Matadeen* and Lord Carnwath in *Gallaher* are so concerned to avoid, by encouraging courts to apply rationality review in an elastic and malleable manner so as to accommodate the normative demands of the equality principle. Jowell had a point in 1994 when he argued that treating the equality principle as a free-standing ground of review would ensure a closer focus on its specific normative requirements, and allow the courts to build up a coherent case-law structured around a direct and systematic engagement with these requirements rather than being refracted through the potentially distorting lens of irrationality.[107]

---

[105] Counsel for both sides argued the case on the assumption that the equality principle was a freestanding ground of review, meaning that the Court was denied the benefit of counsel's opinion on this issue.

[106] M Elliott, 'Consistency as a free-standing principle of administrative law?', *Public Law for Everyone Blog*, 15 June 2018, available at https://publiclawforeveryone.com/2018/06/15/the-supreme-courts-judgment-in-gallaher-consistency-as-a-free-standing-principle-of-administrative-law.

[107] Elliott has made a similar argument in favour of recognising 'consistency' as a free-standing common law principle: see Elliott (n 106).

In general, the Supreme Court's approach in *Gallaher* represents a wasted opportunity. The Court could have elected to treat the equality principle as having a distinct and free-standing status within the common law, and gone on to delineate its substantive and formal dimensions – taking the time to emphasise the greater normative demands and associated higher levels of scrutiny associated with the former as opposed to the latter, along the constitutional significance of equal status and the associated individual right to equality and non-discrimination. This would have helped to remedy the uncertain state of the common law in this context, and provided invaluable guidance to lower courts. It would also have helped to clarify the scope and substance of the equality principle, and given legal actors a better sense of the relative 'demandingness' of its disaggregated formal and substantive elements – which by extension could help minimise the risk of judicial ad hoc decision-making in this context. It would also have moved forward the project of modernising the value system of the common law, by ensuring it adequately reflected the constitutional importance of equal status.

However, in *Gallaher*, the Supreme Court clung to traditional orthodoxy – in interesting contrast to its willingness to develop common law norms in other contexts.[108] This leaves the existing status of the equality principle, and legal protection more generally within the common law for the right to equality and non-discrimination, enmeshed in a messy relationship with rationality review.

VI. Conclusion – Time to Think Again

Does it matter that the status of the equality principle within the common law is less than satisfactory? The Equality Act 2010 and the HRA/ECHR provide extensive legislative protection for equality and non-discrimination rights. This covers much of the substantive dimension of the equality principle, which is generally acknowledged to be more 'demanding' and in need of stronger legal protection than the formal equality concerns that form the subject matter of much of the common law case-law. Given this, and the well-established judicial preference for letting the legislature take the initiative in putting legal flesh on the bones of the concept of equal status, is there really much of a need to be concerned with what was said or not said in cases such as *Gallaher*?

The answer to this is 'yes'. There are grounds to be concerned about the current sub-optimal state of the common law.

To start with, the scope of the Equality Act 2010 and the HRA as it applies to equality and non-discrimination are limited in important ways. The 2010 Act only covers discrimination based on certain 'suspect' characteristics: differential treatment based on any other grounds falls outside of its reach. Also, the

---

[108] See, eg, *Unison* (n 47).

Act does apply to the performance of public functions, but only insofar as the discriminatory behaviour in question is not 'authorised' by primary or secondary legislation.[109] The HRA is wider in scope, with Article 14 ECHR covering all discrimination based on 'status' grounds. However, it only prohibits unjustified discrimination in the enjoyment of other Convention rights, and does not apply to unequal treatment that is not based upon a status ground, ie it has limited applicability to formal equality. The jurisprudence of the European Court of Human Rights has narrowed these limits to the scope of Article 14 ECHR, but they remain a restriction on its reach.[110]

Furthermore, both the 2010 Act and HRA are 'just' legislation, ie they are amendable or repealable instruments, with the HRA in particular being the focus of substantial political hostility. In contrast, the equality provisions of EU law benefit from the supremacy of European law. However, they have limited reach outside of the employment context and/or situations where national law is 'implementing' EU law – and, of course, they will lose their insulated status when and if Brexit happens.[111]

All this means that the common law has a distinctive role to play in protecting the equality principle and the associated right to equality and non-discrimination. At present, it fills gaps left by the HRA and the anti-discrimination legislative framework, especially in relation to (i) breaches of formal equality and (ii) substantive status-based discrimination that falls outside the 'ambit' of other ECHR rights and thus outside the scope of Article 14. By giving legal expression to the constitutionally significant value of equality of status, it also affirms its importance as a key principle of the legal order – thereby also confirming its normative importance as a reference point in interpreting legislation and developing other common law norms in the areas of public and private law. In the future, it may even be called upon to play a greater role in vindicating equality of status, depending on the fate of the HRA and post-Brexit developments.

Given all this, it is unfortunate that the common law equality jurisprudence remains in a less than satisfactory state. Judicial endorsements of the fundamental status of the equality principle have not been matched by a close engagement with its normative specificity, or the distinctions that exist between its formal and substantive dimensions. Instead, it remains enmeshed in a complex and unsatisfactory relationship with rationality review. What Jowell argued back in 1994 thus remains relevant today: it is time to think again about the place of equality and non-discrimination within the common law scheme.

---

[109] See Sch 23 of the Equality Act 2010.

[110] See in general R O'Connell, 'Cinderella Comes to the Ball: Art 14 and the Right to Non-Discrimination in the ECHR' (2009) 29 *Legal Studies* 211.

[111] C O'Cinneide, 'Brexit and Human Rights', in O Fitzgerald and E Lein, *Complexity's Embrace: The International Law Implications of Brexit* (Montreal, McGill-Queen's University Press, 2018) 297.

PART II

The Role and Potential
of Common Law Constitutional Rights

9

The Fundamentality of Rights at Common Law

MARK ELLIOTT*

I. Introduction

The concern of this chapter is with the senses in, and the extent to, which common law constitutional rights can properly be regarded as fundamental. In the context of the UK's constitution, that issue is placed in particularly sharp relief by the (at least superficial) tension between the very idea of fundamental rights and the notion of a sovereign Parliament that, if it really is sovereign, must be capable of limiting or even abrogating rights, however 'fundamental' they might be. A crucial question thus arises about whether rights can in any meaningful sense be regarded as fundamental within in a legal system that adheres to the concept of legislative supremacy.

This, in turn, raises a series of issues that this chapter sets out to interrogate. For instance, it is necessary to consider what it actually means for a right to be 'fundamental' and, in particular, whether any meaningful sense of fundamentality can co-exist with the notion of parliamentary sovereignty. This, in turn, raises questions about the ways in which rights can be protected – and thus potentially accorded a pragmatic degree of, if not absolute, fundamentality – without denying the capacity of a sovereign Parliament to restrict or remove them. It also raises questions – which take us into deeper constitutional waters – about the limits of parliamentary authority, and about whether it remains accurate to conceive of common law constitutional rights as inevitably vulnerable to legislative revocation. In this chapter, I argue that while the answers to some of these questions (perhaps inevitably) remain uncertain, due appreciation of the constitutional context within which common law rights and parliamentary sovereignty sit facilitates an understanding of such rights that accords to them a meaningful, if not an unqualified, form of fundamentality.

* I am very grateful to Kirsty Hughes for her comments on an earlier draft of this chapter.

The analysis set out in this chapter proceeds in three stages. First, the capacity of common law rights to enjoy perceived legitimacy – which, for reasons that will be explained, may in turn bear upon their fundamentality as a matter of legal practice – will be considered. Second, from the discussion concerning legitimacy, three sets of distinctions will be distilled, each of which is relevant to the senses in which common law rights might be 'fundamental'. These distinctions – between what will be termed hard and soft understandings of fundamentality, theoretical and operational senses of the same, and the depth and breadth of common law rights – serve to calibrate more precisely the extent to and the way in which common law rights might properly be considered to be fundamental. Third, the mechanisms through which common law rights' fundamentality is capable of finding expression within the confines of the UK's constitutional framework will be considered. Here, the focus will be on the role of courts as reviewers of the legality of administrative action and as interpreters of legislation. This inquiry will be undertaken in principally empirical, as distinct from normative, terms: that is, the purpose of the chapter is not to argue that the UK constitution ought to be conceived of in a particular way so as to furnish a given degree of protection to fundamental rights; rather, the aim is to examine the capacity of the UK constitutional order, as it is presently understood, to protect rights in ways that render them meaningfully 'fundamental'.

II. Legitimacy

The idea of fundamental, or 'constitutional', common law rights was given a shot in the arm in the 1990s through the extra-curial writings of several prominent judicial figures. Among the most influential contributions to the debate about common law rights and allied constitutional questions were those of Lord Woolf, who would go on to become Master of the Rolls and Lord Chief Justice, and Sir John Laws, who would go on to be a Lord Justice of Appeal. Of current relevance are their papers that appeared consecutively in the journal *Public Law* in 1995. Although very different from one another in many respects, the two articles evidenced, in one sense at least, a shared outlook concerning the very essence of the British constitution – and, pertinently for present purposes, its capacity to accord fundamental status to legal norms, including rights. In his article, Laws sketched a vision of the British constitution in which 'fundamental individual rights' are 'vindicated by a higher-order law'.[1] For his part, Woolf argued that Parliament (like the courts) 'derive[s] [its] authority from the rule of law', such that it is 'subject to' the rule of law and cannot act 'in a manner which

---

[1] J Laws, 'Law and Democracy' [1995] *PL* 72, 85. Laws went on to develop and refine his thesis in many other lectures and articles. See, in particular, the Hamlyn Lectures that he gave in 2013: J Laws, *The Common Law Constitution* (Cambridge, Cambridge University Press, 2014).

involves its repudiation'.[2] It followed, he went on, that if Parliament were to 'do the unthinkable', by legislating contrary to the rule of law, 'the courts would also be required' – not permitted, but *required* – 'to act in a manner which would be without precedent'.[3] In doing so, they would be acknowledging 'that ultimately there are even limits on the supremacy of Parliament which it is the courts' inalienable responsibility to identify and uphold'.[4]

These remarks raise critical questions about the architecture of the UK constitution, and their articulation – now more than two decades ago – by senior judges was, to say the least, striking. The veracity of the constitutional worldview inherent in the writings of the likes of Laws and Woolf is obviously pertinent to the question of the extent to which common law rights can be protected in the face of adverse legislation and so, in that sense, to the question of such rights' fundamentality. Those questions will be examined later in this chapter.[5] For the time being, however, our concern is with a distinct, albeit related, issue that is brought to the surface by views such as these: namely, the legitimacy concerns that they raise, and the relevance, if any, of such concerns to the potential degree of common law rights' legal fundamentality. In that regard, the stinging criticism that Woolf's and Laws's articles drew from Lord Irvine is worth noting. He described the suggestion that judges could set aside Acts of Parliament as an 'exorbitant claim' that 'smacks of judicial supremacism' – a term that he certainly did not intend as a compliment.[6] That Irvine wrote in these terms in 1996, only a year before he was to become Lord Chancellor in Tony Blair's first government, is doubtless significant; at least viewed in retrospect, it amounts to nothing less than an anticipatory ministerial shot across the judiciary's bows. It is also noteworthy that Irvine is credited as a principal architect of the Human Rights Act 1998 (HRA), which erected a carefully calibrated statutory framework around the protection of fundamental (Convention) rights that explicitly denied their priority in the face of incompatible primary legislation.

This exchange of views serves to highlight the risks to which judges may expose themselves in this sphere. When constitutional theses such as those advanced by Laws and Woolf are boiled down to their essentials, and considered with common law rights specifically in mind, they consist of three key propositions: first, that it is for judges to determine, albeit subject to the usual disciplines and constraints of the common law method, what in the first place falls within the 'fundamental rights' category; second, that it is for judges to decide what it means for a right to be 'fundamental', in the sense of prescribing the consequences that may flow from a right's possessing of such a status; and, third, that one of those

---

[2] H Woolf, '*Droit Public* – English Style' [1995] *PL* 57, 68.

[3] Ibid, 69.

[4] Ibid.

[5] See section V below.

[6] D Irvine, 'Judges and Decision Makers: The Theory and Practice of *Wednesbury* Review' [1996] *PL* 59, 77.

consequences may be the invalidation of other legal norms, up to and including provisions contained in Acts of the UK Parliament.

Now, it is certainly possible to construct an argument that supports these propositions – and there is no shortage of such arguments in the literature.[7] Indeed, Laws himself, in the article referred to above, sets about the task of developing precisely such an argument, grounding his thesis in a particular vision of democracy. On this analysis, 'those who exercise democratic, political power must have limits set to what they may do: limits which they are not allowed to overstep', meaning that 'it is a function of democratic power itself that it be not absolute'.[8] That it is possible to envisage laws that could fairly be characterised as incompatible with democratic principles is hard to argue against, even if, paradoxically, such laws emerge from an ostensibly democratic institution. Crucially, however, for Laws this insight sounds in necessarily *legal* terms, meaning that it is not merely open to, but is incumbent upon, courts to articulate and enforce relevant limitations upon administrative and legislative power. One might or (like Irvine) might not find that view persuasive, but my concern here is not to evaluate its persuasiveness. Rather, it is to underline its undeniable contestability, and to consider what the implications of that contestability might be.

In doing so, it is important to be clear about exactly what it is that is contestable (and contested) – or, more precisely, what it is that is *especially* contestable (and contested). Here, it is helpful to draw a broad distinction between, on the one hand, judicial articulation, curation and protection of common law rights and, on the other, judicial insistence – à la Laws and Woolf – upon the ultimate priority of such rights. For a common law judge to identify, say, a right to freedom of expression or of access to court and to take limited steps to uphold it – by, for instance, examining the proportionality of administrative decisions that threaten such rights or, when construing a statutory provision, preferring an interpretation that is sympathetic rather than antithetical to the right – is unlikely to invite great controversy. Indeed, we can go further: courts do such things on a relatively regular basis and this *does not* generally invite such controversy. It would, however, be naïve in the extreme to suppose that the same would be true if a court were to purport to strike down, or decline to apply, a provision contained in an Act of Parliament on the ground of its incompatibility with a common law right.[9] There is, then, a direct relationship between the extent of the fundamentality,

---

[7] The work of Trevor Allan, in advancing the view that there are inherent limitations upon what can properly be regarded as 'law' – and that this view obtains in relation to the UK constitution, its orthodox accommodation of the notion of legislative supremacy notwithstanding – is particularly noteworthy in this regard. See, eg, T Allan, *The Sovereignty of Law: Freedom, Constitution, and Common Law* (Oxford, Oxford University Press, 2013).

[8] Laws (n 1) 81.

[9] For a very helpful discussion of the possible deleterious consequences that the judiciary would face in such circumstances, see D Oliver, 'Parliament and the Courts: A Pragmatic (or Principled) Defence of the Sovereignty of Parliament' in Horne and Drewry (eds), *Parliament and the Law* (Oxford, Hart Publishing, 2018).

in the sense of intransigence in the face of conflicting legislation, that is ascribed to common law rights and scope for concern as to the legitimacy of such rights (thus conceived). This is not to suggest that it would be impossible to construct an argument against lesser judicial interventions. (Whether it would be a convincing argument is a different matter.) But it is difficult to deny that if judges were to insist that common law rights enjoyed unqualified, or 'hard', fundamentality, in the sense of ascribing to such rights absolute priority over *all* other legal norms, they would find themselves on the thinnest of constitutional ice.[10]

Of course, an intellectual case can be made, and many such cases have been made, to the effect that however thin that ice might seem to be, declining to apply laws that offend fundamental rights (and other basic values rooted in the rule of law) is an inherent and non-negotiable component of the judicial role. But whatever the virtues of such an argument might be, it would never command universal – and perhaps not even broad – consent. There is, in the final analysis, no getting away from the fact that imputing a hard-fundamental status to common law rights will always be a deeply controversial position. And this, in turn, points towards an important conclusion: namely, that even if, in intellectual terms, one believes that common law rights ought to enjoy a hard form of fundamentality, the operational reality of common law rights, at least within the particular context of the UK constitution, is – and is likely to remain – different.

Indeed, this is – paradoxically – acknowledged, at least implicitly, by some of those who themselves champion the hard-fundamental thesis of common law rights. For instance, as observed above, Woolf refers to the possibility of the judiciary acting 'without precedent' – by declining to enforce a formally valid provision contained in an Act of Parliament – only if Parliament were to 'do the *unthinkable*'.[11] If this really was as far as Woolf meant to go, then his argument would have little practical application, given that the probability of genuinely 'unthinkable' legislation being enacted must be, or must be close to, zero. In fact, however, Woolf somewhat softens this aspect of his argument, albeit only implicitly, by at least coming close to suggesting that *Anisminic*[12] may be understood in terms of judicial repudiation of the ouster clause that was at stake in that case, thus signalling that the 'unthinkable' is in fact not only practically conceivable but also a historical reality.[13] It may be more accurate, therefore, to

---

[10] By 'absolute priority', I mean a form of priority that ensures that, once a breach of the relevant right has been established, the right takes priority over any conflicting legal norms, including primary legislation. This is a distinct matter from the question of whether a right is, to begin with, 'absolute' or 'qualified'. As I use the term 'absolute priority' in this chapter, it is perfectly possible for a qualified right to take absolute priority: if, for instance, a court were to concluded that an Act of Parliament disproportionality interfered with a qualified right, thus resulting in a breach of the right, the right would override the conflicting Act of Parliament if, to begin with, the right was accorded 'absolute priority' in the sense that that term is used here.

[11] Woolf (n 2) 69.

[12] *Anisminic Ltd v Foreign Compensation Commission* [1969] 2 AC 147.

[13] Woolf (n 2) 69. It is worth noting in this regard that Lord Woolf later went on, in an extra-judicial lecture, to push back strongly in the face of a proposed ouster clause in respect of immigration decisions: H Woolf, 'The Rule of Law and a Change in the Constitution' (2004) 63 *CLJ* 317.

say that Woolf's position is that courts would be entitled, and required, to decline to apply a statutory provision not merely in wholly 'unthinkable' circumstances, but certainly only in extremis: that is, in circumstances that may conceivably arise, and that may in fact already have arisen, but which are nevertheless highly unlikely. The important point is that through these remarks, Woolf clearly acknowledges that, at least in his estimation, judicial negation of legislation on common law rights (or indeed other common law) grounds is to be understood as something extraordinary, in the senses of being both a highly unusual step and one that, if taken, would likely be momentous.

These facets of the exceptionality of judicial repudiation of legislation at common law are closely related, the unfamiliarity of such curial intervention being attributable in the first place to its very momentousness. As to why such intervention should be regarded in such terms, the answer is surely that judges – even if, like Lord Woolf, they are satisfied in an intellectual and legal-constitutional sense of the propriety of such judicial activism – recognise its potential dangerousness in political-constitutional terms, it being impossible to know how matters would play out in the event of such naked confrontation between the judicial and political branches.[14] It is little surprise, then, that judges faced with statutory provisions that potentially conflict with common law constitutional rights prefer to resolve such apparent difficulties interpretively rather than confrontationally, if necessary by – as Lord Phillips put it, in extra-judicial remarks to a parliamentary select committee – assigning to the offending provision 'an interpretation … that it couldn't [linguistically] bear', so as to throw 'the gauntlet back to Parliament'.[15]

Unsurprisingly, we see precisely the sort of approach disclosed by these extra-curial remarks of Lord Phillips and Lord Woolf reflected in judicial decisions. Thus, for instance, in a by-now well-known dictum concerning the constitutional right of access to court, Lord Steyn in the *Jackson* case said that '[i]n *exceptional circumstances* involving an attempt to abolish judicial review or the ordinary role of the courts, [judges] … may have to consider whether this is constitutional fundamental which even a sovereign Parliament acting at the behest of a complaisant House of Commons cannot abolish'.[16] Thus, for Lord Steyn in *Jackson*, as for Lord Woolf in his extra-curial remarks, judicial disobedience to statute is an exceptional step that would be contemplated only in commensurately exceptional circumstances. Meanwhile, Lord Phillips' recognition of the extreme improbability of explicit judicial repudiation of primary legislation, as distinct from interpretive intervention that stops short of outright confrontation, is amply illustrated by authority. Examples are supplied by the Supreme Court's recent

---

[14] On which see Oliver (n 9).

[15] House of Commons Political and Constitutional Reform Committee, *Constitutional Role of the Judiciary if there were a Written Constitution* (HC 2013–14, 802) 16–17.

[16] *R (Jackson) v Attorney General* [2005] UKHL 56, [2006] 1 AC 262, [102].

judgments in *Evans*[17] and by *Privacy International*.[18] In both cases, a majority or plurality of the Justices rendered judgments that accorded notably strong forms of protection to fundamental constitutional rights and allied constitutional principles, but in each case did so by means of statutory construction. Three of the seven Justices in *Privacy International* also expressed doubt about Parliament's capacity to oust judicial review – but, importantly for present purposes, such comments amounted to obiter dicta that were not central to the way in which the case was actually decided. The essential point for the time being, then, is that where courts perceive fundamental rights to be jeopardised by primary legislation, they reach for interpretive tools rather than engaging in a direct face-off with Parliament that would culminate in outright curial disregard of the offending provision. That they do so is implicit, but clear acknowledgment of the legitimacy concerns that would be sparked if they were to proceed otherwise. And while much is made of dicta such as those found in *Jackson* and *Privacy International*, that they remain no more than that is itself telling.

III. Three Distinctions and their Limits

Where does this leave us? It suggests that even those who are prepared to challenge constitutional orthodoxy – which, in this regard, is epitomised by an unvarnished Diceyan conception of parliamentary sovereignty, to which any notion of judicial repudiation of legislation is anathema – make a relatively limited argument as regards the fundamentality of common law rights. To be sure, judges such as Woolf and Laws, along with commentators such as Allan, have not shied away from making the case that common law rights are capable of enjoying a hard form of fundamentality that entails priority over incompatible primary legislation, thus raising the prospect of judicial repudiation of the latter. The same is true of dicta such as those found in *Jackson* and *Privacy International*. At the same time, however, it remains plain that such judicial intervention is far from commonplace (if, in fact, it exists at all), and that those who advance the hard-fundamental position tend, in general, to leaven it by acknowledging that its pertinence is limited to relatively extreme, and thus unlikely, circumstances. The upshot is that even if we were to accept the hard-fundamental thesis as an accurate account of the legal position, it implies a largely theoretical, or in-principle, form of hard fundamentality, as distinct from an operational one. In other words, even if the prospect of ascribing a hard-fundamental status to rights is acknowledged, it remains a possibility that is largely removed from the day-to-day reality of judicial *practice* (certain judicial *rhetoric* to the contrary notwithstanding).

---

[17] *R (Evans) v Attorney-General* [2015] UKSC 21, [2015] AC 1787.
[18] *R (Privacy International) v Investigatory Powers Tribunal* [2019] UKSC 22, [2019] 2 WLR 1219.

The point can be made clearly by contrasting the pragmatic reality (or otherwise) of treating rights as having a hard-fundamental status (on the one hand) as a matter of common law and (on the other hand) under a textual constitutional instrument that accommodates judicial invalidation of legislation. Within regimes of the latter type, such invalidation may well not be common-place, but nor is it, or need it be, wholly exceptional, let alone theoretical. That is so precisely because, under such constitutional dispensations, invalidation uncontroversially lies within the judicial domain, and does not raise the legiti-macy concerns that such intervention would inevitably trigger were judges to engage in it absent the sort of cover that is supplied by a governing constitutional text. In short, the text, within such systems, supplies a roadmap that enables judges, and others, to grasp what the consequences of such intervention will be. As such, it does not reduce to the sort of leap in the dark that would inevi-tably be taken by a judge in the UK who invalidated legislation on common law grounds, and which (whatever one's view as to the intellectual-constitutional position) inevitably serves in the first place as a powerful disincentive to such judicial activism.

A. Theoretical and Operational Fundamentality

The foregoing analysis implicates three distinctions that can be brought to bear when seeking to understand and characterise the nature and extent of common law rights' fundamentality. However, as we will see, while each of the distinctions has some utility in this regard, none of them should be understood in unduly absolutist terms.

The first point, then, concerns the distinction – or, rather, the arguably incom-plete nature of the distinction – between the notions of theoretical and operational fundamentality sketched above. If it is extremely unlikely that a court would ever in practice resort to a form of intervention (eg strike-down) that would depend upon accepting common law rights' hard-fundamentality, it may seem to follow that acknowledging that position at a theoretical level has no bearing upon the operational reality of judicial (or political) practice. However, it would be a mistake to jump to this conclusion, for the reality is probably more nuanced. That is so because, to begin with, the distinction between the theoretical possibility of judicial invalidation and a practical reality in which such curial practice is empiri-cally rare to non-existent is far from watertight. In particular, the characterisation of common law rights as hard-fundamental in constitutional-theoretical terms may bear upon the reality of legal and political practice in myriad ways, even if that does not go as far as the regularisation of the practice of judicial invalidation of statute law.

In this way, the very possibility, however remote, of judicial insistence upon the hard fundamentality of common law rights may at least give the political branches pause for thought when acting in relation to such rights. That is so not because the political branches necessarily accede to the view that invalidation of legislation is an option that is open to the judicial branch in the final analysis, but because the very *existence* of that curial position means that the risk of constitutional crisis (which would likely ensue were the putative judicial option to invalidate to be exercised) is a cost that must be factored in when weighing the political case for legislatively abrogating a fundamental common law right. This suggests that however limited the evidence might be of on-the-ground judicial operationalisation of common law rights' hard-fundamentality, and however much that might suggest that such rights' hard-fundamentality is (at most) 'merely' theoretical, the very inhabitation by (some) judges of that (theoretical) position is *itself* capable of having practical ramifications. The distinction between theoretical and operational notions of common law rights' hard fundamentality is thus not absolute, since the very judicial act of staking out the theoretical position is capable of having consequences that sound in practice in the political realm. To relegate the notion of hard-fundamentality to the realm of the 'purely' theoretical would therefore be to adopt an unduly blinkered view.

B. Hard and Soft Fundamentality

That takes us to a second distinction – between hard and soft notions of common law rights' fundamentality. One way of understanding that distinction is by reference to the question of whether rights can go as far as serving as trumps, such that (among other things) they can serve as a basis upon which to invalidate legislation. However, just as the distinction between theoretical and operational notions of hard fundamentality is not, as we have seen, watertight, so the distinction between hard and soft forms of fundamentality is not itself absolute. In particular, any suggestion that there exists a binary distinction between those notions is surely misguided, the clearly better view being that they represent, by way of loosely describing, different portions of a scale, the 'soft' and 'hard' categories themselves being catholic concepts. From this it follows that even if common law rights in the UK do not, at least in day-to-day operational terms, take effect as hard-fundamental trumps that can straightforwardly and uncontroversially take precedence in relation to and serve to invalidate primary legislation, such rights' status need not necessarily be relegated to a radically inferior category within a taxonomy that is starkly binary in nature.

The better view, then, is that there are degrees of both soft- and hard-fundamentality. For instance, at one extreme, the former category might involve (1) pro-rights statutory construction only in cases of genuine ambiguity as to the relevant provision's meaning; at the other extreme, it might entail (2) very highly creative statutory construction involving the attribution to the provision of a meaning that it cannot (as Lord Phillips put it)[19] linguistically bear.

---

[19] House of Commons Political and Constitutional Reform Committee (n 15) 16–17.

Meanwhile, whereas (3) rights as absolute trumps is the paradigm of the hard-fundamental model, somewhat lesser forms of protection – such as (4) judicial strike-down subject to the possibility of subsequent legislative override via, for instance, re-enactment with a 'notwithstanding' clause – might nevertheless also plausibly be placed within the hard-fundamental category. From this analysis, a further point follows. Just as the two categories accommodate shades of meaning, so they are capable of shading into one another: while approaches (1) and (3) are plainly distinct, the differences between (2) and (4) are far less stark. Whether, as a result, (2) might more properly be placed in the hard-fundamental category or, conversely, (4) in the soft-fundamental category, is debateable – but any such debate would ultimately reduce to a semantic, and largely barren, one. What is important is not whether we label a given approach to the protection of rights as bestowing upon the relevant rights a hard- or soft-fundamental status. Rather, the utility of the distinction between those forms of fundamentality lies in its capacity simultaneously to capture (at the extreme) broad and significant differences between approaches to rights protection and (at the margin) the capacity of forms of protection that might appear to fall short of the 'hard' paradigm to operate, in substance albeit not in form, in ways that may deliver not-radically-different levels of protection.

The foregoing analysis thus suggests that we ought to exercise great caution before dismissing the common law's capacity to invest rights with meaningfully fundamental status merely because it (arguably) does not approach rights, whether theoretically or operationally, in paradigmatically hard, rights-as-absolute-trumps, terms. This, in turn, raises questions about what forms of protection the common law *is* capable of providing, and thus about the *degree* of fundamentality that rights enjoy at common law, even if they fall short of the hard-fundamental paradigm. The remaining two parts of this chapter examine those questions. First, however, it is necessary to address a third distinction, the importance of which – as with the first two – lies as much in its porousness as in its appreciation.

C. Depth and Breadth

The third distinction, then, is between what we might think of as fundamental rights' *depth* and *breadth*. We saw above that hard protection of common law rights through judicial invalidation is generally acknowledged to be a path that, if it is open at all, is (taken to be) available only in extremis. That this is so is important to our understanding of the nature and form of common law rights' fundamentality. The point can most easily be made by way of contrasting the position that appears to apply at common law with that which is generally found under fundamental rights texts. In the latter context, while rights are generally arranged in some form of hierarchical order, such hierarchy usually finds expression in ways that concern matters *other than* the remedial steps that are available in the event of breach. Rather, hierarchy in respect of fundamental rights texts tends to be concretised through such matters as the conception of a given right as absolute or qualified and the extent, if any, of the deference that a court is prepared to exhibit when determining whether a qualified right has been breached. In contrast, once it has been decided that a right has been breached, fundamental rights texts do not generally afford courts weaker remedial options in relation to 'lesser' rights. This is true of texts, such as the US Bill of Rights, under which the nuclear option of strike-down is available, as well as of remedially more conservative texts such as the HRA. Thus, in whatever senses such texts might acknowledge or accommodate a hierarchy of rights, the notion of hierarchy does not tend to extend to the remedial options that are in principle available. On this approach, all rights, once breached, are potential candidates for whatever remedial options are generally open to courts under the relevant text – albeit that the anterior question of such candidacy may be influenced by hierarchy-related considerations that bear upon whether, in the first place, a breach of the right is taken to have occurred.

The position at common law, however, is different: a point that emerges both from the rhetoric of those who countenance hard fundamentality and from the empirical reality of judicial practice. Of course, the absence from the latter of any examples of explicit judicial invalidation of primary legislation casts doubt on whether common law rights can be protected *at all* in that way. But even if one is prepared to take into account the more subtle curial signalling that is found in some of the case law, it appears that the possibility of invalidation is rarely countenanced as something that might be available as part of the standard judicial toolkit for the protection of common law rights. As already noted, it is generally contemplated, if at all, as an exceptional step that might be taken in commensurately exceptional circumstances. As to what might count as such circumstances, the nature of the threatened right and the grossness of its violation appear to be considered to be particularly important. It is clear, for instance, that (whether or not justifiably) English courts have tended to ascribe especial priority to the common law right of access to court, and to have been prepared to go to unusual lengths in order to uphold it in the face of apparently contradictory primary legislation.[20] The already-mentioned majority and plurality judgments in (respectively) *Anisminic*[21] and *Evans*[22] – which, on some analyses, amount or at least come close to implicit judicial invalidation of provisions that appear inconsistent with the right of access to court – are arguably cases in point, as is some of the judicial rhetoric found in *Jackson*.[23] It is noteworthy too that it was the right of access to court that was again in play in *Privacy International*, in which the majority was prepared to bring to bear a muscular interpretive approach so as to protect the right, while the plurality was willing to

---

[20] On the right of access to court, see further ch 3.
[21] *Anisminic* (n 12).
[22] *Evans* (n 17).
[23] *Jackson* (n 16).

go rhetorically further by countenancing the possibility of judicial intransigence in the face of legislative ouster.[24]

However, this sort of approach – that is, judicial practice that might be understood as coming close to de facto invalidation, and judicial rhetoric that contemplates the possibility of, albeit without actually taking, such a step – is far from commonplace. Indeed, prominent dicta concerning the interpretive protection of human rights generally have tended to go hand-in-hand with the express disavowal of any judicial power to go *further* than affording such protection. Take, for instance, Lord Steyn's well-known statement of the 'principle of legality' in *Pierson*, according to which the assumption that 'Parliament legislates for a European liberal democracy founded on the principles and traditions of the common law' is one that 'only has prima facie force' and which can therefore 'be displaced by a clear and specific provision to the contrary'.[25] Similarly, in his exposition of the principle of legality in *Simms*, Lord Hoffmann emphasised that while it 'means that Parliament must squarely confront what it is doing and accept the political cost', it does not detract from the fact that '[p]arliamentary sovereignty means that Parliament can, if it chooses, legislate contrary to fundamental principles of human rights'.[26] The implication is that the crossing of the in extremis threshold – should there be any such circumstances, in which common law rights might conceivably operate as trumps – is likely to occur only when the right in question is especially highly valued at common law and is particularly gravely threatened by the legislative provision in question.

Thus, putting the matter at its (contestable) highest, the position seems to be that only a subset of common law rights – and, perhaps even then, only certain especially important aspects of such rights that would be threatened only by the gravest of legislative incursions – form an irreducible nucleus that may be resistant in the face of implacably incompatible primary legislation. Indeed, we might go further by suggesting that the rights most likely to generate such a judicial approach are those that are in the first place intimately connected with basic constitutional principles such as the separation of powers. On this view, the particular rigour with which courts have shown themselves willing to protect the right of access to justice is explicable, at least in part, by reference to the fact that that right is, in the first place, a reflection of a constitutional principle to which especial curial weight is attached.[27] All of this suggests that, even if common law rights are, at their core, so deeply embedded as to be as ingrained as rights enshrined in a constitutional text that affords judicial strike-down powers, that deep core of common law rights is narrow in scope and – in particular, and in contrast to the way in which rights texts normally operate – does not extend across the full breadth of fundamental rights. Common law rights thus appear, in this crucial remedial sense, to be

---

[24] *Privacy International* (n 18).

[25] *R v Secretary of State for the Home Department, ex parte Pierson* [1998] AC 539 at 587.

[26] *Regina v Secretary of State for the Home Department, ex parte Simms* [2000] 2 AC 115 at 131.

[27] For further discussion of the relationship between the protection of constitutional rights and constitutional structures, see ch 10.

peculiarly hierarchically ordered in a way that textual rights tend not to be, such that only a privileged subset of common law rights might conceivably serve as a basis for invalidation of statute law. This, in turn, suggests that even if common law rights are in principle capable of the same degree of fundamentality as rights contained in invalidation-authorising constitutional texts, that hardest form of fundamentality is reserved to a select fraction of the wider corpus of common law rights.

IV. Operationalisation: Judicial Review and the Separation of Powers

The picture that emerges from the foregoing analysis as to the fundamentality of common law rights is an undeniably messy – or, to put the point less pejoratively, complex – one. Whether such rights can or do take effect within the parameters of the UK's constitutional order in a way that can reasonably be said to be hard-fundamental in nature is a contested and contestable issue – both as a matter of constitutional theory and as a matter of empirical analysis. What *can* be said with certainty, however, is that it is far from generally acknowledged that common law rights enjoy a hard-fundamental status such that they are straightforwardly capable, as a matter of course, of serving to invalidate legislation enacted by the UK Parliament. Yet this should not lead to dismissiveness when it comes to the question of such rights' fundamentality – which question, as already observed, is best understood as one of degree. If, therefore, we wish to build up a picture of the extent of common law rights' fundamentality, it is worth focussing both on phenomena that serve to invest such rights with a (degree of) fundamental status, as well as on structural constitutional features that serve to circumscribe the extent of such fundamentality. It is in the interaction of those phenomena that the true measure of common law rights' fundamentality falls to be perceived. Against that background, this section and the next section of the chapter examine two of the principal vehicles – namely, judicial review and statutory interpretation – in which common law rights can be, and are, legally operationalised within the UK system. Each of these methodologies is capable of ensuring that rights are invested with a substantial degree of protection, but each is also cabined by structural features of the constitutional order – most notably the separation of powers and parliamentary sovereignty – that in turn inform our analysis of the extent to which, and the sense in which, common law rights in the UK can properly be characterised as 'fundamental'.

The suggestion – which is not infrequently made, particularly judicially – that the common law has long served as a vehicle for the protection of fundamental rights must, at the very least, be viewed with caution.[28] It is one thing to say,

---

[28] See, eg, C Gearty, *On Fantasy Island: Britain, Strasbourg and Human Rights* (Oxford, Oxford University Press, 2016).

for instance, that some of the rights found in the ECHR, such as the rights to liberty and property, reflect values that resonate with the English common law tradition. But the question remains whether human rights are protected in ways that render them – at common law – meaningfully fundamental in *practical* terms. Here, judicial practice has not invariably lived up to the promise of judicial rhetoric – a point that emerges with particular clarity from pre-HRA domestic jurisprudence in which claimants pursued strategies designed to circumvent the ECHR's then-unincorporated status. Cases in which such approaches were tried sometimes generated warm judicial words about the common law's affinity with ECHR rights, Lord Donaldson MR's assertion that 'you have to look long and hard before you can detect any difference between the English common law and the principles set out in the Convention' marking perhaps the high-water mark of such thinking.[29] Yet judicial anxiety about incorporating the ECHR by the 'back door',[30] born of Parliament's omission at that time to effect front-door incorporation, meant that (at least on some occasions) rights went largely unprotected at common law. A moment's reflection reveals, however, that such concerns about the propriety of back-door incorporation ought logically to have been beside the point if, as Lord Donaldson appeared to suggest, the ECHR merely reflected rights that were anyway acknowledged at common law. On that view, whether the ECHR had been incorporated, and whether judges ought to have treated it as if it had been, should have been moot, for the common law ought to have been a sufficient vehicle for protection of relevant rights. This, in turn, suggests that judicial rhetoric informed by broad affinities between certain ECHR rights and aspects of the common law tradition was not generally matched by curial preparedness to operationalise fundamental rights by investing them with real remedial bite.

A good illustration of this lies in the courts' general reticence to utilise the proportionality test in pre-HRA human rights cases. Adherence to a rationality test – which, at least at that time, was conceived of as a significantly less demanding standard of review than proportionality – resulted in demonstrably lower levels of rights protection. A well-known but still instructive illustration is supplied by the differential outcomes in the English and Strasbourg courts in the *Smith* litigation, in which the former found that restricting service in the armed forces to heterosexuals was not irrational, while the latter considered it a disproportionate breach of rights.[31] Meanwhile, the perceived constitutional basis for curial resistance to proportionality review is shown nowhere more clearly than in the reliance upon the appeal/review distinction – and thus upon the (particular conception of the) separation of powers which animates that distinction – by Lords Ackner and Lowry in the *Brind* case. The former, for instance, took it as

---

[29] *R v Secretary of State for the Home Department, ex parte Brind* [1991] 1 AC 696, 717.

[30] This term was used in *Brind* (n 29) by both Lord Donaldson MR in the Court of Appeal (at 718) and Lord Ackner in the House of Lords (at 762).

[31] *R v Ministry of Defence, ex parte Smith* [1996] QB 517.

given that applying the proportionality test reduces to asking, 'Is the particular decision acceptable?' – which, he said, would 'involve a review of the merits of the decision' and would therefore be incompatible with the appeal/review distinction.[32] Similarly, Lord Lowry feared that proportionality review would boil down to the 'forbidden appellate approach' and would thus entail 'an abuse of the judges' supervisory jurisdiction'.[33]

Seen through the lens of such judicial practice, the view of Lord Donaldson noted above – that it was hard to find 'any difference' between the common law and the ECHR – appears to take on a positively hyperbolic character. Yet for all those cases that can be cited as evidence of the common law's failure meaningfully to operationalise rights via judicial review, two important qualifications should be noted. The first is that even when such cases were decided in the early to mid-1990s, they did not signify a universally held judicial position. Lords Ackner and Lowry in *Brind* may have greeted the prospect of proportionality review with horror, and it is certainly the case that – doubtless in the light of such castigation at apex court level – the language of proportionality was rarely used prior to the HRA. Nevertheless, the (future) possibility of substantive review along proportionality, not merely *Wednesbury*,[34] lines had already been canvassed (admittedly tentatively) by Lord Diplock in his classical statement of the grounds of judicial review in *GCHQ*.[35] There is also clear evidence of at least elements of the proportionality test being deployed – albeit without the 'p-word' actually being uttered – in judicial review cases that engaged certain rights and other highly-regarded interests. A good example of the former is supplied by *Leech*, in which the legality of secondary legislation engaging the common law right of access to court was tested by reference to whether it fulfilled 'a self-evident and pressing need'.[36] Meanwhile, the courts' willingness to adopt proportionality-style methodology *beyond* the rights context is clearly evidenced by the 'balancing' test developed in the seminal substantive legitimate expectation case of *Coughlan*.[37]

If, then, the first point is that the courts have for some time been *implicitly* willing to go beyond rationality review when it comes to protecting individual rights and other highly-regarded values, the second, related, point is that recent years have seen proportionality emerge more *explicitly* from the shadows at common law.[38] That development is doubtless thanks, at least in part, to the way in which judicial experience applying the HRA has unequivocally demonstrated that deploying proportionality need not cause the constitutional sky to fall in.

---

[32] *Brind* (n 29), 762–63.
[33] *Brind* (n 29), 766.
[34] *Associated Provincial Picture Houses Ltd v Wednesbury Corporation* [1948] 1 KB 223.
[35] *Council of Civil Service Unions v Minister for the Civil Service* [1985] AC 374.
[36] *R v Secretary of State for the Home Department, ex parte Leech (No 2)* [1994] QB 198.
[37] *R v North and East Devon Health Authority, ex parte Coughlan* [2001] QB 213.
[38] See, eg, *Kennedy v The Charity Commission* [2014] UKSC 20 (in particular Lord Mance's judgment); *Pham v Secretary of State for the Home Department* [2015] UKSC 19, (in particular Lord Mance's and Lord Reed's judgments).

In particular, in utilising proportionality in HRA cases, it has become apparent that proportionality review need not eviscerate the appeal/review distinction or undermine the separation of powers doctrine that underpins that distinction. In particular, it is perfectly clear today that when, in *Brind*, Lord Ackner said that proportionality review would involve baldly asking whether the impugned decision was 'acceptable', he was wrong. Now-substantial experience applying the HRA shows that proportionality review need not, and in general does not, entail doing anything as bald or as interventionist as that. Indeed, that that is so is evident both from the structure and content of the proportionality test, as well as from the parallel doctrine of deference that has developed alongside it so as to moderate its application and to ensure that courts are not improperly drawn into the merits of questions of administrative and legislative policy.

In recent years, much intellectual energy has been expended – by both judges and academics – debating whether proportionality ought to replace the reasonableness test.[39] The possibility of its doing so has been acknowledged,[40] but certainly not unequivocally embraced, by judges in the UK, the Supreme Court having chosen in *Keyu* to kick that particular doctrinal can down the road.[41] It thus remains to be seen whether English administrative law will ever reach the point at which rationality is wholly replaced by proportionality in substantive review cases. What is, however, clear is that the terms of the debate have shifted considerably in recent decades. Whereas it once fell to proportionality's proponents to plead its case in the face of profound concerns as to its constitutional appropriateness, it is today those who favour rationality's retention who often find themselves on the back foot, the Court of Appeal itself having suggested – some years ago, now – that *Wednesbury*'s 'burial rites' were overdue.[42] The better view, though, is that to suppose that a choice must be made between rationality and proportionality implies a failure to perceive the true role of and relationship between them: namely, that they are each themselves catholic principles, capable of supplying different levels of scrutiny and of shading into one another at the margins.[43] In any event, the important point for present purposes is that whatever the long-term prospects might be for the reasonableness test in non-rights cases, it is now generally – and rightly – acknowledged that the proportionality test can and does apply when rights and other highly-regarded values are in play at common law, and that it can do so without doing violence to

---

[39] For an overview of the debate and a number of contributions to it, see H Wilberg and M Elliott (eds), *The Scope and Intensity of Substantive Judicial Review: Traversing Taggart's Rainbow* (Oxford, Hart Publishing, 2015).

[40] See, eg, *R (Association of British Civilian Internees (Far East Region)) v Secretary of State for Defence* [2003] EWCA Civ 473.

[41] *Keyu v Secretary of State for Foreign and Commonwealth Affairs* [2015] UKSC 69, [2016] AC 1355, [131]–[132] (Lord Neuberger).

[42] *Association of British Civilian Internees* (n 40) [35].

[43] I develop this argument in detail in M Elliott, 'From Bifurcation to Calibration: Twin-Track Deference and the Culture of Justification' in Wilberg and Elliott (n 39).

constitutional principles. Indeed, that much has been clear since the inception of the HRA, the House of Lords' breakthrough case applying proportionality in a rights context having had at least as much to say about that doctrine's role at common law as under the Act.[44]

This, in turn, has significant implications for any assessment of the UK constitution's capacity to acknowledge and protect fundamental rights at common law. For as long as anything more demanding than rationality review was considered (as in *Brind*)[45] to be constitutionally anathema, any claims about the common law's recognition of fundamental rights were liable to ring largely hollow, its pragmatic protective capacity being significantly limited. Moreover, the fact that in the past only very limited rights protection was supplied via rationality review demonstrates that the common law does not *necessarily* or *inherently* provide a degree of rights protection that enables us to characterise common law rights as meaningfully fundamental in an operational sense. These caveats notwithstanding, recent developments show that the common law is at least *capable* of providing rights with a degree of protection, via proportionality review, that acknowledges their fundamental status. This change is explicable not by reference to any basic constitutional reordering as such, but rather by reference to evolving perceptions of how the unwritten constitutional order is to be understood in terms of what it requires (and prohibits). In particular, it is plain from past judicial aversion to proportionality review at common law that received wisdom used to hold that curial scrutiny of administrative decisions would ride roughshod over the separation of powers if it were to go beyond *Wednesbury* review. That a different view now prevails is indicative of three sets of interlocking changes when it comes to how the constitutional order is understood.

First, the proportionality doctrine is itself perceived in more subtle terms, such that it is not (mis)understood as a vehicle for engaging straightforwardly in 'merits review', but as a device that facilitates closer scrutiny while still taking account of the courts' distinct role as compared to that of the other branches.

Second, the separation of powers is understood in somewhat less doctrinaire terms, such that it no longer operates as a constitutional straightjacket that forbids review on grounds such as proportionality. Such rethinking about the separation of powers was doubtless stimulated in no small part by the HRA, but its implications are not confined to that context. For instance, Lord Sumption – who, in this sphere, is generally regarded as a conservative judge – acknowledged in *Carlile* that while the HRA 'did not *abrogate* the constitutional distribution of powers between the organs of the state which the courts had recognised for many years before it was passed'.[46] Nevertheless, he recognised that 'traditional

---

[44] *R (Daly) v Secretary of State for the Home Department* [2001] UKHL 26, [2001] 2 AC 532.
[45] *Brind* (n 29).
[46] *R (Lord Carlile of Berriew QC) v Secretary of State for the Home Department* [2014] UKSC 60, [2015] AC 945, [28] (my emphasis).

notions of the constitutional distribution of powers have unquestionably been *modified*' by the Act.[47] This aligns with his subsequent recognition in *Pham* that 'although English law has not adopted the principle of proportionality generally, it has for many years stumbled towards a concept which is in significant respects similar, and over the last three decades has been influenced by European juris-prudence *even in areas of law lying beyond the domains of EU and international human rights law*', the upshot being that 'the scope of rationality review' has been increased 'so as to incorporate at common law significant elements of the princi-ple of proportionality'.[48]

Third, it is apparent that any limitations upon the judicial role implied by the separation of powers doctrine are increasingly understood as sitting in relation-ship with the proactive judicial demands made by other elements of constitutional doctrine, most obviously the rule of law. This is certainly not to suggest that greater judicial willingness to protect fundamental rights by engaging in proportionality review implies that (for instance) the rule of law has chalked up a 'win' against the separation of powers. But there are certainly indications that, at the highest judi-cial level, the rule of law today is understood in terms that are sufficiently 'thick' to embrace fundamental common law rights,[49] and that contemporary understand-ings of the judicial role are the product of a triangulation process that is sensitive not only to the limitations implied by the separation of powers but to the judicial obligations imposed by the rule of law thus conceived.

That prevailing understandings of the common law constitution have developed in these ways over recent decades suggests two different, but not contradictory, things. The first is that, as noted above, the relatively high degree of protection provided to rights by the proportionality doctrine is not something that the common law constitution *necessarily* supplies. That much is abundantly clear from the common law constitution's failure, until recently, to provide such protection. The second point, however, is that recent experience demonstrates that the common law constitution is at least *capable* of conferring a degree of operational fundamentality on basic rights via the heightened scrutiny that comes with proportionality review (as distinct from *Wednesbury* review, at least as traditionally understood). It would be naïve to underestimate the role that the HRA played in the constitutional re-evaluation that has brought us to this point. But it would be misguided to say with absolute certainty that that re-evaluation would not have happened without the HRA, not least because the origins of the trend identified by Lord Sumption in *Pham* towards the incorporation of at least

---

[47] Ibid, [29] (my emphasis).

[48] *Pham v Secretary of State for the Home Department* [2015] UKSC 19, [105] (my emphasis).

[49] See, eg, *Daly* (n 44) [30] (Lord Cooke): '[S]ome rights are inherent and fundamental to democratic civilised society. Conventions, constitutions, bills of rights and the like respond by recognising rather than creating them.' More generally, see Lord Bingham, 'The Rule of Law' [2007] *CLJ* 67, 76: 'The rule of law must, surely, require legal protection of such human rights as, within that society, are seen as fundamental.'

'elements' of proportionality can be traced to case law that substantially pre-dates the HRA.[50] It follows that if one of the hallmarks of meaningfully fundamental rights is that their infraction attracts close judicial scrutiny – and, in particular, closer scrutiny than the traditional rationality principle is capable of supplying – the common law constitution's capacity to accommodate such rights is today readily apparent.

V. Operationalisation: Sovereignty, the Rule of Law and Statutory Interpretation

The proportionality test is an important means by which rights infringements can be judicially scrutinised at common law with a degree of rigour that is consonant with characterising such rights as fundamental in the first place. However, for several reasons, it is insufficient on its own to justify that characterisation. First, the proportionality doctrine in and of itself cannot meaningfully contribute to the protection of rights unless, to begin with, the rights in question are recognised with sufficient clarity and certainty by the legal system. Second, proportionality is not in any event a panacea because while it may be insufficient to supply adequate protection of rights – such as the right not to be subjected to torture – that do not fall, or that ought not to fall, to be traded off against competing interests. Third, and more generally, in a system that continues to acknowledge the principle of parliamentary sovereignty, the constitutional space for rights to operate and for proportionality review to bite upon them is necessarily contingent upon legislative acquiescence. If legislation removes a given right in given circumstances, then that is the end of the matter: no question arises about the proportionality of any administrative limitation of the right, because the right, in the first place, is legislatively neutralised. Whether the UK's common law constitution can properly lay claim to a body of fundamental rights thus turns not only upon the rigour with which such rights are protected when they are potentially *in play*, but also, and preliminarily, upon whether there is any mechanism that serves to ensure that such rights cannot in the first place readily be taken *out of play*. This issue ultimately resolves into one concerning statutory construction, and the interplay that occurs in the interpretive arena between the constitutional principles of parliamentary sovereignty and the rule of law.[51]

As we have already seen, there is spirited debate about whether, as a matter of constitutional theory, common law rights are capable of operating in the UK legal order as trumps, such that they may straightforwardly prevail over conflicting provisions in Acts of Parliament. For reasons already considered, that debate is certainly not unimportant. For one thing, it goes to foundational theoretical

---

[50] See, eg, *Bugdaycay v Secretary of State for the Home Department* [1987] AC 514.
[51] For further discussion of, and a different perspective on, this issue, see ch 10.

issues that engage questions about the basic architecture of the UK's constitutional order. And, as suggested above, the mere canvassing of the *possibility* of common law constitutional rights taking priority over primary legislation (at least in extremis) may be viewed as a form of inchoate curial intervention that has indirect implications in the political-constitutional sphere. At the same time, the fact that rights certainly do not unequivocally operate as constraints upon legislative authority should not lightly be assumed to signify that the common law constitution is incapable of operationalising rights in a way that treats them as meaningfully fundamental. A good deal of constitutional space exists, and is in fact inhabited in the UK by common law doctrine, in which meaningfully fundamental rights can operate without necessarily taking effect as straightforward curbs upon legislative authority. Interpretive methodology plays an axiomatic part in that regard.

The question thus becomes what degree of operational fundamentality can be conferred upon rights even if legislative invalidation is not – or is not ordinarily – part of the available judicial arsenal. If our concern to establish whether the degree of fundamentality with which rights can be invested at common law is sufficient to render them meaningfully fundamental, one way of proceeding involves comparing the position at common law with that which prevails under textual fundamental rights regimes. The obvious comparator in the UK context is the HRA. Although it stops short of treating rights as straightforward trumps, the HRA's capacity to confer upon rights a meaningful degree of fundamentality is for present purposes – and, it is hoped, uncontroversially – taken as a given. Against this background, it is instructive to consider how far courts are able and willing to go in rendering rights-consistent interpretations at common law and under the HRA. A means of doing that is by comparing what might reasonably be regarded as high-water mark cases in each context: that is, cases that illustrate the outer limit of what courts are prepared to do. *Ghaidan*[52] and *Evans*[53] are suitable exemplars in the HRA and common law spheres respectively, given that each discloses a particularly bold interpretive approach yielding rights-consistent interpretation of the relevant provision.

In *Ghaidan*, the question was whether the defendant tenant could be evicted from his property following the death of his long-term same-sex partner. That issue turned on whether the deceased partner's status as a 'statutory tenant' under the Rent Act 1977 had been acquired, upon that partner's death, by the defendant. The answer might have appeared to be 'no', for the Act seemed to provide for individuals to succeed only in the context of opposite-sex (married and unmarried) relationships.[54] Thus it referred to statutory tenant status being acquired by the 'surviving *spouse*',[55] a term that was to be read as extending to someone

[52] *Ghaidan v Godin-Mendoza* [2004] UKHL 30, [2004] 2 AC 557.
[53] *Evans* (n 17).
[54] The case was decided before the introduction of civil partnerships and same-sex marriage.
[55] Rent Act 1977, sch 1, para 2(1) (as it was when the *Ghaidan* case was decided) (my emphasis).

'who was living with the original tenant as his or her *wife* or *husband*'.[56] In the face of such gender-specific language rooted in (albeit not confined to) the then exclusively heterosexual institution of marriage, the Act might have been thought to defy a construction that would benefit the survivors of (at that time necessarily unmarried) same-sex relationships. In fact, however, the Appellate Committee of the House of Lords, by a majority of four to one, concluded that the Act could and should be read so as to apply to same-sex relationships, by deeming the legislation to extend to someone who had been living with the original tenant *as if they were* his or her wife or husband. The majority did this in discharge of its obligation under the HRA[57] to interpret legislation, so far as is 'possible', compatibly with Convention rights.[58] As well as being apparent from the effect of the majority's interpretive approach, its potency is evident from Lord Nicholls' explication of it as one that is 'unusual and far-reaching',[59] that may involve 'depart[ure] from the intention of … Parliament',[60] and that may be unconstrained by 'the particular form of words' found in the relevant provision because (in Lord Nicholls' view) undue attention to statutory language would risk turning the discharge of the HRA's interpretive obligation into 'something of a sematic lottery'.[61]

It is unnecessary for present purposes to inquire into whether the House of Lords in *Ghaidan* went too far. The important point is that the interpretive approach adopted was a notably muscular one that clearly ascribed great weight to the rights that were in play. This is underscored by the fact that when the Appellate Committee was presented in *Fitzpatrick v Sterling Housing Association* with the same issue only a few years earlier but (crucially, it would seem) pre-HRA, it concluded that the legislation could *not* be read so as to apply to a same-sex couple.[62] The implication is that the HRA played a decisive role here, and ensured for the relevant rights a degree of interpretive protection that would otherwise have been unavailable. The further implication may appear to be that the degree of such protection available under the HRA outstrips that which is available in respect of common law rights. However, the position is in fact more complex, and the contrasting outcomes found in *Ghaidan* and *Fitzpatrick* should not be taken straightforwardly to evidence the common law's relative incapacity. This point is developed below. First, however, the more general point arises that in the context of certain rights the common law can lay claim to a degree of interpretive muscularity that is at least the equal of that which is apparent in highwater-mark HRA cases such as *Ghaidan*.

---

[56] Ibid, sch 1, para 2(2) (as it was when the *Ghaidan* case was decided) (my emphasis).

[57] HRA, s 3(1).

[58] The germane rights being Arts 8 and 14, which in combination proscribe differential enjoyment, including on grounds of sexual orientation, of the right to respect for private and family life and the home.

[59] *Ghaidan* (n 52) [30].

[60] Ibid, [30].

[61] Ibid, [31].

[62] [2001] 1 AC 27.

As foreshadowed, the Supreme Court's judgment in *Evans* is instructive in this regard.[63] The central issue was the lawfulness of the exercise by the Attorney General of a so-called veto power contained in section 53(2) of the Freedom of Information Act 2000. That power had been exercised in order to (in effect) override a decision of the Upper Tribunal requiring the disclosure of information, the Tribunal having concluded that such disclosure was required under the Act. Bearing in mind that the Upper Tribunal is a superior court of record,[64] the veto power raises obvious and difficult questions about its relationship with fundamental constitutional principle. As Lord Neuberger put it in *Evans*, a power permitting the executive to override judicial decisions with which it disagreed would be 'unique in the laws of the United Kingdom' and would 'cut across two constitutional principles which are also fundamental components of the rule of law': that judicial decisions 'cannot be ignored by anyone', 'least of all ... the executive', and that executive action, 'subject to jealously guarded statutory exceptions', must be subject to judicial scrutiny.[65] Lord Neuberger concluded that broad override powers would 'flout ... the first principle' and 'stand ... the second principle on its head'.[66] Although not explicitly framed in terms of constitutional rights', the relationship between the common law right of access to court and the constitutional values implicated in *Evans* is plain, the integrity of courts' judgments and their immunity from executive veto being essential preconditions for any meaningful right of access to court.

Against this background, Lord Neuberger, giving the plurality judgment, construed the override power very narrowly indeed so as to render it exercisable only in extremely limited (and unlikely) circumstances.[67] Thus an apparently broad power enabling a Minister to override the Tribunal by issuing a certificate 'stating that he has on reasonable grounds formed the opinion that' (in effect) disclosure is not legally required[68] was interpretively transformed so as to be exercisable only in the event of 'a material change of circumstances since the tribunal decision' or if 'the decision of the tribunal was demonstrably flawed in fact or in law'.[69] For the dissentients, this was a step (much) too far: Lord Hughes considered the plurality's interpretation to be 'simply too highly strained'[70] such that it rendered the veto power 'vestigial'.[71] Lord Wilson, meanwhile, said that

---

[63] *Evans* (n 17).
[64] Tribunals, Courts and Enforcement Act 2007, s 3(5).
[65] *Evans* (n 17) [51]–[52].
[66] Ibid, [52].
[67] In a separate majority judgment with which one other Justice agreed, Lord Mance preferred to approach matters applying an administrative law lens by subjecting the exercise of the veto power to notably strict scrutiny which it did not pass, albeit that he conceded (at [130]) that in practice his approach might result in the veto power being lawfully exercisable only 'in the sort of unusual situation' in which its use would be permissible on Lord Neuberger's distinct analysis.
[68] Freedom of Information Act 2000, s 53(2).
[69] *Evans* (n 17) [71].
[70] Ibid, [155].
[71] Ibid, [156].

Lord Neuberger's approach meant that 'for all practical purposes' it would 'almost never' be possible for the power to be lawfully exercised.[72] Indeed, Lord Wilson went as far as implicitly to suggest that the approach of the Court of Appeal – which was upheld by the Supreme Court, and with which Lord Neuberger expressed agreement – was constitutionally heterodox, saying that the Court of Appeal had 'invoked precious constitutional principles', but that 'among the most precious' of those principles 'is that of parliamentary sovereignty', which is 'emblematic of our democracy'.[73]

The disagreement between the Justices in *Evans* demonstrates the essentially contestable nature of the relationship between the key constitutional principles that are in play. For Lord Wilson, the sovereignty of Parliament is the lens through which the rest of the constitution falls to be viewed. The plurality's approach is different. It certainly does not deny, explicitly or otherwise, that parliamentary sovereignty is a fundamental constitutional principle. But it situates that and other constitutional principles, including the rule of law, in a more co-equal relationship, the upshot being that when legislation is, on a plain-words reading, anathema to other fundamental principles, the degree of interpretive latitude that (on this view) can legitimately be exercised so as to render a different, rule of law-compliant construction, is correspondingly greater. This does not imply the making of a choice, as part of a zero-sum game, between constitutional principles, but rather it implies a relational conception of them, according to which their respective meanings and demands fall to be understood by reference to, among other things, one another.[74]

That courts have been willing – as cases like *Evans* and *Ghaidan* illustrate – to go to comparable interpretive lengths in support of (on the one hand) common law values and rights and (on the other) Convention rights under the HRA is in itself significant. In particular, it suggests that there is at least the potential for the common law to offer to fundamental rights a level of protection that approximates to that which is available under the HRA, particularly when the right in question – such as the right of access to court – reflects or is otherwise closely related to fundamental constitutional principles such as the rule of law and the separation of powers. It would tempting, in the light of that, to conclude that the protection of fundamental rights might not suffer unduly if, at some point in the future, the HRA were to be repealed. And, by similar logic, it might be thought that for as long as the HRA remains available, it ought to make little difference whether a case is argued at common law or under the Act. However, the position is in fact more complex than this. Three points, in particular, are worth considering in this regard, each of which serves to illuminate the fundamentality of common law rights relative to rights protected by the HRA.

---

[72] Ibid, [177].
[73] Ibid, [168].
[74] For further discussion, see M Elliott, 'A tangled constitutional web: The black-spider memos and the British constitution's relational architecture' [2015] *PL* 539.

The first reason relates back to the distinction developed in an earlier section of this chapter between the notions of rights' depth and breadth. As we saw, in terms of the remedial options that are available on an in-principle level, Convention rights under the HRA adhere to a one-size-fits-all model: that is, once it is acknowledged that a Convention right is in play, the same remedial options are open to a court irrespective of which particular right it is. In contrast, the preparedness of courts to protect rights at common law may vary according to the right in question. Whereas core common law rights may rest on constitutional foundations so deep as to attract protection coming close or amounting to legislative invalidation, other rights, lying within a broader penumbra, may attract only lesser forms of protection. It follows that even if the common law has the *potential* to offer interpretive protection akin to that which can be afforded under the HRA, whether a comparable level of protection will *actually* be offered may depend on the common law right that is in play. Moreover, this cuts two ways. In some instances, where the common law right lies within the penumbra rather than the core, a court may be unwilling to go as far in terms of interpretive protection as it would if the interpretive obligation under the HRA were engaged. At the same time, however, there may – if some judicial dicta are to be believed – be an elite subset of common law rights that attract *stronger* protection than the HRA can afford, whether by means of interpretive protection that transcends the ascription of merely 'possible' rights-compatible constructions,[75] or outright disapplication of the offending provision.[76] On present evidence, however, that elite subset of common law rights, if it exists at all, is likely decidedly narrow – and confined to rights that are, in the first place, functions of especially highly-prized constitutional principles. This, in turn, helps us to understand the privileged position in which the constitutional right of access to courts appears to find itself.

A second consideration relates to the legal foundations upon which the HRA and common law rights regimes respectively rest, thus implicating questions about their resilience. The rights protected by the HRA rest upon a clear and, in one sense, secure legal foundation. As is well-known, the HRA does not create a domestic legal corpus of fundamental rights as such; rather, it gives effect to an extant body of rights set out in the ECHR. That the Convention is the ultimate foundation of the rights protected by the HRA is important when it comes to considering those rights' legal security in the face of incompatible primary legislation. While the HRA itself explicitly foregoes any claim as to the priority of Convention rights over such legislation, the position is different when viewed from

---

[75] Compare s 3 of the HRA, which requires legislation to be construed compatibly with ECHR rights so far as is 'possible' with Lord Phillips's suggestion that certain common law rights may protected by assigning to apparently irreconcilable statutory provisions meanings that they linguistically 'cannot bear': House of Commons Political and Constitutional Reform Committee (n 15) 16–17.

[76] *Jackson* (n 16).

the vantage point of the ECHR. Understood from that perspective, the Convention rights are binding in international law, meaning that, while it remains a party to the Convention, the UK as a state has no facility lawfully to enact or preserve legislation that conflicts with the ECHR. Judicial remedies rendered under the HRA thus take on a status that exceeds that which the HRA promises as a matter of purely domestic law. Once the role of the ECHR as an international law back-stop is acknowledged, declarations of incompatibility cannot straightforwardly be ignored,[77] just as rights-compliant interpretations rendered under section 3 of the HRA cannot with impunity be legislatively reversed.

The position at common law, of course, is different. In one sense, their legal foundation is perfectly clear: common law rights, self-evidently, are constructs of the common law, and correspondingly it is to the common law that their legal foundations can be traced. Taken at face value, this implies that in hierarchical terms common law rights are inferior to Acts of Parliament, the common law's vulnerability to legislative change or displacement being a characteristic that is necessarily shared by common law rights. However, the difficulty, as we have already seen, is that the status of common law rights (as distinct from the common law generally) is ambiguous, given that some of their leading proponents ascribe to them a degree of fundamentality that renders them immune to legislative interference. The upshot is that the legal foundations of both HRA and common law rights are far from simple. The former, being founded in mere statute law, appear vulnerable to other legislation, but their international law roots in fact imply a greater degree of resilience. Meanwhile, although common law rights may appear to be subject to legislative displacement, it is simplistic to assume that the constitutional status of common law rights is straightforwardly captured by their 'common law' epithet and the relationship with statute law that that normally implies.

The third consideration relates to, but is distinct from, the previous one. The point canvassed immediately above concerns what might be thought of as the day-to-day resilience of rights under the HRA and at common law respectively: that is, the capacity of a given right to remain exercisable in given circumstances in the face of potentially incompatible legislation. A different question, however, arises in relation to what might be termed rights' existential resilience: that is, their capacity to withstand a legislative attempt at wholesale abolition. In this context, the two types of rights are readily distinguishable. Self-evidently, to the extent that ECHR rights have effect in domestic law, that effect is secured by statute. It follows that the availability of such rights within the domestic legal system is contingent upon the HRA, the repeal of which would necessarily, at least to a considerable extent,[78]

---

[77] That is not to suggest, however, that they cannot be ignored *at all*, as the long-running saga concerning prisoners' right to vote demonstrates.

[78] Two caveats need to be entered. First, Convention rights had a limited degree of domestic effect pre-HRA, and there is no reason to suppose that they would have less effect than that if the HRA was

excise the Convention rights from the domestic legal system. In this sense, then, the existential resilience of the HRA regime may be considered relatively limited, given that it is vouchsafed only by Parliament's willingness – for the time being – not to repeal it.

In contrast, the existential resilience of the common law is almost certainly very considerably greater, given that it is an inherent aspect of the legal system in contrast to the HRA which might, on one analysis, uncharitably be characterised as something that has been bolted on. Even if it is the case that the application of a given common law right in a particular set of circumstances is subject to legislative displacement, it is far less clear that a given common law right – let alone the whole corpus of common law rights – is vulnerable to being wholly extinguished for all purposes by legislation. That view arguably plays out on both the legal and the political levels. As to the former, the (contested) argument that common law rights enjoy at least a degree of hard fundamentality would, if accepted, bite with even greater force on the existential level: that is, to the extent that there is a question mark about common law rights' vulnerability to limitation, regulation or displacement by legislation, there must be even greater room for doubt about the capacity of legislation to secure such rights' extinction. Meanwhile, on the political level, while HRA repeal has been countenanced and may soon begin to rise up the agenda again, it is harder to envisage circumstances in which it would be politically feasible to enact legislation seeking to extinguish common law rights, not least because the amount of political capital needed to mount an attack upon rights understood to be an integral part of the English common law would doubtless be greater than that needed to undermine 'European' rights enforced by a 'foreign' (ie the Strasbourg) court.[79] That is not to suggest that a political attack upon common law rights cannot be imagined. Indeed, the pitching of populist forces against a domestic judicial elite that is perceived to favour liberal interests is perfectly easy to contemplate in the present climate, as highly critical reactions[80] to the Divisional Court's judgment in the *Miller* case[81] amply attest. It is nevertheless the case that attempting legislatively to extinguish common law constitutional rights would be a very different sort of project, in both technical and political terms, from repeal of the HRA. It would be rash to argue that such a project could not be in any circumstances accomplished – but it would be equally rash to assume that it could be accomplished readily.

---

repealed. Second, if the HRA were to be repealed, that might very well reveal that ECHR rights had left an imprint upon the common law.

[79] These differences that would sound on the political level are clearly apparent from the way in which the debate about replacing the HRA with a 'British Bill of Rights' played out some years ago, the latter being subject to strong criticism from some political quarters on account – at least in part – of its perceived 'otherness'.

[80] For discussion, see M Elliott, J Williams and A Young, 'The *Miller* Tale: An Introduction' in M Elliott, J Williams and A Young (eds), *The UK Constitution after Miller: Brexit and Beyond* (Oxford, Hart Publishing, 2018).

[81] *R (Miller) v Secretary of State for Exiting the European Union* [2016] EWHC 2768 (Admin).

VI. Conclusions

This chapter has explored the nature of common law rights, and in particular the senses in which they may be considered 'fundamental'. It is hoped that, in the course of doing so, three key points have been demonstrated. The first is that the notion of fundamentality, as it applies in relation to legal rights, falls to be understood as a matter of degree. Certain types of systems for protecting rights – most obviously, perhaps, constitutional bills of rights bestowing powers of legislative invalidation upon courts – may be perceived as investing rights with a paradigm form of fundamentality. (Whether such a model ought properly to be regarded as the, or a, paradigm is arguably debateable – but that is a debate for another day.) It does not, however, follow that any form of rights protection that falls short of – or, less pejoratively, differs from – that 'paradigm' is necessarily incompatible with regarding the rights in question as enjoying a fundamental status. That is so because the more interesting, and salient, question is not whether, according to some binary scheme, rights are or are not fundamental; instead, it concerns the degree to, and the senses in, which rights are accorded a status that sets them apart from other legal norms and which renders rights' violation or displacement a relatively difficult endeavour.

That leads on to the second point that this chapter has sought to establish: namely, that common law rights as they exist under the UK's constitutional arrangements can be regarded as meaningfully fundamental notwithstanding that they attract forms of protection that differ markedly from the 'paradigm' model referred to in the previous paragraph. That much is apparent from the ways in which such rights can be and have been operationalised, the structural limitations of the UK constitution – most obviously the doctrine of parliamentary sovereignty – notwithstanding. All of this said, it is important not to exaggerate or romanticise the common law's capacity in this regard. History – including relatively recent history – teaches that the potential and the reality of fundamental common law rights do not inevitably march hand in hand. A stark reminder of that is supplied by the judicial histrionics manifested in response to the prospect of proportionality review – less than 30 years ago – in *Brind*.[82]

Third, and finally, the somewhat chequered recent history of common law rights – and, in particular, the fact that such rights might today reasonably be regarded as enjoying a greater degree of operational fundamentality than they did three or four decades ago – tells us something not only about the constitutional status of such rights, but about the constitution that, to begin with, accords them that status. As discussed in the previous two sections of this chapter, the operational fundamentality of common law rights is the product of a process of constitutional triangulation that implicates the three key principles – parliamentary sovereignty, the rule of law and the separation of powers – that

---

[82] *Brind* (n 29).

are immanent within the UK's uncodified constitutional order. To the extent that common law rights may be said today (by comparison with earlier times) to enjoy a relatively high degree of protection, this does not connote anything as bald or straightforward as an outright reconfiguration of those basic constitutional principles. There is, for instance, no clear empirical evidence to the effect that those features of the constitutional order – namely, parliamentary sovereignty and the separation of powers – that have tended to constrain the degree of fundamentality that common law rights have been capable of being accorded have now been sacrificed on the altar of a rule-of-law principle conceived in terms so thick as to encompass rights as absolute trumps. Rather, consistently with the evolutive nature a constitution that prizes historical continuity over dramatic rupture, the degree of operational fundamentality today enjoyed by common law rights is a function of changing perceptions of how those principles relate to and shape one another, as distinct from any more radical alteration to the constitutional bedrock. From all of this, it follows that while inquiring into the question of the fundamentality of common law rights is an inherently valuable endeavour, such inquiry is also significant for what it can tell us about the constitutional order itself.

10

Fundamental Common Law Rights and Legislation

ALISON L YOUNG*

There are two main ways in which fundamental common law rights and legislation interrelate. First, the existence of fundamental common law rights affects how legislation is interpreted. This is because of the principle of legality, which states that general words found in legislative provisions cannot remove or restrict, or empower the executive to remove or restrict, fundamental common law rights.[1] Fundamental common law rights can only be removed or limited by clear and specific statutory provisions, or by necessary implication. General words will not suffice. In addition, even when legislation does enable the restriction of fundamental common law rights, any such restriction must be reasonably necessary to achieve a legitimate aim.[2]

Second, there are dicta suggesting that, in extreme circumstances, it might be the case that the courts could possibly refuse to enforce, or perhaps even disapply, legislation which removed fundamental common law rights. The clearest assertion of this possibility is found in *Jackson v Attorney General*, where Lord Steyn, after asserting that parliamentary sovereignty was still the general principle of the UK constitution, stated:

> [i]n exceptional circumstances involving an attempt to abolish judicial review or the ordinary role of the courts, the Appellate Committee of the House of Lords or a new Supreme Court may have to consider whether this is a constitutional fundamental which even a sovereign Parliament acting at the behest of a complaisant House of Commons cannot abolish.[3]

---

* With thanks to Hayley J Hooper and the editors for comments on an earlier version.

[1] *R v Secretary of State for the Home Department, ex parte Leech* [1994] QB 198, *R v Lord Chancellor ex parte Witham* [1998] QB 575, *R v Secretary of State for the Home Department, ex parte Pierson* [1998] AC 539.

[2] *R v Secretary of State for the Home Department, ex parte Leech*, (n 1), *R v Secretary of State for the Home Department, ex parte Daly*, [2001] UKHL 26, [2001] 2 AC 532, and *R (UNISON) v Lord Chancellor* [2017] UKSC 51, [2017] 3 WLR 409.

[3] [2005] UKHL 56, [2006] 1 AC 262, [102].

This dictum was discussed in *AXA General Insurance Ltd v Lord Advocate*, which concerned the extent to which Acts of the Scottish Parliament – and by analogy legislation of the Welsh Assembly and the Northern Irish Assembly – could be reviewed according to common law principles.[4]

Moreover, in *Privacy International Ltd*, Lord Carnwath, with whom Lord Kerr and Lady Hale agreed, suggested, in obiter dicta, a further situation in which courts may refuse to enforce a statutory provision.[5] He argued that there was a 'strong case for holding that, consistently with the rule of law, binding effect cannot be given to a clause which purports wholly to exclude the supervisory jurisdiction of the High Court to review a decision of an inferior court or tribunal, whether for excess or abuse of jurisdiction, or error of law'.[6] In reaching this conclusion, Lord Carnwath regarded the Court's approach to ouster clauses as an exemplification of the principle of legality,[7] reaching is conclusion by balancing parliamentary sovereignty with the rule of law,[8] but distinguishing this from examples of exceptional circumstances, which would apply were Parliament to remove the function of the court, rather than ousting judicial review over a particular tribunal. It is hard to determine, therefore, whether this new possible exception is an exemplification of the first or second relationship between fundamental common law rights and legislation, or a new possible third relationship.

It is relatively easy to describe the principle of legality and dicta regarding when courts might possibly refuse to apply Acts of Parliament. It is much harder to provide an account of the precise scope of application of the principle of legality and to determine when, if at all, courts would be willing to refuse to apply legislation. Moreover, it is also difficult to delineate between fundamental common law *rights*, and fundamental common law *principles*, which sometimes seem to be referred to indiscriminately in the case law and the academic literature. For the purposes of this chapter, fundamental common law principles are more abstract than fundamental common law rights. Principles provide justifications for specific rights. Rights are more precise and provide for a distinct legal relationship between the holder of a right and the individual or institution required to respect or protect the right. Applied to the material in this chapter, fundamental common law rights are linked to the principle of legality. Courts read down legislation to protect a specific right. However, dicta advocating that courts may, in exceptional circumstances, refuse to apply legislation could apply to both fundamental common law rights and fundamental principles of the common law.

This chapter aims to delineate the principle of legality by looking at the case law and by evaluating its rationales. Justifications for the principle of legality are often presented in terms of a perceived tension in the UK constitution between

---

[4] [2011] UKSC 46, [2012] 1 AC 868.
[5] *R (Privacy International) v Investigatory Powers Tribunal* [2019] UKSC 22.
[6] Ibid, [144].
[7] Ibid, [100].
[8] Ibid, [130]–[132].

parliamentary sovereignty and the rule of law.[9] The greater the importance placed on parliamentary sovereignty, the more likely that courts will give a restrictive interpretation of the principle of legality. The more value ascribed to the rule of law, the more likely that courts will use the principle of legality to read down legislation to ensure that it neither removes nor erodes fundamental common law rights. Moreover, if the rule of law is regarded as more important than, or as underpinning parliamentary sovereignty, then it is more likely that the disapplication of legislation which contravenes fundamental common law rights will be accepted as legitimate.

This chapter will re-evaluate this understanding of the principle of legality. It will argue that it is overly simplistic and fails to provide an accurate account of how the principle applies in practice. It will argue, instead, that the principle of legality is best understood as multi-faceted, aiming to protect both democracy and the rule of law without taxonomically prioritising one over the other, the relative importance of these principles being contextually dependent. Moreover, courts are particularly sensitive to protecting the constitutional structures of the UK, especially access to the courts, as well as protecting fundamental rights such as the right to liberty, or those that underpin democracy. It will further argue that, whilst the principle of legality and the potential to disapply legislation are related, and their content depends upon the relative values of democracy and the rule of law, they are best understood as performing different functions. This relies on drawing a further distinction between different types of fundamental common law rights – those designed to protect civil liberties and human rights and those which preserve constitutional foundations. By constitutional foundations, I mean to refer to those fundamental rights and principles of the common law that establish and preserve the distinct constitutional roles of governmental institutions. The principle of legality protects human rights and civil liberties by safeguarding relevant common law rights against inadvertent erosion by the legislature or from erosion by the executive. The potential disapplication of legislation is best understood as a means of protecting foundational constitutional rights and principles.

This understanding provides a more accurate account of how the principle of legality applies in practice and a better normative justification for the relationship between fundamental common law rights and principles, and legislation. The chapter will first provide a more detailed account of the principle of legality and of dicta concerning the possibility of disapplying legislation that would abrogate

---

[9] See, eg, J Goldsworthy, 'Legislative Intentions, Legislative Supremacy and Legal Positivism in J Goldsworthy and T Campbell (eds) *Legal Interpretation in Democratic Statutes* and J Goldsworthy, *Parliamentary Sovereignty: Contemporary Debates* (Cambridge, Cambridge University Press, 2010), ch 9, whose work focuses on linking interpretation, including the principle of legality, to parliamentary sovereignty. For the opposite view, see the work of T Allan, in particular, 'Constitutional Dialogue and the Justification of Judicial Review' (2003) 23 *OJLS* 563, 'Legislative Supremacy and Legislative Intention: Interpretation, Meaning and Authority' (2004) 63 *CLJ* 685 and 'Legislative Supremacy and Legislative Intent: A Reply to Professor Craig' (2004) 24 *OJLS* 563.

fundamental constitutional rights. It will then provide a taxonomy of the rationales for the principle of legality, before evaluating the extent to which these rationales are reflected in the case law. Finally, it will provide an alternative rationale for the principle of legality and explain how this better matches the case law, drawing on distinctions between rights and principles, and delineating those rights and principles of the common law that are constitutional, in the sense of founding the distinct constitutional roles and powers of the institutions of the UK constitution.

I. Interpretation and Potential Disapplication

A. Legislative Interpretation: The Principle of Legality

Although understood as a more recent development of the common law, Lord Hoffmann traced the origins of the principle of legality back to the sixteenth century case of *Stradling v Morgan*.[10] Its most recent iteration can be traced to a trio of cases concerning prisoners' rights and access to the courts: *Leech*,[11] *Witham*[12] and *Pierson*.[13] The courts apply the principle of legality by reading down general legislative provisions to ensure that they do not impede or restrict fundamental common law rights.[14] In *Leech*, Lord Steyn concluded that there was a 'presumption against statutory interference with vested common law rights'.[15] He later stated that '[i]t will be a rare case in which it could be held that such a fundamental right was by necessary implication abolished or limited by statute'.[16] Consequently, although legislation empowering prison officers to censor correspondence with prisoners could empower the enactment of prison rules that required some screening of letters passing between a prisoner and her solicitor, this power was read down in order to protect legal professional privilege, preventing the screening of letters concerning legal matters. In *Witham*, Laws LJ concluded that the right of access to courts was a 'constitutional right', such that the executive could only abrogate the right if a statute expressly permitted the executive to act in this manner, or if this power was found by necessary implication of the statutory language.[17]

Lord Steyn first referred to this presumption of statutory interpretation as 'the spirit of legality' or 'the principle of legality' in *Pierson*, relying on its description

---

[10] (1560) 1 Pl 199. See *R (Morgan Grenfell and Co Ltd) v Special Commissioner of Income Tax and another* [2002] UKHL 21, [2003] 1 AC 563, [8].

[11] *Leech* (n 1).

[12] *Witham* (n 1).

[13] *Pierson* (n 1).

[14] See P Sales, 'A Comparison of the Principle of Legality and section 3 of the Human Rights Act 1998' (2009) 115 *LQR* 598, 610–611.

[15] *Leech* (n 1) 209.

[16] Ibid, 212.

[17] *Witham* (n 1) 585–586.

in *Halsbury's Laws of England*;[18] stating that '[u]nless there is the clearest provision to the contrary, Parliament must be presumed not to legislate contrary to the rule of law'.[19] In the same case, Lord Browne-Wilkinson asserted that

> a power conferred by Parliament in general terms is not to be taken to authorise the doing of acts by the donee of the power which adversely affect the legal rights of the citizen or the basic principles on which the law of the United Kingdom is based unless the statute conferring the power makes it clear that such was the intention of Parliament.[20]

The most influential account of the first component of the principle of legality is found in Lord Hoffmann's pivotal statement placing the principle in its constitutional setting in *R v Secretary of State for the Home Department, ex parte Simms*:

> Parliamentary sovereignty means that Parliament can, if it chooses, legislate contrary to fundamental principles of human rights. The Human Rights Act 1998 will not detract from this power. The constraints upon its exercise by Parliament are ultimately political, not legal. But the principle of legality means that Parliament must squarely confront what it is doing and accept the political cost. Fundamental rights cannot be overridden by general or ambiguous words. This is because there is too great a risk that the full implications of their unqualified meaning may have passed unnoticed in the democratic process. In the absence of express language or necessary implication to the contrary, the courts therefore presume that even the most general words were intended to be subject to the basic rights of the individual. In this way the courts of the United Kingdom, though acknowledging the sovereignty of Parliament, apply principles of constitutionality little different from those which exist in countries where the power of the legislature is expressly limited by a constitutional document.[21]

The Court read down the Prison Service Standing Order 5 of 1996, a policy enacted under section 33 of the Prison Rules 1964. Paragraphs 37 and 37A of Standing Order 5 regulated the access of journalists to prisoners. Paragraph 37 placed a general ban on journalists and writers visiting prisoners for professional purposes. Paragraph 37A did allow for exceptional visits, subject to the permission of the prisoner and of the prison governor. These general policies could be read down, so as not to interfere with the fundamental common law right of freedom of expression; they could not exclude journalists from having access to prisoners in order to pursue stories about potential miscarriages of justice.

The second component of the principle of legality – that any restriction placed on a fundamental right must be reasonably necessary to achieve a legitimate purpose – also stems from *Leech* and the consideration of this case in *R v Secretary of State for the Home Department, ex parte Daly*.[22] *Leech* concerned the interpretation of section 47(1) of the Prison Act 1952, which empowered the Secretary of

---

[18] *Pierson* (n 1) 587–588.
[19] Ibid, 591.
[20] Ibid, 575.
[21] [2000] 2 AC 115, 131.
[22] *Daly* (n 2).

State for the Home Department to make rules for the regulation and management of prisons. The Secretary of State enacted the Prison Rules, including a provision which empowered the governor of the prison to read, examine, or to stop, 'any letter or communication' to or from a prisoner, inter alia, 'on the ground that its contents are objectionable.'[23] Steyn LJ, as he then was, concluded that it was possible to read section 47(1) of the 1952 Act as empowering the executive, by necessary implication, to restrict, to some extent, the general right of confidentiality between a prisoner and her correspondents, where this was needed to prevent escapes from prison, to detect and prevent criminal offences, or to protect national security. However, in order to preserve the free flow of communications between a prisoner and her legal representative, any screening of this correspondence to ensure the pursuit of these legitimate aims must be 'the minimum necessary to ensure that the correspondence is in truth bona fide legal correspondence'.[24]

In *Daly*, a challenge was made to other prison rules allowing for prison cells to be searched by prison officers without the presence of the prisoner. Daly argued that this could breach legal professional privilege if prison officers were to find and read communications between a prisoner and his legal representative found in his cell. As such, he argued that prisoners should be present when prison officers looked through such communications. Lord Bingham cited the approach of Steyn LJ in *Leech*.[25] He accepted that the searching of cells without the presence of the prisoner could be justified due to the risk of intimidation to prison staff were prisoners to be present during a cell search. However, he concluded that, nevertheless, the blanket rule preventing all prisoners from being present, even when looking through legal correspondence, went too far. It would be possible generally to allow prisoners to be present, while excluding those who attempted to disrupt a search, or intimidate a prison officer, or those whose past conduct meant that it was likely that they would do so.[26]

This aspect of the principle of legality was revisited and re-affirmed by the Supreme Court in *R (UNISON) v Lord Chancellor*.[27] *UNISON* concerned a measure of the Lord Chancellor, enacted under section 42(1) of the Tribunals, Courts and Enforcement Act 2007, setting the level of fees for claims before, and appeals to, Employment Tribunals. Section 42(1) specifically empowered the Lord Chancellor to prescribe the fees payable for Employment Tribunals. The Supreme Court concluded that the section did not authorise the Lord Chancellor to impose fees that were so high that they would effectively prevent access to justice.[28] Lord Reed, giving the judgment of the Court, explained that

> even where primary legislation authorises the imposition of an intrusion on the right of access to justice, it is presumed to be subject to an implied limitation ... the degree

---

[23] Prison Rules 1964, r 33(3).
[24] *Leech* (n 1) 217.
[25] *Daly* (n 2) [10].
[26] Ibid, [17]–[23].
[27] *UNISON* (n 2).
[28] Ibid, [87].

of intrusion must not be greater than is justified by the objectives which the measure is intended to serve.[29]

Lord Reed concluded that there was an analogy between this principle and the principle of proportionality; any restriction on the right of access to the court would be 'unlawful unless it can be justified as reasonably necessary to meet a legitimate objective'.[30] The Supreme Court concluded that the fees order was ultra vires as it effectively prevented the right of access to justice.[31] Even if this had not been the case, the fees would also have been unable to be justified as a necessary intrusion on the right of access to justice.[32]

B. Disapplication of Legislation?

It is well-known that the principle of parliamentary sovereignty, as understood by Dicey, means not only that Parliament is unable to bind its successors, but also that courts are not able to strike down legislation on grounds of its lack of constitutionality. Lord Hoffmann's account of the principle of legality in *Simms* reaffirms this view. The principle of legality provides a means of protecting fundamental constitutional rights which fits the traditional understanding of the UK constitution. It is still possible for Parliament, should it wish, to legislate contrary to fundamental constitutional rights protected by the common law, provided it makes its intention to do so clear, so that it can be held to account politically for its actions.

The only circumstance in which, to date, the UK courts have questioned legislation has been in situations where UK law conflicted with directly effective provisions of European Union law. When such conflicts arose, the courts have disapplied legislation.[33] The European Union (Withdrawal) Act 2018 (EU(W)A) preserves the supremacy of EU law as regards legislation enacted prior to exit day (however defined),[34] and modifications of these laws enacted after exit day when this modification includes an intention to preserve the supremacy of EU law.[35] This includes the ability of retained EU law to disapply legislation.[36] However, it does so in a manner which preserves the traditional Diceyan understanding of parliamentary sovereignty. Retained EU law obtains its legal validity through the

---

[29] Ibid, [88].
[30] Ibid, [89].
[31] Ibid, [98].
[32] Ibid, [99]–[102].
[33] See, eg, *Factortame Ltd v Secretary of State for Transport (No 2)* [1991] 1 AC 603, *Vidal-Hall v Google* [2015] EWCA Civ 311, [2016] QB 1003, *R (Davis) v Secretary of State for the Home Department* [2015] EWCA Civ 1185, [2017] 1 All ER 62, *Benkharbouche v Secretary of State for Foreign and Commonwealth Affairs* [2017] UKSC 62, [2017] 3 WLR 957 and *Walker v Innospec Ltd* [2017] UKSC 47, [2017] 4 All ER 1004.
[34] European Union (Withdrawal) Act 2018, s 5(1).
[35] Ibid, s 5(3).
[36] Ibid, s 5(2).

provisions of the EU(W)A, with retained EU law coming into force on exit day. As such, retained EU law would only be capable of disapplying legislation enacted prior to retained EU law coming into force, or where there was an expression of Parliament after exit day that legislation enacted prior to, but modified after exit day, should still be capable of being disapplied by retained EU law. In disapplying legislative provisions that contravene retained EU law in this manner, the courts would be giving effect to the latest will of Parliament. Moreover, there is nothing in the EU(W)A that would prevent its repeal by future legislation wishing to remove the supremacy of retained EU law. Although, if, as seems likely, the EU(W)A is classified by the courts as a constitutional statute, this repeal would either have to be express, or through words that were sufficiently precise as to express an intention to overturn the Act.[37]

As discussed above, dicta suggest a further circumstance in which courts may refuse to enforce legislative provisions. Both relate predominantly to provisions purporting to abrogate or restrict the role of the courts. *Jackson* and *AXA* suggest that it may be possible, in extreme circumstances, for courts to refuse to recognise legislation which abrogates a fundamental common law right. *Privacy International* provides a further specific example of possible circumstances where the court may refuse to apply a statutory provision purporting to remove judicial review over an inferior court or tribunal for excess or abuse of jurisdiction, or for error of law.

In *AXA*, Lord Hope drew on his statement in *Jackson* that 'the rule of law enforced by the courts is the ultimate controlling factor on which our constitution is based'.[38] He went on to state that:

> It is not entirely unthinkable that a government which has that power may seek to use it to abolish judicial review or to diminish the role of the courts in protecting the interests of the individual ... The rule of law requires that the judges must retain the power to insist that legislation of that extreme kind is not law which the courts will recognise.[39]

Lord Hope argued that this principle applied equally to the Westminster Parliament in addition to the Scottish Parliament, although he recognised that it was easier to apply to the Scottish Parliament as the Scottish Parliament is not a sovereign legislator in the same way as the Westminster Parliament. Whilst courts can apply arguments of the rule of law in both, when applying these to the Westminster Parliament, there is a need to balance the requirements of the rule of law against the requirements of parliamentary sovereignty.

It is important to note, first, that the dicta in *Jackson* and *AXA* refer to exceptional circumstances. They are not designed to apply to any situation in which a fundamental right of the common law is *restricted*. Rather, they only apply to

---

[37] *Thoburn v Sunderland City Council* [2002] EWHC 195 (Admin), [2003] QB 151 and *H v Lord Advocate* [2012] UKSC 24, [2013] 1 AC 413.
[38] *AXA* (n 4) [51], referring to his statement in *Jackson* (n 3) [107].
[39] *AXA* (n 4) [51].

the *abrogation* of a fundamental right of the common law. This interpretation was confirmed by Lord Carnwath in *Privacy International*, when he concluded that ouster clauses are not an example of 'exceptional circumstances' as such clauses do not purport to abrogate or derogate from the rule of law and the constitutional protection afforded by judicial review.[40] Ouster clauses may remove judicial review of the decisions of specific inferior courts or tribunals, but they do not remove judicial review completely. In this sense, the difference between the two is one of degree. Yet both may result in the same outcome; a refusal to apply a statutory provision.

In addition, it is unlikely that the dicta in *Jackson* and *AXA* and in *Privacy International* would apply to all fundamental rights of the common law. Both *Jackson* and *AXA* referred to the undermining of the rule of law in a specific manner – that is, by removing judicial review or the ordinary role of the courts. In *Privacy International*, in addition to being understood as a requirement of the rule of law, balanced against the requirements of parliamentary sovereignty,[41] the possible refusal to apply a statutory provision ousting judicial review is also related to a potential logical pre-requisite of parliamentary sovereignty. If Parliament provides a tribunal or inferior court with limited jurisdiction, then it is necessary that a body other than that tribunal or inferior court is required to check that this body acts within its limited jurisdiction.[42] The Investigatory Powers Tribunal, for example, would no longer be a body of limited jurisdiction if it was allowed to determine the scope of its jurisdiction for itself, without the courts checking that it was indeed acting within the limits of its jurisdiction. As such, a clause purporting to remove judicial review for excess of jurisdiction over an inferior court or tribunal with limited jurisdiction would not be given effect to by the courts. Whilst Lord Carnwath appeared to regard this as a potential restriction on parliamentary sovereignty, Lord Sumption regarded this as an aspect of statutory interpretation. Very clear and specific words would be needed to oust judicial review for excess of jurisdiction over an inferior court or tribunal with limited jurisdiction – in essence that would require words to the effect that the inferior court or tribunal was not meant to have limited jurisdiction given that it was specially empowered to determine the scope of its own jurisdiction.[43]

The dictum in *Jackson*, however, may have wider application, extending also to include the right to vote. In *Moohan*, Lord Hodge stated that he did

> not exclude the possibility that in the very unlikely event that a parliamentary majority abusively sought to entrench its power by a curtailment of the franchise or similar device, the common law, informed by principles of democracy and the rule of law and international norms, would be able to declare such legislation unlawful.[44]

---

[40] *Privacy International* (n 5) [119].
[41] Ibid, [130]–[132].
[42] Ibid, [122] (Lord Carnwath) and [208] (Lord Sumption).
[43] Ibid, [210].
[44] *Moohan v Lord Advocate* [2014] UKSC 67, [2015] AC 901, [35].

This dictum was referred to in *Shindler v Chancellor of the Duchy of Lancaster*, although the Court of Appeal concluded that Lord Hodge's statement did not apply to the exclusion from the electoral register for the European Union Referendum of UK citizens who had lived outside of the UK for 15 years or more, as this restriction was not an abusive attempt to entrench power.[45]

Moreover, it is not clear what the remedy would be were the courts faced with exceptional circumstances. Lord Steyn and Lord Hope state that courts would not recognise such legislation, whilst Lord Hodge states that the courts could declare legislation unlawful. Both of these remedies differ from disapplying legislation. Nor is it clear that courts would have the power to disapply legislation in the same manner as is the case for EU law. However, given the ability of the courts to develop their own remedies, it may be the case that, in such extreme circumstances, the courts could develop a remedy which disapplies legislation,[46] especially given that the EU(W)A 2018 specifically mentions the disapplication of legislation as one of the elements of the supremacy of retained EU law, thereby providing recognition by the legislature of the remedy of disapplication of legislation.[47]

II. Normative Framework

The existence of fundamental common law rights may mean that legislation is interpreted differently, and may even give rise to the situation in which legislation is disapplied, given its incompatibility with fundamental common law rights. Both, to a differing extent, rely upon the rationales for the principle of legality and its link to background principles of the constitution. The nature and normative foundation of the principle of legality has received more academic attention in the literature in Australia than it has in the UK.[48] When discussing the rationale for the principle of legality, Brendan Lim distinguishes between a positive and a normative rationale.[49] The positive rationale focuses on the factual reality of Parliament's intention when it enacts legislation. The normative rationale regards the principle of legality as a principle of the constitution, justified on normative grounds.[50]

---

[45] [2016] EWCA Civ 469, [2017] QB 226. The Court also concluded that this was not a breach of Convention rights, as it was not clearly established by the case law of the European Court of Human Rights that the 'right to vote' in Art 1 of the First Protocol extended to a right to vote in referendums.

[46] For an analogous situation, see the development of the declaration of inconsistency with the New Zealand Bill of Rights 1990 developed by the New Zealand courts in *The Attorney General v Taylor* [2018] NZSC 104.

[47] European Union (Withdrawal) Act 2018, s 5(2).

[48] See, in particular, D Meagher, 'The Common Law Principle of Legality' (2013) 38 *Alternative Law Journal* 209, and 'The Principle of Legality as Clear Statement Rule: Significance and Problems' (2014) 36 *Sydney Law Review* 413; B Lim, 'The Normativity of the Principle of Legality' (2013) 37 *Melbourne University Law Review* 372; B Chen, 'The Principle of Legality: Issues of Rationale and Application' (2015) 41 *Monash University Law Review* 329.

[49] Lim (n 48) 373–394.

[50] Bruce Chen relies on this distinction, drawing a similar distinction in his work. See Chen (n 48).

Lim argues that both the normative and the positive rationale are exemplified in Australian case law.[51] This chapter will argue that the same is true of the UK case law. It will also argue that there is a range of both positive and normative justifications for the principle of legality.

With regard to the positive justification, the courts could focus on an assessment of either Parliament's actual or its implied intention when enacting legislation.[52] Parliament's implied intention, in turn, could depend upon a range of factors. Lim focuses on the fundamental nature of the right in question. The more fundamental the right, the less likely that Parliament would have actually wished to remove or erode the right.[53] These implied intentions may arise not just because of the fundamental nature of the right in and of itself, but also because of the development of principles of interpretation by the courts and their recognition and tacit acceptance by the legislature. The legislature does not legislate in a constitutional vacuum and will be aware of the principle of legality, modifying its legislative drafting accordingly.[54] As regards the normative justification for the principle of legality, this may derive not just from a concern to promote democracy,[55] but also from an argument that the fundamental common law rights have greater normative force than democracy, or that they undermine democracy, such that legislation is only legitimate when it reflects fundamental common law rights.[56] Therefore, legislation is only legitimately enforced and applied when this is done in a manner that does not undermine fundamental rights.

The above discussion leads to six possible rationales for the principle of legality. First, the principle of legality could be justified as representing the actual intention of Parliament. Second, the principle could be justified as representing the implied intention of Parliament, it being assumed that Parliament would not wish to legislate in a manner contrary to fundamental common law rights. Third, the principle of legality may be justified as the implied intention of Parliament not to act contrary to a series of interpretative assumptions and presumptions developed by the court, which are accepted by the courts and the legislature as background constitutional principles against which Parliament legislates. Fourth, the rationale for the principle of legality may focus on a normative justification designed to promote democracy. Whilst Parliament may legislate contrary to fundamental common law rights, it may only do so through clearly expressed words, showing a clear intention to act in a manner that overrides fundamental rights which has clear democratic backing. Fifth, the fundamental rights protected by the common

---

[51] Lim argues in favour of the normative justification. See Lim (n 48).

[52] See, Sales (n 14) 600–606.

[53] See also Sales (n 14) 605–6 and P Sales 'Rights and Fundamental Rights in English Law' (2016) 75 *CLJ* 86, 92 and 97–98.

[54] See Goldsworthy (n 9) 242, 245–6 and 308–9.

[55] See D Dyzenhaus, M Hunt and M Taggart, 'The Principle of Legality in Administrative Law: Internationalisation as Constitutionalisation' (2001) 1 *Oxford Commonwealth Law Journal* 5.

[56] T Allan, 'Legislative Supremacy and Legislative Intention: Interpretation, Meaning and Authority' (n 9) and 'Legislative Supremacy and Legislative Intent: A Reply to Professor Craig' (n 9).

law could be regarded as underpinning or conditioning democracy. Sixth, they may be regarded as more important or more fundamental than democracy. This taxonomy of rationales has consequences for the precise formulation of the principle of legality. It also shapes the identification of fundamental rights of the common law, in terms of their source and content, in addition to the methodology used to determine their precise application in a particular case before the court. Furthermore, this taxonomy is relevant to the relative force of the principle of legality.[57]

If the principle of legality is based on the rationale of determining Parliament's actual intention, then we would expect to see courts examining evidence that the legislature was aware that its legislation would modify a fundamental common law right, or that, by enacting a general provision, its legislation would not be capable of modifying a fundamental common law right. This analysis would ensure that the courts interpreted legislation in line with the wishes of Parliament. It would also provide a restrictive account of fundamental rights of the common law. It would only allow reliance on those fundamental common law rights that were recognised at the time Parliament was enacting the legislation falling to be interpreted, in order to determine the real intention of Parliament.[58] Moreover, this list would be narrowed further by the requirement of evidence that Parliament had taken a particular fundamental common law right into account when enacting legislation. There would also be concerns of courts providing detailed determinations of the content of general principles of the common law, particularly if it was felt that this refinement of the content of a principle, in order to determine the content of a common law right, involved the courts taking policy decisions that should best be left to the democratically accountable legislature.[59] It would also be contradictory for a court which adopted this rationale for the principle of legality to conclude that it would be possible for courts to disapply legislation that contradicted fundamental common law rights. If the justification of the principle of legality is to determine Parliament's real intention – whether this be to preserve democracy, or to protect the sovereignty of Parliament – then both would be undermined were the courts to disapply or refuse to recognise legislation, even if this were only in exceptional circumstances.

A principle of legality based on implied intentions will still focus on the wording of legislation, ensuring that legislative provisions interpreted in line with fundamental common law rights are broad and general, and that there are no specific or implied intentions of Parliament to modify or restrict fundamental common law rights. The content of fundamental common law rights will depend upon the arguments used to determine Parliament's implied intentions. If we imply

---

[57] See Meagher (n 48).

[58] See Sales (n 14) 92 and 97–98.

[59] See D Meagher, 'The Common Law Principle of Legality' (n 48) and 'The Principle of Legality as Clear Statement Rule: Significance and Problems' (n 48); P Sales, 'Rights and Fundamental Rights in English Law' (2016) 76 *CLJ* 86; R Ekins and C Forsyth, 'Judging the Public Interest: The Rule of Law vs the Rule of Courts', University of Cambridge Legal Studies Research Paper Series, paper 49/2016.

that Parliament would not wish to legislate contrary to fundamental common law rights, then we would expect courts to focus on determinations of what we mean by *fundamental* rights. The more fundamental the right, the more likely it is that the court will conclude that Parliament would not want to legislate contrary to the right. Moreover, if the courts are focusing on the implied intention of Parliament, there is a need to focus on whether the fundamental right in question was regarded as such at the time the legislation was enacted. However, it may not be the case that such assessments are limited to evaluations of the common law. If it is the case that Parliament's implied intention is connected to the fundamental nature of the right in question, then it is possible for these fundamental rights to be found in other legislative provisions and international law, as well as in the common law.

Theories which analyse the implied intention of Parliament in terms of Parliament's acceptance of fundamental rights as determined by the courts focus less on assessments of what is meant by a *fundamental* right and more on an evaluation of whether a consensus exists between Parliament and the courts as to the content of fundamental common law rights and the need for specific words to restrict these rights. Again, it is unlikely that this rationale for the principle of legality would permit interpretations of legislation that strayed too far from the intention of Parliament, particularly when specific or implied words appeared to enable the restriction of fundamental rights, or to empower courts to disapply legislation.

Rationales for the principle of legality based on a normative justification do not require courts to focus on determining the intention of Parliament. Rather, they apply in a more rule-like or taxonomical manner. Once a fundamental right of the common law has been determined, courts will read down general legislative provisions to ensure the fundamental common law right is neither reduced nor removed by legislation. Whilst courts will focus on the extent to which the right in question is a fundamental common law right, and whether the legislative provision does permit the reduction of the right by specific words or necessary implication, less attention will be paid to ascertaining either the real or the implied will of Parliament. The determination of the content of fundamental common law rights, and their precise application to the situation before the court, will depend upon normative justifications. These may either be distinct, or read into the legislation as constructed interpretations.[60]

A normative justification which focuses on the protection of democracy, ensuring that Parliaments do not inadvertently override fundamental common law rights, may focus more on protecting rights that are vulnerable to erosion by the democratic process, eg minority rights,[61] or on protecting rights foundational to democracy, eg the right to vote, rights to freedom of information, or rights of political speech and political participation. Such a focus may also require an

---

[60] T Allan, 'Legislative Supremacy and Legislative Intention: Interpretation, Meaning and Authority' (n 9).
[61] Lim (n 48).

application of deference when determining the precise content of a fundamental right of the common law.[62] Normative justifications for the principle of legality that rely on the importance of fundamental rights as either underpinning, or as more fundamental than democracy, would again focus on a determination of which rights required protection in this manner. Moreover, courts would be less deferential in the determination of the content of fundamental common law rights, as well as being more willing to accept that legislation which undermined particular fundamental common law rights could be disapplied.

Although we can differentiate between these rationales, it is not the case that they are hermetically sealed. Rationales may be combined, and the distinction, in practice, between the application of a positive rationale which focuses on the implied intention of Parliament and a normative rationale may be more a matter of degree. This often depends upon whether the courts place more or less emphasis on the intention of Parliament, or the normative justification for a specific interpretation of a legislative provision. Moreover, the approach of courts to the application of the principle of legality may by contextually dependent. Courts may be more willing to apply the principle of legality as a rule of the constitution, as opposed to a means of determining the true intention of Parliament, depending on the nature of the fundamental right in question – eg depending on whether this is a deprivation of liberty, or when access to the courts is effectively removed.

III. Interpretative Presumption or Fundamental Principle of the Constitution?

UK case law illustrates that the principle of legality is both a presumption of statutory interpretation and a fundamental principle of the UK constitution designed to protect fundamental rights. Moreover, both the positive and the normative rationales have played a role in shaping the content of the principle of legality. The approach of the UK courts is best understood as contextual, with specific factors influencing the extent to which courts adopt a more normative or a more positive approach. When applying the principle of legality, courts focus on both assumed and actual Parliamentary intentions. The precise wording of legislation, and any evidence of Parliament being aware of the impact of legislation on fundamental common law rights, is used predominantly either to demonstrate that the legislation in question contains specific as opposed to general provisions, such that the principle of legality does not apply, or that the legislation restricts fundamental common law rights by necessary implication. Moreover, legislation can be used to argue against the existence of a purported fundamental common law right. Courts also pay attention to the nature of the fundamental right of the common

---

[62] Meagher (n 48).

law and its importance, as well as whether this right is being balanced against other important interests – eg national security. Courts are also more willing to protect fundamental rights of the common law that directly protect the rule of law or democracy, particularly the protection of the role of courts in judicial review and access to courts more generally.

Lord Hoffmann's iteration of the principle of legality in *Simms* demonstrates the constitutionalisation of the principle. Lord Hoffmann places the principle of legality in its constitutional context, regarding it as the means through which the UK constitution provides a protection for constitutional rights that does not undermine parliamentary sovereignty. At first glance, it may appear that the principle of legality prior to *Simms* was best understood as a presumption of statutory interpretation and that after *Simms* it was better understood as a fundamental principle of the common law, applied in a normative as opposed to positive manner. However, there is evidence of both a positive and a normative approach in the case law prior to, and after *Simms*. This is reinforced when we look more closely at the methodology used by the courts to determine the source, content, and force of fundamental common law rights.

It is not hard to find statements in the case law which regard the principle of legality as a positive principle; an aspect of statutory interpretation designed to ensure that courts interpret legislation in line with Parliament's intention, given its presumed intention not to legislate contrary to fundamental common law rights. These statements can be found in case law after as well as before *Simms*. In *Morgan Grenfell*, Lord Hoffmann states that 'courts will ordinarily construe general words in a statute, although literally capable of having some startling or unreasonable consequence, such as overriding fundamental human rights, as not having been intended to so'. He classified his statement in *Simms* as placing this principle of interpretation in its constitutional context.[63] Similar statements that the principle of legality is just a rule of statutory construction can be found in *AJA v Metropolitan Police Commissioner*, where the principle of legality is referred to as an

> important tool of statutory interpretation. But it is no more than that. When an issue of statutory interpretation arises, ultimately the question for the court is always to decide what Parliament intended.[64]

In a recent Court of Appeal decision, *A-Saadoon v The Secretary of State for Defence*, the Court affirmed that the principle of legality 'is a principle of statutory interpretation, not a broad principle as to how the courts should develop the common law', using this as one reason for rejecting the claim that legislation should be read so as not to override fundamental human rights obligations found in unincorporated Treaty provisions.[65]

---

[63] *R (Morgan Grenfell) v Special Commissioner of Income Tax* (n 10), [8].

[64] [2013] EWCA Civ 1342, [28] (Lord Dyson MR). See also *R (London Christian Radio Ltd and another) v Radio Advertising Clearance Centre* [2013] EWCA Civ 1495, [2014] 1 WLR 307.

[65] [2016] EWCA Civ 811, [198], [2017] QB 1015, quoting and thereby affirming the statement of Leggatt J in the first instance court, [2015] EWHC 715 (Admin), [2015] 3 WLR 503, [269].

However, there is also clear evidence of the normative importance of the principle of legality, and its recognition as a fundamental principle of the UK constitution. For example, recent case law appears to regard the principle of legality as a unifying norm, either through recognising sister principles to the principle of legality, or through explaining earlier case law through the lens of the principle of legality. Both are done in a manner which constitutionalises interpretative presumptions, strengthening the constitutional importance of the principle of legality. In *R v Hughes*, the Court applied the statutory presumption that 'a penal statute falls to be construed with a degree of strictness in favour of the accused',[66] identifying this as a rule of construction that 'is not identical to, but is somewhat analogous to, the principle of statutory interpretation known as the principle of legality',[67] quoting Lord Hoffmann in *Simms*.[68] As such, a long-standing principle of statutory interpretation is incorporated into the same normative justification as the principle of legality, taking on the characteristic of a principle of the UK constitution.

In a similar manner, the Supreme Court classified the way in which courts should interpret Henry VIII clauses as a sister principle to the principle of legality. The Supreme Court had already recognised, relying on a passage from *Craies on Legislation*, that when interpreting a Henry VIII clause, 'the more general the words by Parliament to delegate a power, the more likely it is that an exercise within the literal meaning of the words will nevertheless be outside the legislature's contemplation'.[69] Although the Supreme Court originally referred to this as an application of the normal principles of statutory interpretation, in *Ingenious Media*, the Supreme Court referred to this principle as similar to the principle of legality, again, citing Lord Hoffmann in *Simms*.[70] More recently, the principle of legality has been linked to earlier case law regarding the way in which courts interpret ouster clauses – ie those clauses purporting to remove particular administrative actions from the scope of judicial review. Again, the Court of Appeal,[71] and later the Supreme Court, both cited *Simms*.[72]

The existence of both positive and normative rationales is also evident when we examine the case law more closely to ascertain the methodology used by courts when applying the principle of legality, and when determining the source of fundamental common law rights, their content, and their relative force. The application of the principle of legality is highly context-dependent. First, the nature of the fundamental common law right at play is important. The principle of legality

---

[66] [2013] UKSC 56, [2013] 1 WLR 2461, [26].

[67] Ibid.

[68] Ibid, [27].

[69] *R (Public Law Project) v Lord Chancellor* [2016] UKSC 39, [2016] AC 1531, [26], citing D Greenberg (ed) *Craies on Legislation* 10th edn (London, Sweet and Maxwell, 2012) [1.3.11].

[70] *R (Ingenious Media) v Commissioners for HMRC* [2016] UKSC 54, [2016] 1 WLR 4164, [20]–[21].

[71] *R (Privacy International) v Investigatory Powers Tribunal* [2017] EWCA Civ 1868, [2018] 1 WLR 2572, [21]–[25].

[72] *Privacy International* (n 5) [100].

is more likely to apply where there is clear evidence of the right in case law,[73] rather than when arguments are based on a combination of legislation and case law,[74] or on international law.[75] Courts are also more willing to interpret legislation to prevent the restriction of a fundamental common law right concerning key elements of the rule of law, for example when this removes or prevents access to the courts,[76] or harms the right to a fair trial.[77] Courts are also more likely to read words down when this is required to avoid a large restriction on a fundamental human right, particularly individual liberty.[78] The more a general provision is used to abrogate as opposed to restrict a right, the more the courts will be willing to read down this legislative provision so as to prevent the abrogation of a fundamental common law right. This would appear to suggest that the principle of legality is justified by positive arguments. The more fundamental the right, the easier it is to argue that the legislature would not have wished to inadvertently restrict this right. However, it may also fit a normative justification, the principle playing an important role in ensuring that fundamental rights are protected in the UK constitution.

Second, courts are more likely to read down general provisions in legislation when they are determining the extent to which general legislative provisions empower the executive to restrict fundamental common law rights than when they are interpreting primary or secondary legislation. For example, in *Leech*, Lord Steyn stated that

> [i]t would be a rare case in which it could be held that such a fundamental right was by necessary implication abolished or limited by statute. It will, we suggest, be an even rarer case in which it could be held that a statute authorised by necessary implication the abolition of a limitation of so fundamental a right by subordinate legislation.[79]

The concern for the greater problems that arise when the executive is empowered to abrogate or restrict fundamental common law rights may also explain the connection between the principle of legality and the restrictive interpretation of general words found in Henry VIII clauses. This would appear to prioritise the principle of legality as a constitutional principle, focused on the normative justification of

---

[73] *Cf R (A) v Secretary of State for Health* [2017] EWHC 2815 (Admin), [2018] 4 WLR 2, where the Court concluded that although there was a fundamental common law right to life, there was no evidence for this to include a right to medical treatment in order to save a life, or the right to an organ transplant as opposed to receiving dialysis. This was affirmed in the Court of Appeal, where the Court made no further mention of the principle of legality, *R (BA) v Secretary of State for Health and Social Care* [2018] EWCA Civ 2696.

[74] See, eg, *Moohan* (n 44) and *Re McE, re M and re C* [2009] UKHL 15, [2009] AC 908.

[75] See, eg, *R (Yam) v Central Criminal Court*, [2015] UKSC 76, [2016] AC 771, and *A-Saadoon* (n 65).

[76] See, eg, *Leech* (n 1), *Witham* (n 1), *Pierson* (n 1), *Simms* (n 2), *W (Algeria) v Secretary of State for the Home Department* [2010] EWCA Civ 898, [2010] All ER (D) 321 (Jul), *Home Office v Tariq* [2011] UKSC 35, [2012] 1 AC 452, *UNISON* (n 2) and *Evans v Attorney General* [2015] UKSC 21, [2015] AC 1787.

[77] See, eg, *Tariq* (n 75).

[78] *Ahmed v Her Majesty's Treasury* [2010] UKSC 2, [2011] 2 AC 534 and *B (Algeria) v Secretary of State for the Home Department* [2018] UKSC 5, [2018] AC 418.

[79] *Leech* (n 1) 212. See also *W (Algeria)* (n 76) and *Ahmed* (n 78).

protecting democracy. Even if there would appear to be an intention on the part of Parliament to empower the executive to restrict fundamental rights, the impact on democracy, particularly as regards Henry VIII clauses, is such that the courts will read down primary and secondary legislation to prevent the restriction of fundamental rights. Courts pay less attention to the wishes of Parliament in order to preserve democracy and fundamental rights.

Third, courts pay close attention to the wording of statutory provisions, both in terms of the statutory provision that falls to be interpreted and the statute as a whole. However, this is used predominantly to determine whether there is evidence of a specific legislative intention to restrict or abrogate fundamental common law rights, either from express words or by necessary implication.[80] When carrying out this analysis, courts also pay attention to whether there is evidence of Parliament being aware that the legislation it was enacting would restrict fundamental common law rights, or would empower the executive to do so.[81] Legislative provisions can also be used to reject the existence of a fundamental common law right. The extent to which legislation provides evidence to refute the existence of a fundamental right of the common law depends upon how far it provides an ideation of the content of the purported common law right. The more the scope, application and conditions of application of a right are set out in legislation, the stronger the evidence refuting the existence of a fundamental common law right.

This can be illustrated by the case law surrounding the existence of a common law right to vote.[82] There is case law confirming the importance of the universal right of suffrage, which led to the Supreme Court recognising the classification of the right to vote as 'constitutional'.[83] However, as *Moohan* illustrates, this does not mean that the right to vote has the same status as other fundamental common law rights.[84] Lord Hodge had 'no difficulty in recognising the right to vote as a basic or constitutional right'.[85] However, he did 'not think that the common law has been developed so as to recognise a right of universal and equal suffrage from which any derogation must be provided for by law and must be proportionate'.[86] Lady Hale also stated that, although it 'would be wonderful if the common law had recognised a right of universal suffrage', she agreed with Lord Hodge that 'it has never done so'.[87] Lord Kerr wished to hear more evidence, stating that it

---

[80] See, eg, *R (Gillan) v Commissioner of Police for the Metropolis* [2006] UKHL 12, [2006] 2 AC 307, *W (Algeria) v Secretary of State for the Home Department* (n 76), *Seal v Chief Constable of South Wales* [2007] UKHL 31, [2007] 1 WLR 1910, *Privacy International* (n 5) and *Khaled v Secretary of State for Foreign and Commonwealth Affairs* [2017] EWHC 1422 (Admin), [2017] All ER (D) 119 (Jun).

[81] See, eg, *W (Algeria)* (n 76). Cf *Ahmed* (n 78).

[82] See also ch 6.

[83] *Watkins v Secretary of State for the Home Department* [2006] UKHL 17, [2006] 2 AC 395. This, in turn, referred to *Ashby v White* (1703) 1 Smith's LC (13th edn) 253, 2 Ld Raym 934, 14 St Tr 695 and *Nairn v University of St Andrews* [1909] AC 157.

[84] *Moohan* (n 44).

[85] Ibid, [33].

[86] Ibid, [34].

[87] Ibid, [56].

was 'at least arguable' that a blanket ban on voting for all prisoners breached the common law.[88]

The conclusion of the Supreme Court was influenced by the way in which the right to vote had developed. Although case law existed stressing the importance of democracy and of the right to vote, these cases occurred at a time when the right to vote was severely restricted and there was no universal franchise.[89] There was no long history of case law expanding the right to vote. Instead, the franchise originated in the exercise of a Writ from the King, followed by a series of Acts of Parliament expanding the franchise. The precise content of the right to vote, therefore, is a creature of statute as opposed to the common law. Nevertheless, the right to universal suffrage is a basic right of the constitution, even if this is not a right which can only be restricted by express words or necessary implication in legislation, or which would require express restrictions to be proportionate restrictions on the right to vote. It appears to be more akin to a fundamental principle of the common law, influencing the development of the common law and referred to when interpreting legislation, but not giving rise to a fundamental common law right.

This detailed analysis of statutory provisions and common law precedents would suggest that the principle of legality is more concerned to ensure legislation is interpreted in line with the wishes of Parliament than it is to protect fundamental rights according to their relative normative strength. The right to vote is clearly a fundamental constitutional principle, regardless of whether we adopt a normative justification on the grounds of democracy, or on the claim that parliamentary sovereignty is underpinned or restricted by fundamental rights protected through the rule of law. This is also illustrated by the statements in both *Moohan* and *Shindler* that the complete removal of the right to vote may exemplify an extreme circumstance in which the courts may be willing to refuse to apply legislation. Nevertheless, the role of Parliament's intention in establishing the content of the right to vote means that this right differs from other fundamental rights of the common law when it comes to the application of the principle of legality.

Fourth, courts take account of the specific circumstances of the case when applying the principle of legality. In particular, courts focus on subject matter. Courts are more willing to accept that general legislative words were designed to restrict fundamental common law rights when, for example, this may be required to achieve an important aim – particularly when this involves issues of national security,[90] or where there is evidence of other precise methods in legislative provisions designed to minimise the impact of the restriction on the fundamental common law right.[91] These specific circumstances depend upon what courts perceive to be

---

[88] Ibid, [87].
[89] *Watkins* (n 83) [24]–[25] (Lord Bingham) and [48]–[57] (Lord Rodger).
[90] See, eg, *Gillan* (n 80).
[91] See, eg, *W (Algeria)* (n 76), *Gillan* (n 80), *AJA* (n 64) and *Khaled* (n 80).

the relative roles of the legislature, the executive, and the judiciary and the precise wording of legislation. Again, this would suggest both a concern for a normative justification and to ensure that courts ascertain Parliament's intention.

How this contextual approach applies in practice can best be explained by a paired example, illustrating contrasting outcomes to what may appear, at first, to be similar situations: *Gillan*[92] and *Ahmed*.[93] Both concerned restrictions of the common law fundamental right to liberty. In *Gillan*, both applicants were stopped and searched whilst either taking part in, or recording, a peaceful protest against an arms fair. In *Ahmed*, the applicant had his assets frozen under the provisions of The Terrorism (United Nations Measures) Order 2006.[94]

Both concerned anti-terrorism measures. *Gillan* concerned the Terrorism Act 2000, which provided enhanced stop and search powers in connection with terrorism. These applied irrespective of whether the police constable had grounds to suspect that the individual she stopped and searched was carrying articles related to acts of terrorism. *Ahmed* concerned orders designed to implement UN Security Council Resolutions to suppress and prevent the financing of terrorist acts and actions in preparation of terrorist activities. Both concerned legislative provisions that were similarly expressed, but nevertheless subtly different. In *Gillan*, the Court was asked to construe section 44(3) of the Terrorism Act 2000. This provision authorised the use of stop and search powers in a particular area if the person authorising these powers 'considers it expedient for the prevention of acts of terrorism'. In *Ahmed*, the Court was required to interpret section 1(1) of the United Nations Act 1946, which empowered the enactment of Orders in Council which were 'necessary or expedient' to give effect to measures of the UN Security Council.

The Supreme Court in *Ahmed* was willing to apply the principle of legality, reading down section 1(1) of the United Nations Act 1946. In *Gillan*, the House of Lords reached the opposite conclusion, refusing to apply the principle of legality. Five factors appear to explain this difference in outcome. First, as adumbrated above, the wording of the legislative provisions is different. In *Ahmed* the executive were empowered to issue Orders in Council that were 'necessary and expedient'. In *Gillan*, the authorisation for stop and search powers only needed to be 'expedient'. Counsel for the applicant argued that, given the broad sweeping nature of the powers in question, an authorisation for stop and search powers should only be issued when necessary and not just when expedient. However, the Court focused on the specific choice of words by Parliament. Parliament had used the word 'necessary' in other provisions of the Terrorism Act 2000, but chose to just use 'expedient' for section 44(3). Therefore, the principle of legality would not require

---

[92] *Gillan* (n 80).
[93] *Ahmed* (n 78).
[94] The case also concerned the validity of the Al Qaida and Taliban (United Nations Measures) Order 2006, which will not be referred to for the purposes of this comparison.

the reading of the word 'necessary' into the 2000 Act, especially as 'necessary' has a narrower connotation than 'expedient'. In *Ahmed*, the Supreme Court was willing to ensure that the Terrorism (United Nations Measures) Order 2006 was 'necessary' to implement the Security Council resolution, interpreting this in a very strict manner. The UN Security Council resolution required the freezing of assets of those carrying out terrorist activities, or supporting the acts of terrorism. The 2006 Order required the freezing of assets of those whom the Treasury had 'reasonable grounds to suspect' were carrying out terrorist activities or supporting acts of terrorism. This, therefore, went beyond what was 'necessary' to implement the UN Security Council resolution.

Second, the Court was being asked to do far more in *Gillan* to protect the fundamental common law right than they were in *Ahmed*. In *Ahmed* the Court was able to protect the fundamental right through determining that the general words 'necessary and expedient' did not empower the executive to issue an Order in Council whose provisions went beyond what was strictly required to implement the UN Security Council Resolution. In *Gillan*, the Court was being asked to read words into legislation, transforming an authorisation of stop and search powers when the measure was expedient to also include a requirement that the measure was necessary for the prevention of terrorism. Whilst the principle of legality has been consistently used to 'read down' general provisions, so as not to restrict fundamental common law rights, it has not been used to read words in to legislation in order to protect these rights.[95]

Third, despite both cases concerning the fundamental common law right to liberty, although *Ahmed* did not involve Article 5 ECHR in addition to common law rights, there was a far greater intrusion into this right in *Ahmed* than there was in *Gillan*. In *Ahmed*, the freezing of assets had an impact on those suspected of terrorism and their families, making it impossible for them to have money on which to live, such that they were effectively 'prisoners of the state'.[96] In *Gillan*, the detention by the police during the process of a search was much shorter (one individual being detained for 20 minutes and the other for 5 minutes). Moreover, neither of the applicants had property removed by the police following the search. As such, it was debateable whether any right to liberty had been restricted at all.

Fourth, there was clearer evidence in *Gillan* that Parliament was aware of the potential impact on fundamental rights of the common law when it enacted the Terrorism Act 2000 than there was in *Ahmed* concerning the awareness of Parliament enacting the United Nations Act 1946. In reaching his conclusion in *Ahmed*, Lord Hope remarked on the 'absence of any indication that Parliament

---

[95] This contrasts with s 3 of the Human Rights Act 1998, which allows courts to go further and read words in to legislation in order to ensure its compatibility with Convention rights.

[96] *Ahmed v Her Majesty's Treasury* [2008] EWCA Civ 1187, [2010] 2 AC 534, [125] (Sedley LJ), cited with approval by Lord Hope in the Supreme Court (n 78) [4] and [60].

had the imposition of restrictions on the freedom of individuals in mind when the provisions of the 1946 Act were being debated'.[97] This made it hard to conclude that Parliament would have squarely confronted this possibility, particularly when, at the time, measures of the United Nations tended to be general and did not habitually have an impact on individuals or on individual rights.

By contrast, in *Gillan*, section 44(3) did not stand alone. Rather, it was enacted against a backdrop of other legislative provisions providing constraints on power to issue an order authorising stop and search powers. The order had to be given by a very senior police officer, only being issued when she had reasonable grounds for believing this authorisation was expedient for the prevention of terrorism. The order had to be connected to the aim of preventing acts of terrorism. The authorisation was also limited in time, had to be reported to the Secretary of State who could approve or modify the authorisation, and could lapse if not confirmed by the Secretary of State. Moreover, the authorisation could not be renewed without going through the same procedure, with decisions of the Secretary of State being subject to judicial review. The use of these authorisations was also subject to the general requirement of annual reports on the Act.[98] These specific requirements were used as evidence that Parliament had paid attention to the impact of the requirement on the fundamental common law right to liberty.

Although both provisions were related to actions of the executive, in *Ahmed* the legislation empowered the executive to enact Orders in Council over which there would rarely be any democratic oversight by Parliament. In *Gillan*, the measures empowered senior police officers to authorise specific stop and search powers by police constables. They also required modifications to the statutory code of practice governing the exercise of police stop and search powers.[99] These modifications imposed further guidelines restricting the exercise of these powers.[100] This existence of greater controls over the exercise of power by the executive provided further indication that the legislature was aware of the potential impact of the stop and search power on civil liberties.

It is hard to read the case law as supporting either a purely positive or a purely normative rationale for the principle of legality. Moreover, the case law does not consistently demonstrate an indication that either the rule of law or the sovereignty of Parliament should be regarded as the more fundamental principle of the UK constitution. Both are balanced against each other according to the specific circumstances of the case. Rather than seeing the principle of legality as either normative or positive, it is best understood as a principle of interpretation which performs a constitutionally important function. Its application varies according to the situation in which it is applied, with the courts paying attention to legislative wording, its context, the legislative background, the nature of the fundamental

---

[97] *Ahmed* (n 78) [61].
[98] Ibid, [14].
[99] Code A, issued under the Police and Criminal Evidence Act 1984.
[100] *Gillan* (n 80) [10]–[11].

right of the common law and the extent to which it has been restricted. This conclusion influences the normative justification for the principle of legality, as well as the circumstances in which courts may be prepared to disapply legislation which contravenes fundamental common law rights. This will be examined further in the next section.

IV. Legality and Disapplication Re-imagined

This chapter originally distinguished between a positive and a normative approach to the principle of legality. A normative justification based upon an assessment of fundamental common law rights as underpinning, or as superior to, the will of Parliament provides a stronger justification for the courts to interpret legislation to protect fundamental rights and to refuse to apply legislation which removed fundamental common law rights. However, the more the principle of legality is based upon a desire to discover the actual and real intentions of Parliament, the less likely that courts would be willing to read down legislative provisions. Moreover, this positive rationale would argue against the courts refusing to recognise or apply legislation, even in exceptional circumstances. Similarly, a normative framework based upon the preservation of democracy would point towards a weaker application of the principle of legality, save where required to protect democratic rights or where erosion may occur through the actions of the executive as opposed to the legislature. A democratic-based normative justification would also conclude that courts should not refuse to apply or disapply legislation, unless the democratic foundations on which such legislation was based had been fundamentally undermined.

The position in UK law, however, does not fit one of these rationales. Courts tend to focus more on the normative justification from democracy, as illustrated in *Simms*. However, there are dicta suggesting the possibility of refusing to apply legislation in exceptional circumstances; or as a necessary corollary of the principle of parliamentary sovereignty; or as regards the correct understanding of a balance between parliamentary sovereignty and the rule of law as applied to certain types of ouster clause. Moreover, although courts are more willing to read down legislation which empowers the executive to remove or erode fundamental common law rights, they are less willing to protect the right to vote in this manner. Yet the removal of the franchise is a potential exceptional circumstance where courts might refuse to apply legislation. The extent to which courts are willing to read down general legislative provisions depends upon the importance of the right, the precise statutory wording, and the context of its application. However, courts are more willing to protect not just fundamental common law rights concerning individual liberties or human rights, but also common law rights that uphold constitutional foundations, such as the separation of powers between the legislature, the executive, and the judiciary, particularly protecting access to justice and the role of the courts.

If we are to fully understand the relationship between fundamental common law rights and legislation in UK law, we need to re-visit our normative framework. A better way of understanding this relationship is to realise the extent to which the principle of legality and dicta advocating the refusal to apply legislation in exceptional circumstances serve two complementary purposes. First, they protect fundamental common law rights from inadvertent erosion by the legislature, or removal or erosion by a non-democratically accountable executive body. Second, they protect fundamental constitutional principles that underpin and justify the relative powers of the legislature, the executive, and the judiciary. They are a means through which the courts can both protect the balance between democracy and the rule of law on which the UK constitution is based and the relative institutional powers of the judiciary, the executive, and the legislature on which this delicate balance rests.[101]

These aims are achieved to differing degrees by the principle of legality and dicta concerning the ability of courts to refuse to recognise or apply legislation. The principle of legality is more suited to protecting fundamental common law rights from inadvertent erosion by the legislature or removal or erosion by the executive. It provides a means of balancing the rule of law and parliamentary sovereignty, with the courts applying this in a contextual manner that is sensitive to the relative competences of the judiciary, the executive, and the legislature. In doing so, the courts draw on fundamental constitutional principles and their application to the specific case before the court.[102] Consequently, the precise wording of legislation is more relevant as evidence to refute the existence of a fundamental common law right, or to demonstrate that a legislative provision is specific as opposed to general. This also explains why courts also look for evidence of whether the legislature knew that its legislation would restrict a fundamental right and either faced the political consequences of this action, or legislated in a manner to minimise the erosion of the fundamental right. The focus on necessary restrictions on rights operates in a similar manner to the principle of proportionality, enabling courts to check that any restriction on a right is strictly necessary to achieve the legitimate aim of the legislature. This also explains why courts are more likely to read down legislation empowering the executive to act and the provisions of secondary legislation, than it is to read down broad legislative provisions more generally.

The possibility of disapplying legislation performs a different function. It is more suited to preserving the constitutionally hierarchical relationship between the legislature and the executive and upholding the constitutional role of the judiciary. It can also ensure that the legislature does not abuse its own constitutional position by acting in a manner that would remove or impede the right to vote to such an extent that the legislature could no longer claim democratic legitimacy.[103] This helps

---

[101] AL Young, *Democratic Dialogue and the Constitution* (Oxford, Oxford University Press, 2017).

[102] In earlier work I have referred to this as constitutional collaboration. See Young (n 101) ch 4.

[103] In an earlier work, I have referred to this as constitutional counter-balancing, see Young (n 101), ch 4.

to explain the approach of the Supreme Court in *Moohan*. The Court was not in a position to protect the right to vote in the same manner as it protected other fundamental common law rights, especially given the role of the legislature in providing a more specific iteration of this right. In this sense, the right to vote was more akin to a fundamental common law principle as opposed to a fundamental common law right. Nevertheless there are dicta in the case suggesting that legislation abrogating the right to vote could lead courts to refuse to enforce or recognise such legislation.

It also explains why judicial dicta mention instances where the legislature has severely abused its power, using its power to remove its own constitutional legitimacy or to remove the powers of other institutions of the constitution when determining the possible exceptional circumstances in which courts might refuse to apply legislation. For example, reference is made to a removal of the right to vote by an undemocratic legislature, or one abusing its powers. A further possible exceptional circumstance is the removal of judicial review, or of access to the courts. Courts are only willing to disapply legislation for an abrogation of these rights because of the severe consequences of refusing to apply legislation. Moreover, the principle of legality may provide a better means of protecting these rights from erosion as opposed to abrogation. This also explains why the majority of the Supreme Court in *Privacy International* read down the specific ouster clause, so as not to apply to purported determinations of the Investigative Powers Tribunal as to whether it had jurisdiction to act, in addition to the dicta of three of the seven Justices of the Supreme Court that courts might not enforce a statutory provision purporting to oust judicial review for excess or abuse of jurisdiction, or error of law, from a tribunal or lower court with limited jurisdiction.

The reasoning of Lord Carnwath in *Privacy International*, drawing on *Cart*,[104] appears to exemplify this approach. The Supreme Court was required to interpret an ouster clause which stated that 'determinations, awards, orders and other decisions of the [Investigatory Powers] Tribunal (including decisions as to whether they have jurisdiction) shall not be subject to appeal or be liable to be questioned in any court'.[105] This clause was similar to the ouster clause in *Anisminic*,[106] which stated that 'the determination by the commission of any application made to them under this Act shall not be called in question in any court of law'.[107] The High Court, the Court of Appeal and Lord Wilson in the Supreme Court concluded that the differences between the two – particularly the specific inclusion of determinations of jurisdiction in the ouster clause – was sufficient to distinguish *Anisminic* from *Privacy International*. Consequently, the clause in *Privacy International* ousted the jurisdiction of the Court over decisions of the Investigatory Powers Tribunal (IPT). However, Lord Carnwath, with whom Lord Kerr and Lady Hale agreed, and

---

[104] *R (Cart) v Upper Tribunal* [2011] UKSC 28, [2012] 1 AC 663.
[105] Regulation of Investigatory Powers Act 2000, s 67(8).
[106] *Anisminic v Foreign Compensation Commission* [1969] 2 AC 147.
[107] Foreign Compensation Act 1950, s 4(4).

Lord Lloyd-Jones in a separate judgment, reached the opposite conclusion. They reasoned that the Court in *Anisminic* had concluded that a 'determination' did not include a 'purported determination'. In a similar manner, the ouster clause in *Privacy International* would be read so as not to oust the jurisdiction of the Court over 'purported determinations', including 'purported determinations' made by the IPT as to whether it had jurisdiction.[108]

After analysing the case law on ouster clauses, and the extent to which courts control determinations of inferior courts and tribunals, Lord Carnwath concluded that the case law demonstrates that 'the courts have not adopted a uniform approach, but have felt free to adapt or to limit the scope and form of judicial review, so as to ensure respect on the one hand for the particular statutory context and the inferred intention of the legislature, and on the other for the fundamental principles of the rule of law, and to find an appropriate balance between the two' which Lord Carnwath regards as providing a 'sounder conceptual basis'.[109] Further evidence of this contextual approach is illustrated by the way in which Lord Carnwath draws on the institutional features of the IPT, particularly its composition and its judicial function, which might suggest that judicial review is not needed over the IPT in order to preserve the rule of law. Nevertheless, the majority concluded that the rule of law required that its decisions be overseen by the High Court through judicial review, particularly to ensure that the rule of law was not undermined by the IPT creating its own specialist enclave of statutory interpretations that was not subject to oversight by the courts. The minority also drew on the distinct institutional features of the IPT. However, the minority placed more emphasis on the institutional similarities between the IPT and the High Court, in addition to placing less emphasis on the need for a uniform approach to English law. Nor did they regard the rule of law as applying so generally in this case, focusing on a narrower aspect of the rule of law requiring a check to ensure that the determinations of the IPT, a tribunal with limited jurisdiction, were not beyond the limits of its jurisdiction.

Analysing the principle of legality and dicta concerning the possible disapplication of legislation in this manner also helps to explain the presence of both positive and normative rationales for the principle of legality in the current case law. It provides an alternative rationale, recognising both the importance of the role of the court in protecting fundamental rights, particularly from inadvertent or unintended erosion, whilst providing the legislature with the ability to provide legislative iterations of rights, these iterations being taken into account by courts when applying the principle of legality. Rather than regarding the principle of legality as either requiring a stronger protection of parliamentary sovereignty or the rule of law, which push towards a purely positive or normative justification for the principle of legality respectively, it facilitates a balancing of positive and

---

[108] *Privacy International* (n 5) [104]–[112] (Lord Carnwath) and [164]–[165] (Lord Lloyd Jones).
[109] *Privacy International* (n 40), [130].

normative accounts of the principle of legality. This, in turn, provides an effective means of balancing parliamentary sovereignty and the rule of law; democracy and fundamental rights.

V. Conclusion

This chapter discussed the relationship between fundamental common law rights and legislation. It recognised that the UK courts use both positive and normative rationales for the principle of legality. The principle of legality is both a presumption of statutory interpretation and a principle of the UK constitution. Although courts may not focus predominantly on determining Parliament's actual or implied intention when balancing fundamental common law rights and legislation, they do pay particular attention to the wording of statutory provisions and the broader legislative context. The principle of legality acts as a normative principle, but specific wording can be used to demonstrate that a purported fundamental principle of the common law does not exist. The wording of legislation can also demonstrate that specific as opposed to general words were used to restrict a fundamental common law right, or that Parliament was restricting a right deliberately and not inadvertently. The normative force of the principle focuses predominantly on a democratic justification. This is illustrated by Lord Hoffmann's statement in *Simms*, in addition to the greater willingness of the court to apply the principle of legality when restricting the powers of the executive as opposed to the legislature. It may also explain why principles akin to proportionality are applied by the courts to ensure that specific powers to restrict fundamental common law rights do not go beyond what is necessary to achieve a legitimate objective.

In addition, I have argued that, although connected, the principle of legality and dicta concerning the possible refusal to apply legislation abrogating fundamental common law rights serve different purposes. The principle of legality provides a means of protecting fundamental common law rights more generally, respecting the relative roles of the legislature, executive, and the judiciary in developing and protecting fundamental rights. Dicta concerning the refusal to apply legislation is best understood as protecting foundational constitutional principles. In particular, it upholds the separation of powers, protecting the role of the court as a constitutional safeguard of individual rights, ensuring access to courts and access to justice. Moreover, it is a means by which courts can protect democracy in extreme circumstances – for example if the legislature were to remove the right to vote or restrict the franchise in such a manner that the institution of Parliament no longer had democratic legitimacy. Understanding these principles in this manner provides a better explanation of the case law, in light of the contextual manner in which the court approaches the principle of legality. It also provides a clearer normative justification, explaining how the UK courts balance democracy and the rule of law, both when protecting fundamental common law rights and when upholding fundamental constitutional principles.

11

Common Law Constitutional Rights and Executive Action

JOANNA BELL*

It is well-known that common law constitutional rights have experienced something of a 'resurgence'[1] in public law reasoning in recent case law. This phenomenon, unsurprisingly, has not failed to permeate judicial review of executive action. Thus *Osborn*,[2] for instance, saw Lord Reed emphasising the primacy of the 'common law duty to act fairly'[3] over the Article 6 Convention Right to a fair hearing.[4] Cases such as *Paponette*[5] and *Pham*,[6] furthermore, also indicate that senior judges are becoming increasingly comfortable[7] with the notion that the common law is able to make use of proportionality, a doctrinal tool classically applied in the human rights context,[8] in order to protect the basic rights, interests and expectations[9] of individuals.[10]

Against this background, this chapter explores the relationship between common law constitutional rights and judicial review of executive action. The analysis will be divided into five parts. Part I will tackle a preliminary but tricky

---

* My sincere thanks to the editors for their diligent and thoughtful comments.

[1] R Masterman and S Wheatle, 'A Common Law Resurgence in Rights Protection?' [2015] *European Human Rights Law Review* 57. See further R Clayton, 'The Empire Strikes Back: Common Law Rights and the Human Rights Act' [2015] *PL* 3.

[2] *R (Osborn) v Parole Board* [2013] UKSC 61, [2014] AC 1115.

[3] Language used throughout *Osborn* (n 2). See for instance ibid, 1133.

[4] Convention for the Protection of Human Rights and Fundamental Freedoms (European Convention on Human Rights, as amended), Art 6.

[5] *Paponette v Attorney General of Trinidad and Tobago* [2010] UKPC 32, [2012] 1 AC 1, [38].

[6] *Pham v Secretary of State for the Home Department* [2015] UKSC 19, [2015] 1 WLR 1591.

[7] See further *R (Daly) v Secretary of State for the Home Department* [2001] UKHL 26, [2001] 2 AC 532.

[8] See especially M Taggart, 'Proportionality, Deference, *Wednesbury*' [2008] *New Zealand Law Review* 423; J Varuhas, 'Against Unification' in M Elliott & H Wilberg (eds), *The Scope and Intensity of Substantive Review: Traversing Taggart's Rainbow* (Oxford, Hart Publishing, 2015).

[9] See further *R (Nadarajah) v Secretary of State for the Home Department* [2015] EWCA Civ 1363 and M Elliott, 'Legitimate Expectations and the Search for Principle: Reflections on *Abdi* and *Nadarajah*' (2006) 11 *Judicial Review* 281.

[10] See further *R (Keyu) v Secretary of State for Foreign and Commonwealth Affairs* [2015] UKSC 69, [2016] AC 1355.

definitional issue by making clear what is meant for the purposes of this chapter by 'judicial review of executive action.' The bulk of the analysis will then take place across Parts II, III and IV. These parts will examine the three constituent components of this book's subject-matter and explore their relationship with judicial review. Part II thus considers the extent to which judicial review is an exercise in developing the *common law*, Part III explores the extent to which judicial review is concerned with '*rights*-protection' and Part IV grapples with the problem of whether judicial review or its grounds can be said to be *constitutional*. Part V, finally, will conclude by offering some reflections on what can be learnt from this chapter about the role played by common law constitutional rights within judicial review. Three main lessons will be emphasised here.

The first is that we should not expect too much of the notion of common law constitutional rights. The history of academic writings on judicial review of executive action is replete with examples of a search for the one big idea[11] which is capable of lending it unity.[12] 'Jurisdiction',[13] 'abuse of power',[14] fundamental rights[15] and promotion of the public interest[16] have, for instance, all been put forward as candidates in recent years. Common law constitutional rights, though undoubtedly important in placing limitations on executive action, will not supply us with the missing key which will enable us to understand all of judicial review as a unified whole. Indeed, for a number of reasons, it is highly doubtful that such a thing can be found at all.[17]

The second is that even though they cannot supply the whole, common law constitutional rights, understood in a broad sense at least,[18] supply an important and indispensable part of the picture. There are, more particularly, numerous aspects of judicial review which have taken their shape, to a large degree, because the courts have developed the common law in order to afford a form of legal

---

[11] Dame S Elias, 'The Unity of Public Law?' in M Elliott, J Varuhas & S Wilson Stark (eds), *The Unity of Public Law?* (Oxford, Hart Publishing, 2018) 21.

[12] See also S Nason, *Reconstructing Judicial Review* (Oxford, Hart Publishing, 2017), ch 1.

[13] See especially C Forsyth, 'The Rock and the Sand: Jurisdiction and Remedial Discretion' (2013) 18(4) JR 360; C Forsyth, 'Blasphemy Against Basics: Doctrine, Conceptual Reasoning and Certain Decisions of the Supreme Court' in J Bell, M Elliott, J Varuhas & P Murray (eds), *Public Law Adjudication in Common Law Systems: Process and Substance* (Oxford, Hart Publishing, 2016).

[14] See especially *R v Secretary of State for Education and Employment, ex parte Begbie* [2000] 1 WLR 115 (CA), 1129; S Sedley, *Law and the Whirligig of Time* (Oxford, Hart Publishing, 2018), ch 17. See further P Daly, 'Administrative Law: Characteristics, Legitimacy, Unity' in Elliott, Varuhas and Stark (n 11).

[15] See especially M Taggart, 'Reinventing Administrative Law' in N Bamforth & P Leyland (eds), *Public Law in a Multi-Layered Constitution* (Oxford, Hart Publishing, 2003); T Poole, 'The Reformation of English Administrative Law' (2009) 68 *CLJ* 142; S Elias, 'Righting Administrative Law' in D Dyzenhaus, M Hunt & G Huscroft (eds), *A Simple Common Lawyer: Essays in Honour of Michael Taggart* (Oxford, Hart Publishing, 2009). For a cogent critique see: J Varuhas, 'The Reformation of English Administrative Law? "Rights", Rhetoric and Reality' (2013) 72 *CLJ* 369.

[16] See especially J Varuhas, 'The Public Interest Conception: Its Procedural Origins and Substantive Implications' in Bell, Elliott, Varuhas and Murray (n 13).

[17] As I argue in my forthcoming book: J Bell, *The Anatomy of Administrative Law* (Oxford, Hart Publishing, forthcoming).

[18] This is an important caveat for reasons which will be explained in the conclusion.

protection to individual interests which are regarded as being, in some sense, fundamental.

That being said, the third and final lesson of this chapter is a warning about the difficulties of formulating a neat and accurate explanation of the nature of the protections which the common law has afforded to its values within judicial review to date. One source of difficulty, it will be explained, is that it is possible to look at the issue at both a specific and a general level. At the specific level it seems clear that Parliament is able to override at least certain common law protections, such as the presumption that the executive must give the individual notice before making a decision which will affect their rights or interests.[19] Encapsulating as a simple legal 'test' the inquiry the courts undertake in order to decide whether such a protection has been overridden, however, is a difficult matter. At the general level there are well-known examples of dicta to the effect that the common law's protection of judicial review as a whole is much stronger, such that any attempt by Parliament to do the 'unthinkable'[20] by abolishing it would be met by judicial disobedience.[21] It is, however, extremely difficult to know how significant these dicta are, especially because it is highly unlikely, for both political and legal reasons, that the courts will be faced with a case, the resolution of which will require the courts to rank legislation on the one hand and the common law on the other.

Overall, then, answering the question of what role common law constitutional rights play in judicial review of executive action is both easy and hard. It is easy in the sense that it is clear both that common law constitutional rights cannot explain all of judicial review but that, at least when understood broadly, they supply an important part of the picture. It is much harder, however, to offer a precise statement of the nature of the legal protection the common law has afforded to its values within judicial review to date.

I. A Definitional Issue: What is 'Judicial Review of Executive Action'?

It is helpful to begin the analysis in this chapter by tackling directly a tricky definitional question: what is meant in this context by 'judicial review of executive action'?[22] Defining judicial review is no easy task. One source of complexity is that

---

[19] See, eg, *R (Haralambous) v St Alban' Crown Court* [2018] UKSC 1, [2018] AC 236.

[20] *R (Jackson) v Attorney General* [2005] UKHL 56, [2006] 1 AC 262, [102].

[21] Ibid. See also *AXA General Insurance Ltd v HM Advocate* [2011] UKSC 46, [2012] 1 AC 868, [51].

[22] Note that the language used throughout this chapter is that of judicial review rather than administrative law. To the extent that this chapter is concerned with administrative law that term is understood in a narrow doctrinal sense. This, however, is not to cast doubt on the utility of using the term in a broader sense: see especially C Harlow and R Rawlings, *Law and Administration*, 3rd edn (Oxford, Oxford University Press, 2009), ch 1; N Parillo, *Administrative Law from the Inside Out: Essays on the Themes in the Work of Jerry L Mashaw* (Cambridge, Cambridge University Press, 2017).

'judicial review' has both a procedural and a substantive dimension. Procedurally, judicial review may refer to a process for bringing claims before the Administrative Court first introduced in 1977,[23] known as the 'application'[24] or 'claim'[25] for judicial review.[26] Substantively, judicial review may also refer to a cluster of legal doctrines commonly known as the 'grounds of judicial review'.[27] The procedural and substantive dimensions of judicial review, of course, often converge. Thus courts are frequently faced with legal challenges which have been initiated via the judicial review procedure and which require the application of the grounds of review. It is sometimes the case however, such as where the grounds of judicial review are raised by way of defence in criminal proceedings[28] or where applicants make use of the judicial review procedure to bring a claim founded exclusively on the Human Rights Act,[29] that one of these dimensions of judicial review is present in the absence of the other.[30]

This chapter's focus is primarily on judicial review in the second, substantive sense. Its central concern is the relationship between common law constitutional rights and the grounds of judicial review. The task of understanding this relationship is, however, further complicated by the fact that there is no fixed list of the grounds of review. Thus judges and scholars asked to compile a list of these doctrines would no doubt disagree about whether certain grounds ought to be included[31] and how others ought to be formulated.[32] There is also ongoing disagreement about how the grounds of review are to be arranged or 'classified'.[33] Lord Diplock, for instance, famously suggested that there are three main heads of review – illegality, procedural impropriety and irrationality[34] – and that other grounds are to be understood as emanations of these basic ideas, while others have proposed much lengthier, non-hierarchical, lists of judicial review's basic principles.[35]

---

[23] Rules of the Supreme Court (Amendment No 3) 1977 (SI 1977/1955).

[24] Senior Courts Act 1981, s 31.

[25] Civil Procedure Rules 1998, Pt 54.

[26] For background see S De Smith, 'The Prerogative Writs' (1951) 11 *CLJ* 40; S De Smith, *Judicial Review of Administrative Action* (London, Stevens, 1951).

[27] Note this term is used in a very loose sense to refer to a set of doctrines which can be pleaded before the Administrative Court as grounds for finding executive conduct unlawful. Providing a clearer definition of a 'ground' of review is very difficult for the reasons discussed below. See further J Bell, 'ClientEarth (No 2): A Case of Three Legal Dimensions' (2017) 29 *Journal of Environmental Law* 343.

[28] See especially *Boddington v British Transport Police* [1999] 2 AC 143 (HL).

[29] Human Rights Act 1998, s 8.

[30] This is also the case where the grounds of judicial review were invoked in legal claims brought before the introduction of the 1977 procedural reforms.

[31] For a recent example see *R (Gallaher) v Competition and Markets Authority* [2018] UKSC 25, [2018] 2 WLR 1583.

[32] The most obvious example is the difficulties with formulating substantive review: see especially Elliott and Wilberg (n 8).

[33] Language used for instance in *Council of Civil Service Unions v Minister for the Civil Service* [1985] AC 374 (HL), 410.

[34] Ibid.

[35] See, ie, the list in P Craig, *Administrative Law*, 8th edn (London, Sweet and Maxwell 2016) 17.

A final source of complexity is that judicial review does not stand still; courts may come to recognise new grounds and there is often room for disagreement about whether a new candidate has acquired this status.[36]

While these complexities ought not to be underestimated, it seems fair to say that there is a core cluster of established grounds of review. There is, in other words, a set of doctrines which would, at least in some form, find their way on to the list of most practitioners and commentators. Among them are the following: public bodies[37] must act on a proper understanding of the law;[38] public bodies must act to promote the 'policy and objects'[39] of the legislation which confers their power and not for some other illegitimate purpose;[40] public bodies must take into account all relevant considerations[41] and ignore those which are irrelevant;[42] public bodies must not unlawfully delegate[43] nor fetter[44] their discretion by adopting an unduly rigid policy; public bodies must act and maintain the appearance of acting impartially;[45] public bodies must make decisions in a manner which is procedurally fair[46] including by allowing those whose rights and interests[47] are affected by the decision a fair opportunity to participate;[48] public bodies must at least sometimes offer reasons for their decisions;[49] public bodies must not unlawfully disappoint legitimate expectations;[50] and public authorities must refrain from exercising their powers in ways which are unreasonable[51] and at, least in some circumstances,[52] disproportionate.[53] The language of 'judicial review of executive action' is used throughout this chapter to refer to this cluster of doctrines.

---

[36] A modern example is possibility the question of whether the principle of open justice has acquired the status of ground of review: see especially *Kennedy v Information Commissioner* [2014] UKSC 20, [2015] AC 455; *Dover DC v Campaign to Protect Rural England (Kent)* [2017] UKSC 79, [2018] 1 WLR 108; J Bell, 'Dover DC v CPRE Kent: Legal Complexity and Reason-Giving in Planning Law' (2018) 23 *Judicial Review* 25.

[37] Note the language of 'public bodies' is used throughout because traditionally the courts have regarded the delineating factor between bodies subject to review and those not as being 'publicness' (see especially *R v Panel on Takeovers and Mergers, ex parte Datafin* [1987] QB 815 (CA)). The scope of the principles of review, however, is of course subject to considerable debate. See especially M Taggart (ed), *The Province of Administrative Law* (Oxford, Hart Publishing, 1997).

[38] *R v Lord President of the Privy Council, ex parte Page* [1993] AC 682 (HL).

[39] *Padfield v Minister of Agriculture, Fisheries and Food* [1968] AC 997 (HL), 1030.

[40] *Roberts v Hopwood* [1925] AC 578 (HL); *Wheeler v Leicester CC* [1985] AC 1054 (HL).

[41] *Tesco Stores Ltd v Secretary of State for the Environment* [1995] 1 WLR 759 (HL).

[42] *Associated Provincial Picture Houses Ltd v Wednesbury Corporation* [1948] 1 KB 223 (CA).

[43] *Barnard v National Dock Labour Board* [1953] 2 QB 18 (CA).

[44] *British Oxygen Co Ltd v Minister of Technology* [1971] AC 610 (HL).

[45] *Porter v Magill* [2001] UKHL 67, [2002] 2 AC 357.

[46] *In Re HK (An Infant)* [1967] 2 QB 617 (CA).

[47] *R v Secretary of State for the Home Department, ex parte Al Fayed (No 1)* [1998] 1 WLR 763 (CA).

[48] *Ridge v Baldwin* [1964] AC 40 (HL).

[49] *R v Secretary of State for the Home Department, ex parte Doody* [1994] 1 AC 531 (HL).

[50] *R v North & East Devon Health Authority, ex parte Coughlan* [2001] QB 213 (CA).

[51] 'Unreasonableness' seems increasingly to be the courts' preferred formulation over 'irrationality.' See especially *Pham* (n 6) and *Keyu* (n 10).

[52] See especially *Keyu* (n 10).

[53] See especially *Daly* (n 7); *Pham* (n 6).

II. Is Judicial Review an Exercise in Developing the Common Law?

With this understanding in mind, the chapter can turn to the task of exploring the relationship between judicial review of executive action and common law constitutional rights. It is useful, in surveying this issue, to proceed in the first instance by pulling apart the three constituent notions of this book's subject – 'common law', 'rights' and 'constitutional' – and considering the relationship with judicial review of each notion in turn. The first question which falls for consideration, accordingly, is the extent to which judicial review is an exercise in developing and applying the common law.

In approaching this question, it is helpful to begin by noting an important preliminary point: perhaps unsurprisingly in a common law system,[54] a great deal of scholarly focus in judicial review has been on the common law dimensions of the subject. This is true, furthermore, at both the general-theoretical and specific-doctrinal levels.

At the general-theoretical level, it is notable that one of the most influential accounts of judicial review – 'the common law model'[55] – urges that it is a legal field best conceived of as an exercise in deploying common law standards. The impression this model creates is one where the role played in adjudication by other legal standards, such as legislation, is fairly minimal; where Parliament provides clearly and specifically for an issue, it is said, the duty of the court is to give effect to its manifested intention. But outside of this, the task of the court is to work within an 'undistributed middle'[56] by making use of common law principle to 'supply the omission of the legislature.'[57] It is noteworthy too that the major rival to this theoretical approach – 'modified ultra vires theory'[58] – has evolved substantially over the years, primarily in order to carve out a greater space for the role of the common law.

At the specific-doctrinal level, the core point is that it is very common for commentators to offer accounts of specific grounds of judicial review which focus primarily, if not exclusively, on the common law dimensions of adjudication.

---

[54] Note Elizabeth Fisher's point that in common law systems legislation tends to be seen as 'having second class legal status': see E Fisher, *Environmental Law: A Very Short Introduction* (Oxford, Oxford University Press, 2017) 26.

[55] See especially D Oliver, 'Is Ultra Vires the Basis of Common Law Judicial Review?' [1987] *PL* 543; P Craig, 'Competing Models of Judicial Review' [1999] *PL* 428; P Craig & N Bamforth, 'Constitutional Analysis, Constitutional Principle & Common Law Judicial Review' [2001] *PL* 763.

[56] Language used in for instance Sir J Laws, 'Illegality: The Problem of Jurisdiction' in M Supperstone and J Goudie (eds), *Judicial Review* (London, Butterworths, 1997) 4.18.

[57] Language famously used in *Cooper v Wandsworth Board of Works* 143 ER 414, 420.

[58] See especially C Forsyth, 'Of Fig Leaves and Fairy Tales: The Ultra Vires Doctrine, The Sovereignty of Parliament and Judicial Review' (1996) 55 *CLJ* 12; M Elliott, *The Constitutional Foundations of Judicial Review* (Oxford, Hart Publishing, 2001); M Elliott, 'The Ultra Vires Doctrine in a Constitutional Setting: Still the Central Principle of Administrative Law' (1999) 58 *CLJ* 129.

Consider, for instance, standard textbook accounts of the law on fair hearings.[59] The usual narrative which is offered of this body of law is that of the gradual expansion of the principle of natural justice through to the concretisation of a general 'common law duty to act fairly.'[60] The role played by other layers of law and soft law, such as statutory and non-statutory procedural codes, tends to receive relatively little discussion.[61] A similar point can be made, furthermore, about academic discussion of reason-giving. Thus administrative law scholars are very familiar with the story of how landmark cases such as *Cunningham*[62] and *Doody*[63] marked the incremental recognition of a greater variety of circumstances in which common law fairness implies a duty to give reasons.[64] By contrast, however, very little attention is paid to the continued accumulation of specific statutory duties of reason-giving[65] and the influence of developments such as the Freedom of Information Act.[66]

It is undoubtedly the case that the common law aspects of judicial review are deeply important. There are, more particularly, numerous examples of grounds which have taken their shape to a considerable extent because the courts have developed the common law in order to afford a level of legal protection to some interest or value which is regarded as being of special importance. This is true, for instance, of procedural fairness, where the courts have established a series of common law presumptions which enable individuals whose rights or interests are at stake to participate in the making of the decision.[67] It is true, furthermore, of the law on legitimate expectation which has, to a large degree, evolved as the courts have developed common law doctrine in order to protect the individual from the material[68] and 'moral'[69] harms which result when a specific and directly communicated promise issued by a public authority is later broken.[70] Classic cases such as *Witham*[71] and *Leech*,[72] as well as more recent case law such as *UNISON*,[73]

---

[59] See, eg, T Endicott, *Administrative Law*, 4th edn (Oxford, Oxford University Press, 2018), ch 4.

[60] Language used throughout *Osborn* (n 2).

[61] For a rare example of extended discussion of such codes see P Craig, 'Perspectives on Process: Common Law, Statutory and Political' [2010] *PL* 275.

[62] *R v Civil Appeal Board, ex parte Cunningham* [1992] ICR 817 (CA).

[63] *Doody* (n 49).

[64] See, eg, Craig (n 35) 372–375.

[65] A Le Sueur, 'Legal Duties to Give Reasons' (1999) 52 *Current Legal Problems* 150.

[66] As Elizabeth Fisher has remarked 'freedom of information ... is rarely thought of as "hot"': E Fisher, 'A Decade in the Glasshouse', UK Constitutional Law Blog, 24 June 2015. See further: E Fisher, 'Transparency and Administrative Law: A Critical Evaluation' (2010) 63 *Current Legal Problems* 272.

[67] See, eg, discussion in M Elliott and J Varuhas, *Administrative Law*, 5th edn (Oxford, Oxford University Press, 2017), ch 10.

[68] See especially discussion in *Begbie* (n 14).

[69] *R (Bibi) v Newham LBC* [2001] EWCA Civ 607, [2002] 1 WLR 237, [55].

[70] See further R Williams, 'The Multiple Doctrines of Legitimate Expectations' (2016) 132 *LQR* 639; J Varuhas, 'In Search of a Doctrine: Mapping the Law of Legitimate Expectations' in M Groves & G Weeks (eds), *Legitimate Expectations in the Common Law World* (Oxford, Hart Publishing, 2017).

[71] *R v Lord Chancellor, ex parte Witham* [1998] QB 575 (QB).

[72] *R v Secretary of State for the Home Department, ex parte Leech* [1994] QB 198 (CA).

[73] *R (Unison) v Lord Chancellor* [2017] UKSC 51, [2012] 3 WLR 409.

have also famously made use of the idea that, when assessing whether the executive has overstepped the boundaries of its statutory powers, the courts are to begin from the presumption that Parliament's legislation is to be read compatibly with basic common law values, such as access to justice.[74]

With this point in mind, however, a core point which this part of the chapter seeks to stress is that legal adjudication in judicial review is deeply *legally pluralistic*.[75] While common law notions are highly important in this field and their role should not be understated, ultimately, they constitute one of a numbers of layers of law with which the courts must grapple. The common law, furthermore, does not operate in isolation. Its principles interrelate in a series of complex and varied ways with other layers of law in legal reasoning.

On this matter, three more specific points fall to be made. The first is that to focus only on the common law dimensions of judicial review is to overlook the hugely important role which is played by the *background legislative scheme* in legal adjudication. One way in which legislation comes to play such a role arises because certain of the grounds of review are very 'thin' in the sense that they create legal questions which essentially refer the court to some separate body of law. Consider, for example, what has come to be known as the '*Padfield* principle'[76] or ground. This ground derives from Lord Reid's judgment in the landmark case[77] of the same name and requires that public authorities exercise discretionary power in order 'to promote the policy and objects of the Act'[78] which conferred the power. The important point to be stressed about this doctrine is that it effectively functions as a directive to the court to engage in close analysis of the legislative scheme at the background of the case. Rather than supplying any answers, in other words, this ground begs the, often difficult, question of what the objects of the legislation actually are. Thus when the *Padfield* principle is invoked, judgments usually read as very lengthy and detailed considerations of the statutory background to the case.[79]

Even in the context of grounds of review which are not thin in this sense and in which the common law does a great deal of 'legal work,' the background legislative scheme will still often be central to the adjudication of legal issues. A good example of this is procedural fairness. Procedural fairness is a multifaceted ground of review with a number of different strands. Common to all its aspects, however, is the close and complex way in which its common law components interact with the

---

[74] See also *Daly* (n 7).

[75] See further T Allan, 'The Constitutional Foundations of Judicial Review: Conceptual Conundrum or Interpretative Inquiry?' (2002) 61 *CLJ* 87; T Allan, 'Doctrine and Theory in Administrative Law: An Elusive Quests for the Limits of Jurisdiction' [2003] *PL* 429.

[76] Language used in, for example, *Patel v Secretary of State for the Home Department* [2013] UKSC 72, [2014] AC 651 and *R (Britcits) v Secretary of State for the Home Department* [2017] EWCA Civ 368.

[77] See M Sunkin, '*Padfield v Minister for Agriculture, Fisheries & Food* [1968]: Judges and Parliamentary Democracy' in S Juss & M Sunkin (eds), *Landmark Cases in Public Law* (Oxford, Hart Publishing, 2017).

[78] *Padfield* (n 39), 1030.

[79] The classic example is probably *Bromley LBC v Greater London Council* [1983] 1 AC 768 (HL).

detail of, and policy goals underlying, legislation. Consider, for instance, the issue of disclosure. The common law has long recognised[80] and protected a principle to the effect that where a decision is being taken which will have a significant impact on the rights or interests of an individual and the decision-maker acquires relevant and meaningful[81] new evidence this must be made available to the individual for her to offer comment on.[82] Importantly, however, this is a common law principle with presumptive force only. Where the public authority is able to convince the court that the aims of the legislative scheme at the background of the case necessitates a less generous approach to disclosure this may be capable of overriding the common law starting-point. For present purposes, the most important consequence of this is that, in the course of adjudicating on disclosure issues, one of the major preoccupations of the court will be navigating the relevant statutory scheme in order to extract its underlying policy goals.[83]

The second point to consider is that public authority policies and central government guidance are coming to play an increasingly important role in judicial review. These bodies of 'soft law,'[84] like legislation, interact closely with common law notions. The high-watermark of this trend to date are the important recent cases of *Lumba*[85] and *Mandalia*.[86] In these cases, the Supreme Court articulated a principle to the effect that public authorities must generally 'follow [their] published policy ... unless there are good reasons for not doing so.'[87] Again, the key point is that on its own this ground will rarely determine whether public authority conduct is lawful or unlawful. This is because in the cases which reach the courts there will often be argument concerning the meaning of the relevant policy and whether the public body applied or departed from it in the first place.[88] In cases of this kind, therefore, the major task of the court will be to engage in the often complex task of making sense of the terms and objectives of the authority's own policies.[89]

---

[80] See especially *Bagg's Case* (1615) 11 Co Rep 93b; *Capel v Child* (1832) 2 C & J 558; *Cooper* (n 57). Note however the diminishment of this principle in what William Wade termed the 'twilight years' of natural justice (W Wade, 'The Twilight of Natural Justice? (1955) 67 *LQR* 103): *Local Government Board v Arlidge* [1915] AC 120 (HL); *Nakkuda Ali v MF de Jayaratne* [1951] AC 66 (PC); *R v Metropolitan Police Commissioners, ex parte Parker* [1953] 1 WLR 1150 (DC).

[81] See *South Lanarkshire v Scottish Information Commissioner* [2013] UKSC 55, [2013] 1 WLR 2421.

[82] For recent important examples see *Bank Mellat v HM Treasury* [2013] UKSC 39, [2014] AC 700; *R (Bourgass) v Secretary of State for Justice* [2015] UKSC 54, [2016] AC 384.

[83] See discussion of *Bank Mellat* (n 82) and *Haralambous* (n 19) below.

[84] Language used for instance in G Weeks, *Soft Law and Public Authorities: Remedies and Reform* (Oxford, Hart Publishing, 2016).

[85] *R (Lumba) v Secretary of State for the Home Department* [2011] UKSC 12, [2012] 1 AC 245.

[86] *Mandalia v Secretary of State for the Home Department* [2015] UKSC 59, [2015] 1 WLR 4546.

[87] *Lumba* (n 85) [26].

[88] See, eg, *R (Project Management Institute) v Minister for the Cabinet Office* [2016] EWCA 21, [2016] 1 WLR 1737.

[89] This is certainly true of *Mandalia* (n 86) itself. Note also that a similar point can be made about the well-established principle from *R v Islington LBC ex parte Rixon* [1997] ELR 66 (QB) that local authorities must follow central government guidance in the absence of good reason.

The third and final point to be made here is that there are, perhaps surprisingly in light of the 'resurgence'[90] of common law rights, actually important examples of grounds in relation to which the common law appears to have been playing a *less* important role in adjudication in recent years. There are a number of different ways in which this has been happening.

One is that other layers of law and soft law have been increasingly performing tasks that were once primarily accomplished by the common law. Consider, for instance, the giving of reasons. Several decades ago the courts were regularly faced with instances of administrative decision-making where the public body had outright refused to offer any explanation for its decision.[91] Thereafter, an important body of case law developed in which the principle of common law fairness was deployed to impose a duty to give reasons. In recent years, by contrast, there has been less need for the common law to play this role. Indeed, it has been extremely rare that the courts have been faced with outright refusals to give reasons in modern litigation.[92] A number of considerations explain this development,[93] but the one that is most important for present purposes is the continuing proliferation of specific statutory duties to give reasons in both primary[94] and secondary[95] legislation.[96] Explained briefly, it is extremely common in the modern administrative context for Acts or Regulations to stipulate specifically for the provision of reasons and thus there is a reduced need for the common law to play its gap-filling role. One consequence of this is that, in modern times, the vast majority of legal challenges to administrative reason-giving concern the adequacy of reasons given under a statutory duty[97] which the courts can address with little engagement with common law.

A second factor which may be contributing to a reduction in the role of the common law is growing scepticism, at least in the context of certain grounds, about the utility of thinking in terms of *generalised doctrine*. The clearest examples of this cynicism are the reflections of the Supreme Court in *Cart*[98] on the concept of jurisdiction and of Lord Carnwath in *Jones*[99] on the law-fact distinction.

---

[90] Masterman & Wheatle (n 1).

[91] See especially case law discussed in JUSTICE-All Souls Committee, *Administrative Justice: Some Necessary Reforms* (Oxford, Oxford University Press, 1988), ch 3.

[92] For a very unusual example to the contrary see *Karia v UK Border Agency* [2014] EWHC 4674 (Admin).

[93] See J Bell, 'Reason-Giving in Administrative Law: Where Are We and Why Have the Courts Not Embraced the "General Common Law Duty to Give Reasons?"' (forthcoming).

[94] The most well-known example is Tribunals and Inquiries Act 1958, s 12(1).

[95] See, eg, in the planning context alone, Town and Country Planning (Inquiries Procedure) (England) Rules 2000 (SI 2000/1624), r 11; Town and Country Planning (Development Management Procedure) (England) Order 2015 (SI 2015/595), Art 35(1); Town and Country Planning (Environmental Impact Assessment) Regulations 2017 (SI 2017/571), reg 24(1)(c).

[96] Le Sueur (n 65).

[97] See, eg, *R (MacRae) v County of Herefordshire DC* [2012] EWCA Civ 457, [2012] JPL 1356.

[98] *R (Cart) v Upper Tribunal* [2011] UKSC 28, [2012] 1 AC 663.

[99] *R (Jones) v First-tier Tribunal* [2013] UKSC 19, [2013] 2 AC 48.

These cases arise against the background of a long-standing struggle on the part of both judges and commentators to create and impose general doctrinal structures which will guide the courts when they are faced with a complaint to the effect that a public authority has erred in applying a statutory term to a given set of facts. Concerned to avoid the dreaded 'wilderness of single instances'[100] in which the courts merely intervene when they think they have good reason, academics and practitioners alike have long searched for a technique for demarcating in advance the circumstances in which judicial interference will be deemed proper.

Against this background, the significance of *Cart* and *Jones* lies in the doubts expressed in the judgments that such endeavours continue to be useful. Lord Dyson in the former case, for instance, opined that to strive to structure judicial review in this context by reference to the idea that the courts may intervene to correct only 'jurisdictional' errors is to invoke a distinction that 'is ultimately based on foundations of sand.'[101] In a similar way, Lord Carnwath, in the latter case, expressed cynicism that the distinction between errors of 'law' and those of 'fact' is capable of doing meaningful analytical work in terms of determining whether judicial intervention is appropriate or not. It has long been, for his Lordship, background legal policy considerations which have driven how the courts have applied this dichotomy.[102] This loss of faith in generalist doctrinal structures is deeply interesting[103] and may indicate a renewed focus on the context-specific, legislative aspects of judicial review, and correlatively a move away from the traditional focus on its generalist common law components.[104]

By way of concluding the discussion in this part, it is helpful to think about its importance for the broader question being explored in this chapter: what is the relationship between common law constitutional rights and judicial review of executive action? What begins to emerge from the analysis herein are two of the main lessons which this chapter seeks to emphasise, and which were outlined in the introduction.

The first of these lessons is that we should not expect too much of the notion of common law constitutional rights. As explained above, many scholars and judges have searched for some singular 'master principle or idea'[105] which is capable of serving as the 'organising concept'[106] from which all of judicial review can be seen as flowing. The analysis in this part begins to show why we ought not to, in their 'resurgence,'[107] get swept away into believing that common law constitutional

---

[100] DM Gordon, 'The Relation of Facts to Jurisdiction' (1929) *LQR* 458, 459.

[101] *Cart* (n 98), [111].

[102] See also R Carnwath, 'Tribunal Justice – A New Start' [2009] *PL* 48.

[103] This is not to suggest that this trend is consistently reflected in the Supreme Court's reasoning. See for instance *Gallaher* (n 31) which could arguably be read as signifying the opposite trend.

[104] For recent discussion of this tension see Dame S Elias (n 11) and D Stratas, '"It All Depends on the Circumstances": The Decline of Doctrine on the Grounds and Intensity of Review' in Elliott, Varuhas & Stark (n 11).

[105] Language used in S Smith, *Contract Theory* (Oxford, Oxford University Press, 2004) 11.

[106] Forsyth (n 13).

[107] Masterman & Wheatle (n 1).

rights can provide the missing key to understanding judicial review. It also illustrates why, more broadly, it is doubtful that such a thing can be found at all. Two main reasons for caution in this regard emerge from the discussion above. The first is that legal adjudication in judicial review is deeply pluralistic and the common law, while undoubtedly of the utmost importance in judicial review, is not the only layer of law in play. The second is the importance of remembering that judicial review consists of an array of different grounds, each of which has its own story and may strike the balance between common law, legislation and policy differently from the next.

The second important lesson which begins to emerge from the discussion in this part is that, while common law constitutional rights cannot explain the whole, they do, at least when understood in a broad sense,[108] supply an important part of the picture. There are, more particularly, aspects of modern judicial review which have taken their shape to a large degree because the courts have developed the common law in order to afford protection to an individualised interest which is regarded as fundamental. A major example of this is procedural fairness. As explained above, within the law on procedural fairness the courts have developed a common law presumption that individuals must see and be given the opportunity to comment on new evidence when a decision is being taken which will affect their rights or interests. While this common law presumption is capable in certain circumstances of being rebutted, its existence is deeply important. It is an illustration of the courts' ability to develop the common law so as to provide meaningful protection to the individual.

III. Does Judicial Review Protect 'Rights'?

At this stage, it is helpful to turn to a second constituent part of this book's subject and consider its relationship with judicial review. This part, accordingly, considers the question of the extent to which judicial review is concerned with protecting 'rights'. Three main points fall to be made here.

The first is that there has been, for many years, a good deal of reluctance to make use of the language of 'rights' in the context of judicial review.[109] Thus, for instance, Lord Woolf in a classic article written in 1986[110] suggested that the difference between public and private law is that, while the former is a 'system which enforces the proper performance by public bodies of the duties which they owe to the public,'[111] the latter 'protects the private rights of private individuals or the

---

[108] Note that this caveat is important for reasons discussed in Part 5.

[109] For a further example see for instance *R v Somerset County Council, ex parte Dixon* [1998] Env LR 111 (QB), 121.

[110] Lord Woolf, 'Public Law – Private Law: Why the Divide? A Personal View' [1986] *PL* 220. See further Lord Woolf, *Protection of the Public – A New Challenge* (London, Stevens and Sons 1990).

[111] Ibid, 221.

private rights of public bodies.'[112] In a similar way, more recently, Lord Reed in *AXA*[113] has suggested that, by contrast to an ordinary action in private law, a judicial review claim 'is not brought to vindicate a right vested in the applicant, but to request the court to supervise the actings of a public authority so as to ensure that it exercises its functions in accordance with the law.'[114]

There are perfectly good reasons which can help to explain why judges have sometimes been so quick to expunge the language of 'rights' in this context. The main one is that an undue focus on a particularly narrow understanding of the term 'rights' – namely, as referring to the narrow cluster of 'rights' protected by private law such as contractual and property rights – placed a series of unwelcome limitations on the operation of judicial review for many decades. The throwing off of these constraints has led to some of the most significant achievements of modern public law.[115] One of the most important implications of the procedural reforms of 1977,[116] for instance, was that they enabled the courts to gradually move away from the idea, expounded in cases such as *Boyce*[117] and *Gouriet*,[118] that it was open to a court to issue a declaration or injunction, even if the applicant was able to demonstrate breach of a statutory duty enacted for the benefit of the public,[119] only where she could establish a private law entitlement to the remedies.[120] In a similar way, the classic case of *Ridge*[121] saw the end of an influential line of reasoning according to which an individual can expect a fair hearing only when her traditional private rights are at stake and not when a 'mere' privilege is being withdrawn from her.[122]

The second important point is that even if it is correct and important to emphasise that 'rights', in the narrow sense of rights long recognised by private law, do not play the important structuring role in judicial review they once did this should not lead us to the conclusion that judicial review is unconcerned with 'rights' in a second, broader sense. Consider, for example, some of the writings of Jason Varuhas.[123] Varuhas has sought to draw a distinction between, on the one hand, human rights law and, on the other, common law review. The former,

---

[112] Ibid.

[113] *AXA* (n 21).

[114] Ibid, [159].

[115] See further Lord Diplock's judgment in *R v Inland Revenue Commissioners, ex parte National Federation of Self-Employed and Small Businesses Ltd* [1981] 2 WLR 722 (HL), 737; Lord Diplock, 'Judicial Review Revisited' (1974) 33 *CLJ* 233.

[116] See above n 23.

[117] *Boyce v Paddington BC* [1903] 1 Ch 109 (Ch).

[118] *Gouriet v Union of Post Office Workers* [1978] AC 435 (HL).

[119] A similar issue also plagued the law on mandamus. See especially: *R v Guardians of the Lewisham Union* [1897] 1 QB 498 (DC).

[120] See also *Gregory v Camden LBC* [1966] 1 WLR 899 (QB).

[121] *Ridge* (n 48).

[122] See especially *Nakkuda Ali* (n 80); *Parker* (n 80); C Reich, 'The New Property' (1964) 75 *Yale Law Journal* 733; I Holloway, 'Natural Justice and the New Property' (1999) 25 *Monash University Law Review* 85.

[123] See especially Varuhas (n 8); Varuhas (n 16).

Varuhas suggests, has an 'individualistic rights-based nature'[124] in that its 'primary function... [is] to afford strong protection to and vindicate fundamental, individual, personal interests.' The latter, by contrast, is normatively grounded, not in a concern to protect individual rights or interests but, 'to ensure that public power is exercised properly and in the public interest.'[125] While the operation of some of the grounds of review may incidentally serve to protect individual interests, Varuhas argues,[126] the individual is of secondary importance in this field of law.

This is not the space for a detailed critique of Varuhas' proposed taxonomy.[127] The short point, however, is that notions of individual and public interest closely interact in judicial review adjudication in ways which make it extremely difficult either to draw a neat line between them or to relegate one to the position of 'secondary' importance. Two examples will suffice to illustrate this argument.

Consider, first, *Osborn*.[128] In this case the Supreme Court considered the circumstances in which the Parole Board is required to afford prisoners with an oral hearing in determining applications for release or transfer. Lord Reed's judgment has been read by some as offering an understanding of procedural fairness which, by stressing its important role in protecting individual dignity,[129] offered an essentially 'rights-based' understanding of that ground.[130] To read his Lordship's judgment in this way, however, is to overlook other important dimensions of it. In fact, Lord Reed's conclusion reflects a careful fusion of both the public-oriented purposes underlying the legislative framework at the background to the case and certain individualistic values protected by the common law. Thus, following *Osborn* the Parole Board, in deciding whether a prisoner should be granted an oral hearing must have regard to two broad sets of consideration. First, the extent to which hearing from the prisoner in person will assist the Parole Board in performing its core statutory task of making an individual assessment of the risk she poses to others and thereby protecting both the public at large and the prison population. Second, the importance of treating the prisoner with respect when she has something pertinent to contribute.

By way of a second example, consider the case of *Mandalia*.[131] As noted above, this case served to concretise a principle to the effect that public authorities must generally follow their policies unless there is a good reason not to.[132] In one

---

[124] Varuhas (n 16) 95.

[125] Ibid.

[126] Ibid, 101 and 108.

[127] J Varuhas, 'Taxonomy and Public Law' in Elliott, Varuhas and Stark (n 11), *The Unity of Public Law?* (Oxford, Hart Publishing, 2018). For a critique of Varuhas' approach, see P Craig, 'Taxonomy and Public Law: A Response' [2019] *PL* 281.

[128] *Osborn* (n 2).

[129] See especially ibid, [68]–[70] citing J Waldron, 'How the Law Protects Dignity' (2012) 71 *CLJ* 200. See further T Allan, 'Procedural Fairness and the Duty of Respect' (1998) 18 *OJLS* 497.

[130] See especially J Varuhas, 'Judicial Review at the Crossroads' (2015) 74 *CLJ* 215.

[131] *Mandalia* (n 86).

[132] Note that, although the Supreme Court in *Gallaher* (n 31) suggested that it is improper to think of consistency as a freestanding ground of review, their judgment does not cast doubt on this proposition.

sense, it is clear that the crystallisation of this principle carries significant benefits which extend far beyond the protection of any one individual. If the prima facie position is that public authorities are bound by their policies then this fosters a broader culture of legal certainty in which it becomes easier for all citizens to plan their lives.[133] In another sense, however, the bulk of the case law has a significant 'individual-regarding'[134] element. This is because of a point emphasised above: the principle of the consistent application of policy will rarely by itself generate answers to legal questions, meaning the court will often be required to navigate the detail and underlying aims of a body of soft law. A great deal of public authority policy, furthermore, is focused on regulating the relationship between the public authority and *the individual.* This is true, for example, of *Mandalia* itself. Thus, looking beyond the articulation of the principle of consistency, *Mandalia* is in a sense, what Sarah Nason has termed an 'individual grievance'[135] case in which the applicant argued he was entitled under the Home Secretary's own policy to be informed of the error in his application for visa renewal.

The third important point to be made here is that the analysis in this section is important, not only for its own sake but, because of its relationship with the broader messages of this chapter. Most importantly, for present purposes, the discussion above feeds directly into the first lesson outlined in the introduction. This lesson, as explained above, concerns the importance of not expecting that the notion of common law constitutional rights could come to serve as an 'organising principle'[136] for judicial review. What emerges from this part is another reason why it is highly doubtful that judicial review of executive action could be amenable to this kind of analysis at all: judicial review cannot be reduced to an endeavour to protect one cluster of interests – such as those of the public or those of the individual.[137] These concerns, rather, are closely intertwined in legal reasoning in this field.[138] To imagine, in other words, that it is possible to isolate some singular normative purpose which sits at the heart of judicial review is to underestimate the complexity of its doctrine.[139]

IV. Is Judicial Review 'Constitutional'?

Turning finally to the remaining component of this book's subject, the core question is whether judicial review can be understood to be 'constitutional'. An immediate difficulty incurred here is that there is not necessarily a fixed understanding

---

[133] See further J Raz, *The Authority of Law*, 2nd edn (Oxford, Oxford University Press, 2009), ch 11.

[134] Varuhas (n 8) 52.

[135] Nason (n 12).

[136] Forsyth (n 13).

[137] For an example of these notions being presented as opposing ways of thinking see Harlow & Rawlings (n 22), ch 1.

[138] See further P Cane, 'Theory and Values in Public Law' in P Craig & R Rawlings (eds), *Law and Administration in Europe: Essays in Honour of Carol Harlow* (Oxford, Oxford University Press, 2003).

[139] Nason (n 12) 17.

of what it means to say that something is 'constitutional' in nature and thus there are a number of different possible ways of understanding the question. Consider, for instance, the broad understanding of this notion deployed in the literature on 'administrative constitutionalism'.[140] As Elizabeth Fisher has explained, in this context the language of constitutionalism:

> reflects ... the more traditional connotations of constitutionalism, which is that constitutionalism is concerned with the constituting and limiting of government so as to ensure its principled operation where there are divergences over what this means and entails.[141]

If this is what we mean by 'constitutional' then there is surely no difficulty in using the term to describe the grounds of judicial review. These legal doctrines, after all, are central in the court's endeavours to identify the line between governmental conduct which is permissible and that which is unlawful.[142]

There are, however, thicker understandings of 'constitutional' which make the invocation of this language in relation to the grounds of review more difficult. This part will focus on the understanding of the term which has been most prominent in the literature in recent years. Martin Loughlin has termed this way of thinking the 'modern idea of the constitution'.[143] Explained very briefly, the idea is this: to say that a phenomenon is 'constitutional' is to say that it sits, hierarchically, at the apex of governmental arrangements. This connotes that it has a 'fundamental'[144] status, meaning that it is understood either, at its strongest, as being wholly inviolable by government or Parliament or, at its weakest, as being capable of being overridden by the same only in special circumstances, such as where Parliament expresses a sufficiently clear intention. As Loughlin notes, this understanding of 'constitutionalism' originates and is used more comfortably in states which, unlike the UK, have deliberately adopted a written document which plays this role. Increasingly, however, judges[145] and scholars[146] alike have been experimenting with the idea that some version of it can play a role in the UK context.

---

[140] See especially E Fisher, *Risk Regulation and Administrative Constitutionalism* (Oxford, Hart Publishing, 2007); GE Metzger, 'Administrative Constitutionalism' (2013) 91 *Texas Law Review* 1897; S Lee, 'From the History to the Theory of Administrative Constitutionalism' in N Parillo (n 22).

[141] Fisher (n 140) 24.

[142] Note that one complication here is the unresolved question of the extent to which the grounds of review may also be invoked to regulate the activities of bodies not regarded as public: see especially *Braganza v BP Shipping Ltd* [2015] UKSC 17, [2015] 1 WLR 1661.

[143] M Loughlin, *The British Constitution: A Very Short Introduction* (Oxford, Oxford University Press, 2013) 9. Note that Loughlin juxtaposes this way of thinking with the 'traditional' understanding which underlies much of his own work: see especially M Loughlin, *The Idea of Public Law* (Oxford, Oxford University Press, 2004); M Loughlin, *Foundations of Public Law* (Oxford, Oxford University Press, 2012); M Wilkinson and M Dowdle, *Questioning the Foundations of Public Law* (Oxford, Hart Publishing, 2018).

[144] Ibid, 11 summarising T Paine, *Rights of Man* [1791] (Oxford, Oxford University Press, 2008).

[145] See especially *Thoburn v Sunderland City Council* [2002] EWHC 195 (Admin), [2004] QB 151; J Laws, 'Law and Democracy' [1995] *PL* 72; J Laws, 'The Constitution: Morals and Rights' [1996] *PL* 622; J Laws, *The Common Law Constitution* (Cambridge, Cambridge University Press, 2014); *R (Evans) v Attorney General* [2015] UKSC 21, [2015] AC 1787.

[146] See especially, T Allan, *The Sovereignty of Law* (Oxford, Oxford University Press, 2013); R Masterman & S Wheatle, 'Constitutional Adjudication and the Common Law' in Elliott, Varuhas and Stark (n 11).

Is judicial review 'constitutional' in this sense? There is no easy answer to this question. One major source of difficulty is that it is possible to consider it at both a specific and a general level. At a specific level, the question is whether any or all of the *grounds* of judicial review are 'constitutional' in the sense that they serve to place certain values either off the table entirely or, at least, beyond the easy reach of Parliament. At the general level, by contrast, the question is whether *judicial review* itself, as a broader phenomenon, is protected by the common law in this way.

Considering, first, the question at a specific level, an initial source of complexity is the point stressed above: the grounds of judicial review are not monolithic. It is, in particular, helpful for present purposes to draw a distinction between two different types of ground.[147] Firstly, there are grounds which are focused primarily on *legislation* and on ensuring that the arrangements and policies agreed by Parliament are given effect. Where judicial intervention is based on a ground of this kind it seems rather artificial to describe what has happened as the courts giving effect to some principle which sits higher than Parliament in the constitutional hierarchy. The Court in the well-known case of *World Development Movement*,[148] for instance, did not view itself as giving effect to some external, constitutional principle to the effect that governmental funds cannot be spent on 'economically unsound'[149] projects, which Parliament had failed to exclude by expressing a clear enough intention. The Court, rather, considered that underlying the legislative scheme was a clear policy[150] of funding worthwhile foreign developments and that in intervening it was preventing the government from pursing policies which had not been scrutinised in Parliament.[151]

There are, however, other grounds of review which play a greater role in protecting values that derive from the common law and thus, in at least a sense, subsist outside of the legislation. Even here, however, the 'modern'[152] notion of constitutionalism does not map straightforwardly onto these grounds. Thus consider again, for instance, the common law principle discussed above which requires that information be disclosed to individuals whose rights or interests are affected by a decision so that they can respond. The case law in which this principle

---

[147] See further T Adams, 'Ultra Vires Revisited' [2018] *PL* 31.

[148] *R v Secretary of State for Foreign and Commonwealth Affairs, ex parte World Development Movement* [1995] 1 WLR 386 (QB).

[149] Ibid, 402.

[150] Though note this understanding of the legislation is not universally accepted. See, eg, Lord Sumption, 'The Limits of Law' in N Barber, R Ekins & P Yowell (eds), *Lord Sumption and the Limits of the Law* (Oxford, Hart Publishing, 2016).

[151] This point has a further important implication: because these grounds focus primarily on giving effect to the detail and underlying policies of *Parliament's legislation*, it is therefore very difficult for Parliament to effectively exclude their operation. The classic example of this is *Anisminic v Foreign Compensation Commission & Another* [1969] 2 AC 147 (HL) in which the majority of the House of Lords concluded that an ouster clause did not preclude it from preventing the Foreign Compensation Commission from addressing an interpretive question which Parliament had never assigned to it.

[152] M Loughlin, *The British Constitution: A Very Short Introduction* (n 143) 11.

has been in play cannot be straightforwardly understood through the lens of the understanding of constitutionalism set out above. Thus, in the first place, it is clear that this principle is not regarded by the courts as being wholly inviolable. Cases such as *Bank Mellat (No 1)*[153] and *Haralambous*,[154] for instance, have seen the Supreme Court recognise that a decision could be lawfully taken in the absence of full disclosure.

In the second place, however, nor can it be straightforwardly said that the 'test' for whether Parliament has successfully displaced the common law starting-point is the level of clarity with which the legislature has expressed its intention to do so. Thus consider, by way of illustration, *Bank Mellat (No 2)*. This case concerned the lawfulness of an order issued by the Treasury preventing UK financial institutions from communicating with the applicant Iranian bank. The question which arose before the Supreme Court was whether the Treasury was permitted to make such orders without disclosing to the affected institution the information on which it was acting for comment. Importantly in this case the majority of the Supreme Court did not make use of an all-or-nothing approach to this issue. They did not, that is, proceed by asking whether Parliament had or had not disclosed a sufficiently clear intention to exclude the common law approach to disclosure in this legislative context. The majority's approach, rather, was much more nuanced. The majority gave careful thought to the underlying statutory purposes of the legislative regime and the extent to which accommodation of common law values would facilitate or frustrate the attainment of those aims. The majority recognised that there would sometimes be circumstances in which disclosure of information to a possible subject of an order of this counter would wholly frustrate the objects of the administrative scheme. In such cases, it would be improper for the courts to insist on the common law approach to disclosure. In others, however, such as in *Bank Mellat*, disclosure was not only necessitated by the common law but would actually assist the Treasury in making better and more accurate assessments of whether the legislative goals would be realised by the making of an order.

Taking next the question of whether judicial review is constitutional at a more general level, the analysis which follows is rather different. An obvious place to begin is with the following well-known dictum from the judgment of Lord Steyn in *Jackson*:[155]

> In exceptional circumstances involving an attempt to abolish judicial review or the ordinary role of the courts, the appellate committee of the House of Lords or a new Supreme Court may have to consider whether this is a constitutional fundamental which even a sovereign Parliament acting at the behest of a complaisant House of Commons cannot abolish.[156]

---

[153] *Bank Mellat* (n 82).
[154] *Haralambous* (n 19).
[155] *Jackson* (n 2).
[156] Ibid, [102].

The suggestion in this passage is that, even if the common law values which individual grounds of judicial review protect can be excluded, at least in certain contexts, by Parliament, the broader phenomenon of judicial review itself cannot. Judicial review, rather, is to be regarded as a common law 'constitutional fundamental' in the strongest sense: something which sits above all else in the public law hierarchy and therefore creates hard limitations on what can and cannot be done by Parliament.

It is, however, very difficult to know how significant this and similar[157] dicta are. For one thing, the proposition they embody has gone untested. Importantly, furthermore, it is highly unlikely that a scenario will emerge where a case will turn on the issue of the acceptability of Lord Steyn's suggestion. In the first place, there is the obvious point that it would be extraordinarily politically difficult for Parliament, or perhaps more accurately[158] the government acting through Parliament, to enact legislation seeking to abolish judicial review.[159] In the second, and perhaps more fundamentally, Lord Steyn's dictum imagines a scenario where two legal phenomena – legislation and common law – are taken to be diametrically opposed to one another and where the court's task in deciding the case is therefore to identify which to pledge their allegiance to. This is not, however, how the relationship between legislation and common law is understood in legal reasoning. The question which courts address is always taken to be one of what a given provision *means*, bearing in mind the aims of the piece of legislation it is in as a whole, other legislation and the backdrop of the common law.

Thus imagine, for instance, that Parliament creates a new administrative body ('X') and includes in the empowering legislation a provision which states that 'decisions by X shall not be subject to judicial review'. The effect of such a provision would not be determined by the courts asking which is constitutionally superior: the legislative attempt to exclude judicial review or the common law's protection of the same? A court tasked with ruling on the issue, rather, would proceed by asking what was to be understood in the legal context by the provision '*subject to judicial review*'.

Answering such a question would not be easy. The court would, for instance, need to think about whether 'judicial review' is to be taken as referring to the application for judicial review procedure[160] or whether Parliament is to be taken as purporting to exclude the application of the grounds of judicial review. If the former, the court would be required to consider whether other procedural routes nonetheless remained available for the purpose of legally challenging X's decisions. Could an applicant, for instance, seek to apply for a prerogative writ outside of the application for judicial

---

[157] See also *AXA* (n 21) [51].

[158] A Tomkins, 'What is Parliament For?' in Bamforth and Leyland (n 15).

[159] A famous example of the difficulties of passing a provision purporting to oust judicial oversight is clause 11 of the Asylum and Immigration Bill 2003. See, eg, the reaction of Lord Woolf to this clause in, 'The Rule of Law and a Change in the Constitution' (2004) 63(2) *CLJ* 317.

[160] Senior Courts Act 1981, s 31.

review procedure?[161] What if she were able to frame a claim in private law, could the courts make use of some version of the grounds of review in that context?[162] If Parliament were understood as purporting to exclude the application of the grounds of review would this attempt work in the same way in relation to all of them? As stressed above, for instance, many of the grounds of review[163] are aimed at upholding important aims and features of Parliament's own legislation. Ought a phrase such as 'shall not be subject to judicial review' really be read as permitting X to act in a manner which would fundamentally undermine the broader purposes or structure of the legislation[164] and prevent the courts from stopping this?[165] Or ought the phrase to be read in a manner which is in-keeping with the 'objects and purposes'[166] of the Act as a whole? Similarly, as discussed, an important role of some of the grounds of review is to provide protection to interests or values recognised by the common law. Ought 'judicial review' to be read as excluding these long-standing safeguards? Even if, for instance, the broader aims of the legislation are compatible, and would perhaps even be promoted,[167] by a generous approach to protecting these values?

This is not the space in which to try to address these questions. The main point, rather, is that it is very difficult to regard the dictum of Lord Steyn in *Jackson* as supplying a short and easy answer to the question of whether judicial review is 'constitutional' in the sense of being placed beyond the reach of Parliament. The dictum presupposes a simple legal question – should the courts prioritise legislation or the common law protection of judicial review? – which will probably never arise.[168] This is so for political reasons but also, perhaps more fundamentally, for legal reasons: the courts do not understand their task in such cases as being that of choosing between legislation and common law but of working out what the former means against the backdrop of the latter.

V. Conclusion: Three Lessons Concerning the Role of Common Law Constitutional Rights in Judicial Review

This chapter has been concerned with exploring the role played by common law constitutional rights in the field of judicial review of executive action. It has done

---

[161] See De Smith (n 26); E Henderson, *Foundations of English Administrative Law: Certiorari and Mandamus in the Seventeenth Century* (Cambridge, Harvard University Press, 1963).

[162] See, eg, Lady Hale's speech in *Braganza v BP Shipping* [2015] UKSC 17, [2015] 1 WLR 1661.

[163] Such as the *Padfield* ground (n 39).

[164] See especially *Anisminic* (n 150) and the judgment of Lord Mance in *Evans* (n 145).

[165] See further *R (Cart) v Upper Tribunal* [2009] EWHC 3052 (Admin), [2010] 2 WLR 1012, [38]. For critique see M Elliott and R Thomas, 'Tribunal Justice' (2012) 71 *CLJ* 297, 303–304.

[166] *Padfield* (n 39).

[167] See discussion of *Osborn* (n 2) above. See further D Galligan, *Due Process and Fair Procedures* (Oxford, Oxford University Press 1997).

[168] See also discussion in A Young, '*R (Evans) v Attorney General* – The *Anisminic* of the 21st Century?' UK Constitutional Law Bog (31 Mar 2015).

so by pulling apart the three constituent parts of this book's subject – 'common law', 'rights' and 'constitutional' – and considering the relationship between each and judicial review. The aim of this final concluding part is to tie together some of the loose strands of the earlier discussion by drawing out explicitly and concisely this chapter's three most important lessons.

The first of these lessons is that we ought not to expect too much of common law constitutional rights. We ought, in particular, not to be under any illusion that this notion will supply us with the missing key which will finally enable judicial review to be understood as a unified whole. Indeed, what has emerged from the analysis in this chapter are at least three reasons why it is probably the case that judicial review is not amenable to this kind of analysis at all. First, as stressed in Part II, legal adjudication in the field of judicial review is deeply legally pluralistic; the courts are required to navigate not just one layer of law but many including, among others,[169] common law values, primary and secondary legislation and, increasingly, 'soft law'.[170] Second, as also emphasised in Part II, judicial review, understood in a substantive sense, consists of an array of different grounds. Each of these grounds, in turn, has its own story and strikes a different balance between the different layers of law. Third, as discussed in Part III, judicial review is not unified around protecting one particular cluster of interest. The interests of both the individual and the public, rather, interact in close and complex ways in legal reasoning such that it is not possible to relegate one to the status of secondary importance.[171]

The second lesson of this chapter is that although common law constitutional rights cannot explain the whole, they do, at least understood in a broad sense, supply an important part of the picture. Thus, as emphasised in Part II, there are important examples of grounds of review – including procedural fairness and legitimate expectations – which have taken their shape to a large degree because the courts have developed the common law in order to provide legal protection to individual rights and interests thought to be of special importance.

On the subject of this second lesson, it is worthwhile stressing briefly the importance of the caveat 'understood in a *broad sense*'. The reason for including this caveat is to accommodate for the ambiguities inherent in certain of the constituent components of this book's subject – especially 'rights' and 'constitutional' – which have been drawn out in the course of this chapter. Thus, as explained in Part III, it is important, when making use of the language of 'rights' in the context of judicial review, to be clear that that term is being used something beyond the narrow cluster of private law rights on which judicial review was unduly focused for so long. Similarly, as explained in Part IV, the language of 'constitutionalism' can be

---

[169] Note that this chapter has made no mention of European Union law, nor the case law of the European Court of Human Rights but these, at least presently, provide further layers of law to be navigated.

[170] Language used, for instance, by M Aronson, 'Private Bodies, Public Power and Soft Law in the High Court' [2007] *Federal Law Review* 1.

[171] Cane (n 138).

understood in different senses. While it may be difficult to apply the narrow version of that term described by Martin Loughlin as the 'modern idea'[172] of constitutionalism, the grounds of review certainly operate so as to 'constitute and limit government'[173] and so can be said to be constitutional in at least this wide sense.

The third and final lesson to be extracted from this chapter concerns the difficulties of capturing precisely the nature of the protection which the common law has afforded to its values within judicial review to date. As explained in Part IV, part of the difficulty is that we can ask the question at both a specific and general level. At the specific level, it would seem to be the case that, at least in some contexts, Parliament is able to override the common law protections provided by certain grounds. *Bank Mellat (No 1)*[174] and *Haralambous*[175] for instance both saw legislation displacing the common law presumption of notice and opportunity to comment. Formulating as a neat legal 'test' the approach courts make use of when deciding whether such a protection has been displaced, however, is far from easy and the popular idea that the acid test is one of the clarity of Parliament's expression of intention[176] does not capture the complexity of the court's endeavours.[177] At the general level there are further difficulties. Judicial dicta in a handful of well-known cases suggests that the common law affords strong protection to judicial review as a broader phenomenon, preventing its outright removal by Parliament. It is, however, very difficult to know how significant these dicta are, both because they have gone untested and because it is highly unlikely, for political and legal reasons, that this will change.

---

[172] M Loughlin, *The British Constitution: A Very Short Introduction* (n 143) 9.
[173] To paraphrase Fisher (n 140), 24.
[174] *Bank Mellat* (n 82).
[175] *Haralambous* (n 19).
[176] See Lord Hoffmann's judgment in *R v Secretary of State for the Home Department, ex parte Simms* [2000] 2 AC 115 (HL).
[177] See discussion of *Bank Mellat* (n 82) above.

12

Common Law Constitutional Rights at the Devolved Level

BRICE DICKSON

I. Introduction

The concept of common law constitutional rights is a slippery one. There is no consensus as to when a claim can justifiably be elevated to the status of a right, let alone a constitutional right. Unless both rights and constitutional rights are to be defined purely by the consequences flowing from their breach, which would be somewhat illogical,[1] there is the additional problem of reaching agreement on what those consequences should be. When these difficulties play out at a national level they are difficult enough to resolve, but the difficulties are compounded at a sub-national level. For constitutions, let us remember, are not the preserve of national states. In the US there is not just the federal Constitution dating from 1789 but also 50 state constitutions. Puerto Rico, which is not a state but an unincorporated territory of the US,[2] also has a Constitution (and a Bill of Rights) dating from 1952 and there is an ongoing campaign to get approval for a constitution for a new 'state' of Washington DC. The Russian Federation currently comprises 85 sub-entities,[3] each of which has its own constitution, Parliament and even constitutional court.

The UK is a unitary state, not a federation, but it comprises three separate legal jurisdictions – England and Wales, Scotland and Northern Ireland. This means that these entities each have their own court systems. Scotland and Northern Ireland are not only separate jurisdictions (eg for purposes of private international law) but also regions to which considerable legislative and executive powers have

---

[1] This is one of the problems with the concepts of 'conditions' and 'warranties' in the common law of contract: they are each defined in terms of whether a breach of the clause allows the victim of the breach to bring the contract to an end. We need something more than a purely consequentialist definition.

[2] There are four other permanently inhabited overseas US territories: American Samoa, Guam, Northern Mariana Islands and the US Virgin Islands. All but the last have a constitution of some kind.

[3] This figure includes the sub-entities of Sevastopol and Crimea, the annexation of which by Russia in 2014 is not widely recognised around the world.

been devolved. Significant powers have also been devolved to Wales,[4] and there is now an intensifying campaign for Wales to be granted separate jurisdictional status from England as well.[5]

This chapter explores the viability of the concept of common law constitutional rights at the devolved level in the UK. Do such rights exist? If so, what is their content and does this content differ depending on the devolved area in question? How do these rights sit alongside national common law constitutional rights? If there is a clash, which takes priority? In attempting to answer such questions the chapter will begin by considering the position in each of the three devolved areas before attempting to draw some more general conclusions regarding the viability of the concept of common law constitutional rights at the devolved level. It will then examine the consequences of those conclusions for the viability of the concept at the national level. It will deduce that the concept may be less viable than many commentators believe it to be.

II. The Position in Scotland

In the UK, Scotland is the area to which more powers have been devolved than anywhere else. In the wake of the narrow result in the referendum on Scottish independence held on 18 September 2014,[6] negotiations between the Scottish and UK Governments led to the devolution of further powers to Scotland by the Scotland Act 2016.[7] This could be a reason for suspecting that common law constitutional rights may play a larger role in Scotland than in other devolved areas of the UK, for if the Scottish Parliament and Government have been the most active of all the devolved institutions, it is conceivable that Scottish judges (or even Supreme Court Justices in appeals from Scotland) may have developed common law principles regulating that activism in ways which, directly or indirectly, confer rights on individuals or collectivities in Scotland. If those individuals or collectivities are able to seek vindication of those rights in a court, it could be said that they have acquired common law constitutional rights which are peculiar to the Scottish devolution regime.

Before dismissing such a possibility out of hand, it is worth recalling that Scottish common law does not have to have the same content as the common law of England and Wales. Judge-made law existed in Scotland before it joined with England and Wales in forming the Union of Great Britain in 1707. Moreover,

---

[4] Government of Wales Acts 1998 and 2006; Wales Acts 2014 and 2017; A Sherlock, 'The Continuing Development of Devolution in Wales' (2015) 21 *European Public Law* 329.

[5] G Parry, 'Is breaking up hard to do? The case for a separate Welsh jurisdiction' (2017) 57 *Irish Jurist (ns)* 61.

[6] The 'no' side won by 55.3% to 44.7% of the vote.

[7] The progress made regarding devolution of powers to Scotland is helpfully summarised in a paper available on the Scottish Parliament's website: www.parliament.scot/PublicInformationdocuments/ ListDevolvedPowers0817.pdf.

Scotland's legal system was not thereafter absorbed by the English legal system to anything like the same extent as the legal systems of Wales and Ireland had been from the sixteenth century onwards. It was not merely that the concept of equity was not taken up in Scotland, that arrangements for allowing loans to be secured against property remained different, that different Scottish legal terminology was retained, or that appeals from Scotland to the top UK court were never permitted in criminal cases. There were more fundamental differences, such as the Scots' scepticism of the doctrine of parliamentary sovereignty and their concomitant preference for regarding the Scottish people as sovereign.[8] Even after 1707 there was no edict that the common law of Scotland had to be identical to that in England and Wales, just as there is no assumption that judge-made law in other common law countries which are now independent, such as Australia or Ireland, has to remain the same as that in England and Wales.

A. The AXA Case

The reality is, however, that it is extremely difficult to find strong supporting evidence that judges in Scotland have created any common law constitutional rights specific to Scotland. Some may point to the Supreme Court case of *AXA General Insurance Ltd v Lord Advocate*[9] in this regard, but it does not fit the bill. The appellant insurance companies were challenging the lawfulness of the Damages (Asbestos-related Conditions) (Scotland) Act 2009, an Act of the Scottish Parliament. They argued that the Act was incompatible with their rights under Article 1 of Protocol 1 to the European Convention on Human Rights (the ECHR), which protects the right to peaceful enjoyment of one's possessions and is part of UK law by virtue of the Human Rights Act 1998 (HRA), because the Act declared that asbestos-related pleural plaques and other asbestos-related conditions constituted personal injuries actionable under Scottish law, thereby exposing the insurance companies to greater claims from those who had bought liability insurance policies with them. The companies also argued, relying on the common law, that the 2009 Act was invalid because it was unreasonable, irrational or an arbitrary exercise of the legislative authority of the Scottish Parliament. The Supreme Court dismissed both arguments, holding that, as far as ECHR rights are concerned, the Act pursued a legitimate aim in a reasonably proportionate manner. As regards

---

[8] D Sharp, 'Parliamentary sovereignty: a Scottish perspective' (2010) 6 *Cambridge Student Law Review* 135; G Little, 'Scotland and parliamentary sovereignty' (2004) 24 *Legal Studies* 540; C Kidd, 'Sovereignty and the Scottish Constitution before 1707' [2004] *Juridical Review* 225. In the Scottish appeal which was heard in the UK Supreme Court as part of the ultimately successful judicial challenge to the prorogation of Parliament in September 2019, the Court of Session, in declaring the prorogation of the Westminster Parliament unlawful, did not rely on the concept of parliamentary sovereignty (as the Supreme Court later did) but rather on the concept of parliamentary accountability, whereby Parliament must sit in order to ensure that the government of the day is accountable to it; see *Cherry v Advocate General for Scotland* [2019] CSIH 49, [53]–[60] per Lord Carloway, [89] per Lord Brodie and [116]–[117 and [124] per Lord Drummond.

[9] [2011] UKSC 46, [2012] 1 AC 868.

the common law argument, it stressed that the test for deciding whether an Act of the Scottish Parliament is invalid is not whether it is unreasonable, irrational or arbitrary, but whether it violates the rule of law. Lord Hope put it thus:

> We now have in Scotland a government which enjoys a large majority in the Scottish Parliament. Its party dominates the only chamber in that Parliament and the committees by which bills that are in progress are scrutinised. It is not entirely unthinkable that a government which has that power may seek to use it to abolish judicial review or to diminish the role of the courts in protecting the interests of the individual. Whether this is likely to happen is not the point. It is enough that it might conceivably do so. The rule of law requires that the judges must retain the power to insist that legislation of that extreme kind is not law which the courts will recognise.[10]

Lord Mance agreed, suggesting that a blatantly discriminatory measure by a devolved Parliament or Assembly would be challengeable under the common law 'as offending against fundamental rights or the rule of law, at the very core of which are principles of equality of treatment'.[11] Lord Reed was of the same view. He said that when the UK Parliament passed the Scotland Act 1998 it did not do so in a vacuum: 'it legislated for a liberal democracy founded on particular constitutional principles and traditions. That being so, Parliament cannot be taken to have intended to establish a body which was free to abrogate fundamental rights or to violate the rule of law'.[12]

These remarks, from one English and two Scottish Supreme Court Justices, are very significant. They strongly suggest that, whatever the position vis-à-vis legislation enacted by the UK Parliament, legislation enacted by the Scottish Parliament is reviewable on rule of law grounds, even if a breach of fundamental rights is not also alleged. There is, in other words, a common law constitutional right to review devolved legislation if it breaches the rule of law (or fundamental rights).[13] But the right is not peculiar to Scotland; it exists as regards devolved legislation in Wales and Northern Ireland as well. As yet there is no clear indication that the right exists in relation to legislation enacted by the UK Parliament: there are dicta to that effect from Lord Steyn, Lord Hope and Lady Hale in *R (Jackson) v Attorney General*,[14] but the proposition has not yet formed the *ratio decidendi* of any judicial decision. In recent years a former senior Law Lord and a former President of the Supreme Court have each suggested that parliamentary sovereignty is not so constrained.[15] They see that doctrine as a constitutional fundamental which was not created by and cannot be altered by the courts.

---

[10] Ibid, [51].

[11] Ibid, [97].

[12] Ibid, [153]. At [169] Lord Reed endorsed Lord Hope's view, expressed in *Eba v Advocate General for Scotland* [2011] UKSC 29, [2012] 1 AC 710, [8], that the rule of law 'is the basis on which the entire system of judicial review rests'.

[13] Lord Reed appeared to accept that such review could be called 'constitutional review', the term used by counsel for the Lord Advocate when conceding that devolved legislation is subject to review if it offends against fundamental rights or the rule of law: ibid, [149].

[14] [2005] UKHL 56, [2006] 1 AC 262, [102], [104]–[107] and [159] respectively.

[15] Lord Bingham, in his book *The Rule of Law* (London, Allen Lane, 2010) 167; Lord Neuberger in his Lord Alexander of Weedon lecture, 'Who are the Masters Now?' (6 April 2011) [73].

B. Other Cases on Legislative Competence

It is correct that the view taken by the Supreme Court as to the legislative competence of the Scottish Parliament may differ from the view taken as to the legislative
competence of the Welsh or Northern Ireland Assembly, but if that occurs it is
likely to be a result of variations in exactly what qualifies as a transferred matter in
each of the three devolved areas. It is worth briefly examining the case law of the
Supreme Court (and of its predecessor, the Appellate Committee of the House of
Lords, from 1998 to 2009) to see if any inference can be drawn from it that constitutional common law rights have been recognised at the devolved level. As regards
Scotland there have been at least seven apex court cases on legislative competence,
four of which could be said to have raised rights issues.[16]

In *Whaley v Lord Advocate*[17] two supporters of fox hunting, which had been
criminalised by the Protection of Wild Mammals (Scotland) Act 2002, sought a
declaration that the Act was outside the competence of the Scottish Parliament
because it violated the petitioners' rights under the ECHR[18] as well as other international obligations supposedly binding on the UK.[19] None of the courts which
considered these arguments agreed with them, with the House of Lords unanimously holding that even if ECHR rights had been breached, the breach was
justified and proportionate. There is nothing in the judgments to suggest that any
common law constitutional rights were at issue.

In *Salvesen v Riddell*[20] the Supreme Court found that the rights of the claimant landlord under Article 1 of Protocol 1 to the ECHR had been violated by the
Agricultural Holdings (Scotland) Act 2003,[21] which was therefore outside the
legislative competence of the Scottish Parliament to make. The subsection in
question particularly disadvantaged a group of landlords who had served certain
notices between September 2002 and June 2003. However, the Court took the
unusual step of suspending the operation of its order until the defect in the legislation could be corrected, retrospectively as well as prospectively. This gave the

---

[16] The other three cases are *Martin v HM Advocate* [2010] UKSC 10, 2010 SLT 412; *Imperial Tobacco
Ltd v Lord Advocate* [2012] UKSC 61, 2015 SC (UKSC) 153 and *Re UK Withdrawal from the European
Union (Legal Continuity) (Scotland) Bill* [2018] UKSC 64, [2019] 2 WLR 1. Even if common law
constitutionalism may be said to have played some role in the decision of these cases, common law
constitutional rights certainly did not.

[17] [2007] UKHL 53, 2008 SC (UKSC) 107.

[18] In particular, Arts 8 (the right to a private life), 9 (the right to freedom of conscience), 10 (the right
to freedom of expression), 11 (the right to freedom of association) and 14 (the right to freedom from
discrimination).

[19] These included Art 27 of the Universal Declaration of Human Rights 1948 ('the right to take part in
cultural life'), though of course the UDHR is not a binding treaty; Art 15 of the International Covenant
on Economic, Social and Cultural Rights 1966 (also on the right to take part in cultural life) and Principle
22 of the Rio Declaration on Environment and Development 1992 (the duty on states to enable the effective participation of local communities in achieving sustainable development, again not a binding treaty
obligation): 2004 SC 78, 88–9 (before Lord Brodie in the Outer House of the Court of Session).

[20] [2013] UKSC 22, 2013 SC (UKSC) 236.

[21] s 72(10).

Scottish Parliament time, after undertaking further research and consultations, to formulate reforms that respected the parties' Convention rights. Again, as the case involved only Convention rights it is not possible to draw any guidance from it regarding common law constitutional rights.

Christian Institute v Lord Advocate is a case where the Supreme Court held that, while Part 4 of the Children and Young People (Scotland) Act 2014 was within the legislative competence of the Scottish Parliament to make, it was nevertheless not made 'in accordance with law' as it lacked safeguards for examining whether access to private information was proportionate to the individuals' rights under Article 8 of the ECHR.[22] For the same reason it was incompatible with EU law. As in *Whaley* and *Salvesen*, however, this decision was reached without any reference being made to common law rights.

Finally, in *AB v Her Majesty's Advocate* the appellant successfully argued that the Sexual Offences (Scotland) Act 2009[23] was incompatible with his Article 8 right to a private life because the criminal charges laid against him, which in a later case precluded him from relying on the defence that he thought the girl he had had sex with was 16 or older, did not give him official notice that consensual sexual activity with children aged 13 to 16 was an offence.[24] Once more, common law constitutional rights did not enter the picture.

We can see from these four cases that it can often be difficult to determine whether or not a devolved legislature such as the Scottish Parliament has acted within its legislative competence. The answer will turn on the precise wording of the devolution Act *and* of the proposed devolved legislation. Arguments over legislative competence certainly raise constitutional questions and might even be said to raise common law *constitutionalism* in so far as the judges who are required to answer the questions may find themselves applying common law principles concerning statutory interpretation,[25] the ultra vires doctrine,[26] the legality principle,[27] the concepts of reasonableness and rationality, the doctrine of proportionality[28] or the burden of proof.[29] But in doing so judges are not necessarily engaging with

---

[22] [2016] UKSC 51, 2017 SC (UKSC) 29.

[23] s 39(2)(a)(i).

[24] [2017] UKSC 25, 2017 SC (UKSC) 101.

[25] As in the Northern Ireland case of *Robinson v Secretary of State for Northern Ireland* [2002] UKHL 32, [2002] NI 390, on which see pp 288–89 below.

[26] See, eg, *Aberdeen City and Shire Strategic Development Planning Authority v Elsick Development Company Ltd* [2017] UKSC 66, 2017 SC (UKSC) 67, where the Supreme Court found the SDPA's planning scheme to be ultra vires the Town and Country Planning (Scotland) Act 1997.

[27] See, eg, *Scotch Whisky Association v The Lord Advocate* [2017] UKSC 76, on whether the Alcohol (Minimum Pricing) (Scotland) Act 2012 was contrary to EU law.

[28] For a case where the principle of proportionality was essentially the basis for a ruling that a pharmacist had been unlawfully struck off the register of pharmacists because he had pleaded guilty to three counts of domestic violence, see *Habib Khan v General Pharmaceutical Council* [2016] UKSC 64, [2017] 1 WLR 169. See too *In the Matter of EV (A Child)* [2017] UKSC 15, 2017 SC (UKSC) 67, where the doctrine was applied in a case on whether a permanent adoption order should be made in relation to a child.

[29] In *Sadovska v Secretary of State for the Home Department* [2017] UKSC 54, 2017 SC (UKSC) 38 the Supreme Court held that if an EU state wishes to remove the permanent right of residence of an EU citizen it bears the onus of proving that the alleged abuse of rights or fraud in question has been committed.

common law constitutional *rights*. Unless, as in the *AXA* case already discussed, the appellant specifically relies on a common law right in addition to or instead of a Convention right or some other statutory right, the court's decision cannot provide authority for the existence of a common law constitutional right operating at the devolved level. This is not to deny that devolved institutions can be required to recognise 'general' common law constitutional rights which apply throughout the whole country: such rights might be held to have been baked into the devolution settlements in a way which affects judicial determinations of what is within the competence of any of the devolved legislatures.

Common law constitutional rights are perhaps more easily discernible when administration of the law is at issue. In *Eba v Advocate General for Scotland* seven Supreme Court Justices held, unanimously, that decisions of the Upper Tribunal in Scotland which could not be appealed were nevertheless amenable to judicial review if they raised an important point of principle or practice or if there was some other compelling reason to allow judicial review to proceed.[30] The right of access to justice is a common law constitutional right, as well as a Convention right under Article 6 of the ECHR.[31] But, again, the decision in *Eba* does not create a right which is special to Scotland. The appeal to the Supreme Court was heard alongside two other appeals from English courts which raised the same issue. A separate set of judgments was issued for the English appeals but the net result was the same as in the Scottish appeal.[32] In this context one may refer also to the case of *Davies v The Scottish Commission for the Regulation of Care*,[33] which is an example of the application of the common law doctrine of abuse of process, designed to protect defendants from being subjected to unfair litigation. That too is a nationwide doctrine, not a special Scottish one, so no common law constitutional right specific to a devolved region was at issue in the case.

Ruddy v Chief Constable of the Strathclyde Police may be put forward as another candidate for evidence of the emergence of a common law constitutional right in Scotland.[34] Allowing Mr Ruddy's appeal, the Supreme Court held that he could bring an action, both at common law and under the HRA, for the ill-treatment he allegedly suffered while in a police car. He could also claim that his complaint had not been properly investigated, relying upon Article 3 of the ECHR. He did not need to bring this last claim by way of judicial review, and he could bring it against both the Chief Constable and the Lord Advocate in the same action. Yet again, though, there is nothing specifically Scottish about this ruling. The Supreme

---

[30] [2011] UKSC 29, [2012] 1 AC 710. The appeal resulted in a judgment of the whole Court, handed down by Lord Hope.

[31] *R v Lord Chancellor, ex parte Witham* [1998] QB 575 (Div Ct); *R (UNISON) v Lord Chancellor* [2017] UKSC 51, [2017] 3 WLR 409.

[32] *R (Cart) v The Upper Tribunal* [2011] UKSC 28, [2012] 1 AC 663.

[33] [2013] UKSC 12, 2013 SC (UKSC) 186. The defendant Commission had been abolished; the action should have been taken against its replacement, Social Care and Social Work Improvement Scotland.

[34] [2012] UKSC 57, 2013 SC (UKSC) 126. Again, Lord Hope gave the judgment of the Court.

Court was simply pointing out that what the claimant was seeking to do in this case did not violate the common law principle that a claimant cannot sue two or more people on separate grounds and ask for a lump sum award of damages against them jointly and severally. Here the claimant was not asking for a lump sum. The claims he was bringing were inter-connected and it was in the interests of justice and more convenient to try them together. An appeal from any other part of the UK would, it is submitted, have been dealt with identically.[35]

In a case decided a month after *Ruddy*, the Supreme Court held in *M v Scottish Ministers* that the Scottish Government had acted unlawfully by not ensuring that certain regulations had been issued before the Mental Health (Care and Treatment) (Scotland) Act 2003 came into force.[36] The lack of any regulation defining who was embraced by the term 'qualifying patient' meant that the appellant could not apply for a declaration from the Mental Health Tribunal that he was being detained in conditions of excessive security. Both the Outer and Inner Houses of the Court of Session rejected the appellant's petition because they did not think there was a duty on the government to lay regulations giving effect to an Act unless that Act conferred a right on a specific class of persons. But the Supreme Court unanimously allowed M's appeal. The judgment of the Court, delivered by Lord Reed, relied to some extent on the specific wording of the legislation in question but it also stressed the more general point that there is a basic principle of administrative law that a discretionary power must not be exercised in a way which frustrates the object of the Act which conferred it.[37] This is, surely, an illustration of common law constitutionalism at work but it is not one restricted to the vindication of rights and, more importantly in the present context, not one that is confined to a devolved jurisdiction.

C. Other Candidates for Common Law Constitutional Rights

When considering other possible candidates for the status of common law constitutional rights in Scotland we must of course exclude those rights which have been expressly or impliedly conferred by the *legislation* bringing about the devolution. Thus, the right of Members of the Scottish Parliament not to be sued for defamation in relation to statements they make in proceedings of Parliament is not a common law constitutional right because it is conferred by section 41(1)(a) of the

---

[35] The same could be said of *Moohan v The Lord Advocate* [2014] UKSC 67, [2015] AC 901, where the Supreme Court rejected the argument that under the common law there was a right of universal and equal suffrage. See too *ANS v ML* [2012] UKSC 30, 2013 SC (UKSC) 20, where the Supreme Court held that, if the welfare of a child requires his or her adoption, a parent of the child has no fundamental right to prevent the adoption just because the parent does not consent to it.

[36] [2012] UKSC 58, [2012] 1 WLR 3386.

[37] In support of this proposition Lord Reed (at [42] and [47]) cited *Padfield v Minister of Agriculture, Fisheries and Food* [1968] AC 997; see too *R v Secretary of State for the Home Department, ex p Fire Brigades Union* [1995] 2 AC 513.

Scotland Act 1998. Nor can we automatically categorise as a common law right the enforcement of a duty imposed by devolution legislation. If, for example, the Scottish Parliamentary Corporate Body does not perform its duty to ensure that the Scottish Parliament is provided with the staff required for its purposes, a duty imposed by section 21(3) of the Scotland Act 1998, it does not follow that any individual Member of the Scottish Parliament, or any other person or group for that matter, has a corresponding right to have that duty enforced.[38]

Nevertheless, there are perhaps two specific aspects of the Scotland Act 2016 which might conceivably be viewed as creating common law constitutional rights.[39] The first is the provision which declares that the Scottish Parliament and the Scottish Government are 'a permanent part of the United Kingdom's constitutional arrangements' and that those institutions cannot be abolished 'except on the basis of a decision of the people of Scotland voting in a referendum'.[40] If the UK Parliament were to attempt to abolish either institution without there first having been a referendum, an action could presumably be taken in the courts for a declaration that the abolition is unlawful. If in defence to such a claim the UK Government were to plead the doctrine of parliamentary sovereignty, it would surely be plausible for a court to rule that, while that doctrine might defeat a claim based on section 63A(3), it cannot defeat the common law right which impliedly underlies that provision. Support for this can be found in section 63A(2), which explicitly states that: 'The purpose of this section is, with due regard to the other provisions of this Act, to signify the commitment of the Parliament and Government of the United Kingdom to the Scottish Parliament and the Scottish Government'. This commitment must be seen as having a separate existence from the statutory promise of permanence and is arguably of such a fundamental nature as to have altered the common law of Scotland (and/or the constitutional law of the UK) and thereby to have qualified for protection from the judges. It might even be subsumed within the principle of the rule of law already discussed in the context of the *AXA* case. Quite who would have the standing to vindicate this new common law constitutional right is a difficult, but separate, issue.

The second relevant provision in the Scotland Act 2016 is the one which purports to insert the so-called Sewel Convention into the legal framework of the devolution arrangements. It reads: 'But it is recognised that the Parliament of the United Kingdom will not normally legislate with regard to devolved matters without the consent of the Scottish Parliament'.[41] On the face of it this seems to

---

[38] Presumably the First Minister, as representative of the Parliament, would have the *locus standi* to seek a judicial review of the SPCB's failure to comply with its statutory duty.

[39] The two new aspects have been mirrored in Wales (see p 285 below), but only the second has been mirrored in Northern Ireland (see pp 287–88 below).

[40] Scotland Act 1998, s 63A(1) and (3), as inserted by the Scotland Act 2016, s 1.

[41] Scotland Act 1998, s 28(8), inserted by the Scotland Act 2016, s 2. It is called the Sewel Convention because Lord Sewel, the Minister of State in the Scotland Office, referred to it in July 1998 when the Scotland Bill was before the Lords. But the same convention applied from the time when legislative competence was devolved to the Parliament of Northern Ireland by the Government of Ireland Act 1920: B Hadfield, 'The Northern Ireland Constitution' in B Hadfield (ed) *Northern Ireland: Politics and the Constitution* (Buckingham, Open University Press, 1992) 1, 3.

represent a commitment that the UK Parliament will not trespass on the Scottish Parliament's legislative patch, but the insertion of the word 'normally' is a clear indicator that it was not intended to be a legally binding promise or duty. It simply means that *usually* the Scottish Parliament will be allowed exclusive legislative competence over transferred matters. The wording is very close indeed to that used in the Memorandum of Understanding (MoU) between the UK and devolved Governments, first drawn up in 1999 and supplemented many times since, the purpose of which is to set out the principles underlying the working relations between administrations in the UK, Scotland, Wales and Northern Ireland.[42] The relevant paragraph in the original 1999 Memorandum read: '[T]he UK government will proceed in accordance with the convention that the UK Parliament would not normally legislate with regard to devolved matters except with the agreement of the devolved legislature'.[43] It has remained virtually unchanged ever since. Moreover all of the MoUs have been prefaced with the following statement: 'This Memorandum is a statement of political intent, and should not be interpreted as a binding agreement. It does not create legal obligations between the parties'.[44]

When the applicants in the *Miller* case[45] tried to argue that Article 50 of the Treaty on European Union could not be triggered by the UK Parliament unless it had first obtained the consent of the three devolved legislatures (or at least of the Northern Ireland Assembly, given the importance of the Belfast Agreement and the Northern Ireland peace process) none of the 11 Justices was supportive.[46] The joint judgment of the eight Justices who thought that only Parliament and not the government could trigger Article 50 stressed that the Sewel convention was still a political and not a legal convention and they cited several precedents to support that position,[47] summing up by declaring that:

> The Sewel Convention has an important role in facilitating harmonious relationships between the UK Parliament and the devolved legislatures. But the policing of its scope and the manner of its operation does not lie within the constitutional remit of the judiciary, which is to protect the rule of law.[48]

---

[42] Cm 4444 (1 October 1999). At that time devolution had not yet formally begun in Northern Ireland, so the first MoU dealt only with the UK, Scotland and Wales. Northern Ireland was included in the second version of the MoU: Cm 4806 (26 July 2000). There were subsequent versions published in 2001 (Cm 5240) and 2010 (Cm 7864). Versions produced in 2011, 2012 and 2013 were apparently not given Command Paper numbers. For a short parliamentary debate on the need for an updated MoU, see *House of Lords Debs*, vol 787, 20 November 2017, cols 53–68.

[43] Para 13; it is para 14 in the latest (2013) version.

[44] Para 2 in the latest (2013) version. It goes on to say: 'Nothing in this Memorandum should be construed as conflicting with the Belfast Agreement', a sentence first inserted in the 2000 version.

[45] [2017] UKSC 5, [2018] AC 61.

[46] Ibid, [136]–[151] (per the majority) and (282) (per Lord Hughes).

[47] *Re Resolution to Amend the Constitution* [1981] 1 SCR 753 (Sup Ct of Canada); *Madzimbamuto v Lardner-Burke* [1969] 1 AC 645 (Privy Council); *Attorney General v Jonathan Cape Ltd* [1976] 1 QB 752 (High Ct).

[48] [2017] UKSC 5, [151]. At [146] the same judges said: 'Judges … are neither the parents nor the guardians of political conventions; they are merely observers'.

We can conclude from *Miller* that in Scotland no *common law* constitutional right flows from the Sewel convention, regardless of whether it is considered as a mere constitutional convention that has developed through custom and practice or (since 2016) as a legislatively endorsed fundamental constitutional principle. In truth, although the devolution arrangements in Scotland are more developed than in Wales or Northern Ireland, and have been inserted into a legal system which was already more divergent from the English legal system than were the legal systems of Wales and Northern Ireland, it is difficult to point to any common law constitutional rights in Scotland which are peculiar to that jurisdiction. That of itself is not a basis for concluding that no common law constitutional rights are peculiar to Wales or Northern Ireland either, but it would certainly suggest that there would need to be something very specific about one or other of those two regions for such a right to be deemed to exist.

Summing up, none of the cases on the legislative competence of the Scottish Parliament, on other human rights issues, or on the Parliament's subordination to Westminster, can plausibly be cited as an authority in favour of the existence of constitutional rights at the devolved level in Scotland. The furthest one can go, it is submitted, is to raise the *possibility* that two such rights might be emerging. The first, relying on the *AXA* decision, is a common law constitutional right applicable in all three devolved areas of the UK, namely the right to challenge an Act of a devolved legislature on the grounds that it violates the rule of law. As yet such a right does not exist at the national level because of judicial deference to the doctrine of parliamentary sovereignty, although there are judicial dicta which hint that in appropriate circumstances the Supreme Court might recognise it at that level too. The second *possible* common law constitutional right, which could perhaps be seen as part and parcel of the first to the extent that it overlaps with the concept of the rule of law, is the right to challenge the validity of Westminster legislation which threatens the permanence of the Scottish Parliament.

III. The Position in Wales

Devolution in Wales has been very much a work in progress since 1998. Initially the Government of Wales Act 1998 provided for a model of devolution whereby the Welsh Assembly could not enact 'primary' legislation comparable to the Acts of the Scottish Parliament and the Northern Ireland Assembly. It could merely create secondary legislation on a range of specified matters that were transferred to it by the UK Parliament. The roles of the Assembly and the Executive within the Assembly were closely inter-twined. They were not formally separated as legal entities until, partly as a result of recommendations made by the Richard Commission in 2004,[49] this was provided for by the Government of Wales Act 2006. This Act allowed the

---

[49] *The Commission on the Powers and Electoral Arrangements of the National Assembly for Wales.*

Assembly to make 'Measures', but the subject areas which could be legislated for in that manner were still highly restricted.[50] Further powers could be devolved either through the UK Parliament providing for such devolution in sections of Acts or through that Parliament and the Welsh Assembly approving 'Legislative Competence Orders'. The 2006 Act made it clear that all the potentially devolvable powers could be transferred if the people of Wales voted for that in a referendum and in 2011 that is exactly what they did. As a result, the Assembly which was elected two months later acquired the power to legislate in all those areas through Acts.

The Wales Act 2014 brought about even greater devolution by implementing recommendations of the Silk Commission which issued Part 1 of its Report in 2012.[51] Responsibility for stamp duty, business rates and landfill tax was devolved and permission was given to the Assembly to replace these taxes with different taxes if it so wished. It was also agreed that responsibility for other taxes could be devolved following negotiations between the Assembly and the UK Government. Moreover, if the people of Wales were to so decide in another referendum, the Assembly would be able to exact an element of income tax and acquire new borrowing powers. In a nod to the prospect of Wales becoming a separate jurisdiction from England, the 2014 Act also required the Law Commission for England and Wales to provide Welsh Ministers with advice and information on matters of law reform which those Ministers have referred to the Commission.[52]

No further referendum took place and the Wales Act 2017 removed the need for such a referendum prior to income tax powers being devolved.[53] The more general aim of the 2017 Act was to implement those parts of the St David's Day Agreement 2015 which required legislation. That Agreement had been arrived at on the back of Part 2 of the Silk Commission Report published in 2014.[54] The 2017 Act changed the devolution model from a 'conferred powers' model to a 'reserved powers' model, similar to that which applies in both Scotland and Northern Ireland, meaning that in Wales there is now a clearer dividing line between powers which have been reserved to Westminster and all the other powers (which are deemed to be transferred). Amongst the powers which have been newly devolved is the power to run Welsh Assembly elections. A new Schedule 3A to the Government of Wales Act 2006 sets out the powers which can be exercised concurrently or jointly by Welsh Ministers and Ministers of the Crown. The reserved powers are listed in a new Schedule 7A to the same Act and further general restrictions relating to those reserved powers are set out in a new Schedule 7B (to which there are in turn some general exceptions). In 2017 the Assembly Commission of the National Assembly of Wales recommended that from 2020 the Assembly should

---

[50] Between 2008 and 2011 the Assembly passed 22 Measures.
[51] Commission on Devolution in Wales, *Empowerment and responsibility: Pt 1 Financial powers to strengthen Wales* (2012) and Pt 2 *Legislative powers to strengthen Wales* (2014).
[52] Wales Act 2014, s 25(2).
[53] Wales Act 2017, s 17.
[54] See n 51 above. It was also preceded by a White Paper entitled *Powers for a purpose: towards a lasting devolution settlement for Wales* (Cm 9020).

be renamed the Welsh Parliament (*Senedd Cymru*),[55] and later that year an Expert Panel on Assembly Electoral Reform proposed that the voting age for elections to that Parliament should be reduced from 18 years to 16 years.[56] At the time of writing no legislation had yet been introduced to implement either recommendation.

Just as in the case of Scotland, it is difficult to discern within the current arrangements for devolution in Wales any common law constitutional rights that are peculiar to the region. The most that can be claimed is that as a result of some of the constitutional changes some additional rights have been impliedly conferred on those who have the standing to exercise them. Such rights, by definition, are primarily statutory in nature but it is possible that one or more of them may also reflect an underlying common law right. Thus, as in Scotland, the amended Government of Wales Act 2006 declares that the Assembly and the Welsh Government cannot be abolished except on the basis of a decision of the people of Wales voting in a referendum[57] and it enshrines the so-called Sewel Convention.[58] Arguably the former of these provisions has confirmed a constitutional common law right which would prevent Westminster from abolishing the National Assembly of Wales without a referendum.

A. Cases on Legislative Competence

In Wales there has not been as much litigation relating to devolution as there has been in Scotland, but still three cases on the Welsh Assembly's legislative competence have gone as far as the UK Supreme Court. The first was *Attorney General v National Assembly for Wales Commission*,[59] where the Attorney General for England and Wales argued that the Local Government Byelaws (Wales) Bill 2012 – the first Bill which the Welsh Assembly tried to enact under the new powers conferred on it as a result of the referendum in 2011 – was not within the Welsh Assembly's competence. Only five Justices sat to hear the case, but they unanimously held that the Bill's removal of the Secretary of State's power to confirm local council byelaws was merely incidental to or consequential on the Bill's primary purpose of removing the need for confirmation of byelaws by Welsh Ministers and it was therefore not outside the Assembly's competence.

The Attorney General for England and Wales made a further reference in 2014, this time of the Agricultural Sector (Wales) Bill.[60] The Bill's main purpose was to establish a new Agricultural Wages Panel, replacing an Advisory Panel which had been abolished by the Enterprise and Regulatory Reform Act 2013. The Welsh

---

[55] 'Assembly set to be renamed Welsh Parliament' BBC News, 13 June 2017: www.bbc.co.uk/news/uk-wales-politics-40263684.

[56] *A Parliament that Works for Wales* (Nov 2017).

[57] Government of Wales Act 2006, s A1(3).

[58] Ibid, s 107(6).

[59] [2012] UKSC 53, [2012] 1 AC 792.

[60] *In re Agricultural Sector (Wales) Bill* [2014] UKSC 43, [2014] 1 WLR 2622.

Government argued that it had competence to make legislation which 'relates to' agriculture, while the Attorney General argued that the Bill related to employment and industrial relations, which were not devolved matters. Again the Supreme Court held unanimously that the Bill fell within the Assembly's competence. In an important aside the Court stressed that while the Government of Wales Act 2006 was an Act of great constitutional significance, it had to be interpreted in the same way as any ordinary statute.[61]

In *In re Recovery of Medical Costs for Asbestos Diseases (Wales) Bill* it was the Counsel General for Wales (effectively Wales' own Attorney General) who had doubts about the Assembly's competence to enact the Bill.[62] This time the Supreme Court agreed with the referring official because, although the Assembly had competence to legislate for the 'organisation and funding of [the] national health service', this could not include the imposition of new forms of liability for economic loss on persons not directly connected with the national health service, such as employers and insurers.[63] Through obiter dicta all five judges agreed that the Bill was also incompatible with the rights of employers and insurers to the peaceful enjoyment of their possessions under Article 1 of Protocol 1 to the ECHR, in the absence of any special justification having been proffered for the interference with these rights. The decision is analogous to that reached by the Supreme Court in the Scottish case of *AXA*.[64]

In these three cases no mention was made of common law rights, constitutional or otherwise. Given that one of the distinguishing features of Wales is that there are many inhabitants whose first language is not English but Welsh, the National Assembly of Wales has understandably taken steps to enhance the protection afforded to that language[65] (as Scotland has in relation to Gallic, although to a lesser extent[66]), but again it is not easy to see the relevance of any *common law* constitutional rights in this context. The common law's commitment to equality could conceivably be cited to support a general claim that speakers of Welsh should not be disadvantaged vis-à-vis speakers of English, but there is no clear precedent for such a claim. Although not entirely analogous, in *R (Bibi) v Secretary of State for the Home Department*[67] the Supreme Court made no reference to such a common law principle when two appellants unsuccessfully challenged the validity of an amendment to the Immigration Rules requiring a foreign spouse or partner

---

[61] Ibid, [6], per Lords Reed and Thomas CJ (with whom the other three Justices agreed). They cited in support *Attorney General v National Assembly for Wales Commission*, n 59 above, [80] (per Lord Hope, with whom Lords Clarke, Reed and Carnwath agreed).

[62] *In re Recovery of Medical Costs for Asbestos Diseases (Wales) Bill* [2015] UKSC 3, [2015] AC 1016.

[63] Lord Thomas CJ and Lady Hale dissented to the extent that they did not think it was beyond the Assembly's competence to impose liability on employers.

[64] See the discussion in the text at n 9 above.

[65] Welsh Language (Wales) Measure 2011; National Assembly for Wales (Official Languages) Act 2012.

[66] Gaelic Language (Scotland) Act 2005.

[67] [2015] UKSC 68, [2015] 1 WLR 5055. See too the decision of the Northern Ireland Court of Appeal in *Mac Giolla Cathain (Caoimhin) v Northern Ireland Courts Service* [2010] NICA 24, an unsuccessful attempt to invalidate the Administration of Justice (Language) Act of 1737, which requires all proceedings in Northern Ireland's courts to be conducted in English.

of a British citizen or person settled in the UK to pass a test of competence in English before coming to live there.

We are forced to arrive at a similar conclusion to that reached in relation to Scotland: there are no common law constitutional rights specific to residents of Wales, with the possible exception of the right to challenge devolved legislation because it breaches the rule of law, or Westminster legislation because it threatens the permanence of the devolved legislature.

IV. The Position in Northern Ireland

Devolution has a much longer and more complex history in Northern Ireland than in any other part of the UK. It functioned between 1921 and 1972 and then intermittently from 1999 until today. For substantial periods since 1999 it has been interrupted due to the inability of local political parties to reach consensus on controversial issues. The Northern Ireland Act 2000 made provision for the re-imposition of direct rule by UK Government order if deemed necessary, but that mechanism was repealed as a result of the St Andrews Agreement of 2006,[68] meaning that today, if the Assembly and Executive are not operating, direct rule cannot resume unless a new Act is passed at Westminster to that effect. Since the collapse of the Northern Ireland Executive in January 2017 there has been no government in Northern Ireland but also no direct rule from Westminster. The running of the territory has been the responsibility of civil servants, with the UK Parliament having intervened on three occasions to ensure that a budget is approved to allow public expenditure to take place.[69]

The Sewel Convention has not been expressly written into the devolution legislation, where there is still a provision saying that devolving legislative competence to the Northern Ireland Assembly 'does not affect the power of the Parliament of the United Kingdom to make laws for Northern Ireland'[70] but, as in Scotland and Wales, Standing Orders have been drawn up to govern the handling of 'legislative consent motions' whenever the agreement of the Northern Ireland Assembly is sought to the UK Parliament considering provisions in a Bill which deal with a devolution matter.[71] Likewise, unlike in Scotland and Wales the permanence of the Northern Ireland institutions has not been guaranteed because of the ongoing

---

[68] Northern Ireland (St Andrews Agreement) Act 2016, s 2(5) and Sch 4.

[69] See the Northern Ireland Budget Act 2017 and the Northern Ireland Budget (Anticipation and Adjustments) Acts 2018 and 2019.

[70] Northern Ireland Act 1998, s 5(6).

[71] Standing Order 42A, inserted in 2012. See too the Scottish Parliament's Standing Orders Rule 9B.2 and the National Assembly of Wales' Standing Orders 29.6–29.8. Up to May 2018 (from May 1999) there had been 79 legislative consent motions in the Northern Ireland Assembly, 88 in the National Assembly of Wales and 173 in the Scottish Parliament: 'Brexit and the Sewel (legislative consent) Convention', Institute for Government, 17 May 2018, available at www.instituteforgovernment.org.uk/ explainers/brexit-sewel-legislative-consent-convention.

political dispute as to the long-term constitutional future of the area. This is reflected in the Northern Ireland Act 1998, which begins by specifically allowing Northern Ireland to leave the UK altogether if a majority of the people of Northern Ireland vote for that option in a referendum.[72]

The length and complexity of Northern Ireland's experience of devolution have not, however, resulted in any greater role for common law constitutional rights in the region. The Northern Ireland Act 1998, which aimed to implement many of the provisions in the Belfast (Good Friday) Agreement, is often described, even by judges, as a constitutional document, but it is hard to identify within it any indisputable constitutional rights (which would in any event be primarily statutory) and judges have certainly not supplemented it with a set of related rights under the common law. The Agreement, and subsequent corresponding legislation, did 'recognise the birthright of all the people of Northern Ireland to identify themselves and be accepted as Irish or British, or both, as they may so choose' and it accordingly confirmed that 'their right to hold both British and Irish citizenship is accepted by both Governments and would not be affected by any future change in the status of Northern Ireland'.[73] However that was not a new right, simply the recognition of an existing one, and the term 'all the people of Northern Ireland' was left undefined. It has recently come to light, incidentally, that people who identify themselves as Irish may still be deemed to be British too even though they do not wish to be.[74]

A leading case is *Robinson v Secretary of State for Northern Ireland*,[75] where Peter Robinson, a Democratic Unionist MP, challenged the election of David Trimble and Seamus Mallon as First and Deputy First Ministers of Northern Ireland because it had taken place outside of the six-week period required by the 1998 Act.[76] By three to two the Law Lords held that, despite the non-compliance with the Act, the election of the two Ministers was valid. Lord Bingham, one of the judges in the majority, said:

> The 1998 Act does not set out all the constitutional provisions applicable to Northern Ireland, but it is in effect a constitution. So to categorise the Act is not to relieve the

---

[72] s 1 and Sch 1.

[73] Para 1(vi) of the 'Constitutional Issues' section of the Agreement Reached in the Multi-Party Negotiations and Art 1(vi) of the Agreement between the British and Irish Governments annexed to the Multi-Party Agreement. Under the Irish Nationality and Citizenship Act 1956, s 6A (inserted in 2004) a person born in Northern Ireland can acquire Irish nationality only if one of his or her parents has, during the four-year period preceding the birth, been resident in Ireland for not less than a period aggregating three years. The residence, it seems clear, has to have been in the Republic of Ireland.

[74] *Secretary of State for the Home Department v De Souza*, a decision of the Upper Tribunal (Immigration and Asylum Chamber), Appeal Number EA/06667/2016, 14 October 2019, available at https://tribunalsdecisions.service.gov.uk/utiac/ea-06667-2016.

[75] [2002] UKHL 32, [2002] NI 390. For commentary see M Lynch, '*Robinson v Secretary of State for Northern Ireland*: interpreting constitutional legislation' [2003] *PL* 640. More generally see J Morison and M Lynch, 'Litigating the Agreement: Towards a New Judicial Constitutionalism for the UK from Northern Ireland?' in J Morison, K McEvoy and G Anthony (eds), *Judges, Transition and Human Rights* (Oxford, Oxford University Press, 2007) 105.

[76] Northern Ireland Act 1998, s 16(8).

courts of their duty to interpret the constitutional provisions in issue. But the provisions should, consistently with the language used, be interpreted generously and purposively, bearing in mind the values which the constitutional provisions are intended to embody.[77]

Given that this decision deprived the people of Northern Ireland of what could be viewed as their statutory constitutional right to another Assembly election, one might even conclude that the *Robinson* case negated a constitutional right, unless one labels the right to have a functioning government as an overriding constitutional right, a right so fundamental that under the rule of law as it operates in a devolved context it trumps an express statutory right. In truth the case is not so much about a common law constitutional right as about a common law right to have a statutory provision (which happens to have constitutional significance) interpreted in a purposive manner.

The House of Lords again had to interpret the Northern Ireland Act 1998 in a case concerning the powers of the Northern Ireland Human Rights Commission. The Commission had wanted to intervene in inquests concerning 29 people who were killed by a bomb in Omagh in 1998. The High Court and a majority of the Court of Appeal in Northern Ireland interpreted the Act restrictively, denying the Commission any power to intervene. But by a majority of four to one the House of Lords reversed the Court of Appeal's ruling.[78] The majority felt comfortable in holding that the capacity to make submissions to a court was 'incidental' to the powers expressly conferred on the Commission to review the adequacy and effectiveness in Northern Ireland of law and practice relating to the protection of human rights and to promote understanding and awareness of the importance of human rights in Northern Ireland.[79] Once again this was really just a decision on statutory interpretation and it tells us very little if anything about common law constitutional rights *per se*. In 2018 the UK Supreme Court had further occasion to look at the powers of the Human Rights Commission, this time holding that in the absence of any actual or potential victim the Commission could not abstractly challenge primary legislation dealing with abortion on the basis that it was in violation of the ECHR, but speaking obiter the majority then said that if the Commission had had that power they would have found the primary legislation on abortion[80] to be in breach of Article 8 of the ECHR.[81]

The *Miller* case, on Brexit and Article 50,[82] included consideration of five questions *referred* from Northern Ireland, one by the Court of Appeal and four by the Attorney General. Two of the questions had in effect already been answered in the part of the judgment dealing with Ms Miller's application. A new

---

[77] [2002] UKHL 32, [11].

[78] *In re NIHRC's Application* [2002] UKHL 25, [2002] NI 236.

[79] Northern Ireland Act 1998, s 69(1) and (6).

[80] Offences Against the Person Act 1861, ss 58 and 59.

[81] *In the matter of an application by the NIHRC for Judicial Review* [2018] UKSC 27, [2019] 1 All ER 173.

[82] [2017] UKSC 5, [2018] AC 61.

question was whether, if only Parliament could trigger Article 50, the consent of the Northern Ireland Assembly was also required. As already mentioned,[83] the Court held unanimously that it was not, because the 'Sewel' convention operates only at the political level and not the legal.[84] A second new question was whether the equality provisions in section 75 of the Northern Ireland Act 1998 imposed any constraints on the triggering of Article 50 and again the Justices unanimously ruled that they did not.[85] The final new question was whether the triggering of Article 50 without first obtaining the consent of the people of Northern Ireland somehow violated section 1 of the Northern Ireland Act, which declares that Northern Ireland remains part of the UK unless a majority of the people of Northern Ireland vote to the contrary in a border poll. Here too the Supreme Court saw no merit at all in such a proposition. Neither the Attorney General for Northern Ireland nor any other counsel in the case was able to point to any common law constitutional right to support their stance in this case.

Some might observe that a common law constitutional right appears to underpin two recent decisions by High Court judges in Northern Ireland which suggest that commitments made in a devolved government's Programme for Government are judicially enforceable by individuals or groups who are disadvantaged by non-fulfilment of those commitments. In *The Committee on the Administration of Justice's Application* a non-governmental organisation convinced the judge that Northern Ireland's Executive (ie, the multi-party Government) was in breach of the law by not having adopted an identifiable strategy for tackling poverty, social exclusion and patterns of deprivation, based on objective need.[86] The judge referred to the lengthy documentation which showed that the Office of the First and Deputy First Minister had considered and even acted upon some plans for reducing poverty and promoting social inclusion, but he did not think these efforts amounted to anything like a strategy. Two years later a different judge reached a similar conclusion in *Conradh na Gaelige's Application*,[87] where what was at issue was the Executive's failure to adopt an Irish language strategy.

The commitment to produce these two strategies had been set out in the inter-party and inter-governmental St Andrews Agreement of 2006.[88] Vitally, the commitment was then included in the legislation which implemented parts of that Agreement.[89] Only a poverty strategy was mentioned in the Programme for Government for 2008 to 2011, agreed by the parties which formed the mandatory

---

[83] See above, Part II.C.

[84] [2017] UKSC 5, [136]-[151], [242], [243] and [282].

[85] Ibid, [133], [242], [243] and [282]. Section 75 requires new laws and policies to be screened for their effect on equality of opportunity and good relations as between various groups in Northern Ireland, eg religious groups.

[86] *CAJ's Application* [2015] NIQB 59 (Treacy J).

[87] [2017] NIQB 27 (Maguire J).

[88] St Andrew's Agreement (2006), Annex B, p 12, although the word 'strategy' was not explicitly used in relation to the Irish language.

[89] Northern Ireland Act 1998, ss 28D and 28E, inserted by the Northern Ireland (St Andrews Agreement) Act 2006, ss 15 and 16.

coalition Government after the Assembly elections in 2007,[90] but no such strategy was ever formally adopted. A 20-year strategy dealing with the Irish language was eventually published in 2015 after a public consultation, but again no further steps were taken to implement it.

The key point here is that the duty to produce these strategies was imposed by legislation, so the common law played no role in the cases other than providing a remedy for the applicants – a declaration in judicial review proceedings. In the Irish language case, for example, Maguire J concluded that the purpose of the legislation in question had been frustrated and 'robbed of any practical effect'.[91] To that extent the decisions are but illustrations of the nationwide principle that failure to comply with a statutory duty can be the subject of a judicial declaration.[92] It is submitted, therefore, that the two Northern Ireland cases do not provide support for the existence of any common law constitutional rights in this context: what the judges did was apply standard judicial review principles, albeit in a novel context. There was no 'devolved' dimension to their rulings.

By way of summary, despite the very special circumstances surrounding devolution arrangements for Northern Ireland, no more convincing a case can be made for the existence of common law constitutional rights specific to residents of Northern Ireland than it can be for their existence in Scotland or Wales.

V. Conclusions Regarding Common Law Constitutional Rights at the Devolved Level

The three foregoing sections provide little evidence to support the assertion that there are common law constitutional rights operating at the devolved level anywhere in the UK. Such regional constitutional rights that do exist are based in legislation rather than the common law, and such common law constitutional rights that do exist are operative throughout the country and not just at a regional level. An excellent example of a Supreme Court decision reasserting the constitutional right of access to justice is *R (Unison) v Lord Chancellor*,[93] where the Employment Appeal Tribunal Fees Order 2013[94] was held to be contrary to the common law, to statute law and to EU law. As Elliott observes, the principle of legality (a part of the rule of law) was powerfully harnessed by the process of statutory construction

---

[90] Northern Ireland Executive, *Programme for Government for 2008 to 2011* (2008) 11 and 35.
[91] [2017] 17 NIQB 27, [18].
[92] See, eg, *R (Child Poverty Action Group) v Secretary of State for Work and Pensions* [2012] EWHC 2579 (Admin), where the judge ruled that before issuing a child poverty strategy the Secretary of State should have complied with the statutory duty to consult with the Child Poverty Commission (even though it did not exist!); *R (Clientearth) v Secretary of State for Environment, Food and Rural Affairs (No 3)* [2018] EWHC 315 (Admin), on the unlawfulness of the UK Government's Air Quality Plan.
[93] [2017] UKSC 51, [2017] 3 WLR 409.
[94] SI 2013/1893.

in that case in order to secure a fundamental constitutional right.[95] To that extent the case is an excellent illustration of the kind of fundamental common law right described by Trevor Allan in his seminal article in this field:

> It will be suggested that since enactment cannot change the weight of pre-existing rights – and introduce new rights if they are intended to be fundamental – constitutional adjudication, under a written charter, will inevitably, and legitimately, reflect the scope and force of "constitutional" rights at common law.[96]

When such fundamental common law rights are threatened only at a devolved level the resulting litigation may well provide further illustrations of how specific challenges to those rights can be overcome, but this does not turn those rights into common law constitutional rights operating only at the devolved level.

An interesting attempt to build on the special constitutional arrangements devised for Scotland, Wales and Northern Ireland was made in *R (Rotherham Metropolitan Borough Council) v Secretary of State for Business, Innovation and Skills*.[97] A large local council in England argued that, compared with the UK regions to which powers had been devolved, it was being discriminated against in the allocation of EU Structural Funds. While all seven Justices who heard the case in the Supreme Court agreed that this was a field in which judges should tread carefully because the decisions in question reflected, to some extent, political choices, they nevertheless ruled that the matter was indeed justiciable. But they were severely split as to what view should be taken of the allocation of funds in this particular case. Applying the standards of review familiar to challenges of executive decisions on economic matters, they found by four to three that the allocation was lawful.[98] The three dissenting judges thought that the decision by the Secretary of State for Business, Innovation and Skills was unlawful because he had given priority to irrelevant considerations, failed to treat like situations alike and treated unlike cases alike.[99] In Lord Carnwath's words:

> I conclude that the criticisms made by the two regions of the decision-making process ... have not been satisfactorily answered ... It matters not, in my view, whether this is expressed as an issue of unequal treatment or lack of proportionality under European law, or inconsistency and irrationality under domestic law, the anomalies are in my view sufficiently serious to have required explanation which has not been given, and which renders the resulting decisions "manifestly inappropriate" under EU and domestic principles.[100]

---

[95] M Elliott, '*Unison* in the Supreme Court: Tribunal Fees, Constitutional Rights and the Rule of Law', Public Law for Everyone, 26 July 2017.

[96] T Allan, 'Constitutional Rights and Common Law' (1991) 11 *OJLS* 453, 456. See too his *Law, Liberty, and Justice: The Legal Foundations of British Constitutionalism* (Oxford, Clarendon Press, 1994) ch 6.

[97] [2015] UKSC 6, [2015] 3 All ER 1.

[98] The majority comprised Lords Neuberger, Sumption, Clarke and Hodge; the minority comprised Lady Hale and Lords Mance and Carnwath.

[99] [2015] UKSC 6, [162], per Lord Mance (with whom Lady Hale agreed).

[100] Ibid, [187].

The term 'manifestly inappropriate' derives from *R (Sinclair Collis Ltd) v Secretary of State for Health*,[101] where Arden LJ showed that it had been used not only in decisions by the European Court of Justice with regard to implementation of the Common Agricultural Policy but also in decisions by national legislatures and others.[102] In the same case Laws LJ concluded that the test did not differ materially from the principle of proportionality.[103] However, even if the dissenting judgments in the *Rotherham MBC* case had been the majority judgments, the result would not have amounted to the assertion of a new common law constitutional right, let alone a constitutional right vesting in UK regions, but would simply have been a further illustration of how the principles underlying judicial review – which remain common law creations – often operate in ways which protect people against apparently unjust decisions.

In her 2014 lecture entitled 'Constitutionalism on the March?' Lady Hale observed that the Supreme Court had recently taken the opportunity to underline the view that the natural starting point in any dispute concerning fundamental human rights should be domestic law and not the Human Rights Act 1998. But none of the examples she provides in support of this observation are cases with a regional dimension.[104] Richard Clayton has analysed the same cases, amongst others, but he too makes no suggestion that some common law constitutional rights apply only in one or more of the devolved regions of the UK.[105] I have myself argued that the existence of a category of common law constitutional rights is still contestable, at least if we mean by such rights claims that can withstand an express inconsistency with an Act of Parliament,[106] but I have not yet seen any firm evidence that if there is such an embryonic category it comprises regional constitutional rights.

However, let me repeat that there may be two exceptions to what has just been stated. The first arises when legislation is proposed or enacted at the devolved level but is challenged on the ground that it is seeking to do something which is contrary to the rule of law, such as abolish the right to bring judicial review proceedings in relation to certain decisions. This can be deduced, arguably, from the *AXA* case.[107]

The second potential exception relates to the guarantees concerning the permanency of the devolved institutions. In Scotland and Wales the guarantees are declaratory in nature and, as such, may not obviously give rise to constitutional

---

[101] [2011] EWCA Civ 437, [2012] QB 394 (CA).
[102] Ibid, [115]–[137], citing, eg, *R v Minister for Agriculture, Fisheries and Food, ex parte Fedesa* Case C-331/99, [1990] ECR I-4023.
[103] n 101 above, [47].
[104] They were *R (Osborn) v Parole Board* [2013] UKSC 61, [2014] AC 1115; *Kennedy v The Charity Commission* [2014] UKSC 20, [2015] AC 455; and *A v BBC* [2014] UKSC 25, [2015] AC 588.
[105] 'The empire strikes back: common law rights and the Human Rights Act' [2015] *PL* 3.
[106] 'Repeal the Human Rights Act and rely on the common law' in K Ziegler, E Watts and L Hodson (eds), *The UK and European Human Rights: A Strained Relationship?* (Oxford, Hart Publishing, 2015) ch 7.
[107] See above, Part II.A.

rights vested in individuals or institutions. In Northern Ireland the guarantee is also declaratory, but the declaration is conditional and makes it clear what will happen if the condition is fulfilled. Declaratory legislation, it is submitted, is best categorised as 'political legislation' rather than legally enforceable legislation. By this I mean that if it is breached the consequences are usually, at least in the short term, political and not legal. But no government likes to be politically embarrassed by a failure to adhere to legislative aims and sometimes the embarrassment may develop into unconstitutionality if, through judicial review, the failure is highlighted in a court of law. Thus, if at some future point the UK Government were to seek parliamentary approval for a Bill which compromised the permanency of the devolved institutions in Scotland and Wales, or altered the conditionality attached to the status of Northern Ireland as a part of the UK, there could be challenges to the constitutionality of such legislation, the argument being that the Bill would be unlawful because it would be in breach of a common law constitutional right vesting in residents of the devolved regions, a right encompassed by, or supplementary to, the doctrine of the rule of law.

13

The Reach of Common Law Rights

THOMAS FAIRCLOUGH*

I. Introduction

The British constitution faces many challenges. Many of those arise from the 2016 referendum concerning the UK's membership of the European Union. That is not to say, however, that the constitutional lawyer's focus should only be on 'Brexit'. The British constitutional landscape is in constant flux. Successive governments have sought to use their political power to shift the constitutional architecture of the state. Attention on Brexit should not be permitted to obfuscate another constitutional change that has been on the political agenda (in some quarters) for some time: the repeal of the Human Rights Act 1998 (HRA). The purpose of this chapter is to look at the power of the common law in assuring the rights currently located in the HRA. In doing so, I look at the context in which the debate on common law rights takes place; that is, in the face of HRA repeal there has been recurring judicial encouragement of a revisiting of the common law. However, far from being enthused, the response from the academic community has been sceptical; the general argument has been that the common law does not protect people's rights in the same way as the HRA because the rights it recognises are narrower than those under the HRA.

This is an empirical claim predicated on the common law being exclusively what the case law *says* it is; more specifically, the approach taken by those I call the common law sceptics is to report what rights cases *have* recognised and, if a right has not *in fact* been expressly recognised in a reported case, then that right does not exist at common law. This chapter argues that this approach is flawed and so the current debate about how far the common law reaches is, similarly, a flawed debate. The consensus reached in the literature thus far is, I argue, wrong by virtue

* Thanks are owed to Trevor Allan, Mark Elliott, and Kirsty Hughes for reading earlier versions of this chapter. Likewise, thanks are owed to the participants of the 'Human Rights Post Brexit' British Academy Funded Workshop held in Cambridge in March 2017, where an earlier version of this piece was presented. Further still, thanks are owed to my *viva voce* examiners, Alison Young and Lord Reed, for all of their invaluable comments (this chapter being based on my doctoral thesis).

of a problematic working methodology. A focus only on the empirical case law ignores the dynamic, principle-orientated approach that the common law should and does take. On this approach, the principles underlying rights that have already been explicitly recognised can equally account for other rights; there is no reason to suppose, therefore, that these rights would not be recognised. Recognition of a right is, of course, generally a judicial function but the judiciary are doing just that: *recognising the right that already exists.* An absence of prior recognition does not mean that the right does not already exist at common law; existence and recognition are separate matters. In this sense I argue that the superior courts' function vis-à-vis common law rights is diagnostic not constitutive.[1]

In short, this chapter argues that the empirical view is too narrow and pessimistic an account of the common law's reach; a principled approach looking for reasoned consistency in law is both more theoretically coherent and more optimistic about the common law. Whilst I do not purport or attempt to catalogue all of the rights that the common law protects, I will use some examples of previously unrecognised common law rights as rights that one can argue nonetheless exist at common law. This will reveal that the potential of the common law to protect rights is far more wide ranging than has been previously supposed. The chapter concludes by looking at the operation of the common law in comparison with the rights arising under the European Convention on Human Rights (ECHR) as enunciated by the European Court of Human Rights (ECtHR). I argue that in fact there is little to choose between the two approaches to legal human rights and so a repeal of the HRA would not fundamentally narrow the range of human rights available in the domestic legal system.

II. Constitutional Context: HRA Repeal and the Common Law Revisited

The common law was largely forgotten about with the coming into force of the HRA. As Lord Neuberger, extra-judicially, put it: '[T]he attitude of many lawyers and judges in the UK to the Convention was not unlike that of a child to a new toy. As we became fascinated with the new toy, the old toy, the common law, was left in the cupboard.'[2] In this sense a kind of 'common law inertia'[3] set in vis-à-vis utilising the common law to protect human rights. This gained judicial support

---

[1] I borrow this terminology from G Letsas, 'The Scope and Balancing of Rights: Diagnostic or Constitutive?' in E Brems and J Gerards (eds), *Shaping Rights in the ECHR: The Role of the European Court of Human Rights in determining the scope of human rights* (Cambridge, Cambridge University Press, 2014).

[2] Lord Neuberger, 'The Role of Judges in Human Rights Jurisprudence: A Comparison of the Australian and UK Experience' (8 August 2014) [29].

[3] R Masterman and S Wheatle, 'A common law resurgence in rights protection?' [2015] *European Human Rights Law Review* 57, 58.

in *Watkins v Secretary of State for the Home Department*[4] where Lord Rodger suggested that now that the HRA incorporates the ECHR the common law does not need to go to lengths to protect rights; indeed, Lord Roger went as far as to say that where something falls within a ECHR right then 'a claimant can be expected to invoke his remedy under the Human Rights Act rather than seek to fashion a new common law right'.[5] Brice Dickson observes that this saw 'the coffin lid of constitutional rights ... well and truly screwed down'.[6] The reasoning for this apparent casting aside of the common law is based on epistemological ease; the common law does not provide clear, definitional, listed rights. Unlike the HRA[7] the common law, whilst saying it protects rights, often does 'not explain what that means'[8] and was never explained with systematic rigor by the House of Lords or the Supreme Court.[9]

Specifically, as Rogerson Masterman and Se-shauna Wheatle point out there is 'no complete list of rights which the common law ranks as constitutional ... by contrast ... [the HRA and ECHR] provide a codified statement of what those rights are ... There is no comparable definitive statement of common law rights'.[10] However, this 'inertia' has tended to dissipate in the face of threats to the HRA; judicial support for a revisiting of common law rights has been endorsed at the highest level.[11] Indeed, Lord Mance has made clear that:

> There has too often been a tendency to see the law in areas touched on by the Convention *solely in terms* of the Convention rights ... the Convention rights represent a *threshold protection* ... In some areas, *the common law may go further than the Convention*, and in some contexts it may also be inspired by the Convention rights and jurisprudence ... But the natural starting point in any dispute is to start with domestic law.[12]

Further, Lord Toulson has argued that the ability of the common law to protect rights 'has not ceased on the enactment of the Human Rights Act 1998'[13] and Lord Reed has noted that the common law's 'application should normally meet the requirements of the Convention, given the extent to which the Convention and our domestic law in this area walk in step, and bearing in mind the capacity of the

---

[4] [2006] UKHL 17, [2006] 2 AC 395.

[5] Ibid, [64] (Lord Rodger).

[6] B Dickson, *Human Rights and the United Kingdom Supreme Court* (Oxford, Oxford University Press, 2013) 28. It is clear that a common law approach to rights' protection was largely abandoned in favour of using the HRA. I do not here attempt to quantify this though it is something that would perhaps be useful from a socio-legal point of view in the future.

[7] I leave aside here the issue of the scope of ECHR rights. These are far from certain.

[8] *R v Lord Chancellor Ex p Witham* [1998] QB 575, 585 (Laws J).

[9] Dickson (n 6) 26.

[10] Masterman and Wheatle (n 3) 59.

[11] See generally *Kennedy v The Charity Commission* [2014] UKSC 20, [2014] 2 WLR 808; *Osborn v Parole Board* [2013] UKSC 61, [2014] AC 1115; and *A v BBC* [2014] UKSC 25, [2014] 2 WLR 1243. For a brief comment on the history of this renewed focus see T Fairclough, 'Black Spiders and Public Lawyers: Constitutionalism Revisited?' (2016) 21 *Judicial Review* 44.

[12] Emphasis added. *Kennedy* (n 11) [46] (Lord Mance).

[13] Ibid, [177] (Lord Toulson).

common law to develop'.[14] These cases 'emphasise the common law as guarantor of human rights'.[15]

This has led to a view, certainly amongst some members of the judiciary, that the common law has the ability to protect human rights to an extent roughly equal to that of the HRA. If this is so, then, we might ask, to what extent is a codified Bill of Rights necessary for the efficacy of rights' protection? It is that question which this chapter seeks to answer, at least in part. There are various vectors against which one can measure the potential of common law rights against their statutory counterparts found in the HRA. Mark Elliott has noted that these include *which* rights are protected; the *rigor* of their protection; and their *constitutional resilience* in the face of legislative hostility.[16] I do not take issue with these vectors here but only wish to explore the first of their number; namely, to what extent are the rights incorporated by the HRA replicated in the common law? This says nothing of the rigor of their protection nor about their ability to weather a hostile political and legislative environment. Whilst both of these are clearly important space precludes their examination here.[17]

A. The Academic Debate

As might be expected, the judiciary's renewed focus on common law rights has prompted a large amount of academic commentary.[18] Much of this commentary has been surprisingly sceptical of the common law's ability to adequately match the reach of the HRA.

Richard Clayton QC says 'a number of recent decisions ... suggest that common law rights are ... centre stage' and as such 'some will, no doubt, argue that using domestic law rights can achieve much the same as the HRA'.[19] As such, Clayton

---

[14] *A v BBC* (n 11) [57] (Lord Reed).

[15] *The Commissioner of Police of the Metropolis v DSD and NBV* [2015] EWCA Civ 646, [27] (Laws LJ).

[16] M Elliott, 'Beyond the European Convention: Human Rights and the Common Law' (2015) 68 *Current Legal Problems* 85.

[17] This leaves the evaluation of the overall power of common law rights as compared to the HRA incomplete. This chapter does not purport to be a complete picture. It evaluates one aspect of the debate. Discussions about *Wednesbury* and proportionality, s 3 HRA and the principle of legality, and the degree of constitutional entrenchment of the common law and HRA would each easily occupy chapters of their own.

[18] Including Lady Hale, 'UK Constitutionalism on the March' (2014) 19 *Judicial Review* 201; Masterman and Wheatle (n 3); R Clayton, 'The empire strikes back: common law rights and the Human Rights Act' [2015] *PL* 3; S Stephenson, 'The Supreme Court's renewed interest in autochthonous constitutionalism' [2015] *PL* 393; A Straw, 'Future Proofing: Running Human Rights Arguments under the Common Law' [2015] *Judicial Review* 193; C Gearty, 'On Fantasy Island: British Politics, English Judges, and the European Convention on Human Rights' [2015] *EHRLR* 1; Elliott (n 16); Fairclough (n 11); E Bjorge, 'Common Law Rights: Balancing Domestic and International Exigencies' (2016) 75 *CLJ* 220; and S Boyron, 'The Judiciary's Self-Determination, the Common Law, and Constitutional Change' (2016) 22 *European Public Law* 149.

[19] Clayton (n 18) 3.

says it is 'opportune to reflect on the scope for utilising fundamental common law rights'.[20] However, almost immediately Clayton argues, 'problems remain about how we identify common law rights and how common law rights will impact in practice, as a result of their *traditional limited status* in English law',[21] before going on to *list* the rights he says the common law protects.[22]

Likewise, Conor Gearty describes common law rights as a 'fantasy'.[23] Gearty has suggested that in the past the common law has shown a 'partisanship ... for property and contract rights over gender and racial equality; an hostility to trade unions and the Labour party so severe that neither could have survived without legislation directly overturning judicial malevolence; the common law's service as a base for the serial abuses of liberty'.[24] In a way similar to Clayton's piece described above, Gearty seems to rely on what the common law explicitly and narrowly *has done* as constitutive of what the common law *is*.

Further, whilst Lady Hale has, extra-judicially, stated 'the common law ... is a rich source of fundamental rights and values'[25] her Ladyship went on to state that there are difficulties with the identification of common law rights by suggesting 'no two lists ... would be the same'.[26] Indeed, Lady Hale went on to agree explicitly with Clayton and observed 'identification of less well-established common law rights is more difficult'.[27] In addition, judicially, Lady Hale has denied the common law is concerned with the right to vote; speaking frankly, her Ladyship stated: 'It would be wonderful if the common law *had* recognised a right of universal suffrage. But ... *it has never done so*'[28] – and so, it seems, for Lady Hale it cannot or, at least, does not recognise such a right now.

Finally, Mark Elliott has argued 'it is hard to dispute the proposition that such rights as could be inferred from the case law appeared to occupy a terrain substantially narrower than that occupied by the Convention rights'.[29] All of these pieces share a common characteristic: they empirically catalogue the rights explicitly protected by the common law and see that as constitutive of what the common

---

[20] Ibid.

[21] Ibid, 4 (emphasis added).

[22] Clayton lists the rights from Woolf et al (eds), *De Smith's Judicial Review*, 7th edn (London, Sweet and Maxwell, 2015).

[23] C Gearty, 'On Fantasy Island: British politics, English judges and the European Convention on Human Rights' UK Const L Blog (13 November 2014). The suggestion might be that Conor Gearty's focus is not on the methodological side of common law rights but is instead expressing a *distrust* of common law judges and their will to uphold rights. Indeed, he focuses in large part on the judges themselves and not their judgments. Though this is a socio-legal question I would simply suggest that it would be the same judges who have acted under the HRA. The HRA allows enough latitude to the judiciary that, if they really did want to avoid protecting rights, they would do so.

[24] Ibid.

[25] Hale (n 18) 201.

[26] Ibid, 201.

[27] Ibid, 205.

[28] Emphasis added. *Moohan and Another v The Lord Advocate* [2014] UKSC 67, [2015] AC 901, [56] (Lady Hale).

[29] Elliott (n 16) 4.

law protects; indeed, Elliott explicitly claims, 'the normative reach of common law rights is an ultimately *empirical* question'.[30] Since this is apparently lower than what the HRA explicitly protects it is, according to these writers, the case that the common law does not reach as far as the HRA. If this approach is correct[31] then, it would seem, it is hard to disagree with these writers and dispute the proposition that the common law does not occupy the same terrain as the HRA vis-à-vis *which* rights are protected. It will be useful here to look at the rights found under the HRA and the rights that have been explicitly recognised in domestic common law judgments.

B. Rights under the HRA

The HRA gives effect in domestic law to Articles 2–12 and 14 of the ECHR, Articles 1–3 of the First Protocol, and Article 1 of the Thirteenth protocol.[32] This includes various civil and political rights, which, for reasons of space, are not listed here.[33]

Whilst these rights are abstract in wording the ECtHR has generally taken an expansive view of how they ought to be given effect. Whilst a descriptive account of the reach of each right is impossible within the parameters of the present discussion a general overview of the principles governing the area covered by the ECHR rights (and therefore the reach of the HRA) will be useful. The general approach of the ECtHR has been to treat the ECHR as a living instrument, with the meaning and reach of the rights not fixed at the time the ECHR was made but instead understood in line with the contemporary moral understanding(s) of their points or purpose.[34]

Originally the ECtHR looked at consensus amongst contracting Member States to see what each right meant in practice. Over time, a loosening of the consensus approach occurred[35] and eventually gave way to one that looked at 'elements of international law other than the Convention, the interpretation of such elements by competent organs, and the practice of European States reflecting their *common values*'.[36] An example of how this works can be found in *Rantsev v Cyprus and Russia*,[37] which revolved around whether or not human trafficking

---

[30] Ibid, 11 (emphasis added).

[31] As stated above, the argument developed in this chapter is that this approach is not correct.

[32] HRA, s 1(1)(a)–(c).

[33] The full wording of each of these rights can be found in Sch 1 HRA.

[34] For example, the ECtHR changed its position on adoption of children by homosexual couples; it used to say that this did not fall within Arts 8 or 14 ECHR but this understanding of the rights was re-evaluated and changed in *EB v France* (2008) 47 EHRR 21, [70]–[73] and [91]–[93]. This approach has been taken in other jurisdictions such as Canada, see *Edwards v Canada (A-G)* [1930] AC 124 (PC).

[35] See G Letsas, 'The ECHR as a Living Instrument: its Meaning and its Legitimacy' in A Follesdal et al (eds), *Constituting Europe: The European Court of Human Rights in a National, European and Global Context* (Cambridge, Cambridge University Press, 2013) 115–7.

[36] *Demir and Baykara v Turkey* [2008] ECHR 1345, [85] (emphasis added).

[37] App No 25965/04.

falls within the prohibition on slavery for the purposes of Article 4 ECHR. The ECtHR noted that 'sight should not be lost of the Convention's special features of the fact that it is a living instrument which must be interpreted in the light of present-day conditions ... There can be no doubt that [trafficking] threatens human dignity and fundamental freedoms ... and cannot be considered with ... the values expounded in the Convention'.[38] In *Hirst v United Kingdom* the ECtHR all but abandoned consensus as the determinative factor, stating that 'even if no common European approach to the problem can be discerned, this cannot in itself be determinative of the issue'.[39] To understand how interpretation of ECHR rights occurs the following passage from George Letsas, after considering the many cases (some of which are mentioned above), is useful. He says the:

> Court treats the ECHR as a living instrument by looking for *common values* and *emerging* consensus in international law. In doing so, it often raises the human rights standard *above* what most contracting states currently offer. It reasons mainly by focusing on the substance of the case.[40]

The supranational court treats the rights found in the ECHR as expansive; the expanded view of these rights is linked to the best understanding of the values underpinning the rights. Consensus can be evidence of these values but not constitutive thereof. The task of delimiting the scope of rights does not centre around what the framers of the ECHR would have thought the extent of the rights would be; nor do we look at what Member States signing the ECHR would have thought the scope of the rights would have been and say that this is constitutive of the scope of those rights; nor again does the task focus on how the rights would have been understood by the general populations at the time the ECHR was agreed. Instead, the ECtHR takes a value first approach to rights interpretation, seeking to ensure that the rights are understood by the values that underlie them.

C. Empirically Recognised Common Law Rights

What follows is not designed to be an exhaustive list of empirically recognised common law rights but is instead designed to give a flavor of their breadth; even on an empirical view it is obvious that the common law has recognised many of the rights found in the HRA. Perhaps the most classic example of a common law right is access to the courts. In *Raymond v Honey*,[41] when examining whether a broad statutory provision gave the Secretary of State for the Home Department the ability to refuse a prisoner access to the courts, Lord Wilberforce stated that there was nothing in the Act that conferred powers to stop 'unimpeded access to the courts'. His Lordship decided the Home Secretary could not do this since

---

[38] Ibid, [282].
[39] App No 74025/01.
[40] Letsas (n 35) 122.
[41] [1983] 1 AC 1 (HL).

access to the court is 'so basic a right'.[42] Likewise in *A v B (Investigatory Powers Tribunal: Jurisdiction)*[43] Collins J noted: 'The courts of this country have always recognised that the right of a citizen to access a court is a right of the highest constitutional importance'.[44] A related right is a right to a fair hearing; as Lord Steyn puts it in *R (McCann) v Manchester Crown Court*,[45] 'under domestic English law [citizens] undoubtedly have a constitutional right to a fair hearing'.[46] Likewise, in *Osborn v The Parole Board*[47] not only did Lord Reed urge a refocusing on the common law but he specifically noted that the requirements of Article 5(4) ECHR go no further than that of the common law (or, to put it another way, if a public body satisfies its common law duty to give a fair hearing it will also satisfy its Article 5(4) obligation).[48]

Further, the right to life was recognised at common law at least 15 years before the HRA came into force. In *R v Secretary of State for the Home Department, ex parte Bugdaycay*[49] Lord Bridge held that: 'The most fundamental of all human rights is the individual's right to life and when an administrative decision under challenge is said to be one which may put the applicant's life at risk, the basis of the decision must surely call for the most anxious scrutiny'.[50] Related to the right to life is the right to be free from torture: Lord Bingham makes clear that 'from its very earliest days the common law of England set its face firmly against the use of torture'[51] due to it being 'totally repugnant to the fundamental principles of English law'[52] and 'repugnant to reason, justice, and humanity'.[53] Hence the common law will not admit evidence procured by torture; not, as might be thought, just because of a rule of evidence but also because of 'constitutional principle'.[54]

The right to liberty has also been expressly recognised by the common law since at least the nineteenth century.[55] More recently, Roskill LJ held that when

---

[42] Ibid, 12–13 (Lord Wilberforce).

[43] [2008] EWHC 1512 (Admin), [2008] 4 All ER 511.

[44] Ibid, [12] (Collins J).

[45] [2002] UKHL 39, [2003] 1 AC 787.

[46] Ibid, [29] (Lord Steyn).

[47] *Osborn* (n 11).

[48] Ibid, [112]–[113] (Lord Reed). The broader discussion of the Art 5 case law takes place at [101]–[113].

[49] [1987] AC 514 (HL).

[50] Ibid, 531 (Lord Bridge). I leave aside the question of what 'anxious scrutiny' is for the purposes of this chapter as that falls within the purview of the rigor of the protection of rights.

[51] *A and others v Secretary of State for the Home Department (No 2)* [2005] UKHL 71, [2006] 2 AC 221, [11] (Lord Bingham). Though illegal at common law torture did take place in England in the 16th and early 17th centuries; however, this did not take place with the authority of the common law but rather by virtue of the Royal Prerogative in cases (generally) dealing with offences against the state. This pre-dates the English civil war. Now, of course, the prerogative, if incompatible with the common law, must give way.

[52] D Jardine, *A Reading on the Use of Torture in the Criminal Law of England* (London, Baldwin and Cradock, 1837) 6.

[53] Ibid, 12.

[54] *A and others* (n 51) [13] (Lord Bingham).

[55] In *Bowditch v Balchin* (1850) 5 Exch 378, 381, it was held that: 'In a case in which the liberty of the subject is concerned, we cannot go beyond the natural construction of the statute.'

a court 'has to consider a matter involving the liberty of the individual, it must look at the matter carefully and strictly, and it must ensure that the curtailment of liberty sought is entirely justified by the statute relied upon by those who seek that curtailment.'[56] Most succinctly, in *R (Juncal) v Secretary of State for the Home Department*[57] Wyn Williams J made clear that 'the citizens of this country do enjoy a fundamental or constitutional right not to be detained arbitrarily at common law.'[58]

Further, freedom of expression has been recognised at common law. In *Attorney General v Observer Ltd*[59] Lord Goff boldly stated that he wished:

> to observe that I can see no inconsistency between English law on this subject and article 10 of the European Convention on Human Rights. This is scarcely surprising, since we may pride ourselves on the fact that freedom of speech has existed in this country perhaps as long as, if not longer than, it has existed in any other country in the world.[60]

Likewise, in *R v Secretary of State for the Home Department, ex parte Simms*[61] Lord Steyn held that: 'The starting point is the right of freedom of expression. In a democracy it is the primary right.'[62]

It seems at least highly arguable that the common law has not recognised[63] the same breadth and/or depth of rights as the HRA does. Certainly, as Lady Hale pointed out, it has not regularly recognised a right to universal enfranchisement[64] nor can it be said that the case law has enunciated a right to family and private life in the common law.[65] If all that matters is what the case law *says* then one can certainly see that the common law does not go as far as the HRA vis-à-vis the reach of rights; as such, if the HRA were repealed the common law would not, on this approach, replicate the rights lost from the statute book.

III. A Principled Approach to Rights' Identification

The contention of this chapter is that the conclusion in the preceding paragraph rests on an approach to legal identification that is flawed. My argument is that the

---

[56] *R v Thames Metropolitan Stipendiary Magistrate, ex p Brindle* [1975] 1 WLR 1400 (CA), 1410 (Lord Roskill).
[57] [2007] EWHC 3024 (Admin).
[58] Ibid, [47] (Wyn Williams J).
[59] [1990] 1 AC 109 (HL).
[60] Ibid, 283 (Lord Goff).
[61] [2000] 2 AC 115 (HL).
[62] Ibid, 125 (Lord Steyn).
[63] I use the word recognised in its strictly empirical sense: ie what the cases *actually say* the common law protects.
[64] *Moohan* (n 28) [56] (Lady Hale). Cf *Watkins* (n 4) [61] (Lord Roger): 'Although embodied in a statute, in a system of universal suffrage today the right to vote would fall within everyone's notion of a "constitutional right". And, doubtless, the principle of legality would apply in construing any statutory provision which was said to have abrogated that right.'
[65] Thus, there has not been a direct analogue to Art 8 recognised under common law jurisprudence.

empirical view – on which common law rights are dependent upon judicial enunciation for their realisation, such that anything that cannot be seen in the case law is not a common law right – is flawed as it fails to take account of the role that legal principle plays in legal identification.

As TRS Allan says, 'the common law constitution is chiefly characterized by its dependence on legal principle'.[66] The argument in this section will be that the common law sceptics have failed to take into account the role that the rule of law plays in shaping the common law. Whilst judicial recognition of the common law is inherently limited by what is litigated and to what level, I argue that that is not the same as saying that *decided* cases are exhaustively *constitutive* of the extent of the common law. Nor is it the same as saying that the decided cases are necessarily correct or the end of any given question vis-à-vis common law rights. A better view is that the principles underlying the common law, specifically the rule of law, exist due to their normative status, not because a case says they do.[67] These principles shape common law discourse and condition the reach of rights; whilst we may have finite *iterations* of rights in the case law that does not mean the reach of the common law is in any way *limited* to such decisions.

A. The Rule of Law as the Controlling Factor

The starting point in this argument against the common law sceptics is that they sideline the role the rule of law plays in public law debate and the normative condition of the common law.[68] At the most general level Lord Hope tells us: 'The rule of law enforced by the courts is the ultimate controlling factor on which our constitution is based.'[69] This tell us that the powers of the state must be conditioned by the rule of law; what rights we have at common law are, in part, determined by the rule of law (as opposed to merely and wholly dependent on judicial recognition). As Allan puts it:

> [W]hen we point to the rule of law as a basic principle of British government, we identify our constitutional foundations with the value of law itself ... the rule of law is not merely an ideal or aspiration *external* to the law ... it is a *value* internal to law itself, informing and guiding our efforts to ascertain ... legal rights.[70]

---

[66] TRS Allan, 'The Moral Unity of Public Law' (2017) 67 *University of Toronto Law Journal* 1, 2.

[67] See R Dworkin, 'The Model of Rules' (1967) 33 *University of Chicago Law Review* 40 on this point.

[68] A broader version of this claim is made in T Fairclough, '*Evans v Attorney General*: The Underlying Normativity of Constitutional Disagreement' in S Juss and M Sunkin (eds), *Landmark Cases in Public Law* (Oxford, Hart Publishing, 2017).

[69] *Jackson v Her Majesty's Attorney-General* [2005] UKHL 56, [2006] 1 AC 262, [107] (Lord Hope). A thorough theoretical examination of this claim is in S Lakin, 'Debunking the Idea of Parliamentary Sovereignty: The Controlling Factor of Legality in the British Constitution' (2008) 28 *OJLS* 709.

[70] Emphasis original. TRS Allan, *The Sovereignty of Law: Freedom, Constitution, and Common Law* (Oxford, Oxford University Press, 2013) 88.

The rule of law is something at the core of law; any discussion of legal powers, rights, and responsibilities must take account of the rule of law. It is a discussion that must be more than a mere reporting exercise of what previous cases have said. To ignore or sideline this inherent and important point is to engage in a mistaken exercise and conclusions gained from that exercise are themselves built on shaky foundations.

This should not come as a surprise. Many cases relating to common law rights depend on the rule of law for their justification. In *Simms* Lord Steyn says that not only is freedom of speech an important constitutional right but that it is so because 'without it an effective rule of law is not possible'.[71] Likewise in *A v B* Collins J makes clear that removing the right to a fair hearing is '*prima facie* contrary to the rule of law'.[72] Further, Laws J in *Witham* states that common law rights are 'logically prior' to the democratic political process[73] and therefore somehow inherent in law. Finally, Lord Reed in a recent judgment on access to justice[74] states that 'access to justice is not an idea recently imported from the continent of Europe, but has long been embedded in our constitutional law. The case has … been argued … on the basis of the common law right of access to justice'.[75] Indeed, not only is the right 'embedded' in the domestic constitution but it seems to be embedded because the 'right of access to the courts is *inherent* in the rule of law'.[76]

The rule of law conditions common law rights and the courts often follow this analysis. Therefore, difficulty sets in when academics try to present the extent of the common law as a solely empirical question determined entirely by what previous case law says in a narrow sense.[77] It is, in fact, in part a normative question about the best conception of the rule of law, which underpins legal practice. Elliott is therefore wrong when he says that a distinction 'needs to be drawn between values associated with the common law and rights protected by it'[78] and that a way to reconcile the opposing views of TRS Allan and Conor Gearty is to see that the former is concerned mainly with theoretical values whereas the latter focuses on 'tangible protection'. Elliott separates value and doctrine; his point seems to be that to know what the common law *actually* protects we just look at the case law in a narrow sense but, if we want to know what the common law *could* protect then we look at the values underlying the common law and use them to justify *changing* the law. In this regard, Elliott acknowledges the

---

[71] *Simms* (n 61) 125 (Lord Steyn).

[72] *A v B* (n 43) [12] (Collins J).

[73] *Witham* (n 8) 581 (Laws J).

[74] *R (UNISON) v Lord Chancellor* [2017] UKSC 51, [2017] 3 WLR 409. Note that Lords Neuberger, Mance, Kerr, Wilson, Hughes and Lady Hale all agreed with Lord Reed.

[75] Ibid, [64] (Lord Reed).

[76] Ibid, [66] (Lord Reed) (emphasis added).

[77] That is, says about the right in question in the particular case not what it says about the rule of law more generally.

[78] Elliott (n 16) 5.

potential for common law *legal change* in line with values when he says there is
'no *a priori* reason why the body of such rights should not develop in a way that
over time yields a degree – perhaps a very high degree – of convergence with
the Convention'.[79] Elliott therefore suggests that principles/values are relevant to
changing or *developing* the law; what the law *actually is* at any given time depends
solely on decided case law understood in a strict, narrow sense. For Elliott, to
answer the question 'is there a common law right to vote?' we just look at the
case law and see if the courts *have in fact* recognised such a right. This does not
preclude the Supreme Court answering the question 'should there be a right to
vote at common law?' such that they may, on Elliott's account, *change* the law to
incorporate such a right but, for Elliott (and presumably the other common law
sceptics), the Supreme Court would be doing just that: using values they say are
associated with the common law (though external to it) to *change* the law. There
is not, on their account, currently a common law right to enfranchisement and
to say that there is would, on their approach, be wrong.

This is, again, too narrow a view of the common law and how we know what
it is.[80] A report of 'doctrine' cannot sideline principle; doctrine is nothing but the
specific crystallisation of principle that comes from a (normative) understanding of that principle.[81] Put another way, the values underpinning doctrine do
just that: they underpin doctrine. Trying to separate value and doctrine proves
difficult since the two are intertwined and interdependent; as I argue elsewhere
we understand law by reference to a dialogue between its features and values.[82]
The nexus between value and practice is something that the common law sceptics
sideline and treat, at best, as relevant to common law *change* but not identification
of what the common law *is*. Thus, the picture of the common law they present is
incomplete because it ignores the fact that *principles* are currently part of the law
and constrain judicial discretion; any attempt to know what the law is should take
account of these principles. A judge, when adjudicating on a seemingly novel
point, does not just look at the empirical case law to see what the law is and then
reaches for values 'associated' with the common law to change the law if she so
desires. Instead, a judge facing a situation in which there is no clear established
'rule' is obligated to take into account relevant principles when making her decision; to fail to account for principle in making a decision leads to criticism that

---

[79] Ibid, 11.

[80] For a non-common law rights example see *In re Spectrum Plus Ltd (in liquidation)* [2005] UKHL
41, [2005] 2 AC 680 where the House of Lords was asked, if they were minded to overturn a previous
decision, whether they would do so with prospective effect only. That is, their Lordships were asked to
'change' the law from the date of their determination but not apply the 'new' law to contracts entered
into before said decision (including the case before their Lordships). The House of Lords declined to
do so on the basis that the House of Lords would, if it overturned the previous case, be recognising the
law as it was, and dismissing what 'the law ... was generally thought to be ... [the newly recognised law]
operates retrospectively as well as prospectively' [6]–[7] (Lord Nicholls).

[81] See SR Perry, 'Judicial Obligation, Precedent, and the Common Law' (1987) 7 *OJLS* 215; and Allan
(n 70).

[82] See also Fairclough (n 68) 302.

the judge was *legally wrong* in the outcome they reached.[83] More specifically, for our purposes, a judge, tasked with deciding whether there is a common law right to, say, enfranchisement, would be wrong if she failed to take account of the rule of law when making her decision since it and the values it contains control legal decision making.[84] It would be an abdication of judicial responsibility to merely *report* past cases as exhaustive of the law. Allan puts this point best in the British constitutional setting when he says 'the judicial enforcement of rights may make great intellectual demands on judges, who are required to exercise *judgement* in what may often be finely balanced disputes, but it does not involve *discretion*, in the sense in which other state officials may enjoy a legitimate freedom of choice between competing alternatives'.[85] It would not be enough for a judge to say, as Lady Hale did in *Moohan*, that there is no common law right to voter enfranchisement because the common law has not (thus far) recognised such a right; instead, adjudication must account for values underlying the law. There is little discretion in making such decisions; judicial adjudication is bound by the relevant legal principles governing a case. In this way, Lord Hodge's approach (though not his conclusions) in *Moohan* better accords with the best framework:

> I have no difficulty in *recognising* the right to vote as a basic or constitutional right .... It is also not in doubt that the judiciary have the constitutional function of adapting and developing the common law through the reasoned application of established common law *principles* in order to keep it abreast of current social conditions.[86]

Likewise, the Supreme Court's recent judgment on tribunal fees[87] gives implicit support to this view. Here, Lord Reed states that 'many examples can be found of judicial *recognition* of the constitutional right of unimpeded access to the courts'.[88] Again, it seems that Lord Reed sees the judicial role, even in the Supreme Court, as recognition of a right in line with constitutional principle (as stated above he sees the right as linked to the rule of law) and he uses previous cases as 'examples' of that recognition not as constitutive of the right itself.

Pausing here, it is worth emphasising why this distinction is important. It may be that common law sceptics agree with my argument but, in response, could say that it does not matter.[89] We currently have the HRA. The common law's rights will only come into play on repeal of the HRA; even then, they would only matter if the proposed British Bill of Rights is significantly weaker than the HRA. Therefore, they might say, there is little practical utility in examining approaches for the identification of common law rights. This argument is, however, difficult

---

[83] R Dworkin, *Taking Rights Seriously* (Harvard, Harvard University Press, 1977) 35. I leave aside here the slightly more complex issue of when can principle rescind a well-established rule.

[84] See *Jackson* (n 69) [107] (Lord Hope) and Lakin (n 69).

[85] Allan (n 70) 279.

[86] *Moohan* (n 28) [33] (Lord Hodge) (emphasis added).

[87] *UNISON* (n 74).

[88] Ibid, [76] (Lord Reed) (emphasis added).

[89] I am grateful to Alison Young for pointing out this argument.

to sustain for four reasons. First, the judiciary has directed advocates to argue common law rights *now* not in the event of HRA repeal.[90] Second, there is value in knowing what the common law is. Our understanding of domestic, common law rights provides insight into the wider workings of the common law constitution, which has both intrinsic and instrumental value. Third, the argument I am presenting, that when assessing the reach of the common law we must look to the rule of law not just narrow case law, is relevant to shifts in understanding outside of rights cases or even administrative law. The role of the rule of law can be applied equally to private law doctrine and problems.[91] Finally, the difference between myself and the sceptics is that I am assessing what the common law *currently protects* by reference to the rule of law; as argued above, the sceptics seem, at best, to see the rule of law and its associated values as being relevant only to *changing* the law. Therefore, my argument is that the instant the HRA is repealed (if it is) the common law is *already there* to protect one's rights;[92] it does not require a change in the law.[93]

A response to this final point may be that the common law has not in the past protected rights; some would say that the common law finds its basis in 'a heavily class-bound, patriarchal society in which most people had no right to vote, religious difference was not tolerated, and radical political debate was routinely limited by persecution and imprisonment'.[94] Whilst it is true that some common law judges have in the past tolerated such injustices, it is worth pointing out that the approach to the common law that I am advocating requires one to see the common law in light of morality; it is implicit here that morality has an objective meaning. That is, there is a right answer to moral questions. For this reason, I broadly agree with Allan when he says that:

> The common law inevitably reflects the society and polity within which it is imbedded; but its susceptibility to enlightened change, in conjunction with altered perceptions of justice in society at large, is a product of its intrinsic dependence on the moral judgment and vision of all who participate in legal analysis.[95]

That is, whilst the common law may have been used to justify unjustifiable results in the past its reflective nature, dependent on our own views of morality, means that it will not give the same unjustifiable results now. As our understanding of

---

[90] *Osborn* (n 11).

[91] See LM Austin and D Klimchuk (eds) *Private Law and the Rule of Law* (Oxford, Oxford University Press, 2014).

[92] It is also there to protect one's rights whilst the HRA is in force.

[93] This, of course, ignores the socio-legal point about the need for litigation to have rights vindicated and recognised by the senior courts.

[94] G Kennet, 'Individual Rights, the High Court, and the Constitution' (1994) 19 *Melbourne University Law Review* 581, 611.

[95] TRS Allan, *Constitutional Justice: A Liberal Theory of the Rule of Law* (Oxford, Oxford University Press, 2001) 249.

morality shifts so too does our understanding of the rule of law; since the rule of law is linked to which rights we have at common law our (newer) understanding or recognition of morality change what rights we identify at common law.[96]

B. Identifying Rights with the Rule of Law: Non-Arbitrariness and Equality

Even after arguing that the rule of law is relevant to the identification of common law rights and that this is of significant value a question arises: what values does the rule of law encapsulate and how do these values map onto rights hitherto unrecognised as part of the common law? At its core, the rule of law 'promises protection ... against the arbitrary exercise of power'.[97] The rule of law reflects consistency in principle; it constrains decision making when one sees that it is concerned with equality before the law.[98] This means that the law 'must itself be non-arbitrary, in the sense that it is justified in terms of a *public or common good*- one that we can fairly suppose favours a similar freedom for all'.[99] The rule of law, in this sense, is against arbitrary distinctions between persons or groups; instead, objective legitimate justification for action is needed.[100] This goes further than saying that law is concerned only with the uniform application of rules regardless of their content; the rule of law provides for equality in principle, not just mere consistency in application.

There is plenty of judicial recognition of this principle, which gives support to the interpretation I endorse: Lord Donaldson MR held that 'it is a cardinal principle ... that all persons in a similar position should be treated similarly'[101] and Lord Bingham held that 'decision makers ... should act in a broadly consistent manner'.[102] Indeed, the insistence of equal treatment before the law seems to have affected one of the most fundamental changes to administrative law of the last century: the erosion between jurisdictional and non-jurisdictional errors of law.[103] Whilst these cases may be said to deal with formal equality a more

---

[96] This could be read as suggesting that the rule of law and morality are on a linear progression of enlightenment. I make no claim as to the same; such a suggestion is a question of legal and political sociology. There is the risk that judges will make the *wrong* decisions and fail to adequately recognise what the rule of law mandates (as described below). Such a risk occurs because the rule of law and its objective moral demands fall to be interpreted by humans, who can make errors in the decision-making process. This is not an argument against the common law any more than it is against statutes that require interpretation; it is a recognition of the fallibility of lawyers.

[97] GJ Postema, 'Fidelity in Law's Commonwealth' in Austin and Klimchuk (n 91) 17.

[98] R Dworkin, *Law's Empire* (Cambridge, Mass, Harvard University Press, 1987) 227.

[99] Allan (n 70) 93.

[100] See generally, R Dworkin, 'Is there a right to pornography?' (1981) 1(2) *OJLS* 177.

[101] *R v Hertfordshire CC, ex parte Cheung, The Times*, April 4, 1986 (Lord Donaldson MR).

[102] *R (O'Brien) v Independent Assessor* [2007] UKHL 10, [2007] 2 AC 312.

[103] See *R v Hull University Visitor, ex parte Page* [1992] UKHL 12, [1993] AC 682.

substantive principle has also played a part in administrative law decisions. As far back as the nineteenth century Lord Russell held that byelaws could not provide for differing treatment between differing classes.[104] Likewise Lord Denning held that the courts 'will not allow a power to be exercised arbitrarily or capriciously or with unfair discrimination, neither in the making of rules or in the enforcement of them'.[105] The broadest statement of principle comes from Lady Hale, who tells us that arbitrary treatment '[i]s the reverse of the rational behaviour we expect from government and the state. Power must not be exercised arbitrarily. If distinctions are to be drawn, particularly upon a group basis, it is an important discipline to look for a rational basis for those distinctions.'[106] In short, the rule of law looks for differences to justify different treatment but not all differences are acceptable to legitimate different treatment for the rule of law. That is, not all reasons are good enough to satisfy the rule of law. As Lady Hale says, distinctions must be *rational*.[107]

Once we appreciate the foregoing, we can see a new dimension to how identification of common law rights can proceed. Rather than focusing on what has been decided in the past the debate should turn to look at the values the rule of law encapsulates and what rights they justify. If the rule of law, which underlies such common law rights as freedom of speech, a fair hearing, and freedom from retrospective punishment, can underlie a previously unrecognised right there is no reason to suggest that the courts should not recognise such a right when asked to by counsel in appropriate litigation. It is through the reasoned application of principle and justification for differing treatment between cases that we establish common law rights.

That is not to say that the courts *will* do so, which involves legal sociological issues involving predicting judgments. Instead, the focus here is on what the law *actually is*, which I suggest is not entirely dependent on judicial enunciation. A fact and knowledge of the fact are independent of one another; knowledge of a fact does not create the fact itself. A judge saying a right has not been violated does not mean that the right *has not* been violated. It merely means that that judge *thinks* it has not been. This is, in essence, the distinction that George Letsas draws between constitutive and diagnostic questions. Courts usually act by using diagnostic tests to determine whether rights *have in fact* been violated; their saying they have (or have not) does not mean that they have (or have not) been violated.[108]

---

[104] *Kruse v Johnson* [1889] 2 QB 291 (CA).

[105] *Edwards v SOGAT* [1971] Ch 354.

[106] *Ghaidan v Godin Mendoza* [2004] UKHL 30, [2004] 2 AC 557, [132] (Lady Hale).

[107] Ibid. Baroness Hale does not mean *Wednesbury* reasonableness here.

[108] Letsas (n 1). See further R Dworkin, *A Matter of Principle* (Cambridge, Mass, Harvard University Press, 1985) 120 where he says legal problems have 'a right answer. It may be uncertain and controversial what that right answer is, of course, just as it is uncertain and controversial whether Richard III murdered the princes. It would not follow from that uncertainty that there is no right answer to the legal question, any more than it seems to follow from the uncertainty about Richard that there is no right answer to the question whether he murdered the princes'.

C. Non-Arbitrariness and Common Law Rights

This leads us to a fresh but key question: what counts as a difference capable of justifying differential treatment as between persons and what does this mean for rights at common law?[109] The answer to this question will help us to identify rights at common law. As stated throughout this section, not all differentiation is *justified* differentiation for the purposes of the rule of law. As such, we need to know what does count as justified differentiation. To understand this and therefore what rights exist at common law we have to recall what was pointed out in the previous section: the rule of law, which is the controlling factor in the constitution, is concerned with non arbitrariness, which in turn displays or reflects the value of equality of concern. Such a form of equality is, fundamentally, the antithesis of arbitrariness; it reflects consistency in principle at its deepest level, which is what the law is concerned with.[110] As we saw above there is plenty of judicial support for this view. The principle of equality of concern is fundamental to the identification of rights in the common law constitution. It grounds the rights found at common law. This is *not* the same as saying that there is a crude prohibition on different treatment; it is only to say that such treatment must be open to justification in line with constitutional principles, with equality being central to that.[111]

The starting point, therefore, is equality of concern; it is about respecting the equal dignity of each individual. As Letsas puts it, it is about 'the right to be treated with equal respect and concern by one's government, and the right to be treated as someone whose dignity matters and matters equally to those of others'.[112] In short, this formulation of equality provides a basis of how state power works: it demands that state power should show equal concern for citizens in its use. Since the common law is predicated on the rule of law, which in turn encapsulates an idea of anti-arbitrariness, and the opposite of arbitrariness is the value of equality of concern then we ought to see the common law in this light. Once this idea takes hold it is easy to see that individuals have an abstract, yet concrete, right to be treated as equals. Law, which is fundamentally about equality of concern, intrinsically provides for this. So, we must be treated as equals whose dignity matters and the state cannot use law in a way that does not show such equal concern.

What does this mean? More specifically, what rights does this ground? In short, non-arbitrariness in the form of equality of concern, which the rule of law

---

[109] Do note that this is different (though clearly related) to the *assessment* question of how we and who should assess whether a particular difference is one that warrants differentiation in treatment. This broadly concerns institutional competence and deference as well as more broadly considering the relationship between the judiciary, executive, and legislative branches of the state.

[110] Allan (n 95) 123.

[111] Ibid, 122.

[112] G Letsas, 'Dworkin on Human Rights' (2015) 6 *Jurisprudence* 327, 333.

demands, acts as a 'trump' against certain types of reasons for state action. On this account the common law respects decisions one makes about one's own life and actions, and also does not allow interference with somebody's choices on the basis of one's own external preferences.[113]

Thus, legal power cannot be used to ban or limit political action by, say, communists because society thinks that they are morally bad, nor to stop homosexuals adopting children because of a preference for the traditional nuclear family, nor again can stop ethnic minorities or women or transgendered people from serving in the military because white male serving officers would not want them to serve and so on. All of these actions rely on external preferences; that is, preferences about how others are treated without any objective justification, which is the cornerstone of the rule of law. A system that respects the rule of law requires objective justification for differentiation in treatment.

The argument is that there is one general right: to be free from arbitrary state interference.[114] Legal action must be objectively justified in the sense that it does not rely on the idea that someone or some course of conduct is not worthy of equal respect.[115] Instead, such differentiation in treatment must rely on, for example, evidence that a particular person or group should be treated differently because the rights of others need to be protected and the only way to do this is to seemingly limit the liberties of the first person.[116] This is why, for example, it is permissible to restrict the right to liberty if someone has committed a crime: he or she is incarcerated, at least in part, so as to protect others. It is also why it is impermissible to incarcerate someone because you *suspect* (but cannot prove) they have committed a crime. It is also why, for example, the Communist Party must have a freedom to demonstrate or to free expression but cannot burn down property or riot in Whitehall; rights do not extend to infringing others' rights.[117] In short, the common law certainly does not categorically *list* or *prescribe* a set schedule of rights but, instead, works on the basis of equality of concern or non-arbitrariness; it is concerned with the dignity of persons. It is not the case that the common law necessarily lists rights to vote or to freedom of assembly; rather, as Letsas puts it, citizens 'have a right not to be deprived of a liberty on the basis that their conception of the good life is inferior. Specific rights therefore exist only when, and to the extent that, there are liberties of individuals that the majority is likely to attack motivated by hostile external preferences.'[118]

One might respond to this by saying that it sets the threshold of government action too low: if the state can show that it was acting with equal concern but there was an objective reason for action that did not take account of external

---

[113] This is itself explained by the principles of intrinsic value and personal responsibility: see R Dworkin, *Is Democracy Possible Here?* (Princeton, Princeton University Press, 2006) 9–10.

[114] Dworkin (n 100) 198.

[115] Dworkin (n 83) 238.

[116] Ibid, 202.

[117] Ibid, 201.

[118] G Letsas, *A Theory of Interpretation of the European Convention on Human Rights* (Oxford, Oxford University Press, 2007) 114.

preferences, then would it not be acting in accordance with rights? What is to stop the state torturing a terrorist for information? By virtue of being a terrorist and the need for the safety of its citizens why can a state not torture him at common law? Dworkin's response is to say that some practices are so clearly wrong that they cannot be justified; even if purportedly showing equal concern for the dignity of the individual the practice simply cannot do so: 'some acts of government are so obviously inconsistent with the principles of human dignity that they cannot be thought to be justified by any intelligible conception of those principles'.[119] That is, when judging whether the government is acting in good faith we do not look at whether the government *thinks* that it is showing equal concern for the dignity of its citizens; rather, we look, objectively, at whether it is *in fact* doing so.

D. The Recognition of Common Law Rights

As stated throughout, the aim of this chapter is not to catalogue the rights that the principles underlying the common law justify. The aim is far more modest: to demonstrate that the current debate has taken place on a flawed premise and demonstrate the richer role the common law plays in human rights adjudication using select examples of rights that, whilst unrecognised, do exist at common law. The principles underlying the common law justify far more rights than the common law has *in fact explicitly* recognised in past decisions and here I will demonstrate just two of them (albeit controversial ones).

First, the right to vote is a useful example. We all suppose that, generally, in a Western liberal democracy participation in that democracy is essential. This shows equal concern for citizens; something that the rule of law is itself concerned with. Thus, the context of the UK is that, generally, citizens are able to vote in elections for those that govern and participate in the law making process. Any deviation from this approach would be arbitrary to the extent that it could not be objectively justified. Unjustifiable differentiation in treatment between persons is the antithesis of the rule of law[120] and so law can, and more importantly *should* (in the sense of putting the judiciary under a legal obligation) recognise a general right to enfranchisement, which can only be limited for objectively legitimate reasons. A good example would be the voting age: having it at 18 is objectively justified on the premise that those under this age are deemed to not have enough experience to participate in the democratic process. A degree of variation of the age limit to vote (eg lowering it to 16, or increasing it to 21) is therefore justified. Thus, this differentiation in treatment does not offend the rule of law. However, removing the vote from, say, one gender, or giving it only to land owners, or to those of a particular ethnic origin would be a violation of the rule of law; it would not be

---

[119] Dworkin (n 113) 36.
[120] See Postema (n 97).

objectively justified within the context of a liberal democracy. As a result, since the rule of law underpins the common law, controls its content,[121] and places the judiciary under an *obligation* to decide a case a particular way we can say, with confidence, that the common law supports a right to enfranchisement and that a judge, tasked with deciding this point head on, would be legally obligated to decide as such. This is not the same as saying it will be easy; human rights cases, as pointed out above, often require difficult questions of judgement on competing arguments of principle. However, as stated throughout a lack of epistemological ease in the judicial role does not mean that that role does not exist or should not be carried out properly; it merely means that we need judges who are well equipped to decide the cases brought before them, which is a question of legal sociology and not of law per se.

Another example is the right to end one's life with the help of another person. That is, is there a right to euthanasia? Clearly, the state is empowered (and indeed is under a duty) to protect its citizens. Preventing people's lives from being ended prematurely by others is objectively justifiable when conceived of as a safeguard for vulnerable people who might be persuaded to say they want to end their own lives so they will no longer be a burden or for the financial gain of their next of kin. It does not follow, though, 'that an *absolute* rule is morally acceptable'.[122] There will, of course, be genuine cases of people wishing to have help in ending their lives. If these situations exist – that is if these people are not vulnerable to manipulation and are of sound mind – then it is difficult to see what the rationale is for preventing them from doing so or for criminalising those who do help. The only reasons commonly put forward are those regarding the sanctity of life, but this is an external moral consideration about how others ought to think or feel, which equal concern does not permit. Further, as I have stressed throughout this chapter consistency of treatment is key and fundamental to the rule of law. As Allan suggests, evidence of an ill person's right to dignity and their autonomy vis-à-vis medical treatment is clearly present in our own system. We allow, for example, a hospital patient to refuse medical treatment. As Lady Hale points out in *R (Nicklinson) v Ministry of Justice*[123] we have recognised that there are cases where those who are terminally ill but of sufficient mental capacity to give informed consent can decline assistance without which they will die.[124] As Allan says, if we recognise the freedom to end our own lives by refusing medical treatment or by suicide we should not differentiate between those cases and those who lack the 'physical independence' to end their own lives.[125] Whilst of course recognising that a ban on assisted suicide is, in *general*, justified to protect those who cannot consent it is only justified to the extent of a legitimate difference; you

---

[121] See *Jackson* (n 69) and the common law rights cases quoted above.

[122] Allan (n 66) 23.

[123] [2014] UKSC 38, [2015] AC 657, [303] (Lady Hale).

[124] See *Re B (Consent to Treatment: Capacity)* [2002] EWHC 429 (Fam), [2002] 1 FLR 1090.

[125] Allan (n 66) 25.

cannot use a general ban to unjustly treat one group (here the physically incapacitated) as compared to another group (eg terminally ill but physically able). To not recognise that such differentiation does not turn on justified principle is a breach of the obligation to treat citizens with equal concern; as such, equal concern, which lies at the heart of the rule of law, recognises a right to end one's own life in limited circumstances.[126]

Recalling our discussion above of the ECHR will also be useful here because we can see how ECHR rights operate in a similar way to domestic rights' interpretation and application. There is therefore an analogy to be drawn. Throughout I have argued that common law sceptics are incorrect when they say that the common law does not recognise the same rights as the HRA because it has not done so in the past. I have therefore rejected an empirical view of the common law and instead demonstrated that the common law is focused on *principle*; that is, the judiciary's function is to give judgment on difficult cases but in doing so they do not and should not just look to the past narrowly defined. Instead, they look to constitutional principle for their inspiration (specifically, the rule of law and all it entails).

We can recall how the ECtHR originally looked at empirical consensus in deciding the reach of rights found under the ECHR. As pointed out above the ECtHR looked to 'present day standards' in interpreting the ECHR rights. However, we also then went on to discuss how the ECtHR has now started to look for *values* underlying rights; that is, it now takes a far more *principled* approach to rights' identification.

Where, then, is the difference between the common law and the ECHR's approach to rights' identification? In recognition of rights, at least, we can see the two as being far closer than one would think. As pointed out above, almost by definition the common law does not give a catalogue of the rights it recognises. However, even whilst the ECHR and the HRA purport to do just that the meaning of those abstract rights only comes about after reflection on constitutional principle; this is exceptionally similar to the common law methodology. Both the ECHR and common law, both sets of rights, are best understood as concrete iterations of general constitutional principle and values, both recognise that substance is more important than form; it is therefore difficult to see too much substantive difference between them once this is understood.

It is important to note that this must be understood for it to work; as I suggest throughout this chapter, what the common law rights *are* and what the judiciary *says* common law rights are, are not wholly identical; there will be times when the judiciary fail to uphold or recognise a right that does exist at common law. One can recall Lady Hale's lack of engagement with the constitutional principle in *Moohan* to demonstrate this point. Whether or not the judiciary will uphold

---

[126] For a longer discussion on this issue see Allan (n 66) 23–6. See also R Dworkin, *Life's Dominion: An Argument about Abortion and Euthanasia* (London, Harper Collins, 1993). I stress again that this does not discuss enforcement of any such right, which is a separate, though important, issue.

common law rights is a question of legal sociology: it depends on the judges and their backgrounds and training (indeed, as said this may well be why Conor Gearty is sceptical of common law rights). However, given their exposure to human rights due to the HRA, we can hope that judicial awareness of principle and rights is now such that, absent the HRA, they would boldly protect the rights of the citizens against the state.

IV. Conclusion

This chapter looks at which rights we can say we have at common law. The aim was neither to be prescriptive nor to give a list; instead, the aim was far more modest in that I suggested that the majority of writers on common law rights took a flawed approach to the identification of rights. They use a narrow, empirical approach to try and catalogue rights. This, I have argued, does not properly reflect how the common law works. Instead, the focus ought to be on the primary normative underpinning of the common law: that is, with the cardinal requirement that state action must be in accordance with law. This, I argued, reflects a commitment to anti-arbitrariness, which in turn recognises equality of concern for the dignity of citizens by the state. I then argued that whilst common law rights cannot be catalogued or listed, each right that the common law has recognised is a specific manifestation of principle; moreover, there is evidence that the judiciary recognise what they are doing because they rely on the rule of law to justify the recognition of a right at common law. By reflecting on the idea of equality of concern for the dignity of citizens we can see a vast array of common law rights; treating citizens with an equality of concern means we cannot stop them protesting just because we disagree with their views; we cannot stop people voting because they are somehow undesirable characters or because most people think a certain type of person should not vote; and, provided they are of sound mind, we cannot stop someone who wishes to do so from ending their life, or punish their family for helping them to do so. Of course, there are situations where it is permissible to stop such actions but these must be objectively justified; that is, the state must show equal concern for the dignity of its citizens when it stops citizens from exercising a purported liberty. Thus, you can stop citizens protesting in a certain way if you know the protest is going to result in a large amount of violence; you can stop people voting if they are below a certain age; and you can stop them ending their own lives with assistance if there is a real risk they might have been unduly influenced to do so (thus meaning it is not a real choice).

The law, in its role as a protector against arbitrariness, should recognise all of these rights and more *even if* it has not already done so; what has been done in the past is not constitutive of the entire legal landscape now. Our understanding of the common law, its nature, and its content, evolves as our understanding of the principles underlying the common law develops. Yet such principles do not exist because they are acknowledged; they are acknowledged because they exist.

INDEX

More than the Sur

A study of a multi-agency chil

Valerie Wigfall and Peter Moss

JOSEPH
ROWNTREE
FOUNDATION

NATIONAL
CHILDREN'S
BUREAU

making a difference

The National Children's Bureau promotes the interests and well-being of all children and young people across every aspect of their lives. We advocate the participation of children and young people in all matters affecting them. We challenge disadvantage in childhood.

NCB achieves its mission by

- ensuring the views of children and young people are listened to and taken into account at all times
- playing an active role in policy development and advocacy
- undertaking high quality research and work from an evidence based perspective
- promoting multidisciplinary, cross-agency partnerships
- identifying, developing and promoting good practice
- disseminating information to professionals, policy makers, parents and children and young people

NCB has adopted and works within the UN Convention on the Rights of the Child.

Several Councils and Fora are based at NCB and contribute significantly to the breadth of its influence. It also works in partnership with Children in Scotland and Children in Wales and other voluntary organisations concerned for children and their families.

The Joseph Rowntree Foundation has supported this project as part of its programme of research and innovative development projects, which it hopes will be of value to policy makers and practitioners.

The views expressed in this book are those of the authors and not necessarily those of the National Children's Bureau or the Joseph Rowntree Foundation.

Published by National Children's Bureau Enterprises Ltd, 8 Wakley Street, London EC1V 7QE

ISBN 1 900990 63 6

National Children's Bureau Enterprises Ltd is the trading company for the National Children's Bureau (Registered Charity number 258825).

Front cover photograph of children at Collingham Gardens Nursery by Niki Sianni

Typeset by LaserScript Ltd, Mitcham, Surrey CR4 4NA

Printed and bound in the United Kingdom by Bath Press

Contents

Acknowledgements

This research project has been both a challenging and a rewarding experience. We have greatly valued our involvement with the Campus, and have learned so much over the two and a half years working there. Many people have helped with the study, and while we are anxious that no individual effort should go unacknowledged, it would take too long to list by name every person who has contributed.

We are indebted to the Campus staff for always finding time to talk to us, and for assisting so willingly with all of our surveys and interviews. The research would not have been possible without their cooperation. We should like to thank especially Gillian Pugh, Maggie Bishop, the governors and staff of Coram Family, Georgette Davies and the staff of Collingham Gardens Nursery, Lucy Draper and the staff of the Coram Parents' Centre, Georgie Anderson and the staff of the Field Lane Homeless Families' Centre, Beverley Dawkins, Angela Woodley and the staff of KIDS, Dominic Fox, Helen Drake, and the staff of King's Cross Homelessness Project, Bernadette Duffy and the staff of the Thomas Coram Early Childhood Centre, and Christine Asbury and the staff of TreeHouse.

From the statutory sectors, we acknowledge the contributions of Lesley Whitney and Philip O'Hear of Camden LEA, Amy Weir and Campus social workers from Camden Social Services Department, Sarah Timms of the Camden and Islington Community Health Trust and Yvonne Millar of the Primary Care Child Psychology Service.

In the local community, we were helped by Sandy Wynn of Coram's Fields, Clare Gilhooly of Bedford House Community Centre, Mark Blundell and Sioned Williams of King's Cross and Brunswick Neighbourhood Association, Cieran Rafferty and Louise Gates of the Calthorpe Project, and Noelle Vickers of William Goodenough House.

We could not have wished for a more dedicated and loyal team to help us with the fieldwork. Organisationally, it was far from easy, and they rose to the challenge with energy and commitment. For interviewing, interpreting and transcribing, we are grateful to Jeasmin Begum, Oleksei Hronskiy, Fiona McAllister, Bet McCallum, Farhana Mazumder, Susan Stocker and Janet Turner. Also Alison Clark, though working on the Listening to Children component of the study, took time to help with the interviewing, and has been a much valued colleague throughout the project. For computing help, we are grateful to Charlie Owen of TCRU.

The support of the Joseph Rowntree Foundation was essential for funding the research, and we are particularly grateful for the guidance of Susan Taylor, their Senior Research Manager. We have benefited greatly from the support of an expert Advisory Group, convened by the Joseph Rowntree Foundation. Those members not already mentioned include Tricia Cresswell, Iram Siraj-Blatchford, Teresa Smith, Lonica Vanclay and Margy Whalley.

Finally, we owe an enormous debt of thanks to all of the families who have shared their experiences with us, for the purposes of our study. For this we are especially grateful, and hope that they, and other families with young children, may derive benefit from the results of the research.

1 Introduction

This report describes a study of the Coram Community Campus, a unique and innovative multi-agency child care network located in the King's Cross area of London. The research was part of a wider programme sponsored by the Joseph Rowntree Foundation that addressed 'the prevention of family breakdown through mainstream services'. Our project commenced in July 1998. It provided an opportunity over a two-year period for us to work closely with a wide range of stakeholders – the practitioners, statutory authorities, local community workers and, not least, the families who used the services – in order to monitor the Campus as it evolved. At its core, our research aimed to examine how the Campus functioned as a particular model of service provision, to explore what difference this approach was making for practitioners and users, and to assess its wider replicability.

Background to the research

Compared with most other countries in the European Union, the UK has a poor record in developing early childhood services (Moss, 1996). For too long, children's services here have been narrowly conceived, compartmentalised and fragmented (Hodgkin and Newell, 1996), focusing on 'one need or providing one function in isolation, addressing one item on the agenda of one agency' (Moss and Petrie, 1997). However the needs of children and their parents can seldom be divided up into neat categories such as health, education, leisure, employment, although services in the past have tended to be organised and offered as if they were (Pugh, 1988; Ball, 1994). More often, what is required is a combination of services from a number of agencies (Pugh and McQuail, 1995).

Alongside this record, research has increasingly indicated the importance of children's experiences during their early years, when foundations are laid for later development (Sylva and Wiltshire, 1993; Ball, 1994). Results suggest that a high percentage of children's learning takes place in the first five years of life, during which time the role of parents is also critical.

A further body of research has pointed to the long-term benefits, in both human and financial terms, of preventive work with parents and young children (Schweinhart, Barnes and Weikart, 1993; Pugh, De'Ath and Smith, 1994; Utting, 1995). Simple, relatively inexpensive measures, put into effect early, can save the need for more complex and costly interventions later. It is thought that, wherever possible, support is best provided within open-access, mainstream services (nurseries, health centres, etc.) in the local community, rather than through specialist referral services (Statham, 1994; Smith and Pugh, 1996; Sinclair, Hearn and Pugh, 1997). This approach similarly has looked to cross professional boundaries and work in partnerships in order to address the holistic needs of children and families.

The development of the Coram Community Campus endorses these twin themes of prevention and integration, whilst recognising the importance of high quality early education. Its launch in 1998 was timely, within the context of current social policy, as government has at last begun to accord priority to services for the youngest children. The Campus provided an opportunity to translate twenty years' thinking into practice. Our report sets out to 'tell the story' of the early growth of the Campus, from the varied perspectives of the stakeholders, highlighting both the successes and the failures which have emerged along the way, from which the viability of the model for wider replication might be assessed.

The study

The aims of the project were:

1. To describe and evaluate the development of the model of service provision – the Coram Community Campus as a multi-agency child care network – both in terms of its ability to meet its broad goals and from the perspective of the families concerned, in particular concerning its

accessibility for different groups of families, sensitivity and responsiveness to meeting their needs and circumstances.

2. To contribute to its development.
3. To assess its replicability.
4. To develop and apply methods of evaluating the service provision from the perspective of young children and to contribute to the development of a service that enables and is responsive to the 'voice' of the child.

In our efforts to make sense of the Campus concept, we had to remind ourselves constantly that the object of the study was the *'Campus'* and not an evaluation of the *individual* services which it comprises. In evaluating the Campus as a 'whole', we wanted to assess whether it became 'more than the sum of its parts'. Thus, our primary concern was the way the various services fitted together, their relationships, the network that was produced beneath the 'umbrella' of the Campus framework, not the way the individual services themselves functioned. At times it was difficult to maintain this perspective, particularly when services tended to view things from within their own boundaries. It was not always easy for them to 'think Campus' when their sights were so clearly focused on their own service provision. Yet for projects to reap the benefits of collaboration and cooperation that the Campus was intended to promote, an important step was to be aware of the wider context and to be prepared to cross boundaries. We shall come back to these issues in Chapter 4.

From the outset, we recognised that the concepts of integrated services and 'joined up' thinking that underpinned the Campus were already widely acknowledged and had become accepted in social policy both nationally and locally. With this in mind, we saw our task not so much as assessing the effectiveness of multi-agency working *per se*, but rather exploring how it can happen and what are the difficulties that have to be addressed. Our objective then was to unravel how the Campus functioned within the context of a world which is not 'joined up', where resources are scarce, where services come from different positions of strength, and social exclusion is still a fact of life for many of the families using the services.

Our overall approach to the research was firmly based in the naturalistic tradition of democratic evaluation (MacDonald 1974). We wanted to discover how the programme was experienced and interpreted by those directly engaged in the whole process, that is the policy makers, managers, staff, and users within the Campus boundary, as well as those operating outside it, in other agencies or in the local community. The research was also formative (Patten, 1987) in the sense that we were seeking to improve practice, by feeding back the results as they emerged in the course of the study. From our position, as outsiders to the Campus, we were well placed to look in and observe what was happening, piecing together the evidence gathered from the different sources while also exchanging information between the participants, and thereby endeavouring to promote better understanding for them.

The current wave of government initiatives has been accompanied by a growing preoccupation with monitoring and evaluation, not least in the field of early years. Increased investment has brought with it the growing burden of accountability, via objective measurement, targets, impact assessment, cost appraisals, standards and guidelines. Our focus in this project has been rather different, in that we were looking not for measurable criteria based upon a simple process of cause and effect, but for a deeper insight, 'making sense of what is going on' (Dahlberg, Moss and Pence, 1999). We set out to examine the process outcomes – the impact of services working together, the differences made to families – while locating these outcomes within a context of time and place, and also maintaining an awareness of the diverse stakeholders. In seeking understanding, rather than objective measures, we wanted to accommodate complexity and diversity. This approach was, in our view, more appropriate, given the multi-faceted nature of the Campus and ultimately would, we felt, be of greater value when considering replication.

The project comprised three main components, each involving different methods.

1. A case study of the development of the Campus over its first two years.
2. Interview based work with families, including a survey of families using Campus services and case studies of families from three subgroups: homeless families, lone parent families and fathers in traditional families.
3. An exploratory study on how to give meaning to the 'voice of the child'.

This report describes and analyses the results of the first two components. The third has been written up separately.[1]

The methodology adopted was primarily qualitative. We undertook documentary analysis, attended key meetings and used observation and interviews. We conducted two rounds of semi-structured interviews, at the start and at the end of the project, the latter covering two-thirds of those originally interviewed. The interviewees, 42 in total, comprised project heads, staff members, and parent representatives, as well as representatives from the statutory authorities and local community groups. The qualitative work with users comprised eighteen in-depth interviews with parents from each of the three specific subgroups. We collected quantitative data via a census of Campus users conducted over a two-week period. This highlighted demographic details and patterns of use. It covered a total of 332 families. We also completed a survey of 137 users based upon a semi-structured questionnaire administered in personal interviews. Finally, we undertook a limited survey of 56 non-users, to find out why the Campus was not being used, and to explore use of alternative services.[2]

Report structure

Our report looks back to the origins of the Campus, then picks up the strands to analyse the Campus over the two years of our study. It aims to be both descriptive and interpretive, setting down our perceptions, as researchers, which are themselves based on the views of the participants in the study.

In Chapters 2 and 3, we document the process of evolution, from the early planning of the Campus through to its realisation in its present form. We set out the organisational structure and composition of the Campus in Chapter 2, focusing on the relationships, the management, and the role of Coram Family, in order to gain an understanding of Campus dynamics. In Chapter 3, we highlight the enabling factors that have facilitated the development of the Campus, together with some of the constraints which have made it difficult.

---

1 – The results of this part of the research may be found in a separate report, *Approaches to Listening to Young Children*, by Clark, A. and Moss, P. (2001), Joseph Rowntree Foundation/National Children's Bureau.
2 – See Appendix 2 for a more detailed account of methodology.

In Chapter 4 we examine the difference the Campus has made for the service providers. We explore the degree to which services are beginning to work together, establishing partnerships within the Campus via both the formal structures that have been set up, and the informal mechanisms, and we consider some of the barriers that have impeded services from working together more effectively.

The voluntary/statutory partnership upon which the Campus is founded forms the subject of Chapter 5. Health services, social services and the local education authority are examined in turn, highlighting the aspects which have proved successful, and those which have proved more problematic.

Chapters 6 and 7 shift the focus to the users of the services, the families. In Chapter 6, we map out who they are, how they find out about the Campus, and ways in which Campus services are attempting to reach families who might not know what is available. Chapter 7 then looks at the ways families use the Campus, the impact that services have had for them, and the extent to which users, both parents and children, are able to influence provision.

Finally, in Chapter 8, we draw the findings together to consider the policy and practice implications. We review whether the Campus is indeed proving to be more than the sum of its parts, and what the implications have been so far. We look at lessons to be learned from the Campus experience for planning and implementing multi-agency working, and indicate some of the conditions that might contribute to successful outcomes. We conclude by considering whether this particular network model, or parts of it, is replicable more widely.

The report relies heavily on the words of our participants, quoting extensively from the interviews conducted. Quotations are shown in the text in italics. We identify the specific Campus projects associated with each quotation but where references are made to users, their names have been changed to preserve anonymity.

2 What is the Coram Community Campus?

> 'The Coram Community Campus is a group of voluntary and statutory organisations working together to provide a "one-stop shop" for local families in the King's Cross area of Camden.' (Coram Family, 1999)

> 'The opportunity is here to set up something high quality for children and responsive to parents.' (Coram Family, Interviewed in 1998)

Introduction

The term 'Campus' generally denotes a spatial arrangement whereby a number of buildings share a common site, often linked to an educational input. But over and above this, at the Coram Community Campus, it is an organisational arrangement, the aim being a multi-agency network in which all of the parts are linked together, working in partnership to a common purpose, this being the provision of comprehensive, open access and flexible services to meet the needs of parents, carers and young children in the local community. At the heart of the concept is the notion of the 'one-stop shop' for families and young children, incorporating a whole range of services that are relevant to need and are provided on one site.

With its emphasis on partnership and integration, the Campus vision pre-dated many current policy initiatives, notably the Early Excellence Centres and the Sure Start projects. In its realisation, there is nothing in the Campus that is inherently new. Indeed, multi-agency early years centres have been in existence for some time, for example, Hillfields Nursery Centre, which opened in 1971, or the Pen

Green Centre in Northamptonshire, which opened in 1983 (Whalley, 1994; Makins, 1997). What is new at the Campus is the idea of bringing mainstream services, supplied by a range of public sector and voluntary agencies, into a network of more closely integrated relationships, coordinated by one agency, Coram Family, as the catalyst and facilitator. It is this model of service provision, created from a public/private partnership and headed by a voluntary organisation, which potentially might be replicated more widely.

Location

The Campus is located on a three-and-a-half acre site in the King's Cross Ward of the Borough of Camden. Using the Jarman indices of deprivation, it is the most deprived ward in the borough, and amongst the most deprived in London. The last census data (ONS, 1991) showed that 35 per cent of its population were from ethnic minorities, particularly Bangladesh, and 22 per cent were unemployed. Only 16 per cent were owner-occupiers, compared with a national figure of 69 per cent (ONS, 1999). There is a high level of homelessness and occupancy of bed and breakfast accommodation, accompanied by an increasing number of refugees and asylum seekers. Many of the families in the catchment area of the Campus face major economic and social challenges that may place them at high risk of breakdown. It is unquestionably an area of high need. At the same time, like many other parts of London, the area is also very mixed, with a significant number of middle class families, as well as a large student population.

The Campus site in itself could be said to be unique. It incorporates a number of buildings that have been on the site for years, dominated perhaps by the refurbished red brick building in the centre. The open space surrounding the buildings is spacious and includes an ecological garden attached to one of the nurseries together with well-equipped children's play areas. One side of the Campus borders a former cemetery, now a park. The other side flanks Coram's Fields, a seven-acre site which also traces its origins back to the original Foundling Hospital.[1] Surrounded beyond by

---

1 – Coram's Fields is owned and managed by a charitable trust which is quite separate from Coram Family, although the site is similarly dedicated to families and children, offering extensive play areas, a nursery and drop-in.

dense inner city development, the setting of the Campus is peaceful, away from the traffic and problems of King's Cross, a *'calm oasis'*, described as a *'safe haven away from the bustle of life but at the same time in with it'*.

Service providers

In our research, we focused upon seven individual service providers which together constitute the Coram Community Campus[2] (Figure 2.1). Some of these were already located on the site before the Campus came into being. Others moved there specifically, attracted by the idea of being a part of the Campus concept. A third group was newly created and tailored to the Campus. The seven projects, briefly described below, are:

Thomas Coram Early Childhood Centre (TCECC) – A 108 place nursery school maintained by Camden LEA and part funded by an annual grant from Coram Family, providing education and day care to children aged six months to five years. It was created by merging two nurseries formerly on the site: St Leonard's, a Camden LEA nursery school, and Coram Community Nursery Association (CCNA), a parent managed voluntary sector nursery. TCECC was designated an Early Excellence Centre by the Department of Education and Employment (DfEE) in 1999.

Coram Parents' Centre (CPC) – A parents' centre newly created on the Campus by Coram Family, largely funded by the Government Office of London under a grant from the Single Regeneration Budget (SRB). The CPC shares early excellence status with TCECC, as a result of which it also shares a governing body.

Collingham Gardens Nursery (CGN) – A 20 place parent managed community nursery, funded by grants from Camden LEA and Leisure and Community, providing education and day care to children aged two to five years. It has been located on the site for over 30 years.

---

2 – The Campus also accommodates the headquarters of Coram Family, together with a number of its pre-existing projects. These were not included in the study. This distinction underscores one of the problems encountered in the research, namely which projects constitute 'the Campus'. In the event, we adopted the criteria of community-based projects. This corresponded with services that had signed up to the Campus principles, as discussed in Chapter 3.

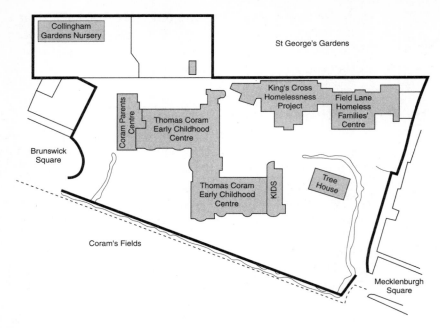

Figure 2.1 Coram Community Campus

KIDS – A special needs charity working with children with disabilities and their families. Based formerly in North Camden, KIDS relocated to the Campus in September 1998 and subsequently restructured to become KIDS London.

Field Lane Homeless Families' Centre – A voluntary sector family centre offering practical help and support for homeless families, asylum seekers and refugees. The centre has been a tenant on the site since 1988.

King's Cross Homelessness Project (KCHP) – A former Coram project incorporated into KCHP, an existing voluntary sector project. Providing advice and outreach to families living in temporary accommodation, KCHP has been a tenant on the site since 1995.

TreeHouse – A small school for children with autism or related communication disorders, a registered charity supported by Camden LEA. The school moved temporarily to the site in December 1998.

Other outside agencies are partners in the Campus and have representation on the site. Those included in the study were:

Camden Local Education Authority – Managing the TCECC, linked through the governing body to the CPC, and also supporting a number of the other voluntary sector organisations on the site.

Camden and Islington Community Health Trust – Committed to three rooms in the CPC, intended to serve as a base for the work of the child development team, the child psychology team and health visitors.

Camden Social Services – Committed initially to one room in the CPC, and the provision of two part time social workers. Camden Social Services also funds one of the deputy head posts in the TCECC and supports 20 per cent of the places for special needs children.

The last two agencies provide specialist 'add-on' services to the other service providers on the site. Though physically located in the Parents' Centre, they are available to users across Campus services. As we show in Chapter 3, this adds a complicated dimension to the network.

Range of service provision

Together, the providers offer a wide range of community based services and activities located across the Campus, what was described as a *'pick and mix'*. Some activities are situated within specific projects, others overlap across projects. They include:

- Provision for **children** – both nursery and day care, after school and holiday clubs for primary children, and support for children with special needs.
- Provision for **parents and carers** – drop-in, parent support in the task of bringing up children, and opportunities to access training and employment.
- **Health and Social Care** – Campus services working in partnership with the health trust and social services to promote family and child health and welfare, including the services of a child psychologist and social worker.
- **Creative arts** – building on a long tradition on the site and recognising the value of arts in therapy. Future development plans include a dedicated community arts centre on the Campus.
- Provision for **training and research** – the Campus acting as an early years training base in Camden.

Figure 2.2 sets out the range of activities offered at the Campus. It illustrates the holistic approach to service provision.

Origins of the Campus

The origins of the Campus go back in time, and are rooted in the history of Coram Family and the site which it owns. The

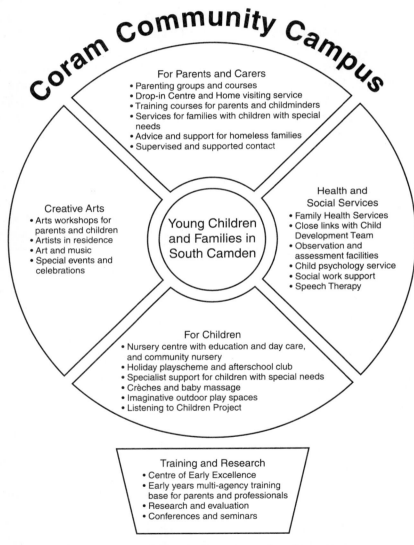

Figure 2.2 Activities offered at the Campus

Foundling Hospital for the 'maintenance and education of exposed and deserted young children' had been established on the site by Thomas Coram in 1739 under Royal Charter. Today, the Thomas Coram Foundation (renamed Coram Family), is a widely recognised charity with a reputation for its innovative and pioneering work with vulnerable children, notably in the fields of adoption and fostering, contact and leaving care. Over the years the King's Cross site has accommodated a number of family services, including the Coram Children's Centre, itself one of the first combined nursery and day care centres in the UK, founded by Jack Tizard in 1974.

The idea of creating a multi-agency child care network on the site, which would not only incorporate but also add to the existing provisions, offered Coram Family an opportunity to broaden its strategy. It enabled the organisation to move beyond its work with vulnerable children, into preventive work, in line with a growing movement in this field (Carnegie Trust Force, 1994; Audit Commission, 1994). It also allowed Coram Family to shift its focus of activity to the local community, with the aim of providing the best possible services for local families and children. Coram saw this commitment fitting within its wider aim of operating at the cutting edge of innovative services that might be replicated.

Early development

The 'Campus' as it came to be known, was an ambitious project which involved drawing together many stakeholders operating at many different levels. The conditions which laid the foundation for the project were:

- A site which was ready for redevelopment.
- A well-established voluntary sector organisation, Coram Family, committed to integrated service provision, and prepared to take the lead in masterminding the programme.
- A collection of diverse family services, both statutory and voluntary, operating independently, but willing to collaborate as neighbours on the site.
- A local authority and health authority willing to support multi-agency working.

The process of implementing the Campus project was complex and extremely challenging, spanning several years. Critical stages within the programme are shown in Figure 2.3. Our research started in July 1998, as the Campus was poised to take physical shape, shortly before the reopening of the main building on the site following its extensive refurbishment. The abbreviated synopsis of the Campus development shown in Figure 2.3 belies the huge amount of preparatory work that preceded it, planning and negotiating, reconciling vested interests, securing funding, setting up structures, establishing new partnerships. As the lead agency, Coram Family conceived and held on to the vision. It had the power, and also access to the resources to make it achievable. For a voluntary sector organisation to undertake such a role was

---

- **Appointment of a Project Development Manager** (1994) to direct and support the development programme, later renamed Community Services Manager (1997).

- **Consultation** with families, existing tenants of the site, funding agencies, local child care establishments and community groups, initially to establish needs and subsequently to explain redevelopment proposals.

- **Multi-Agency Working Party** (1994) set up, including representatives from Health, Education and Social Services, to develop a model and plan a strategy.

- **Applications for funding**, both unsuccessful (Lottery, 1995) and successful (SRB, 1997).

- **Campus Steering Group** (1997), including existing tenants of the site, funding agencies, users, workers and managers, Coram governors – to implement the strategic plan and oversee the development process, later to become Campus Coordinating Group (1998).

- **New Chief Executive for Coram Family** (1997) who brought *'national clout'* to the project as a result of her high reputation in the early years and parenting fields.

- **Consultation/negotiation** (1997–98) with statutory agencies to seek contribution to establishing integrated service.

- **Coram Parents' Centre established** (1997) funded by the SRB grant, a partnership between existing nurseries and Coram Family, managed by Coram Family.

- **Thomas Coram Early Childhood Centre established** (September 1998) – created by amalgamating St Leonard's LA nursery school and Coram Community Nursery Association, voluntary sector nursery.

- **Completion of first phase of construction programme** (December 1998) for site redevelopment.

Figure 2.3 Campus development stages

unusual, particularly when it came to forging working partnerships with statutory authorities. The implications of this strong leadership have been far-reaching, though not always positive for the Campus, as we go on now to show.

Organisation and management structure

As well as creating the vision and acting as the catalyst of everything that has taken place at the Campus, Coram Family continues to operate in the role of coordinator, drawing the service providers together, and ensuring that they act in collaboration. Without this coordination, the Campus would never be more than a collection of services working in physical proximity. However, coordination carries also a notion of control, which has been hard to reconcile within the organisational structure of the Campus.

Figure 2.4 illustrates Campus management and demonstrates the complexity of the relationships and the lines of accountability. (In Figure 2.4, the solid lines with arrows represent accountability, the dashed-lines represent landlord–tenant relationships, with the one exception of Collingham Gardens Nursery, which owns its own building, but leases the land from Coram Family, a relationship that is shown here by a dotted-line.) The CPC is the only Campus project directly managed by Coram Family. It shares Early Excellence status with the TCECC, although the latter is accountable to Camden LEA. There is an integrated planning structure for these two projects, via a joint governing body, although as yet this does not have delegated funding. The links between these projects are close, and the relationship with Coram Family is clear and comfortable. The other Campus service providers are accountable to their individual management bodies. As a result, they come with a degree of independence and autonomy which most wish to preserve. *'We certainly have had to strive sometimes not to have Coram Family on our wall or on our board outside in the signage. We have never wanted that, we are KIDS, and we are here on the Campus but we are an independent organisation, and I think it is v important that we remain so'* (KIDS).

This raises the question as to how far services can be integrated or can engage in joint working if providers are not under the same management, which we will consider when we look at the services working together in Chapter 4.

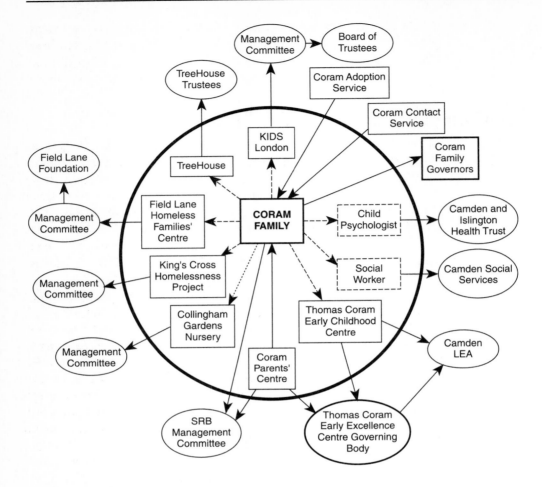

Figure 2.4 Campus management

The contribution of Coram Family as the lead agency at the Campus has been significant as creator and coordinator. Coram Family has facilitated participation in the shared vision of the Campus, and encouraged the different organisations to work together, even though it does not manage them directly. At the same time, as owner of the site, it is the landlord to most of the Campus projects. Effecting a partnership between organisations which have such strong identities, of which they are very protective, under an umbrella organisation of the size and strength of Coram Family, overlaid for many by a landlord–tenant contractual relationship, is inherently difficult.

Further afield, beyond the boundary of the Campus, Coram Family is one of the oldest child care charities in England, well-respected and recognised for its work with vulnerable children. This strength has given the organisation credibility in seeking support and funding for the Campus. It has also brought its own problems. At the start of the research, we were aware of a deep-seated distrust among Campus projects. There was a suspicion that Coram Family might be 'using' the Campus to enhance its national reputation, and in doing so, might be 'using' some of the projects. For instance, in promoting Campus work with disabled children or with the homeless, it was suggested that Coram Family might gain recognition for work done by others. Similarly, some local community groups were suspicious of Coram Family's motives in setting up the Campus, fearing that it would compete with, rather than support their work.

Consultation went some way towards alleviating these fears, involving groups in the planning process, allowing them to have a voice, although even this was tinged with the suspicion that it was purely notional, and that views expressed were not always being listened to. Our role as researchers was significant in enabling many of the anxieties to be shared and concerns to be brought out into the open and discussed, *clearing away the baggage*, as it was described. The interim research report provided a much needed opportunity for collaborative reflection.

Summary

- The first major goal for the Campus network was assembling the component parts, establishing a structure and laying the foundation.
- The Campus involves a number of related services, some new, others longer established, providing a wide range of activities for families and children.
- The partnership spans the statutory and voluntary sectors, but the parts are not equal, nor do they share common accountability.
- The organisational structure is complex, with Coram Family, as the lead agency, playing a strategic role, further complicated by its joint role as landlord.

3 Making it happen

> *'We need little steps into what might be a big meeting. Otherwise how are we really going to get to know one another.'* (KIDS, interviewed in 1998)

> *'I have had a lot of laughter and listening to all of the different people who have different views on different things over the year, because we are never all going to agree about everything. And I genuinely believe in partnership, I think it is the way forward, but I do get quite frustrated with the time that everything takes. It just takes so long and the families need help now.'* (Field Lane, interviewed in 2000)

Introduction

No one underestimated the challenge that lay ahead as the Coram Community Campus begun to take shape back in 1998. Robert Owen (1836) described how 'the practice of everything new however trifling requires time and experience to perfect it ... as in every other attempt by human means to unite a great many of the parts to produce one grand result many partial failures may be anticipated'. His advice seems as relevant today when attempting to understand the processes by which the Campus has evolved in its first two years.

The Campus achievement was acknowledged by the Chief Executive of the Field Lane Foundation at the start of our research – *'I am lost in admiration that they have done it. It is so difficult to do.'* In this chapter, we shall explore some of the enabling factors which helped to make the Campus happen and outline some of the reasons why it was so difficult.

Shared vision

A clear vision of what the Campus is aiming for has been essential for its realisation. As we showed in Chapter 2, Coram Family's vision is focused on creating a 'one-stop shop' for families and young children, with multi-agency services offering high quality, open access, mainstream provision. Coram Family's vision extends wider than the Campus in its ambitions – *'it wants to be at the cutting edge of services that can be replicated'.* Though its underpinning aim is local services for local people, *'it wants to be able to do the same thing in Hackney, and Greenwich, and Tower Hamlets, and everywhere else'* (Coram Family). There is a sense that Coram Family is taking everyone else along with it, but most people at management level that we interviewed felt they shared the overall vision and that it accorded with their own. *'I think they've got another agenda ... that is the perception of having multi-faces of education, training and childcare, from nought upwards, and everything that a parent or family could want to be better at, all that support. And yes, I do wholeheartedly welcome that and think it is a wonderful thing to strive for'* (CGN).

It seemed that smaller projects sometimes find the shared vision a constraint – *'it is hard enough struggling to keep the organisation alive, without having to worry about a wider perspective on what you are doing'* (KCHP), or simply find it harder to prioritise – *'rents and the realities of the day to day get in the way sometimes of what is going to happen in the future'* (CGN).

The vision has been translated into a shared value base, known originally as the Campus principles, subsequently reworked into aims and objectives (Figure 3.1). The Campus Coordinating Group jointly worked out the principles in the early planning stages. Acknowledging the need for a shared identity, they were intended to define a set of common goals, what might be termed the 'operational definition' of the Campus vision, to which all Campus service providers would subscribe. Initially groups signed up to them as a condition of tenancy when they took on their leases at the Campus, although the legal status was never clear. The principles, while linking Campus groups into a shared identity, also had to take account of the multi-agency structure of the Campus. They had to accord therefore with the objectives of the statutory agencies supporting the Campus.

Campus Aim

The aim of the campus is to offer an integrated and flexible service to parents, carers and children in the local area. It is offered in such a way that users can both influence and benefit from a range of care, education, health and social support related to their individual needs.

Campus Objectives

- To provide a safe and stimulating environment, both indoors and out, and to actively promote children's learning and development.
- To support parents as partners in their children's early learning and development.
- To support parents in gaining access to training and employment.
- To provide advice and support to families, including homeless families and those whose children have special needs.
- To contribute towards a multi-agency training resource for early years staff on the Campus and in Camden.
- To integrate the arts within the environment and services provided and through specialist therapy.
- To promote equality of access and opportunity based on a policy of inclusion.
- To involve users (children, parents and carers) in planning and managing services.
- To complement local services and work in partnership with the local community.
- To provide accessible health and social work services.
- To evaluate the development of the Campus.

(July 1999)

Figure 3.1 Campus aims and objectives

The practical task of formulating a shared valued base as principles or objectives was in itself a valuable exercise in joint working, forcing projects to examine shared understanding of concepts and practice. However, there was no evidence of changes in practice resulting, largely because most projects considered they already embraced similar objectives individually. *'Anybody in the country working with children and families is going to subscribe to that set of objectives. They are just a description of good practice really'* (CPC). *'They were always there; we have always worked that way. We very much agree with them, but they haven't made a difference'* (CGN).

Certainly, at senior level, service heads were aware of the Campus objectives, having shared in their formulation, and generally supported them. Given the diversity of Campus projects, it was acknowledged that both the vision and the objectives have to be broad, but that different people would access different bits, and follow different routes to achieve them. *'To integrate the arts is not a particularly important objective for KIDS, we would promote it if possible, but to promote equality of access and opportunity based on a policy of inclusion is vital for KIDS' work, so they have different weightings'* (KIDS).

We found less awareness among lower level staff or users of either the vision or the objectives. *'Things don't always filter down'* (KIDS), *'People who coordinate the different parts of the Campus are more attuned to what the vision is. People working in one specific centre or parents perhaps haven't quite such an idea of what it is meant to be'* (TCECC). One staff member suggested that the Campus objectives might usefully be given to prospective job applicants, to raise awareness of the Campus from the first encounter.

Statutory support

Securing the support of the statutory community authorities, Camden Council and Camden and Islington Health Trust, was absolutely critical to enabling the Campus to proceed. Working with senior managers and winning their support was the key which unlocked so many other doors. In Camden, it was the deputy leader of the council who, as chair of the Under Eights Committee, was responsible for initiating a complete turnaround for the Education Department, from the potential withdrawal of funding, as a result of the proposed closure of the existing nursery school, to an increase in funding to support the new children's nursery on the Campus. This in turn unlocked support from Social Services and Leisure, as well as endorsing the financial support from Coram Family governors. Coram Family was *'pushing on an open door'* at Camden Council, given its existing commitment to integrated child care and education. The revenue funding it provides for the TCECC gives it a secure base, as well as demonstrating a confidence in the Campus in wider circles. Coram Family's commitment to 'quality, innovation and replication' has been central to its development of the Campus, and as such, this approach accords with Camden's own philosophy, certainly at senior level.

Camden Council was itself helped by the external conditions in terms of the national strategy for joined up thinking, child care partnerships, children's service plans, and the general impetus to work collaboratively – *'the external environment began to be run in different ways and it made it much easier'*.

The support of senior managers from Social Services and Health was equally critical in enabling the Campus to be multi-agency, although in practice the Campus has perhaps not moved as far as it might have done in achieving this, for reasons which will be explored further in the Chapter 5.

Bringing in the key figures from health, education and social services during the planning stages of the Campus underscored the partnership and was important for breaking down barriers. For the Early Excellence Centre that input continues through representation on the governing body and has been very positive for the TCECC and the CPC. It has strengthened their combined identity. The ambition initially was that the entire Campus should be given early excellence status, but its innovative structure proved too complex to fit into the DfEE framework. As a result, there is now a tendency for the statutory services to think of the Early Excellence Centre as 'the Campus', overlooking its links with the other Campus service providers.

Resources and funding

Initial funding from an SRB grant marked the turning point for the Campus – *'there was a sudden burst of energy. It was all taken and given a push. They were given money and things got going.'* Subsequently, government policy for families and young children has made a lot of additional funding available. Securing early excellence status for the TCECC and the CPC has been significant, and although the Campus has not benefited directly from Sure Start, outreach workers and the training officer have been funded indirectly as a result of it.

Beyond the two projects in the Early Excellence Centre, the struggle for funding continues to be a constraint. Some service providers feared that, because of the Campus, the association with Coram Family might operate to their detriment when competing for scarce resources. *'There is confusion from outside agencies, they still have a view that we are all under*

Coram Family, it seems to be a hard scenario for some to grasp, that we are all autonomous, but on the land, and all working together' (CGN). Potential funders might either assume Coram Family was supporting them, or they might withhold funding if they have already donated to Coram Family separately. In fact, the fund-raising efforts of Campus projects have not apparently suffered over the period of the research, and on the positive side, the benefits of early excellence funding are beginning to reach other Campus projects, for example, with opportunities to tap into the training programme.

Individuals and roles

The efforts and achievements of particular individuals at the Campus have to be acknowledged. All of the Campus projects have extremely competent leaders, and this has been both enabling and constraining. Strong personalities are part of it, but equally the project leaders bring a variety and wealth of experience which has helped pull the Campus together. Where it has been possible for organisations to overlap, such as when a representative of one serves on the governing body or management committee of another, there have been mutual benefits.

While Coram Family as an organisation has been the catalyst for everything which has taken place at the Campus, its Chief Executive and Community Services Manager have been the individual catalysts within Coram Family. The Community Services Manager has been the link person on the ground who has tied everything together. It is difficult to see how the Campus would have happened without someone taking on this role. Her time has been dedicated to Campus matters, ensuring it a priority that no one else, with busy individual agendas, could give to it. She was instrumental in the early preparatory work, but also later in maintaining the energy, oiling relationships, both within and outside the Campus, and continuing to steer the Campus on its course. She has initiated and facilitated much of the collaboration between groups.

Higher up, the 'partnership' between the Coram Family's Chief Executive and the Campus has been mutually beneficial. The Campus has gained from her personal background and influence. She has been the key to unlocking the high level doors, securing support and accessing funding. The deep respect which she commands has helped to restore trust in Coram Family and greatly enhanced its reputation while moving the Campus forward. *'Gillian Pugh has a lot of background in child care ... her expertise is an asset. It is refreshing to have someone heading Coram who is focused on children'* (TCECC). *'Her national reputation brings credibility, just with her being there. The publicity the Campus has got, and the nursery becoming a centre of excellence are to do with her profile'* (Community group representative). For her part, the Campus has been a vehicle for translating into practice everything she has been advocating and campaigning for in the early years field. *'It is a tremendous privilege, all the research evidence that I have gathered together and all the work that I have done has been about advising people to set up services like this, and here I was, in a position to be able to do it'* (Coram Family).

Location

The site has obviously been significant in enabling the Campus concept to be translated into practice. We will consider the importance of location when we examine the replicability of the model in drawing together our conclusions. The renovation of the main Campus building has consumed an enormous amount of time, energy and resources, although again it has affected different service providers in different ways. In the early phase, the physical challenge often took precedence over the practical challenge of integration, though it did bring services together in the process of dealing with the building and site issues and contributed to a sense of ownership. The new building provides a good focal point for showing people that early years services are valued.

Summary

- A shared vision translated into a shared value base was important for carrying the Campus forward.
- Lower level staff and users were less aware of the vision or the objectives.
- The external environment was receptive to Coram Family's Campus project, both nationally, and locally in Camden.

- The commitment of senior management in health, education and social services underscored the multi-agency partnership.
- Progress was driven by strong personalities, particularly the Chief Executive and Community Services Manager of Coram Family.

4   Services working together

'There seems to be a dedicated and tangible emergence of a committed project and there is an element of inter-connectedness which is clearly visible now and is clearly beginning to work.' (KCHP)

'You are part of something called a Campus. There is an expectation that we will all work together, which is not to say that if we were simply round the corner we wouldn't. It sort of puts an onus on you to work together rather than not.' (TCECC)

Introduction

We have moved from the origins of the Campus, to its structure, and then through the processes of its early evolution, focusing upon the overall concept and what enabled it to become established. In this chapter, we step back at the end of the two years research to review some of the outcomes of the Campus model of service organisation for the service providers. Our concern here is to establish whether indeed services are working together, what forms this is taking, by what mechanisms it is being achieved, and what difference, if any, it is making.

We have been aware that working collaboratively demands a new approach. At the Campus, providers offer a range of services to different client groups. They operate in different ways, in terms of leadership, management, internal and external accountability. They come with different philosophies. Quite apart from the practical difficulties of bringing such a diverse group together and trying to work in a 'joined up' way on the ground, the Campus has had to respond to local authority agendas which are themselves imposed by broader government agendas. The dilemma is working within this wider context and reconciling all of these potential differences. Two years is not long to implement quite radical changes but the research has allowed us to assess what movement there has been, and identify what has worked at the Campus and what has proved to be problematic.

Relationships on the Campus

The relationship between some of the service providers pre-existed the Campus, notably the homelessness projects, Collingham Gardens Nursery and the two former nurseries. These projects had been accustomed to working as neighbours. Over the years, they had developed informal ways in which they helped and supported each other, from the most basic tasks, such as sharing equipment, to referring families from one project to another. With the exception of the former local authority nursery, the projects were all voluntary sector, and hence had flexibility to develop their own procedures. They did not share a building but were physically close enough on the site to meet informally and to 'pop in and out of each other's houses'.

Identity with the Campus has brought changes in many of those existing relationships. Obviously, the most radical change was the merger of the old nurseries into the new TCECC and its move into the newly refurbished building. This has created a much bigger organisation (108 places) with all of the implications such an increase in size brings with it. Perhaps because of its size, the TCECC has the strongest presence on the Campus. The new head confronted the daunting challenge of amalgamating two very different early years regimes, bringing the two staff teams of the former nurseries to work together within a totally new structure. The level of stress generated by the changes, both for staff and users, was immense. Inevitably, the early energy of the TCECC was focused upon getting established in its own right rather than forging links beyond its own boundaries. Larger scale requires tighter organisation. Much of the informality and flexibility of the former voluntary sector nursery has given way to formal practices and procedures required by the statutory sector, such as admissions criteria and attendance requirements.

Whereas the TCECC in its early life has had to look inward in its endeavours to consolidate its internal affairs, in contrast the Coram Parents' Centre from the start has looked outward to the Campus and beyond. It was the first project created specifically for the Campus and is therefore firmly rooted in the ethos of partnership and collaboration. Because it started with nothing, the CPC had to be creative in forming links at all levels as a means of becoming established. In the process, it has built up good relationships and developed valuable contacts on a formal and informal level with most of the service providers on the Campus, and also with groups in the wider community as it has extended out. Many of the 'add-on' services such as the child psychologist and the social worker are located in the CPC which again helps to make it the hub of the Campus for both staff and users. The CPC is not in competition with any of the other Campus services providers, and operates thus as an effective linking organisation. It was described as *'the jewel in the crown'* of the Campus, and widely regarded as a flagship project.

Over and above this general linking role, the CPC is closely tied with the TCECC as a result of the Early Excellence Centre status they share. The relationship between these two projects is close-knit, cemented by the requirements of this common status. The governing body, the Early Excellence evaluation, joint training and outreach work have all generated a common identity from the start. Even so, it was suggested that integration was still not as great as it might be – *'the staff badly need to know each other better, we are meant to be in this Early Excellence Centre together and half of them don't even know each other's names'* (CPC). Early Excellence status also has an impact on the families who use the centre, promoting greater movement of users between the CPC and the TCECC. We will look more closely at this when we come to consider users later in the report.

The relationship between TCECC and CGN is unusual in as much as the two nurseries are very different in size, style, and structure, yet in many ways they are working in competition. In electing not to amalgamate with the new nursery, CGN risked its own survival, but in reality the threat has proved to be less than feared. The head of CGN serves on the joint governing body of the TCECC and the CPC, endorsing a relationship which has proved mutually beneficial – *'Being a governor has given me an insight into a much larger organisation and how it functions, and that has been very useful for CGN as a smaller charity'* (Head, CGN); *'She has a real eye on our services and I find that very helpful'* (Head, CPC); *'She brings a perspective that we wouldn't otherwise get'* (Head, TCECC).

It is not surprising that relationships between the other service providers are somewhat looser. The two homelessness projects have always been linked, and they continue to work closely together, strengthened by a shared outreach worker, and with a steady movement of families between the two. Much of KCHP's work takes place in communities at some distance from the Campus. Locally, it is primarily an advice-based service. Thus, it shares less common ground with other Campus projects, although there is evidence of a *'trickle'* of clients passing between them. Field Lane, on the other hand, has always tried hard to refer its clients to local agencies, and the variety of what is available on the Campus has increased the potential. It maintains fairly strong links with other Campus projects, but there are practical difficulties in integrating homeless families into mainstream services, which we will come on to later, and these limit the possibilities. The two disability projects retain their autonomy while recognising the loose links that connect them. KIDS came to the Campus with high expectations of building stronger relationships with other projects. Some limited progress has been made, but the pace has been slower than anticipated. TreeHouse, on the other hand, came with equally high expectations, only to be frustrated by its temporary status on the Campus – *'I think people don't see us as part of the Campus in the way everything else is. So we sometimes miss out on things because of that'* (TreeHouse).

The relationships between the Campus service providers are therefore diverse, as Figure 4.1 demonstrates, with some projects more closely linked than others. Our evidence suggested that identification with the Campus does seem to have strengthened ties between projects – *'it's pulled together more in the last year, it's more focused. There seems to be less threat about individuality'* (CGN), bringing an *'element of inter-connectedness'* (KCHP) which was less apparent when they were simply neighbours.

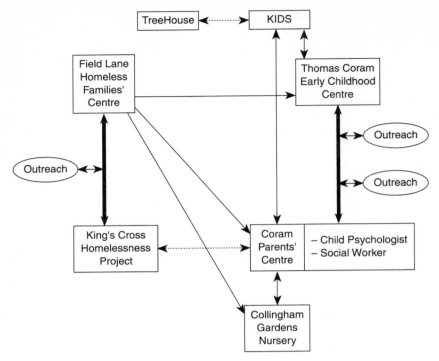

The weight of line indicates the strength of the relationship. Arrows denote the main direction of relationship, via referrals.

CGN and KIDS are also linked to TCECC and CPC as a result of membership of the governing body, CGN as a partner in the SRB funding for CPC, KIDS as Campus representative.

Figure 4.1 Relationships between Campus service providers

Collaboration and cooperation

We indicated earlier that the impetus toward integration and so-called 'joined-up thinking' has been gaining momentum. The 'coordination debate' lays an emphasis on services cooperating, developing partnerships, breaking down boundaries, working flexibly, in the interests of addressing the child or the family holistically, rather than tackling needs in isolation. In a study for the National Children's Bureau (McQuail and Pugh, 1995) three different models of organisation were identified within the context of local authority children's services:

- Integrated – the most coherent, unified under a committee with delegated authority;

- Coordinated – formal arrangements between departments at member and officer level;
- Collaborative – few formal arrangements beyond ordinary corporate management procedures.

Although the NCB study identified the integrated approach as the most effective if universal services offering care and education to children were the aim, it acknowledged that more often a mixed economy exists, reflecting different political, demographic and historical traditions. Research conducted by the National Foundation for Educational Research for the Local Government Association (Osgood and Sharp, 2000) used the same models to investigate the organisation of local authority services for children under five since the introduction of the National Childcare Strategy in 1998. It too concluded that, 'while joined-up working practices may well be best, there are several ways of joining up practice, many of which still allow a local authority to deliver its service well' (p. 27).

The Campus network is in many ways more complex in its organisation than the local authority structures which these studies addressed. As we pointed out in Chapter 2, Campus services do not come under common management, nor, as we showed in Chapter 3, do they have assured sources of funding. Not surprisingly then, we found evidence of a 'mixed economy' in terms of the degree of integration, collaboration and cooperation which is taking place between them, linked closely to the strength of the relationships described above.

We would stress again that integration is made harder by the fact that Coram Family coordinates, but does not own the Campus projects. *'Because we are all autonomous, it is really the land that is holding us together'* (CGN). Projects are learning how to work together to maximise the potential which the Campus offers but of necessity reconciling this with individual priorities. *'I think each organisation, including Coram Family, the CPC, and the TCECC, they all have their own identities and make use of it when it is more appropriate to be seen as an independent organisation. It is a bit of a balancing act. And it is being able to identify the times when it is really appropriate and really beneficial to work in partnership, for example a joint funding application, or a joint piece of work that will benefit all of the children on the Campus, but also feeling it is alright when you want to do something on your own'* (Field Lane).

Our interviews with Campus service providers revealed a whole range of ways in which projects are joining up, sharing and collaborating, some of which continue to be a reflection of simple neighbourly proximity, such as existed before the Campus came into being – *'if we have some cakes left over from a party, we might pop them over to Field Lane'* (CPC). Others are more far-reaching, embracing a greater degree of integration within a coherent and unified structure, such as the examples already given of the CPC and the TCECC under the auspices of the Early Excellence Centre. Once again, the evidence suggests that even where there was a high degree of integration, collaboration occurred more often at higher management level. Lower down, it tends to be dependent upon individual initiative – *'It is almost as if anyone who has an interest can go and talk to someone in that field, which is quite nice, but it is a case of finding motivation and time to go and do that'* (TCECC).

Organised structures

A number of organised structures have developed or are in process of being developed which might serve to re-enforce the corporate identity of the Campus and strengthen the links between the individual service providers.

Campus Coordinating Group

From the beginning, the Campus Coordinating Group, which meets every two or three months, has been the single platform which brings all Campus groups together. It is chaired by the Community Services Manager, and includes a number of representatives from Coram Family, acting in its capacity both of coordinator and landlord, as well as representatives from the statutory agencies based on the Campus and heads of all the service providers. In terms of communication and consultation, it fills an important role and makes a major contribution to the planning and administration of the Campus – *'For the heads of organisations who tend to go to it, it is a very quick way of finding out what is going on elsewhere, and what opportunities are coming up. If somebody has got something to offer, they can come and talk to that group, and it puts them in contact with everybody'* (KIDS). It provides a useful focus.

The Coordinating Group endeavours to strike an acceptable balance between issues related to the Campus as a whole, contributions from outside bodies with a relevance for Campus activities, and estate management issues. Most people felt it worked well as a means of information sharing at senior management level, but suspected that the information does not percolate down to staff. As a vehicle for strategic planning, it was suggested that the Coordinating Group at times works less well, in that it can feel like paying 'lip-service' to consultation, rather than an opportunity for views to be openly expressed as part of a democratic process. This is primarily because the partners are not equal and Coram Family's voice is so much stronger than the others.

Seminars

As a means of bringing Campus groups together, the programme of seminars has been less successful. These are open to all members of staff working at the Campus. The early ones were intended to bring staff together in a fairly informal way, rotating around the Campus projects, enabling staff to get to know each other and to share information about respective work. Both late afternoon and lunchtime seminars have been attempted, with equally disappointing results. As long as attendance is voluntary, it seems that staff show little inclination to give up their spare time – *when you work full time with children, you want to relax in your spare time'* (KIDS).

As far as introducing staff to other Campus projects, induction at the start of a new appointment offers an opportunity. However, ideally it requires time spent within each project, getting to know them, rather than an intro-ductory tour around the Campus. Alternatively, projects could 'exchange' staff from time to time, in order to gain insights about practices and procedures – *'one of the nursery workers could work in our playroom for an afternoon and vice versa. We are all involved in child care, of one kind or another, but it is all very different'* (Field Lane).

The Campus Open Day

While some questioned that Campus energy should be spent on organised social events such as the Campus Open Day, this event provided a unique opportunity for projects to work together in putting on a joint celebration of the Campus, which most people regarded as a great success. The importance of such an occasion should not be underestimated, despite the amount of time and effort taken up in its organisation. The burden fell on the Community Services Manager to pull it all together, to 'bully' and persuade everyone to do their bit. Inevitably, the workload was not evenly distributed, but the Open Day did include *all* of the Campus projects. Its significance was in some ways greater for those projects less closely involved in Campus affairs, operating on the margins.

The benefits were real for everyone who participated. For the staff – *'I was very enlightened to be working with all of these workers in the same field, in the endeavour to create an open day, just the communication and the conversation ... for years you pass them by, but you don't know their names, or who they are ... The open day was a model of cooperation and coordination between people'* (KCHP). Equally, it was valuable for the children to step outside their own boundaries, and to mix with the other children on the Campus – *'Especially for our children, they could just go out of the gates and do something. We weren't sure how they would react because they don't like change of routine but most of them loved it'* (TreeHouse). *'How often do the children from Field Lane get to meet with the children from the nursery, for the children from CGN get to meet with the children from TreeHouse or from KIDS? We don't have enough opportunities for us to feel like one group'* (Field Lane). And not least for the families – *'once they get to mix with each other in a social environment they feel much more a part of one thing, and the distance between the doors becomes less'* (Field Lane).

Joint training

In our early interviews, many people saw joint training as one of the most exciting prospects which the Campus offered, and from which all projects stood to benefit. It serves both as a means of crossing boundaries and furthering professional development – *'Just by being on training with somebody, you are learning together which is good, but you have your coffee time and have a chat and talk to people about what they do, and as a way of sharing information about how you work, that can be very good'* (TCECC). It enables people to see the world through other people's eyes. In so doing, it helps to build trust, which is an important stage in growing together with greater understanding.

While acknowledging the diversity of Campus service providers, and consequently their different training needs, there clearly are some common areas which might be served by joint programmes, such as first aid or health and safety. So far, the programme of joint training has been modest. But again, it comes down to time and resources. One suggestion was that projects might build into their annual budgets some contribution to a common Campus 'training pot', buying into as much or as little training as needed.

A training coordinator has recently been appointed through Early Excellence Centre funding, with the remit of developing the Centre as a Camden-wide resource for training both staff and parents. This appointment opens up possibilities for Campus service providers, in that they will be the first beneficiaries outside the Centre to whom programmes will be offered. To date, the training coordinator's work has focused upon developing a strategy to complement the existing Camden training programme, and setting up pilot initiatives, largely centred upon the projects of the Early Excellence Centre. It is still at an early stage, but the indications are already encouraging – *'it is a positive thing for us ringing up the new training coordinator to ask if there is any possibility of us accessing some training put on in the Children's Centre and the answer was "yes", there was no question about who you are, or what is your contribution, and that's been lovely'* (CGN). The potential is there to build upon while the resources exist.

Common data collection

Service providers, while subscribing to the collective identity of the Campus, have nevertheless retained responsibility for their individual record keeping, tailored to their own specific requirements. Where our task was to evaluate the Campus as an entity in its own right, we realised during the early phase of the research that what was missing was a common information system across the Campus. Without this, there was no way of knowing generally how many families were using Campus services, where they came from, their sociodemographic and economic characteristics, how they used services and for how long. Such information could play an important part both collectively and individually in management, monitoring and accountability.

The Campus Census, conducted in the first year of our research, was an attempt to monitor the families using Campus services over a two-week period, to create a 'snapshot' of the Campus, against which subsequent changes of use might be compared. It produced some common data, albeit of limited value, due to its incompleteness, but the actual process of undertaking it proved valuable for discovering the practical difficulties of such a collective exercise.

One of the problems related to the different methods used for data collection; some projects administered the census form in person, while others referred to existing records for the information. In the latter case, the diversity of the record keeping systems resulted in widespread gaps in the data. There were difficulties finding time to gather the information together, particularly in the smaller projects with only limited staffing, as well as ethical issues concerning the sharing of confidential data. Finally, there was a problem of multiple counting when the same families use more than one Campus service.

The intention was that the census would serve as a pilot study, and if successful, the Campus would itself take over the administration on future occasions. However, given the difficulties, it was decided in the Campus Coordinating Group not to repeat the exercise for the present time. Essentially, the census required projects to 'cede a little sovereignty' in order to see the wider Campus perspective, *'to lose a bit of the thing they thought was theirs for the greater good'*. The failure to do so, and the subsequent absence of any Campus-wide overview, illustrate the problem of developing a collective identity.

Shared activities and resources

We identified many examples of sharing which were already taking place, or were planned for the future. These extended both Campus-wide and within specific parts of it. We highlight some examples below.

- Campus newsletter, coordinated by CPC, prepared two or three times per year, distributed across Campus and to local community groups.

- Joint bid for Healthy Living Centre funding, initiated by Field Lane, but extended to include both Campus and non-Campus groups, King's Cross wide.
- Joint Inset Days – primarily between the CPC and TCECC, but also including CGN and KIDS, covering topics such as bilingualism, equal opportunities, and creativity.
- Shared use of outdoor playspace for the holiday and afterschool playschemes.
- Shared use of meeting rooms, parents' room, computers, as well as facilities such as washing machine, photocopier, etc.
- Toy Library organised by the Early Excellence Centre, available for all families, on and off Campus.
- Regular collaboration between homeless families centre, CPC and nurseries to allocate special places in afterschool/ holiday playschemes and nurseries.
- Joint parent support course offered by CPC and KIDS, located off Campus, for families with disabled children.
- Courses and events for fathers, offered by CPC, but open to fathers Campus-wide.
- Shared posts – between the Early Excellence Centre projects, shared outreach workers, training officer, and one shared staff post. Also outreach worker shared between the two homeless families projects.
- Shared meal service – TCECC cooks lunches for Tree-House children.
- Research projects, such as the Coram Family 'Listening to Children' project, which is externally funded and extends across Campus and also to other community-based locations.

Future plans for shared activities and resources include a shared minibus, a communal woodland area, a sensory garden to be jointly developed by CGN and CPC, a soft play and sensory room in the TCECC for wider use, and the reinstatement of an interpreting service, to be free for the homeless families projects, with a nominal charge for other Campus projects. The Field Lane fund-raiser has also worked on some shared initiatives on behalf of the Campus, notably a proposal for shared display panels and another for a volunteer coordinator, responsible for volunteer work across the Campus.

Sharing resources is a form of cooperation which in the first instance benefits the service providers, though ultimately improves services for families. Opportunities for sharing and working together are *just beginning. Lots of things are still being sorted out'* (CGN). Some Campus projects are collaborating more than others. Clearly, the Early Excellence Centre generates the closest exchanges between its two projects, whereas services dealing with special client groups, such as the homelessness projects or the disability projects would have less scope for working together. We were aware that initially issues to do with the building had consumed a lot of common energy – *'to do with the toilets and the car parking'* – but there is a feeling that things have moved on, and even though it is just beginning, *'it is a very positive and creative time'*.

Community resource

We have already referred in Chapter 2 to the potential threat which the Campus posed to local groups during its early life, a product of the perceived power of Coram Family and the apparent ease with which it achieves success. In terms of working with local community groups, the perception of the Campus without question improved over the two years of our research, and the feeling is that it has become established as a valuable community resource. The CPC in particular is thought to have made a huge impact locally.

The threat of closure for other local facilities because of the Campus has not materialised, although there have been some changes in local provision because of it – *'there is no point in trying to duplicate that, when there is a huge Campus that is well resourced and managed'* (Field Lane). At the same time it would not be true to say that the Campus is working in close collaboration with all local groups, nor would it necessarily wish to do so. The fact that Campus projects work with each other in some ways reduces this need. The links are there where appropriate, such as between the Bengali professionals, who form a close-knit network providing support for the Bengali community, or when there is collaboration for specific joint initiatives, as happened between Coram Family and Coram Fields, its neighbour, for the co-production of a summer musical play.

The local community in the area is described as very confident, with families moving around services, establishing their own networks to keep abreast of what is available. The Campus, on the other hand, puts a priority on reaching the families who are outside these networks, and we will consider this further in Chapter 6.

Barriers to working together

If collaboration and joint working between Campus projects have not progressed as fast as some might have hoped, what has prevented this? There was general agreement that the Campus lacks opportunities for informal contact between projects and individuals. This was seen as *'the icing on the cake'* by one project, while another commented that it is down to the individual to be sociable and it is not everyone's choice. But for those who want more contact, there is no social gathering space where people can come together to talk or to share a cup of coffee, *'just to sound off outside your own four walls'*. At senior levels there is perhaps more informal interchange, rooted in some long-term connections, most of which pre-date the Campus. For the rest, *'there is no joint area where we meet. We don't go through the nursery or the building, they don't come here. We meet "over the garden fence" or else effort is required'* (KIDS). A Campus café, which could be parent run, would fill the gap and encourage people to *'come outside their own boxes'*. This is an idea currently under consideration for the next phase of development.

Another barrier which has constrained services from working more effectively together is the absence of what in education terms is known as 'non-contact time', that is time away from the children for staff to reflect or plan together. Other Centres, such as Reggio Emilia in Italy, or the Pen Green Centre in Northamptonshire, built this in at the start. Indeed, the TCECC included it for its own staff when setting up its procedures, ensuring that they meet once a week. This shared time has undoubtedly helped ease the TCECC through its teething stage and contributed to establishing an early identity. For the Campus as a whole, some kind of 'non-contact time' could have been incorporated at the initial planning stage, although for projects already operating on the site and separately managed it might have been difficult to implement. What is important is providing an opportunity for 'thinking time', when people can both reflect on their practice and be in dialogue with others about it.

This links to another constraint, described as *'individual agendas of busy-ness'* (CPC). Not only is there an absence of 'non-contact time' but also virtually everyone on the Campus is working to tight schedules, meeting targets. There is so much scope and potential for joint things to happen, but the reality is that the pressures within immediate boundaries take precedence – *'how much time and energy do you devote to the common good, because the stuff that is sitting in your face everyday tends to take priority?'* (Field Lane). All of the different initiatives generate their own workloads – *'by the time you include inspections and filling in things for the Government Office of London and so on, monitor, monitor, monitor ... people are really overburdened'* (Coram Family).

Another essential ingredient for working together successfully is clear and open lines of communication, especially when there are so many things going on. The Campus Coordinating Group as we have indicated has been an important vehicle for sharing information and communicating generally at senior management level. Certainly, communication between projects has improved concerning practicalities, the day-to-day things, if there is a class running or a new piece of work. Having said this, it is hard to keep up with all of the new projects and initiatives. In our role as researchers, we kept closely in touch with activities on the Campus, but on several occasions we found that projects, both staff and users, were unaware of significant developments taking place elsewhere on the Campus from which they might have benefited. No doubt the dust will settle as the pace of change steadies. Even so, when there was clear overlap in work, for example developing outreach programmes, communication was not as good as it might have been. It is important to share ideas at the 'vision' stage and where appropriate to combine energy. Again, it is a case of striking a balance between working independently and working collaboratively, working in cooperation and not in competition.

Communication could also improve at a strategic level in relation to Coram Family as the coordinator of the Campus, and the individual service providers. Every project has its own three or five year development plan, but little mutual consideration is given to how they fit together – *'we are all talking about how we can fit into Camden's strategy for children and young people, and how we can fit into the health action zones, and all the different things in the wider borough and London-wide, but we are not looking into how we fit into each other's strategies on the Campus. I don't think it is a lack of will, I think it is a lack of opportunity, a lack of energy, and a lack of time to fit everything in'* (Field Lane). In moving the individual organisations forward, Campus services need to be aware of the strategies others are developing, so that they can link into things when they become available – *'if I don't have an understanding of what their forward thinking is, and vice versa, everybody is going to miss opportunities'* (Field Lane).

Summary

- Campus projects are working together more and there is a mutual exchange going on as service providers and the other groups in the local community learn how to respond to the Campus challenges.
- Organised structures have been developed which strengthen corporate identity, some more successful than others.
- The risks of subscribing to the Campus concept generally were less than was feared originally, and were outweighed by the benefits.
- Working together has been constrained by lack of opportunities for informal interaction, absence of dedicated 'non-contact time' for reflection and planning, and pressured individual workloads. Information sharing could have been better.
- The potential is there for the Campus to develop further in terms of projects collaborating.

5   Voluntary/statutory partnership

> *'The partnership with Camden has been one of the really most gratifying and exciting things about the whole enterprise. It can always improve.'* (Coram Family)

> *'Once people get to know one another, the links can be much better, and so we can talk about the development of children's services across agencies and sound each other out about things ... It is good to have voluntary agencies to canvass or talk to. It gives a different slant.'* (Camden and Islington Community Health Trust)

Introduction

Recent policies relating to children and families stress the importance of partnerships. Yet the difficulty of working across voluntary/statutory boundaries is acknowledged – *'Whenever you bring voluntary and statutory agencies together there is always difference and conflict. Unless all parties are actually willing and committed to overcoming these differences, then you won't overcome them'* (Camden LEA). The success in creating the statutory/voluntary partnership at the Campus was largely due to the willingness and determination of all the participants to make it happen. Having achieved the partnership, we now examine in this chapter how it is working in practice, and whether the multi-agency network is indeed breaking down some of the traditional boundaries between the sectors.

As we have indicated, a lot of work went on during the planning stages to bring the various groups together and secure a commitment to the Campus. Initially, statutory support tended to be education led, dictated by the urgency to get the new nursery up and running, but maintaining the support of Health and Social Services at senior level was equally important. A strong voluntary organisation like Coram Family is in a good position to coordinate the statutory agencies, its main advantage being that it is not in competition with any one agency. On the ground, as we go on to show, the results have been more variable.

Health services

Perhaps the most outstanding success of the health input has been the child psychology service. This was moved to the Campus from a conventional clinic setting, initially as a six-month pilot project. Though it was slow initially to get established, the psychologist has seen her appointment uptake rise from 70 per cent attendance in a clinic setting to 93 per cent at the Campus, which she described as *'phenomenal'*. The ability to respond to a request for an initial appointment without a long wait was thought to encourage attendance. Parents can obtain help with serious problems, or simply seek reassurance with difficulties related to routine developmental stages *'without feeling a failure'*. They can easily self-refer, without the need for an intermediary. There is opportunity for informal exchanges over a cup of tea. Accessibility, ease of keeping appointments, and the non-stigmatising nature of the service have meant that the child psychologist has become a popular, accepted and normal part of Campus life. As a result, the service is reaching more families, such as refugee families, many of whom would not otherwise have access.

The child psychologist has built the service up from nothing. Its success is in part due to her personal dedication and effort. In addition, her status is sufficiently senior to enable her to know clearly what she is aiming for and to pursue her objectives with confidence. Her presence at the Campus has also been boosted by a grant from the Princess Diana Fund linked to Great Ormond Street Hospital. Building upon the solid foundation already established, this funding supports a community-based family intervention project which fits well with the Campus ethos.

The sort of universal health services originally envisaged for the Campus have proved more difficult to achieve. The

Health Trust committed at the outset to three rooms in the Parents' Centre. The precise use for these rooms was never formalised. Early ideas included basing the southern 'spoke' of the child development team on the site, together with a drop-in and health advice service with child developmental checks and immunisation. It was anticipated that the nature of the service would evolve over time, according to needs. But apart from the child psychology service, baby massage is the only one to have materialised so far, save for a brief attempt at a speech and language therapy service, described more fully below.

Primary care, which might have made the first inroad at the Campus, has in practice proved a difficult area to break into because of apparent wariness at field level. The local health centre is located round the corner from the Campus but the health visitors there appear reluctant to venture in. Their involvement with the Campus extends to little more than referring clients when appropriate, which is clearly important, but does not actually bring down any boundaries. One explanation suggested was that the health visitors believe families currently using Coram services are getting all the support that they need. They prefer to concentrate on families who do not have access to the Campus, but fail perhaps to recognise that the Campus might operate as a community resource for *all* local families. The idea of incorporating a community child health centre on the Campus, including GPs, is one which is currently being explored for the next phase of development.

The health input has had greater success in the homeless families' centre, where a dedicated health room has been created, supported by the Health Trust. In this case, the provision comes under the umbrella of services for excluded families, with the remit of making health care accessible to those who might not have access to a conventional health centre. Hence, there is less risk of conflict. The health personnel appear to be comfortable in providing this service as an alternative to a mainstream service. It is, however, specific to the homeless families' centre, rather than a Campus-wide service.

Among specialist health services, a speech and language therapy service was introduced mid-way in our research, in response to an expressed demand from Campus service providers. It offered a drop-in session, once a month, for parents to discuss with a therapist any worries they might have about their children's talking. But with eight referrals in three months, only one of which warranted assessment, the clinic was deemed not viable, and was not continued. The feedback from parents who had used the service was very positive in that they were reassured that their children were developing along the expected lines, yet these referrals were deemed 'inappropriate' by the health service.

This rather short-lived experience raises a number of issues and makes an interesting comparison with that of the child psychologist. Firstly, only one session per month makes it difficult for a new service to become known. Secondly, the viability of the service was measured on the basis of the number of 'appropriate' referrals generated, that is those which warranted further assessment. Yet accessibility to specialist help, and the resulting relief of anxiety, could be seen as equally valuable in terms of family support. In addition, the ease of self-referral to the Campus therapist contrasts with similar consultations in a conventional health centre setting, accessed via professional referrals. It would seem that in the community setting of the Campus there might be scope for a more flexible approach, if prevention or reassurance are seen to be as valid as problem solving.

Despite the disappointments, the Health Trust readily acknowledges the benefits the Campus has brought so far, notably in improving the dialogue across children's services and enabling them to share in policy making at management level. The more fundamental changes will take longer to develop – 'the opportunities have been there, and it is our fault if we haven't been able to take advantage fully yet, but I am hopeful it will happen' (Health Trust).

Social Services

Like the health services, there has been support from Camden Social Services at senior management level, but this has proved difficult to operationalise. In this case, changes in high-level personnel within Social Services have been disruptive, and there has been no single senior person committed to seeing the service get established on the ground. For some time, Social Services committed to a room in the Parents' Centre, but provided no staff. Eventually, two part-time workers were assigned, to provide two half-day sessions.

The community setting, with its emphasis on prevention rather than crisis intervention, calls for a different approach, endorsed by the difference between the statutory and the voluntary sectors – *'the former is much more constrained, and has to operate within stricter frameworks. The latter can be more flexible, but this often produces conflict'* (Social Services).

Perhaps not surprisingly, it has proved hard for the service to operate within these parameters. Uptake for social work consultation was slow from the start. Coming in so late in the day, the staff has had to be creative, establishing a role for themselves, demonstrating what they can offer. Equally, the existing Campus services have had to learn how best to use the social work service. Social work still carries a stigma, which almost certainly contributes to the problems of take up. If these difficulties can be overcome, the Campus setting has clear benefits over the conventional social work setting, as the following example illustrates – *'I had a woman who came to see me who would not give me her name, but she wanted advice in relation to domestic problems she was having. I was able to respond to her hypothetical "what if" questions, which I would not have had time to do in the normal setting ... it is less formal here, there are no Social Services files, creating a record, as usually happens, and they don't have to give their name, so the service should be much less threatening'* (Social Services).

Because of the disappointing results, the social work service has been halved, to one worker for one half-day session per week. As the Parents' Centre has outgrown its existing space, so the social work room has been taken over for other purposes, and the social worker now fits in wherever is available. Nevertheless, it is felt that the scope exists to develop more family related work at the Campus. This is currently being explored, linked to the general rethinking on the delivery of children's services. Discussions are under way with senior social services staff on the new multi-agency assessment framework, in which the Campus could play a key role. Campus based social workers, supported by other Campus services, might undertake general assessments of children in need. The Campus could conceivably then come close to meeting its original aim, supporting the neediest children, in terms of assessment and provision. It is a case of gradually unlocking the potential which the Campus offers in these areas.

Education Services

The partnership between Coram Family and Camden Education that dominated the early planning stages continues to underpin the TCECC, and LEA funding is critical to the nursery's functioning at the core of the Campus. Building such an effective partnership has been a great achievement. *'The relationship between Camden and Coram has made a difference, people in the early years field see it as something different and exciting'* (TCECC).

This partnership with the Education Authority has brought its own problems, but these relate primarily to accommodating the nursery within an existing early years structure in which it does not quite fit. In Camden's procedures, the TCECC is the odd one out. It is the only school with a head teacher in the Camden Early Years service; as such it gets much greater funding than the other early years centres, while being exempt from the registration and inspection of services for the under threes required under the Children Act. The legal and technical difficulties are complex. They are not in themselves Campus issues, but they have implications for replication.

Equally, there are implications of Early Excellence status relative to other Camden provision in terms of the additional resources that the TCECC receives – *'as soon as something is successful, then there will be other things that are seen as less successful, and other people won't like you for it'* (Coram Family). Many people we interviewed, both on and off Campus, questioned the notion of superiority which the status of early excellence conveys. Even so, it was suggested that there might be a slight but subtle shift in Camden generally, *'from people thinking "that horrible organisation that gets all the money and does all these things and we hate it", to "they are doing very well, maybe we could identify with them a bit"'* (CPC).

Summary

- Securing senior level support of the statutory services for the Campus is clearly only one part, albeit an important one, of what is a complex and difficult partnership to achieve in practice.
- Coram Family has been instrumental in bringing the partnership together.

- For it now to be effective, it requires flexibility and often a different approach from the field workers.
- Senior management must remain committed to the Campus principle, and dedicated to exploring new ways of working in order to realise its full potential and ensure that Campus services best serve the needs of their users.

6   Families using services

> 'The fact that it is open to everybody in the community gives a message which is really important about its accessibility and its openness, which is great.' (TCECC)

> 'Our focus is to try and find families who aren't using other facilities, and this is what our outreach workers work at. We have only been partially successful, that is our focus for the future.' (CPC)

Introduction

The services the Campus provides are intended to be inclusive and accessible, reaching out to the most vulnerable families. In this chapter, we will look at who is using the Campus, and how it reaches them.

Our interview-based work with families comprised a user survey and 18 in-depth interviews. For the in-depth interviews, we focused on three particular groups, each of which has specific needs – fathers, single parents and homeless families.[1] The groups were located in four Campus services – the Parents' Centre (CPC), the Early Childhood Centre (TCECC), Field Lane Homeless Families' Centre, and Collingham Gardens Nursery (CGN).

However, where we encountered difficulty in getting service providers to 'think Campus', the problem was even greater for users. Many of them were using only one Campus service, and their comments therefore related specifically to that service

---

1 – The selection of these groups was influenced by the focus of the Joseph Rowntree programme.

rather than the Campus. We have endeavoured to pull out the strands which we feel have a bearing on Campus issues.

Who uses the Campus?

It is estimated that the Campus provides for some 600 local families in Camden (Report to Coram Governors, September 1999). Our Campus Census was intended to provide complete collective data on all users over a two-week period. It covered a total of 332 families. However, for the reasons already outlined (see Chapter 4), it proved far from satisfactory, with missing data ranging from 4 to 54 per cent. Therefore, we refer below to our survey data to give an indication of who is using the Campus. The user survey was administered to 137 individuals (121 women, 16 men), across all Campus services.

Demographic details

- *Age*: More than half (60 per cent) of the parents were over 30 years of age.
- *Ethnicity*: Around a third were white British, with another third white non-British, of whom more than a half came from Eastern Europe. The largest non-white group was Black African (13 per cent), followed by Bengali (10 per cent).
- *Language spoken*: Almost a half (46 per cent) stated that English was *not* the language spoken most frequently at home.
- *Residence status*: Just over three quarters (78 per cent) of families were permanently resident, 17 per cent were refugees or asylum seekers.
- *Living situation*: Just over a quarter (27 per cent) of families were living in temporary accommodation, just over a half (52 per cent) were living in rented accommodation, 14 per cent were owner-occupiers.
- *Benefits*: Just over a half (57 per cent) of families received some kind of state benefit, other than child benefit or disability benefit. The proportion was significantly higher in the homeless families projects.
- *Family type*: Two thirds of those we surveyed were living with a partner, husband or wife. Just over a quarter (27 per cent) were lone parents.

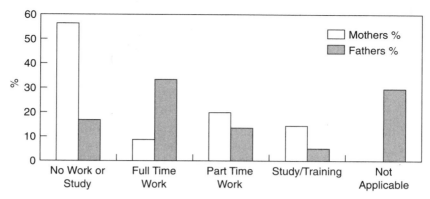

Not Applicable = no resident father

Figure 6.1 Parents' work status

- *Work status*: Just over a half (56 per cent) of the 137 families surveyed had a mother who was neither working nor studying, and just under a fifth (17 per cent) had a father in the same category (see Figure 6.1).

Accessibility

The success of the Campus in promoting equality of access and opportunity, based on a policy of inclusion, depends upon making itself known in the community and ensuring that those who would benefit most do in fact come. The individual services however operate different policies, such that the accessibility of the Campus may not be the same for all.

The admissions policy for the TCECC is determined by Camden Education Authority, which specifies clear-cut criteria based upon need (20 per cent designated for children in need or with special needs), siblings or proximity to the centre. It was suggested by the head that this admissions criteria, though stricter than that operated by the former parent managed nursery, is in fact fairer, more transparent and more inclusive. The TCECC currently has a waiting list of over 300 families, and although it is recognised that many of these have applied to more than one nursery, inevitably there will be disappointments when what is offered as an accessible local service is not actually available.

Other Campus projects operate an open-access policy, but like the nursery, this too can be tempered if demand exceeds supply, as has happened with some of the CPC programmes. Notably, for its holiday club and some of the more popular classes, it has had to revise its admissions policies and procedures in an effort to ensure that its services reach the most needy families, rather than those who know how to plan ahead in order to get to the front of the queue. However, a tension can arise between reaching those in need and providing a reliable service that people can plan around when places have to be rationed due to over demand. A single mother of an eight-year-old son with behavioural problems described her fear of losing his place in the holiday club:

R: *'He has been coming for about a year and a half or so now. I don't think the demand was as great then as it is now. But now the way it works is that you have to apply every school holiday.'*

I: *'Has that posed a problem?'*

R: *'Well, it has and it hasn't. I worry that he is not going to get in, and I've been lucky that he has got in.'*

I: *'But you never feel absolutely sure?'*

R: *'No, and I've got nobody to look after him when I go to work those two mornings ... And not only that, because he is difficult, I need a break from him and he needs a break from me ... so if he didn't get in it would be awful for our family and for the older children as well, absolutely awful.'* (CPC)

This issue highlights an ongoing dilemma for the Campus, namely its aim to support the most vulnerable families set alongside its commitment to provide open-access, non-stigmatising, mainstream services. The problem is common to most open-access family centres (Pithouse and Holland, 1999; Statham, 1994). To reach the vulnerable, such as the homeless, or to attract particular, under-represented groups, such as fathers, services must be targeted, yet this could be said to contradict an open-access policy. On the other hand, the Campus fulfils an important community development function in a deprived neighbourhood, which might in the long term produce greater benefits than targeting those in greatest need (Holman, 1987). It is a difficult balance to achieve.

Finding out about services

Accessibility links also to knowing what is available. Individual Campus services undertake their own promotion.

The longer established ones have already acquired a reputation in the local area, whereas the CPC, as a new service, has gone to some length to publicise itself, particularly when newly set up. At a broader level, the Campus newsletter is circulated to a wide range of local groups, and Coram Family produces a Campus brochure describing all of the services. We were interested to find out if families who had accessed individual services were aware of the Campus itself. Of the families we surveyed, three quarters knew that the service they came to was part of a larger group of services, but over a third (37 per cent) stated they had not heard of the Coram Community Campus as such. The users of the nurseries were most likely to be aware of the Campus.

In our research, we undertook a limited random survey in the neighbourhood (in local primary schools, a community centre and health centre) aimed at identifying non-users. The purpose was to find out whether local families knew about Campus services, how they had found out about them, and whether they used any other local family services. We found that just over two thirds (68 per cent) had never heard of the Campus and this was the main reason given as to why they had not used any of the services – they simply did not know about them, either individually or collectively. Those who did know of Campus services either just knew about them from living locally, or had been told about them by others. However, over a third of the non-users interviewed thought they would definitely use the Campus in the future. Just under two thirds of the 'non-user' sample were using other local family services, which included nurseries and community groups.

Our work with Campus users enabled us to find out how people had heard about the service they were using. In most cases (64 per cent) it was by word of mouth, usually recommendations from friends or neighbours – *'I think most people learn about things that way, because in this area there are focal points – Coram's Fields, the park – you meet people there, you get to say hello, and it is just "oh, have you been to such and such?" And that's where I went'* (CPC).

For the homeless families in particular, almost all of the users had come as a result of a personal recommendation, usually another resident in the bed and breakfast hotel, or the manager, or a professional such as the health visitor. *'We were just discussing in the kitchen with some other women. One woman from Sierra Leone said to me there is a place, Field*

Lane, where you can take your baby, a place where you can be happy and not all the time in the hotel' (Field Lane). *'My health visitor, when she visit me she saw that I was always inside depressed. She said I need to go out. She say someone come to visit me at my hotel, to bring me here'* (Field Lane).

Nursery users, on the other hand, were more likely to be aware already of local provision, either as a result of living in the area, or through the library or the council offices. For some, it was a case of putting a child's name down at several nurseries, and taking whichever offered a place first. Others described a process whereby they had researched what was available until they found the right nursery – *'I'd seen a few small nurseries and I went to visit a couple of others. I was passing by and saw the sign and just walked through the front gates. I don't know, I just had this kind of feeling that I had found the place, because it was such a kind of peaceful, very welcoming place'* (CGN). The TCECC, as a Camden nursery, offers a free core day for children aged three years and above, for which there is heavy demand. For working parents, the full-day fee based option which both nurseries offer is an equally sought after resource. Probably the greatest shortage is places for under-twos, of which the TCECC has only twelve. At the time of our survey, siblings of children admitted under the former admissions criteria filled many of these.

Networking is effective between local community groups, as well as between individuals. CPC users were more likely to have come via this route, recommended by another Campus service, usually the TCECC, or some other early years provision such as a local playgroup. Some of these referrals came specifically because of a specialist provision offered at the Campus, and from that initial introduction users then discovered other activities. For example, a mother came to consult the child psychologist in the CPC on the recommendation of her child's nursery teacher (not Campus). Her use of Campus services has grown from this.

I: *'So you made that gradual increase of involvement by starting off seeing the psychologist to bringing him in to the afterschool club and then joining classes yourself and bringing him to the holiday play scheme?'*

R: *'Yes, exactly, and it's all here ... and that means you see the same people all the time. I think that is important with a child like David. You know the people who are looking after him, and you are comfortable with them, and he is comfortable here'* (CPC).

Just as the users had been encouraged to come by others, so too they had recommended Campus services to their own friends. Four out of five users had recommended the service they used, and two thirds of these recommendations had been followed up.

Reaching families in need

In its first year, the Campus was very much preoccupied with sorting out its internal organisation and adapting to the new physical space. Once things had settled, it was recognised that services, although successful in terms of numbers, might not be reaching some of the most vulnerable families. These might be families who were not involved in local networks, who had not been long enough in the locality to know what is available, who did not speak English well enough to find out information for themselves, who did not have the self-confidence to venture into new situations. It was felt that special strategies were needed to make contact with these hard-to-reach families who might not otherwise come.

Outreach work was identified as a way of targeting these special groups. Mid-way through our research, two outreach programmes were set up, one by the homelessness projects, funded under the King's Cross SRB grant, the other by the CPC/TCECC, under early excellence funding. The early evidence suggests that both outreach projects are achieving results. In nine months, the homelessness outreach worker has brought in more than 110 new families. They are now coming at a rate of five a week. The worker visits some of the most isolated families living in temporary accommodation, does an initial needs assessment, gives them information about the Campus homelessness services, which is translated into nine languages, and if necessary escorts them on their first visit to the Campus, where they move initially between Field Lane and KCHP, and then on to other Campus services if appropriate. The investment in translation and interpreting is high, but it is an essential part of communicating with these families if they are to benefit from the services that are available.

The CPC and the TCECC share two designated outreach workers who have been visiting families in the local estates and also following up referrals from other community projects. As well as bringing families in to the Campus, they aim to provide ongoing home support if appropriate and needed. They have been targeting especially the Bengali community, in which women tend to be very isolated at home, and the children rarely attend children's services. As a result, the number of Bengali users coming to the Parents' Centre has increased. The impact so far on the nursery has been less evident, but new admissions are linked to waiting lists and specific entry dates, thus it may take time for the effect to filter through.

The CPC/TCECC outreach workers have in addition recently launched a toy and book library which is proving to be very successful. Available to all families at the Campus, the workers also take it out to isolated families in the community, in the hope they might be encouraged to come to the Campus.

The CPC has been running classes and sessions in several local primary schools for some time, in an attempt to spread services more widely. This too has generated a two-way passage, by making families more aware of services available on the site.

Of course it is impossible to know whether families reached through outreach would have found out about the Campus in any other way. Longer-term study might identify changes in the pattern of Campus users, but unfortunately the initiative came too late in the research for the real impact to be assessed. Clearly, there is potential for the outreach workers to adopt a proactive role on the Campus, introducing families to the range of services available and encouraging movement between them.

Summary

- Both nurseries have long waiting lists, while the CPC has had to ration places for some activities.
- The Campus has to balance an open-access policy alongside its aim to reach vulnerable families. For the latter, outreach programmes attempt to reach families who might not otherwise come.
- Networking was the main route for finding out about individual services, although knowledge of the Campus generally was limited.

7 Meeting family needs

> 'It's great when you arrive at a set of buildings and you get an understanding about what is happening ... It is a big support network, each unit has only limited resources, but you feel your needs are covered at the Campus.' (CGN user)

> 'Everyone expects to win the lottery, I pay £1 but I am chuffed when I win £10. And this is what is happening here. I paid my £1 to come in, and I've got three numbers instead of one!' (TCECC user)

Introduction

To be a parent raising young children in an inner city area of London is stressful. Add to this the strain of being single, or working, or living in temporary accommodation, and the stress is immediately multiplied. Campus services, as we have indicated, aim to support the individual needs of families living in the inner city, and in so doing to improve the quality of their lives. The potential the Campus offers was aptly summarised – *'a family, whatever their circumstances, coming onto that site can immediately have access to a very wide choice of services without having to go anywhere else. If you are a chaotic family, if you are a very distressed family, if you are homeless, if you are a refugee, you don't speak English, you have no money, you can come onto that site and speak to someone and you will be sent in the direction where somebody will meet your needs. I can't think of a family for whom that would not be the case on the Coram Campus'* (Camden LEA).

'One-stop shop'

The Campus sets out to be a 'one-stop shop', a term defined as 'satisfying all of a customer's needs within a range of goods or services' (*Oxford English Dictionary*, 1998) in one place. Our user survey and interviews allowed us to examine this concept in relation to family needs and multiple use of the services on offer.

In the survey, 18 out of a total of 137 respondents were using more than one service at the time they were interviewed. Two-thirds of these (12) were users of the CPC and the TCECC, that is the Early Excellence Centre. A further 32 respondents had used another Campus service at an earlier point in time, and indeed two of these had used more than one such service. Thus, just over a third (35 per cent) of those interviewed had experience of more than one Campus service provider. Several others stated that they had their children's names on the waiting lists for one of the Campus nurseries, and hence might become multiple users in the near future. Multiple use of services was however rare for homelessness families or for users of the projects for children with disabilities.

We were aware that the concept of a 'one-stop shop' at the Campus could however operate at different levels. It could involve families accessing services across projects, as above. But it could also apply to families engaging in a number of different activities within one project, depending upon availability and need. For example, a family could be using the drop-in, attending classes and obtaining health and welfare advice, all within Field Lane Homelessness Centre. Looking therefore at activities people were engaged in, as distinct from services they were using, we found that just over half (51 per cent) of our respondents had engaged in at least three activities since they had been coming to the Campus, many within the same project. Furthermore, whereas homeless families had rarely used other services on the Campus, within the homeless families' centre, 'one-stop shop' provision meant that 71 per cent of the users had engaged in three or more activities.

However, when we asked respondents if they preferred having activities all on one site or spread around the local community, opinions were almost equally divided, with the users of the large nursery being the most in favour of having everything on one site and the most likely to say that experiencing this on the Campus had made a real difference to them. Other respondents were in favour of a combination. This is, in fact, already happening, for example the CPC sessions in local primary schools, or their hospital-based classes for prospective fathers.

Case Study 1

Perhaps the most impressive example of 'one-stop shopping', both between and within services, was the family whose pattern of use is mapped in Figure 7.1. This family comprised the father, his Spanish wife, and their two children, a son who has been diagnosed with Asperger's Syndrome and Attention Deficit Disorder and a younger daughter.

Their son first attended the former local authority nursery school on the site, before his disability had become apparent. At that time, his parents simply thought he was a *mischievous boy*. The parents were encouraged by the nursery teacher to go to the Parents' Centre next door, which

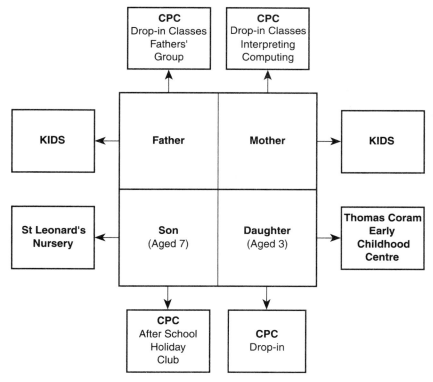

Figure 7.1 One family's use of Campus services

was just starting up. They found it *'a nice friendly place where you could meet and talk and do crafts and learn about different cultures. It was a respite, a place where you could learn child management, where parents could have a cup of tea and get to know each other.'* Later on the father went to a fathers' group meeting, which he described as *'sharing fatherly problems'*, but indicated nothing more had come of this, other than a fathers' football match, in which he was unable to participate.

The son's problems were picked up at nursery so that by the time he moved on to mainstream primary school the family was receiving help from both the health and education authorities. As a child with special needs, he was offered one of the designated places in the After School and Holiday Club at the CPC. The daughter was given a place in the TCECC where she is getting special help with her slow speech development. Meanwhile, the mother has continued going to the Parents' Centre, taking classes in computing and a community interpreters' course. The family has also linked up with KIDS, via a recommendation from a worker on another holiday scheme which their son attended. Contact with KIDS has been *'reassuring ... to know that there are other parents with exactly the same behaviour difficulties with their children'.*

This family had received over time a huge amount of support from a variety of Campus services, which they readily acknowledged and valued. In the absence of close family, and with friends who find their son's challenging behaviour difficult to cope with, this couple could not imagine how they would have managed without the Campus – *'I find it reassuring that they accept our son ... no matter what he does, he will still be there, welcomed. His behaviour would be different to most other children and I don't ever feel that my wife and I are the cause. They make us feel they want to help us.'* Yet, when asked if having everything on the one site had made a difference to them, the response was *'I hadn't thought about it, but now you have made the point I realise it would have been very difficult if you had to keep going to other places.'*

'One-stop shop' for the homeless

Both the CPC and homeless families projects could be said to operate as 'one-stop shops' in their own right, given the variety of activities which each offers. For the CPC, this operates along with a steady two-way movement of families between other Campus services. The homeless families projects, on the other hand, tend to be more self-contained. A comprehensive service for homeless families offers everything from laundry to complicated legal advice, from drop-in to health checks, with just a few steps between them all. They try hard to refer families on to other agencies, believing firmly that they are as entitled to all the resources as any other families. But their users are in some ways a special group with particular needs.

In theory the Campus should have made it easier to refer families on to other agencies on the site, and the other agencies try very hard to accommodate them. For instance, places for the children of homeless families are reserved in the holiday club, and the CPC worker liaises with the Field Lane staff to allocate them. However, the reality is that homeless families often have to go through a slow process before they are at a stage where they are willing or able to take up some of the wider opportunities, largely due to the stigma which homelessness carries and the lifestyle which accompanies it. A single homeless mother described to us how she tried going with her young baby to the Parents' Centre – *'they said that they teach you baby massage and that also it's a social sort of activity so I said, "Why not, instead of sitting in the hotel and being depressed and staring at four walls – go outside and try and get a life"'* (Field Lane). She gave up after a couple of visits, preferring to stay with her friends from the hotel at Field Lane, where she felt more comfortable with others who shared her situation.

Case Study 2

A second example, Figure 7.2, illustrates a different pattern of 'one-stop shopping'. This Kosovan family had arrived at the homelessness centre having lost everything – *'you don't know language, you don't know place, you don't know everything there, you are like shock, you know, day after day you have to learn'* (Field Lane/TCECC). The centre had been their lifeline, helping them to piece their lives together. It obtained a place for their three-year-old son in the TCECC on the Campus, which enabled the parents to attend English classes, first at Field Lane, but graduating later to a further education

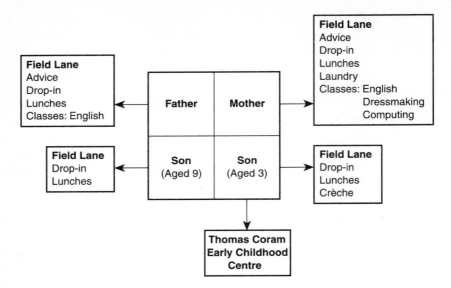

Figure 7.2 A homeless family's use of Campus services

college. The family also took advantage of many of the activities on offer within Field Lane. When interviewed, they had progressed to the stage where they were beginning to look ahead, to think about getting jobs and having a permanent home. *'My life now is here ... It is good luck we found the homeless families' centre and the nursery. This is luck.'*

Effectiveness

Campus services aim to be high quality and effective. In our survey, we asked whether the Campus services had made a difference to the way people felt. Interviewees were invited to tick as many aspects as they felt appropriate from a list which included feeling 'Less Anxious', 'More Confident', 'Less Stressed' and 'Happier'. They could, if they wished, tick *all* items. However, although the question referred to *'Campus services'*, for the majority of respondents who had experienced only one service, responses almost certainly related to that service, rather than the Campus.

'Feeling Happier' (60 per cent) was the aspect ticked most frequently, closely followed by 'Feeling Less Stressed' (52 per cent). Responses varied according to service provider. The families from the homeless families' centre overall were more positive in their responses, with 90 per cent feeling happier. In addition, they were more likely to tick 'Feeling Less Anxious' and 'More Confident' as a consequence of using the service. We also asked which *one* of these items was most important for the interviewee, for which they could tick only one item (Figure 7.3). In this case, it was 'Feeling Less Stressed' which was ticked most frequently, by 27 per cent of the sample, although again there were variations between services.

Concerning effectiveness for children, respondents were invited to tick ways in which Campus services had been helpful. Again, they could tick *all* of the items if they wished. The responses were very positive for all of the items specified with 'Making Friends' and 'Learning New Things' the two most frequently ticked (81 per cent and 82 per cent respectively). The homeless families once again were more positive about 'Happiness' for their children, although the differences with users of the other service providers was not as great as the previous question. Overall, the one single item most frequently identified as of greatest importance for children was 'Making Friends', (Figure 7.4), ticked by almost a third of the sample.

Many of these sentiments were enlarged upon in our in-depth interviews. Across all of the Campus services, parents talked positively about their importance, both for themselves and for their children. For example, a homeless mother explained how *'this centre contributed 100 per cent. It's*

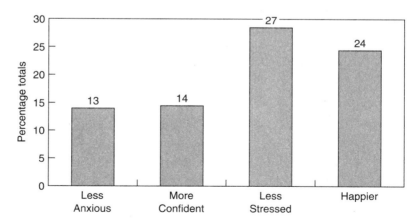

Figure 7.3 Single aspect thought most important benefit for users

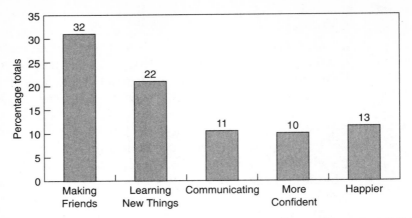

Figure 7.4 Single aspect stressed as most important for child

contributed joy in me. All the stress went. It keeps me happy as I never thought ... it changed my life. It has brought full happiness in me, surprising me' (Field Lane). Another mother with a special needs child in the TCECC, as well as twin babies at home, acknowledged the benefits for her son, plus the support she had received from both the nursery and the Parents' Centre – *'I'd be tearing my hair out now if I had Tom with the twins, all at home ... I wouldn't be able to cope. But the nursery does so much for Tom. He learns a lot there, he's happy and it helps me because it gives me time, it gives me a break while he is there ... Then you've got all the other things'* (TCECC/CPC).

In a separate question, 'Happiness', 'Friendliness', 'Learning New Things', 'Getting a Break' were once again the items mentioned most frequently as the most enjoyable aspects of coming to services on the Campus, yet as qualities, they are difficult to measure in any formal way using official targets.

The measures we have used suggest Campus services are perceived as effective in relieving stress and improving well-being. The question remains as to how much is due to the *Campus* and how much is due to the *individual services* themselves. For instance, the mother who described how leaving her baby in the crèche in Field Lane enabled her to relax and catch up on sleep, and *'that helped me to be sort of like a good mother in terms of not being irritable because I am tired'* could have done this without any of the other Campus services. Alternatively, the secretary of the small parent managed nursery – *'The nursery has opened up areas where if I hadn't been there, or maybe if I had been somewhere else, I don't know what would have happened. It has opened up areas where I was able to tap into this.'* She had not benefited from any other Campus service, though clearly could have done so in her situation, had she been aware of what was available.

Partnership and participation

Our findings indicate that users feel they and their children are benefiting from Campus services, but are they as positive about their ability to influence those services, as the Campus objectives suggest they should be doing? In our work with families, we endeavoured to explore the extent to which Campus users wanted to be partners with the service providers, to have a voice in shaping the provision, and whether they considered they were able to do so. (Our questions had to relate to specific services, in the absence of opportunities for user participation in the Campus as a whole.) We also wanted to find out their views about listening to children's voices, as well as the importance they accorded to recognising their rights.

Four out of five respondents in the survey considered it was very important to seek adults' views and to act on their wishes when deciding on policies and practice. A slightly lower proportion, just under two-thirds, considered the same thing was very important for children. Only one respondent thought it was not important for adults, and three thought it was not important for children to be consulted in this way. However, the notion of participation was difficult for some to comprehend, particularly the homeless families, perhaps due to language difficulties.

Questioned on how satisfied they were that the projects they used actually did seek adults' and children's views, almost a half (48 per cent) were 'very satisfied' regarding adults' views, and almost a quarter (23 per cent) were 'quite satisfied'. Thus, seven in ten were satisfied to some degree. One in five had no specific view in response to this question. Concerning satisfaction with seeking children's views, nearly half of the respondents, spanning all Campus services, had no opinion to express. Almost all of those who did express an opinion were satisfied to some degree, most 'very satisfied'.

Asked about their current level of involvement, just over a third (38 per cent) of our sample volunteered to help with activities and slightly fewer than this (33 per cent) attended meetings related to the running of the service. Only eight respondents in our survey were serving as representatives on the management committees or governing body. Parental involvement was significantly higher in the two nurseries.

When asked if they would like to be involved more in planning and running things at the Campus, just over half (57 per cent) of those questioned said they would. Just over a quarter (27 per cent) stated that they specifically did not wish to be involved, while the remainder had no view or considered the question inappropriate. Users of the small parent managed nursery (CGN) were the most enthusiastic about getting involved, while users of the homeless projects were the least likely to want this.

For many of the homeless families the difficulties concerning participation relate to language. It is hard to get involved if you don't speak English. Even where language is not the issue, the fact remains that these families are probably the most vulnerable on the Campus, and need to build their self-confidence before they can take on significant responsibility. Thus participation for them came in different guises. For instance they are invited to become involved with the lunches; they plan the meal, purchase the ingredients, and then cook it. It is a modest level of participation, but serves an important function – *'It makes me feel better when I am not happy and I come here and talk with someone, you can cook dinner here and that … it gives you a little bit of confidence in yourself'* (Field Lane). Though they are not actively involved in running it, the users of the homeless families' centre acknowledged that the service is not 'imposed' upon them, and valued this – *'there is a lot of freedom, no restrictions when you come'* (Field Lane).

Obviously it is much easier to achieve partnership if the organisation is smaller. In this respect, the small parent managed nursery has a clear advantage over some of the other Campus services. It has a high level (almost 50 per cent) of parent representation on the management committee, and has no trouble finding people with special expertise to fill the various roles. Parents feel that they are in control, working in close collaboration with the staff. The 'organiser', as the head is titled, serves on the management committee, but does not have a vote.

In a similar way, the disability project, KIDS, has gone out of its way to include parents in its service – *'KIDS always looks to how to solve problems, and is very much led by parents, not policies and documents, which larger organisations like social services tend to be led by. KIDS becomes your "friend", therefore lots of people who use them put something back'* (KIDS).

The expansion of numbers in the TCECC which resulted from the merger of the two former nurseries has brought some major changes in parental input, particularly for former users of the community nursery. Where previously, almost half of the parents had served on the management committee, there are now only four parent governors out of a total of 108 families who use the service. Many parents therefore saw this as a retrograde step. They felt, certainly initially, that they had lost power, and that their voice on the governing body was a mere token to parental involvement – *'it is a less familiar environment, it is more anonymous . . . when you were involved as a parent, part of the management committee, your opinion was much more important than it is now'* (TCECC). Re-establishing some level of parental involvement, albeit of a different kind, has taken time but it is beginning to happen. It is now much more to do with parents working alongside staff in the nursery, or learning from them how to participate in their children's learning. To begin with parents were not familiar with this culture and the dedicated parents' room was empty most of the time. However, there have been some successful workshops, and the new training officer is now running courses in parent volunteering, aimed at encouraging parents to get involved in this way.

The growth of the Parents' Centre has meant that it too has encountered some difficulty involving users in decision-making. The governing body of the Early Excellence Centre requires two parent governors from the CPC, yet the nature of the Parents' Centre does not lend itself to this type of representation. The families are diverse. They include users of the drop-in and baby massage, as well as those attending classes, plus parents of children in the out of school activities. Families tend to be involved for a shorter time than the nursery users. Thus it is not easy to recruit parent governors. Once appointed, it is hard for them to keep in touch with the users in order to represent their views. The CPC holds regular meetings to promote user participation, but a further difficulty has been the burden posed by a barrage of monitoring requirements. The centre provides data for a total of 19 different evaluations, internal and external (Draper, 2001). There is a limit to how often users might reasonably be asked for their views and a danger that overload in this respect might actively discourage participation. However, we found parents seemed satisfied that, when called for, they could talk to the staff and would be heard sympathetically – *'If I had any complaints myself, not that I have, but if I did, the staff are approachable here and that's what I like about the place. Whereas I don't think I've got much confidence in myself and somewhere else I would probably just stop going, here I would go and voice my complaint'* (CPC).

We have referred above to the fact that nearly half of the respondents in our survey had no view to express concerning their satisfaction with the degree to which children's views are sought and acted upon. Increasingly, Campus services have been incorporating 'listening to children' as good practice, encouraged perhaps by research activities on the site.[1] Yet it seemed that the notion of children's rights was unfamiliar to many of the users. In our interviews, only one parent responded directly to this question:

I: *'Do you think children's voices are heard? Do you think of the things your son has been part of on the Campus that he has been listened to, if he has wanted to say anything about it?'*
R: *'Oh, he says a lot. Oh yes, they are good at that, they are focused on empowering children'* (CPC).

It is a difficult concept to convey in an interview, particularly when English is not the first language. The problems may well have been due to unfamiliarity with the terminology as much as with the concept. On the other hand some parents we talked to, while seeming to understand the notion, rejected it as inappropriate for very young children. It may be that Campus services will need to work more closely with parents, to make them aware that young children are capable of expressing views in various ways and should be listened to, both at home and in the nursery.

---

1 – Notably the 'Listening to Children' element of our study, and the externally funded Coram Family project.

Summary

- The campus operates as a 'one-stop shop' across and within services, though the majority of families use only one service.
- The potential exists for Campus services to make a real difference when users take advantage of the range of provision on offer.
- Users were very positive about Campus services, but their views tended to relate to individual services rather than the Campus as a whole.
- Parental participation was acknowledged as important and was generally thought to be satisfactory at the Campus. It took different forms across Campus services.
- The concept of children's rights was unfamiliar to many users and therefore difficult for them to comment upon.

8   Conclusions

> *'Things don't just stop at one point. There is a future after the future which has been reached now.'* (CPC)

> *'There is a broad wish to be able to develop a community campus that would provide a whole range of services to accommodate the needs of the local community. Everybody would be able to understand that. But as to what the stages are that we are going through, how we will know that we have reached it, how we are going to measure the achievement ... it's almost like "suck it and see".'* (Field Lane)

We have described the context within which the Campus is located and explored in some detail how it functions, both from the viewpoint of the service providers and the families who are using it. Our conclusions are drawn at a particular moment in time, when the Campus is still in its infancy. Clearly, it will continue to evolve and grow as services respond to changing needs and circumstances. This fact should be borne in mind as we review the findings of our study.

Our task in this final chapter is threefold. Firstly, we want to review the concept of a multi-agency network and assess the extent to which the Campus has achieved this status. Next, we want to draw out the broad lessons that might be learned from the Campus experience where they have relevance for practitioners and for policy makers. Finally, building on these lessons, we want to consider the replicability of the Campus model as a type of network, or of elements within it, in order to determine the extent to which it could or should be repeated.

What constitutes a multi-agency network?

We might define the distinguishing features of a multi-agency network as a range of different services which have some overlapping or shared interests and objectives, brought together to work collaboratively towards some common purposes. The network requires coordination of its different services in order to relate more closely to each other and so become 'more than the sum of its parts'. **Networks may vary in a number of ways:** their interests and purposes; the services and agencies they bring together; the relationship between the services, including physical proximity (for example, from sharing the same site to being spread across a particular locality) and the degree of autonomy and integration; organisation, including measures to support coordination; and whether they are established as part of a national programme (for example, Sure Start partnerships) or consist of more ad hoc arrangements involving particular services in a particular place.

The potential benefits of working in this way, of becoming more than the sum of the parts, are multiple. The participating organisations, in uniting to work together toward common goals, may achieve more coherent, comprehensive services. They may gain strength from working in partnership. There are possible benefits from sharing ideas and pooling resources, from joint working and training, and from mutual support. Collaboration across agencies makes it easier to work with families in a holistic way, and facilitates cross referral. This in turn benefits the users, who also enjoy a wider range of provision, with easier access to general and specialist services, addressing all of their family needs.

Viewed within this broader context, the Coram Community Campus is by no means the first example of a multi-agency child care agency: variations of the network theme are increasingly common. But as we noted in Chapter 2, the Campus has certain distinctive features, notably the way it combines mainstream services, in a public/private partnership, coordinated and headed by a voluntary organisation.

How far has the Coram Community Campus achieved this status?

In creating a Campus, the foundation has been laid for developing a particular kind of multi-agency network. It brings together a range of services, both statutory and voluntary, all of which work with families and young children, and share as their primary aim meeting local needs. It thus has the potential to become 'more than the sum of its parts'. However, our findings suggest that it still has some way to go in the process.

Campus services are beginning to learn from each other, share skills, enjoy a cross fertilisation of ideas. Indeed, as we have shown in Chapter 4, there are already a number of practical links, and more of these are planned. But **if the Campus is to be more than a collection of family services sharing a site, more work needs to be done in terms of services feeding in to one another** by way of cross referrals, developing more areas of joint working and training, pooling resources and producing Campus-wide information.

What then are the constraints that appear to be impeding the greater integration of Campus services? We can identify three of particular significance, none of which are probably peculiar to the Coram Campus: indeed, they seem likely to be issues facing any attempt to build an effective network. **First, finding and maintaining a balance between the autonomy of individual services and collective action and identity is a difficult and delicate process**. At the Campus, the 'parts' are neither equal, nor do they all share the same relationship with Coram Family. Most are accountable to their own managing boards, which are outside the Campus structure. It is probably better that services retain their autonomy, and in any case few if any services are likely to be prepared to surrender their independence: but at the same time, it makes it harder for them to work in a 'joined up' way. More widely, individual services have individual perspectives and separate agendas, the result of their internal concerns and of external demands, not least the particular perspectives and separate agendas of the different policy areas to which each service relates. Faced by these concerns and demands, collective action and identity can easily take second place: the history of unsuccessful attempts to collect information at a Campus-wide level, about users and their use of the Campus, is one striking example.

Second, participating services and their staff, at all levels, have limited space and time to devote to the Campus. Funding of individual services allows little or no time for Campus-related activities. These might involve opportunities to discuss the concept, principles and plans for the Campus, and their implementation, and to participate in joint training programmes. Or, to take another example, they might involve visiting, or working, in other services, or otherwise spending time with staff in other services discussing and reflecting on practice as a means to deepen understanding of different perspectives and understandings, and to seek new, shared understandings.

Third, there are the external forces which may hamper coordinated work. The Campus, no more than any other network, does not exist in isolation, but within a larger context. Government agendas and funding attempt to encourage 'joined up' thinking and actions in some respects, and there are increasing examples of government supported networks and partnerships. But Government policy can sometimes work against effective networks, through for example introducing too many initiatives, projects, targets, funding schemes and other mechanisms specific to particular services. The structuring of the workforce employed in children's services is fragmented, with diverse training. Funding of services pays little attention to the need for staff to have 'non contact' time for their personal development, as well as to devote to collaborative work, or for other forms of support for more ad hoc networks which fall outside national programmes.

The Campus brings many different opportunities to parents and children on the one site. Our findings suggest that **the strong links between the services and their proximity can ease the passage of families between them**. Families, in turn, acquire trust in individual services, from which they gain confidence to move around services, deriving added benefits that might not have been possible without the Campus structure. The examples where this is happening, though relatively few in number, indicate how effective it can be.

But from the perspective of the users, it is hard to evaluate how far the Campus has achieved the status of a multi-agency network when so many have experienced only one Campus service, and are satisfied with what they are getting from it. **That more families are not exploiting the potential that the Campus offers may be due to the early stage of its development, together with a lack of awareness**.

Families will have to learn how to use it, encouraged by the service providers. The interest in the Campus that our questions aroused suggests families are receptive to the idea of the network, and keen to see it developed further.

Outside the Campus, **it will take time for its corporate identity to become clearer**. The notion of a 'Campus' is not one which is familiar to many people, at least outside the university world. The Campus tends to be perceived as a 'product' of Coram Family, with all of its services coming under Coram's umbrella. Indeed, the term 'collective' might be easier to understand, stressing as it does the element of working together whilst retaining autonomy, though it perhaps underplays the potential for becoming more than the sum of its parts.

What are the conditions needed?

The evidence of the research highlights some of the issues associated with setting up and implementing the Coram Community Campus as a multi-agency child care network. As one of our interviewees said, *'You can't just stick everybody together and hope it works'* (TreeHouse). The path so far has not been entirely smooth, nor have the problems encountered all been resolved. Nevertheless, tension can be viewed as constructive, and lessons learned from the experience. Some key pointers for policy and practice can be drawn out.

Planning

Our research has demonstrated that, at its core, multi-agency working requires a programme that sets specific goals while devising well thought out means for achieving them. The essential requirements in such a process would appear to be:

- **Vision** – establishing and maintaining a clear vision, which all participants acknowledge and support, of what the multi-agency network (over and above its individual service components) is aiming for, the contribution of each service and agency to the network, and how the success of the venture might be judged.
- **Principles** – a shared value base as the operational definition of the vision, which underpins the approach to working and to which all participants subscribe.

- **Corporate strategic planning** – at the Campus, this has had to accommodate diverse individual services, allowing them autonomy to develop in their own way, whilst endeavouring to exploit the potential their differences offer for working together.

Translating the plan into practice

Once devised, our evidence suggests that the plan for multi-agency working requires a democratic approach to implementation which is inclusive and which draws all of the stakeholders into the process. Above all, translation into practice requires the following:

- **Coordination** – can come from one of the participant agencies, or from an outside body with no other interest within the network, and can be externally funded or jointly funded. A voluntary organisation works more effectively in this role, because of its independence. The Campus has benefited from Coram Family serving this role, including the provision of a community services manager as the link person to pull the network together. Ideally, however, the roles of coordinator and landlord are best separated.
- **Communication** – structures need to be built in at all levels to facilitate clear lines of communication and visibility in order to establish trust between participants and increase awareness. Above all, opportunities should be provided to confront, to challenge, and to disagree, without being destructive.
- **Consultation** – everybody's views must be taken on board and thought through, including the staff of the different agencies and services, groups working in external organisations outside the network, and the users, both parents and children. The consultation process can slow a programme down, but its importance should not be underestimated.

Resources and support

A programme cannot be divorced from its context. Time and place inevitably have a part to play. Resources that will contribute to successful outcomes include:

- **Time for the process of organisational change** – both to set up the network, and to get it 'bedded in' and established. Government time scales often fail to take account of the need for participants, both individually and collaboratively, to talk, to share, and to listen to concerns, especially at the outset of new programmes.
- **Time for staff development and shared activities** – built in from the outset, time should be set aside regularly to provide opportunities for reflection, visiting, discussion, reading, and training, so that staff might learn about other services and practice.
- **Funding the network** – this is the bedrock for successful multi-agency working. Time and other resources, including personnel, to support the development of a network inevitably cost.
- **Statutory support** – the partnership between Coram Family as a voluntary sector agency, and the statutory agencies of health, education and social service has been fundamental to the Campus, and is likely to be so for any other network. Future success will depend upon maintaining this good relationship and developing it further with field staff.
- **Quality staff** – multi-agency working calls for greater professional skill. The stability and strength of service leaders and staff at the Campus has certainly contributed to the progress achieved thus far. Future success will depend upon sound systems being in place to sustain the network when personalities change, both within the services and in the statutory agencies.
- **Evaluation** – continuous evaluation plays an integral part in new initiatives. There is a need to be reflective and self-critical, to be flexible and responsive, in terms of both the planning and the practice. An outside agent may validate self-evaluation. An important part of evaluation is a cross-network system for monitoring use and users of the network.

Replication

Given the increasing attention paid in policy to partnerships, and the growing numbers of networks, our evaluation of the Campus is timely in the opportunity it presents to consider the replicability of this particular model of multi-agency working. In many ways, the Campus is the product of a unique opportunity. A major voluntary agency has developed a substantial inner city site, in partnership with a number of smaller voluntary organisations and a London borough that was already committed to multi-agency working, within a political climate which recognises the importance of early years. To this extent, the Campus, or any other network, could never be replicated in its entirety. Every network is unique in its particular circumstances. It seems, therefore, more appropriate to consider aspects of the Campus network that might be replicated and incorporated into some of the partnership programmes that are currently emerging, using 'replicate' to mean a concept, an approach or method of working which might be worked with and adapted to other circumstances.

To start with, we might consider the replicability of the general concept: **of services coming together to work in collaboration, linked by a common value base, with some kind of overall coordination, aimed at providing more effective services to meet needs**. The precise services in the network can vary, reflecting the local conditions and needs, as might the lead agency, again depending upon the local context. The Campus shows that projects do not have to relate to one another in the same ways; some may overlap more than others in their shared working, as we saw in Chapter 4, Figure 4.1. Services at the Campus are devoted to families and young children, but **there is no reason why a multi-agency network should not be equally replicable for other groups**. For example, a network might focus upon provision for older children, offering services to support parents and teenagers, with input perhaps from workers in the crime prevention field. A school or schools might form part of such a network.

A Campus implies a network with a shared site. The Coram Community Campus has created a dedicated environment that enhances the corporate identity of the network, and facilitates services working together. **A shared site may have particular advantages, but is not essential: a network of services spread across a locality might also achieve much**. For the professionals, it would require greater commitment if they were not seeing one another regularly, both formally and informally. At the same time, the Campus is itself having to move beyond its shared site, extending its services beyond its boundaries, taking them out into the community, through home visiting and work in local primary schools and community groups. This too is important for replication, in terms of reaching families who do not live in the immediate area of the site: whatever the network, it cannot confine its activities to the site or sites of its constituent services.

A feature of the Campus that might be replicated is having a key service at the core of the network, such as an early childhood centre or a family centre. A **core project might operate as a 'one-stop shop'** within the overall network, itself incorporating a range of services. But in addition to offering a range of services itself, this **'core project' might also serve as a gateway or introduction from which families might then move on to other services**, although it need not be the only route to these other services. Given the broad scope of its activities, and its effectiveness as a link between projects, the Parents' Centre has performed this role on the Campus. Indeed, it is hard to imagine how the Campus network could have functioned without this core agency. Where we are seeing so much government money going into inner city regeneration, the example of the Parents' Centre at the Campus could serve as a worthwhile model for community capacity building.

Within the network, the Campus has pointed to how **services can work both independently and collaboratively**, responding to needs, complementing rather than duplicating each other – though the Campus also shows how challenging it is to achieve a good balance. Perhaps a feature that distinguishes the Campus is the freedom which service providers have had to develop in this way, retaining their autonomy. This again is something that might be replicated, particularly in a community development context, though the coordination of autonomous services as opposed to their incorporation into one structure may slow down or limit the development process.

Many families may use only one service, as we found at the Campus, and this should be expected, while others may tap into the various parts of the network as needed. **What is important is that the opportunities are there for users to access a range of services**. Services therefore need to publicise themselves so that local families know what is on offer, but in addition they should be actively steering users to whatever network provision might be appropriate. Above all, users should feel comfortable moving around services; the approach should be 'seamless' in terms of ease of transition.

Looking ahead

In the long term, the effectiveness of the Campus network as a model will be felt in the community, when local people know of its existence, have access to the services, and are supported, enabled and empowered by what is offered. They will come to the Campus because it gives them what they want. It will be 'buzzing' and people will talk about it. The potential exists for the buildings to be used much more, in the evenings and on the weekends, as it becomes an established community resource and local people begin to feel some sort of ownership.

At this stage, our findings can relate only to the short term. Our research has shown how difficult it is to set up and work as a multi-agency network. The sentiments generally coming through from service providers after just two years conveyed a commitment to the notion of the multi-agency network, a belief that it can be achieved, that it brings benefits to users and providers, but that the Campus is not there yet. From the users' perspective, what is already on offer at the Campus is clearly valued. Without exception, Campus services are individually outstanding, providing excellent high quality family support that is meeting need and exceeding official targets. Services have grown stronger as the Campus has matured and are working together more collaboratively. They will no doubt become even more effective as they continue to learn how to exploit fully the opportunities that the multi-agency network presents.

Appendix 1 Coram Community Campus Projects Glossary

CGN	**Collingham Gardens Nursery**
CPC	**Coram Parents' Centre**
Field Lane	**Field Lane Homeless Families' Centre**
KCHP	**King's Cross Homelessness Project**
KIDS	**KIDS London, working for children with special needs**
TreeHouse	**TreeHouse School for children with autism and related disorders**
TCECC	**Thomas Coram Early Childhood Centre**

Appendix 2 Research methodology

Case Study of development of Campus

In the first phase of the research, commencing July 1998, we established the background to the site and to Coram Family (then the Thomas Coram Foundation), in order to gain an understanding of the origins of the Campus. Our early tasks included documentary analysis and initial visits to meet with project heads, conducted at the point when the Campus partners were first coming to work together on the site. We also started attending key Campus meetings, which included the Campus Coordinating Group, the Joint Governing Body of the TCECC and the CPC, together with its sub-committees, the Campus seminars, and health planning meetings.

The first round of semi-structured interviews took place with personnel from each service provider on the Campus: heads, a selection of staff and parent representatives. Lasting up to an hour, they covered the following issues: the Campus concept, Campus objectives, anticipated achievements, benefits and opportunities it presented, worries and concerns of being part of the Campus, and expectations for the future. A high level of tension was apparent at this time. Interviews provided an opportunity for frankness and sharing of anxieties. Given this sensitivity, we decided that tape recording would be inappropriate.

We also interviewed representatives of six local community groups: Coram's Fields, King's Cross and Brunswick Community Centre, the Calthorpe Project, Bedford House Community Centre, the Community Development Officer of the King's Cross Partnership, and William Goodenough Nursery; also representatives of the statutory authorities: health, education and social services.

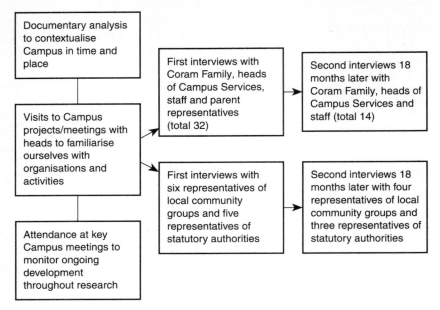

Case Study of development of Campus

Results of this early work were analysed and written up in an Interim Report, which was presented to the Campus and to the local community groups in two feedback/dialogue sessions at the end of the first nine months of research. After all of the early tensions, this experience was described as cathartic. It allowed some of the defensive barriers to come down, and generated a much more positive outlook for taking the Campus forward.

Follow-up interviews were conducted with approximately half of the original interviewees some 18 months later. In the second round, we excluded parent representatives, having by then completed the user survey and in-depth interviews. We also excluded heads and staff who had moved on to other posts in the interim period. Like the first, these second interviews were semi-structured. They expanded many of the earlier issues. The schedule included sections on experiences working within the Campus structure, differences it had made, overall benefits and risks, and views on replication and success. This time we asked if we might tape record the interviews; only two people refused. Interviews were then transcribed, entered into NUD*IST and coded for the final analysis.

Campus Census

From the outset, the absence of any Campus-wide statistical data about users caused us concern. Although not part of the original research proposal, we therefore undertook to carry out a 'census' of family users as a pilot exercise for developing a more permanent means of record keeping. This was conducted over a two-week period in the spring of 1999. The exercise threw up a number of problems, largely as a result of the diversity of the services and their varied systems of record keeping. Briefly summarised, the problems were:

1. **Census format** – the difficulty of designing a set of base questions to 'fit' services which operate in different ways and with different users.

2. **Method of collection** – one project, the CPC, collected census data in person, but was unable to cover all its users; others referred to their own records but could not provide all of the information requested. The homelessness projects were unable to conduct the census at the specified time because of staff shortages, and then had difficulty providing the data retrospectively from records. One project, KIDS, provided data on only a very small number of its users.

3. **Multiple use** – post-codes were requested in the census, which, together with family name, might help identify those families who were using more than one service. However, many post-codes were incomplete or missing, as was the family name for the users of one project, due to confidentiality issues.

4. **Missing data** – because of the above problems, varying but significant amounts of the data requested was missing: for example, family type (lone parent, two parents, etc.), 10 per cent missing; receipt of income support, 29 per cent missing; mother's work status, 34 per cent missing; father's work status, 54 per cent missing.

The results of the census were far from satisfactory, largely because it lacked consistency and was not comprehensive in its coverage. The data produced was of limited use in our research, though we felt the exercise in itself was revealing. The overall numbers served as a guide for sampling when preparing our user survey.

Interview-based work with families

User Survey

The survey took place in October 1999 and extended across the seven core Campus services covered by the research: The Coram Parents' Centre, Collingham Gardens Nursery, Field Lane Homeless Families' Centre, King's Cross Homelessness Project, KIDS, the Thomas Coram Early Childhood Centre, and TreeHouse School. In addition to the two researchers working on the project, we had a team of four experienced and competent interviewers, including a Bengali interviewer.

The original proposal was for a sample of 170 families: 100 mothers and 70 fathers. This was estimated to represent between 1 in 3 and 1 in 4 parents using services. Though we were aware that it was incomplete, the numbers from the census (total 332 families) suggested a need to rethink this target. We therefore reduced the sample number to 135 as more closely approximating 1 in 3 users. In addition, the Census had indicated that fathers represented a very small proportion of active Campus users. We suspected that it would be difficult to achieve a sample of 70 such fathers in total. We decided then to leave the gender of the interviewee open, focusing instead on the most active user from the family.

Part of the problem in determining total numbers was that patterns of use varied so greatly. In the nurseries, the population was clearly defined, whereas the use of the other projects was much harder to establish. Furthermore, while we had included off-Campus use in the census, we decided that we should limit the survey to on-Campus users, to ensure at least some experience of the 'Campus'.

Random sampling

We needed to obtain a random selection of interviewees from services which operated in different ways, further complicated by the issue of multiple use of services (the same family might thus be selected twice, via different services). For the nurseries, classes at the Parents' Centre, the After School and the Holiday Club, we decided to interview every third person from the registers. With the drop-in at the Parents' Centre, interviews were conducted randomly during sessions at the service, reflecting we hoped the random pattern of use.

Both KIDS and TreeHouse had such a small number of users that random selection proved more difficult. We ended up with just three families representing each service.

The homeless families projects required a slightly different approach. Here, the problems of language may have impinged on the selection process. KCHP, as an advice-based service, operates by appointment. Virtually none of its users were capable of being interviewed in English. Over time, KCHP had attracted a large number of Polish/Slovak families (approximately 80 per cent). We therefore used the services of a Polish/Russian interpreter while attending a number of advice sessions, at which we invited clients to be interviewed, either before or after their appointment. Virtually all agreed to participate. In addition, our Bengali interviewer conducted two interviews with Bengali users.

At Field Lane, we resorted to more subtle procedures, one of the most successful being the laundry list. Potential interviewees were identified from it and invited to be interviewed while they waited for their washing. We also spent time at the drop-in, randomly interviewing users. The process was a little unpredictable because of language difficulties. In some instances, one user translated for another. For the most part, there was a great deal of goodwill and support for the survey, linked, perhaps, to the loyalty users had for Field Lane.

Since the number of users of both homelessness projects was not clear-cut, we set a target figure for these interviews, based upon an estimate of users in an average week.

Languages

The Census had alerted us to the fact that for many Campus users English was not the first language, yet we had no way of knowing when a particular language might be required. In practice, the language issue was less problematic than initially feared, We were able to cope reasonably well with English (over 80 per cent) with the help of Bengali, Polish/ Russian and Albanian interpreters for the rest.

The Questionnaire

The design of the questionnaire was a collaborative process, which involved working closely with the service heads. Amongst other things, the questions covered:

- knowledge of the Campus and use of services;
- users' home location and use of other community services;
- parent and child participation and involvement in services;
- parenting support and effectiveness of services;
- demographic details.

The format of the questionnaire was essentially fairly tight, with only a few open-ended questions. Like the census, a comprehensive design proved problematic, due to the diverse nature of the services. For example, questions on parenting seemed inappropriate for certain users of KCHP, who came for specific practical advice, often without children.

The user survey broken down by gender and Campus service providers is shown in the accompanying table, alongside the census totals.

User survey

	Men	Women	Total survey completed	Census totals
TCECC	5	31	36	100
CPC	4	50	54	126*
CGN	2	6	8	22
KIDS	0	3	3	9*
TreeHouse	0	3	3	10
Field Lane	2	19	21	33*
KCHP	3	9	12	32
Total	16	120	137	332

*Census figures did not cover total users.

Interviews took around 30 minutes, and were conducted at the Campus. The quantitative data was analysed using SPSS.

We were generally surprised by how few users declined to be interviewed (around 8 per cent). Where we were able to compare the demographic details with the census figures, our sample appeared to be representative, save for slightly under-representing the Bengali families. However, we suspect the inclusion of off-Campus users may have swelled the numbers of Bengali families in the census.

Survey of non-users

In addition to the user survey, we decided to undertake a limited survey in a number of locations close to the Campus. We wanted to get some kind of measure of the families who might be *non-users* of Campus services: who they were, where they lived, why they did not come, etc. For this exercise, we designed a brief questionnaire which we administered to parents identified with young children, taking no longer than five minutes to complete. We used a Bengali interviewer because we were aware of the high number of Bengali families in the locations we were targeting. The survey took place during the first two weeks of March 2000, focusing on parents attending clinic sessions at the local health centre, in reception classes at two local primary schools, at the local shopping centre and a local community centre. It covered a total of 56 families, comprising 11 fathers and 45 mothers.

In-depth interviews

The 18 in-depth interviews focused on three groups of Campus users: single mothers, fathers (all of whom were in traditional two-parent families) and homeless families using the Field Lane Centre (see accompanying table). In the proposal, the third group was to have comprised refugee families. However, it was evident from our user survey that Field Lane Homeless Families' Centre was reaching a wider range of families than just refugees. We felt it was important that these other homeless families should be included in the study in view of the particular needs they clearly had.

In the user survey, we had asked respondents to indicate if they were willing to be interviewed again. Most had responded positively. We selected the subjects for the in-depth interviews very carefully, reviewing their individual circumstances and endeavouring to represent a balanced cross-section of the various services provided on the Campus. In the event, we limited the interviews to users of the two nurseries, the Parents' Centre and Field Lane, because these were the largest user groups, most of whom lived in the local area. Users of KIDS, TreeHouse and KCHP tended to come from a wider catchment area, and to use a single Campus service only. However, we included two families who had children with special needs and had used the services of KIDS in the past.

In-depth interviews

	Fathers	Single mothers	Homeless	Total
CPC	2	3	0	5
CGN	2	1	0	3
TCECC	2	2	0	4
Field Lane	0	0	6	6
Total	6	6	6	18

We compiled a set of broad themes around which the interviews were loosely structured to take account of the range of services and situations. Our aim was to construct a 'picture' of the interviewee and his/her family, starting out with a profile of early upbringing to set the context, followed by a review of present circumstances and parenthood, leading in to the particular part played by Campus services. With the latter, we referred back to responses given in the earlier survey for expansion.

Ideally, we wanted to conduct these interviews in the subjects' homes, in order to gain an insight into home circumstances, but more often interviewees preferred to be interviewed at the Campus. We were assisted in the interviewing by one of the interviewers who had worked on the earlier survey. Interviews lasted generally about an hour and were tape recorded, with the interviewee's consent. Following transcription, the data was entered into NUD*IST for coding, in preparation for the qualitative analysis.

Ethical Policy

Throughout the research, we have endeavoured to balance the public 'right to know' with the individual 'right to privacy' (MacDonald and others, 1975), by a process of consultation and negotiation, based upon the criteria of fairness, relevance and validity. Our ethical policy was one of 'informed consent' whereby everyone whose view was sought was well informed, fully aware of the purpose and nature of the research and freely chose to participate. Where anonymity could not be assured, we invited comment and obtained individual consent before publishing the material.

References

Audit Commission (1994) *Seen But Not Heard: Coordination of Community Child Health and Social Services for Children in Need*. HMSO

Ball, C (1994) *Start Right: the Importance of Early Learning*. Royal Society of Arts

Carnegie Task Force (1994) *Starting Points: Meeting the Needs of Our Young Children*. US: Carnegie Corporation

Dahlberg, G, Moss, P and Pence, A (1999) *Beyond Quality in Early Childhood Education and Care*. Falmer Press

Draper, L (2001) 'Being evaluated: a practitioner's view', *Childhood and Society*, 16, 1

Hodgkin, R and Newell, P (1996) *Effective Government Structures for Children: Report of a Gulbenkian Foundation inquiry*. Gulbenkian Foundation

Holman, R (1987) 'Family Centres', *Children and Society*, 1, 2

MacDonald, B 'Evaluation and the control of education', *in* MacDonald, B and Walker, R eds (1974) *SAFARI: Innovation, Evaluation, Research and the Problem of Control*. Centre for Applied Research in Education, University of East Anglia

MacDonald, B and others (1975) *The Programme at Two*. Centre for Applied Research in Education, University of East Anglia

McQuail, S and Pugh, G (1995) *The Effective Organisation of Early Childhood Services*. National Children's Bureau

Makins, V (1997) *Not Just a Nursery . . . Multi-agency early years centres in action*. National Children's Bureau

Moss, P 'Perspectives from Europe' *in* Pugh, G ed. (1996) *Contemporary Issues in Early Childhood*. National Children's Bureau

Moss, P and Petrie, P (1997) *Children's Services: Time for a New Approach*. Thomas Coram Research Unit

Office for National Statistics (ONS) (1991) *1991 Census of Population*. The Stationery Office

Office for National Statistics (ONS) (1999) *Housing in England 1997/98*. The Stationery Office

Osgood, J and Sharp, C (2000) *Developing Early Education and Childcare Services for the 21st Century.* National Foundation for Educational Research

Owen, R (1836) *A New View of Society, and Other Writings,* 1927 edn. Everyman Library

Patten, M (1987) *How to Use Qualitative Methods in Evaluation.* Sage Publications

Pithouse, A and Holland, S (1999) 'Open access family centres and their users: Positive results, some doubts and new departures', *Children and Society,* 13, 3

Pugh, G (1988) *Services for the Under Fives: Developing a Coordinated Approach.* National Children's Bureau

Pugh, G, De'Ath, E and Smith, C (1994) *Confident Parents, Confident Children: Policy and practice in parent education and support.* National Children's Bureau

Pugh, G (1999) *Developing the Coram Community Campus: a discussion paper.* Coram Family

Pugh, G and McQuail, S (1995) *Effective Organisation of Early Childhood Services Summary and Strategic Framework.* National Children's Bureau

Schweinhart, L, Barnes, H and Weikart, D (1993) *Significant Benefits: The High/Scope Perry Preschool Study through Age 27.* US, Michigan: High/Scope Press

Sinclair, R, Hearn, B and Pugh, G (1997) *Preventive Work with Families: The Role of Mainstream Services.* National Children's Bureau

Smith, C and Pugh, G (1996) *Learning to be a Parent : A Survey of Group Based Parenting Programmes.* Family Policy Studies Centre/Joseph Rowntree Foundation

Statham, J (1994) *Childcare in the Community: the provision of community based, open access services for young children in family centres.* Save the Children Fund

Sylva, K and Wiltshire, J (1993) 'The impact of early learning on children's later development', *European Early Childhood Education Research Journal,* 1, 1

Utting, D (1995) *Family and Parenthood: Supporting families, preventing breakdown.* Joseph Rowntree Foundation

Whalley, M (1994) *Learning to be Strong.* Hodder & Stoughton

Index